THE HORNET STRIKES

The Life and Times of a Royal Air Force Fighter Squadron

"Irritatus Lacessit Crabro"

Frank M Leeson

Copyright 1998 by Frank M Leeson

Published in Great Britain by

Air-Britain (Historians) Ltd
12 Lonsdale Gardens, Tunbridge Wells, Kent

Sales Dept: 19 Kent Road,
Grays, Essex, RM17 6DE

Correspondence to:

J.J.Halley, 5 Walnut Tree Road,
Shepperton, Middlesex, TW17 0RW
and not to the Tunbridge Wells address

All rights reserved. No part of this publication may be reproduced, stored in a retrieval system or transmitted, in any form or by any means, electronic, mechanical, photocopying, recording or otherwise, without the prior permission of Air-Britain (Historians) Ltd

ISBN 0 85130 272 6

Printed by Halstan & Co Ltd
2-10 Plantation Road
Amersham, Bucks
HP6 6HJ

Front cover: Sgt M E Croskell in his Hurricane AK-F over southern England in the summer of 1940. The original painting by Geoffrey Nutkins now hangs in the Crypt Bar of the Officers' Mess, Bentley Priory, and is reproduced by kind permission of the President of the Mess Committee

Back cover: Fg Off A G R Ashley in his Mustang III attacking a German barge on the Danube, 19 October 1944. The original painting by Cpl Frank Wright, an Engine Fitter with No.213 Squadron, was commissioned by Roy Ashley while serving with the Squadron, and is reproduced here with his kind permission.

CONTENTS

Foreword		5
Chapter 1	Naval Origins 1916 - 1917	7
Chapter 2	The Royal Air Force 1918 - 1919	17
Chapter 3	With the B.E.F. in France	35
Chapter 4	Dunkirk	47
Chapter 5	The Battle of Britain, Exeter, No. 10 Group	54
Chapter 6	The Battle of Britain, Tangmere, No. 11 Group	64
Chapter 7	Farewell to England	73
Chapter 8	The Desert Air Force	87
Chapter 9	Victory in the Desert	99
Chapter 10	A Very Special Operation	113
Chapter 11	A Waiting Game	121
Chapter 12	The Balkan Air Force	131
Chapter 13	The Middle East	156
Chapter 14	The Second Allied Tactical Air Force	176

APPENDICES

A	Battle Honours	194
B	Commanding Officers	195
C	Squadron Bases	196
D	Squadron Aircraft	198
E	Squadron Aircrew	200
F	Account in Cypriot Press	208
G	Copy of "Blood Chit"	210
Author's Note		211
Scrapbook		213
Index		221

This History of
213 Squadron, Royal Air Force
is dedicated to
the memory of
the late
Group Captain P T Bayley
Commanding Officer 1959-1961
without whose initiative, interest and support
it would not have been written,
and to all the Officers and Men who
served with the Squadron on the ground and
without whom the aircraft would not have flown.

FOREWORD

By The Late Air Vice-Marshal R Graham CB, CBE, DSO, DSC and Bar, DFC, JP,
Her Majesty's Lieutenant for the County of Bute.

This history of No.213 Squadron - "The Hornets" - covering the first fifty years of its existence, is a simple, sincere and factual account of the courage and integrity of young men who undertook their duties with selfless determination in the face of odds. We must be grateful to those responsible for compiling, with care and understanding, this record of lighthearted valour, self-sacrifice and great achievement.

As an illustration of the stuff the men were made of, the flight of 'two thousand miles on one fan' over the Mediterranean to an unknown destination from an aircraft carrier without the normal flight preliminaries takes a lot of beating, even when compared with combats against superior numbers and hazards of weather and desert. "Follow the Fulmar" is a phrase not likely to be forgotten in the Squadron.

The pilots of 213, when called upon, dominated the air, land and sea by virtue of their enthusiasm, training, discipline and team spirit and, above all, by their confidence in their aircraft. A confidence that was, and always will be, a tribute to the men and woman engaged in the design, construction and maintenance of the equipment. In their turn, these men and woman will forever be proud of the pilots who proved, beyond a shadow of doubt, the worth of their work.

Although No.213 was only one of the many squadrons to achieve greatness, it will always be the best of squadrons to those who had the honour to serve in it. May all who read this history find in it, as I have done, encouragement to follow the path of those whose record is that of endeavour crowned by achievement.

"Per Ardua ad Astra"

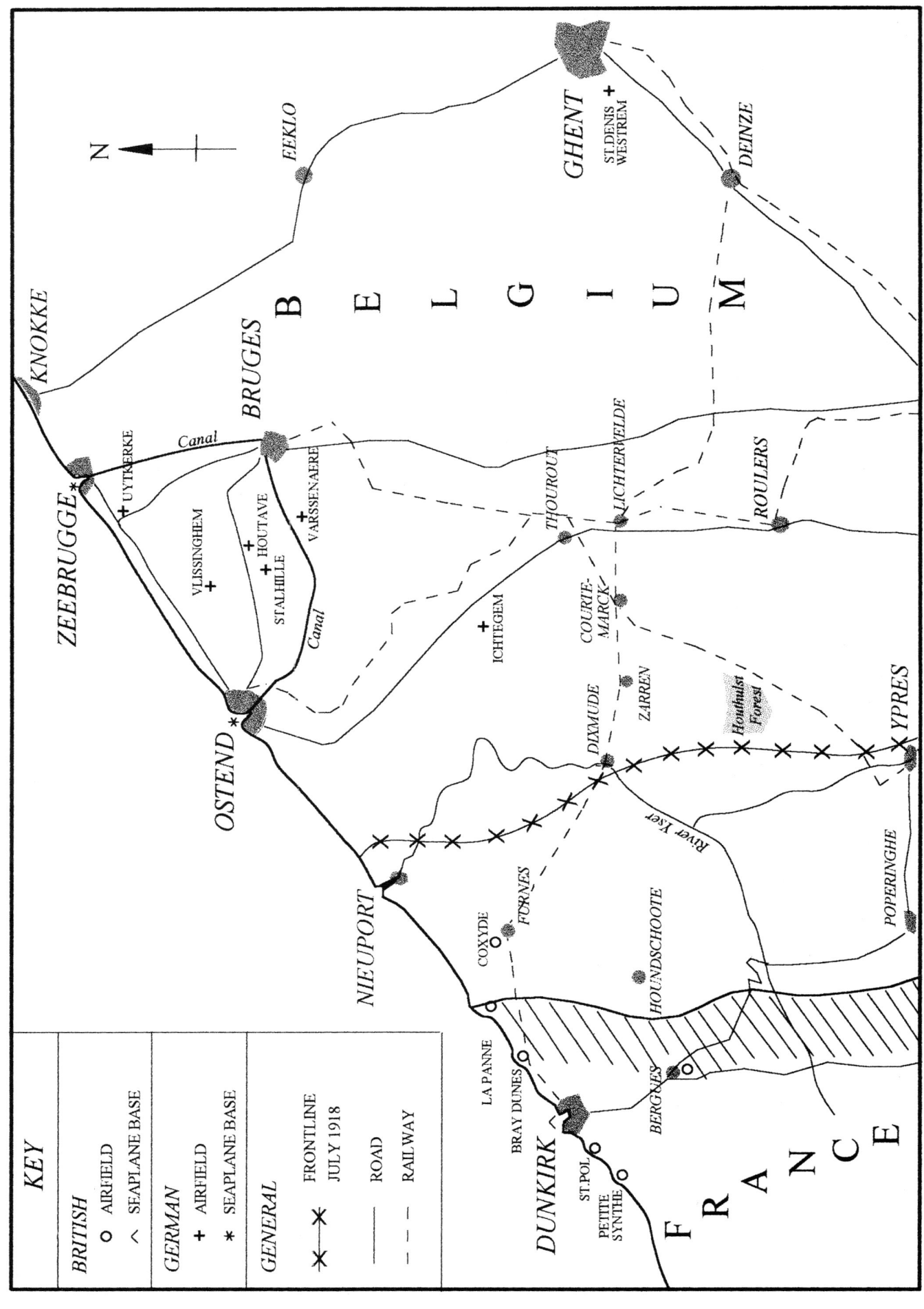

Flt Sub-Lts L H Slatter, P S Fisher and J E Potvin with Flt Lt R Graham standing in front of a Sopwith Baby seaplane at the Dunkirk Seaplane Base in the Spring of 1917. (F Cheeseman)

CHAPTER ONE - NAVAL ORIGINS 1916-1917

Flying from the Seaplane Base at Dunkirk, Naval pilots had, since 1915, been providing essential air services for the Dover Patrol. This Patrol consisted of a mixed number of mine-laying and mine-sweeping vessels, and was supplemented by destroyers, monitors and P-boats which operated in the eastern approaches to the English Channel. The commander of this force in the latter part of the war was Admiral Sir Roger Keyes, KCB, CMG, CMVO, DSO, RN who had succeeded Admiral Sir Roger Bacon, KCB, KCVO, DSO, RN at the beginning of the last year of the war.

Freedom of passage for merchant ships in the Channel was essential, not only to keep Britain supplied with raw materials from abroad, but also to keep the British Army fighting in France. Everything had to cross this narrow strip of water. The task of the Dover Patrol was to guard the eastern end of the Channel against any enemy raiders. The chief threat came from submarines and destroyers sneaking out from ports in North Germany, and even more dangerously, from the captured Belgian ports of Zeebrugge and Ostend. Apart from the essential sea-lanes that required protection, there were for most years of the war, thousands of tons of merchant shipping anchored off The Downs as a result of the British Government's policy of searching neutral shipping for contraband of war. Admiral Bacon's answer to the problem of maintaining freedom of passage across the Channel, because of the lack of destroyers or other fast surface craft, and also the limited methods of submarine detection then available, was to attempt to blockade the entire Belgian coast. To this end, the Belgium Coast Barrage was constructed. This considerable enterprise, first laid down in the summer of 1916, consisted of mines, both deep set and surface, attached to mile upon mile of netting which blocked the passages through the shoals off Dunkirk. It then continued along the French-Belgian coast, some eleven miles out to sea, until Dutch territorial waters were reached.

An essential addition to this static barrage was a force of destroyers and torpedo-boats which set out at dawn each day to patrol the seaward side of the barrage while shallow-draft monitors provided bombardment support . These daily sorties operated primarily against the submarines based on the ports of Zeebrugge and Ostend, and were supported by patrols flown from the Seaplane Base at Dunkirk. The work of these air patrols was hazardous and unrewarding; looking for submarines in the muddy waters off the Belgian coast proved more difficult than looking for needles in an haystack. Apart from their spotting function, the aircraft were equipped with bombs for attacking any submarines caught on or near the surface. Spotting duties were also carried out for the monitors shelling the German coastal positions, although without a radio link this proved to be a very frustrating business.

Flt Sub-Lt R Graham's Sopwith Baby Phyllis. *(F Cheeseman)*

Seaplanes were used for these anti-submarine patrols since most of the flying was carried out over the sea and the reliability of the early aero-engines was not particularly good. Short two-seaters were used and were unarmed apart from the bombs they carried.

In addition to the natural hazards and technical difficulties of the early days of flying, the Dunkirk seaplanes were confronted with very formidable opposition provided by two German seaplane units, one based at Zeebrugge and the other at Ostend. At Zeebrugge, Seeflug I was the main unit which consisted of thirty-seven Friedrichshafen FF-33 biplanes and Brandenburg KDW single-seat and W 12 two-seat high-speed floatplanes. In March 1917 this force was increased when Seeflug II, with ten more aircraft, commenced operations from Ostend. German seaplane design had reached a more advanced stage than the British, and their aircraft always had the edge on the types operating from Dunkirk. The Friedrichshafen was a two-seat fighter carrying one fixed machine-gun and a two-way radio and was powered by a 200 hp Benz engine. The Brandenburg KDW was a single-seat aircraft with one fixed machine-gun while the W 12 had one or two fixed guns and one movable gun. Against such opposition it soon became apparent that the unarmed Short seaplanes could not operate by day without an escort. To fill this role at Dunkirk, Sopwith Babies were introduced as single-seat fighters. Even so the German aircraft still had a marked superiority in speed, rate of climb and manoeuvrability as the British aircraft were handicapped both in the air and on the water by the presence of a tail-float. The four flights of six aircraft at Dunkirk had the additional disadvantage of being consistently outnumbered.

Since August 1915 Cdr C L Lambe RN had been in command of the Naval air forces at Dover and Dunkirk. He had repeatedly warned that more fighting seaplanes were needed if the work along the Belgian coast was to continue. The establishment of Seeflug II in March 1917 worsened an already grave situation. Repeated combats with superior enemy forces and increasing bomber raids from the German land bases around Zeebrugge had created a parlous situation at Dunkirk. The Seaplane Base could muster only five fighting seaplanes - and two of these were under repair. The French had even fewer aircraft. When the situation was reported to the Admiralty, nine more Sopwith Babies were sent to Dunkirk but proved to be no real answer to the problem.

In June 1917 Cdr Lambe proposed a radical solution to the problem when he suggested that the fighting seaplanes should be replaced by more advanced landplanes. He suggested that Sopwith Pups fitted with flotation bags might be the answer. Admiral Bacon was also aware of the deficiencies of the seaplanes under his command and in a memorandum to the Admiralty he wrote:- "The seaplane is an inferior aeroplane, considerable advantages being sacrificed by providing it with the power of floating on the water. This flotation is entirely unnecessary provided the engines are reliable. The engines of aeroplanes, I consider, are sufficiently reliable to make the addition of floats unnecessary." In his report he continued to stress the importance of speed and the ability to fight the German aircraft on equal terms in all aspects of the work of the air services supporting the Dover Patrol.

While Cdr Lambe's proposals were still under consideration by the Admiralty, there occurred an engagement which illustrated the point that both Bacon and Lambe were making. Playing a leading role in this episode was Flt Lt R Graham (later Air Vice-Marshal R Graham CB, CBE, DSO, DSC and Bar, DFC, JP) who was to command the Seaplane Defence Flight from its formation until the Armistice, by which date it had become No.213 Squadron, RAF. Ronnie Graham was born in Japan on 19 July 1896, and was studying medicine when hostilities commenced. In 1915 he joined the Royal Naval Division and in September of that year was transferred into the Royal Naval Air Service (RNAS) as a Flight Sub-Lieutenant. In 1916 after his training he commenced his service flying at the Dover Seaplane Base and in 1917 moved with his unit to Dunkirk to give cover to the North Sea Fleet and the Belgium Coast Barrage.

At 06.00 hours on 19 June 1917 a Short seaplane, escorted by two Sopwith Babies, set out on a mine and U-boat spotting patrol. The two Sopwiths were flown by Graham and Flt Sub-Lt J E Potvin. About one hour after the patrol had left its base at St. Pol, with a storm raging over Dunkirk, a bell in the base's pigeon loft rang signalling the return of a bird with a message. Two pigeons were found there with messages from Graham. The messages, brief and to the point, gave the outline of a sad story. "Short shot down - Potvin? Ten miles NNE Nieuport. One Hun shot down. My tanks shot. French TBD on its way. Send fighters." The second message added a few more details. "Short landed O.K. down NNE Nieuport Potvin? I shot one down but he did not crash. My tanks no good can't climb. French TBD on its way. Send more fighters quick." The officers in the Short were Flt Sub-Lt L P Paine and Lt T Rodgers. At 07.20 hours a further pigeon arrived carrying a message from Paine. "Am shot down. Hit in tank radiator. Rodgers dead. Please send CMB at once."

The events of the day are on record. Twelve miles north-east of Nieuport the patrol had been attacked by three German fighting seaplanes flown by Lts Bieber, Backmann and Dyck from the seaplane base at Ostend. Dyck, after a short engagement, shot Potvin down into the sea. At the same time he himself came under attack from Graham and was so badly wounded that he was forced to land his aircraft on the water. Meanwhile Bieber had been attacking the unarmed Short, killing Rodgers the observer and piercing the tank and radiator. In further fighting with the two remaining German seaplanes Graham's aircraft sustained more damage and, with a failing engine, he was obliged to break off the encounter. Turning back along the coast he made for the Base at Dunkirk, but when the Sopwith's engine finally cut out completely, Graham put his aircraft down in the sea alongside a French destroyer. Lt Bieber was also committing his aircraft to the water in an attempt to rescue his wounded companion Dyck. Despite the difficulty of moving the wounded man, Bieber eventually manhandled him aboard his

Sopwith Baby 8157, the first aircraft flown by Flt Sub-Lt R Graham following his unit's move from Dover to the Dunkirk Seaplane Base in 1917. (F Cheeseman)

aircraft and made off for Ostend. His gallantry was, however, in vain as Dyck died on the way to hospital.

At Dunkirk, Graham's message caused some alarm since the storm that was still blowing prevented the despatch of any more aircraft. A hurried consultation was held to discuss the possibility of sending one of the still secret fast Coastal Motor Torpedo Boats (CMBs) that had only recently arrived at Dunkirk. Soon two of these craft were on their way, but further trouble was in store. The engines of one of the boats started to give trouble shortly before they were engaged by four German destroyers. Despatching its torpedo at the approaching enemy, the serviceable boat turned for home. The fate of the other boat was sealed; without engines she fell prey to the Germans and her crew under Lt W Green RN were taken prisoner. Paine, the survivor in the badly damaged Short seaplane, was also picked up. This singularly unfortunate patrol resulted therefore in the loss of one secret naval vessel and two aircraft plus a third damaged, with one pilot killed, one observer killed and one pilot captured.

Paine, who but for this unfortunate incident would no doubt have been part of the Seaplane Defence Flight when it was formed, spent the rest of the war in a prisoner-of-war camp. A post-card from him, in the Officer's Prison Camp at Freiburg, Baden, to Ronnie Graham dated 4 October 1917 leaves a lot unsaid between the lines:-

"Thought perhaps you'd like a line from me. Parcels are beginning to come along & things are not too bad now. We are not badly treated here (....censored.........).I certainly do not recommend being taken prisoner. Thank Slatter for coming out & having a look see at me. Some kit turned up for me last week & was a welcome change. Send me a line now and then & let me have local news. Green is fit and sends his chin chins. I suppose you know poor old Tim Seven went west.

L Philip Paine"

The supply of improved fighting aircraft had become imperative if the work of the Seaplane Base was to continue. In the latter part of June 1917 the news came that Lambe's proposals had been accepted. A Seaplane Defence Flight was to be established. As suggested, the aircraft to be used was the Sopwith Pup carrying flotation bags which were thought to be necessary despite the handicap they imposed.

The unit that was eventually to become No.213 Squadron, RAF, had been created. On 3 July 1917, four pilots of the fighting seaplanes, Flt Lts R Graham, P S Fisher and G W Price and Flt Sub-Lt L H Slatter (later Air Marshal Sir Leonard Slatter, KBE, CB, OBE, DSC & Bar, DFC), picked up four Sopwith Pups from the aircraft depot at Dunkirk and flew them the few miles to nearby St. Pol. This airfield, which was to be the Flight's home for the remainder of the year, adjoined the western edge of the town of Dunkirk and was bounded on the northern side by the lines of sand-dunes which fringe that coast. Accommodation was provided for the flight personnel in standard Naval wooden huts while the aircraft were housed in canvas Bessoneau hangars. A photographic reconnaissance unit, No.2 Squadron RNAS, was already operating from this small field.

The conversion from sea- to land-based aircraft presented no great difficulties for the pilots as they had all been trained on landplanes. The short flight to St. Pol had been made longer to give the pilots the chance to become

Sopwith Pup flown by Flt Sub-Lt L H Slatter. (N Franks)

Flt Sub-Lt L H Slatter in the cockpit of his Sopwith Pup Mina. (N Franks)

better acquainted with their new aircraft. The Pup was a fast light fighter, just what was required on the Belgian coast. In the following days more pilots arrived, in July - Flt Lt F G Horstmann, Flt Sub-Lt L C Pinscott and Flt Sub-Lt J R Allen, and in August Lt C P Brown (later Air Vice-Marshal C P Brown, CBE, DFC) and Flt Sub-Lt P Duggan. All came from the Seaplane Base at Dunkirk.

On 16 July 1917 two of the Flight's four original pilots were awarded the Distinguished Service Cross. Flt Lt Graham's award was in recognition of his part in the action with the three German seaplanes and six days later he was promoted to the rank of Flight Commander and assumed command of the Seaplane Defence Flight The other recipient of the DSC was Flt Lt Fisher whose experiences illustrate very well the fluctuating fortunes of war. Returning from combat on one occasion he found almost one hundred bullet holes in his aircraft and the landing wires were shot away. As the aircraft slowed after landing the wings drooped forlornly onto the ground. Fisher himself had not a scratch. The very next day he was hit once, by a tracer bullet, which pierced his knee and thereafter he walked with a limp.

Early July saw the first fighter patrols airborne. The very first, on 11 July, was flown by Graham, Price and Slatter, three pilots whose names recur frequently in the combat reports of the following months. Slatter was one of the many pilots from the Dominions who flew with the Squadron in both World Wars. Born on 8 December 1894 and educated in South Africa, he trained as a civil engineer. On the outbreak of war he served initially as a despatch rider with an armoured car unit. In 1916 he joined the RNAS as an observer and flew with the Seaplane Squadron at Dunkirk. In July 1916 he was selected for pilot training and, after completing the course, returned to the Seaplane Base in February 1917 as a fully qualified pilot. He served with the Seaplane Defence Flight from its inception until July 1918 when he was transferred to No. 4 ASD Pilot Pool to train pilots up to operational standards. In 1919 he served with 47 Squadron in Russia. Choosing to remain in the service after the war he commanded Nos.19, 111, and 43 Squadrons before becoming Station Commander at Tangmere in 1935. Because of his former service with the RNAS, Slatter was frequently involved with the naval side of the RAF's operations. During the Second World War he commanded No.15 Group Coastal Command before becoming Commander-in-Chief Coastal Command in 1945.

During the winter of 1916/1917 the complex defence works of the Belgium Coast Barrage had fallen into disrepair. The severe weather had not only broken up the nets and displaced the mines but had also prevented the daily sorties of the Belgium Coast Patrol, thus allowing the Germans to come out and dismantle large sections of the barrage. In July 1917 a large collection of naval vessels arrived in Belgian coastal waters to commence the work of relaying the mines and nets. The first task of the Flight was to protect this fleet against attacks by the powerful German seaplane units. For the remainder of the month patrols of between five and seven aircraft were in action along the coast. A high patrol was flown at 17,000 feet, without the benefit of oxygen, and a low patrol at 7,000 feet. It was soon discovered that the flotation bags fitted to the Pups expanded at altitude and imposed an even greater handicap on the aircraft. Their removal restored the Pups to their original performance and was welcomed by all the pilots.

Operating in an offensive fighter role, the Pup was seen to its best advantage and the patrols had considerable freedom of action. On 12 August 1917 Graham flying together with Fisher and Slatter destroyed a Friedrichshafen over the sea off Ostend. This aircraft was operated by Seeflug I and was flown by Flugmaat Paatz and Vizefeldwebel Putz, both of whom were killed in the engagement. As the effectiveness of the Flight's operations were noted, other tasks were quickly assigned to it. One of the less congenial tasks was escorting the slow and cumbersome Curtiss H 12 flying-boat that arrived at Dunkirk for long-range spotting duties. Without an escort the Curtiss was an easy target for the German seaplanes but, even when stretching the endurance of the Pup escort to the limit, the range of the spotting patrols was severely limited. Nevertheless numerous patrols were flown until the flying-boat was damaged and the work ceased.

Another diversion from fleet protection work was provided on 22 August when the Flight was ordered up to intercept Gotha bombers returning to their bases in Belgium after a raid over Dover and Sheerness. In fact the Pup had an insufficiently high operating ceiling to interfere seriously with the high flying Gothas, however numerous engagements were fought with the enemy fighters that had come up to escort them on their last leg home. Thus it soon became clear that there was plenty of work to be done along the Belgian coast by a unit equipped with fast, light, manoeuvrable fighters.

On 21 September the Flight was expanded and renamed the Seaplane Defence Squadron. This change of designation followed quickly after a change of aircraft when the Pups had been exchanged for the more famous Sopwith Camel. The

Camels B6410 and B6397 of the Seaplane Defence Squadron, Bergues, France, December 1918. (F Cheeseman)

Camel was probably the most effective allied fighter on the Western Front and those equipping the Squadron had the added advantage of a Bentley rotary engine rather than the standard Clerget rotary. The Camel's armament consisted of two Vickers guns firing through the propeller; it was the "hump" housing the firing mechanisms of the guns just forward of the pilot's cockpit that gave the Camel its name. Although considered difficult to fly its speed, rate of climb, manoeuvrability and lightness on the controls made its reputation. The RNAS Bentley-powered 2F.1 Camels had a single Vickers and a Lewis on a movable mounting above the wing.

During the thirteen months that the war had to run the Squadron would operate over one hundred Camels, nearly three-quarters of these were built by two manufacturers, the Sopwith Aviation Company Limited at its factory at Kingston-upon-Thames, and Clayton & Shuttleworth Limited of Lincoln. This latter company had a number of contracts to provide Camels for RNAS units before the creation of the RAF. The third major manufacturer of the Camels flown by the Squadron was the Nieuport & General Aircraft Company Limited of Cricklewood, London. It should not be supposed however that the ninety-four aircraft supplied by these three companies came to the squadron directly from the factory. The aircraft first arrived in France at No.4 Aeroplane Supply Depot, near Guines a few miles outside Calais, from there they were allocated to operational units. It was also to Guines that the aircraft returned after flying accidents or receiving damage in combat that could not be dealt with in the Squadron's workshops. Some aircraft made the journey from St Pol or Bergues to 4 ASD on a number of occasions, serving with a variety of different units. Only two of the Squadron's aircraft, part of an order of five hundred, were complete rebuilds, that is having been completely reconstructed at one of the number of Aircraft Repair Parks established in France, after suffering major damage in combat or accidents.

The experience of a patrol flown on 22 September illustrated both the frustrations and hazards, other than enemy action, that faced the aircrew of the First World War. A mixed patrol of Pups and Camels was put up as an escort for a Short Seaplane on a bombing mission over Zeebrugge. The formation proceeded safely along the coast to the target area and located some German destroyers in the harbour. However as the Short approached to bomb the destroyers it stalled on turning and spun into the sea. Unable to afford any help to the luckless crew, the escort returned to Dunkirk.

In the early days of flying, spinning was a hazard that was not well understood, indeed a set spin recovery action was only taught from 1917 onwards. Before that an aircraft more likely than not crashed if it entered a spin. Graham however had been more lucky in an experience earlier in the war. He was airborne over the sea in a Short two-seater in company with another, when he turned to look for the other aircraft. So critical was the balance of the Short that it quickly fell into a spin and as no parachutes were carried he prepared for the expected crash. His first thought was for his observer and he shouted to him to tighten his straps. However due to the noise of the engine and the wind in the wires his observer did not hear, so releasing the control column Graham demonstrated what he wanted him to do. With the controls now free the aircraft's natural stability brought it out of the spin and Graham flew carefully back to Dunkirk. Such incidents were eagerly discussed by the pilots in the Mess but the reasons for spinning and the precise actions needed to correct a spin remained obscure before 1917.

A serious problem presented itself while the Squadron was still at St. Pol. While practising air-to-ground firing at a target moored in a small lake near the airfield, a pilot was killed when his Camel dived straight into the water. For a time the cause of the accident remained a mystery; it seemed that no attempt had been made to pull out of the dive. Some days later, Graham was carrying out attacks on the same target when, with his aircraft in a steep dive and the throttle closed, his elevators suddenly became sloppy and ineffective. It seemed to Graham that the previous accident was about to repeat itself. Thinking that if he was going to crash he would rather be killed than maimed or seriously injured, he put on full power. Almost immediately the elevators became effective again and the Camel roared out of its dive skimming the surface of the lake. Back at St. Pol the explanation soon became clear. A test pilot at the depot had reported that some

Major R Collishaw, DSO and Bar, DSC, DFC, one of the most successful Naval fighter pilots on the Western Front. Flew as a Flight Commander with the Squadron from November 1917 until January 1918.

Lt D S Ingalls, DSM, DFC, a US Navy pilot who joined the Squadron in March 1918. Served for two short periods during which he shot down five enemy aircraft and a balloon. He was the only US Navy pilot to score five victories in the First World War and the first to win the DFC. (N Franks)

of the Camels were flying tail heavy and the tailplane had been re-aligned to correct this. The adjustment however meant that when the Camel was in a steep dive with the engine throttled back the elevators were blanked-off and became useless. Graham's action in opening up his engine had restored the airflow over the tailplane and so once more restored elevator control. Such were the trial and error methods by which the facts about flying were learned.

The daily sortie of the Belgium Coast Patrol on 25 September was given the special task of escorting the monitor HMS *Terror* which had been brought up to shell the dock installations at Ostend. As the smoke screen, laid to protect the ships from return fire, was clearing and the monitor was turning away out to sea, Graham and Slatter arrived overhead in their Camels. Soon they saw four Brandenburgs and two Friedrichshafens approaching from the east. Manoeuvring to gain an advantageous position Graham and Slatter dived from above onto the Germans. On the first pass Graham shot down a Brandenburg of Seeflug I flown by Vizeflugmaat Plattenburg and Lt. Brettmann, while Slatter gave chase to a Friedrichshafen that was making for the coast and forced it down into the sea. As the other aircraft withdrew towards Ostend, Graham and Slatter returned to the Fleet to inform it of the action and direct it to the spot where the damaged Brandenburg had landed. On returning to the scene of the action, the pilots found that the single-seat Friedrichshafen had sunk, and that one of the remaining Brandenburgs had

landed on the water in an endeavour to pick up the crew of the one that was damaged. However, owing to the extra weight, it had been unable to take off and Graham and Slatter were able to empty all their remaining ammunition into this unfortunate aircraft. A triumphant return to Dunkirk was quickly curtailed when Graham's engine, protesting at the loss of oil from a bullet hole, failed just north of Malo-les-Bains and he was forced down into the sea off Dunkirk. Once again he was picked up by a passing ship. A rope was passed around the propeller boss of his damaged aircraft, and the ship set off at a good speed in the direction of Dunkirk. Unfortunately, due to the rough sea, all that remained of the Camel by the time the harbour was reached was the propeller on the end of the line.

The evening report from the Admiral hardly contained a full account of the action. It stated only that "Several hostile aircraft were seen manoeuvring overhead"; no mention was made of the friendly ones.

By 1917 the military situation on the coast had become fairly static. The great line of trenches that stretched across northern France ended here in the town of Nieuport, roughly half-way between Ostend and Dunkirk. The air forces of both sides had established bases behind the immediate front line and were increasing their effectiveness almost daily. On the Allied side, most of the squadrons of the Flanders Command were concentrated near Dunkirk, at St. Pol or Bergues, or a

Left to right: Ensigns E T Smith, D S Ingalls and K A McLeish USN standing in front of the CO's Office, Bergues, France, April 1918.

little further up the coast at Bray Dunes, Furnes, Coxyde and Petite Synthe. The German airfields were sited, in the main, a mere forty miles north-west between Zeebrugge and Bruges at Stalhille, Uytkerke, Varssenaere, Houtave, Vlissinghem and further inland at St. Denis Westrem. Apart from bombing raids mounted from these bases Dunkirk was also within range of the batteries of heavy guns established by the Germans around Ostend. Fortunately St. Pol was just out of range.

The aircrew of the Seaplane Defence Squadron experienced for the first time that strange contrast between fighting and death in the skies over the Front Line and life in a normal town that was to become so familiar to aircrew in the great air battles over Great Britain and Western Europe during the Second World War. The average age of the pilots, including the CO was between nineteen and twenty. All were teetotallers through habit and choice and their aircraft each carried a girl-friend's name.

In the Autumn of 1917 the bombing power of the Flanders Command reached its peak with squadrons of D.H.4s and Handley Pages flying from the airfields at Bray Dunes and Petite Synthe. Much of the bombing was carried out at night against the German airfields and it brought swift retaliation. The pace of the air battle increased.

Although somewhat unsuited for the work, the Pups and Camels of the Squadron were pressed into service as night fighters. On moonlit nights, patrols were sent up to intercept raiders over Dunkirk although at St.Pol the facilities for night-flying consisted only of two rows of paraffin flares. On the night of 19 September, Slatter, airborne in his Pup, picked out the shape of a twin-engined Gotha against the lights of Malo-les-Bains. For an instant he lost it, but then he saw the flames from the engine exhausts and found that he was able to keep it in view. As he closed in behind the unsuspecting German his light Pup was all but thrown out of control by the propeller wash of the big machine ahead of him. Then quickly regaining his position he held his Pup in the turbulent wake and emptied a drum from his Lewis gun into the Gotha. After a further attack, he had the satisfaction of seeing the raider crash into the sea in flames. At least one Pup - N6179 - had certain modifications carried out to make it a special night-flying machine. Slatter tested this aircraft on 20 and 25 September and then carried out patrols in it on 25, 27 and 29 September and on 1 and 2 October before it was returned to England. On the night of 29 September Slatter attacked another Gotha, killing one of its gunners and damaging one of its engines, forcing it to land at Nieuport.

With the approach of winter, bad weather seriously hampered the Squadron's flying with fog and mist often forming over the low-lying sandy coast. But this did not prevent seaplanes from the base at Dunkirk returning two by two for much needed rest periods to Walmer. In the early days of the Squadron's existence the pilots had continued to fly seaplanes at night in addition to their normal duties in day fighters; however the Squadron itself had not been rested.

On 17 October 1917 Flt Lt J W Pinder, who had been posted in from 9 Squadron RNAS as a Flight Commander, destroyed a seaplane three miles north of Zeebrugge. Before leaving the Squadron at the end of August 1918 on transfer to 45 Squadron, Pinder was to claim a further eight German

WO II John Wesley, who was later commissioned and flew with the Squadron from 21 January 1918 until the end of the war. Trained as a carpenter, he was also the Squadron's Rigging Officer.

aircraft either driven down out of control or destroyed. In doing so he was able to join thirteen other pilots who claimed five or more victories that contributed to the one hundred and ten enemy aircraft brought down by the Squadron during the First World War.

The Camels had become an essential part of the air defences along the coast. In order to contribute towards the cost of the war various parts of the Empire set up funds to pay for aircraft which were then presented to the RNAS or RFC. On 20 October two such Camels arrived on the Squadron, B6399 *Punjab No. 43 Jhang Gujaret Si* and B6400 *Lady Ho Tung* subscribed by Hong Kong. With the increase in bombing operations the fighting had been fierce, and in the month of October alone sixty-one pilots had been lost from the bases around Dunkirk. Despite such losses, the Squadron continued to have successes, on 27 October Slatter shot down an Albatros D III which crashed into the sea north-west of Ostend. In another engagement, typical of the Squadron's operations in the closing months of 1917, Flt Sub-Lts Brown, Lawson and Mayle destroyed an Albatros D V east of Nieuport. Brown was a particularly able and aggressive pilot. In 1918 he became a Flight Commander and was awarded the DFC and Bar for the fourteen victories he achieved during three hundred and seventy-four hours of operational flying. He later served throughout the Second World War and retired from the Service with the rank of Air Vice-Marshal.

In December Flt Sub-Lt G C MacKay recorded the first of his eighteen victories with the Squadron; this total made him the highest scoring of the Squadron pilots in the First World War. Born in Toronto on 17 May 1898, MacKay initially joined the Seaplane Defence Flight on 2 November 1917 and stayed with the unit until the end of the war. Promoted to Flight Commander in 1918, he amassed over three hundred hours of operational flying, was twice wounded, and received the DFC, the Belgian Order of Leopold and the Croix de Guerre. On 4 December, together with Pinder, he destroyed an Aviatik C III in the Houthulst-Zarren area. The next day accompanied again by Pinder and also Flt Sub-Lts M L Cooper and J deC Paynter an Albatros two-seater was destroyed four miles NW of Wenduyne. Again, on 19 December, when MacKay was in action flying Camel B6407, he caught another Albatros and forced it down out of control between Ostend and Zeebrugge.

There was no precise or uniform procedure during the First World War for the submission and recording of claims for aircraft brought down. The RNAS allowed claims for German aircraft driven down out of control and also allowed shared claims crediting each pilot engaged with the victory. The daily records amalgamated at Headquarters were also less than totally reliable since the activities of some squadrons, particularly those of No.5 Group based on the Belgian coast, were not included in the daily communiques of aerial activity. The published daily and weekly totals of enemy aircraft destroyed accordingly did not include those involving the pilots of Nos.4, 9, or 13 Squadrons RNAS. This situation continued for the whole of the Squadron's service with No.5 Group.

Eventually the weather brought some respite from combat; three days before Christmas 1917 the weather clamped in completely and no operations interfered with the seasonal festivities.

The New Year opened with the CO in hospital as the result of a flying accident on 29 December. Flying a new Camel that had only been delivered two weeks before, and following a series of low-level aerobatics, he had crashed into the hospital where his fiancée was a nursing sister and for whose benefit he had been performing. As one of his Flight Commanders pointed out later, at least he had crashed where he was sure to receive the best medical attention and tender loving care. Following this accident, the first few weeks of 1918 found the Squadron under the temporary command of Flt Cdr R Collishaw DSO, DSC (later Air Vice-Marshal R Collishaw CB, DSO & Bar, OBE, DSC, DFC). Collishaw, known as "The Canadian Ace", already had thirty-eight victories to his credit, largely secured with Nos.3 and 10 Squadrons RNAS, when he arrived at St. Pol on 24 November as "A" Flight Commander.

Earlier in the year, in the middle of July, he had crashed just inside the Allied lines as the result of a bizarre accident in a Triplane. A fragment of a shell casing from German anti-aircraft fire - "Archie" - had struck the nose of his aircraft and cut the wire cable which helped to secure two large metal side plates extending back from the engine cowling. Both plates flew off, and while one of them disappeared harmlessly, the other lodged itself vertically between the leading edges of the two starboard lower mainplanes. With his aircraft in an almost uncontrollable state, only his first class airmanship enabled him to regain the Allied lines before putting the Triplane down in a controlled crash that tore off its undercarriage.

Five days later Collishaw was awarded the DSC, and less than two weeks afterwards he received, in recognition of his thirty-eight victories, the DSO. At the end of July he was given three months leave in Canada and on his return to France he joined the Seaplane Defence Squadron.

He was soon back in action and on 10 December, after a number of flights to familiarise himself with the Camel, he drove down out of control an Albatros D V over Ostend. Nine days later, while leading a section of three aircraft escorting D.H.4s which were spotting for ships shelling shore targets, two Albatros two-seaters were encountered between Ostend and Zeebrugge. MacKay, who was flying one of the other Camels, followed an Albatros down and fired two bursts. The observer was seen to stand up in his cockpit, hold both of his arms up in the air and then fall right out of his machine which went down out of control. The other Albatros escaped but later the section met a formation of four Albatros and Collishaw surprised one of them and sent it down out of control.

During December and January the Squadron frequently found itself providing fighter cover for the aircraft spotting for naval guns bombarding Ostend. On one such occasion, on a bitterly cold day, Collishaw was leading the Squadron at 20,000 feet over Ostend when a formation of German fighters was seen coming up to challenge them. As he led one flight down onto the enemy and attempted to open fire, nothing happened as both guns were frozen and nothing he could do would clear them. Collishaw decided that although he could not shoot at anyone, he would continue to lead the Squadron. As the Germans came up the Camels dived down onto them, and each time the enemy dived away. On landing Collishaw discovered that not only had his guns been frozen but so had those of all of the other Squadron aircraft. Each pilot had assumed that only his guns were unserviceable and had stayed to support the others, adding to the show of strength. Years after the end of the war, Collishaw met the pilot who had led the German formation. He discovered that the Germans had been in exactly the same situation; every aircraft's guns had been frozen. Each pilot had thought that only his guns were not working, but had stayed to support his comrades. As Collishaw says in his autobiography "It was surely one of the fiercest and most harmless combats of the war".

In January, with the return to flying duties of Ronnie Graham, Collishaw was posted to take command of No.3 Squadron RNAS, the unit he had served with briefly in early 1917.

The New Year also brought yet another change of name. Already the existing designation, Seaplane Defence Squadron, had become out-dated, since for some months the Squadron had been carrying out all the tasks of a typical fighter unit and had not merely been engaged in seaplane defence work. In mid-January 1918 the Seaplane Defence Squadron became No.13 Squadron, RNAS. The superstitions associated with this number seemed all too well founded as the first days under the new designation brought weather that precluded all flying. When the weather did lift, the aircraft were flown to the Squadron's new base at Bergues which had been assigned to it at the same time as its new name. The distance flown was not very great as Bergues, where the Squadron was to stay until almost the end of the war, was only six miles south-south-east of St. Pol. The move was necessary since, as the air services at Dunkirk had expanded, the small field at St. Pol had become rather overcrowded.

Bergues was a considerably larger airfield; roughly triangular in shape, it housed one squadron in each corner. The two other units on site were the old partners from St. Pol, No.2 (photo-reconnaissance) Squadron and No.17 (anti-submarine) Squadron which had also been formed from the Seaplane Base at Dunkirk. The airfield at Bergues was situated on a slight rise in the ground that enabled it to drain a good deal better than the surrounding low-lying countryside. This enabled the light Camels to operate from its natural grass surface even in the wettest conditions.

On 29 January, a formidable patrol consisting of Flt Cdr L H Slatter and Flt Sub-Lts M L Cooper, J E Greene, G C MacKay and J deC Paynter attacked and destroyed a seaplane which crashed in flames one hundred yards off Blankenberghe Pier. The next day Paynter was flying with Flt Cdr M J G Day when the two-seater seaplane they attacked exploded in mid-air, the wreckage falling just north of Ostend.

The first weeks of 1918 spanned the operational career of one of the most remarkable pilots to fly with the Squadron; his life and death reflect the spirit that carried so many young men to the Western Front in the years 1914-1918. Miles Jeffrey Game Day had already proved himself a first class pilot testing aircraft at the Royal Navy's Isle of Grain establishment. He was, however, not only an excellent pilot but he also had a gift for poetry, and his verses on flying had gained for him an increasing reputation. Admirers of his work wished him to give up flying completely and devote himself entirely to writing, which promised him a secure future. For Day, such promise for his future only caused an uneasiness which became a conviction that, if his future was so secure, then his work at Grain was making an insufficient contribution to winning the war. Accordingly he volunteered for combat duties.

On 19 December 1917 he joined the Squadron as Acting Flight Commander. During the five-week period preceding his death in action, he gained six victories in engagements with enemy aircraft and was awarded the DSC. On 3 January he forced down what he believed was a Rumpler two-seater out of control over Dunkirk. While leading his section on patrol over the Fleet on 25 January, a two-seater seaplane was seen and chase given. This pursuit soon brought the patrol into action with six Fokker Triplanes and two Albatros scouts. The trap, if such it was, failed and, during the engagement, Day forced one of the Fokkers down out of control over Standen. On 30 January, together with Paynter, he destroyed another Rumpler two-seater two miles north of Ostend. On 2 February he forced down yet another Rumpler, which was captured near Oostkerke, and on 19 February, while leading his section of Paynter and Flt Sub-Lts, J C Stavin, E V Bell and G D Smith, a seaplane was shot down in flames east of Ostend. It was clear that Day brought to combat flying the same flair and single-mindedness that had made him such a successful test pilot.

On 27 February his short but illustrious career came to an end. Once again he was leading his flight, when more than six enemy aircraft were seen some distance away. Giving his Camel full throttle, he signalled to attack and soon drew ahead of his companions. He engaged the German patrol single-handed and a fierce dog-fight ensued. Before the remainder of his Flight could join the action, the overwhelming odds had prevailed. Day's aircraft was shot down in flames over the sea twenty-five miles off Dunkirk by a seaplane of Seeflug II flown by Flugmeister Dreyer and Leutnant Franz. Even though he had been so briefly with the Squadron, his death was keenly felt by his fellow pilots at Dunkirk, and to the end of its existence a copy of his book of poems remained one of the Squadron's cherished possessions.

In February 1918 came the first of a small group of American Naval pilots who were to serve with the Squadron when Lt C Meyer arrived from the US Aviation Instructional Centre at Dunkirk. Although he flew only a few patrols before returning to the Centre on 5 March his attachment marked the beginning of a mutually beneficial relationship.

US Naval flying corps had been authorised in 1916, but when America entered the war in April 1917 little had happened, and the strength of the corps was 48 officers and 239 enlisted men equipped with 54 training-type aircraft. The first overseas unit arrived in Europe in June 1917, and a base was established at Dunkirk on 1 January 1918. The outstanding unit contributing to the early growth of US Naval Aviation was the First Yale Unit, an unofficial privately-sponsored organisation of college students formed in 1916 to produce naval aviators. After initial training at West Palm Beach, Florida, and Huntington Bay, New York, and further training in France, two members of the First Yale Unit, Ensigns D S Ingalls and K McLeish, soon to be joined by a member of the Second Yale Unit, E T Smith, were sent to the RFC training school at Gosport for instruction as scout pilots. After instruction at Gosport, the three Americans completed their training at the RFC gunnery school at Turnberry, Scotland, and arrived at the US Naval Air Station at Dunkirk on 21 March 1918, the same day that the Germans under Major General Ludendorff launched their powerful Spring Offensive, the "Kaiserschlacht".

After a short sharp artillery and gas barrage, the German Army, reinforced by divisions transferred from the Russian Front, over-ran the Allied trenches and strong points, and broke into open country, advancing as much as forty miles along a seventy-mile-wide front. Amiens was threatened, and General Sir Hugh Gough's Fifth Army was all but destroyed. During the aerial fighting, Allied losses of aircraft and pilots reached the highest levels ever. At the end of March, Ludendorff attacked again, striking at the British First and Second Armies along the River Lys, less than thirty miles from Dunkirk. Although the Squadron was not directly engaged in the fighting over the Front, the effects of the heavy losses were felt as four experienced pilots, Flt Sub-Lts W J MacKenzie, F C Stovin, E V Bell, and R N Ball, who had all come from 12 Squadron RNAS at the end of 1917 and the beginning of 1918, left for 9 Squadron, RNAS, which had recently returned to France, with its Bentley-powered Camels, to reinforce the hard-pressed RFC squadrons over the Western Front. Flt Sub-Lt W A Moyle was also posted away to 3 Squadron, RNAS, now commanded by Ray Collishaw, and attached to the RFC, while Flt Lt P E Beasley went to join 11 Squadron RNAS which had reformed as a bomber unit based on the French coast in January. Flt Sub-Lt L C Messiter had a close shave on 24 March, when he was forced down into the sea by a Pfalz D III, and his aircraft sank in the West Deep off Nieuport; fortunately he was picked up by a French torpedo-boat.

As the Allied losses mounted, the Commanding Officer of the US Naval Station at Dunkirk, Lt G Chevalier, offered the services of some of his pilots to the squadrons stationed at nearby Bergues. The offer was immediately accepted, and on 29 March 1918 three Ensigns, Dave Ingalls, Kenneth McLeish and "Shorty" Smith, were assigned to the Squadron. They were joined by Lt W P Havilland who had served with the Escadrille Lafayette, and was currently Chief Pilot at the American base.

Reinforced by the Americans, and with the pilot strength standing at fifteen, the Squadron was ready for its next task in the war. The complement of each RNAS and RFC squadron had originally been twenty pilots. This had initially been reduced to eighteen, but so heavy had been the losses in the heavy fighting of 1917 that by the opening of the last year of the war a squadron's pilot strength had been officially reduced to fifteen.

As the British and French Armies prepared for their own Spring Offensive, a complete reorganisation of the air forces on the Belgian coast was undertaken. In March 1918 it was decided that No. 61 Wing of the Flanders Command, which consisted of Nos. 1, 2, 10, 13 and 17 Squadrons RNAS, should be attached permanently to the Dover-Dunkirk Command for operations with the Naval forces. However, due to the shortage of fighter squadrons at other points along the Western Front, Nos. 1 and 10 Squadrons RNAS were detached from the Wing and indeed never returned. As the projected American squadrons had some difficulty in forming, No. 13 Squadron RNAS remained the only fighter unit in the Command.

The Squadron's last significant bombing operation against the enemy as a naval unit took place on the night of 26 March, when Slatter led eight Camels against the seaplane base at Ostend. The main target was the heavily protected hangar complex surrounding the inner basin of the harbour. Each aircraft carried one 50-lb bomb slung under the fuselage and the attack was delivered from between 100 and 500 feet. Over the target, twelve large searchlights lit up the sky and gave ample scope to the numerous anti-aircraft and machine-gun positions around the base. Although at the time no results could be ascertained due to the intensive ground fire, it was estimated that six of the eight bombs had fallen on the target. Aerial photographs later showed that considerable damage had indeed been inflicted on the hangars. On the return trip, Slatter, always eager to harry the enemy, attacked the German airfield at Vlissinghem and succeeded in extinguishing the airfield lights.

On 30 March a Low Fleet Patrol flown by Lt C P Brown and Flt Sub-Lts G F C Hopewell and R I Whiteley saw two two-seat Rumplers and two two-seat seaplanes at 1,000 feet ten miles north-west of Zeebrugge. The Camels climbed into position, and as they attacked the enemy aircraft turned inland towards Blankenberghe. The Camels pursued them, continuing to attack, and fired some 1,100 rounds in all but without decisive effect.

The first raid in which the Americans took part was a rather more domestic affair which took place on the night of 31 March/1 April 1918 to mark the passing of the Royal Naval Air Service. Bad weather had washed out any flying on 31 March, and the target for the evening was the Mess of No. 2 Squadron, RNAS. Having exhausted that squadron's supplies of alcohol all the chairs, windows, pictures and glass were destroyed, following which the process was repeated at No. 17 Squadron's quarters. Here the damage was compounded when a red-hot stove was knocked over. When it was set up again, someone crawled onto the roof and dropped a smoke bomb down the chimney which succeeded in blowing the stove all over the room, blinding the combatants and ruining everyone's uniform. The party finally broke up when No. 2 Squadron unlimbered two fire extinguishers which were discharged at the invaders; the Squadron's journey back to its own quarters was enlivened by everyone pushing each other into the small canal that ran along the side of the road. Two of the party disappeared from view entirely. The first patrol as an RAF unit took place the next day.

Camel B7234, frequently flown by Flt Sub-Lt R I Whiteley. (J M Bruce/G S Leslie Collection)

CHAPTER TWO - ROYAL AIR FORCE 1918-1919

In November 1917 the Royal Air Force (Constitution) Bill received the Royal Assent, and on 1 April 1918 the world's first independent Air Force came into being. No.13 Squadron RNAS attached the prefix two hundred to its number, as did all other RNAS squadrons, and assumed its new designation, No.213 Squadron, Royal Air Force. The ranks for officers in this new arm of the services were not introduced until 27 August 1919 and, for the remainder of the war, Army ranks were used, Sqn Cdr Graham taking the rank of Major. Air Force Memorandum No 2, published in March 1918, set out the regulations for this new service, and on 15 September 1919 a new blue/grey colour was approved for the new uniforms; prior to this date it had been decided that khaki would be worn as Service Dress but would not be compulsory until existing RFC and RNAS uniforms were worn out. Flanders Command became No.5 Group, RAF, and the four squadrons at Bergues formed No.61 Wing.

Despite the activities of the previous evening that distinguished the passing of the Royal Naval Air Service, the Squadron marked the first day of its new existence as a unit of the Royal Air Force in appropriate style. The morning Low Fleet Patrol, airborne at 09.30 hours, consisting of eight Camels flown by Greene, Cooper, McKay, Horstman, Gray, Beasley, Brown and D G Smith, returned at 11.15 hours with nothing to report. Later three of the newly-arrived American pilots, Havilland, McLeish and E T Smith, carried out test flights in the local area. It was left to a Low Fleet Patrol flown between 13.35 hours and 15.25 hours by the experienced trio of Lts Greene, Cooper and McKay, who had been heavily engaged in the raids of the previous evening, to make the day memorable with the destruction of three enemy aircraft over Zeebrugge. Two of these were from Seeflug 1; one aircraft, flown by FlugObermaat M Behrens and Lt D R Hauptvogel, was shot down in flames by Cooper, and the other, flown by Flugmaat Fricke and Lt zur See Tornau, was probably shot down by Greene. John Edmund Greene, born in Winnipeg on 2 July 1894, had joined the RNAS in 1916 and arrived on the Squadron at the end of October 1917. During the final year of the war, he brought down fifteen enemy aircraft, the majority being the formidable Fokker D VII. The last of his successes was achieved on 14 October 1918 when, together with Lt K MacLeish USN, a Fokker D VII was forced down out of control over Ardoye. Later the same day, he was shot down over the Belgian lines, probably by pilots of Jasta 43. He was buried close to the spot where his aircraft crashed.

A patrol on the following day, Kenneth McLeish's first over enemy lines, was less eventful, but nevertheless instructive. As McLeish admitted in a letter home: "I took it more or less for granted that any bus I saw over the lines would be a Hun!". He continued; "We spied some Hun seaplanes off in the distance and proceeded to climb and get into the sun. When we had our position we nosed down and dove at them. I had mine all picked out, and became so

Left to right: Lt J A C Tayler, Lt W E Gray, Capt F G Horstman, Lt J W Pinder, Lt R A Talbot, Lt S M N Hancock, at Bergues, early May 1918. (J M Bruce/G S Leslie Collection)

absorbed in my sights that I forgot to look at the leader. When I looked, he had come out of his dive and was turning away. This sort of rocked me, as I was all alone. I decided not to open up, but to get back into formation. The old Huns were diving away like blazes for shelter. I flew directly over one with my eye on him all the time, and keeping both height and the sun. I was just praying that he would open on me, as I had him cold, but nothing happened. Thank the Lord I didn't fire! They turned out to be Allied machines!".

Attachment to the Dover - Dunkirk Command for operations with the Royal Navy meant that, in the next two months, much of the Squadron's flying was to consist of High and Low Fleet Patrols as well as High and Low Offensive Patrols inland.

However the early part of April was marked by periods of particularly bad weather, which on a number of days precluded all operational flying; rain, fog, mist, and bone-chilling cold were often more hazardous than enemy activity. A special patrol planned for 7 April had to turn back due to bad weather over the patrol lines, however not before Lt K R Cole had become separated from the formation at 15,000 feet, and had been shot down ten miles north-west of Zeebrugge, becoming a prisoner-of-war. As the weather was too bad for fighter operations in the Squadron's target area, some of the Squadron's pilots were pressed into service flying the D.H.4 bombers of 217 Squadron, which was also based at Bergues. On such days the pilots returned wet, but above all cold. McLeish wore a pair of silk gloves as a first layer, covered by a pair of rubber gloves, and then a pair of fur-lined, fur-covered flying gloves. This he believed was the warmest possible combination. Yet two of his fingers still froze absolutely solid, and his thumb and one other finger were frostbitten when he landed; the damage was such that he was off flying for four days. At first the altitude of the high patrols, 20,000 feet, also caused severe headaches combined with nausea and dizziness after half an hour or so these effects wore off leaving only the splitting headache. Despite the introduction of the electrically-heated Sidcot flying suit, the intense cold induced by long hours on high altitude patrols remained a problem. A pilot of 202 Squadron flying photographic reconnaissance sorties had his nose, lips and both cheeks frozen so badly that they "turned brown and peeled off." To combat the affliction he grew a moustache.

The first of the American pilots left the Squadron on 16 April 1918, when Lt Havilland returned to the US Seaplane Base at Dunkirk en route to a staff position in Rome as part of the Americans campaign to support the Italian war effort by sending both Army and Navy pilots to Italian bases in the Mediterranean. Much to their annoyance, the end of their attachment was also in sight for the three Ensigns who returned to the US Seaplane Base on 20 April, as Kenneth McLeish saw it:- "We were all sent back to the base. The RNAS could use us, but the RAF are too good for us." The Squadron's regular establishment had been brought up to strength earlier in the month when Lt J A C Tayler had been posted in from the former RNAS base at Freiston, and Lts F L Cattle, C H Denny and J Reid had arrived from 212 Squadron on 7 April.

The Squadron's fighting strength still stood at fifteen pilots, with the same number of aircraft, of which normally

Camel B 3782 flown by Capt J deC Paynter in the Spring of 1918. (F Cheeseman via F L Cattle)

Lt G S Hodson, who served with the Squadron from 29 August 1918 until 17 March 1919. Later Air Marshal Sir George Hodson, CB, CBE, AFC. (J M Bruce/G S Leslie Collection)

between sixty and seventy per cent were serviceable. Co-operation with the Royal Navy also meant that the Squadron was closely associated with raids against Zeebrugge and Ostend. Although these operations were mainly naval in character, they do represent an early attempt at combined operations, and 213 Squadron, together with 202 Squadron, which carried out the preliminary photographic reconnaissance work, were the two RAF units chiefly involved.

Continual bombing and shelling of the harbour at Zeebrugge had persuaded the Germans to build their main repair base and maintenance depot for ships and submarines at the more distant town of Bruges. Early in 1918, aerial reconnaissance had shown that they were building ferro-concrete submarine pens, which were virtually bomb-proof, in the old harbour of the town. Bruges itself lies about ten miles inland and is connected to the North Sea, at both Zeebrugge and Ostend, by a canal which has an outlet in each harbour.

As early as 1915, plans had been drawn up to block Zeebrugge harbour and, with it, one entrance to the Bruges canal, but these had not been put into effect since it was hoped that a successful advance by the Army would put the harbour in Allied hands. However, following the collapse of Russia in 1917 and the German break-through on the Western Front, this prospect receded and, with the Army's opposition withdrawn, attacks on Zeebrugge and Ostend were given the go-ahead. By the time the final plans were drawn up, Admiral Bacon had been replaced as Commander of the Dover Patrol by Admiral Keyes, and the detailed plans previously drawn-up were modified.

The raid on Zeebrugge, as finally planned, was to have three inter-related and simultaneous actions taking place under the cover of darkness and a heavy smoke-screen. Over one thousand, seven hundred seamen and marines were to storm the Mole from the old cruiser *Vindictive* and capture the gun batteries mounted on the head of the Mole. At the same time, two old submarines loaded with explosives were to be used to destroy the railway viaduct which was supported by an iron framework of girders some six hundred yards long and which connected the Mole to the shore. As these actions were taking place, the three blockships were to enter the harbour and be sunk across the entrance to the Canal. At Ostend the block-ships, once through the smoke-screen, would steam straight for the canal entrance without the benefit of any support or diversionary activity.

On 11 April 1918, the attacking ships, seventy-four in all and under the command of Admiral Keyes, joined up off the Goodwin Sands some sixty miles from Zeebrugge. Whilst the ships were steaming across the Flanders Bight, elements of Nos.61 and 65 Wings, RAF, carried out the planned preliminary aerial bombardment. Between 1400 and 1525 hours Paynter led five Camels, flown by Hopewell, Horstmann, G D Smith, Slatter and McLeish, on a special bombing operation against the Zeebrugge Mole. Each aircraft carried a 50-lb bomb with a 2½-second delay fuse. The cloud base over the target was 1,000 feet and the plan was for the raid to approach as close as possible to Zeebrugge before climbing into the cloud; then, when judged to be directly over the Mole, to dive down to about 300/400 feet and release their bombs. The plan worked well, particularly for the first aircraft; after that the anti-aircraft fire became progressively more intense, and by the time McLeish, flying the last aircraft, made his attack, all hell seemed to have broken loose. The rapid-fire pom-poms were putting up a barrage in front of him, and he watched the tracer bullets "doing loops and split turns round my neck". There was so much smoke that he lost sight of the target and pulled back up into the cloud base; he eventually dropped his bomb on another target and returned to Bergues having learned never to fly as the last machine in a daylight, low-level, bombing raid. Despite the heavy anti-aircraft and machine-gun fire, bombs from the other five aircraft were seen to fall near sheds 1 and 3 on the Mole and on two large steamers moored near shed No.3.

On the same day, 217 Squadron flew its D.H.4s on anti-submarine and reconnaissance patrols and 202 Squadron photographed the harbour from its D.H.4s. Despite worsening weather, two bomber squadrons from No.65 Wing carried out night-bombing attacks, although only two aircraft from 215 Squadron took part in the raid. In the event, a critical shift in the wind direction that would have made an effective smoke-screen impossible, led Admiral Keyes to abandon the raid at 00.45 hours when the attacking fleet was only some sixteen miles from Zeebrugge.

The raid was now planned for the night of 22/23 April, St. George's Day. In the intervening period, the German breakthrough in Belgium led to the redeployment of the squadrons on the more advanced airfields, and to the Handley Page squadrons, Nos.207 and 215, being withdrawn from the area. The loss of this strong bombing force meant that the fighter-bomber work of the Squadron assumed an even greater importance.

During the afternoon of 22 April, although the weather deteriorated considerably, the wind remained in the right quarter - north-east - for an effective smoke-screen to be laid, and the order was given for the raid to proceed. The deteriorating weather, however, prevented the planned initial aerial attacks, and the naval action commenced around mid-night. The attack by the seamen and marines on the Mole

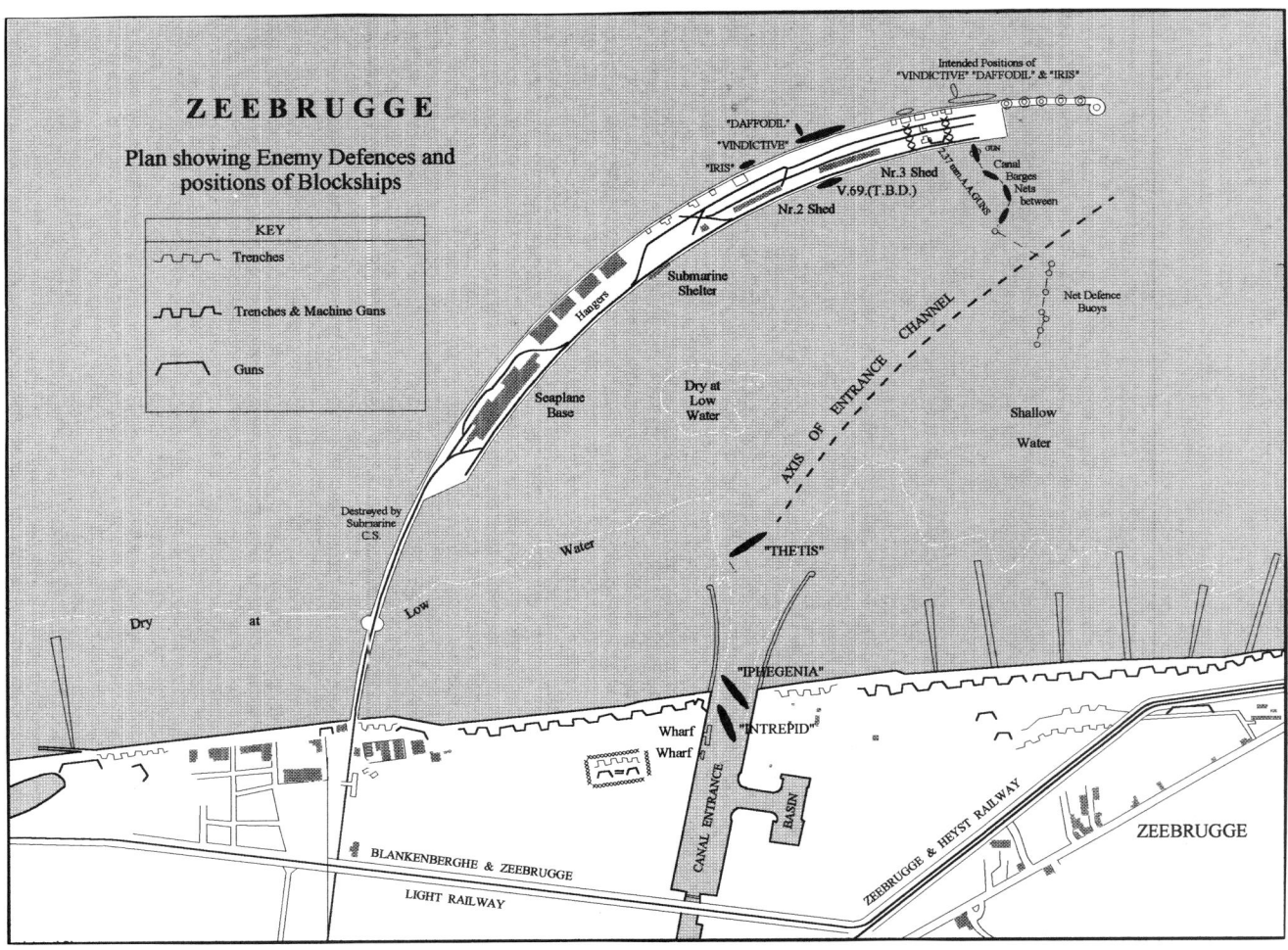

itself has become a byword for gallantry and courage even though the Mole was neither secured nor the gun batteries on it captured as intended. As the blockships entered the harbour, a huge explosion announced that the submarine *C3*, under the command of Lt Sandford RN, had rammed the viaduct and had been successfully detonated, destroying all communications between the Mole and the shore.

The first of the three blockships, HMS *Thetis*, was severely damaged by gun fire and her propellers were fouled by the protective netting through which she cut on her way towards the mouth of the Canal. The action on the Mole, however, was engaging most of the Germans' attention which enabled HMS *Intrepid* and HMS *Iphigenia* to move in well past the piers that marked the entrance to the Canal and to be sunk there as planned.

At Ostend, the blocking attempt failed completely since the crucial Stroon Bank marker buoy, from which the course to the Canal entrance was to be set, had been moved a mile to the east. In the darkness, and shrouded in the dense smoke-screen, this was not apparent and the ships grounded well to the east of the harbour entrance.

With first light on 23 April, and despite low cloud and poor visibility, photo-reconnaissance patrols were flown which showed the blockships across the Canal entrance at Zeebrugge. These photographs did not however tell the full story and after twenty-four hours, during which the Ostend entrance was used, submarines were again able to leave and enter the Canal at Zeebrugge, albeit not at all states of the tide.

On the day following the raid, as the weather improved, a series of raids was planned to hamper the German salvage work, and for the first time the Camels carried 112-lb bombs. The Squadron launched four attacks in the course of the day. At 1100 hours four aircraft, with Pinder leading Lts W E Gray, F G Horstmann and W A Windsor, attacked the Mole from between 700 and 2,000 feet and hits were scored, although Windsor was forced to jettison his bomb over the sea. At 13.10 hours, Slatter and Cooper arrived over Zeebrugge, but the presence of hostile aircraft prevented them from making a low-level attack. They released their bombs from 9,000 feet and intervening cloud obscured the results. Approximately one hour later Paynter, leading Smith and Lt J A C Tayler, who was carrying four 20-lb bombs, attacked from 1,000 feet. On the return flight to Bergues, the trio was attacked by enemy aircraft and Tayler evaded his pursuers by the unorthodox manoeuvre of spinning into cloud. Fortunately he was able to regain control of his machine and returned safely to base at Bergues, as did Paynter and Smith. In the early evening, between 17.00 and 17.10 hours, Graham led seven Camels flown by Pinder, Brown, Greene, Cooper, MacKay, Windsor and Lt G F C Hopewell on the final raid of the day. Once again hits were scored on the Mole. The raid seemed to come as a surprise to the Germans as the anti-aircraft and return machine-gun fire were lighter than in the earlier attacks, and no enemy aircraft were seen. Following the Squadron's good work, both Graham and Slatter were mentioned in dispatches for the outstanding part they had played in the follow-up raids.

The remains of the Squadron hangars and aircraft after a German bombing raid on 29 June 1918.

The Camel of Lt J A C Tayler entangled in a Bessoneau hangar after low-level aerobatics, 7 August 1918.

A further bombing raid planned for 27 April had to be diverted because of bad weather over Zeebrugge harbour. As an alternative, the aircraft which took off at 1400 hours led by Paynter and flown by Pinder, MacKay, Hopewell, Greene and Brown, attacked targets of opportunity as they occurred. An aircraft stores depot at Lisseweghe was bombed and shot up together with the nearby railway sheds, permanent way and canal. Over Houtave airfield, intense machine-gun fire was encountered, and as the attack was pressed home from between 150 and 500 feet Pinder noticed that a football match was in progress. Hits were scored on the hangars - not the players! In the vicinity of Uytkerke airfield, the flight was attacked by enemy aircraft and Brown drove down an Albatros D V out of control. While he was over the airfield at 500 feet, he had seen an Albatros taking off, and as he released his bomb he was attacked from above and ahead by the Albatros. A circling match ensued and eventually Brown was able to fire thirty rounds from above and behind at point-blank range. The Albatros went into a vertical dive and was at 200 feet when last seen by Brown as he himself was chased out to sea by three more enemy aircraft.

In the ensuing days, pressure was maintained against both harbours. Fifteen aircraft attacked the Zeebrugge Mole again on 2 May, when hits were scored both on the Mole itself and the seaplane sheds nearby. Four days later the Ostend seaplane base was the target for eight Camels led by Paynter. Pinder hit some sheds and saw that fires had been started; Paynter, Brown and Hopewell did not reach the target but jettisoned their bombs over the sea in order to pursue enemy aircraft they had seen in the distance. Paynter reported that he could see the fires started by Pinder's attack from two miles out to sea. On 10 May, Graham led MacKay, Greene, Windsor and Lt J Reid on a combined reconnaissance and bombing sortie over Ostend and Zeebrugge. The aircraft were carrying the now usual 112-lb bombs, which on this occasion were armed with a 2½-second delay fuse. Hits were recorded on the Mole and the sheds by the three aircraft that arrived over Zeebrugge. Windsor had been forced to turn back over the sea with engine trouble, and Reid had lost formation and so returned to base.

On 8 May, in between these bombing raids, Brown was in a flight carrying out an observation patrol over Wenduyne, when six enemy aircraft were seen; the flight dived in formation from 15,000 feet. Brown fired one burst at the left-hand machine, when two more enemy aircraft were seen climbing into sun behind the flight. The attack was then concentrated on these aircraft and Brown fired a sixty-second burst at 100 yards, but was then immediately attacked by three more Albatroses coming from the direction of Wenduyne. He fired a short burst with both guns into the cockpit of an Albatros D III which seemed to behave curiously for a moment, and then started to spin, at first slowly but soon faster and faster; it was claimed as driven down out of control. As the combat report of Capt Paynter sets out, he was even more successful during this attack.

As the naval raid against Ostend had not achieved its objective, a second plan was devised which entailed using the now badly-damaged cruiser *Vindictive* as a blockship by sinking her across the narrowest part of the channel into the harbour. When further bad weather delayed this operation, initially planned for the night of 27 April, another series of bombing raids was directed against the seaplane base at Ostend. In an attack on 6 May, a flight led by Paynter scored direct hits on the hangars which started fires that could be seen two miles out to sea. Paynter also destroyed an Albatros D V in the vicinity of Wenduyne.

Eventually, despite low cloud and lingering mist, final preparations were made for the raid on Ostend to take place on the night of 9/10 May, when the next high water occurred. The naval forces sailed from Dunkirk and Dover as darkness was setting in. Just as the blockships were leaving Dunkirk roadstead, Commodore Lynes was informed that all the buoys off Ostend had been removed. He called for confirmation of this unwelcome news, which had been obtained at the last moment by No.202 Squadron on a coastal reconnaissance patrol. These buoys were important because they not only indicated the positions for laying the smoke-screen, but they also served as starter-markers from which HMS *Vindictive* would set course. In the gathering darkness, Graham and MacKay set off from Bergues on a low-level reconnaissance mission over the mist shrouded coast. They thoroughly reconnoitred the approaches to the harbour, satisfying themselves that the buoys had indeed been removed. As soon as their report was received by the Naval command, prompt steps were taken to site a special lighted buoy at the crucial spot which, in the event, formed a good focal point for the raid. Once again, although nothing was spared in terms of bravery and courage, and although *Vindictive* entered Ostend harbour, it proved impossible to sink her squarely across the main channel. A low reconnaissance patrol reported that she was lying high out of the water between the piers marking the entrance to the canal and obstructing only one third of the channel.

The following day, five aircraft set out on a sortie with

Two of the many Canadians who flew with No.213 Squadron Capts W J Mackenzie and G C MacKay.

Lt H H Gilbert, who flew with the Squadron from 14 October 1918 until 16 March 1919.

Lt A B Rosevear in RAF uniform.

Lt F T Sargeant in his Sidcot flying suit.

Capt L H Slatter, OBE, DSC and Bar, DFC. One of the original pilots who formed the Seaplane defence Flight at St Pol in June 1917, he continued to fly with the Squadron until 2 July 1918. (N Franks)

Capt W E Gray, who flew with the Squadron from 16 December 1917 until 19 October 1918.

the combined objectives of reconnoitring Ostend harbour and bombing Zeebrugge. In the event only Graham, Greene and Mackay made it to the target area; Windsor had to return after developing engine trouble over the sea and Reid lost formation and so returned to base. Once again, hits were scored on the Mole and the sheds at Zeebrugge.

Under the combined weight of these aerial attacks and shelling by the monitors, the once-powerful seaplane units Seeflug I and II were withdrawn from the Belgian coast and established farther north, out of harm's way, at Kiel and Wilhelmshaven. The withp

23drawal of these two units and the opening of the Allied offensive on the Western Front brought a considerable change to the Squadron's operations. Although fighter patrols were still mounted, more and more of the flying was to be in a ground-attack role in support of the Belgian Army.

Hitherto the bulk of the flying had been in support of the Belgian Coast Patrol. It was due to the commander of this force that the Squadron acquired the hornet for its badge. As far as Cdr. Lynes was concerned, the fast fighters of the Squadron were his "hornets" that drove off the attacks of the German seaplanes. This *nom-de-guerre* appealed to the pilots and they quickly took it as their own. Thus when a badge was adopted, the hornet was taken as the centre-piece with the motto "*Irritatus Lacessit Crabro*", which is probably best translated as "When roused the hornet strikes".

After Zeebrugge, Admiral Keyes maintained the bombing strength of his command at a high level and impressive tonnages were dropped as the summer drew on. The main target area lay between Ostend and Bruges where the Germans had established numerous airfields. However these raids brought swift retaliation, and a snap raid on Bergues devastated the Squadron's corner of the airfield. This raid was delivered on the night of 29 June 1918, at the same time as an attack on Dunkirk itself. Direct hits on the hangars started fires which destroyed them and the twelve aeroplanes parked inside. There was no loss of personnel, however, as everyone was dispersed in huts on a farm some two miles from the airfield. By the following morning, despite the serious nature of the damage, the ground crews, assisted by working parties from the ships in Dunkirk harbour, had cleared the debris and the pilots had flown in replacement aircraft from the depot at Calais. The replacement of the aircraft had actually taken less time to complete than the paper work accounting for their loss. The crews of the German reconnaissance aircraft who flew over in the after-

```
                COMBATS IN THE AIR.(No.24)

Squadron No: 213                 Date: 8th. May 1918.
Type and No. of Aeroplane:       Time: 19.50
    Sopwith Camel B7254.
                                 Duty: O.P.
Armament: 2 Guns Vickers.        Height: 15,000 feet to G.L.
Pilot: Capt. J. de C. Paynter.          (Destroyed.........Three:.........
Observer: _____                Result {Driven down out of control......
Locality: Wenduyne.                     (Driven down.....................


REMARKS ON HOSTILE MACHINE:- Type, armament, speed, etc.
Albatross Single Seater Scouts. D.3.


                      NARRATIVE.
     I dived with formation of 5 Camels on six E/A Single
Seaters at 19.50. I attacked the leader who did a right hand hoick
and rolled into a spin. I followed him down, and attacked him again
when he flattened out. After stunting round one another for several
minutes I got on his tail at about 3,000 feet and fired a burst
with both guns. He staggered and fell into the sea, with left wing
down and engine on. I flattened out and was almost stalling while
trying to get my engine when I was attacked from behind and above
by another E/A. He shot past me and I regained my engine and hoicked
over him. After a few circles the E/A broke away and I fired a long
burst right down into his cockpit, he rolled upside down and fell
into the water. Immediately afterwards I was again attacked from
behind and above by a third E/A who also overshot me about 50 or 60
feet above me. I stalled under him and fired both guns right along
his fuselage which was ripped right open and he burst into flames
and fell in the sea. I then came home having expended all my
ammunition.
                           (Sgd.) J. de C. Paynter.
                                      Captain.

                           (Sgd.) R. Graham.
Certified true copy.                  Capt.
                                 Commanding Officer.
1939.                              No. 213. Squadron.
Original extracted for permanent
retention by the Squadron, see
A.M. File 655640/37.
```

noon must have been surprised and disappointed when they saw the Squadron's aircraft lined up as usual in full strength.

Every squadron had its share of pets and mascots, and the Squadron had an assortment of dogs of different shapes and sizes. One particularly intelligent animal, known as "Fritz", had been down in the bomb-shelter so often that he knew the sound of approaching German bombers and what it meant. With a dog's keen hearing, he could detect a raid approaching, and would make for the shelter well before any of the pilots, thus providing a very effective air-raid warning system.

During a daylight raid on 18 June, Capt J de C Paynter decided not to take shelter, and was fatally wounded by bomb fragments; five airmen were also injured. Paynter had joined the Squadron on 2 November 1917 on a posting from 9 Squadron, RNAS. Born on 17 May 1898 in Southsea, Hampshire, he initially saw service with 6 Squadron RNAS early in 1917. He was injured in a crash at Hinges and, on recovery, joined 9 Squadron RNAS. In the spring of 1918, following his transfer to 13 Squadron RNAS, he was appointed a Flight Commander. He destroyed or drove down out of control, sometimes with assistance, nine enemy aircraft and was awarded the DSC on 1 June, just seventeen days before he was killed.

Lt H H Gilbert sitting in the cockpit of his Sopwith Camel, 1918.

A group of Squadron Officers sitting on the steps of the chateau at Varssenaere that had served as the Officer's Mess for the German airfield which had been attacked by the Squadron on 13 August 1918. Back row left to right: Lt A B Rosevear, Capt W J MacKenzie, Lt G C Garner. Front row from left: Lt A H Turner, Capt Maine (Gunnery Officer), Lt H C Smith, Lt A H Pownall.

Combat in the air during June brought further losses, albeit that the month started on a successful note when, on 2 June, Pinder, Gray and Tayler forced a Pfalz D III down out of control over Moorslede. Towards the end of the month the news was less good; all contact with Lt K W J Hall was lost at 19,000 feet north-east of Nieuport on 21 June. He had joined the Squadron only the previous month, and eventually he was reported as a prisoner-of-war. Pinder also had his problems on 21 June when his propeller flew off while he was returning to base at 2,500 feet; he eventually made a forced landing just east of Bergues. On 27 June, Lt W G Evans, who had also only arrived on the Squadron in May, was posted missing having last been seen in a spin four miles north of Blankenberghe following an attack by four enemy aircraft of Marine Jasta 2; his loss was credited to Flugmaat Zenses. Two days later, in an encounter with aircraft from Jasta 52, Lt F L Cattle's aircraft collided with the Camel of Lt F P Pemble while being attacked by Vizefeldwebel Wadowski, both aircraft crashed near Les Moeres, and both pilots died later from their injuries.

Since early in the war, the Squadron had been engaged in low-flying attacks on enemy installations, even before the aircraft were modified to carry bombs. One such raid was carried out by Paynter on 25 January 1918. Operating from between ground level and fifty feet, he reported that he had found about eight men and, apparently, an NCO whom he attacked from about eight feet and fifty yards. He noted that for much of his patrol he was accompanied by a French Nieuport flying at about the same altitude and firing at everything in range. The effectiveness of such ground-attack sorties in the destruction of both materiel and morale has been well attested in subsequent accounts of the fighting on the Western Front. The dangers of such operations, and the high level of losses sustained by those involved, has also been well documented.

On 30 July Cooper was leading an High Offensive Patrol over Bruges when he saw five silver-sided Albatros D Vs at 16,000 feet. In the initial attack, he shot one down at close range, and the Camels then turned and flew towards the Allied lines, pursued by three German fighters. Four miles south-east of Ostend, Cooper's patrol was about to turn and attack its pursuers, when a patrol led by Capt. Pinder dived down on the Germans from the north. Again, in the initial attack, Pinder forced one of the Albatros D Vs down out of control. He then climbed again to join Gray, who was making a head-on attack on another enemy aircraft which went into a spin, levelled out at 6,000 feet, and then dived away towards Ostend. The next day Colin Brown forced a Rumpler two-seater down into the sea eight miles north-north-east of Nieuport, the crew being rescued by a Royal Navy destroyer

A flying accident on 7 August demonstrated the ever present danger of low-level aerobatics, when Lt J A C Tayler's aircraft became inextricably entangled with a Bessoneau hangar as the result of such activity. He is buried in the grounds of the military hospital at Coudekerque. He had joined the Squadron in April 1918 as a Flight Sub-Lieutenant from Freiston, the RNAS training establishment.

On 9 August 1918, the now-promoted Lt D S Ingalls returned to the Squadron after a period at the US Navy base at Dunkirk flying seaplanes, followed by an attachment to 218 Squadron, equipped with Handley Page bombers. During this second attachment to the Squadron, David Sinton Ingalls (later Rear-Admiral D S Ingalls DSM, DFC, USN) became the only American Naval pilot to destroy five enemy aircraft during the First World War. He also became the first American to win the newly-created Royal Air Force decoration - the Distinguished Flying Cross - which replaced the DSC for RNAS pilots and the MC for those serving with the Royal Flying Corps. He was soon back in action, and on 11 August, together with Colin Brown, he forced down out of control an Albatros two-seater seven miles north-east of Dixmude. On the same patrol over the front lines, another Albatros was brought down three miles east-south-east of

Squadron pilots and "Visitors", Stalhille, Belgium 1918. Seated: two Belgian Officers and two unidentified pilots. Standing Unknown, Lt P C Jenner, Capt J W Pinder, Unknown, Lt W E Gray, German Prisoner, Unknown, Maj R Graham, Unknown, German Prisoner, Unknown, Unknown, Lt C P Brown, Unknown, German Prisoner, Capt W J MacKenzie, Unknown, Unknown.

Dixmude by Lts C P Sparkes, W E Gray, A H Turner and E Toy.

The value of low-level bombing raids had been amply proved against the ports of Ostend and Zeebrugge and now the Squadron suggested that their scope should be extended. The plan was based on the simple idea that such raids should be mounted when weather conditions precluded normal offensive patrols, and when it was likely, for the same reason, that enemy aircraft would be grounded. From the study of operational records, and the Squadron's own experience at Bergues, it became clear that a well-planned and concentrated attack against an airfield could inflict damage out of all proportion to any likely losses.

When it was learned in July that strong German reinforcements were about to arrive at the important airfield of Varssenaere, an obvious target presented itself. A plan to launch a large-scale attack was carefully prepared, and Command gave its seal of approval. The attack was to be delivered at dawn from a low level by fighter aircraft. During the first two weeks of August, the Squadron carried out intensive practice in formation flying. The detailed plan involved Camels from Nos.210, 213 and 17 US Aero Squadrons in the first wave, to be followed an hour later by D.H.9 bombers of Nos.211 and 218 Squadrons. Fighter cover for the raid was to be provided by 204 Squadron at 5,000 feet.

All preparations were completed by 13 August, and eighteen of the Squadron's Camels took off at dawn. Two dropped out early on, one developed engine trouble and one lost formation and returned. Only thirteen of 210 Squadron's original eighteen aircraft took part, as two crashed on take-off, one suffered engine failure and two failed to pick up the formation. The twenty-nine remaining Camels of Nos.210 and 213 Squadrons formed up over Dunkirk with 17 US Aero Squadron, so that some fifty Camels in all set off in two long lines, flying parallel to the coast seven miles out to sea. On approaching Ostend, Lt. W E Gray of 213 Squadron, who was leading the raid, gave the signal and the whole force turned in towards the coast diving onto the target from about 5,000 feet. As the pilots swept in towards the airfield, they could see three flights of Fokkers lined up on the ground with their engines running and officers and mechanics standing about talking. For ten minutes chaos reigned as the fifty Camels unloaded ninety-six 25-lb and six phosphorous bombs on to the ill-fated airfield. The hangars and machines on the west side of the airfield were the Squadron's main target and they were largely destroyed either by explosions or the resulting fires. A Fokker biplane was set on fire together with half of a Gotha hangar. Once the bombs had been released, the aircraft remained over the target strafing the Fokkers and any personnel caught in the open. Lt C P Sparkes was close enough to note a Fokker biplane with a yellow wasp-like fuselage and silver and grey mottled wings. Between them, the Squadron's sixteen aircraft fired 7,500 rounds at ground targets. Despite the return fire, which caused some damage, all the aircraft returned safely to Bergues.

The report from the CO No.61 Wing to the GOC No.5 Group stated that the raid had been a complete success and had surprised the enemy. No hitch had been encountered. The escort work of 204 Squadron had been excellent, although its

Pilots of "C" Flight standing in front of Mackenzie's aircraft, 2nd Lt F T Sargeant, Lt G S Hodson, Lt H E B Holden, Capt W J MacKenzie, OC "C" Flight, 2nd Lt L A Coombes, 2nd Lt W S Phelps, Lt A H Pownall and 2nd Lt R A Pearce holding insignia from his aircraft.

Sopwith Camel, No.213 Squadron, Bergues, France, 1918.

aircraft had been heavily fired upon and most of them sustained hits. The Camels of 17 US Aero Squadron, it was noted, had descended well below the level of the hangars to shoot up ground targets. Many of Nos.210 and 213 Squadrons' machines had been hit by splinters of bombs and machine-gun fire. Great credit was due to Lt W E Gray for his good leadership.

Over forty aircraft had been destroyed and Varssenaere remained disorganised for a considerable period. Command was suitably impressed and further attacks on similar lines were encouraged.

Information subsequently obtained concerning this raid was set out in another letter:-

"The owner of the chateau at Varssenaere who was interned in Bruges for 4 years and was doing "hard labour" in the docks visited his old home on 22 Oct. 1918 and said that 20 Gothas and 18 Fokker Biplanes were destroyed and about 60 personnel killed.

The woman who keeps the estaminet adjoining the aerodrome said that 20 Gothas were destroyed and about 20 scout machines were destroyed or damaged and over 50 persons killed. Considerable damage was done to a large dump in the vicinity."

On 15 August a report by Capt J W Pinder on the performance and effectiveness of the Salamander (an armoured Sopwith Snipe with a 240 hp B.R.2 engine which he had tested at Brooklands) was sent to Headquarters No.61 Wing. He noted that the particular virtue of the aircraft was its armoured plating, which weighed six hundred pounds, and was arranged in the shape of a bath, enclosing the pilot, petrol, oil and ammunition tanks as well as the controls and engine pipes. Its weight made it heavier on the controls than the Camel and, although easy to fly, visibility was poor. He thought that it could almost be used, below 10,000 feet, for fighting the Albatros Scouts. It could reach 10,000 feet in approximately twelve minutes; the armour plating, which was between six and eleven millimetres thick, could stop a German armour-piercing bullet at 150 feet, except at the sides and all the plating would stop anti-aircraft shrapnel. The Salamander was armed with two fixed machine-guns and carried seven hundred and fifty rounds per gun; its bomb load was the same as the Camel's, four 20-lb Coopers or one 112-lb bomb. It was to be used primarily for trench strafing and attacking kite balloons, but Pinder thought that it would be admirable for the low-level bombing of Ostend or Zeebrugge. Practically the only way it could be brought down was to be hit by an explosive bullet in the main spar, thereby severing two flying wires, or by a direct hit from anti-aircraft fire. In view of the operations on which the Squadron was soon to become engaged, it was unfortunate that it was never equipped with this aircraft.

The success of the raid on Varssenaere airfield had been such that plans were soon put in hand at Bergues for a solo raid by the Squadron against the German airfield at Uytkerke, just outside Zeebrugge. The raid was scheduled for the first day when low cloud covered the area and so would give protection to the attacking formation. The site of the airfield was ideal for the raid, since it was near the coast, and the attackers could approach undetected out to sea before diving onto the unsuspecting target. Using aerial photographs of the airfield, the raid was carefully planned. It was timed to arrive over the airfield at 13.30 hours when it was hoped that most of the German machines would be on the ground, their crews having lunch. In the lead aircraft was Capt C R Swanston, who was subsequently awarded the DFC for his part in leading the raid. The Squadron's Bombing Report for 15 September 1918 sets out the story succinctly:

"Machines crossed target at 13.30 and 80 bombs dropped in close proximity to sheds. 11 direct hits on hangars and huts. One in north group burst into flames set fire to next. Workshops behind hangars also in flames, bomb right through middle.

Each of four flights took a different group of hangars so bombs were equally divided. Swanston and Gray DFC attacked A/A battery on a train with M/G. Ingalls and Hewett confirmed one truck in flames when firing ceased. Ingalls and Smith shot down a Rumpler on return.

MacKay slightly wounded in arm and leg.

Nelson slightly wounded in arm.

All machines on target, all bombs exploded, all machines returned.

80 bombs dropped   2210 rounds fired."

Lt D S Ingalls, USNRF was also awarded the DFC for his part in this raid, the first to be won by a US Navy pilot. As an Acting Flight Commander, he had led five aircraft in the formation of twenty, had obtained direct hits on his assigned targets, and had attacked six enemy aircraft single-handedly, driving one down out of control. In his

2nd Lt F T Sargeant sitting in Capt F W MacKenzie's Camel which is carrying the Squadron markings, representing a flash of lightning, and white elevators

Lt F T Sargeant of "C" Flight in the cockpit of his Sopwith Camel, F3121, in which he flew all of his combat sorties.

recommendation for the award, Graham wrote "His keenness, courage and utter disregard of danger are exceptional and are an example to all. He is one of the finest men the Squadron has ever had."

The letter confirming the details of the raid on Varssenaere also covered the Uytkerke raid :-

"Lt A R Talbot crashed into the sea off Mole 19.10.1918, he swam ashore and was taken to Blankenberghe. He obtained from various inhabitants the following information re the low bombing raid on 15 September by 213 Squadron on Utykerke Aerodrome.

110 German mechanics were killed. Considerable damage was done to most of the machines and many fires were started. The Huns compelled Belgian civilians to extinguish the fires. No Belgians killed or even injured.

Two young women, who were on very intimate terms with many of the German pilots, said that the German squadrons had moved as follows:-

    from Vlissinghem to Ghent
         Stalhille to Allemand
         Varssenaere to Anvers
         Uytkerke and Houtave to Mariakerke-pres-de-Gand
         Ichteghem to St Denis Westrem
         Zeebrugge to Wilhelmshaven
         Ostend to Kiel

Most of the airmen have gone to Cologne. Flt Cdr Saxenburg who was at Varssenaere claimed to have shot down 27 allied machines."

These two raids against airfields were only a part of the new plan adopted by the Allies as the Flanders Offensive opened on the Western Front. The Battle of Flanders was the last in the series of battles designed to break the German Army's fighting capability. The left wing of the attack, under the command of the King of the Belgians, was mounted by the Belgian Army supported by some French units and the British Second Army along a front extending from Dixmude to St. Eloi, just south of Ypres. The Belgians were short of aircraft and, as no other units could be spared from the Front, the Dunkirk Command was called upon to help. Thus No.5 Group, comprising No.61 Wing, which consisted of Nos.202 and 207 Squadrons flying D.H.4s, and Nos.210 and 213 Squadrons flying Camels, and No.82 Wing with No.38 Squadron flying F.E.2bs, No.214 Squadron flying Handley Pages and No.218 Squadron flying D.H.9s, was selected to support the Belgians in the field. II Brigade, made up of a further seventeen squadrons, was attached to General Plummer's Second Army. Bombing sorties were flown to disrupt the Germans' communications, and offensive patrols were mounted in direct support of the troops. During August and September these offensive patrols most frequently engaged Fokker D VIIs, widely regarded as one of the most effective of the German fighter aircraft and as having a definite edge over the Camel except when the latter was in the hands of experienced pilots. The Fokker was faster in a dive and could out-climb the Camel which was, however, much lighter on the controls and, being more manoeuvrable, could always turn inside its adversary. But such flying needed skill and experience.

On such a patrol, farther inland than usual, on 12 August, both Mackay and Greene drove down Fokker D VIIs out of control four miles south-east of Ypres. There were losses to come later on in the month. On 15 August, Lt C H Denny was on patrol when the formation was attacked by fifteen enemy aircraft and he was shot down and killed over the front-line between Dixmude and Ypres. On 21 August Lt W A Rankin was airborne with a patrol that was attacked by eleven enemy aircraft and his Camel was so badly shot up that he had to force-land near an aerodrome outside Roulers, from which experience he escaped unhurt. With the same problems as Rankin, Lt L C Scroggie chose the beach at Malo-les-Bains on which to land his badly damaged aircraft. Lt J Wooding was last seen being heavily engaged by enemy aircraft over the coast, and it was eventually learned that he was a prisoner-of-war. On 25 August, in a fierce engagement over Ostend, Mackay, Brown and Greene, all experienced and aggressive pilots, accounted for three Fokkers driven down ten miles east of the town. In this engagement, Lt E C Toy, who had only arrived on the Squadron the previous month, was shot down and killed.

In the second half of September, as the date for the big Flanders Offensive drew near, the pace of the aerial activity over the front-lines increased. On 18 September, David Ingalls, assisted by Lts H C Smith and G S Hodson, brought down a kite balloon in flames; the burning debris fell onto a hangar starting a fire which then engulfed two further adjoining hangars. Five days later, Lts Gray, Sparkes, Talbot and M H Hancock shared in forcing down a Fokker D VII east of Dixmude. The next day Hodson had further successes when, on patrol at 14.45 hours, he drove down a Fokker D VII out of control, then while attacking another saw it turn onto its back and crash onto the road one mile west of

Mitswaere. Later the same afternoon, when flying with Ingalls, they attacked a Rumpler over St Pierre Capelle and shot it down in flames. However, on 25 September an evening patrol was attacked by seven Fokker D VIIs three miles west of Thourout, and in the ensuing engagement 2nd Lt G Iliff was killed; he had joined the Squadron almost exactly one month previously. 2nd Lt J C Sorley was last seen attacking an enemy aircraft at 10,000 feet five miles south-east of Ostend, and his aircraft subsequently crashed north-west of Roulers after a prolonged dog-fight with Lt zur See Achilles of Marine Jasta 5; Lt C P Sparkes was also shot down, by Flugmaat Zenses of Marine Jasta 2, and became a prisoner-of-war. During the same encounter, Lt C J Sims and 2nd Lt R A Pearce attacked a Fokker D VII which fell into a spin, collided with another Fokker, and both crashed five miles south-west of Ostend. These two victories brought Sim's total of enemy aircraft destroyed to five in three months, and he was awarded the DFC. He received his commission in the RNAS on 23 October 1917, just two months before his eighteenth birthday, and joined the Squadron on 23 May 1918. He continued on operations until the end of the war, bringing down eight enemy aircraft and destroying one kite balloon.

The bombing area of No.5 Group consisted of the country north of the railway line from Courtemarck to Zarren and Lichtervelde. The distant offensive patrols, on which the Squadron was mainly occupied, were flown eastwards from the coast and north of a line from the sea to the Houthulst Forest. The main objective of the Belgian Army's land offensive was Ghent, the German's most important base in the area, and the Squadron's patrol lines therefore crossed the German's main supply and communication routes. Operating at extremely low altitude, these offensive patrols were very effective in spreading confusion among the convoys and troops moving up to the front. It was in this role that the RAF made its greatest direct contribution to the fighting on the ground; but it was here also that casualties were the heaviest. The pilots pressed home their attacks in the face of the severest return fire, while lack of experience in this type of operation and lack of practice in aircraft recognition among the ground forces combined to make the situation even more hazardous.

As secrecy was essential to the success of the opening of the ground offensive, there was no abnormal aerial activity preceding the attack on the morning of 28 September. During the night low cloud and rain covered the area, and only limited bombing activity was carried out by the D.H.4 squadrons against the German rail communications.

At 02.30 hours, the opening bombardment commenced and continued for three hours, until fifteen minutes before zero hour. The opening attack was made by nine Belgian Divisions, seven in the front-line, on a frontage of fifteen thousand yards from the junction with the British Second Army just north of Ypres to Lake Blankaert, some two miles south of Dixmude, against Passchendaele Ridge and Houthulst Forest. The day was one of uninterrupted success; the German artillery was weak, and soon died away under counter-battery action. By the evening of the first day, only the north-eastern tip of Houthulst Forest remained in German hands and the limits of the old battlefields of 1917 had been reached and passed.

The main targets for the squadrons of No.5 Group were the communication centres of Thourout, Courtemarck and Lichtervelde. The Squadron was heavily engaged on the opening day. Eight ground-attack sorties were flown in support of the advancing troops, the targets being German reinforcements and supply convoys moving up to the Front.

At 07.15 hours, Swanston led a formation of eight Camels, each carrying four Cooper 20-lb bombs, which succeeded in bombing a supply convoy and a train. The cost of such air support was high, however, and three pilots, Lts P C Jenner, shot down by Lieutenant M Lampel, W A Rankin, and 2nd Lt A Fletcher failed to return. Lt S M N Hancocks returned with his longeron shot through as did Lt R A Pearce with his aileron damaged by machine-gun fire. All three missing pilots, it was subsequently learned, were prisoners-of-war. On occasion, this information was provided by German pilots flying over the Allied lines, and dropping a bag containing lists of RAF pilots shot down, indicating whether they were unharmed, wounded or killed.

At 08.15 hours, a further thirteen aircraft, led by the CO, took off to continue the harassment. Two aircraft, flown by Greene and Lt G C Garner, had to return as they were unable to keep up with the formation. Lt J C Stone lost his way and landed at Bray Dunes, and his misfortunes continued when he crashed on take-off. Graham himself had to force-land at Lampernisse owing to engine trouble. The remaining nine aircraft attacked, as their first target, the camouflaged German camp at Pralt Bosch where three ammunition wagons were destroyed. Direct hits were also recorded on four field guns, and thirty horses were stampeded. On the Courtemarck to Thourout road, many men and horses were killed, and a large artillery battery on the edge of Courtemarck was bombed and shot up. A number of the Camels were hit by return machine-gun fire.

Swanston led his second sortie of the day at 10.15 hours, with the eight pilots who had returned from the first operation. In the course of the eighty-minute patrol, four trains were attacked, two of which were heading towards the Front.

The 11.30 hours patrol again had mixed fortunes; Brown and Lt H E B Holden had to return with engine trouble, while Lt A F Chick had to force-land at Lampernisse with three bullets through his windscreen and an engine that had seized up as the result of a bullet through the oil-tank. The remaining five aircraft bombed German Army billets at Wercken and also scored hits on Thourout railway station. The anti-aircraft and machine-gun emplacements protecting the camp at Pralt Bosch were also shot up, when a number of the patrol's machines were hit by ground fire.

Capt Cooper led the 13.15 hours sortie of seven aircraft, which revisited the army billets at Wercken and the railway station at Thourout. This town formed the northern apex of the important Zarren-Thourout-Lichtervelde triangle, which stood at the heart of the railway network between Ghent and the Front.

Capt Brown was again in the air at 14.30 hours, leading six Camels, although only four reached the target area. Lt H C Smith had to land at Hondschoote with engine trouble, and Lt W G Pearson had to return to base for the same reason. The remaining aircraft found four ammunition wagons loading at an ammunition hut near Wercken, and used their bombs and guns to disrupt the proceedings.

In the late afternoon, Graham was again in action leading six Camels, which bombed and shot up a train west of Lichtervelde, leaving it in flames. Many direct hits were also scored on some Nissen huts that were left smouldering near Courtemarck. As usual, the attacks were delivered from between 100 feet and 200 feet.

The last patrol of the day, airborne at 17.10 hours and consisting of Greene, Brown, Ingalls, Garner, Holden and 2nd Lt A B Rosevear, reported that no German troops were

2nd LT F W Radford standing by his overturned Camel, March 1919.

Camel C200 at Stalhille, Belgium. Arrived on the Squadron 14 November 1918, left for No. 11 Aircraft Park, Ghistelles 24 February 1919.

visible on the Gitsberg-Hooglede road itself, but wagons were attacked on a side-road and direct hits scored on a barn in which German soldiers were sheltering. In a last attack, twelve horse-drawn transports were bombed and shot up, killing twenty-five men and thirty-five horses. The combat report concludes "nothing was left standing".

By 16.00 hours, when the daily report to Wing HQ was drawn up, 185 bombs had been dropped and 6,600 rounds expended. It is clear that flying at such intensity could not be regarded as normal. Nevertheless, this special effort on the opening day of the Flanders Offensive does illustrate the disruption caused by the aggressive ground-attack sorties flown by the RAF squadrons in support of the advancing Armies and the hazards encountered in those operations. In recognition of his part in leading the Squadron in support of the Belgian and French Armies, Graham was awarded the Belgian Order of the Crown and the Croix de Guerre.

The Belgian Divisions resumed the attack at 06.00 hours the next day, encountering stiff resistance, particularly in the north of their sector. To the south, progress was better and the leading units reached De Ruiter, only two miles south-west of Roulers. In the north Dixmude, which had the same significance for the Belgians as Ypres had for the British Army, was captured by a wide turning movement from the south. Bad weather prevented the same level of air support being given as on the opening day, and it was not until the afternoon that the first patrol was airborne. A low offensive patrol of eighteen aircraft, sweeping east across the area immediately behind the German lines, caught a horse-drawn convoy of fifty wagons moving south into the battle area near Roulers. As the Camels went in, the convoy was completely broken up by bombs and machine-gun fire, and the wagons that were not destroyed were left scattered in the fields. Having disposed of the convoy, the patrol moved on to attack the railway station at Roulers. One mile east of the town Brown drove down a Fokker D VII.

Bad weather, with heavy rain, set in overnight and continued throughout 30 September, precluding any effective air support for the Armies, which continued to make good progress. However, by the following day, the bad weather and appalling road conditions slowed the advance which was also meeting increased resistance as the Germans brought six new divisions into the line.

As the weather improved during the first days of October, the Squadron resumed operations, harassing the retreating German troops from between 20 and 300 feet. The price, however, was high, and losses to the intense ground fire mounted. On 2 October, the Squadron lost one of its long-serving members when Capt M L Cooper's aircraft was hit by machine gun fire and spun straight into the ground while he was bombing a train north-east of Gitsberg. Maurice Lea Cooper was only eighteen years old when he joined the RNAS as a Flt Sub-Lt on 29 April 1917. He was initially posted to 9 Squadron, RNAS, and joined the Seaplane Defence Flight on 7 November 1917. Between December 1917 and July 1918 he destroyed one enemy aircraft, and shared in the destruction of three others, and was involved in driving two down out of control; he was awarded the DFC in June 1918. After serving as a Flight Commander, he was posted away from the Squadron to No.5 Group Headquarters on 17 September 1918. Although officially serving at Headquarters, he was still based at Dunkirk, and he continued to fly on operations as the Flanders Offensive opened. It was one of the cruel facts of operational life that flying skill and experience contributed less to the chances of survival in the ground strafing role than they did in aerial combat with enemy fighters. Another aircraft was lost when 2nd Lt W H Herd experienced engine failure over the sea; while attempting a forced landing alongside the Royal Navy monitor *General Craufurd*, he actually ran into the side of the ship and his aircraft sank; fortunately he was rescued.

These low-level patrols contrasted with the high-level offensive patrols, flown above 10,000 feet, to combat the sweeps of the German fighters. Such patrols often encountered the formidable Fokkers, whose pilots fought no less fiercely as their armies retreated towards the Rhine. Much of the opposition encountered by the Squadron came from the Fokker D VIIs of Marine Feld Jagdgeschwader Flandern, commanded by Oberleutnant S G Sachsenburg, who at one time had been based at Varssenaere. Two encounters on 4 October illustrated the point.

The first patrol, airborne at 08.20 hours, initially engaged fifteen enemy aircraft, which were soon joined by five more. It was noted that five Spads remained circling above the fight for the whole of the engagement. The great success of the day fell to Brown, who shot down three Fokker D VIIs over Rumbeke. Greene destroyed another east of Roulers and Lt A H Turner shot down a fifth in flames, as well as driving down a two-seat Rumpler which was seen to land heavily in a field also near Roulers. To complete a most successful encounter, Chick forced another Fokker down out of control which crashed into a field. Several other enemy aircraft were engaged although no further claims were made.

An eighth aircraft was observed in flames, and a ninth was seen to crash, but at the time it was not known if these were friendly or enemy aircraft. When the patrol returned to Bergues, Lts K G Ibison and W G Upton were missing and it was realised that Upton's aircraft was the one seen in flames north-west of Roulers.

In the afternoon, fourteen Camels took off on an high offensive patrol, although within half-an-hour three had had to return to base with engine trouble. The remaining eleven saw nine Fokker D VIIs over Thourout at 17,000 feet and turned towards them, despite the German's height advantage, and engaged at 12,500 feet a few miles further on over Roulers. Greene was one of the first to score when the Fokker he engaged crashed into a field and burst into flames. He then turned his attention to another, which he drove down out of control and which crashed near his first victim just north of Iseghem. Chick drove another down and followed it until it disappeared, spinning, into a bank of cloud at 2,500 feet. Holden was attacked by eight Fokkers and went into a spin from which he recovered at 80 feet. As he pulled out, he stalled and shot down one of his pursuers who had inadvertently overshot. He was then attacked by another Fokker which also overshot and flew straight into the ground near Lampernisse. 2nd Lt J N Marchbank, who had joined the Squadron only six days earlier, crashed and finished the day in No. 14 General Hospital at Wimereux. With eleven enemy aircraft accounted for on two patrols, 4 October stands out as probably the Squadron's most successful day of aerial combat in the First World War.

The Camel, B7270, flown by Greene on his sortie, had something of a distinguished record. It was the aircraft in which Capt A R Brown DSC, of 209 Squadron, had shot down Rittmeister Manfred von Richthofen, Commander of Jasta I, on 21 April near Vaux-sur-Somme. Richthofen had in fact been killed by a single machine gun bullet, which the nearby Australian troops also claimed to have fired. Capt W J Mackenzie, who had first served with the Squadron as a Flt Sub-Lt from the middle of December 1917 until 27 March 1918, when he was posted to 9 Squadron RNAS, had also been involved in this famous air battle, in which he had been wounded. He returned to the Squadron on 8 October 1918 and continued to serve with it until after the end of the war.

After the initial successes of the first three days of the offensive, the poor state of the roads and the disorganised supply services of the Belgian and French Armies brought the advance to a halt. For just over a week the Armies paused to regroup and reorganise. By 14 October, the order of battle of the Group of Armies of Flanders pitched twelve Belgian Divisions, six French and ten British, with four cavalry Divisions in support, against the twenty-four Divisions of the German Fourth Army commanded by General Sixt von Armin. The battle plan was for the British Second Army to form a flank guard to the south and the Belgians to the north, while two French Corps were to make the principal attack in the centre to gain the Roulers - Hooglede Plateau extending north-north-east of Roulers, and then press on eastwards towards Ghent. Zero hour was 05.35 and the attack met with immediate success; besides the ground gained, up to two miles including the town of Roulers, over six thousand prisoners were taken.

The weather was fine and bright, but cold with ground mist that hampered air operations until about 11.00 hours. The three patrols flown on this day showed the other side of the coin from the successes of 4 October, and just how terribly dangerous bombing and offensive patrols were - whether high or low. A virtually full-strength patrol of twenty-three aircraft took off at first light, 06.00 hours, to carry out low level bombing raids on the town of Lichtervelde and the roads running south and east from it. Marchbank, who had returned to the Squadron from hospital only the day before, crashed on take-off but was fortunately unhurt. Lt F C A Thorpe was less lucky, and as a result of his crash on take-off he finished the day in Queen Alexandra's Hospital. Over the target area, intense machine-gun fire was encountered and the three aircraft flown by Graham, Greene and Owen were hit but completed the operation. Lt H C Smith shot down an LVG which crashed east of Gits, but was himself wounded in the leg. In the course of the raid two convoys were shot up and bombed, and a total of one hundred and fifty-four 25-lb Cooper bombs was dropped.

At 09.30 hours the second sortie of the day, a high offensive patrol with bombs, was flown by nineteen aircraft. All the bombs had been dropped near Ardoye when the patrol saw fifteen Fokker D VIIs and two Fokker Triplanes at 16,000 feet. As the Camels climbed, the Fokkers pulled away and then dived to attack. In the ensuing dog-fight Greene and McLeish each helped the other in the destruction of two Fokkers. It is noteworthy that these two were experienced pilots. For the inexperienced it was a different story. By the end of the engagement, in which it was always clear that the Camels were too low at the outset, and hampered by bombs when the enemy aircraft were first seen, three pilots were missing - Lt W T Owen, whose aircraft had been damaged on the earlier patrol, 2nd Lt J C J McDonald who had joined the Squadron only nine days before and Lt L B McMurtry who had joined only five days before on 9 October.

The third patrol of the day, another high offensive patrol, this time without bombs, was airborne at 13.30 hours and returned at 15.10 hours. After patrolling for an hour, and when they were at 11,000 feet two miles north of Dixmude, the fifteen Camels saw eleven Fokker D VIIs at 8,000 feet with three more above at 12,000 feet. The Camels dived onto the enemy below and a fierce dog-fight ensued. Lt C J Simms destroyed two Fokkers and forced down another that was last seen, still spinning at 400 feet with white smoke streaming from its fuselage. Lt F W Radford shot down another which he followed down to 800 feet, where its spin took it into cloud over Eesen. After his first attack, Hodson saw the wing come off his target and it crashed near Beerst. MacKay found another Fokker in a vertical dive; he fired a short burst at it, the tail broke off and it went straight down over Zevecote. During the engagement two Camels were seen in flames and when the Squadron returned to Bergues three pilots were missing - Capt W E Greene, whose aircraft crashed at La Panne, and who was taken to the hospital at Penvyse with a fractured skull, from the effects of which he subsequently died, Lt K McLeish USN, who had only returned to the Squadron the previous day after a spell at the RAF training establishment at Eastleigh, and 2nd Lt F L R Allen. There was some mystery concerning MacLeish's disappearance and it was not until after the war had ended, and an aerial search was conducted on 30 December 1918 by a group of pilots, led by MacKay and consisting of Gilbert, Hancocks, Rosevear, Garner and Turner, that the wreckage of his Camel was found close to an old building in the flooded area near Penvyse. His body was then finally recovered and given a full military funeral.

In the course of the day, the three patrols had lost six pilots listed as missing, with a further two injured, one severely. Greene had flown on all three patrols and with fifteen victories to his credit he was the Squadron's second highest scoring pilot in the First World War.

The airfield at Stalhille after the Armistice.

Lt L A Coombs.

Clearly 14 October 1918 was a black day for the Squadron when it experienced the highest losses ever recorded in one day's operations. The problem of finding replacement pilots experienced earlier in 1916 and 1917 was now a thing of the past, and the same day seven new pilots were posted in from No.4 Aeroplane Supply Depot Pilot Pool at Guines.

In the middle of the month, another raid on a German airfield was planned, but in the event the raid on the primary target could not be carried out, and the CO led the Squadron on a roving mission to attack targets of opportunity as they appeared. Once behind the front line, a German troop train was found travelling east across the flat Belgian countryside. Taking full advantage of this unexpected opportunity, Graham led the Squadron round in a large circle allowing each aircraft in turn to come in and make its attack right over the on-rushing engine. However it was not until Sims came in low and dropped his bombs that spectacular results were achieved. His first bombs burst on either side of the track and then the locomotive itself exploded in a huge ball of smoke, with steam and debris flying in all directions as Sims flashed over it and pulled away into a climb. His claim that one of his bombs had fallen straight down the funnel of the engine was corroborated by Graham who was flying low alongside the train. The force of the explosion toppled the locomotive off the tracks, and as the whole train came to a shuddering halt. The German soldiers began jumping out and crawling from the overturned carriages before running in all directions to seek cover from the circling Camels, which continued to dive and attack the wreckage of the train.

At the front, the Armies had made the vital break-through, and mile by mile the Germans were pushed back out of south-western Belgium. By 15 October, having lost the battle for Roulers, they broke contact and retired to the east seeking to establish a new defensive line extending south from Bruges to Thielt.

By 17 October, the Belgian cavalry had reached the Bruges - Ostend canal, and the Belgian 5th Division entered the town of Ostend itself. Although bad weather once again prevented more than slight aerial activity for the Squadron, casualties continued to mount and both Lt E J Whitewell and 2nd Lt W G Fleming were wounded and taken to Queen Alexandra's Hospital.

One of the two replacement pilots who arrived on 26 October was 2nd Lt F T Sargeant, an American citizen from Brewer, Maine, who had joined the RFC on 17 October 1917 in New York. While working in the Remington arms factory in Bridgeport, Connecticut, he had seen a picture in the *Saturday Evening Post* of a pilot climbing up through clouds in a fighter aircraft; from that moment he had only one ambition. Although America was not at war, there was a British Recruiting Mission for the Royal Flying Corps on Fifth Avenue, New York, so, armed with a letter of introduction from a man who was a friend of Theodore Roosevelt, he presented himself for an initial interview. A week later he was sent to Toronto, with other American volunteers, where they swore an oath of allegiance, making them British citizens for the duration of the war, and subject to British military discipline. Thus, having pledged his allegiance to King George V, Sargeant became a cadet in the RFC, with the rank of Air Mechanic - Third Class.

The initial ground instruction was carried out at Toronto University, and at Deseronto, near Kingston, Ontario; the flying training took place at Taliaferro Field No.2, located between Dallas and Fort Worth, Texas. Having successfully completed his flying training, he returned to Canada, and on 14 May 1918 he was commissioned as a Second-Lieutenant in the newly-created Royal Air Force. The final phase of his training on Avro 504s, and his conversion on to Pups and Camels, took place at No.204 Training Depot Station, based at Eastchurch on the Isle of Sheppey in Kent. The conversion onto Camels included spin recovery action, which was not only a practical lesson in itself, but also instilled confidence in flying the tricky and sensitive Camel, which had something of a reputation, after the stable and reliable Pup. The first solo in a single-seat Camel was a cause of some apprehension as so many students were killed on this first trip. After finishing at Eastchurch, Sargeant was selected as a Camel fighter-pilot, the most sought-after posting, and sent to No.5 Pilot Pool at Wissant, just outside Calais. From there he moved a few miles inland to No.4 Aeroplane Supply Depot at Guines which was the central reserve for both Camels and pilots for the squadrons in the Flanders Command. On arrival at Bergues, the first pilot he met was MacKenzie who detailed him to be one of his wing-men. As far as Sargeant was concerned, this was a fortunate meeting as flying as wing-man to a Flight Commander - MacKenzie led "C" Flight - was much safer than flying at the end of the vic-formation in which a Flight operated, the position which usually fell to the lot of a new pilot.

On 19 October, the CO shot down an LVG in flames near Somergem, and four days later Capt J W Pinder, who had arrived from 9 Squadron, RNAS in the summer of 1917 as a Flight Commander, recorded his fourteenth and fifteenth victories when he drove down two Rumpler two-seaters in the space of twenty minutes, the second of which landed near Corcieux, and was captured by Allied troops.

Two High Offensive Patrols on 30 October produced nothing but a brief skirmish with five Fokker D VIIs at

19,000 feet over Ghent, which was quickly broken off by the German pilots spinning down and flying away to the east. Notwithstanding that the pilot's cockpit was located very far forward in the Camel, and only a fire wall separated the pilots feet from the engine compartment, the open cockpit remained bitterly cold at such altitudes particularly in winter, and the "Fug-boots", sheepskin boots which reached to the tops of the pilot's legs, only slightly lessened the discomfort.

One particular weather hazard which caused problems for the pilots operating along the Belgian coast was the low cloud and fog that could roll in quite suddenly off the cold waters of the Channel. Holden and Sargeant encountered just such conditions, as they climbed out over the sea before turning in towards the German lines, on 30 October, having taken-off on a low-level bombing and strafing sortie. Soon Sargeant could no longer see Holden's aircraft, nor the ground, nor anything else outside the limits of his own Camel. Realising that under these conditions the sortie would have to be abandoned, he decided to let down gradually until he could see the ground again. He then headed north until reaching the coast, where he turned south-west to keep the Channel on his right, which would take him away from the enemy lines. After a while he saw, by chance, right underneath him a canal that he knew ran right by the airfield at Bergues. Turning inland he let down even lower to see things more clearly, and flew alongside the narrow waterway. After a short distance, he was abruptly reminded of the first of two things he had forgotten in the excitement and anxiety of returning safely to base. The radio mast situated close to the airfield suddenly loomed out of the fog, and he pulled up sharply, barely in time to avoid it. Then directly in front of him was the airfield, and he landed directly ahead, ignoring any slight wind that there might be, and ran his wheels along the ground with his tail up, taxying towards the hangars, pleased to be down in one piece.

As he approached the flight-line, a figure standing near the hangar entrance suddenly turned and ran away from the approaching aircraft as fast as he could. Sargeant throttled back, brought his Camel to a halt, switched off the engine, and as the propeller slowed and twitched to a stop he climbed out of the cockpit, stepped out onto the wing, and jumped down to the ground. As he was pulling off his flying helmet, the ground-crew sergeant, who had last been seen running away, came back breathlessly and reminded Sargeant of the second thing he had forgotten that morning. Walking around the wing of the Camel, he pointed to the fuselage under the cockpit and said "Sir, did you know that you still have all your bombs in the rack?". Sargeant then realised that he had been so absorbed in returning to base that he had forgotten both about the radio mast and his load of bombs. He replied somewhat facetiously that he wanted to keep them as souvenirs, but now remembered all too clearly the orders to jettison bombs over the sea if for any reason pilots had to return from a raid with them still in the racks. A crash or hard landing could easily dislodge the bombs from the racks and create a nasty situation. As it was, Sargeant's was the only Camel to make it back to base that day; the rest of "C" Flight, that had taken off before Holden and Sargeant, all landed elsewhere, Mackenzie and a few others putting down on the beach.

As the last month of the war opened, a period of bad weather severely restricted flying. On 7 November, after remaining at stand-by all day, with only a weather check to confirm that the bad weather in the vicinity of the airfield extended inland towards the operational area, the Squadron stood down and the CO organised "a Binge" in a private room in a large restaurant on the quay fronting the harbour in Dunkirk. The champagne was flowing freely when about ten o'clock the head-waiter burst into the room to announce that the war was over. The celebrations had hardly started when Ronnie Graham came into the room to say that everyone had to report back to the airfield. Around midnight back at Bergues, the sad truth that the report was a false alarm, and that the Squadron would continue to operate as usual, was explained by the CO.

The next morning, the full Squadron, made up of all three flights, consisting of eighteen aircraft set off on a High Offensive Patrol. The large amounts of cloud encountered en route severely restricted visibility and made formation flying difficult, a task not helped by the previous late night. After a couple of hours of arduous wheeling around in a murky sky over the enemy lines, the patrol returned to Bergues having seen no signs of any enemy aircraft.

The morning offensive patrol on 9 November encountered a formation of four lozenge-camouflaged Fokkers about ten miles east of Ghent, and a brief but vicious fight ensued. One enemy aircraft was seen to go down, and then suddenly the fight was over and the sky was clear of enemy aircraft. As the patrol continued, moderate amounts of inaccurate anti-aircraft fire were experienced over Ghent, where fires could be seen in the docks below. Some five miles north-west of the city, Lt C J Sims brought down an observation balloon. On the afternoon patrol, MacKay, leading "A" Flight, shot down a Fokker D VII ten miles south-east of Ghent. The next day the city was occupied by the Belgian and French forces.

The penultimate day of hostilities saw the Squadron engaged on a special mission, the details of which were withheld until the aircraft had moved up to the forward airfield at Varssenaere to be refuelled. As the pilots gathered around Graham, a dark green limousine drove onto the airfield, and two men, one dressed in the uniform of a Belgian general, stepped out. At this point the CO disclosed the details of the mission, which was to act as escort to the general, who was in fact the King of the Belgians, and his aide-de-camp, who were to inspect the front lines in that sector from the air. As the pilots were briefed and dispersed to their aircraft, the King and his aide were equipped with flying-suits, goggles etc., and assisted into the observer's cockpits of two D.H.4s. Then, refuelled and fully armed, the Squadron took-off, formed up at various levels around the royal entourage and set off towards the front lines.

With all heads constantly turning, and eyes continually searching the skies for any hostile aircraft, it was not surprising that one was soon spotted, a low flying two-seater nosing into the area of the Squadron's protective responsibility. The four Camels of "A" Flight flown by MacKay, Rosevear, Gilbert and Chick were somewhat lower than MacKenzie's "C" Flight and therefore reached the enemy aircraft, which turned out to be an LVG, first. The German pilot immediately dropped down to tree-top height in an attempt to evade his attackers, and the rear-gunner opened up with brisk and accurate return fire, which was all the more effective as the Camels could only attack from above, and were forced to pull away in vulnerable climbing turns as they finished their attacks. As a result nearly all of the attacking aircraft suffered some damage from the accurate shooting of the German observer, despite the erratic movements of his aircraft. Nevertheless, with the air around the LVG full of flying bullets, the eventual outcome was inevitable; after a well placed burst of fire, claimed by Rosevear, the observer dropped out of sight into his cockpit and the firing ceased.

Squadron Officers at Stalhille, Belgium early 1919 grouped in front of the Squadron's Operations Room. From the left to right back row: Lts H E B Holden, J Wesley, E A Hodson, L A Coombs, A B Rosevear, R A Pearce, G C Garner, A F Chick, A M Taylor,, Capt J R Swanston, Maj. A G Taylor, Capt. Spellings (Recording Officer and Adjutant), Capt. G C MacKay, Lts S M N Hancock, and A H Turner. Front row: Lts F W Radford and E R Huston. Not present for the photograph were Capt. W J MacKenzie, Capt. Maine (Gunnery Officer), Lts J P Stewart-Burton, H H Gilbert, W S Phelps, A H Pownall, and F T Sargeant. (Photograph courtesy of the Department of Defence, Ottawa.)

Under further attacks from the Camels, the German pilot attempted to make a forced landing. His aircraft struck the ground, bounced, skidded along, and finally came to rest with its nose buried in a furrowed field and its tail pointing towards the sky.

During the attacks on the LVG, Sargeant's aircraft had been hit by a burst of anti-aircraft fire and it was with some difficulty that he nursed it back to Varssenaere where he was soon joined by the other more or less badly damaged aircraft of "A" and "C" Flights. MacKay had sustained more damage than anyone else; half of the control wires that worked the tailplane, rudder and ailerons had been shot away, and it was something of a miracle that he had managed to make it back at all. Sargeant also had four bullet holes in one blade of his propeller and three in the other. The flight had lasted one hour, forty-five minutes. Rosevear's aircraft was so badly damaged that it was no longer serviceable.

The two D.H.4s and the rest of the Squadron had not yet returned, and two very shiny visored and braided military caps belonging to the King and his aide were spotted on the back-seat of the limousine. Like high spirited school-boys, the pilots tried the caps on, striking poses of mock dignity. All was returned to order before the D.H.4s and the Camels of "B" Flight came into sight and landed one by one. After being assisted from the observer's cockpit, the King came over to inspect the damage sustained by the Camels in the combat with the LVG. Clearly impressed by the stark evidence of the fight that had taken place, he shook hands with MacKay and said "Captain, you are a very brave pilot." Once the royal party was out of sight, MacKay ran over to the other pilots shouting "Hey Boys, shake the hand that shook the hand of the King of Belgium." which they did. MacKay was in fact awarded the Order of Leopold by the King for his part in this action.

Having consumed a Spartan lunch of bully-beef and hard-tack biscuits, the pilots whose aircraft were still considered airworthy climbed back into their cockpits ready for another patrol. However, after the excitement of the morning, the afternoon sortie, airborne at 13.20 hours and returning at 15.55 hours, was something of an anti-climax. At 12,000 feet, somewhere between Ghent and Antwerp, eleven Fokker D VIIs were spotted at 18,000 feet, but notwithstanding their height advantage, after following for a few miles, the enemy formation dived away to the east. Although it was not realised at the time, this was to be the Squadron's last patrol of the war, and the destruction of the LVG in the morning was the last victory credited to an aircraft of No.5 Group. All the pilots knew was that they had survived another day of hostilities. At dinner in the evening there was some discussion as to when the war would end, but most of the conversation revolved around the morning's mission with the King of the Belgians.

The day of the Armistice started in the early morning darkness - around 05.30 hours - with the Orderly Sergeant pounding on the doors of the Officers' Quarters and announcing, in what was meant to be a cheerful voice, "Gentlemen, wake up, wake up, the war is over!". The pilots response was anything but cheerful, and was along the lines that they had heard that all before. The news that the CO wanted all pilots to report to the Mess immediately suggested that their scepticism might be unwarranted. By the time the short lorry ride had deposited them at the Mess, the CO was already there with a smile on his face. As they gathered round, and Graham sat once more on the soap-box that he used for briefings, he told them "I have a signal from Group Headquarters stating that an armistice is to be signed at 11 o'clock this morning." The burst of jubilation that greeted this news was brought to an abrupt halt as Graham said that the entire squadron was to carry out an High Offensive Patrol that morning on a line from Bergues to Lille, remaining on the Allied side of the lines. His instructions continued "At five minutes to eleven you are to turn your planes toward the German lines and give the Bloody Hun one final good blast. Don't come back here with any ammunition in your guns.".

The weather did not look at all promising as the final preparations were made for the last patrol. Several aircraft had already taken off in deteriorating conditions when fog started to roll in from the coast, moving silently across the field and reducing visibility to a dangerous level. Finally the CO, who had been standing on the field without his tunic and his hands in his pockets looking first towards the Channel and then at the darkening sky, turned towards the aircraft of "C" Flight and waved his arms signalling that the patrol was cancelled. Mackenzie fired a red flare from his Very pistol into the clouds signalling to the pilots circling above that the mission had been cancelled. With a curious mixture of relief and disappointment, the aircraft were taxied back to the hangars. As the full meaning of the momentous occasion dawned on them, the pilots climbed from their cockpits and grabbing their Very pistols began to fire off red flares into the air. Three of the Camels which had taken off landed and their pilots were soon adding to the barrage of soaring Very lights which were now aimed at the sole remaining airborne Camel flown by 2nd Lt J C Stone, who seemed reluctant to end his wartime flying in other than a spectacular fashion. He then proceeded to beat-up the airfield, repeatedly diving at the pistol firing party on the ground, skimming the hangars and the Officers' Mess and generally giving vent to an accumulation of built-up tension that had been necessarily held in check until this final moment.

However the exuberance of those on the ground was gathering momentum, and several near misses by glowing Very cartridges convinced Stone that he should land. Between the excitement of the moment and the deteriorating visibility he misjudged his landing approach and wound up hanging somewhat ignominiously from his straps. He was quickly retrieved from his inverted position, happily unhurt, but somewhat embarrassed by the merciless ribbing of his rescuers. The group of pilots now separated into two sections facing each other across the open space of the aerodrome and began firing away at each other with reckless abandon. Before long some of the shimmering balls of red fire landed against one of the canvas hangars which started to burn; happily the Squadron fire section was quickly on the scene before any real damage was done. At this point the CO calmed things down, ordering the Squadron to stand to until eleven o'clock, after which celebrations could continue.

As eleven o'clock arrived, a bugler sounded the last post, and then a different noise arose from the surrounding countryside as near and far the church bells started to ring in celebration of the end of hostilities. Suddenly, everyone was dashing for the lorries with the same idea in mind, to go into Dunkirk. As the lorries circled round the town square Mackenzie saw a newspaper-boy on the pavement and bought his entire stock of papers, then standing in front of the statue of the famous French Admiral Jean Bart, he proceeded to give them away to cries of "La guerre est fini! Journal! La guerre est fini!" He had had quite a few drinks and was feeling no pain. The celebrations in Dunkirk were brought to a sudden halt as the result of a complaint made to the Provost Marshal, that men wearing the uniform of the Royal Naval Air Service were behaving in a manner unbecoming to officers and gentlemen. So all Squadron personnel were rounded up irrespective of the uniform they were wearing, RNAS, RFC, Army or RAF and the celebrations continued back at Bergues out of sight and out of mind of the Provost Marshal.

Soon after the Armistice, the pilots moved from their snug, wooden huts on the farm into uncomfortable metal Nissen huts on the airfield itself. The huts had no proper floors, were without any form of heating, and the metal walls were punctured with numerous gashes and holes, a testimony to the German bombing raids of a few months previously. Fortunately the time spent in these uncomfortable quarters was limited and on 27 November the Squadron moved up to the captured German airfield at Stalhille, just outside Ostend. Here the buildings were much more substantial, being of wood and brick construction, and close to the Bessoneau hangars that housed the aircraft. When the news of a move first came it was hoped that the Squadron would move up to Varssenaere and a visit was paid to the chateau that served as the Officers' Mess, but these hopes were dashed and it was at Stalhille that the Squadron spent its last months in Belgium.

With the coming of the Armistice, Maj Graham, who had commanded the unit from its beginnings as the Seaplane Defence Flight and had been awarded the DSO, DSC and Bar and the DFC while leading it in action, returned to the UK to take over 233 Squadron at Dover. Command of the Squadron then passed to Maj A G Taylor on 21 November 1918. Maj Taylor, who had a Royal Flying Corps background and no combat flying experience, came to the Squadron from commanding No.204 Training Depot Station, based at Eastchurch on the Isle of Sheppey. Any new CO would have had a difficult task in following the very highly respected and immensely popular Ronnie Graham. Taylor had a particularly difficult time, especially in coming to terms with the number of Naval terms still in use such as "ship's office" instead of orderly room and "the number of Camels on deck", rather than the number of Camels in service. His attempts to change some of these terms met with little success, and did little for his popularity.

While the living conditions at Stalhille were comfortable, the amount of flying carried out was somewhat restricted, partly by the poor weather conditions and for some pilots by inclination. Theoretically, each pilot had to fly a set number of hours to maintain his proficiency. Some, however, having survived the dangers of war-time flying, had no desire to continue, and those who still enjoyed the experience stood in for them. During January, flights were made along the coast as far as Calais and Boulogne, both to accrue air time and to keep in practice; even at this time it was still not known for certain if the Armistice really would mark the final end to hostilities. Finally, on 25 February 1919, those Squadron aircraft which were not to return to England were flown to No.11 Aircraft Park at Ghistelles, where they were to be burned. The pilots collected various parts as souvenirs, and 2Lt J W Radford deliberately crashed his aircraft rather than hand it over to be destroyed.

The Squadron remained in Belgium for a further month, and then in the middle of March 1919, when many other RAF units returned to England, No.213 Squadron came home for the first time. The home-coming however was a sad one. The Squadron was split up, and the remaining aircraft flown to Scopwick Lines in Lincolnshire, which later became Digby. Here the Cadre was to remain until 31 December 1919, when the Squadron was finally disbanded.

A flight of the Squadron's Gloster Gauntlet IIs, showing their peace-time markings, airborne from Northolt in 1937. (A Thomas)

CHAPTER THREE - WITH THE B.E.F. IN FRANCE

The disbandment of the Squadron in 1919 was only one amongst very many, as the large and well-equipped Air Force of some two hundred and eighty squadrons, that had been built up in the four previous years, was dismantled. The war to end all wars had been fought and won, and the Air Force that had played so large a part in that victory was thrown, almost literally, on to the scrap heap. Only twenty-eight squadrons were retained, and those were largely stationed outside the United Kingdom. Little or no thought, it seemed, was given to any future, save that of continuous peace as hailed by the politicians.

By 1922, when the first flush of victory was over and the Government was looking again at the country's defences, the contingency against which they were to be measured was a hypothetical war with France. In the spring of that year, after considerable military pressure, the Government announced plans for the creation of a Metropolitan Air Force of fourteen bomber and nine fighter squadrons. Almost immediately, however, this plan was modified and a scheme introduced to provide parity with France, requiring fifty-two squadrons by 1928. So started the whole series of plans for the expansion of the RAF that were devised in the inter-war years. Yet even this scheme, which made all due allowances for economy and the Ten Year Rule, which postulated that Britain would be involved in no major war for ten years, was modified on the return of the negotiators from Locarno. The date for completing the formation of the fifty-two squadrons was moved from 1928 to 1936.

It was left to the Defence Requirements Committee of 1933 to recognise, at last, that "the ultimate potential enemy" was Germany. The Committee also estimated that Germany would be ready for war by 1938/1939, and urged rapid completion of the fifty-two squadrons scheme.

When Germany's plan for the creation of an air force of 1,368 machines by 1936 was disclosed, the fifty-two squadron scheme was abandoned. To replace it, and in the hope that it would give pause to the war-like preparations of the Germans, a more ambitious scheme was drawn up to provide forty-three bomber squadrons and twenty-eight fighter squadrons. It soon became clear, however, that this scheme had completely failed to discourage the Germans, and a plan to provide real opposition was adopted.

This accelerated plan was to be completed by the Spring of 1937, and would provide thirty-five fighter squadrons. The aircraft for these squadrons was to be the Gloster Gauntlet, and it was intended to replace these later by a more powerful aircraft then under development. As part of this accelerated plan to provide Britain with an effective fighter defence, No.213 Squadron was reformed. After eighteen years of silence, "The Hornets" were to be back in the skies once more.

So it was at Northolt, on the morning of 8 March 1937, that the Squadron was reborn. The initial equipment of aircraft was, as planned, Gloster Gauntlets. The pilots in the

Air Marshal Sir Humphrey Edwardes Jones, KCB, CBE, DFC, AFC who, as a Squadron Leader, came from the Aeroplane and Armament Experimental Establishment at Martlesham Heath to command the Squadron when it was reformed in 1937.

main came initially from No.111 Squadron, being the bulk of that squadron's "B" Flight, together with Flt Lt J E J "Jackie" Sing and Plt Off R P R Powell from "A" Flight. To complete the pilot establishment came Fg Off W A K Igoe and Plt Offs W N Sykes and R W Denison together with Sgts C Grayson and L A Bates from 23 Squadron and Acting Plt Offs J Ellis and B J E Lane from 66 Squadron. To command came Sqn Ldr J H Edwardes Jones (later Air Marshal Sir Humphrey Edwardes Jones, KCB, CBE, DFC, AFC) from the Aeroplane and Armament Experimental Establishment at Martlesham Heath. Known to all the Squadron pilots as E J, he had flown as a test pilot, developing the original Spitfire.

The Gauntlet was the last open-cockpit fighter to go into service with the RAF. Fitted with a Bristol Mercury air-cooled engine which developed 645 bhp at altitude, and with a top speed of 230 miles per hour, it was for a time the fastest aircraft in service. A metal-framed, fabric-covered aircraft, armed with two Vickers machine-guns mounted just below and forward of the pilot's cockpit, it had a wing span of just over thirty-two feet and an overall length of some twenty-six feet. At the height of its career, it equipped fourteen fighter squadrons. As the flow of pilots from training units and other squadrons commenced, some of the No.111 Squadron pilots returned to their original unit, but others stayed.

The life of a fighter squadron in the later nineteen-thirties had a quality all its own and Northolt, on the edge of London, was the place to enjoy it to the full. With an old reputation to live up to and a new one to make, nothing but the best was good enough, on the ground and in the air. The prevailing fighter tactics of the period meant that immaculate close formation flying was essential; here, also, much of a squadron's spirit of camaraderie and one-ness was built up.

The pilots were young and single and their lives revolved around their aircraft. The excellent results of the early weeks of hard work were first seen by the public at large on 29 May 1937, when the Squadron sent flights to Catterick, Odiham and Hendon to take part in the annual Empire Air Day programme.

When the Squadron was reformed, ideas concerning camouflage were still being developed, and initially the aircraft were finished in silver. Across the top of the upper mainplane and along the length of each side of the fuselage ran broad stripes of black-yellow-black, the Squadron's colours. It was at this time that the hornet was officially adopted as the Squadron's badge, and the motto "Irritatus Lacessit Crabro" registered with the Chester Herald, Inspector of Royal Air Force Badges. By December 1937 the order was given that all fighter aircraft should be camouflaged, and the aircraft re-emerged from the hangars with green and brown upper surfaces and painted silver underneath.

After spending the first two months of its new life with No.11 Group at Northolt, the Squadron moved north, on 1 July, to the airfield at Church Fenton, in Yorkshire. Still in the process of completion, this station came under No.12 Group, whose main responsibility lay in the area along the East Coast. The airfield was one of the many being constructed under the great expansion scheme now that it was realised, almost too late, that economy was not the mark against which to measure the scale of the air force required to defend the country. The Squadron found itself leaving its comfortable, well-established, home near London for its new quarters still in the process of construction; tents temporarily formed the Officer's Mess until permanent buildings were completed. Later a large house on the edge of the airfield, eventually to become the Station Commander's residence, was taken over as the Squadron Mess.

Once settled at its new base, the Squadron was soon making full use of its initial establishment of twelve aircraft. This time was spent to such good effect that the Squadron qualified to represent No.12 Group in the Sassoon Trophy. This competition was held annually among the squadrons of Fighter Command, each Group being represented by its chosen unit. The competition was held in October and, despite having only been in existence for some eight months, the Squadron successfully carried off the Flight Attack Competition. Just how useful this training was to be, in the war that was about to be fought, is open to question. With the experience of aerial combat from the First World War still a recent memory for many senior RAF officers, it now seems incomprehensible that the training for fighter pilots concentrated almost exclusively upon three main Fighting Area Attacks:

No.1 Attack: A succession of fighter aircraft, usually three or six flying in vics, attacking from astern, against a single bomber aircraft.
No.2 Attack: Two or more fighter aircraft attacking in line abreast, against a single bomber aircraft.
No.3 Attack: Three fighter aircraft attacking a single bomber simultaneously from the rear, beam and rear quarter.

Flying in the cumbersome vic formation of three aircraft not only limited manoeuvrability, but also restricted the keeping of a good look-out. The set attacks all assumed a single bomber and two or more fighters, an equation that was seldom achieved when the fighting really started. With the speed of the bombers almost as great as that of the fighters

Gauntlet K5302 overshot landing at Wittering and overturned, 11 August 1938 (W Hughes)

attacking them, a stern attack was usually the only option open to the fighter pilot. The more flexible German fighter "Schwarm" of four aircraft, later adopted in the RAF as the "finger-four", took some time to be recognised as the best grouping of the basic fighting unit, a pair of aircraft, a leader and his wing-man.

The following months were spent in the normal round of training, notably in formation flying and gunnery, interspersed with the annual competitions at other airfields and Army Co-operation Exercises. Having successfully opened Church Fenton, the Squadron ended its ten-month stay there on 18 May, with a move to the old-established airfield at Wittering, which was destined to remain its base until June 1940.

The last year of peace passed very much as the year before. The Squadron now knew itself and its aeroplanes; something had been achieved, the value of which would only become apparent with the first clash of combat. The return trip from an armament practice camp at Aldergrove, in Northern Ireland, showed the pilots and the CO to good advantage. Once airborne from the shores of Lough Neagh, a fleeting glimpse of the Irish Sea was all that was seen of the country beneath, since the cloud cover was complete. Eventually the CO gave the order to descend, and the whole formation disappeared into the cloud below. The cloud base was something below one thousand feet and the visibility poor, nevertheless soon after breaking cloud the familiar spire of Stamford Church emerged through the mist, and a neat formation landing concluded a most satisfactory trip. In the days before radio direction finding and radar controlled approaches, this was the flying that bound a squadron together. The year 1938 saw the same round of Empire Air Day flypasts, of competitions and Army exercises, while almost to a man the Squadron aircrew remained unchanged.

In January 1939, however, one fundamental change did take place, when the biplanes were exchanged for Hurricane Is. These aircraft were to be flown throughout the most exacting part of the coming war, over France, during the withdrawal from Dunkirk, throughout the Battle of Britain, and all through the great battles in the Western Desert. The first Hurricanes that reached Wittering, on 16 January, were not in fact quite the same aircraft as were used later. They had the Merlin II engine but did not carry VHF radios, and only mounted a fixed-pitch propeller. The aircraft's electrical system was powered by twelve-volt accumulators which required changing every other day, while the radios that were fitted, TR9Ds, required fresh two-volt accumulators every day, and 120-volt accumulators weekly. The aircraft were parked on the far side of the airfield at Wittering, which meant that the two Wireless and Electrical Mechanics, Ted "Smugger" Smith for "B" Flight and "Jimmy" James for "A" Flight were kept busy. The aircraft were started by trolley accumulators, and as there was no mechanical transport, these had to dragged back and forward between the aircraft and the hangars where the only charging points existed. The radio itself had a rather poor performance and range, as well as a tendency to drift off tune. In theory the radio had a direction-finding capability, which involved a clock in the cockpit which had to be set to a checked zero every hour; it was not relied upon.

These aircraft arrived in the standard wartime camouflage, matt Dark Earth (brown) and Dark Green on the upper surfaces applied in a specific pattern. Two patterns were used, Schemes A and B, the second being a mirror image of the first; these patterns were applied to alternate

Three of the Squadron's Gloster Gauntlets, with K7806 in the foreground.

Gauntlet K7810, flown by the CO, Sqn Ldr J H Edwardes Jones, at Northolt in 1937. (A Thomas)

aircraft off the production line. In accordance with the decision taken in September 1938, the undersides of the aircraft were painted black and white, the order stipulated black for the under surface of the port mainplane and white for the starboard; however, at least one squadron used the reverse colour scheme. There was also confusion as to where the two colours should meet. In practice, this was sometimes along the aircraft's centre-line, and sometimes at the wing root. To make the RAF roundels clearly visible, a yellow surround was added; however this was removed in March 1939, when Type B roundels were introduced with a red centre and blue outer ring. In October 1939, Type A roundels, blue, white, red were re-introduced under the extreme wing-tips of many machines, and this became standard practice up to the present day. Also at this time, squadron code letters or, more officially, unit identification letters, were introduced for signalling and in-flight identification purposes; they were to remain in use into the fifties in one form or another. These were applied in mid-grey paint, two letters ahead of the roundel on the port side of the fuselage and two letters aft on the starboard side. When hostilities commenced, all Fighter Command's squadrons changed their unit identification letters - except No.213 Squadron, which kept the letters 'AK'.

To assist in the transition from biplane to monoplane, Douglas Blackwood was posted to the Squadron as a flying instructor. In 1934 he had flown one of the Furies that had given the famous aerobatic performance at Hendon during which the aircraft remained tied together. He was also the last of his family to edit the famous Blackwood's Magazine.

The change from the old-fashioned biplane to the modern monoplane went off smoothly, and without incident. Soon the Squadron was experimenting in ways of penetrating cloud in formation; such flying soon led naturally to an even higher standard of formation flying. The CO, in his spotless white flying-suit, would lead the Squadron in a formation take-off, twelve aircraft in four vics of three across the width of Wittering's wide grass airfield, in the poorest weather conditions. After a short period on top, everyone would disappear back into the cloud, to emerge from the overcast once more close to the airfield, and still in immaculate order. Unfortunately, the report containing the results of these experiments was never published, due to the war which was soon to break over Europe.

Sometimes new exercises with this fast new monoplane did not go entirely according to plan. On his first night-flying practice, Wilf Sizer noticed that the flares laid out by the duty pilot from No.23 Squadron, a night-flying Blenheim unit, forming the runway lighting, were flashing past at a particularly high speed as he came over the runway threshold. Going round again only repeated the experience. The Tower called up to ask if he was having any trouble and he explained his predicament. He was advised to fly more slowly. Feeling that if he flew much more slowly the Hurricane would fall out of the sky, he came round again and touched down as near the end of the runway as he could. The flares still flashed by all too quickly, and eventually the Hurricane finished up on its nose blocking the Great North Road, and disturbing the mainly lorry traffic between Wansford and Stamford. The incident also made him very unpopular with the ground staff, who had to cut the wing bolts in order to remove the mainplane from the road. The explanation for the high ground speed on the approach, and Sizer's salvation as far as the CO was concerned, was that the 23 Squadron duty pilot had laid out the flare path down-wind as the weather forecast indicated a change of wind direction by the time that squadron's Blenheims would be returning.

The coming of Autumn also brought the noise of war, even though it was only the phoney war, a term that came to have a special meaning for the Squadron. Orders to mobilise were given on the night of 1 September 1939, but preparations already in hand made this almost a formality. The Squadron had been engaged in the annual exercise during August, and was already in a high state of readiness. Some RAFVR pilots were with the Squadron completing their Summer Camp, and they stayed on to learn to fly the Hurricane. A dual-control Fairey Battle was used when it was serviceable. One of these part-time pilots, Sgt Lishman, became lost on one occasion above cloud while on a Sector recce. At length, seeing an airfield through a break in the overcast, he descended and landed, to find himself on the airfield at Cranwell. The VR pilots had no "Wings", and he was accordingly placed under arrest on suspicion of being a spy. A telephone call to Wittering did not in itself clear up the problem, and Wilf Sizer had to fly over to identify the unfortunate VR pilot. Later "E J" gave them their Wings, and Sgts Howe and Lishman joined "B" Flight.

In early September, the pilots were engaged in building sand-bagged aircraft pens at dispersal points on the airfield, much to the delight of the ground crews. Already an advanced flight of six aircraft was stationed during the day at West Raynham, a grass airfield nearer the coast, guarding against sneak raids from the sea. This flight was airborne from Wittering at dawn, returning at 2000 hours. As both

An early Hurricane I, L1770, revving up at Wittering. (A Thomas)

Flights contained at least four bridge players, the timetable enabled them usefully to while away the waiting hours. For eight pilots on the Squadron, the war thus started with a very early morning flight to a game of bridge in a field in Norfolk. In October, No.610 (County of Chester) Squadron, an Auxiliary unit, flew down to Wittering from its home base at Hooton Park with its newly-acquired Spitfire Is, remaining until April 1940.

Much to the Squadron's chagrin, the phoney war lived up to its name and little enough occurred to disturb the everyday routine. Some excitement was experienced by "B" Flight Commander, Flt Lt R D G "Widge" Wight, when on an air test the propeller of his Hurricane flew off while he was over Boston. Fortunately he had sufficient height and skill to make a "dead-stick" landing back at Wittering. The Squadron's Operations Record Book (ORB) sets down with evident disappointment the fact that "no enemy aircraft have been reported active in this sector so far". The advance flight at West Raynham became a permanent fixture, with the duty of protecting convoys passing along the East Coast, but this also provided little action.

West Raynham itself was a Bomber Command station. It was a Coastal Command Hudson, returning from a shipping patrol off the Norwegian coast, that afforded some of the pilots of the Squadron their first taste of war. With the pilot and the rear gunner dead, the aircraft was landed at the second attempt by the navigator, on instructions from the tower. The numerous bullet holes in the wings and fuselage, through which blood was pouring onto the grass, afforded a sobering sight. The phoney war came to have a grimmer meaning.

In the absence of the real thing at Wittering, dummy attacks by Wellingtons were arranged with 38 Squadron from Marham, and were intercepted with some success. Increased enemy air activity over the North Sea led the whole Squadron to move to West Raynham during daylight hours, whenever a convoy was passing across the front of the Squadron's sector. Even so - and despite numerous reports and three moves to West Raynham - enemy activity remained confined to the northern sectors, and October passed with nothing more to offer than false alarms and fruitless searches.

The last weeks of 1939 passed in this way, and non-operational flying showed a marked increase as flights departed regularly to Sutton Bridge for air firing practice. As the RAF expanded, rapid promotion came to some members of the Squadron, but it meant that, even before action was joined, the Squadron was to lose some of the benefits of its two years together. Fg Off W A Toyne, who had joined the Squadron in 1937, was posted to 264 Squadron as a Flight Commander, and acting Flight Lieutenant. With twenty-eight pilots on its establishment, the Squadron was able to put two formations of twelve aircraft into the air simultaneously. By the end of February, the Squadron was still training hard, with the Hurricanes now in full fighting trim, equipped with variable pitch propellers and VHF sets - TR1133As.

The Hurricane I flown by the Squadron in France, over Dunkirk and throughout the Battle of Britain, was a compromise aircraft that in some respects linked the old world of the biplane with that of the modern fighter. In designing the Hurricane, Sydney Camm sought to utilise, on grounds of economy, as many as possible of the existing jigs and tools that were already in the Hawker factory. Thus the aircraft was, in many ways, very traditional in design; the fuselage was built with wooden formers and stringers covered with fabric, stiffened by a strong metal tubular frame. By early 1940, however, stressed metal skin wings had been developed. In actual combat the "wooden" fuselage was found to have greater durability and resistance in the face of exploding cannon shells than the metal frame and stressed metal skin of the Spitfire. Statistically, the Hurricane was outperformed by the Messerschmitt-designed Bf 109E, against which it was pitted over France, and in the Battle of Britain. However in the hands of a skilled and experienced pilot, it was a very effective fighting machine.

Powered by a 1,030 hp Rolls Royce Merlin III twelve-cylinder liquid-cooled engine, the Mk.I Hurricane had a maximum speed of 328 miles per hour at 20,000 feet, a service ceiling (the height at which an aircraft's rate of climb falls below 100 feet per minute) of 34,200 feet and a range of just over five hundred miles. Its armament consisted of eight Browning .303 machine-guns, mounted in the wings, together capable of firing 1,200 rounds per minute; the magazines carried 300 rounds per gun. This compared with the slightly smaller and less robustly-built Bf 109E, which was powered by a 1,150 hp twelve-cylinder liquid-cooled Daimler-Benz engine, which gave it a maximum speed of 357 miles per hour at 12,300 feet, a service ceiling of 36,000 feet and a range of four hundred and twelve miles. It was armed with two Rheinmetal 7.9 mm machine-guns, mounted on the engine crankcase and firing through the propeller, each supplied with 1,000 rounds, and two 20 mm cannon, one in each wing, with sixty rounds per gun. The 18-lb weight of a three second burst from a Bf 109E's machine-guns and cannon compared with 10 lbs from the Hurricane I's eight machine guns.

The greatest weakness of the Bf 109 was, probably, that its lightweight airframe and high-lift wings meant that it was a comparatively delicate aeroplane, which the German pilots were less prepared to push to its limits, particularly in contrast to the rugged Hurricane.

While the Bf 110 never lived up to its reputation, and its lack of manoeuvrability and poor acceleration put it at a great disadvantage to the Hurricane in a dog-fight, nevertheless it was a formidable opponent. Faster than the Hurricane, with a top speed of 349 miles per hour at 23,000 feet, it also had powerful armament. The Bf 110C mounted four 7.9 mm machine-guns (each supplied with 1,000 rounds), and two 20 mm cannon (each with 180 rounds) in the nose, and one rear-firing machine-gun in a dorsal position. When attacking from above and behind, diving in with speed advantage, and with its formidable armament, the Bf 110 was a potent enemy.

The "phoney war" ended as dawn broke on Friday, 10 May 1940, when one hundred and thirty-five German divisions attacked across the frontiers of Luxembourg and Belgium, and paratroops descended upon their objectives in Belgium and the Netherlands. At the same time, the Luftwaffe attacked airfields in Belgium, France and the Netherlands. Such opposition as was put up was quickly overwhelmed; in the north the Dutch Air Force was virtually destroyed by 13 May, and on 15 May the Dutch Army was ordered to surrender. As the German Panzers pushed through the Ardennes and on to Sedan, they encountered little opposition. Crossing the Meuse on the night of 11/12 May, the German armour, supported by the Stukas of the Luftwaffe, made straight for the Channel ports, splitting the Allied forces in two. These events were soon to draw the Squadron south into the maelstrom.

In London, the argument between Lord Dowding and the War Cabinet over the disposition of Fighter Command's few precious squadrons, was reaching a critical stage. The outcome of this argument would decide 213's immediate future. Already six fighter squadrons were in France, four (85, 87, 607 and 615) forming part of the Air Component of the British Expeditionary Force, under the command of Air Vice-Marshal C H B Blount, OBE, MC, and two Squadrons (1 and 73), were with the Advanced Air Striking Force. The French reverses on the Meuse, as the German Panzers drove westwards, soon prompted the call for yet more aerial support. The French Prime Minister, M. Reynaud, personally appealed for another ten squadrons to be sent across the Channel. In Dowding's view such dispositions would be the height of folly; ever since the opening of hostilities, he had insisted that all fighter production should be reserved for building up Fighter Command at home, to face the expected knock-out blow from the Luftwaffe. He likened the sending of squadrons abroad in piecemeal fashion to the opening of a tap, through which ultimately the whole of the output of Hurricanes would be drained away. Any squadrons now sent to France would necessarily be Hurricane units, as the only servicing facilities available were for this type of aircraft. On hearing of the French call for ten more squadrons, Dowding appeared before the War Cabinet to register his objections personally, and gained a short respite. However further news of the plight of the French Army on 16 May produced a compromise by which eight half-squadrons were to be sent.

The distinction of being the first Squadron pilot to engage the enemy probably belongs to Plt Off J M Strickland of "A" Flight, who had been with the Squadron since October 1937, and had flown a Hurricane over to Amiens/Glisy, the initial assembly and supply point for replacement Hurricanes being supplied to the squadrons in France. Early on the morning of 16 May, he delivered one of six Hurricanes being supplied to 87 Squadron at Lille/Marcq. As there were no 87 Squadron pilots available to fly these aircraft, the pilots who had flown them in elected to stay. They went into action immediately and only two survived to return to the UK, Strickland being one of the survivors.

The effect of the decision to send eight half-squadrons to France was immediately felt at Wittering. That same evening, 16 May, "B" Flight consisting of Flt Lt "Widge" Wight, Plt Offs H D Atkinson and W M Sizer and Sgts S L Butterfield, J A Lishman and Valentine departed for Manston. Some of the accompanying ground-crew personnel travelled in a Bombay, a twin-engined bomber/transport aircraft, and some in an Ensign air liner. At Manston, where they spent the night, the Flight found numerous other units ready to cross the Channel.

Early on the morning of 17 May, at 06.15 hours, the transport aircraft, the Bombay and the Ensign carrying twenty-eight ground crew, took-off, each with its accompanying gaggle of fighters. "B" Flight, together with "A" Flight from 601 (County of London) Squadron, was bound for Merville, some fifteen miles west of Lille, where it arrived in two sections, Blue at 07.35 hours and Green a little later. En route, other aircraft peeled off to their respective destinations. The airfield at Merville, just to the south of the town, and the River Lys, was only distinguished from the surrounding countryside by the presence of a wind-sock and a few Nissen huts. The groundcrew were accommodated in tents in a field on the edge of the village, and fed from a field kitchen. As an AC1, Ted Field had acquired a section, which consisted of AC2 Carney, Electrician 2 and AC2 Major, Wireless Operator.

Already in residence was 79 Squadron, to which "B" Flight was attached, and 3 Squadron, which was being reinforced by the flight from 601 Squadron. These two squadrons, 3 and 79, had arrived in France on 10 May to form the air echelon of No.63 Wing of the Air Component. On the same day they had been joined by "A" Flight of 615

Douglas Blackwood who, as Flt Lt D Blackwood, flew with the Squadron as a Flying Instructor during the conversion from Gauntlets to Hurricanes in 1939. He was the great-great-great grandson of William Blackwood, the founder of Blackwood's Magazine, *and the last member of the family to edit the publication.*

Squadron, which had flown in from Le Touquet.

For the Squadron, the days of training and gleaning information of the Germans from reports were over, and the oft-expressed wish for action was to answered later that morning. At 14.30 hours Green Section, Wight, Atkinson and Valentine was ordered to patrol Landrecies - Avèsnes - La Capelle - Wasigny, with top cover provided by nine Hurricanes of 3 Squadron, but no hostile aircraft were seen. During the patrol, Valentine became separated from the section and, after crash-landing, finished the day in Le Touquet hospital with a broken arm.

Also at 14.30 hours, Lishman, together with seven Hurricanes from 79 Squadron, encountered and attacked seven Dorniers ten miles north east of Arras. The enemy aircraft were flying at 6,000 feet, in tight formation of sections line astern, heading east. The Dorniers dived down to ground level and Lishman followed, giving one a long, fifteen-second burst from 250 yards, closing to 75 yards. Pieces flew off the enemy aircraft's cowling and black smoke began to pour from the starboard engine. Experiencing considerable return fire from the Dornier's rear turret, Lishman broke away with his ammunition exhausted and claimed one enemy aircraft destroyed, the Squadron's first recorded victory and the forerunner of many in the course of the Second World War.

At 15.30 hours, a lone Do 215 reconnaissance aircraft was reported over Merville, and Wight was ordered up to intercept it; unfortunately it turned south-east while in cloud at 20,000 feet when Wight was searching to the north-east. In the late afternoon, Wight was leading Blue Section of "B" Flight, Butterfield and Lishman, on patrol between Gravelines and Furnes at 12,000 feet when he saw four Bf 109s one mile to the south, at the same altitude and flying in the same direction. As he called up on the R/T and commenced his attack, he saw eight to ten more 109s at 14,000 feet. He opened fire at 150 yards and his target half-rolled and began to emit white smoke. As Wight followed it down and fired another burst, the hood flew off and the pilot half-rolled his aircraft again and baled out successfully, some five miles east of Dunkirk. Once more Wight climbed, and this time attacked the topmost flight of eight Bf 110s; he caught one in a diving turn with a burst of fire, causing black and white smoke to pour from one of the engines. The Bf 110 turned onto its back and the hood flew off, allowing the pilot to escape from his burning aircraft which continued its dive towards the ground. After another patrol at 19.25 hours, between Brussels and Bain-le-Compte, which passed off without incident, the Flight settled down for its first anxious night in France.

While "B" Flight was officially based in France, "A" Flight, without its Flight Commander Flt Lt J E J Sing, and consisting of Fg Offs W A Gray, R A Kellow and E G Winning, Plt Off LG E Stone and Sgts M E Croskell and P P Norris, flew down to Biggin Hill, arriving at 11.50 hours on 17 May. Jackie Sing, much to his disgust, was in hospital having his appendix removed. Taking off again at 13.15 hours, the Flight escorted a Bombay of 271 Squadron across the Channel and arrived at Abbeville at 14.25 hours. Also operating from Abbeville during the day were 32 and 151 Squadrons, "B" Flight of 111 Squadron and "B" Flight of 601 Squadron. In the late afternoon, the Flight left Abbeville for Merville to refuel, and at 17.45 hours was airborne again on patrol over Brussels and Verde - Brain until 19.50 hours, before returning to Biggin Hill, not having encountered any enemy aircraft during its patrols from Abbeville.

At Wittering, after "B" Flight had left, another transport aircraft had arrived; rather than send it away empty, and perhaps with memories of the First World War, the Station Commander had all the pilots personal kit loaded on to it. The pilots being billeted in an estaminet, and complete with Mess Kit, tennis rackets and a xylophone, were well prepared to uphold the traditional idea of Englishmen going to war. Needless to say, when the time came to return to England, transport aircraft were less available, and the tennis rackets and xylophone were left for the use of the Luftwaffe; this no doubt helped them to appreciate their opponents who went to war so well equipped.

The two Flights had left Wittering, but the CO, Edwardes Jones, was, much to his annoyance, still there. However his lonely state was not unnoticed, and he came south to join the battle. Flying from Hawkinge, 17 Squadron's CO was missing, so Edwardes Jones took command. Thus he had the probably unique distinction of commanding two squadrons in action at the same time.

In a generally confused situation, 18 May remained a relatively quiet day for the Squadron, although on the ground the rapidly advancing German armoured thrust reached the Cambrai - St Quentin line. "A" Flight led by Tim Winning flew to Lille/Marcq, and fighter patrols were mounted throughout the day, while a section of "B" Flight acted as escort for some Blenheims on a bombing raid. The rapid collapse of the ground forces in France meant that the airfields of the Air Component were in danger of heavy and prolonged attack, if not actual occupation by the German

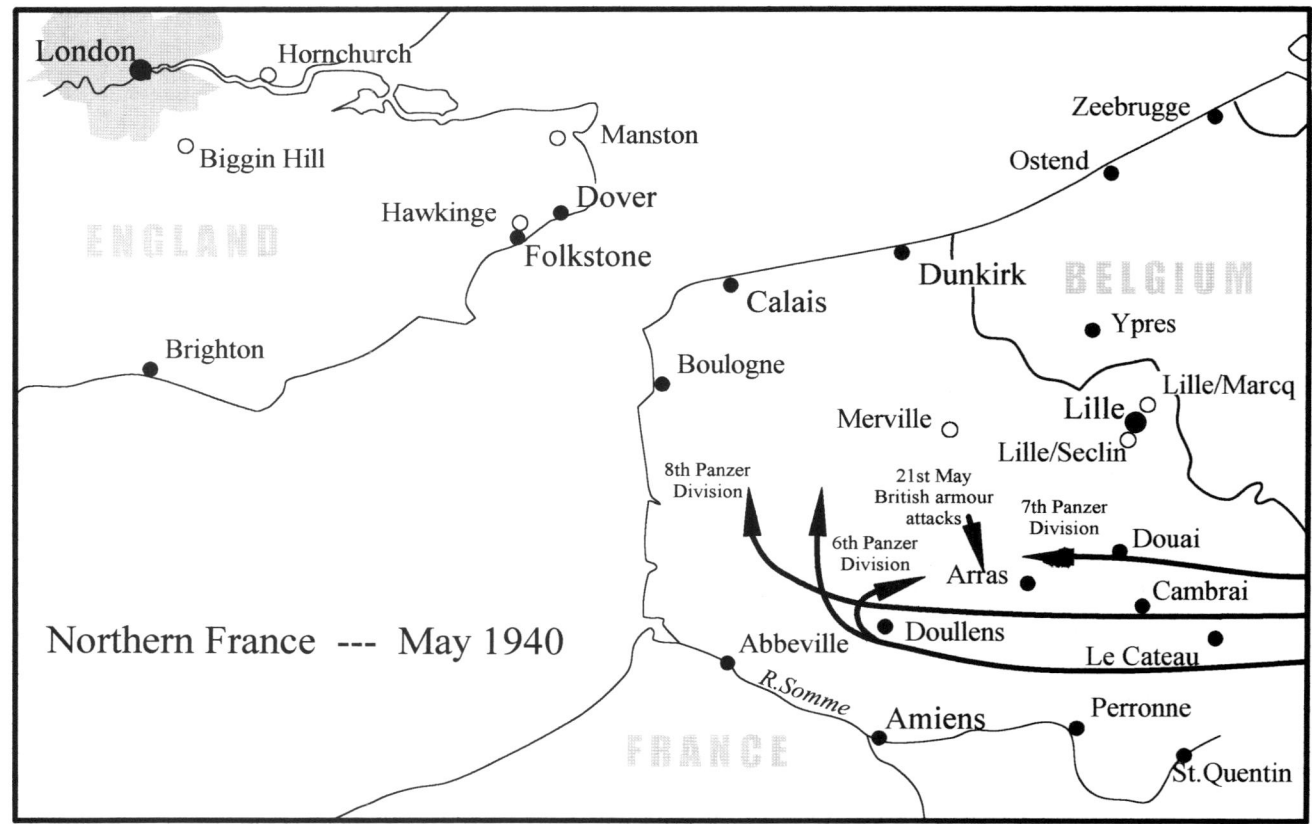

Army. At Merville, a Control Centre as such did not exist, the Flight's only contact with the rest of the front being a solitary telephone in one of the huts. Patrols were therefore flown on a strictly *ad hoc* basis - apart from the escort duties, which were organised by an higher authority. Contact with the Luftwaffe, which also seemed to lack a strong directing authority, was largely a matter of luck.

Early in the morning, Green Section was airborne, with a section of 79 Squadron, to engage seven Do 17Zs of 5/KG 76, and by the time Atkinson and Lishman came up with the German bombers they were ten miles north-east of Arras. The section of 79 Squadron had already launched its attack, and smoke was seen issuing from the second aircraft in the rear section of the enemy formation. Atkinson attacked the third aircraft in the rear section, and encountered return fire which hit his Hurricane. Lishman, flying as Green Three, carried out an attack on the Dornier on the extreme right-hand side of the formation. After a thirteen-second burst, he saw large amounts of black smoke coming from the German bomber's starboard engine, and he broke away to port.

Wight was ordered to fly an airfield defence patrol, as a single aircraft and, once airborne from Merville, he saw ack-ack bursts over Arras. He climbed initially to 5,000 feet, and then, when he saw eight or nine Bf 110s at 6,000 feet, he continued to climb in order to attack. He fixed his sights on one enemy aircraft, but his guns did not fire. As the leading Bf 110 opened fire at Wight, he dived vertically towards the ground doing aileron turns on the way down. Once he had landed back at Merville, it was discovered that the aircraft had not been rearmed after its previous sortie. It should be pointed out that the Hurricane was in fact one of 79 Squadron's, which Wight was flying as those of "B" Flight were all unserviceable.

At 15.25 hours, aircraft from 79 Squadron and "B" Flight joined up over Douai at 18,000 feet, and then flew on as part of an escort of thirty-six Hurricanes for the Blenheims of 18 Squadron which were bombing targets near Avèsnes, but no enemy aircraft were encountered. On his last patrol of the day at 18.30 hours, Atkinson did, however, claim a Bf 110.

In contrast to the calm and peace of England, France seemed a panic-stricken cauldron. Not least among the disquieting features was the presence of fifth column agents in the area. Returning from one patrol, the pilots noticed, some miles from the airfield, a large arrow ploughed into a grass field pointing directly at Merville. Nevertheless, even with such aids, a small grass field, distinguished only by a wind-sock, was no easy target to find. A formation of Do 17s proved the point when they flew directly over the field without releasing its bombs. The Flight, on the ground at the time, dived for the slit trenches beside their aircraft, and the bombers - fortunately - only identified their target in time for the rear-gunners to fire off a few rounds as the formation swept overhead. The greatest threat came, in fact, not from the air, despite the short distances separating the two air forces, but from the advancing German Army. On 18 May, it was ordered that no more squadrons were to be sent to France, and that all units there would be withdrawn within the next two days, and continue to operate from bases in South-East England. In the evening, "A" Flight returned to Biggin Hill, landing at 20.30 hours.

By Sunday, 19 May the advancing German forces had reached Péronne, some thirty-five miles due south of Lille, where the reorganised French 7th Army was detraining to reinforce the front, which stood along the Somme and Ailette between Péronne and Coucy-le-Chateau, straddling the River Oise. Operating in accordance with the War Cabinet's plan, "A" Flight, which Strickland had now rejoined, returned to

Lille/Marcq early in the morning. Just after midday, all five aircraft were scrambled as the airfield was attacked. The French ack-ack opened up, and a Hurricane, not one of the Squadron's, was hit and the pilot baled out. The Flight climbed to 12,000 feet over Lille, where it was attacked by two Bf 109s which fired as they dived past, and then started to climb again. As one pulled up, Stone fired a five-second burst and saw pieces falling off it and white smoke started to pour from the engine. The Messerschmitt then dived almost vertically down to ground level. Stone looked around for the second 109 but could not find it, and returned to land at Lille/Marcq.

In the afternoon, Stone was once again on patrol between Douai and St Armand, in a section of three, when at 10,000 feet he saw three Ju 88s and called the others to attack. He dived upon the leader and closed to one hundred yards, but then the Ju 88's rear gunner opened fire, badly puncturing the Hurricane's radiator, causing glycol to pour into the cockpit and obscure the windscreen. Stone's first attempt to force-land at an airfield between Orchies and St Armand was frustrated when the nearby ack-ack battery opened fire. For his second attempt he picked an unguarded field near Nomain and landed safely. There, to his surprise, he found Strickland, injured after being shot down by ack-ack fire. Having arranged for him to be taken to a Casualty Clearing Station, Stone then telephoned his position to No.60 Wing at Lille. Although the Wing could not provide any transport, 48 Division proved most helpful in producing a car and driver, and Stone was taken back to Merville where, in the evening, he joined up with "B" Flight. The remaining aircraft of "A" Flight returned to Biggin Hill.

The morning of "B" Flight's third day at Merville, 19 May, started early for Atkinson when he was airborne at 05.00 hours, together with nine aircraft from 79 Squadron, on a defensive patrol. Some ten miles north-east of Arras, the patrol encountered seven Dorniers, which were immediately attacked, and one Dornier was seen to drop its bombs harmlessly over open country. Atkinson attacked the third aircraft in the rear section with two eight-second bursts, closing from three hundred and fifty to two hundred and fifty yards and causing white smoke to pour from the port engine. In the attack, however, Atkinson's aircraft was hit by an incendiary shell on its spinner, which then lodged in the port cylinder block, while another struck the oleo-fairing and cut the pipe to the brake.

At 12.00 hours he was airborne again, flying as Number Two in Yellow Section, with Sizer leading and Butterfield flying as Number Three. The section was ordered to patrol between Tournai and Oudenarde at 12,000 feet. After some thirty minutes, ack-ack fire was seen north of Tournai. On investigation, Atkinson spotted a single aircraft north-east of the town, and informed his leader as he went down for a closer look, followed by Sizer and Butterfield. As he approached, the enemy aircraft, - a Henschel Hs 126 used by the Germans for spotting and reconnaissance duties - twisted and turned as it dived down to a height of only fifty feet above the ground. As Sizer opened fire from two hundred and fifty yards, the rear cockpit caught fire and the rear gunner standing up in the open collapsed dramatically over the side of the aircraft. It seemed to Sizer that this, his first combat, was all too much like something he had seen at the cinema. Butterfield flying slowly continued the attack and used all his ammunition. Under this weight of fire, the Henschel's tail-plane broke off and, as Sizer attacked again, it half-rolled into the ground and exploded.

In the afternoon, Atkinson was ordered to patrol base at 20,000 feet, as a single aircraft on a defensive patrol. As he climbed up through 12,000 feet, he saw gun-fire to the east. At full throttle, he went to investigate and saw twenty-five He 111s flying in sections, line astern. Picking on a straggler, he made three attacks from 250 yards, closing to 100 yards, and experienced return fire only on his first attack. Other Hurricanes arrived as Atkinson was leaving, with one He 111 pouring black and white smoke from its port engine and with pieces of cowling and metal being thrown off.

In his first action of the day, Wight was on patrol with seven aircraft at 8,000 feet over Oudenarde when a Hs 126 was seen below. He dived to attack, fired a four-second burst, and then immediately pulled up to look for any accompanying escort. Butterfield flying as Blue Three continued the attack, with his throttle closed he made a deliberate attack after four other Hurricanes had fired. By now the Henschel's engine was failing badly and, as Butterfield fired a few more bursts at close range, the rear gunner ceased firing. Wight, having found no escort, returned to make a beam attack which caused the Henschel's engine to stop, and it fell into a belt of trees.

Wight's next engagement was somewhat inconclusive. While on patrol over the airfield at 15,000 feet, he saw ack-ack fire over Arras. He climbed into sun, and at 20,000 feet saw six Bf 109s about five thousand feet below. He dived to attack the nearest, in a stern attack from slightly below, firing a three/four second burst. He then broke-off, thinking that the aircraft were French Curtiss Hawks, and climbed back into sun. The aircraft he had attacked half-rolled, emitting white smoke, dived vertically to about 2,000 feet and then continued in a more shallow dive towards the south still smoking.

In the evening, at 17.00 hours, six Hurricanes from "A" and "B" Flights were on patrol when ack-ack fire was observed fifteen miles south-east of Oudenarde. The target was another Hs 126. Individual attacks were made as it dived steeply turning to the left and right. Two bursts from Lishman silenced the rear gunner and the unfortunate aircraft continued on its way down until it crashed. Later in the evening "A" Flight returned to Biggin Hill.

On the morning of 20 May, "A" Flight flew down to Manston to refuel and then acted as escort to twenty-four Blenheims on a raid to Arras and Cambrai. While a good deal of flak was encountered, no enemy aircraft were seen. The Flight then landed at Merville and operated in conjunction with "B" Flight. The small grass airfield at Merville was rapidly becoming overcrowded as the two airfields closer to Lille were abandoned and Nos.85 and 87 Squadrons flew in. There were now some fifty Hurricanes scattered around, far too many for the ill-equipped and understaffed Operations Room. The Control Centre was the former flying club hut, and the half-dozen or so telephones that had been installed to provide communication with the forward observation posts; all had exactly the same ringing tone. This led to somewhat farcical scenes as calls came in and the airmen struggled to determine which instrument to answer. At the same time the local area knowledge of both the pilots and the controllers was scanty, to say the least, so it is not surprising that interceptions were largely a matter of chance.

Nevertheless, as the Germans drew closer, actions became more frequent and the morning patrol of "B" Flight's last day at Merville saw the section led by Wight destroy a Do 17. He was leading nine aircraft on a patrol line from Oudenarde to Kerkhove, when a single enemy aircraft was seen after ack-ack bursts were observed over Courtrai. As Wight closed for a beam attack, which developed into a stern attack, the Do 17 flew up-sun and the rear-gunner opened fire at four hundred yards. Firing short bursts, Wight closed to 250 yards when he opened fire again, causing pieces to fly off the damaged aircraft and the port engine to stream oil and white smoke. Atkinson's was the second aircraft to attack and, after two bursts from short range, the enemy aircraft began to dive away for the ground, riddled with bullets, and with both engines smoking. Atkinson's aircraft was covered in oil and hit by a bullet which entered through the escape panel, ricocheted off the armour plating and smashed the voltmeter on its way out of the starboard side of his cockpit. Butterfield was a long way behind when the Do 17 was first spotted, and only came up after six Hurricanes had already attacked. He thought that he saw a gun firing backwards from the starboard engine, (presumably sparks from damage inflicted earlier) and concentrated his fire on this. The "gun" ceased firing and the enemy aircraft slowed down, with oil and smoke coming from its starboard engine, as Butterfield passed above it. Lishman also joined in the attack and, firing a single fifteen-second burst as he closed from 250 yards to 75 yards, saw smoke coming from both engines. Sizer, normally a "B" Flight pilot, but flying with Red Section, also attacked, and saw black smoke and petrol vapour coming from the port engine. A pilot of 79 Squadron later reported having seen the Dornier crash. The unfortunate aircraft was, in fact, a Do 215 of 3(F)/ObdL.

By 10.00 hours, Gray was airborne again, with a formation of six aircraft led by Wight, when at 10,000 feet over Arras an enemy aircraft was seen flying very low south-east of the town. All six Hurricanes, including Sizer's Red Section, dived to the attack and Gray pulled up after a five-second burst, closing fast. After a second burst from Atkinson, the Henschel Hs 126 dived down and landed on a road near Neuville. The crew escaped and the aircraft, from 2(H)/23 Pz, spotting for 1 Panzer Division, was strafed by Butterfield, leaving it completely unserviceable.

In the afternoon, at 17.00 hours, Wight, Atkinson and Lishman in a formation led by Wg Cdr H Broadhurst, the Station Commander of Wittering, became heavily engaged with about thirty Bf 110s. Wight's combat report tells his part of the story:

"I was leading 3 of my aircraft and 3 of 79 Squadron when I saw 5 Me 110s at 15,000 ft followed by about 25 more at 18,000 ft about half a mile behind. I climbed so that I could attack the top lot and attack from the rear. When the section leader of 79 Squadron broke away and attacked the bottom lot or in other words the bait I continued climbing with 213 who stuck with me until I gave the word to attack; after an extensive dog-fight of about five or six minutes an E/A stall-turned in front of me, and I gave him all my remaining ammunition in a burst of about 10 secs.; he flew straight into the burst and fell out of the sky in a floppy manner, but I could not watch him go down as I had to leave myself. I dived vertically to ground level aileron turning on the way down."

Atkinson, flying as Wight's Number Two in Blue Section, picked out a target for a beam attack, but his deflection was wrong, so he selected another and made two head-on attacks. As the two aircraft passed each other he fired two long bursts, with the enemy fighter returning cannon fire but recording no hits. The 110's port engine began to stream black smoke and what was possibly petrol vapour. Atkinson did not have time to see if it crashed, as with his ammunition exhausted, he half-rolled his aircraft, dived down to 2,000 feet at full speed, and headed for home.

Lishman, Blue Three, gave his selected target two seven second bursts of fire from two hundred and fifty yards in a beam attack after it had broken away from the formation and had begun to straggle. He claimed it as a possible, noting that it had opened fire with its cannon at a range of about one thousand yards.

With the CO flying from Hawkinge, leading 17 Squadron over France, and "A" and "B" Flights flying operations from Merville, life back at Wittering continued with its routine as three recent arrivals on the Squadron, Fg Off New and Plt Offs P O P Allcock and Bowen, carried out local area familiarisation flying.

By the evening of 20 May, when "A" Flight returned once more to Biggin Hill, the position at Merville had become critical. Shells could be seen and heard bursting nearby, and the roads became choked with refugees. Finally, all the flights were ordered to leave Merville; a number of the unserviceable aircraft were pushed together, and some of the armourers and fitters set fire to them. Shouted orders told the groundcrew to evacuate the airfield, and an Ensign flew in to pick them up. The pilots of the various flights were strapped in their Hurricanes, ready to take off and escort the Ensign back to England. Straight from the end of its landing-run, the Ensign taxied to the nearest flight and loaded all the personnel. As it taxied around the airfield perimeter, the loading process was repeated, until only "B" Flight remained. But now, to the consternation of both pilots and ground-crew, the Ensign swung into wind, and proceeded to roar across the airfield and take-off, already badly overloaded.

For the groundcrew it was a bitter moment, as it was known that this was the last transport aircraft to leave Merville. The Germans could be heard fighting their way towards the airfield. An even more bitter anguish perhaps was felt by the pilots, as the men who had serviced their aircraft started them up for the last time, and sent them off on their thirty-minute journey to tea at Northolt. Minutes previously, these men had seen the aircraft sent to take them back to England struggle into the air without them. Now, with nothing in their faces to show their disappointment, they wished the pilots luck and saw each Hurricane safely into the air, as they had so many times in the past.

The airfield soon merged into the distant landscape, as the Hurricanes overhauled the Ensign, and escorted it back to its destination in southern England. As the aircraft crossed the coast, the familiar landmarks of the peaceful countryside slipped below. When the dark mass of London appeared on the horizon, the aircraft lost height and dropped down to the neatly laid-out airfield at Northolt, where the Squadron had been reborn such a short time previously. As the tattered, scarred Hurricanes taxied in, the carefully-cut grass in two shades of green, which surrounded the immaculate flower-beds and the unscarred buildings, bore witness that they had returned to a different world. In the quiet of the Mess, the war seemed very distant, but nothing seemed quite so far away as that field with its wind-sock at Merville, where the ground-crew had seen them off so short a time ago. In the evening the Flight returned to Wittering.

Back at Merville, once the aircraft were safely away, Flt Sgt Dave Davenport, a determined NCO of the old school, set about extricating the groundcrew from their parlous position. The first task was to re-mobilise the transport, that minutes before had been rendered unserviceable. With this task accomplished, and against a background of gun-fire, the whole party set off in a small lorry in the direction of Dunkirk, through streams of refugees, and via a short cut which took them into Belgium. Eventually, after being strafed by a German aircraft, the party arrived at the coast. Here,

A Squadron Hurricane I in a makeshift dispersal.

however, the situation seemed to Davenport to be somewhat confused, so the party proceeded southwards, along the coast, to the small port of St. Valéry-en-Caux. Here the lorry was dumped, and Dave Davenport managed to secure a passage for everyone aboard a destroyer bound for England. Eventually, after a very crowded, but otherwise uneventful crossing, the whole party arrived back at Dover. Here they were given a mug of tea, a sandwich and a piece of cake before being handed over to the Military Police, who put them on a train for Tidworth, where the Army had billets prepared, beds made up and food prepared. Having split up into groups of two or three en route to Tidworth from Dover, the next morning was spent on the parade ground re-assembling. From Tidworth, the party returned to Biggin Hill, and immediately went to work servicing the aircraft, using borrowed tools, their own tools and personal kit having been abandoned at Merville, Ted Smith recalls that "his" tool-box had "242" painted on it.

Alan Hill, who had joined the Squadron as an AC2 Instrument Repairer in September 1939 - for a period he was the only 'instrument basher' on the Squadron - had no-one to blame but himself for the perilous position in which he found himself at Merville on 20 May. At Christmas 1939, he had been given the choice of a posting to Canada or Christmas leave. Thinking that nothing much was happening in Canada, he had chosen Christmas leave. When the groundcrew party to go to France was being made up, there was one airman who had only recently married and was reluctant to leave England, so Alan Hill, universally known as Hill Sixty, volunteered to go in his place. The response of Flt Sgt Davenport, to whom he put his request, was that he did not care who went as long as the paper-work was in order.

At Merville, he found the excitement he had been looking for, both by day and night. One evening, lying on the starboard wing-root of a Hurricane while changing an oxygen bottle by the light of a shaded torch, he felt something poking his rear-end. It turned out to be the business end of a bayonet wielded by a soldier who looked scared stiff and who thought the oxygen bottle was a bomb and that Hill was a fifth-columnist.

On 20 May, together with George 'Jedd' Carney, he had been given a few hours off and told 'Don't go far'. They were in a small *estaminet* near the airfield when a despatch-rider appeared and asked them for their unit. On being told, he replied 'Get back fast, they're pulling out'. On returning to the airfield, they found Flt Sgt Smith with half-a-dozen airmen, a truck and a supply of petrol. They edged their way into the stream of refugees and slowly made their way, not towards Dunkirk, which was cut off, but to Boulogne.

On arriving later at night, they were told to 'Push the truck into the harbour but keep your tin hats'. They were then taken to a hut built on stilts on some marshy ground behind the docks where they had no difficulty in falling asleep on the bare boards. Early next morning, in the course of a German air raid, the stilts at one end of the hut were destroyed and about thirty 'erks' and 'squaddies' finished up in a heap at the lower end.

Eventually, they all joined an enormous queue waiting to board the only vessel in sight, a very curious-looking coaster, perhaps a collier; but it looked like a cruise liner to those waiting on the shore. Finally, packed like sardines, the party endured another visit from the German Stukas before setting sail for Dover, and then on to Tidworth.

After one night as guests of the Army, they moved on to

Biggin Hill to join up with 'A' Flight which was already there. Arriving in the middle of the night, they found that no food was available in the Mess. One of the group, 'Swede', who in his civilian life in Norfolk was a poacher, disappeared across the airfield and returned with two rabbits which, by about 13.30 hours, had been turned into a pie fit for a king.

For "A" Flight the show was still on, and sweeps were flown over the French coast which was becoming increasingly hostile. The afternoon of 21 May saw the most significant British counter-attack against the advancing German armoured divisions, when an armoured brigade, supported by two territorial infantry battalions, some garrison troops and field artillery commanded by Major-General Harold Franklyn, and designated "Frankforce", clashed with the infantry and tanks of Rommel's 7 Panzer Division to the north of Arras, while 8 Panzer Division pushed on westwards south of the town. After two days of heavy fighting, during which time elements of 8 Panzer Division reached the Channel coast, the British counter-attack came to a halt and had to withdraw. For the next two days, Rommel's division was halted for rest and repairs and only continued its advance again on 26 May.

After the early morning trip down to Manston on 21 May, "A" Flight again escorted some Blenheims, this time on a raid in the Boulogne/Le Touquet area, and landed at Le Touquet. Following the return to Manston at 14.15 hours, a fighter sweep with 151 Squadron was flown at 17.25 hours in the same vicinity, when again a good deal of flak was encountered. Winning, Plt Off Fisher and Sgt Cooney each registered claims against luckless Henschel Hs 126s spotting for the German Army. The Flight returned to Biggin Hill in the evening, landing at 19.45 hours.

On 22 May, the Flight flew down to Manston after lunch. It then took off for France and escorted a Bombay back to the UK, as the squadrons in France were withdrawn. Two patrols were flown, one in the late afternoon that caught a lone Hs 126 near St Pol, which Winning claimed as a possible. At 19.40 hours, a further patrol was flown but no enemy aircraft were seen, and in the evening the Flight returned once again to Biggin Hill.

The next morning, the Flight returned to Wittering, landing at 11.15 hours, to find "B" Flight already there. Apart from the wandering groundcrew, the Squadron was once more reunited. During this period of respite the Hurricanes were upgraded, VHF radios were fitted, and aircraft with Rotol constant-speed propellers were flight tested; the Hurricanes originally received had been fitted with the DH two-speed propeller.

The first clash with the Luftwaffe was over, but the respite was very much in the nature of the calm before the storm. The Squadron's appetite for action had been whetted, and it was ready for more. The worth of the Hurricane, and its eight machine-guns, had been proved to the hilt. Only the Bf 109 could compare with it. In speed and rate of climb the 109 was, in fact, definitely superior, but the Hurricane could always out-turn its adversary, and in dog-fighting manoeuvrability meant safety. The point was graphically illustrated to Edwardes Jones, when he lead the Squadron over the Channel and it was bounced by one hundred plus Bf 109s. Quickly whipping into a tight turn, he was soon leading five Germans line astern in a neat circle. With a high rate of turn, he even found himself gaining on the fifth Bf 109. However before the biter was bitten, the Germans broke off the engagement and the CO was able to return safely to Biggin Hill.

The Squadron had found itself outnumbered, but not outfought. When confronted by superior numbers, as was to happen time and time again over Dunkirk, it was found that a full-blooded attack, from above and behind if possible, did most to restore the odds. The great mass of enemy fighters immediately broke into many single units, and then for five or ten minutes the air would be full of aircraft in every conceivable attitude. Then, just as suddenly as the attack had started, the fight would be over, and the sky empty. It was then down to wave-top height, and home if no ammunition or insufficient fuel remained, or up to find the rest of the Squadron and reform for another attack.

The much-discussed conflict between Churchill and Dowding concerning the use of Home Defence fighter squadrons in France was never quite as black and white as it has often been portrayed. Both men understood that, operationally, Fighter Command's front-line squadrons should not be frittered away in France. Nevertheless, under the strongest political pressure from France, Churchill gave some ground, and by the time all RAF units were withdrawn all but three of Fighter Command's Hurricane squadrons had operated from the other side of the Channel, either as a whole or in part. The reasons for not sending the squadrons across the Channel were practical; that is, they were operational and technical, since the infrastructure required to operate them effectively did not exist. There was no proper control system to make effective interceptions possible. The airfields, in the main, and certainly including Merville, were literally grass fields with no proper control tower or runways, and certainly no form of defence from attacks by land or air. The reasons for sending the squadrons to France were political and, as is so often the case, the political reasons overrode the practical.

Other factors also hampered the effectiveness of the RAF squadrons in France. The training for air combat that had prevailed throughout the nineteen-thirties was dangerously flawed, with the emphasis being given to tight formation flying to the detriment of gunnery and effective fighter tactics. In the event, the Hurricanes in France had been frittered away, being used too often in flight - or section - strength to oppose mass formations of German aircraft. In the final analysis, the twelve No.11 Group squadrons that reinforced the Advanced Air Striking Force and the Air Component in France lost fifty-nine Hurricanes, with eleven pilots killed, seven lost as prisoners-of-war and five injured, while claiming ninety-seven enemy aircraft destroyed and thirty-nine as probably destroyed. The Squadron fared better than many, losing only two Hurricanes and with two pilots injured, one of these as the result of a flying accident. Against this, the Squadron had made claims for six and three-quarters enemy aircraft destroyed, and two probables.

CHAPTER FOUR -

DUNKIRK

Air Marshal Sir Hector McGregor, KCB, CBE, DSO, who as Sqn Ldr H D McGregor, DSO, commanded the Squadron from 27 May 1940 until 25 August 1940. (Ministry of Defence)

On Sunday 26 May 1940 the British Expeditionary Force, together with elements of the French Army, were pinned down and surrounded in the seaside town of Dunkirk. Under the code name "Operation Dynamo", the great withdrawal of the troops from the beaches commenced.

Five days after the return of "B" Flight from France, the Squadron moved south once more to Biggin Hill, and flew patrols over the Belgian coast covering Ostend and Zeebrugge. Despite their protests, Nos.32 and 79 Squadrons were sent north to rest and Nos.213 and 242 Squadrons arrived to operate over Dunkirk, while No.229 Squadron came to fill the gap in the home defences. Although the decision to withdraw from Dunkirk had been taken on 26 May, the order came too late to affect No.11 Group's dispositions for that day. The real air battle over the beaches of Dunkirk was therefore fought on the last four days of May and the first three days of June.

By 2 June, when the British rearguard was withdrawn, some 338,226 Allied troops had been evacuated from the beaches, over seven times more than the 45,000 that it had been thought possible to rescue when Dynamo was conceived. Over France, from 10 May, and during the period of the evacuation up to 4 June, the RAF lost four hundred and thirty-two Hurricanes and Spitfires. The spirit of the pilots at Dunkirk has been recorded for posterity in a letter, written at the height of the battle, by "Widge" Wight, "B" Flight Commander, to his mother:-

"Well, another day is gone and with it a grand lot of blokes. Got another brace of 109s today, but the whole Luftwaffe seems to leap on us - we were hopelessly outnumbered. I was caught napping by a 109 in the middle of a dog-fight, and got a couple of holes in my aircraft, one of them filled the office with smoke, but the Jerry overshot and HE'S dead. If anyone says anything to you in the future about the inefficiency of the RAF - I believe the BEF troops were booing the RAF in Dover the other day - tell them from me that we only wish we could do more. But without aircraft we can do no more than we have done - that is our best, and that is fifty times better than the German best, though they are fighting under the most advantageous conditions. I know of no RAF pilot who has refused combat yet - and that sometimes means combat with odds of more than fifty to one. Three of us the other day had been having a fight, and we were practically out of ammunition and juice when we saw more than eighty 109s and twelve Ju 87s, all the same we gave them combat and they left us alone in the end - on their side of the Channel too. This is not a tale of stirring heroism, it is just the work we all do. One of my Sergeants shot down three fighters and a bomber before they got him - and then he got back in a paddle steamer. So don't worry, we are going to win this war even if we have only one aeroplane and one pilot left - the Boche could produce the whole Luftwaffe and you would see that one pilot and the one aeroplane go into combat. All that sounds very involved, but I am trying to convey to you something of the spirit of "Per Ardua ad Astra" today. The spirit of the average pilot has to be seen to be believed."

Having flown down to Biggin Hill from Wittering on the evening of 26 May, dawn the following day found the Squadron, accompanied by six aircraft of 242 Squadron, acting as escort to Blenheims operating against St. Omer, where the Germans were pressing hard against the defensive perimeter. With the escort duties safely over, the aircraft took up a patrol line from Gravelines to Nieuport, where they came under heavy but inaccurate anti-aircraft fire from our own guns. The patrol returned to Manston at 07.50 hours. The Squadron flew in four vics of three; Edwardes Jones, Croskell and Boyd leading "A" Flight, consisting of Red and Yellow Sections, with Winning, Gray and Stone, while Wight, Atkinson and Grayson led "B" Flight, made up of Blue and Green Sections, with Sizer, Butterfield and Lishman.

At 09.25 hours the same formation, minus Butterfield, flew a patrol over the Eccloo - Maldegem area but no enemy aircraft were encountered, nor was any ground activity seen.

The main action of the day involved the nine aircraft, led by the CO, which took-off at 16.10 hours to patrol from Gravelines to Furnes at 12,000 feet. While over the beaches, Atkinson saw four Bf 109s approaching from the south, followed by eight more, and alerted the CO. The Bf 109s were escorting a force of He 111s en route to bomb the ships in Dunkirk harbour. As Atkinson dived to attack, the Bf 109 formation broke up, and he followed one round in a wide circle; when it turned south again he gave it a long burst in a quarter attack. The 109 started to climb, pouring white smoke, and he gave it another long burst from abeam, at which it rolled slowly onto its back and dived down smoking furiously. Another pilot saw burning wreckage two miles south of Bombourg, which could have been the aircraft attacked by Winning of "A" Flight, who selected one of the four Bf 109s as a target and followed it into a right-hand climbing turn. At 17,000 feet the German reversed his turn, and Winning saw his bullets strike their target. The Messerschmitt was last seen diving away into the smoke over Dunkirk.

At the final reckoning, two kills were credited to Wight (details of the combats no longer exist) and one each to Atkinson and Winning.

Wight had the legendary eyesight of the fighter pilot. When to others the sky was a blank, he could discern distant specks; when others picked up the specks, he could identify the type of aircraft. With such an advantage the Squadron was often able to take up a good attacking position before launching itself onto the enemy.

The weather on the morning of 28 May was dull with huge masses of thundery cumulus cloud building up in the sky. The Squadron was airborne at 05.45 hours escorting six Blenheims on a bombing raid over St. Omer. With escort duties over, a patrol line established, once again, between Gravelines and Nieuport, covered the beaches north and south of Dunkirk. At 07.10 hours Wight saw an He 111 dropping bombs; he flew to engage it but the bomber suddenly slowed down, causing him to overshoot; Sammy Butterfield however scored hits before it disappeared into cloud. Five minutes later, while at 6,000 feet, the patrol was attacked from above by six Bf 109s, which came in from the north and passed across in front of the Squadron before wheeling round to attack from the rear. Turning into the attack, Wight opened fire causing the tail of one to burst into flames and subsequently break-off; the 109 crashed just south of Middelkerke. As another enemy aircraft crossed in front of Sizer, he dropped in behind it and chased it inland. After a few bursts it began to trail smoke and rolled over; looking back as he passed over it Sizer saw the Messerschmitt crash into a wood.

However, the engagement was not all one-sided. Tim Winning, the Squadron Adjutant, failed to return, while Boyd crashed into the sea but was picked up and returned safely.

By mid-morning, after a quick bite to eat at Biggin Hill, the Squadron's ten remaining Hurricanes, in company with the mostly-Canadian 242 Squadron and with 229 Squadron as top cover, were heading once more towards the great pall of smoke that marked the town of Dunkirk like a beacon. From Dover to the French coast, the Channel was like a broad highway carrying a continuous stream of boats across the water. Since it was impossible for the squadrons to fly and fight together due to the cloud and smoke, they soon became separated, and some elected to patrol on top while others, including 242 Squadron, lost height and flew beneath the clouds.

Towards the end of the patrol, action was joined with approximately thirty Bf 109s, which appeared out of the mist escorting Dorniers, He 111s and Ju 88s, which were just starting their bombing runs over the beaches. Wight saw the Bf 109s coming and turned to attack, sending one down trailing smoke. He then joined up with the CO, and headed for home. However he then saw some eighty aircraft, which he initially thought were Blenheims and Spitfires, but which actually turned out to be Ju 88s and Bf 109s. The two Hurricanes turned to attack, and engaged four 109s. Wight caught one in a stall turn and used all his remaining ammunition on it. Edwardes Jones, in a tight turn followed by six Bf 109s and after hearing Wight say that he was returning to base, at last found a 109 in his sights, only to discover that his guns were still on "safe".

Gray climbed up to attack two Bf 109s at the rear of the formation. He hit one with several short bursts in the course of a quarter attack, the 109 fell away and dived to the ground. Gray did not follow as he came under attack from abeam and astern by two more Bf 109s; having no remaining ammunition, he climbed into cloud and returned to base.

Elsewhere in the sky Atkinson, flying as Blue Four, climbed to engage the fighter escort, which he first saw south of the Squadron and some 2,000 feet above. Several Squadron aircraft climbed and each selected a target. Atkinson's quarry dived for cloud cover after receiving his initial burst. He then saw another Bf 109 diving steeply and heading for the German lines. A final burst of gunfire brought smoke from the departing enemy aircraft and it crashed eight miles behind the German lines.

Lishman also claimed a Bf 109 destroyed. Within five minutes, despite the great odds, seven enemy aircraft had been knocked down, several more damaged and the bombers scattered. Five of the victims were Bf 109s, and the other two were an He 111 and a Bf 110. In the course of this engagement three Hurricanes were lost but Lishman, who was wounded, and Butterfield were picked up in the Channel and were soon back in action. Plt Off G G Stone, who was dead when picked up, was buried at sea with full Naval Honours. Butterfield's combat report gives some idea of the pace of the battle:-

"I was Blue Two in a formation of nine (ten) aircraft patrolling Dunkirk. Towards the end of our patrol about nine Me 109s were sighted. A dog-fight ensued and an Me 109 sailed in front of me and started climbing away from me. I opened fire at 100 yards and the second burst set him on fire. I then turned, right onto another Me 109 and fired one burst from astern; his port wing folded up. As I levelled out a Ju 88 flew across my path. I did a quarter attack on him. His starboard engine emitted black smoke and he half-rolled into the sea. I was then hit underneath by a cannon shell and did a turn to the right and saw an Me 110 fly past. I did a beam

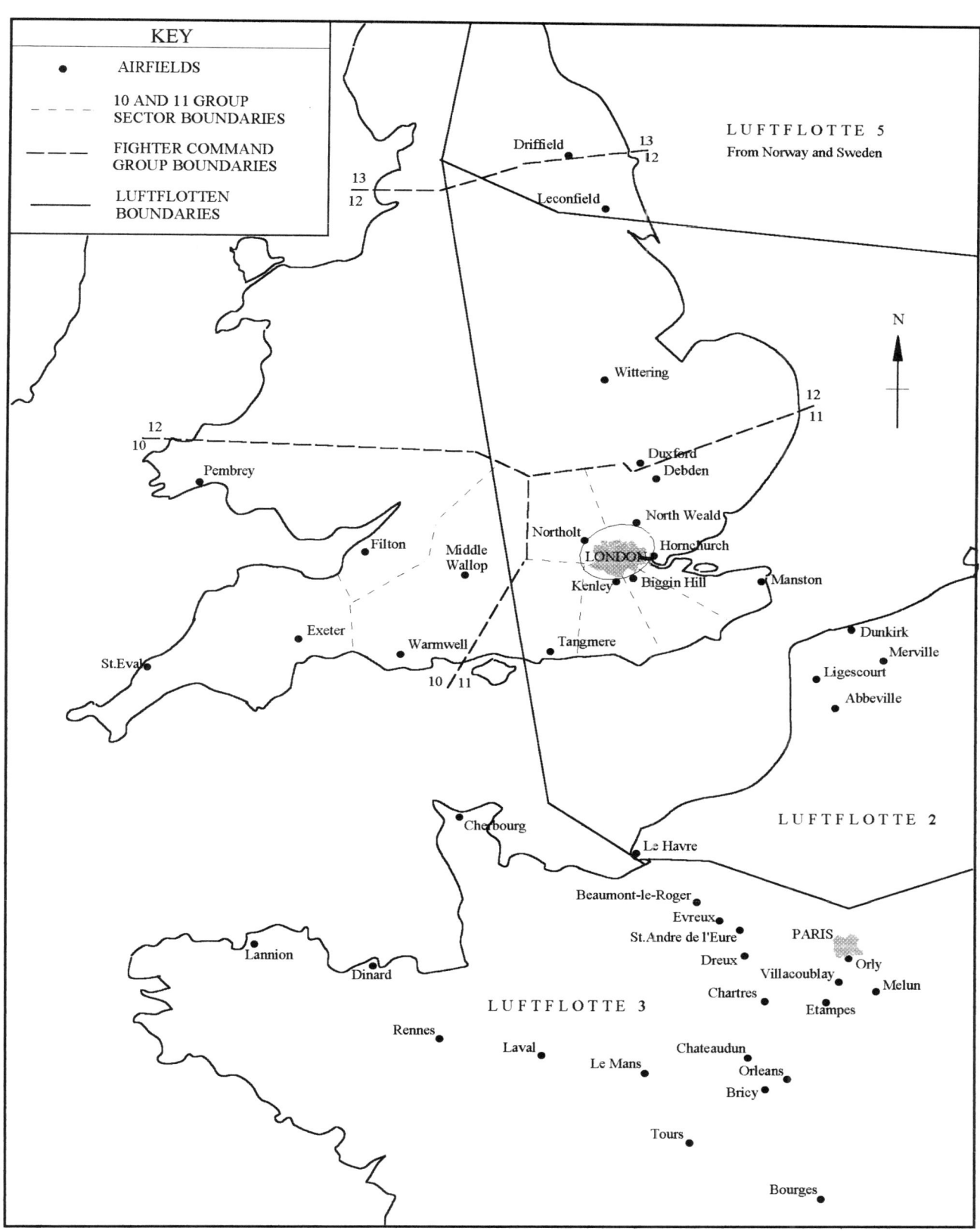

DUNKIRK AND THE BATTLE OF BRITAIN - 1940

attack on him and his starboard engine smoked and he turned on his back and fell into the sea. I then turned to the right and saw a large number of enemy aircraft proceeding from the direction of Dover. A number of them immediately turned upon me and I pulled the plug and headed for home, twisting and turning. Which ever way I turned I ran into incendiary fire and the aircraft was hit a number of times. Two shells smashed the instrument panel and three more struck underneath and the engine stopped and flames appeared over the wing roots. I was at 400 ft. and tried to get out but couldn't, so I pulled the stick back from a crouching position on the seat. As the aircraft stalled I got over the port side and took a header off the mainplane. I was being fired at so I delayed pulling the rip-cord until I was about 200 ft. above the sea. I left the aircraft at 800 ft. The parachute worked perfectly and my life-jacket held me up with one deep breath in it. I was picked up by the paddle-steamer *Sundown* and landed at Margate."

The evening sortie, airborne at 19.45 hours, and again led by the CO, found the six remaining Hurricanes over the beaches until 21.40 hours. During the day two hard engagements had been fought, and four aircraft were missing. Now late in the day, in thick weather and raining hard, six of the same pilots who had flown the dawn sortie at 05.40 hours were on patrol once more. The bad weather, however, was sufficient to discourage the Luftwaffe, and no contact was made with the enemy. During the day, a total of 321 sorties were flown over the beaches by the squadrons involved at Dunkirk. Four of the squadrons had flown three patrols each at maximum strength. The order of the day had been "to ensure the protection of the Dunkirk beaches (three miles either side) from first light until darkness by continuous fighter patrols in strength". Nothing had been spared in the execution. In the main, the Luftwaffe had concentrated its efforts on bombing the town and port of Dunkirk; this was due in no small part to the increased RAF air cover, as well as the poor weather, and the heavy pall of smoke that covered the area for most of the day.

In these latter days of May, Sqn Ldr Edwardes Jones usually led the Wing flying from Biggin Hill. He was always on the look out for "trouble", and the long patrols he led caused not a few anxious moments, not due to concerns about enemy activity, but to the low fuel state recorded and whether or not the aircraft would make it back to base.

The third morning of the operation, 29 May, brought some respite to the pilots at Biggin Hill as the dawn patrols were flown by Nos.19, 41, 222, and 616 (South Yorkshire) Squadrons operating from Hornchurch. So it was not until mid-day that the eight available Hurricanes took off for the advanced airfield at Manston. Only two patrols were flown this day, in line with Air Vice-Marshal Parkes's declared policy of flying fewer missions, but each in greater strength. On both patrols the Squadron found heavy concentrations of enemy bombers.

Patrolling with Nos.56 and 151 Squadrons, eight Hurricanes flew as top cover to twelve Defiants of 264 Squadron, which were deliberately operating at a lower altitude on the look-out for German bombers. As a formation of five Bf 109s attacked, perhaps mistaking the Defiants for Hurricanes, four were shot down as they closed in on the Defiants flying steadily in line astern. Some ten minutes later, six He 111s appeared from the south at 14,000 feet, three thousand feet above the Squadron. In the first pass Edwardes Jones damaged three He 111s, which were subsequently further attacked by other members of his section and claimed as possibles.

Wilf Sizer was over Dunkirk, leading Green Section with Atkinson as his Number Two, followed by Blue Section. As he dived down to attack the third He 111 in a section of three, he lost Atkinson. Soon black smoke was pouring from the enemy aircraft Sizer had attacked, and no return fire was coming from the rear gunner; after he had attacked a second time the Heinkel's starboard engine blew up and it disappeared into the black smoke above Dunkirk with one engine on fire.

Having become separated from his leader, Atkinson climbed up to attack a straggler, making several beam attacks. The Heinkel had already been attacked once, probably by the CO, and was smoking slightly. By the end of Atkinson's last attack the Heinkel's port engine was pouring black smoke with a flicker of flame, and the propeller was idling. Atkinson was forced to turn away as he had used all his ammunition, and he could also see Bf 109s approaching.

Flt Sgt C Grayson climbed to attack another He 111; opening fire at three hundred and fifty yards, he put in two three-second bursts as he closed to one hundred yards. White, and then black, smoke came from the Heinkel's starboard engine, and though Grayson throttled back he was unable to maintain his position behind the damaged enemy aircraft. He therefore broke away to starboard to give cover to the Defiants as they climbed to engage six Do 215s. Before that engagement could take place however, he saw a formation of forty Stukas, about 3,000 feet below and approaching Dunkirk from the sea. He carried out a quarter attack on the rearmost bomber and, after firing a four-second burst, smoke appeared from his target followed by a red glow from the cockpit. As it dived steeply away Grayson turned his attentions to another Ju 87 but when he tried to fire his guns nothing happened. He then returned to base and landed, where it was discovered that a bullet had entered through the leading edge of his starboard mainplane, and had lodged inside his number two starboard gun ammunition tank.

Llewellyn shot down a third He 111 before engaging the fighter escort and destroying two Bf 109s. On the earlier patrol he had already shot down an He 111 and a Bf 109.

Gray, flying as Red Two, climbed to engage the enemy aircraft, and fired at one He 111 in a stern attack; black smoke poured from its engine and it dived away towards the ground. Gray broke away and, as he pulled up, he found a Ju 87 directly in front of him; he fired the rest of his ammunition and, as the enemy aircraft disappeared into the mist over Dunkirk, he could see that it was trailing black smoke.

Mike Croskell had been unable to maintain his position as Red Three in "A" Flight when the Squadron climbed to attack the Heinkel formation, due to a faulty engine. However, when he saw below him some thirty Ju 87s about to bomb Dunkirk harbour, he followed one Stuka down and attacked it as it pulled out of its dive. It immediately turned over on to its back and dived towards the sea, smoke coming from its engine. Croskell did not have time to see if it crashed as he was immediately attacked by a Bf 109 which he "had great difficulty in avoiding".

On the evening patrol, again with eleven Defiants of 264 Squadron, the Squadron was airborne at 19.00 hours returning at 21.00 hours. On this patrol Llewellyn shot down his third He 111 of the day.

Five minutes after reaching Dunkirk, the patrol spotted several Ju 88s bombing the beaches. Despite strong anti-aircraft fire from the ack-ack posts and the destroyers in the harbour, no aircraft seemed to be hit. Gray, Red Leader,

Also involved in the opening days of the German offensive on 10 May 1940 were fighters of the Belgian Air Force, in this case Fairey Firefly IIMs

attacked one Ju 88 and after several short bursts it began to emit black smoke, and then escaped into cloud.

Atkinson, on patrol as Blue Four, saw the Ju 88s out to sea, and closed for a beam attack. Despite return fire from the rear cockpit, he closed in and used all his ammunition in one long sustained burst. As he broke away he saw another aircraft making an attack. These successes were achieved without loss to the Squadron, and eight Hurricanes were again serviceable for the following day.

Fighter Command's efforts on 29 May received greater recognition on the ground, and a most appreciative signal was received from the Vice Admiral Dover, Bertram Ramsay, "I am most grateful for your splendid co-operation. It alone has given us the chance of success". The only regret on the part of the pilots was the limited amount of time they were able to stay on patrol over the beaches. Inevitably it seemed that an attack had just finished when they arrived, or that one developed when lack of fuel forced them to return to England. Patrolling at economical cruising speed gave the Hurricane approximately forty minutes over the beaches, but any combat when full power was required cut this time drastically.

On 30 May the weather took a decisive hand, and the three hundred German bombers, waiting to take off with their fighter escorts, were kept on the ground by total cloud cover between 300 and 3,000 feet. Fog and sea mist also rolled in over the coast which, mingling with the smoke from the beleaguered town of Dunkirk itself, made high level bombing very difficult, and dive bombing by either the Ju 87s or Ju 88s totally impossible. In the afternoon spasmodic raids developed, and Parkes's policy of flying patrols in strength was fully implemented. With the CO once more up front, the Squadron's eight remaining Hurricanes led the Biggin Hill Wing of four squadrons on patrol at 12,000 feet. Above at 25,000 feet was 264 Squadron flying Defiants, whilst 56 and 151 Squadrons gave top cover. Shortly after 15.00 hours a lone Do 17 was seen, and the CO ordered "Blue" Section led by Wight to engage. The enemy aircraft was flying at 5,000 feet approximately one mile east of Dunkirk. Wight dived to the attack with the sun behind him. His first burst caused an explosion halfway along the Dornier's fuselage which was visible to Edwardes Jones still some 10,000 feet above. Pieces flew off, the pilot appeared to be losing control, and intermittent flames were also seen to be coming from the port engine. Wight closed in, and saw that the Dornier was riddled with holes and no return fire was coming from the upper turret. The section made further attacks until the damaged bomber disappeared into cloud at 1,000 feet. Two hours later the four remaining serviceable Hurricanes were again over the beaches, in very thick weather, and returned to Biggin hill without having contacted any enemy aircraft. Here they were joined by the rest of the pilots and the other unserviceable aircraft.

These were some of the earliest Wing formations flown, and several problems presented themselves. Not only did each squadron operate in its own particular style, but also no training had ever been carried out with such large formations. No.213 Squadron normally split into two flights once over the beaches and then operated as two independent units. Some squadrons had difficulty in maintaining formation when climbing through cloud, and there was little planning as to how a Wing should operate. In the very beginning, each squadron took it in turn to lead; once Edwardes Jones discovered that, due to losses in one squadron, a Flying Officer was due to lead not only his own squadron, but the whole Wing.

Notwithstanding the comparative lull in aerial activity on the 30 May, a signal was sent by Lord Gort, VC, DSO, MVO, MC, Commander-in-Chief of the BEF, praising the efforts of the RAF. The contents of this signal, together with a message from the Chief of the Air Staff, were then sent to all Commands and subsequently distributed to all squadrons directly or indirectly involved in the air operations over Dunkirk.

MESSAGE FROM LORD GORT AND FROM THE CHIEF OF THE AIR STAFF.
30th May 1940.

Message from Lord Gort:

"Extremely grateful for valuable work of RAF. Presence and action of fighters is of first importance in preventing embarkation being interrupted and is having most heartening effect on troops".

Message from Chief of the Air Staff.

"I wish to express to you my warmest congratulations on the successes achieved by all Units during the critical period of the last forty-eight hours and my profound appreciation of the effort which you have been able to sustain. The messages from Lord Gort and VA Dover will show you clearly how vital a factor air-support is during the continuance of the present operation, and I count on all ranks to continue to do their utmost to help the Navy and the Army, who are fighting most gallantly under conditions of extreme difficulty."

Under the cover of the cloud, mist, haze, fog and smoke, and with the limited activity of the Luftwaffe interrupted by the Hurricanes and Spitfires of No.11 Group, almost fifty-four thousand Allied soldiers had been evacuated during the day. Thus far over 126,000 troops had been taken off the beaches, far more than the planners had ever imagined could be saved.

By the morning of 31 May the weather had cleared and, after the early morning mist had gone, the day remained clear and fine. The Luftwaffe's main objective this day was to be the allied shipping, rather than the town of Dunkirk itself. The morning remained relatively calm, but the afternoon saw some of the heaviest fighting of the whole operation. Though not all beaten back from the harbour area, the raiders were so harassed that much of their bombing went astray; only one vessel was sunk by a direct air attack.

The morning trip from Biggin Hill to Manston was duly completed and, after refuelling, the Squadron put up ten aircraft on patrol once more, together with 264 Squadron in its Defiants. However, on this occasion, some brilliant tactician had decreed that the positions of the two squadrons should be reversed, which led to disaster for both units.

This patrol was led by Wight, as the CO was forced to remain at base to catch up with his administrative duties. His successor, Sqn Ldr H D McGregor, DSO (later Air Marshal Sir Hector McGregor KCB, CBE, DSO, C-in-C Fighter Command 1959-1962), had arrived at Biggin Hill. Allaying the doubts of Edwardes Jones, McGregor borrowed his helmet and parachute and went along with the Squadron to see how it operated. One mile north of Dunkirk a mass of over one hundred enemy aircraft was sighted, a mixed bag of Bf 109s, Bf 110s, and He 111s.

The scores mounted rapidly as a fierce dog-fight developed with the fighter escort. Wight destroyed two Bf 109s, while Fg Off K N G Robinson, Sizer and Butterfield each downed one; Butterfield also claimed one probable. Sgt Norris reported shooting down an He 113, a new type for the Squadron. Indeed a new "type" altogether for, although a number of these aircraft had been reported as being shot down, no such aircraft existed. The He 113s that appeared in German propaganda were in fact He 100 prototypes that had been painted in various spurious squadron markings and colour schemes, and posed in a line to appear as if they were in operational service. The "He 113s" that were shot down were almost certainly Bf 109s.

On landing back at Biggin Hill, Wight discovered to his horror that only five of the Hurricanes had returned. Somewhat ashen in appearance, he reported to Edwardes Jones that he had lost five aircraft, and the new CO, in the process of shooting down seven enemy aircraft.

In fact Sizer had landed his blazing aircraft just south of Dunkirk, and arrived back at Dover late in the afternoon. Robinson had parachuted onto the beach and he also made his way back to Dover with the ships that seemed to be going in that direction. But Fg Off W N Gray and Sgt T Boyd had been killed in action, and McGregor's adventures by the time he returned to Biggin Hill had been somewhat protracted.

Quite early on in the engagement his aircraft had been set on fire by cannon shells and he baled out well out to sea. Once in the water, remembering Edwardes Jones's request to "look after" his parachute and head-set, he wrapped the shroud lines of the parachute several times around his arm. Fortunately his descent into the sea had been observed by a destroyer, which promptly hove to a little distance from him. By loud hailer he was informed that he had descended into the edge of a minefield, and, as the destroyer could not approach any closer, he would be cast a line. Having secured a firm grip on the line, McGregor signalled the destroyer which slowly steamed off dragging him clear of the minefield; but at some discomfort since the parachute tended to act as a sea anchor as it was dragged through the water. Once on board, his troubles were not over as the ship was proceeding towards Dunkirk and not Dover. Thus his afternoon was spent uncomfortably amid the crash of bombs and the whine of shells, interrupted by occasional explosions as one of the losers of the aerial battle above plunged into the troubled waters he had so recently left. Evening found him once more back in England.

Sizer had also spent the day more or less uncomfortably on the beaches at Dunkirk. While putting the final touches to the destruction of a Bf 109 travelling north over the beaches, he had found himself under attack from behind. After a shattering crash, the windscreen and canopy of his aircraft became covered in glycol and oil. His first reaction was to leave his badly damaged aircraft, and to this end he climbed into a crouching position on the seat. However, the rows of "little white electric light bulbs" that continued to stream past his canopy persuaded him that he was still receiving the full attention of his attacker. Accordingly he slipped back into his seat, and dropping low over the sandy beach of La Panne, just up the coast from Dunkirk, he put his Hurricane down in the soft sand which brought it to an abrupt halt. With his straps still undone from his attempt to bale out, he was stunned and bleeding from cuts on his nose and chin when he climbed from his stricken aircraft.

Once clear, the first thing that attracted his attention was the noise of the engine - still running, and driving the propeller-boss, minus blades, round and round in its sandy bed. So he returned to the aircraft to switch off the engine, and retrieve his parachute. This latter task seemed particularly important, as being Squadron Parachute Officer he felt that to return without it would be more than his life was worth. With his wounds roughly dressed at a nearby casualty clearing station, he set off in the direction of the beaches, looking for a quick return to England. Unlike some other pilots, who received a rather chilly reception from the Army, it seemed to Sizer that his return was given considerable priority. He assumed that this was probably due to the belief that his place was in the sky overhead, and that the sooner he was back there the better.

Once at Dunkirk, he was about to board a destroyer, when a naval officer at the gang-plank pointed out that the neighbouring Clyde paddle-steamer *Plynlimon* would leave first, and that he would be better off aboard her. That officer probably saved Sizer's life. For as the *Plynlimon* churned her way out of the harbour, a swarm of Ju 87s concentrated their attack on the waiting destroyer, and a direct hit seemed to rip her apart at the seams. Back at the hospital in Dover, one of Sizer's first visitors was McGregor, who had also just arrived back from his own short sea voyage.

After this engagement, the returning aircraft landed at Manston at 15.35 hours, and in the evening returned to Wittering.

The new month saw the Battle of Dunkirk nearly over as far as 213 Squadron was concerned. On 1 June, four new squadrons were made available to Air Vice-Marshal Park, AOC 11 Group. No.43 Squadron had arrived at Tangmere from Wick, 66 Squadron had come from Coltishall to Kenley, 72 Squadron at Acklington had come down to Gravesend and 266 Squadron at Wittering was ordered to readiness, having recently arrived from Martlesham Heath. Some of the existing squadrons had been weakened sufficiently to warrant their withdrawal from the front line; others needed to be relieved after a longer than usual period of operational duty. However, there seemed little rhyme or reason as to why some squadrons were withdrawn from the front line and others remained. Both 54 and 74 Squadrons had performed well and, although tired, were operating increasingly effectively when they were withdrawn. On the other hand 17 and 19 Squadrons had been in action continuously since well before Dunkirk, and would remain.

On 1 June one aircraft flew to Henlow, and that was the only flight that day. On 2 June, flight tests were carried out and at 13.15 hours four aircraft flew to Kenley and returned immediately. At 16.30 hours two aircraft flew to Northolt, and in the evening a patrol of five aircraft flew over the Dunkirk beaches, and returned with nothing to report.

The Junkers Ju 87, popularly known as the 'Stuka', was widely used for dive-bombing during the campaign in France and Belgium

The two following days saw the Squadron on patrol in strength between Manston and Deal, returning from Manston to its old base at Wittering in the evening of 4 June. One forty-five minute trip had removed the crews, once again, from the war-torn skies of the Channel to the peaceful fields and quiet countryside of Northamptonshire. Here the Squadron rested for five days, practising combat and formation flying. On 7 June Edwardes Jones flew his last trip with the Squadron, and departed to Sutton Bridge.

On the last day of the Squadron's rest, 8 June, five aircraft were airborne practising combat, and two formations totalling thirteen aircraft were also airborne. Wight was selected to take a Hurricane to Farnborough, where he carried out practice combat with a captured Bf 109 to assess its strengths and weaknesses. Early in the evening of the following day, thirteen aircraft flew south once more to Biggin Hill for "operational purposes". These purposes proved to be fighter sweeps over the coastal areas of Northern France. With Dunkirk taken at last, the Germans turned their attention towards the rest of France, and especially Paris.

On 10 June the Squadron's first trip of the day, as in the past, was to a forward airfield, this time Hawkinge. From there, escort was provided for twelve Blenheims *en route* to bomb Rouen. The trip lasted one hour and fifty minutes, most of which was flown at just above stalling speed to conserve fuel. On these missions, the same problems arose which were later to cause conflict between the fighter and bomber forces of the Luftwaffe during the Battle of Britain. As the bombers took their time forming up and circling at the rendezvous, the fighters' precious reserve of fuel was being whittled away. Dog-legs on the way to the target added to the fighter pilots'

anxieties, as did long approaches from the far side of the target area. Very often, even a short period of combat meant that insufficient fuel remained for the return to base. Even more seriously, it sometimes became necessary for the fighters to leave their charges before the target area had been reached. For the RAF, the initial raiding period was short, and the problems were thus shelved, but for the Luftwaffe during the Battle of Britain the effort was on a larger scale and no adequate solution ever evolved. In the afternoon of 10 June, a fighter sweep was mounted over Rouen and, as in the morning, no opposition showed itself.

For the next four days, until 14 June, the same pattern unfolded. Numerous fighter sweeps covered the French coast from Le Havre up to Calais, taking in Rouen and "A" Flight's sometime base at Abbeville. On two occasions enemy aircraft were seen in the distance, but they were not engaged. On the last day of this type of operations a bomber escort was provided once more, this time to Béthune.

At Biggin Hill, with the first period of intense air activity over, the Station Commander - Gp Capt Grice - organised a party to end all parties, which was also designed to help reduce the stocks in the cellar of the Officer's Mess, in case of an invasion. The Squadron acquitted itself with its usual *élan*. The party expanded as the night wore on and, led by the CO, the pilots departed for the Savoy and were soon singing well-known Air Force ballads to the accompaniment of Mr Carol Gibbons at the piano. The return to Biggin Hill was by courtesy of London taxi-drivers, one of the early occasions that later developed into something of a tradition for the pilots of this famous station.

The Hurricane's main opponent in the Battle of Britain, the Messerschmitt Bf 109E, on this occasion in a field near Aldington, Kent, on 5 September 1940

CHAPTER FIVE - THE BATTLE OF BRITAIN - EXETER, No. 10 GROUP

The Battle of France was over, and in the warmth of the early summer days the Luftwaffe prepared for its next passage of arms. Proud and confident after its crushing victories in the campaigns against Poland, Denmark, Norway, The Netherlands, Belgium and above all France, the German High Command planned for the final thrust against Britain. As the Army over-ran northern France, so the Luftwaffe ground parties moved into the captured airfields and prepared the forward bases for the great "Luftkrieg gegen England". For a month the victorious war-machine was restored and re-primed. Facing the British Isles from Norway to Brittany, three great Luftflotten were poised and waiting while the Commanders debated when, and at which targets, the attack should be launched. For the Luftwaffe was now venturing into the unknown, and a new pattern for victory was needed; a plan that would make the most of its great superiority in numbers when fighting against the aircraft and men of Fighter Command.

In southern England the problems were legion, and one that had already been foreseen now existed in reality. The chain of radar stations, upon which depended the efficient use of the RAF's small fighter force, had become outflanked, notably in the south-west. The German long-range bombers based in Brittany now had a comparatively clear run up to the aircraft factories sited at Bristol, and in the Midlands. Even before the war such a situation had been foreseen, and a new fighter group had been planned for the south-west, in order to free No. 11 Group for the exclusive defence of London and the south-eastern counties. Accordingly construction of a new Headquarters for this new Group, No. 10, had been started at Rudloe Manor, Box, near Bath, in February 1940.

In June, as the air fighting in the south lulled before the coming storm, the squadrons of Fighter Command were re-deployed to face the encircling enemy. On the morning of 18 June, 213 Squadron left Biggin Hill for its home base at Wittering, and then in the afternoon flew south once more to the tiny civilian airfield at Exeter. So one month almost to the day since the Squadron had first taken-off from Wittering to go to war, the Hurricanes left its wide open spaces for the last time en route to their new base in the Filton Sector, which thus received its first squadron. In tight formation, low over the town, 213 made its presence known to the citizens of Exeter.

The airfield itself, set on the eastern side of the city alongside the road to Honiton, was a small domed grass field used by Rapides providing an air service to and from the Channel Islands. The main building was the Whitney Straight clubhouse, which was taken over as the Squadron Office. Refuelling facilities consisted of one pump, basically an ordinary garage pump, but twenty feet high.

Once having arrived, the main problem was accommodation; various solutions presented themselves. The NCOs soon made the clubhouse their own, which kept them near both the aircraft and a ready supply of ale. Initially, the officers settled in a large country house complete with silk sheets, and dinner served by a butler, at eight. However the owner required the pilots to be in by ten-thirty. The CO decided therefore that such quarters were a little too unmilitary and a section of The Rougemont Hotel in Exeter was commandeered. The permanent residents were soon able to vouch for the Squadron's high morale as closing time became a thing of the past, with the connivance of the local police - and to the delight of the shapely barmaid.

The sergeant pilots were put in an open truck and driven into the residential area of Honiton Clyst, where local residents volunteered to accommodate them.

Finding quarters for the airmen was the most pressing problem. Most of the local farmers, seen by the CO and the party he took with him to look for likely buildings, were unable to produce anything other than homemade cider especially brought out in their honour. The airmen were finally accommodated in tents in an orchard at the side of the airfield. LAC A R Henry was one of the first of the war-time intake of tradesmen to arrive on the Squadron. On being called up, he was determined not to be mustered in a clerical post, which would merely repeat his job in civilian life. At his initial interview at Uxbridge he therefore steered the conversation round to the intricacies of the two-stroke engine, with which he had just made an acquaintance in the magazine *The Motorcycle* that he had picked up on the train. He was duly sent for training as a mechanic, although as it turned out, he served as a Flight Mechanic (Airframe) rather than Flight Mechanic (Engines). After six months training in a bus garage at Morecambe, where the only aircraft he saw was an old Fairey Battle that did not fly but was used to give instruction in the hand signals required to taxi an aircraft, he passed out as an LAC with the appropriate two-bladed propeller badge on his arm.

He therefore arrived at Honiton Clyst late one evening in July, in charge of nine men. By midnight, they had found the airfield, were directed by an RAF Policeman through a gap in the barbed wire perimeter fence and told to "Follow that star and you will come to a bell-tent". The directions were good, and all the new arrivals settled down for their first night on an operational Squadron, twenty feet all touching the centre-pole. Waking up next morning, they found themselves at the Hurricane dispersal point of "B" Flight. Any trepidation Henry felt on his first day was not due to being on an operational squadron as such, but to the fact that, even though he was an LAC, he had never worked on a "real" aeroplane, and now he was among regular airmen, AC1s and AC2s who had been in the service for a number of years in some cases, and had plenty of Hurricane experience.

Already the shortage of fighter pilots was critical, and the Squadron's losses at Dunkirk were made up from a variety of sources. At this time also, front-line squadrons had their establishment of pilots increased in readiness for the long gruelling struggle ahead. In the first few days of July eleven new pilots arrived at Exeter. Three, who arrived on 1 July, were Fleet Air Arm pilots on loan to the RAF from the Royal Navy. Sub-Lts H G K Bramah and D M Jeram were relatively experienced pilots. However Sub-Lt W J M Moss had only been awarded his wings at 7 FTS, Peterborough on 17 March 1940. After completing his course on 26 May he was loaned to the RAF and, on 15 June, posted to 7 OTU, Hawarden, for a Hurricane conversion course. Plt Off A G Osmand also joined in the early days of the month.

With Flt Sgt C Grayson, who had been a pre-war airman pilot, came six Sergeant Pilots, G D Bushell, R D Dunscombe, P P Norris, E G Snowden, S G Stuckey and G N Wilkes. Little is on record concerning their background, other than in the case of Sgt Stuckey, another pre-war airman pilot who had served with 73 Squadron in France.

Towards the end of the month on 23 July, before the battle spread to involve 12 Group's squadrons in serious fighting, two experienced pilots, Plt Offs M S C H Buchin and J A L Phillipart arrived from the Belgian Air Force.

As the Squadron was once more established at full strength, so 10 Group as a whole was finally equipped with the remaining units that would make up its full fighting complement. By 9 July, one day before the Battle of Britain is reckoned to have commenced, the Group became fully operational and took over responsibility for the south-west. No. 10 Group consisted of three sectors, with Sector Stations at Pembrey, Filton and St. Eval. Only four squadrons could be spared for these three sectors. No.92 Squadron flew its Spitfires from Pembrey, No.234 Squadron operated the same type from St. Eval, and Nos.87 and 213 Squadrons flew their Hurricanes from Exeter. Later in the battle, in August, No. 10 Group also took responsibility for the Middle Wallop Sector and the squadrons under its control. Just as serious as the lack of squadrons, however, was the incomplete state of the Sector Stations, and the fact that neither the radar network nor the establishment of the Observer Corps posts was complete.

Across the Channel the Luftwaffe had moved into its newly-acquired airfields. Facing No. 10 Group was Luftflotte 3, with its bases in Brittany and the Cherbourg Peninsula. Commanded by General-Feldmarschall Hugo Sperrle. Luftflotte 3 had been allocated the area of the Channel and Great Britain west of a line stretching from Le Havre to Selsey Bill, and then north to Oxford and Birmingham. This line, in fact, coincided almost exactly with the eastern boundary of No. 10 Group's area. In practice, of course, such arbitrary boundaries lost most of their significance once the squadrons were in the air.

The main fighter strength of Luftflotte 3 consisted of one hundred and eighteen Bf 109s, one of the outstanding fighters of the early war years. These aircraft came from Jagdgeschwader (JG) 53 based at Rennes, Dinant, and Brest, and JG 27 flying from Carquebut, Crépon and Plumetôt, bases located along the northern coast of the Cherbourg Peninsula. They were supported by aircraft from JG 2 based at Beaumont-le-Roger and Le Havre, which operated with both Luftflotte 3 and Luftflotte 2. Supplementing the Bf 109s was Zerstörergeschwader (ZG) 76 equipped with Bf 110s, based at Le Mans and Laval. This aircraft, known by the Germans as the "Zerstörer" ("Destroyer"), was surrounded by an aura of invincibility when the Battle of Britain commenced. Designed as a twin-engined long-range escort fighter, it was intended to sweep clear a path for the following bomber streams. Its crews were hand-picked and constituted an elite corps. In fact the Squadron scored its greatest successes against this aircraft; the Bf 110 suffered from structural weaknesses in the tail section, and from a lack of manoeuvrability and acceleration.

The main bomber force of Luftflotte 3 consisted of some 527 aircraft, almost entirely He 111s and Ju 88s, two of the best of Germany's albeit poor bomber force. The He 111s belonged to Kampfgeschwader (KG) 27, based at Tours, Dinard, Bourges and Rennes, and KG 55 based at Dreux, Chartres and Villacoublay. The Ju 88s came from **Lehrgeschwader (LG) 1 based at Orleans/Bricy** and Châteaudun, KG 51 at Mélun, Orly and Etampes and KG 54 at Evreux and St. André-de-l'Eure. A small number of Do 17s and He 111s plus thirty-seven Ju 87s, "Stukas", based in

Brittany, provided a subsidiary dive-bomber capability. By the third week of July the Germans were ready to attack in force, and the units in France were ordered to assume a state of immediate readiness.

Throughout the month 213 Squadron had been engaged once more in the frustrating work of convoy protection and coastal patrol work and, although the early German attacks were directed against shipping, contacts were nil. Convoys were normally picked up somewhere off Portland Bill and given continuous cover in section strength until they were well past Start Point. The only relief from the boredom of these patrols was to orbit somewhere near Start Point, where the BBC sometimes broke through on the high-frequency radio, providing a welcome diversion.

The Squadron's account in the Battle of Britain was opened by one of the Fleet Air Arm pilots while on a lone patrol. On 15 July a small force of Luftflotte 3 bombers attacked the Westland aircraft factory at Yeovil and other targets in the area. Although heavily outnumbered by the Ju 88s, Bramah pressed home his attack, scoring numerous hits before he himself was forced down by heavy return fire.

On 31 July "A" Flight with Jackie Sing, Mike Croskell, Norris, Phillipart and Beguin set off for what was known as Hullavington's forced landing ground, to fly night patrols over Bristol, sorties which lasted for about one hour forty five minutes. The Flight spent a week there, with no facilities whatsoever. To take a bath required sixpence, and a visit to the hotel in the local town.

On the evening of 8 August Sing and Norris were patrolling as Red Section, some fifteen miles north of Guernsey, when Norris saw two Bf 109s flying below them. As he dived to attack Sing tried to find the second enemy aircraft, which had climbed up into sun. He saw Norris open fire, and his bullets strike the Messerschmitt's auxiliary fuel-tank, but no other damage was inflicted. Unable to find the second Bf 109, Sing then attacked the aircraft hit by Norris, and shot it down in flames. He then saw the second 109, caught up with it, and managed one short burst before running out of ammunition.

As the final plans for the invasion of Britain, "Operation Sealion", were being drawn up, a conflict in the German High Command became apparent. Hitler had ordered all preparations to be completed by mid-August, but the Navy, on whom the greatest burden would fall, wished to postpone the operation until the spring of 1941. Finally at a conference with Hitler, Grand-Admiral Raeder agreed, under pressure, to a date in September 1940. In order to gain the required air supremacy, the German Air Staff proposed, with unabashed optimism, to devote four days to the destruction of the air defences south of the Thames, and a further four weeks to the subjugation of Fighter Command as a whole. Thus the date for "Adler Tag" ("The Day of the Eagles"), the day when the major air onslaught on Britain would begin, was fixed for 11 August. As the first phase of the Battle of Britain drew to a close on 7 August, it became clear that the main burden, so far, had fallen on the squadrons of 11 Group in the south-east.

Towards the end of the first week of August, the German High Command became preoccupied with the launch of the great air assault and, although the date had been moved to 13 August, large formations were still sent across on the original date for "Adler Tag".

For 213 Squadron this was it. Its own personal battle started in earnest once more. On this day, 11 August, the two early morning patrols had made no contact in a cloudy sky. Then at 10.09 hours as a feint was made towards Dover, a large raid making for the Weymouth area was identified on the radar screens. The one telephone in the Squadron's quarters was soon ringing and the Hurricanes, when scrambled, were ordered to Portland at 10,000 feet. The reception for the German raiders was going to be warm since six other squadrons were also put up to intercept. Even so the Germans had a numerical advantage for there were approximately one hundred and fifty enemy aircraft consisting of Ju 88s and He 111s escorted by Bf 109s and 110s, a typical raid.

First contact fell, as usual, to Blue Section led by Wight who, with Butterfield and Snowden, attacked between fifty and sixty Bf 110s of I/ZG 2 fifteen miles south-west of Portland Bill, at 16,000 feet. As the dogfight developed, individual attacks were made on the centre of the formation which made a gentle left-hand turn, apparently intending to form a defensive circle. Snowden took a deflection shot at one Bf 110 which, after a second burst, turned on its side and went down. Deflection shots at two other Bf 110s also silenced both rear gunners, however by then he had used all his ammunition and his Hurricane was on fire from cannon shells which had struck the underside of his aircraft, bursting an oil pipe. He therefore dropped out of the fight and spiralled down to land on the Lulworth tank ranges, where soldiers said that they had seen four Bf 109s crash into the sea.

Strickland called Green Section to follow him as he climbed seaward of the German formation to attack the leading section. The Ju 88s immediately dived away breaking formation, and dropped their bombs wide of the town. Strickland picked out one bomber and gave it two short bursts and, as it dived away, its port engine started to smoke. It then continued down to 2,000 feet. After two more bursts from a quarter attack, the rear gunner ceased firing and the starboard engine seemed to fail. By now, the enemy aircraft was losing height rapidly, and after two further bursts it crash-landed on Portland Bill, where the three crew members were taken prisoners by the Army. Strickland noted that the only evasive action taken by the Ju 88 was to throttle back, and use its dive-brakes as it turned inwards, which caused him trouble as he tended to overshoot.

Sub-Lt D N Jeram was leading Green Section when the formation of Ju 88s was first seen; he closed with one and silenced the rear gunner. The bomber then dived away, letting out what Jeram took to be a length of wire attached to a parachute. As it continued its dive, trailing oil and smoke, Jeram broke away and opened fire at another target, the starboard engine of which caught fire as it dived away towards Chesil Beach.

McGregor attacked a Ju 88 in the leading section from abeam with a two-second burst, which caused the rear gunner to stop firing. Another two-second burst into the starboard engine set it on fire and the aircraft crashed in flames on the west side of Portland Bill. He then attacked the second aircraft in the leading section of three Ju 88s and saw petrol streaming back from the damaged aircraft. He delivered another attack on the third enemy aircraft as it was about to drop its bombs, but his ammunition ran out before he could see any result.

Sgt. M E Croskell, in "A" Flight, was just savouring the sight of a German crew baling out of their fiercely blazing bomber when he was attacked by five Bf 109s. By taking full advantage of the Hurricanes superior manoeuvrability he evaded the first attack and then, fastening onto the tail of one of his assailants, sent the Bf 109 down into the sea.

Sgt R T Llewellyn, flying as Yellow Three in "A"

One of JG 26's Bf 109E-4s in a field at Alcombe, Kent, on 31 August 1940

Flight, saw the German aircraft as they dived to bomb Portland. He attacked the nearest enemy aircraft from dead astern and fired a four-second burst which seemed to cause an explosion inside the fuselage, and the aircraft was engulfed in flames.

Plt Off A I Osmand attacked a Ju 88, setting its port engine on fire when he was attacked by a Bf 109; he broke off with damage to his hydraulics and crash-landed back at base.

It was a good day for the two Belgian pilots in their first real combat with the Squadron. Buchin flew as Number Two in Red Section led by Phillipart, and both registered claims against Ju 88s. Phillipart opened his account with a stern attack on the leader of a formation of Ju 88s. Initially, as the German pilot opened his airbrakes, Phillipart overshot, but his second attack forced the enemy aircraft very low, and after numerous hits it struck the sea and disintegrated. Phillipart nursed his aircraft home with bullets in the oil-tank and cooling system. When the Squadron returned to Exeter, the final tally was nine enemy aircraft claimed as destroyed.

Yet even in this first harsh clash the losses were grievous. Both Wight and Butterfield failed to return from their battles over the sea. These were losses that could not be replaced. From the first battles in France and over Dunkirk, both pilots had shown the indispensable quality and spirit which made Fighter Command an elite force. Their experience of battle conditions was irreplaceable; between them, even before the battle had been fairly joined, they had destroyed or helped to destroy a total of twenty-two enemy aircraft. Both represented the traditions of the peace-time Air Force which, inevitably, bore much of the brunt of the early fighting.

Ronald Derek Gordon Wight, from Skelmorlie in Ayrshire, had joined the RAF in April 1934. After his flying training he was posted to 208 Squadron at Heliopolis in Egypt, where he also served for a short time with 64 Squadron. In November 1936, he returned to the UK, and served for a year at Martlesham Heath before joining 72 Squadron. He was posted to 213 Squadron in February 1938, and then, in April, to 80 Squadron. However he was on sick leave when 80 Squadron moved overseas, and so rejoined 213 Squadron, becoming a Flight Commander in February 1939. After the air fighting over Dunkirk, he was awarded the DFC in recognition of the ten enemy aircraft he had destroyed, four in France and six while flying from England.

Samuel Leslie Butterfield was a pre-war regular, and was serving with the Squadron when war broke out. Of his total of five enemy aircraft destroyed, he shot down four in one single sortie over the Dunkirk beaches on 28 May. On 14 June he had been awarded the DFM. Before the age of the "Ace" arrived both had passed on. A new grimness pervaded Exeter as the harsh reality of the losses was realised.

In the evening Jackie Sing was airborne, leading Red Section on patrol at 15,000 feet over Portland Bill, when he saw fifty enemy aircraft made up of thirty Bf 110s escorted by twenty Bf 109s. Climbing through cloud they lost contact with Red Three before approaching the enemy bomber formation from above. In the ensuing dog-fight with the Bf 109 escort, the two Hurricanes became separated and Sing managed two four-second bursts at a Bf 110 which burst into flames.

The tempo of the Battle was now reaching one of its fierce climaxes, since 12 August was an important day for the Germans. An approaching ridge of high pressure heralded a period of fine weather over the British Isles, and Luftflottes 2 and 3 were ordered to be ready for the big attack on the next day. In preparation for this, large scale raids were to be mounted against radar sites and airfields in southern England. Once again the Squadron's early patrols had proved fruitless, but at mid-day all the aircraft were scrambled to Portland Bill. The radar station at Poling had picked up a very large formation approaching Brighton from the south. This formation was made up of the whole of KG 51, almost one hundred Ju 88s, plus ZGs 2 and 76 totalling one hundred and twenty Bf 110s. Above them, as escort, came twenty-five Bf 109s from JG 53, the elite "Pik As" Geschwader named after the Ace of Spades emblem carried on their aircraft. As the formation approached Spithead, all but fifteen of the approximately two hundred and forty-five aircraft turned north towards Portsmouth, passed through the gap in the balloon barrage over the harbour, and launched a fierce attack upon the town and the docks.

Approaching from the west, the Squadron's Hurricanes avoided Portsmouth, where they could mark the progress of the German formation by the intense anti-aircraft fire colouring the sky. As the Germans turned away from the target area making for their bases in France, the Squadron attacked.

South-east of the Isle of Wight the Squadron intercepted a force of seventy-plus enemy aircraft. Once again a fierce dog-fight developed, and the Germans received a severe mauling; already the much-vaunted Bf 110s were forming defensive circles when attacked. The Kommodore of the Edelweiss Geschwader, Oberst Dr. Fischer, flying his Ju 88 back the way he had come, was shot down south of the Poling radar station and crashed into the sea.

Flt Lt J E J Sing (later Wg Cdr J E J Sing, DFC), leading Red Section, found the Bf 110s flying in a large circle and led his section in trying to find a suitable target. While thus engaged he was himself attacked by a Bf 109 and blacked out in an evasive turn, losing his section. Having successfully eluded the unwelcome attentions of his assailant, and some twenty miles out to sea, Sing finally picked up twelve enemy aircraft that had broken away from the main formation and were making for home at 2,000 feet. With throttle wide open, he went after them and attacked the rear machine, which crashed into the sea. As he climbed away, he saw another formation of seven aircraft at 200/300 feet and again attacked the rear machine. As he attacked, the two rear machines turned outwards and the next two made climbing turns outwards. Two others stayed where they were but seemed to throttle back, while the leader turned sharply round to an almost head-on position. This manoeuvre left Sing almost in the middle of the Bf 110s and he received cross-fire from a number of cannons. As he broke away, the leader crossed his sights and Sing managed two short bursts, which set the Bf 110 on fire, and it dived into the sea. He had used only one hundred and thirty rounds per gun, but as he was nearly out of fuel he broke away and returned to base, where he landed with just ten gallons in his tanks.

Bushell lost his leader during violent evasive action, and he then saw a Bf 110 climb up in front of him. He pulled his Hurricane into a climb after it, and despite his superior speed which caused him to over-take it rapidly, he managed to fire one short burst. As smoke and flame came from the Bf 110's port engine he had to break away to avoid a collision. When last seen the Messerschmitt was burning fiercely. He then saw another Bf 110 diving out to sea and he followed it at 2,000 feet for a long time, apparently unobserved. Having closed to within three hundred and fifty yards, he commenced a dive and came up close astern. His first short burst seemed to have no effect, but a longer burst, using the remainder of his ammunition, set the port engine on fire and the German aircraft was last seen very low over the water burning and pouring smoke. Bushell returned to land at Warmwell low on fuel and with a bullet through his starboard tank, a cannon shell through the end of his starboard wing which had severed the electrical under-carriage wiring system, and two more lodged in his port elevator.

Yellow Section soon fell behind the rest of the Squadron as Strickland, Yellow Leader, was suffering from engine trouble. His section was therefore alone when they made contact with the seventy or so enemy aircraft. Some made off towards France, while another fifteen formed a defensive circle. As Strickland could not manoeuvre into a reasonable position he kept his section above in the sun and waited. When he saw a Bf 109 at sea-level he dived to attack and chased it to within fifteen to twenty miles of the French coast. He fired a good long burst at two hundred yards from dead astern and the 109 gave off a large cloud of smoke. To keep the enemy aircraft in sight, Strickland pulled away to one side and as the 109 pulled up to 800 feet he gave it another short two-second burst. The pilot baled out and the aircraft crashed into the sea.

Atkinson was leading "B" Flight on patrol over the Needles when he saw a mass of enemy aircraft at 17,000 feet south-south-east of Portsmouth. He attacked his first Bf 110 in a prolonged quarter stern attack, firing a seven-second burst which set the port engine on fire whereupon it dived into the sea. He then attacked another from underneath and after a five-second burst it dived away out of control; Atkinson believed that it must have hit the sea. He then attacked a third enemy aircraft on a quarter attack, but his ammunition was exhausted after a short two-second burst. When he landed he discovered bullet holes in his port wing and the trailing edge of his port flap.

Once the enemy formation had been sighted, Plt Off H W Cottam quickly became detached from the rest of "B" Flight, and made quarter attacks on three German aircraft without noticeable effect. He then fired on a fourth, which was in a stall-turn, at a range of one hundred yards; as he closed to fifty yards his ammunition ran out, and pieces began to fall off the Bf 110, which then started to smoke and spin.

Flt Sgt C Grayson, leading Green Section, was ordered to patrol Portland at 15,000 feet and then, moving progressively westward, Swanage and the Needles. He became separated from his section while investigating anti-aircraft fire over Portsmouth. Eventually he found a dog-fight in progress over the south-east of the Isle of Wight and joined in, attacking a Bf 110. Having forced it down to sea level he then broke away, and looking back saw a large splash in the water.

For the eleven German aircraft claimed as destroyed, two Hurricanes, flown by Sgts S G Stuckey and G N Wilkes, failed to return to Exeter.

With the dawning of "Adler Tag" itself, 13 August, the first warning of an impending attack came at 05.30 hours when enemy aircraft were reported forming-up over Amiens. As these formations began moving north, two other raids were picked up. One of these, of particular interest to No. 10 Group, was detected just north of Cherbourg. The Squadron had been allotted a patrol line at 12,000 feet, running from Portland to Swanage, then on to St. Catherine's Point and Portsmouth. At 06.30 hours, in the misty dawn, the Hurricanes took off from the sleeping airfield. However, despite the cloudy conditions to the east, the raids there had been severely mauled and though accompanied by a strong fighter escort, the bombers from Cherbourg turned back long before reaching the coast. So, ninety minutes after becoming airborne, the Squadron returned to breakfast without having seen any combat.

The next action of the day occurred a little before noon when about twenty aircraft were picked up on the radar, again near Cherbourg. These aircraft were a formation of Bf 110s which were intended as the fighter escort to the Ju 88s of KG 54, which were supposed to be headed for the Royal Aircraft Establishment at Farnborough and the nearby airfield of Odiham. Unfortunately the bombers failed to put in an appearance and the fighters came on alone. To meet them, squadrons were put up from Tangmere, Warmwell and Exeter. No.213 Squadron from Exeter had the most distance to cover, and only arrived over Portland Bill after the initial attack had been delivered from an advantageous position. Nevertheless, the arrival of a third squadron to join the dog-fight settled the issue for the badly mauled Bf 110s, and they turned helter-skelter for home.

Strickland's Blue Section was last off, as they were at thirty minutes readiness, and they only caught up with Red Section of "A" Flight over Portland at 15,000 feet as the German formation was retiring. Larichelière, flying as Blue Two, saw his leader dive towards a Bf 110, and as he followed he saw a Ju 88 through a gap in the clouds. He turned on to the German bomber's tail and, with two short bursts, hit the starboard engine, which then started to emit black smoke. He followed his adversary for some fifteen minutes, playing hide and seek with him through the clouds. Eventually he caught the Ju 88 in a clear patch for long enough to put two more bursts into its port engine setting it on fire, and the enemy aircraft dived into the sea. Larichelière could see a small motor-boat rushing towards the wreckage of the aircraft. While thus engrossed he was surprised by a Bf 109 and immediately broke upwards in a climbing turn to reach cloud cover. He then headed south for a few minutes thinking that he would not be followed. Then he returned to find the Bf 109 inspecting the wreck; now the boot was on the other foot and Larichelière made no mistake. After a short burst of three seconds, the 109 gave a sudden upward jerk, stalled, and dived into the sea approximately five hundred yards from the wreckage of the Ju 88.

Later in the afternoon the Germans repeated their two-pronged attack of the morning, but this time the strongest attack was mounted in the west. Group Headquarters made hasty preparations to meet formations of fifty-plus, thirty-plus, twenty-plus and thirty-plus coming in from the Cherbourg Peninsula. The Squadron arrived with No.238 to join No.152 in their Spitfires over the coast off Portland at 1526 hours. Later, sections of other squadrons joined the fray. 213 had sections patrolling both above and below the cloud layer that covered the area between four and six thousand feet. The German bombers, making up the raiding force, were drawn from Lehrgeschwader 1 equipped with Ju 88s from Orleans/Bricy, and from Stukageschwader 3, part of Fliegerkorps VIII, equipped with Ju 87s from Brittany. As these bombers approached, a large formation of fighters was seen to draw ahead of the main body of aircraft. When the fighters drew nearer it was possible to identify forty Bf 110s and a further twenty Bf 109s. This force was immediately attacked by the Squadron's Hurricanes and the Spitfires of 152 Squadron.

The first aircraft to make contact were the seven above the cloud led by Sing. For Atkinson, on patrol with Green Section below the cloud, the first indication of events up above was the sight of two aircraft falling from the base of the cloud into the sea. Climbing above the cloud to 10,000 feet he saw that the fighting was even higher still, so he turned and climbed into sun. There he waited above the melée until he saw a straggling Bf 109; after five short bursts, pieces fell off and it dived out of control into the sea. Having climbed back to 10,000 feet he used the rest of his ammunition on another Bf 109, but without visible effect; he then dived into the cloud for cover and returned to base.

Larichelière, flying with Blue Section of "B" flight, also below the cloud cover saw what he thought was a bomb drop into the sea beneath him. He decided to investigate and climbed up to 10,000 feet. After passing through a thick layer of cloud he found himself in a dense formation of forty Bf 109s and a further forty 110s. Directly in front of him was a 110; he fired a short burst and escaped back into the cloud after seeing the German fighter explode in pieces.

Osmand's first indication of the action above the cloud came when he heard the cry of "Tally Ho" from "A" flight; he climbed up and saw a circle of fifty Bf 109s and 110s. He dived on a stray 109 and soon found himself surrounded by five more. One passed in front of him at close range and he fired two bursts; black smoke streamed back from its engine. As he followed it down through the cloud he saw signs of three aircraft having being shot down into the sea, two quite recently, fifteen miles south of Portland.

While this battle was going on, the Hurricanes of 238 Squadron attacked the remaining Bf 110s, which were acting as close escort to the Ju 87s. Later 609 (West Riding) Squadron came to join the battle in their Spitfires and found some luckless unescorted Ju 87s just below them and took their chance; the Spitfires superiority was underlined in no mean fashion. Thus was fought out one of the biggest aerial battles of the war so far.

Back at Exeter, the score was seven enemy aircraft claimed as destroyed for the loss of Sgt P P Norris, who was shot down off Portland. A good contribution to Fighter Command's total for the day, which finally stood at a very satisfactory thirty-four enemy aircraft destroyed for the loss of thirteen.

After two days of intensive operations, 14 August gave some respite to both sides and Luftflotte 3 pursued a novel plan of its own which eventually earned a rebuke from Goering. Sperrle's plan was to send over small high-level raids to attack a wide variety of targets in south-west England. This plan is reflected in the Squadron's flying for the day, when eight patrols were flown but each only in section strength. In the cloudy conditions, contacts were few, and successes hard to achieve.

The difficulties became evident early in the day when Llewellyn, who was on a lone patrol between Seaton and Bridport, saw enemy aircraft just below a layer of cloud at one o'clock and four miles south of Seaton. Concealed in cloud, he dived to investigate. As he emerged from his cover, he saw half-a-mile away on his port side an aircraft which he recognised as a Do 17. He circled for a beam attack, and opened fire at six hundred yards. The Dornier dived away into a cloud bank with black smoke coming from its starboard engine.

Late in the evening, Green Section was patrolling overhead Seaton at 16,000 feet when Atkinson, flying as Green Two, saw three He 111s flying just below them in a north-westerly direction through the tops of a rough layer of cloud. He called the leader and turned to attack the third aircraft in the formation from astern. After making three attacks as best he could through the clouds, smoke started to come from the German bomber's port engine and Atkinson had to break upwards in order to avoid losing his target in the cloud. He then saw the undercarriage fall down and the whole of the He 111 was hidden in smoke. After one more burst, an engine stopped and caught fire and the aircraft crashed four miles south of Lyme. The crew of four jumped and were captured. From the return fire, however, he received shell splinters in his arm. Llewellyn, on patrol once more, had another frustrating engagement when he stalked a Do 17 through the clouds, and registered several hits before it disappeared into a large bank of clouds trailing smoke.

With a spell of fine weather the air fighting continued at a high intensity; nothing now existed outside the flying and fighting that constituted the Squadron's own personal battle. To have sufficient pilots and Hurricanes ready for the next day was all that mattered. The pilots had soon adapted to the small confines of the airfield at Exeter, although initially strange compared to the wide open spaces of Wittering. However for the ferry pilots it could prove a different matter. On one occasion, when serviceable aircraft were in desperately short supply, the arrival overhead of six brand-new Hurricanes with Rotol variable-speed propellers was hailed with delight. Minutes later only two remained undamaged, as four of the pilots came to grief on Exeter's small hump.

The domed shape of the airfield also had other consequences. On one occasion, having watched the Squadron scramble in line abreast from the flight-line, and disappear over the hump the groundcrew were surprised to see, only seconds later, twelve Hurricanes roar low over their heads still picking up their wheels. Unbelievably 87 Squadron, the tenants on the other side of the airfield, had been scrambled at exactly the same moment. As knights in the lists, the two squadrons had met half-way across the airfield, both just on the point of take-off. Incredibly no aircraft was damaged; passing through the gaps, over or under each other, both squadrons became safely airborne with nothing more than a missed heart-beat to mark the occasion.

Thursday 15 August saw the heaviest day's fighting of the battle; though many long and hard days were still to come the Luftwaffe never again matched the effort of this day. Every available fighter and the major part of the bomber and dive-bomber force were used to mount some 1,786 sorties. For the first and last time, raids were mounted simultaneously by all three Luftflotten. The most significant feature of the days operations was that only 520 of these sorties were flown by bomber aircraft. The remaining 1,200 or so were flown by the fighters in a final effort to destroy Fighter Command.

In the south-west the big raid built up in the evening. A force of seventy to eighty bombers, escorted by a large number of single and twin-engine fighters, was located approaching the south coast. At 17.16 hours eighteen Hurricanes, from 213 and 87 Squadrons, were once again taking up the regular battle line over Portland Bill at 20,000 feet. After half an hour on patrol Sqn Ldr J S Dewar, DSO, DFC the CO of 87 Squadron, who was in the process of handing over command to Sqn Ldr Lovell-Greg and who was on this occasion leading Blue Section of 213 Squadron's "B" Flight, saw the enemy approaching in waves of fifty-plus aircraft. The bombers, Ju 87s and Ju 88s, were stacked in layers at about 15,000 feet with the Bf 110s and the Bf 109s above them as top cover at 25,000 feet. The now familiar pattern soon established itself as the Hurricanes clashed with the massed formations of Germans. The twenty Bf 110s from V Gruppe (Zerstörer) Lehrgeschwader 1 based at Ligescourt almost immediately formed their defensive circles which, while making them more difficult to attack, completely nullified their effectiveness as escorts to the forty Ju 87s of I Gruppe, Stukageschwader 1 and II Gruppe, Stukageschwader 2 from Lannion.

The Squadron was led by Jackie Sing, "A" Flight Commander, leading Red Section. At 20,000 feet the Squadron was at roughly the same height as the Bf 110s and Sing carried out a quarter attack on one which immediately burst into flames. He then attacked a Ju 87 from behind and that also burst into flames; he then engaged another Bf 110 which burst into flames after a prolonged attack. Plt Off M S H C Buchin, one of the two Belgian pilots, who was flying with Red Section, was shot down and killed in this engagement. Having served as an instructor in the Belgian Air Force, Maurice Simon Henri Charles Buchin escaped to France in May 1940 and was employed as a ferry pilot. In mid-June he flew to Bayonne and then sailed in a Dutch freighter to England, arriving in Plymouth on 23 June. After a Hurricane conversion course he joined the Squadron on 23 July 1940.

Phillipart, the other Belgian pilot, was leading Yellow Section over Portland Bill when he attacked the last Bf 110 in a formation; after a short burst it flick-rolled, and spun into the sea. He was then attacked from astern by four Bf 110s. Seeing tracer fire coming past him he pulled into a tight turn and positioned himself on the tail of one of his attackers. After two bursts the Bf 110's starboard engine caught fire and it went into a slow gliding turn. Breaking off from that engagement, Phillipart next attacked the second Bf 110 in an echelon starboard of three aircraft in formation; it turned over onto its back and went into an inverted dive, shedding pieces as it went. He then engaged a single Bf 110 in a dogfight in the course of which he damaged its starboard engine which stopped; the German fighter then dived away into patchy cloud while Phillipart remained up above. When the German fighter re-appeared, the rear gunner opened fire as Phillipart attacked again, but as he followed the damaged aircraft down below the cloud base he saw that the rear gunner had ceased firing. Sing, who had seen Phillipart's attack, observed that the port engine was also emitting black smoke and running intermittently. On returning to base Phillipart found that he had one bullet in his tank and another in the cockpit.

Bushell was flying as Yellow Two, when he saw a Bf 110 break away from a mass of circling enemy aircraft and dive towards the sea. He followed it down in a steep dive and rapidly overtook it. The rear gunner opened fire and Bushell fired a long burst, but his deflection must have been faulty and there appeared to be no result, except perhaps that he killed the rear gunner as firing ceased. Closing once more, he held the enemy aircraft in his sights and fired the remainder of his ammunition; pieces fell off and the Bf 110 dived into the sea. With his ammunition exhausted Bushell returned to base.

Llewellyn's combat report records the early moves of Yellow Section:-

"As Yellow Three I patrolled as ordered and we engaged the enemy aircraft. Prior to coming into actual combat I followed Yellow Leader into sun. From there I carried out a diving attack on an Me 110 about 6,000 feet below. Before I was in range of my objective I saw an Me 110 to port carrying out a climbing turn to attack a Hurricane. I changed my direction and fired when the enemy aircraft was nearly stalled and I was approximately 50 yards range. I saw my burst hit below the pilot and the aircraft went down in flames. I climbed back into sun and then carried out an attack (beam) on a second enemy aircraft. The tail and rear end of this aircraft disintegrated and the aircraft dived and spun irregularly into the sea. I didn't see anyone abandon the aircraft. I then carried out an attack on a third enemy aircraft from above and astern. Smoke came away from the front section of the fuselage and the port wing root. The crew of two immediately abandoned the aircraft by parachute. As my ammunition was expended I returned to base."

Strickland, leading Green Section at 20,000 feet over Portland Bill, saw Dewar dive into a formation of Bf 110s below them and he followed him down. Picking one out as a target, he gave it a short burst from behind and it went straight into a terrific dive. As Strickland followed it down he saw the hood come off, and the two crew members bale out, landing in the sea. He then climbed up again to look for more enemy aircraft and came head to head with another Bf 110 just above a layer of cloud. After a short burst, it dived away into the cloud and Strickland went below to look for it, but with no success. He then suddenly saw a Ju 87, and came up beneath it; after two short bursts the crew baled out and the Stuka hit the water one mile off Chesil Beach where it burst into flames. He had fired six hundred rounds so climbed up once more to look for further action, but finding no more enemy aircraft he returned to base.

Sizer was flying as Number Two to Strickland when he was attacked by a large number of Bf 110s. Although he was unable to make a good attack on his first target, he saw pieces falling off it and the port engine seemed to be stopping as it dived away. At 8,000 feet he saw a large number of Ju 87s and attacked one, causing its engine to stop and the crew to bale out. Another pulled up into a stall-turn as he attacked and then fell into the sea. After these successes, he chased a Bf 110 but did not see any strikes as he used up the remainder of his ammunition.

After attacking three enemy aircraft with short bursts of fire, Dewar himself came under attack from a determined Messerschmitt and his cockpit rapidly filled with smoke following repeated hits in his engine. Ducking out of the raging dogfight and throwing back his hood, he nursed his ailing Hurricane back to the forward airfield at Warmwell. Taking a deep breath as he turned onto his final approach he put his head back into the cockpit and managed a successful landing. This safe return he noted "...was very fortunate as the aircraft is not seriously hit except in the engine and wings".

Laricheliére, flying with Blue Section, heard Dewar's warning of the presence of enemy aircraft, and immediately saw to his left and below a Bf 110 going in the opposite direction. He stall turned and dived after it; once on its tail he put in a short burst at the port engine which began to give off black smoke. As the 110 dived away, the hood flew off and the crew jumped out; Laricheliére followed the stricken aircraft down and saw it crash into the sea a mile or so south of Portland. He immediately climbed up again, and as he was passing through a thin layer of cloud at 4,000 feet he saw a Ju 87 trying to escape to the south-east. He immediately flattened out and, after a few minutes of dodging in and out of cloud, he managed to position himself on its tail; after two short bursts the Stuka started to spin. Laricheliére saw all sorts of pieces flying off it as he followed it down until it crashed into the sea near the coast east of Portland. For a second time he climbed up again. At approximately 7,000 feet he met another Bf 110, and after a certain amount of dodging about he found himself directly underneath it at less than thirty yards range. He pulled up into a stiff climb and fired a long burst into its port engine and centre section. The Bf 110 seemed to cartwheel and then spin, finally crashing into the sea, again very near the coast of Portland Bill. As he had by now used all his ammunition he returned to Exeter.

Sgt R D Dunscombe's day was less successful. He closed to one hundred yards to attack a Bf 110 and saw it go down. However, he was then attacked himself from behind and his port wing was hit by a cannon shell; he pulled out of the resultant spin and returned to base.

Moss took off independently at 17.25 hours, and air-tested his aircraft before proceeding to a position south of Portland, where he saw a burning machine crash into the sea. He climbed into sun and levelled off at 20,000 feet. From this height he dived and attacked a Bf 110, silencing the rear gunner and causing the starboard engine to smoke badly.

In this one engagement, on the day that was meant to see the final destruction of Fighter Command, the Squadron claimed eleven Bf 110s destroyed and four possibles, plus five Ju 87s destroyed, for the loss of one pilot and Hurricane plus a number of others damaged. As Exeter was the home of the Armament Division of the Royal Aircraft Establishment, 213 Squadron was one of the first, if not **the** first, to use De Wilde explosive .303 ammunition, at a ratio of one to twenty. A hit was indicated by a small blue flash, and it was quite a useful addition to the armoury. In this day's fighting, Laricheliére had used it to good effect in destroying three enemy aircraft and a good deal of his success he credited to the new ammunition. Among other things he noted that strikes were easier to observe, and thereby to determine if the shooting was on target.

Friday 16 August was yet another day of maximum effort by the Luftwaffe, and by mid-day the radar plotted some three hundred and fifty aircraft between Yarmouth I.O.W and Portland. The Squadron pilots had been in heavy engagements on five successive days; now once more they were making their way to Portland to meet the attackers at 15,000 feet. Considerable amounts of cloud over southern England made the task of interception difficult. A scrappy dogfight ensued as the Germans sought the protection of the clouds, and many of them succeeded in making their way through to their targets.

On patrol between Swanage and St. Catherine's Head at 12,000 feet, Blue Section was jumped by three Bf 109s. Atkinson broke away upwards and followed one with a red spinner; after three bursts of machine gun fire it went straight into the sea pouring black and white smoke. In the stiff combat with others of the fighter escort, the Squadron lost Laricheliére, the first of the many Dominion pilots who were to fly with it in the Second World War, just as they had in the First. Joseph Emile Paul Laricheliére was a French-Canadian from Montreal who had joined the RAF on a short service commission in 1939. After attending No.22 Elementary and Reserve Flying Training School at Cambridge, he was initially posted to 504 Squadron on 18 May, joining 213 Squadron one week later. On two days in August, the thirteenth and fifteenth, he destroyed six enemy aircraft before being shot down himself over the Isle of Wight.

In the previous days the German losses had been heavy, and the wear and tear on Fighter Command great. Now a period of poor weather gave the Luftwaffe an opportunity to reduce the level of its attacks and review the situation. Regular patrols were still mounted by the Squadron's aircraft, but often only in pairs.

On 18 August, while on patrol over the Isle of Wight at 15,000 feet, the Squadron was "investigated" by a squadron of Spitfires which came in from the rear on to the tails of the Hurricanes. The patrol was abandoned lest the Spitfires mistook them for Bf 109s. Atkinson climbed 2,000 feet above the rest of the Squadron to keep an eye on the Spitfires, and he saw one come in, right through between the sections, and on to the leader's tail. While waiting for the Spitfires to leave the Squadron alone, Atkinson saw a single aircraft 2,000 feet below them heading south. He called up on the R/T and dived down; the enemy aircraft descended to sea level, but in the dive Atkinson closed to within 350 yards and put in one long burst. The Bf 109 started to smoke and then slow rolled into the sea, seven miles from Ventnor. As he turned away, he saw another twenty Bf 109s, four of which chased him back towards the coast. He shook them off by turning tightly and fired a quick burst into one of his erstwhile pursuers, but with no discernible effect. As he was now low on fuel, he returned to base having failed to contact his section leader.

The next day, Red Section, on patrol over the south Devon coast at 13.17 hours, intercepted an enemy aircraft which quickly disappeared into the cloud cover. Red Leader, Jackie Sing, sent Llewellyn below the cloud layer to see if the raider emerged, but he saw nothing. Then Sing ordered the Flight to meet up over Exeter at cloud base. On coming out of the cloud, Llewellyn saw what he thought was Red Leader about one mile distant flying in a south-easterly direction. As he closed up, he saw that the aircraft had two engines; he reported to control and went in to investigate. At 800 yards he came under fire and returned this with a short burst when he had closed to 600 yards. The Ju 88, for such it was, climbed into cloud and as it emerged above Llewellyn made a beam attack from 250 yards closing to 150; the crew of the Junkers seemed unaware of his presence. After a three-second burst, black smoke came from the enemy aircraft's fuselage and then the glow of a fire appeared as it fell through the cloud; no one baled out as far as Llewellyn could see.

During the second half of August, four new pilots arrived to fill the gaps made by the heavy fighting. On 17 and 19 August the first two Polish pilots to fly with the Squadron arrived at Exeter. Fg Off Marian Duryasz had joined the Polish Air Force in 1932. He arrived in the UK after the defeat of Poland, in January 1940, and joined the Squadron on 17 August, just two days before his fellow countryman Sgt Antoni Wojcicki. Fg Off H D Clark, who had been a King's Cadet at the Royal Air Force College, Cranwell, from where he had graduated in 1938, joined on the same day. Sgt G Stevens had joined the RAFVR on 5 July 1937, and had been called up to full-time service on 1 September 1939. After serving as an instructor at No.6 OTU, Sutton Bridge, he converted to Hurricanes and joined 151 Squadron at North Weald late in August just as it was about to move north to Digby for a period of rest. Not wishing to be out of things again, he asked to be posted to a front-line squadron in the south of England and in total fulfilment of his request he was sent to join 213 Squadron at Tangmere.

On 20 August two aircraft of Red Section, flown by Sing and Llewellyn, were again on patrol when three Ju 88s were seen at 11,000 feet. Just as Sing was about to open fire at the third enemy bomber, the rear gunners opened fire and the formation dived into cloud line astern. The Hurricanes were not able to position themselves for a further attack until the bombers were over Newton Abbot, diving at full speed to bomb the railway station. Sing attacked the leading aircraft as it broke away from its bombing run, but although he managed to inflict some damage he did not see the Junkers crash. Llewellyn closed in to attack another of the bombers as it was heading back towards the coast; after his third attack large pieces fell off, and an enemy aircraft was reported to have crashed into the sea off Dawlish. As the report was made by a civilian, the claim was logged as unconfirmed.

Despite the cloudy, squally conditions on 22 August, Phillipart, leading a pair of aircraft from Yellow Section at 20,000 feet over Exmouth, saw an unidentified aircraft coming in from the south. On investigation it turned out to be a Ju 88 and, followed by his Number Two, Phillipart made a beam attack diving vertically, followed by a stern attack. The German bomber caught fire between the starboard engine and the fuselage; the four crew members crew jumped out one by one and all their parachutes opened. The aircraft, on which Phillipart noticed that the black crosses were inside a white circle, dived into the sea.

This victory somewhat compensated for the nasty experience of the previous day, when the Squadron had been hurriedly scrambled as a lone Ju 88 flew in from the south at low level and planted a stick of bombs across the airfield. Such raids were particularly disturbing as the groundcrew were still living in tents near the airfield. The freak effects of the blast from such raids could not always be relied upon to be as kindly as on the occasion when a tent was blown away from over the heads of six sleeping airmen.

Looking back on the Battle of Britain as a whole, it can now be seen that these few days of comparatively limited activity marked the end of the second phase of the fight.

On the German side the pause was marked by a reassessment of the targets allocated and a readjustment, to the detriment of the freedom of action of the fighters, of the system of escorts. The most significant action however was the withdrawal of the Ju 87 from the battle. Units equipped with this aircraft, which had proved slow and cumbersome in comparison with modern fighters, had suffered great losses and Fliegerkorps VIII, with the vast majority of the Stukas under its control, was withdrawn from the Cherbourg Peninsula.

On 24 August, as the weather cleared, the third phase of the battle opened with the Germans concentrating their attacks more than ever on the airfields and radar stations in the south of England. The attacks in this phase were to be concentrated on a much narrower front than heretofore, and the only heavy raid to penetrate into the south-west came on 25 August. After this date, much of the strength of Luftflotte 3, already weakened by the loss of its Stuka units, was transferred to Luftflotte 2 in the Pas-de-Calais; the remaining units concentrated their efforts on the less risky business of night raids.

The big raid of 25 August built up in the afternoon as a force of one hundred aircraft was identified on the radar screens assembling off St.Malo. Between 16.00 and 17.00 every squadron from Tangmere to Exeter was scrambled, not only to oppose the raiders but also to ensure that none of them were caught on the ground and damaged by bombs or gunfire. Thus eight of the Squadron's Hurricanes were soon in position over Warmwell at 20,000 feet. Despite the presence of two other squadrons in the area, the Germans were as usual in considerably greater strength with about forty-five bombers, Ju 88s and Do 17s, escorted by upwards of two hundred fighters. The Squadron's position over Warmwell put it right at the heart of the attack as the raid was bound for that very airfield.

Early contact was made; Strickland had led Blue Flight up to 22,000 feet when he saw sixty Bf 109s and 110s below them at 18,000 feet. He led his section in to attack, and fired a short burst at a Bf 110 which slowed considerably as its port engine started to smoke. Strickland broke away as the 110s started to form a defensive circle. He then patrolled alone, about half-a-mile inland from the circling enemy fighters, where he found a formation of twenty Ju 88s. He attacked one with a long burst from astern, but seemed to inflict no damage. After following a Bf 109 down until it crashed into the sea, he turned to patrol about half-a-mile off Chesil Beach. As he did so he realised that a Bf 109 was trying to formate on his wing tip then, realising his mistake, the German pilot flew out to sea as fast as he could. Strickland managed to overhaul him and shot him down in flames into the sea; the pilot baled out at 700 feet but his parachute failed to open.

Llewellyn, on patrol with "A" Flight, had become separated from the rest of the Squadron while climbing up through cloud, to 22,000 feet over Warmwell. He saw six Hurricanes patrolling about one mile away, and went over to join them, but while he was still three-quarters of a mile away they dived to attack the enemy formation. As the Bf 110s formed a circle he flew in and attacked from below and against the rotation. A Bf 110 caught fire and dived towards the sea. Llewellyn broke away and decided that it was inadvisable to attack the circle of Bf 110s again. He then saw a Spitfire with a Bf 109 on its tail, so dived and made a stern attack; the 109 fell away, caught fire and crashed in a field three miles north-west of Portland. As the air pressure for his guns had failed, he returned to base.

Snowden arrived on the scene only after the fight had started, following a quick refuelling stop at base after a previous sortie. Initially, therefore, he evaded the fighter screen and came up with a large formation of Ju 88s. While engaged in shooting down one of these, he himself came under fire from a Bf 109 approaching from astern. Committing every sin in the book, the Messerschmitt dived past Snowden and pulled up in front of him; a long burst sent the Bf 109 crashing into the sea off Swyre. A party of officers from the Durham Light Infantry had seen a Ju 88 already on fire being attacked again by a Spitfire at 1,000 feet just before it crashed into the sea. The initial attack on the Ju 88 had caused some considerable damage to Snowden's aircraft and, picking out a suitable field, he made a forced landing near Burton Bradstock. Snowden was not the only casualty on this occasion for the heavy fighter escort, with a large number of Bf 109s, had put up a strong fight.

Two pilots were missing when the Squadron returned to Exeter. Plt Off H D Atkinson, who had been with the Squadron since the early days, and had been awarded the DFC in June for his part in the fighting in France and over Dunkirk, had been shot down in the combat over Warmwell. Harold Derek Atkinson, from Wintringham in Yorkshire, had attended the RAF College at Cranwell from September 1937 until July 1939, being posted directly to 213 Squadron on graduation. Between 19 May and 18 August, while flying with the Squadron, he had destroyed nine enemy aircraft and shared in the destruction of three others; he also had two unconfirmed as well as a share in one damaged.

Phillipart was also missing. Jacques Arthur Laurent Phillipart was somewhat older and had considerably more flying experience than most RAF pilots in the Battle of Britain. Born at Mont-St-Guibert, Belgium, on 11 January 1909 he was already a well known pilot of the Aéronautique Militaire when war broke out, having been sent to the UK in 1938-1939 in connection with the reorganisation of the Belgian flying schools. With the occupation of Belgium, he went to France and served on the staff of General Legros, travelling frequently to the UK as a liaison officer. Crossing to England in June, he was sent to No.7 OTU, Hawarden, on 7 July to learn RAF fighter operations before joining 213 Squadron on 15 July. In the fourteen-day period from 11 to 25 August, he destroyed six enemy aircraft, the first Belgian pilot to reach this total, and claimed one possible. He was shot down by Hauptmann Hans-Karl Mayer of I/JG 53 and, although he baled out, he did not survive, and it was not until three days later that his body was recovered from the sea. So both of the gallant Belgian pilots, fighting amongst friends but in a foreign country, had finally settled their accounts with their enemy.

Two days after this fierce engagement, Sqn Ldr McGregor flew his last sortie in command of the Squadron, leading a flight, appropriately enough over Warmwell. Tragically Sub-Lt W J M Moss was killed on this patrol when he lost control of his Hurricane over the sea. Moss had joined the Fleet Air Arm on 3 July 1939 and commenced his flying training at 14 EFTS, Castle Bromwich. On 11 December 1939 he was posted to 7 FTS, Peterborough, where he gained his wings. He was loaned to the RAF on 15 June 1940 and completed a Hurricane conversion course at No.7 OTU, Hawarden; he joined the Squadron at Exeter on 1 July 1940.

For the final stages of the Battle of Britain and throughout all the subsequent moves that finally took it into the Western Desert, the Squadron was commanded by Sqn Ldr D S MacDonald (later Gp Cpt D S Wilson-MacDonald DSO, DFC). He had joined the RAF Reserve in 1934 and was granted a short service commission the following year, after learning to fly in a Tiger Moth at Filton, just outside Bristol. His first posting was to 41 Squadron, temporarily flying Hawker Demon fighters in the Middle East. After a period as a flying instructor, he took command of 213 Squadron on 28 August 1940.

A 213 Squadron Hurricane joins a line-up at Upwood for inspection

CHAPTER SIX -

THE BATTLE OF BRITAIN -

TANGMERE, No.11 GROUP

Plt Off G H Westlake in his Hurricane in dispersal at Turnhouse, April 1941. (G H Westlake)

Throughout the third phase of the Battle of Britain, the Germans concentrated their attacks more and more upon the narrow front guarded by No. 11 Group. As the field of conflict was reduced to the skies above Kent, Sussex and Surrey, so some of the battle hardened squadrons that had hitherto been guarding the flanks were moved into No. 11 Group's area. On 4 September a surprise attack on the factory and airfield at Brooklands moved the C-in-C Fighter Command to ask for maximum cover for factories in this area in the coming weeks. As the existing No. 11 Group squadrons were already fully committed, new units were needed. So on the morning of 7 September, the eve of the fourth phase of the battle, popularly known as "The Blitz", 213 Squadron flew its battle scarred Hurricanes into Tangmere to replace 601 (County of London) Auxiliary Squadron. After fighting in France, over Dunkirk, and while flying from Exeter, the Squadron was to remain in the forefront of the battle until the very end. Goering's over-confidence in the success of the Luftwaffe raids, and a fit of rage by Hitler, switched the attack at this juncture to London itself; the Battle of Britain was nearing its climax.

Nevertheless the first few days at Tangmere were frustrating ones for the Squadron. The problem of combating the night raids of the Luftwaffe was assuming greater proportions as more of its bomber force was switched to this task. With only a limited number of night-fighters available the experiment of using Hurricanes at night was tried. For the first four days at Tangmere the Squadron operated, somewhat unhappily, in this role. Night patrols were flown over the south coast led by Sing and Fg Off R W Kellow, but a great deal of effort resulted in very little reward. On 9 September, after a night patrol on a line from Selsey Bill to Dungeness, Croskell had four gallons in his tank, and Sing just one gallon, when the aircraft landed. After three successive nights with still nothing to show for full-scale operations the experiment was stopped. Thus the Squadron was operating in its natural day fighter role when the Luftwaffe launched its final series of daylight bomber raids against London.

The day of Hitler's first postponement of a decision concerning "Operation Sealion", 11 September, saw the Squadron engaged in its first big action since coming to Tangmere. Two German formations from Luftflotte 3 coming in from Cherbourg and Seine Bay linked up over Selsey Bill and flew on towards their target at Southampton, the Squadron's twelve Hurricanes met the raids shortly after they had joined together. The engagement was fierce and the Squadron became heavily engaged with the fighter escort. It was an accepted fact that, whenever MacDonald was leading, the Squadron always found fighters and bombers, never just the latter. Although he was a first class shot, he had been runner-up to Sqn Ldr H Broadhurst in the pre-war RAF gunnery competition, easy pickings from unescorted Ju 87s or other bombers never came his way throughout the whole war. With the CO in the lead combat could be counted on with one or other of the types of German fighters.

The two Flights, led by the CO and Sing, were ordered into the air at 15.45 hours to patrol base, and were then vectored towards Selsey Bill, where they saw twenty Bf 110s at 15,000 feet. As Red, Yellow, Blue and Green Sections made quarter attacks in turn, the German fighters formed the now familiar defensive circle. Before Jackie Sing, Red Leader, could make a second attack, he was hit and had to bale out..

Llewellyn, flying as Red Three, saw fifteen Bf 110s four to six miles south-east of Selsey Bill. As the Squadron attacked he fired a two-second burst from one hundred yards at a Bf 110 started to smoke and Mike Croskell, Yellow Two, saw it dive vertically into the sea. Looking north Llewellyn saw fifteen of the bomber versions of the Bf 110 (referred to in combat reports as Jaguars) cross the coast, and then turn inland west of Portsmouth. He climbed into sun, and when about five hundred feet above the last enemy aircraft, which was flying to and fro as a look-out, he made a beam attack. He opened fire at three hundred yards closing to seventy-five; after three or four bursts of fire smoke and flames appeared, and when last seen the bomber was burning furiously.

Fg Off R W Kellow, Yellow Leader, singled out another Bf 110, and after he had made a quarter attack it dived into the sea. Yellow Three, Fg Off M Duryasz, achieved precisely the same result with another quarter attack. The third member of the section, Bushell, flying as Yellow Two, waited above the circle until it split up and the enemy aircraft

Plt Off W M Sizer, DFC, drawn by Cuthbert Orde, 26 October 1940, and included in his book "The Pilots of Fighter Command".

Flt Lt W D David, DFC and Bar, who flew with the Squadron as a Flight Commander in October and November 1940, drawn by Cuthbert Orde, 6 December 1940

turned for home; he then attacked the rear aircraft from above on a beam attack. It entered into a steep dive and crashed into the sea.

In "B" Flight, Blue Leader, Strickland, Blue Two, Plt Off H W Cottam, as well as Green Three, Sgt R D Dunscombe, all made quarter attacks on Bf 110s and each claimed one damaged. At the final reckoning four Bf 110s were claimed as destroyed, one each by Kellow, Duryasz, Croskell and Llewellyn, and five damaged by MacDonald, Sing, Cottam, Sizer and Snowden. For reasons that remain unclear, the claims of Strickland and Dunscombe were not allowed. Sgt A Wojcicki was last seen making for the centre of the enemy formation, when his Hurricane was hit and burst into flames, it crashed into the sea one mile off Selsey Bill. Antoni Wojcicki was born in Poland on 1 August 1914, and had joined the Squadron at Exeter on 19 August 1940; he is remembered on the Polish Air Force Memorial, Northolt.

When the Squadron finally returned to base after this running battle along the south coast, in addition to the loss of Sgt Wojcicki both Sing and Strickland were missing. The latter turned up quite quickly, but as the days passed and no news came it began to look as if a invaluable Flight Commander had been lost. In fact Jackie Sing had been picked up from the Channel by a tanker en route from the USA. Being an inveterate smoker, and with his own cigarettes soaked through, his first request was for a cigarette. He was told quite firmly that smoking was forbidden as the tanker's cargo was one hundred octane petrol, and that the ship was in a convoy bound for Shellhaven. By the time the tanker docked, having been attacked all the way round to the Thames Estuary, he was a nervous wreck, not so much from the embargo on smoking but from the knowledge that he was sitting on thousands of gallons of aviation fuel. While the crew assured him that they would never feel safe dashing about the sky in a Hurricane, Jackie Sing had absolutely no doubt where he felt the most safe, and he was anxious to be back there. So it was not until the tanker had docked, and everyone had almost given up hope for his safe return, that he was finally able to make his way back to Tangmere.

On 12 September, as low cloud obscured much of the south coast, the Germans paused before yet another all out assault. Nevertheless Blue Section found a lone Ju 88 and chased it for twenty minutes before shooting it down. Snowden, flying as Blue Three, saw the German bomber just above a layer of cloud, and dived to make a stern attack. Pieces flew off the Ju 88, and the rear gunner stopped firing. Snowden last saw it as it disappeared into the clouds with Blue Leader on its tail still firing. After a further quiet day on 13 September, the German High Command concluded that air superiority was not beyond their grasp and that another few days might clinch the battle. So following an indecisive day on 14 September, when two patrols in Squadron strength were flown without coming into action, the Luftwaffe launched its last great daylight attack.

The dawn of Sunday, 15 September, now annually celebrated as Battle of Britain Day, saw a fine summer's day break over southern England. For the pilots at Tangmere Sunday was no different from any other day. The Hurricanes stood ready in the dispersals and the aircrew sat around waiting.... As the day wore on, clouds built up over the Weald of Kent and a fine opaque screen covered the whole of southern England between four and six thousand feet. Fighting commenced a little before mid-day but the Squadron, though having patrols airborne throughout the morning, was not heavily engaged.

Just after mid-day the first engagement took place, when Blue Section met twenty Bf 109s over the centre of the isle of Wight at 23,000 feet. Plt Off B Wlasnowolski, Blue Three, attacked one in a climbing turn, first to starboard then to port, as it tried to hide up sun. He then saw another pair of 109s a long way off below him, and he dived to attack. After five short bursts from above and behind one of the German fighters stall-turned and dived vertically to ground level, with smoke pouring from its engine.

Soon after 14.00 hours, the second and heavier attack developed. Though the warning was shorter than in the morning, six pairs of squadrons were scrambled to meet the raiders, flying towards London..

At 1410 hours, with Jackie Sing leading Red Section of "A" Flight, the Squadron took off with 607 (County of Durham) Squadron. The raiders came in with no feints or subterfuge, stepped up in mass formations from 15,000 to 26,000 feet. The two squadrons were vectored onto two enemy formations over Edenbridge at 13,000 feet, each consisting of approximately forty Do 17s, flying in squadron vics, with only a light fighter escort. A formation of Bf 110s was seen five miles to the east, but this might have been part of another raid - they were of little help to the Do 17s.

The fighting commenced at 14.50 hours and the German formations quickly broke up under the initial attack. By the time the last section dived onto the luckless Dorniers, the sky was filled with a confused mass of aircraft.

Sing picked out a target and shot away the whole of its nose, including the pilot's cockpit, in a head-on attack. The enemy aircraft went into a steep dive, and was claimed as a probable. Sub-Lt D N Jeram, Green Two, and Duryasz, Red Three, went right through the bomber formation, and then turned back and attacked an enemy aircraft from astern; each claimed one Do 17 destroyed, having followed it down and seen the crew bale out. Charlie Grayson, one of the most experienced pilots on the Squadron, leading Green Section, made a stern attack on another and saw it go down in a vertical dive; it was claimed as another probable. Snowden, Green Two, also drove one down in a stern attack.

After three Bf 110s and three Do 17s had been shot down, the remaining bombers were seen to be jettisoning their bombs over open fields, and retiring southwards. While fuel and ammunition lasted, the remnants of the formation were pursued out to sea. After his initial engagement, and as the battle developed, Snowden made his way towards Dungeness where he found a Bf 110, and shot it down into the sea with a deflection shot.

In Blue Section Cottam dived vertically onto a Do 17 and damaged it, before flying south towards Dungeness where he saw a Spitfire attacking a Bf 110. He joined in and helped to shoot it down into the sea. Throughout the engagement visibility had been good with ten-tenths cloud cover at 13,000 feet; the enemy formation had been intercepted just above the cloud layer. However the engagement had not been fought without losses; Mike Croskell, Yellow Three and Reg Llewellyn, Yellow Two, who had a bullet in his shoulder, had both to bale out and finished the day in hospital.

Reginald Thomas Llewellyn, born in Bristol on 25 March 1914, had joined the RAF as an Halton apprentice, in January 1930. He was serving with 27 Squadron in India when selected for pilot training, which was carried out in the UK. In November 1939 he joined 263 Squadron as a Sergeant Pilot before being posted to 41 Squadron in January 1940, and then moving to 213 Squadron in March. In rapid succession he had flown Gladiators, Spitfires and Hurricanes. Between his first action over Dunkirk late in May, and his last when he was shot down and suffered serious wounds to his right arm, he had destroyed thirteen enemy aircraft, plus one unconfirmed, one probable and two damaged.

The Squadron's tally in this engagement was three Do 17s destroyed, one each by Jeram, Llewellyn and Duryasz, two probably destroyed, by Sing and Grayson, two damaged, by Bushell and Cottam and two Bf 110s destroyed by Snowden and Cottam, this last shared with an unknown Spitfire pilot.

In all the day's operations, so fierce had been Fighter Command's reaction that the order was given to the German High Command postponing the invasion indefinitely. The great air onslaught on the British Isles had been defeated in its major objective, the achievement of air superiority over the Channel and south-east England.

After the heavy losses of 15 September, Goering once more switched his attacks back to the installations of Fighter Command and the ratio of fighters to bombers was also increased still further. As summer faded and the weather reduced the scale of operations, the battle moved into its fifth and final phase which is taken as ending on 31 October. As September drew to a close, the Luftwaffe began to restrict its bomber attacks to the hours of darkness, the daylight sweeps being confined to large formations of fighters.

As a presage of things to come the Squadron was jumped by a strong force of Bf 109s and 110s while patrolling Redhill at 22,000 feet on 17 September. Only after a stiff fight were the Germans driven off without loss. In such combats the advantage lay very much with the Bf 109s. The net result of the new German tactics was that, while large numbers of RAF squadrons were still being scrambled, fewer were coming into action.

On 18 September, Strickland was leading "B" Flight, as Blue Leader, on the more mundane duty of convoy patrol at 17,000 feet, just below a layer of cloud, and from this altitude he had a good view of the convoy as it steamed past Selsey Bill some ten miles out to sea. Control called up to warn the Flight of an approaching enemy aircraft. Soon anti-aircraft fire was seen coming from the convoy, and then a Ju 88 was identified just about to start its bombing run. Strickland led the Flight down and fired one short burst, using deflection as he dived vertically on the German bomber. He then turned into a quarter attack, and finally made a stern attack, but the enemy aircraft was moving fast, and he had to open fire out of range. Green Two had already made two attacks when, after another long burst, the perspex dome of the rear turret broke off, and the port engine began to idle with a piece of the cowling missing. The German raider was last seen at twenty feet flying over the sea on one engine. It was noted that this Ju 88 carried a red stripe on its fuselage similar to those encountered over Portland on 11 August.

On 25 September Sing damaged a Do 215 while on patrol at 14.55 hours. On an evening patrol the next day, while off the coast twenty miles south-west of the Needles at 14,000 feet, Sgt E G Snowden saw an unknown number of Do 17s or 215s, preceded by about fifty Bf 109s flying in a south-westerly direction away from Southampton. As he climbed into sun he was attacked by six of the escorting fighters, which dived down upon him in line astern. He turned in behind the last one and fired three short bursts

Left: Fg Off L H Schwind, who flew with the Squadron for one week in September 1940. (The Wildernesse Club)
Above: The plaque erected by the members of The Wildernesse Club, Sevenoaks, Kent, to mark the spot on the Wildernesse Golf Course where the Hurricane flown by Flt Lt L H Schwind (his promotion only came after he was killed) crashed on 27 September 1940. (The Wildernesse Club)

which sent it down vertically, giving off smoke. As more Bf 109s came down Snowden broke away, and flew into nearby cloud cover.

Throughout the later half of September, a steady flow of pilots, with previous squadron experience, arrived to make good the losses suffered in the fierce fighting of August and the first two weeks of September. From 85 Squadron at Martlesham Heath came Fg Off J Lockhart, who was to stay with the Squadron until January 1942, eventually taking command. The next day saw the arrival of the Squadron's third Polish pilot, Plt Off B A Wlasnowolski, who had not only fought against the Germans with the Polish Air Force in 1939, but had also flown with 32 Squadron from Biggin Hill, and with whom he had destroyed three German aircraft in three days in August 1940.

Another experienced pilot arrived on 19 September, when nineteen year old Plt Off R Atkinson joined from 600 Squadron at Manston. He had been with 242 Squadron at Biggin Hill in May, and had moved with it to the French airfield at Châteaudun to cover the Army's retreat to the Channel coast. Two more pilots arrived on 20 September, Sgt H J R Barrow and Fg Off L H Schwind. Barrow had been with 607 Squadron at Usworth in June 1940 and had moved to Tangmere on posting to 43 Squadron in August. Schwind, who had joined the RAF on a short service commission in 1937, had carried out his flying training at Wittering and had flown Gauntlets with 54 Squadron at Hornchurch and Vickers Vincents with 55 Squadron at Dhibban in Iraq before returning to the UK, serving in Scotland and then joining 85 Squadron at Martlesham Heath.

To complete the list of new arrivals came Plt Off James MacGill Talman, from Dunbartonshire, who had won a DFC while fighting over France in May 1940, and Plt Off G H Westlake (later Gp Cpt G H Westlake, DFC) who had spent a week with 43 Squadron at Usworth, but who was to spend almost two years with 213 Squadron rising in that time from Plt Off to CO. Westlake was born in Rangoon on 21 April 1918. He joined the Royal Air Force Volunteer Reserve in September 1937, when a student at De Havilland's Aeronautical Technical School. Called up at the outbreak of war he was initially posted to Ansty as an *ab initio* flying instructor. In April 1940 he attended OTU before being posted to 43 Squadron on 21 September 1940.

On 27 September at 08.40 hours, the Squadron was ordered to patrol the Mayfield Line, and at 09.55 hours intercepted an attacking force of Bf 110s over Gatwick. As the fighting moved westward Sing damaged a Bf 110 over Mayfield. The Squadron had already split up, when dived on by a squadron of Spitfires, before the enemy aircraft were engaged, and Strickland leading Blue Section found himself alone with his Numbers Two and Three Lockhart and Barrow. He then heard from a London ground station that enemy aircraft were crossing the coast, so the section set off in the direction of Dover. Strickland then saw twelve Bf 110s flying above them in line astern and climbed to attack the leader from below and ahead. After a short burst which seemed to cause little or no damage, he broke away and saw anti-aircraft fire in the sky towards London. On investigation he found about thirty Bf 110s in a circle, with fifty Bf 109s above them. He pulled off to one side and waited until he saw a chance to attack. He then caught a Bf 110 by surprise and following a quarter attack it fell out of the circle. As Strickland continued to attack it all the way down, three other Hurricanes also joined in. After two good bursts at 1,500 feet the port engine went on fire, but at the same time the rear gunner put some cannon shells through the radiator and fuselage of Strickland's Hurricane and he had to force land, wheels up in a field at Horne, near Redhill. Fortunately he was unhurt. It was reported later that the Bf 110 had crashed in flames at Whitchurch.

Having seen many enemy aircraft milling about over Redhill, Barrow waited until the anti-aircraft fire had ceased and then made a head-on attack on a Bf 110. A three-second burst from three hundred yards caused pieces to fly off from the front of the fuselage and wings. After breaking away, he saw another Bf 110 with a Hurricane on its tail, and he followed them down. When the Hurricane broke away Barrow attacked, firing two three-second bursts, opening fire at three hundred yards. Black smoke came from the German fighter's port engine and, after a further attack by another Hurricane, it crashed on the edge of Gatwick aerodrome. During the engagement Fg Off L H Schwind, who had flown his first patrol with the Squadron only three days earlier, and was flying with Sizer and Jeram as Green Section, was shot down and killed. His aircraft crashed into Chance Wood, on Wildernesse Golf Course, near Sevenoaks. In 1970 a memorial plaque was erected on the spot where his aircraft crashed. Harold Schwind - the name is almost certainly of Danish origin - was due to be married the following day. He had in fact been promoted to Flight Lieutenant on 3 September 1940 but it seems unlikely that he ever knew of his promotion.

Airborne at 13.40 hours on 28 September, with the CO leading Red Section, the Squadron was ordered to patrol Camberley at 20,000 feet accompanied by 602 (City of Glasgow) Squadron. On reaching the patrol line the formation was ordered to return to base at 16,000 feet. Once overhead, MacDonald was informed that sixty enemy aircraft were approaching over Selsey Bill at 18,000 feet. On sighting the enemy formation, MacDonald led the two squadrons into sun and reached a position slightly behind them at 20,000 feet. An attack was made on the rear of the formation, which seemed to come as a surprise since the Bf 110s broke up and had difficulty in reforming any sort of regular pattern. MacDonald attacked and followed his target down until it crashed into the sea. He was joined by Sgt Redhill who confirmed the kill. There had been considerable return fire but it was erratic and out of range. In this same engagement Talman claimed another Bf 110.

The new pattern of operations, standing patrols on set patrol lines at 20,000 feet plus, became fully established as October heralded the coming of winter, and the strain on the pilots increased rather than diminished. For ten weeks the Squadron had been in the front line of the greatest air battle ever fought. Seven of the pilots still flying had been with the Squadron since before Dunkirk, they were Flt Lts J E J Sing and R W Kellow, Plt Offs H W Cottam and W M Sizer, Flt Sgt C Grayson and Sgt E G Snowden and R D Dunscombe. Sgt. M E Croskell had flown with the Squadron during the fighting in France, over Dunkirk and during the Battle of Britain, until 15 September when he was wounded and taken to hospital, returning in December. By that time so great had been the changes in personnel that the only pilot he knew was the CO. Sgt R T Llewellyn had also been with the Squadron since March 1940, and had flown throughout the spring and summer months until he too was injured in the fighting on 15 September.

Though the disparity in numbers was not so great when the Squadron came into action during these last weeks at Tangmere, and engagements themselves were fewer, it was the nature of the flying that imposed new strains. The fast, high sweeps of the German fighters called for even greater vigilance, and longer hours on patrol, if interceptions were to be made. In the brief spells of good weather the Luftwaffe attacks multiplied rapidly. It was now found necessary to abandon one of the cardinal principles that had been applied in the early stages of the battle. The practice of keeping the aircraft on the ground until a raid actually developed now had to be abandoned in order to maintain standing patrols over the Kent coast to catch the high flying raiders. Patrolling and fighting now at high altitudes, above 20,000 feet, with poor weather conditions below was a new and unpleasant experience. Thus, as the German raids became more sporadic and the weather worsened, the Squadron's flying time increased rather than diminished. Two or three patrols were flown each day in Squadron strength according to the new instructions. Trailing long white condensation-trails across the sky, the Squadron soon became familiar with a whole new set of land-marks, Beachy Head, St Catherine's Point and Selsey Bill. These landmarks on many days constituted the patrol line.

On patrol over Portland at 20,000 feet, on 30 September, with the CO leading, fifteen enemy aircraft were encountered flying in a southerly direction just above a ten-tenths layer of cloud. The Squadron formed into line astern and commenced a diving turn that brought it to within one thousand feet of the German formation. As an echelon attack was delivered, MacDonald saw the starboard rudder of his target Bf 110 collapse. He then saw an aircraft on his tail and suspected an attack from a Bf 109, so he pulled away to port, and lost sight of the aircraft he had attacked. He was told later by some of the pilots that they had seen an enemy aircraft without a tail-plane and it was assumed that it was his. After breaking away he attacked another Bf 110, which dived away towards some clouds and reached them before he was able to open fire. He then returned to the scene of the fight and flew around at 2,000 feet to see if he could see any pilots who had baled out; all he found was the wreckage of two aircraft which he could not identify.

Barrow was flying as Green Two when he saw the formation of Bf 110s some 5,000 feet below. He followed down into a stern attack, and opened fire at three hundred yards with two three-second bursts, pieces broke off the tail and the rear of the fuselage as the 110 dived away into cloud. Stevens, Yellow Two, followed his leader down attacking one and silencing the rear gunner; he then attacked another and after three bursts, black and white smoke came from the port engine and, once again, the enemy aircraft dived away into the clouds.

A day of bright periods, 5 October, brought the German fighters and bombers out in force. Green Section with Wilf Sizer leading was ordered to patrol base at 20,000 feet. While they were still climbing up through 12,000 feet, Control warned of enemy aircraft approaching Beachy Head ten thousand feet above them. Once over Beachy Head the section was vectored 010 degrees as the German formation moved north. The first Ju 88 Sizer saw was already being chased by a Hurricane just below a layer of cloud. He joined in the pursuit with Green Two in close attendance. As Sizer opened fire pieces began to fall off the German bomber and its port engine started to smoke by the time Sizer has used up all his ammunition both engines were smoking badly. The Ju 88 pulled into a climbing turn, and managed to avoid Green Two, but to no avail as it was later shot down into the sea by aircraft of 253 Squadron.

A patrol later in the day ran into a larger raid. The Squadron was protecting Southampton and Portsmouth when two raids approached the former from Cherbourg. Many of the bombers turned back before reaching the target area, but a fierce fight developed with a formation of Bf 109s sporting yellow spinners. With no bombers to worry about the German pilots appeared to be itching for a fight. The situation eventually resolved itself into a stalemate and no claims were made or losses sustained.

On 9 October, Snowden was ordered to patrol base below the cloud cover as Number Two in Yellow Section, and then ordered to Selsey Bill above the cloud. As he emerged on top he saw a Ju 88, which flew past him, and then opened fire from the rear turret. Snowden fell in behind, and made two stern attacks followed by a beam attack, as the two aircraft dropped down from 6,000 to 2,000 feet over the sea. By this time Snowden had used all his ammunition, and he saw the Ju 88 flying south with pieces falling off it until it crashed into the sea approximately thirty miles south of Selsey Bill.

The next day, as Ron Atkinson was climbing up to intercept a formation of enemy aircraft over Brighton, he saw a lone Dornier crossing in over the coast some 8,000 feet above him. He continued his climb, turning so that he intercepted the raider ten miles north-east of base. He fired a two-second burst from astern and then lost it as it flew into cloud. Atkinson continued his climb and caught the raider as it emerged on top of the cloud layer, when he attacked again from above and behind with two three-second bursts, and saw bullets entering the fuselage and wings. The Dornier went into a steep turn, and half rolled into cloud, after which all contact was lost. The Observer Corps reported seeing a Dornier heading towards France, smoking badly and losing height.

Patrolling between base and Southampton ten days later, the Squadron intercepted a formation of Bf 109s on its way to London. Bushell flying as Yellow Two saw a Bf 109 come down on his Leader's tail; he opened fire at fifty yards range and pieces flew off the German fighter's starboard wing as it dived away. He then saw two more on his own tail, which were firing at him so he dived away after his Leader, Kellow, who was hit and in obvious distress. The two Bf 109s followed for a short while, but then made off. Bushell continued to circle until Kellow managed to crash-land in a field. He was then ordered to return to base; he noted that the Messerschmitts had yellow markings on their tail fins where British fighters carried the red, white and blue flashes. Kellow made it back to Tangmere later, and uninjured.

Although the German fighters had greater freedom of action without formations of bombers to protect, and with their two-stage superchargers which gave the Bf 109s an advantage over even the Hurricane Mk.II, the German pilots were still meeting their match when they encountered the Squadron, even though it was still flying the Hurricane Mk.I.

On 17 October the Squadron was again jumped while on an evening patrol over Portland at 20,000 feet. The German fighters had been climbing almost continuously all the way across the Channel, and so were able to arrive with height in hand. The Squadron was flying in two sections of six led by the CO flying as Red Leader, and Sing. The CO saw seven Bf 109s on a southerly course below and to the port of the Squadron and, as he turned in their direction, the Squadron was attacked from above and behind. MacDonald singled out a target and attacked, opening fire at close range and the 109 went into a left hand turn leaving a trail of white smoke. It then dived for cover in cloud and MacDonald could not follow as he was again being attacked from behind.

Barrow, as Red Three, followed his leader as he broke away from the initial attack, and then dived to attack a Bf 109. He then saw another German fighter below and as he made a beam attack firing a two-second burst from two hundred and fifty yards range, the enemy aircraft took little evasive action. He then made another quarter attack from ahead, closing from two hundred and fifty to one hundred yards, and saw his ammunition striking the target and pieces falling off as the German fighter entered cloud in a spiral dive. Barrow followed it down and broke through the cloud base but had lost contact.

Sgt Bushell, flying as Yellow Two, followed his leader also as he broke away from the attacking fighters. Both saw a yellow-nosed 109 flying south and Yellow Leader fired all his ammunition in a prolonged stern attack. As the German fighter continued to dive away out to sea Bushell gave chase, and, making a quarter attack, he closed to about one hundred yards from which distance he opened fire, causing a thick white substance to stream from the front of the enemy aircraft. The German took only feeble evasive action and Bushell saw his bullets strike both wings; as he turned away his Hurricane was covered in oil. Bushell attacked once more and the now badly-damaged fighter disappeared into the haze at 10,000 feet losing height rapidly, with oil and glycol streaming from it.

Plt Off R Atkinson failed to return from this fierce engagement, his aircraft crashing at Weeks Farm, near Pluckley, Kent. Sgt Geoffrey Stevens' aircraft was also damaged over Ashford, Kent, and he realised that to abandon it could result in considerable damage and loss of life if it crashed onto the town. The fire in his engine went out so he stayed with his aircraft, and crash-landed it on the outskirts of the town. Although at the time the report recorded "pilot unhurt", Stevens had in fact injured his spine, from which injury he has suffered ever since. Once again the three or four enemy aircraft destroyed did something to redress the balance.

On 19 October Flt Lt W D David, DFC and Bar, who had been posted in from 87 Squadron as a Flight Commander on 16 October, shot down a Ju 88 four miles north of Manston in Kent.

As he led "B" Flight off the ground at 10.55 hours to carry out practice flying in the local area, operations called up to ask him to investigate a plot. Green Section landed and David led Blue Section off to the east for some minutes before swinging round on to a course of 100 degrees. Eventually the section came out of cloud near Manston, and picked up a speck 2,000 feet below and four miles to the north. The section dived to attack, and the enemy aircraft immediately started to climb away. David then led a beam attack from the rear, and at one hundred yards he saw hits striking behind the starboard engine; the wing caught fire and the fuselage started to glow. The badly damaged Ju 88 then dived away into misty cloud which covered the sea at 800 feet about thirty miles, on a heading of 140 degrees, from Manston. None of the Section's aircraft was hit by return fire.

Although this was to be David's (later Gp Cpt W D David, DFC and Bar) only victory with the Squadron - he was posted to 152 Squadron in November 1940 - he was to be the highest scoring pilot to have served with the Squadron during the war. He was officially credited with destroying fifteen enemy aircraft, sharing two others and with five unconfirmed and four damaged. The majority of his victories were achieved with 87 Squadron during the fighting in France, for which he was awarded his DFC and Bar.

Apart from the increased ferocity that seemed to mark these battles the worsening weather added other problems. The very next day saw the Squadron patrolling over Brighton with the cloud base at ground level. Two other squadrons at Tangmere refused to become airborne in such conditions. During one period of particularly bad weather an attempt was made to move "B" Flight the short distance to the nearby airfield at Ford. The ground crews moved off and awaited the arrival of the aircraft but, as each one taxied in, it sank into the soft ground. The ground crews spent the rest of the day pulling the Hurricanes out of the quagmire with tractors before they were all able to return to Tangmere.

By the end of the month a new series of operational directives from Air Vice-Marshal Park meant that the Squadron was usually airborne as one of a pair with one of the other units in the Tangmere Wing; either 602 (City of Glasgow) Squadron or, later, 145 Squadron which came down with its Spitfires from Dyce in Scotland.

A last convulsive effort by the Luftwaffe on 28 and 29 October saw the month out, and brought the Battle of Britain officially to its close. On the first of these days while over Tangmere at 20,000 feet, the Squadron was once more attacked by a force of Bf 109s that came in with height advantage. The familiar pattern soon established itself. As the Bf 109s came diving in from above, the formation broke up into a series of individual dog-fights, in which each side attempted to take advantage of the, by now well-know, weaknesses and tactics of the other. With both height and speed the Bf 109s had the initial advantage but, once the dog-fight commenced, the superior manoeuvrability of the Hurricane evened out the chances.

However, in the first attack, Plt Off R R Hutley's Hurricane was hit by a long burst from one of the German fighters and crashed into the sea off Selsey Bill. He was picked up unconscious by the Selsey life-boat, but died without recovering consciousness. Tommy Thomson was bounced by three Bf 109s. He was successful in avoiding the attentions of two of them but seemed to have the third permanently in his mirror. Eventually he was hit, losing bits and pieces off his port wing, and having his left arm and side peppered with shrapnel. His arm was paralysed, which made maintaining control of his aeroplane rather difficult, but he nevertheless made a successful forced landing in a field on the outskirts of Fareham. By the time he returned to Tangmere, after fourteen months in The Royal Victoria Hospital, Netley, near Southampton, the Squadron had moved on.

Thomas Russell Thomson had joined the RAFVR in 1939 at Prestwick, and commenced his flying training on Tiger Moths, but with the outbreak of war he was called to full time service. After completing his flying training and conversion to Hurricanes at Hullavington, he joined 607 (County of Durham) Auxiliary Squadron at Tangmere on 9 October, moving to 213 Squadron on 21 October. When he returned to active service in 1942 he specialised in the operational control of flying, and in 1945 as a Wing Commander he became the Chief Flying Control Officer, Fighter Command. He was mentioned in dispatches in 1945, and left the service to join the Ministry of Aviation in 1946.

On the last official day of the battle a formation of Bf 109s was intercepted while carrying out dive-bombing attacks on Portsmouth. In a short sharp engagement both the CO and Kellow were successful in bringing down enemy aircraft but the popular Polish pilot, Plt Off B A Wlasnowolski, was shot down over Selsey Bill and killed when his aircraft crashed onto the Liphook Game Farm, Stoughton, Hampshire. Boleslaw Andrzej Wlasnowolski was born on 26 November 1916, was awarded the VM (5th Class) and the KW, and is buried in Chichester Cemetery, Sussex.

At the time it was not at all clear that anything substantial had changed, as October gave way to November. On the first day of the new month, the Squadron was on patrol late in the afternoon when the CO saw sixteen Bf 109s flying towards Portsmouth at 26, 000 feet. On reaching the coast the enemy formation split into two groups; one of these carried on towards Portsmouth and made a dive bombing attack on the town, while the other swung round, and came in behind the Squadron. MacDonald isolated one enemy fighter, and followed it down in a dive, but was unable to close with However at 15,000 feet it reduced its angle of dive while it. continued down until it reached a position approximately three miles south of the Isle of Wight. MacDonald closed up and delivered a shallow quarter attack, and the enemy fighter, taken by surprise, took no evasive action, and after a short burst dived into the sea.

As November drew on patrols were recalled more frequently as the weather closed in at Tangmere, and interceptions became even more rare. To replace the missing pilots new faces appeared in the crew-room and it was at this time that the two French Commandants, Beguin and René Deport arrived. René Deport, always known on the Squadron as Claude, was an excellent guitar player, and had stood in with the famous Hot Club de France band of Grapelli and Rheinhart fame. Plt Off Schou from Norway also arrived to add to the international air that prevailed at Tangmere.

Other changes saw the departure of Jackie Sing, who had been awarded the DFC on 22 October, and the command of "A" Flight passing to Fg Off Billy Drake, before he also left to form one of the first "Jim Crow" flights at Hawkinge. The loss of Strickland had deprived "B" Flight of its leader and command now passed to Wilf Sizer, who had flown with the Squadron since the very earliest days. During November his aircraft was damaged by the rear gunner of a Ju 88, which he was attacking with George Westlake. His aircraft was hit in the radiator, oil cooler and undercarriage, which subsequently jammed with one wheel up and one down; on instructions from Control he baled out.

The last battles, fought while the Squadron was still in the front line, occurred in November, when on three occasions patrols came to grips with high-flying formations of Bf 109s.

On 6 November the Squadron was ordered to patrol base at 30,000 feet together with 602 (City of Glasgow) Squadron. At 22,000 feet Sgt Dixon saw about thirty Bf 109s approaching the Portsmouth area from the south. As they drew near they turned and made their final approach to the town from the north-east. As the Squadron attacked the enemy formation broke up and formed a defensive circle. Dixon's section broke up in the ensuing dog-fight. He quickly found a Bf 109 on his tail but managed to shake it off without sustaining any damage. When he next saw his attacker it was in a vertical climb almost in his gun-sights. Dixon fired and saw his bullets entering in the vicinity of the cockpit. During a second attack his guns did not fire, so he broke away and returned to base; he noted that most of the Bf 109s had yellow spinners.

Snowden, flying as Yellow Leader in "A" Flight, made a climbing turn inside a formation of twelve Bf 109s that were flying in a wide circle around the Squadron. He saw one enemy machine pass on the outside of a turn and prepare to attack Red Leader, so he cut across the circle and attacked with four short deflection bursts at three hundred yards. The German fighter dived away towards some thick cloud over the Isle of Wight, streaming glycol to such an extent that it seemed highly unlikely to Snowden that it could make it back to base in view of the long sea crossing. He returned to rejoin the Squadron having lost Yellow Two and Three in the fight.

This was Snowden's last success before leaving the Squadron; since his first victory on 11 August he had destroyed five enemy aircraft, damaged two and claimed one probable. However Sgt H H Adair was shot down, by Major

"B" Flight outside the dispersal hut, Driffield, January 1941.

Helmut Wick of J/G 2. His aircraft crashed into a chalk hillside at Pigeon Farm, Widley near Portsmouth. The aircraft struck the hillside with such force that his body was never recovered, and he remained listed as missing in the Squadron's records.

Again on 15 November the Squadron was attacked by about twenty plus Bf 109s some twenty miles south of Selsey Bill. As the Squadron broke up Westlake, who was flying as Green Leader, tried to join up with another Hurricane chasing a Bf 109 out to sea, but lost contact with them in cloud. Then, seeing a smoke trail above him, he climbed and an aircraft dived past him. He then saw two more Bf 109s approaching dead ahead and 400 feet above him. He climbed inside them and, as they turned, he fixed one in his sights and fired two short bursts; the 109 burst into flames and black smoke came out of the cockpit. The other German fighter was now behind Westlake and he saw him firing, but with no results. As Westlake turned towards him, the German made off towards France outdistancing the Hurricane.

On 22 November Red Section was airborne at 09.30 and at 09.50 Kellow and Stevens sighted a Do 17 north-east of Guildford. Kellow engaged and shot it down. Finally, leading 602 (City of Glasgow) Squadron on 28 November, an action was fought over Bembridge in which Sgt H J R Barrow was shot down off St. Catherine's Point and killed. This action marked the end of the Squadron's stay under No. 11 Group's control.

Many pilots had come and gone in the course of the Battle, and it was a very changed Squadron that flew north from Tangmere on the first day of December 1940. The move was planned to take place after a last dusk patrol, the aircraft to be refuelled for a night take-off and a dawn landing at Leconfield. In the event one aircraft needed maintenance on one of its oleo-legs. The groundcrew working in the dark and without lights discovered, when the work was done, that petrol had been used instead of oil in the oleo. More frantic work was carried out to have everything put to rights before take-off.

The fighting was over for a brief period, and for almost the first time since July the Squadron was airborne but not on an armed patrol. Led by Sizer, eight Hurricanes headed for Leconfield in Yorkshire. Wilfred Max Sizer, who was soon to leave the Squadron on posting as an Instructor to 55 OTU, had been with the Squadron since May 1939. During this time he had shared in the flying and fighting in France, over Dunkirk and throughout the Battle of Britain; he had destroyed seven enemy aircraft, damaged three and shared another Ju 88 destroyed with 253 Squadron. He had been awarded the DFC on 8 October 1940.

At Leconfield, in 12 Group, the Squadron was rested together with 303 (Polish) Squadron, which had been operating in the later stages of the battle from Northolt. Resting was only a relative term, for as new pilots arrived a busy training programme was soon under way. Among the new arrivals at Leconfield was Sgt A Hancock. Allan John Hancock, from Wallingford, Berkshire, was born in Lahore, India, in 1918. He joined the RAF early in the summer of 1940 and trained at Marshall's Flying School, Cambridge and No.7 FTS at Peterborough. He was graded "Above Average" throughout his training and after attending No.56 OTU was posted directly to the Squadron.

Apart from the normal training routine, formation flying

was carried out over the nearby town of Kingston-upon-Hull to help bolster civilian morale. As in the early days of the phoney war, air-firing practice was once more carried out at Sutton Bridge where Wg Cdr J H Edwardes Jones DFC was now commanding No. 6 Operational Training Unit. A busy December kept the log-books well filled, but was marked by a particularly tragic loss. Sgt G D Bushell, who had been with the Squadron since early July and had shot down three Bf 110s in the course of the Battle, was killed when his Hurricane crashed in a snowstorm at Risby Park on the last day of the year. January saw a succession of days on which the weather was so atrocious that no flying at all was possible.

In the middle of the month another move was made, but this time only a few miles north to the nearby airfield at Driffield in 13 Group, a mere few minutes flying time across the Yorkshire Moors. The timing of the move was fortuitous, as the day after the Squadron left Leconfield it was the target for a heavy German bombing raid which caused considerable damage. At Driffield the same routine was carried out as at Leconfield, and after a great period of change and adjustment the Squadron was building up once more as a new team. However the month was marred by two fatal accidents in the course of training.

Soon enough a new task was found and the end of the first week in February found the Hurricanes flying north once more, this time bound for the most northerly airfield on the mainland - remote, snowbound Castletown in Caithness. This airfield had been hurriedly constructed exactly one year earlier, to provide a base for the squadrons protecting the great naval base at Scapa Flow. Lack of accommodation on the airfield meant that most of the ground-crews were billeted in an Infant's School almost on the coast near Dunnet Head, where all the facilities were child-sized and there was plenty of hot water but no cold. Here at last a use was found for the plentiful snow.

By the beginning of February 1941 the Luftwaffe units based in Norway had become so discouraged that raids seldom disturbed the peace of this northern spot. Mike Croskell remembers the intense loneliness of night patrols flown over Orkney and Shetland with no lights in sight, only the two banks of exhaust flames on either side of the engine, which in fact made night interceptions almost impossible despite the deflector plates that were eventually fitted to the upper front part of the fuselage. On the whole, due to the adverse conditions and the lack of enemy activity, flying duties were considerably curtailed. For a fortunate few who had been granted home leave, the heavy snow falls that curtailed flying had the advantage of preventing their return for over a week since the railway lines north of Aberdeen were blocked.

One operation mounted from Castletown was the detachment of "A" Flight to Sumburgh in the Shetland Isles. Here, another hundred or so miles to the North again, the Flight had a watching brief over a huge expanse of northern ocean. The intended quarry was the large four-engined Focke-Wulf 200 Condor, which was used as a long-range reconnaissance aircraft. The long patrols over the sea resulted in only three engagements with these aircraft and it seemed to the pilots, who had become used to the devastating effects of their machine-guns against other fighters, that the Browning .303s had very little effect on the large Condors. As far as they could see, the Germans flew on almost undisturbed back to Norway

After about one month of this unrewarding work the Flight departed from Sumburgh and returned to Castletown. Here regular patrols were worked in with the training routine, and on the night of 17 March a section led by Westlake was scrambled to intercept an enemy aircraft over Wick. As was more often than not the case at night, no contact was made.

So occupied, the Squadron waited and prepared for its next task in the war after the most intensive period of action in its history. In the course of the Battle of Britain and the fighting over Dunkirk, the Squadron had claimed over one hundred and thirty enemy aircraft destroyed for the loss of a little over thirty pilots.

The headstone, in Chichester Cemetery, marking the grave of Plt Off B A Wlasnowolski, who was shot down and killed on 1 November 194

*The Squadron's pilots and officers, Nicosia, Cyprus, Summer 1941. Front row left to right: Fg Off Bill Allen (Intelligence Officer), Sgt Wally Lack, Doc Brocklebank (Medical Officer), Plt Off Bert Houle, Fg Off George Westlake, Sgt Hank Hancock, Sgt J D Ritchie, Fg Off Eddie Edmunds, WO Wally Wallace, unidentified pilot in sunglasses.
Middle and back rows: Sgt Marshal, Sgt Henderson, unidentified pilot half hidden, Flt Lt Tem Temlett, DFC, Fg Off John Sowrey, Bertie Webb (Adjutant), Flt Lt Jimmy Lockhart, Plt Off Logan Briggs, Sqn Ldr Duncan MacDonald, unidentified pilot in shadow, Sgt Tug Wilson, Plt Off Duffy Douthwaite, Sgt Ken Sissons, Sgt Freddie Wilson, Sgt Steve Stephenson, RCAF.
(J A Sowrey)*

CHAPTER SEVEN - FAREWELL TO ENGLAND

For two months, the Squadron's Hurricanes flew over the bleak moors and rocky coasts of Caithness. Then, in the middle of April, came the mysterious news that the Squadron was to be moved overseas to an unknown destination. The two French pilots were exchanged and the number of aircrew brought up to full strength. From 17 Squadron, which had recently come north to Castletown from Croydon, came Fg Offs J A Sowrey (later Air Cdre J A Sowrey, DFC, AFC) and C B Temlett, DFC, both of whom were to stay through many and varied adventures. Temlett had joined the RAF as an apprentice at the Electrical and Wireless School from where he had won a scholarship to the RAF College at Cranwell. He passed out at the end of a shortened course in December 1939, was posted to an Army Co-operation Squadron, and had fought with it in France. In the course of this fighting, flying a Lysander, he had shot down a Bf 109 and had been awarded the DFC. Having volunteered for Fighter Command, he had been posted to 17 Squadron. John Sowrey had also attended Cranwell in 1939 and, on passing out, had been posted to 613 Army Co-operation Squadron in 1940. As the last elements of the BEF had pulled out of France, he had taken part in the dropping of supplies to the troops defending Calais. While dropping canisters filled with food, water and ammunition, the Lysanders had come under murderous ground fire and losses were high. In March 1941 he had joined 17 Squadron to become a fighter pilot, and had thus arrived at Castletown.

To further the work of preparation, a move was made on 21 April 1941 to Turnhouse, near Edinburgh, commanded by Wg Cdr The Duke of Hamilton and Brandon, a somewhat more accessible location than remote Castletown. The journey south was carried out in very bad weather, and to at least one of the new arrivals it seemed to be a case of every man for himself. Some of the aircraft followed a course down the east coast whist others chose the west coast; eventually everyone arrived safely. Here Sgt W R Henderson, known generally as

The Squadron's Hurricanes taxy out for take off; Fg Off J A Sowrey's aircraft is the last in the line-up. (J A Sowrey)

Ray or "Hindoo", transferred in from 602 Squadron. The Squadron's groundcrews were also reinforced; the new arrivals included Jack Walton, an armourer who arrived from Leuchars and stayed with the Squadron until the end of the war, and a new Armament Officer, Plt Off Burgess. These new arrivals were never to arrive at Turnhouse, but were billeted in a house in Edinburgh until it was time to move overseas.

At Turnhouse the pilots were given the opportunity to try out a tropicalised Hurricane I with a forty-five gallon drop tank slung under each wing. The Squadron put two and two together, and Malta soon became established as the firm favourite for the most likely destination. In two weeks, during which time the Squadron was non-operational, preparations were completed for the move overseas. Vaccinations and inoculations were followed, for the fortunate few who lived near Edinburgh, by forty-eight hours leave. Then finally, as the main party moved down to Liverpool for embarkation, the news came that the destination was to be North Africa.

The situation there was critical, not only from the immediate military standpoint but also from the supply position. With the fall of France and the arrival of the Germans in Libya, sailing convoys through the Mediterranean had become a major naval operation - and a risky one at that. To obviate this difficulty, two alternative routes to Egypt, the bastion in the Middle East, had been devised. These were longer and more arduous than the short Mediterranean route but, it was hoped, less dangerous from the point of view of enemy activity. So, not wishing to risk all of such valuable eggs as the Squadron and its aircraft in one or even two baskets, the three parties into which the Squadron was divided each travelled by a different route.

Four pilots, including Sowrey and Plt Offs Pain and P Pound, made up the Advance Party, which was to go by sea to the Gold Coast (now Ghana), and then fly their aircraft overland across Africa and up the Nile Valley. The Main Party, consisting of the CO and the majority of the pilots plus aircraft, was to proceed by aircraft carrier to a point east of Gibraltar, and then fly off to Malta and so on to Egypt. The third party, consisting of the Squadron doctor and the groundcrew, was to take the longer route round the Cape of Good Hope and so arrive in Egypt via the Red Sea and the Suez Canal.

Early in May, in the middle of an air raid on Liverpool, the first element of the Squadron slipped away on board H M Transport *Highland Princess* with the aircraft, Hurricanes and Tomahawks, stacked in crates down in the holds. The sea trip proved eventful; having successfully eluded the Luftwaffe at the start the *Highland Princess* was later chased by the battleship *Bismarck*, but once again any contact with the Germans was avoided. Naturally enough when, later in the voyage, the news was received on board that the *Bismarck* had been sunk, the champagne flowed freely in celebration; what was left at the end of the party was "hoovered" out of the glasses by the Mess stewards. Eventually the party disembarked in lighters at Takoradi in the Gold Coast, the sea terminus of the almost four-thousand-mile route to Egypt.

The "Takoradi Route" had been set up in July 1940 when Gp Cpt H K Thorold, with a small group of ground personnel, arrived to begin work on the installations that would be necessary to establish a route which would cross Africa and be capable of handling heavy reinforcement traffic for Middle East Command. The bare essentials for such traffic already existed in the form of the staging posts of the weekly passenger and mail service set up in 1936. The main construction party arrived in Africa in August 1940, and eventually over seven thousand men were employed in servicing the route which, when fully developed, was capable of handling 120 aircraft per month. By the end of August 1943, over 5,000 aircraft had passed that way. It has been

The Sergeant Pilots of the Squadron, Nicosia, Cyprus, Summer 1941. Left to right: Eddie Edmonds, Hank Hancock, unidentified, Tug Wilson, Freddie Wilson, Hindoo Henderson, unidentified in shadow, Steve Stephenson, RCAF, J D Ritchie, unidentified with helmet, Ken Sissons, Wally Wallace. (J A Sowrey)

well said that "victory in Egypt came via the Takoradi route".

When the *Highland Princess* arrived off Takoradi harbour, there was already something of a bottle-neck created by more than two hundred Curtiss Tomahawks which were already there, albeit minus spares and tool kits. The newly-arrived short-range fighters, mostly Hurricanes and more Tomahawks, were removed from their crates and assembled for their first and probably most testing flight. Until the last moment it remained a matter of some doubt as to which aircraft the pilots would be given. Sowrey had his first flight in a Tomahawk, and fervently hoped that he would not have to fly one all the way to Egypt. Finally, to his relief, the decision was made in favour of the Hurricane.

Flight tests over, and all preparations made, the aircraft, led by a Blenheim, took off and climbed to between 10,000 and 15,000 feet for the first two-hour flight covering the 375-mile leg along the palm-fringed coast to Lagos. The following day, a further two hour twenty minute flight over hilly jungle brought the aircraft to Minna for an intermediate refuelling stop. Then, pressing on to the north-east, another leg of one hour thirty minutes brought the aircraft to Kano. From here the course lay almost due east for fifteen hundred miles. Maiduguri three hundred and twenty-five miles and one hour fifty minutes further on, marked the boundary of Nigeria. The next six hundred and eighty-nine miles to El Geneina lay over Free French territory consisting of sand, marsh scrub and again mile upon mile of sand; four hours of boredom tinged with anxiety. Two such legs constituted more than enough flying for one day. Having arrived at El Geneina in the Anglo-Egyptian Sudan, with French Equatorial Africa behind them, a night's rest prepared the pilots for two more legs totalling 754 miles, one to El Fasher with a flying time of one hour thirty minutes and the other 500 miles on to Khartoum, which brought the party back once more to the "luxuries" of civilisation.

The most difficult part of the journey was now over, and after a night stop the aircraft flew almost due north for one thousand and twenty-six miles along the Nile. On 10 June a single leg of three hours ten minutes brought the formation to Wadi Halfa. The overnight stop at the Wadi Halfa Hotel encountered some inter-service discrimination when the Greek manager of the hotel closed the bar to everyone other than the Army. Flt Lt Tommy Farr and John Sowrey tackled this head-on by throwing him into the Nile - twice! The four hour thirty minute flight the next morning, to Abu Sueir in the Canal Zone, served to remove them from the ire of the army Provost Marshal which the events of the previous evening had not unsurprisingly provoked. Here the Advance Party climbed out of their aircraft on 11 June 1941 to find "A" Flight already in residence.

The route taken by the Main Party had indeed been a good deal shorter but, at the same time, even more hazardous than the flight across Africa.

The party embarked in HMS *Furious* at Liverpool on 11 May 1941 in company with Nos.229 and 249 Squadrons. Below decks were sixty-three Hurricanes packed nose to tail, minus wings and propellers. The great adventure was on. Each of the squadrons aboard the carrier had been in the thick of the fighting during the Battle of Britain. With the crisis at home over, they were now off to grapple once more with the Luftwaffe in the skies of North Africa. As the Squadron left the UK, never to return, the Nominal Roll of its pilots was:-

Sqn Ldr D S MacDonald, DFC

"A" Flight	"B" Flight
Flt Lt Gould	Flt Lt J Lockhart
Fg Off C B Temlett, DFC	Plt Off G H Westlake
Fg Off J A Sowrey	Plt Off Downie
Plt Off J L Briggs	Plt Off Lynch
Plt Off Pain	Plt Off Crowther
Plt Off Douthwaite	Plt Off P P Pound
Sgt P P Wilson	Sgt F A W J Wilson
Sgt Marshall	Sgt R J Wallace
Sgt K N R Sissons	Sgt A J Hancock
Sgt Edwards	Sgt Gledhill
Sgt W A Lack	Sgt W R Henderson
Sgt Sims	
Sgt Boyd	

Exactly one week after leaving Liverpool, *Furious* arrived at Gibraltar without interference from the Kriegsmarine or Luftwaffe. Here the carrier joined with HMS *Ark Royal* (to which 249 Squadron transferred), the cruisers *London* and *Sheffield*, and eight escorting destroyers. As dusk fell the whole convoy steamed south-westward along the Moroccan coast past the port of Tangiers. Then, under the cover of darkness, course was altered 180 degrees and full speed was made into the dangerous waters of the Mediterranean.

At the early morning briefing, the pilots were told to be prepared to fly-off at dawn the following day, destination Malta. For the three squadrons the real part of the journey was just beginning and the prospects were forbidding. Although the convoy represented a powerful force, the Royal Navy was still anxious to keep its exact position a secret. Accordingly no information as to their whereabouts was given to the pilots - no point of departure, no course to steer, no flight plan or map was provided; the only instructions were to "Follow the Fulmar". This was the single-engine two-seat fighter aircraft provided by the Navy to lead each flight to the island. Not surprisingly, such precautions were thought to be a little too stringent by the pilots on the squadrons, so they set about preparing some unofficial navigation aids. The first need was for some sort of chart; the relevant page from the atlas in the Wardroom library filled the bill. Secondly, some estimation of the point of departure was needed, and by various means this was calculated to be more or less opposite the North African port of Bône. This turned out to be a fairly accurate estimate.

Equipped with these aids, the flight planning for the trip went ahead. Even so, the fates seemed to have all the ace cards very much in their own hands. The aircraft were only to be assembled finally below deck just prior to take-off; this made anything in the nature of a test flight out of the question. Swinging the compasses of the aircraft after fitting the wings and propellers was also impossible due to the confined space.

Apart from the navigational uncertainties, there were doubts about the fighting capabilities of the aircraft, since in their long-range configuration the Hurricane's combat performance was severely limited. The under-wing tanks fed through pipes which wound uncomfortably close to the wing-mounted guns. This meant that the two outer guns could not be fired at all, while the ammunition for the inners was necessarily limited. The two innermost guns had only one hundred rounds of ball ammunition, while their neighbours had a mere fifty.

Already the eight hundred miles or so of hostile Mediterranean, to be flown at sea level, looked an awfully long way. To put the finishing touch to the trip, intelligence sources reported that the Germans had positioned over one hundred Bf 109s on the island of Pantellaria to prevent the squadrons reaching Malta. The whole operation revealed a skeleton in the cupboard, since the previous attempt to fly aircraft in to Malta in this way had come to grief because the RAF worked in miles-per-hour and statute miles, while the RN's calculations were in knots and nautical miles. All but two of the aircraft involved had run out of fuel well before reaching the island.

With perhaps some of these thoughts in their minds, the Squadron pilots strapped into their aircraft on the flight deck in the chill dawn of 21 May 1941. The moment for their first deck take-off had arrived. A brief run-up, followed by a quick check of the special pumps that drew the fuel up from the long-range tanks, and the aircraft were ready to go. Soon the first flight was airborne, without mishap, in the wake of its navigating Fulmar. Almost at once however a fault developed in the Fulmar, and the flight roared around over the carrier in tight formation while the Fulmar was landed on again and a replacement took-off. Even so, *en route*, the replacement was unable to retract its wheels completely, but apart from this the three hours and thirty-five minutes flight passed as bearably as the cramped cockpit of the Hurricane allowed.

The flight led by Flt Lt R Lockhart was less fortunate in its experiences. Initially all went well and the flight soon formed up and set course in the wake of its leading Fulmar. To conserve fuel as effectively as possible throttle movements had to be kept to a minimum holding 1850/1950 rpm. and 1½ lb. boost, which produced an indicated airspeed of approximately 135 mph. Unfortunately, after about an hour into the flight, the Fulmar pilot decided he was lost and returned to the carrier. So, after nearly two hours airborne, the formation set off once again in what was hoped was the direction of Malta. Now, of course, fuel reserves were more critical than ever and gauges were studied anxiously as the miles of blue sea slipped below.

On nearing the island of Pantellaria, while no Bf 109s were encountered, it soon became very clear that the formation would pass extremely close to the shore and the Italian anti-aircraft gunners opened fire - more however in hope than in anticipation! To make the gunners' task more difficult, Lockhart took the flight down to wave-top height. Here the Squadron sustained its only casualty of the whole operation. Plt Off Downie's aircraft was seen to strike the water while he was looking at his "map". Fortunately he recovered, but a few miles further on he struck the sea again and his aircraft disintegrated. One of the sergeant pilots in the formation reported that he had seen a dinghy and the sea stained with marker-dye. However there was nothing that could be done, and the remaining Hurricanes pressed on to Malta. Four days later, it was heard that Downie had been picked up and was a prisoner-of-war; this was later confirmed by the Italian radio while the Squadron was in Cyprus. As the last of the formation touched down at Luqa, its engine cut out. The only other loss was one of the Fulmars that developed engine trouble *en route* and made for the North African coast, where the crew was interned by the Vichy French.

On arrival at Luqa the crews were met by Sqn Ldr Mould and, as soon as the aircraft were dispersed in the sand-bagged pens around the airfield, the pilots departed for a much-needed lunch. Early in the afternoon, while being shown round one of the huge underground air-raid shelters,

Fg Off J A Sowrey showing off the underside camouflage of one of the Squadron's Hurricane Is, Cyprus, Summer 1941. The camouflage was that applied to Hurricanes in the UK used as night-fighters in accordance with an Air Ministry directive.
(J A Sowrey)

the island was attacked by fighter-bomber Bf 109s from Sicily and some of the Squadron's aircraft were damaged.

It was soon learnt that, notwithstanding the long flight in the morning, the day's flying was not over, and as soon as the serviceable aircraft were refuelled and made ready they would push on to Egypt. Thus once again with a navigating escort - this time a Beaufighter flown by Sqn Ldr R F Yaxley - a long flight over the Mediterranean was the order of the day. Sweating it out in their blue tunics and a temperature of eighty degrees Fahrenheit, the pilots of the serviceable aircraft were strapped in for stage two of the journey. The difficulties of flying a Beaufighter at the slow speed that the Hurricanes required to make the most of their fuel meant that soon the formation was strung out in a fifty- mile line. After about an hour, the CO and the last three Hurricanes had no longer the faintest contact with the escort and so turned back to Malta. Shortly after this the Beaufighter turned around, presumably to pick up the stragglers, and in doing so succeeded in losing the rest of the Squadron. Nevertheless, after three hours forty-five minutes flying, Westlake and Plt Off Crowther and Sgts Hancock and Wallace made landfall.

By the time the Hurricanes had covered half the distance, the aircraft's courses were gradually diverging as each pilot believed in his own compass. Plt Offs J L Briggs and Groves crossed the coast near Gambut, some thirty miles inside German occupied territory, and made it to Mersa Matruh shortly after the first party.

After their safe arrival, the pilots' recuperation after the day's flying was aided by long draughts of strong Tiger XXXX beer, generously provided by an Australian Army Ack-Ack Mess. The reception over, the pilots made their way carefully to their tents hoping that they would never again have to cross nearly two thousand miles of water on one "Fan" in a single day. Over the next few days the remainder of the Squadron flew in from Malta and, staging through Amriya, everyone finally assembled at Abu Sueir, the oldest permanent RAF station in the Nile Delta. Here the Main Party rested for ten days awaiting the arrival of the Advance Party from Takoradi. With excellent quarters, the comfort of khaki-drill and plenty of swimming and sunbathing, the pilots were soon sufficiently bronzed to be indistinguishable from the old sweats.

By the beginning of June the Ground Party's journey was only nearing its halfway point. On Thursday 22 May 1941 they had embarked in the converted passenger liner *Georgic* at Greenock destined for a long sea voyage. Initially the course lay north towards Iceland; fortunately for the nerves of those on board they were unaware that Germany's most powerful warship, the *Bismarck* had been sighted by HMS *Suffolk* in the Denmark Strait, between Iceland and Greenland, in the evening of 23 May. On Saturday 24 May, the day on which HMS *Hood* was sunk west of Iceland, the convoy was attacked by a lone German bomber which caused a certain amount of panic, but no damage, being brought down by the guns of HMS *Exeter* before the carrier *Argus* could launch its aircraft. It was now common knowledge that the *Bismarck* was in the area, and while the *Georgic* steamed out into the Atlantic, to within two days sailing of the Gulf of St.Lawrence, two of the escorting destroyers, *Cossack* and *Zulu*, were detached from the convoy to help in the search

Loading the guns of a Hurricane I, Nicosia, Cyprus, Summer 1941. (J A Sowrey)

after the Navy had lost contact early in the morning of 23 May. It was thus with some considerable relief that the news was heard, on 27 May, that the *Bismarck* had been sunk in the eastern Atlantic, following an engagement with the battleships *Rodney* and *King George V*, and the cruisers *Suffolk* and *Dorsetshire*.

Once out of range of the German Air Force, and with the danger from the *Bismarck* past, over-riding boredom took hold. The extreme overcrowding, with layered hammocks slung below decks, and the feeling of sea-sickness were relieved to some degree by sleeping on deck as the *Georgic* entered warmer latitudes, steaming south back across the Atlantic making for Freetown. The official means of combating boredom was to mount guards twenty-four hours a day at the end of every corridor, or every deck, those on duty serving two hours on and two hours off. LAC Henry noted from the ships notice board that an issue of library books was to be made to each squadron. Presenting himself at the appointed time, he was relieved to see that no other representative from 213 Squadron was present. The Sergeant to whom he reported with his parcel of books did not seem very interested, so Henry took charge of the Squadron library, thereby relieving some of his boredom and also avoiding Guard Duty. After an initially eventful thirteen days at sea the convoy reached Freetown on 4 June.

Leaving Freetown on 6 June, the *Georgic*'s course took her once more across the Atlantic, crossing the Equator on 9 June, almost to the coast of South America, then re-crossing the South Atlantic. The journey was broken, on 20 June, when a three-day stop was made in Durban. As the reluctant travellers disembarked they saw lines of motor cars waiting, the owners only too happy to pick them up and spend the day showing them the sights of their city. Then on Monday 23 June, after a farewell parade, the *Georgic* set sail on the last leg of its journey which, after a brief call at Aden, finally ended after seven weeks at sea at 08.00 hours on 8 July at Port Tewfik at the southern end of the Suez Canal. On disembarking the party proceeded to the Middle East Pool at Kasfareet. There everyone was kitted out with khaki drill uniforms topped off with over-large topees, and informed that to be seen not wearing these in daylight hours was a chargeable offence. On 10 July the news came that the *Georgic* had been hit and sunk in a raid by Ju 88s; nobody admitted being the first to cheer. The whereabouts of the Squadron's aircraft and pilots remained a total mystery; the groundcrews were to rest and acclimatise for a few weeks. Resting soon turned to boredom, relieved only by visits to Ismailia and raids by Italian bombers, which led to the seemingly endless digging of slit-trenches. The pattern for the remainder of July was set.

Early in June 1941 Hurricanes were as rare as corn in Egypt, and five in the air together were considered a large formation. Collishaw, the Air Officer Commanding, asked that pilots in his Command always flew low over towns to boost the civilian population's morale. Thus the Squadron's twenty-one aircraft were needed in many quarters. Also, as the ground party was still en route in the *Georgic*, operations as a self-contained unit could not start at once. So, even before the Advance Party had arrived at Abu Sueir on 11 June 1941, the Squadron's two flights went their separate ways, and one was then further sub-divided.

The situation in the Western Desert was critical. Longmore had lost the confidence of Churchill and was called to London on 3 May, never to return to Egypt, and on 1 June Air Marshal A W Tedder was confirmed in his appointment as Longmore's successor as Air Officer Commanding-in-Chief, Middle East Command. After the initial successes of Maj Gen R N O'Connor and Air Cdre R Collishaw, DSO, OBE, DSC, DFC, against the Italians, the Germans, under Rommel, had pushed the British line back again to the Egyptian frontier. Here lay the key to the Middle East, and it was here that the Squadron experienced its first action in the desert. The main party, led by the CO and designated "B" Flight, moved up to the fighting in Syria, while the other half of the Squadron was divided into "A" and "C" Flights, which were attached to 274 and 73 Squadrons respectively.

"A" Flight, which largely consisted of Plt Offs J L Briggs, Gould, and Lynch and Sgt Marshall, moved westward from Abu Sueir into the desert to the forward landing ground at El Gerawla. Here they found 274 Squadron, which had been based there ever since Rommel's advance had been halted at the frontier. With the arrival of "A" Flight, the pilots of 73 Squadron and 1 SAAF Squadron who had been attached to 274 Squadron returned to their own units, although some pilots of 229 Squadron remained on attachment. This first taste of desert conditions revealed how completely different the war was from that being fought in Europe. Here control from an Operations Room was practically unknown. Each pilot had to rely on his own interpretation of what was required. A vast territory was covered by only six or seven squadrons, each of which, over-committed, under-manned and plagued by serviceability problems, had to perform a multitude of tasks. The milk-chocolate and beige camouflaged Hurricane Is, with which they were equipped and which formed the front line fighter defence, suffered from over-strained engines, sand-choked controls and every type of machine-gun stoppage as well as the penalty of long-range tanks. Nevertheless, the spirit that was to epitomise the Desert Air Force overcame all this as well as the Luftwaffe and the Regia Aeronautica.

The great reorganisation and expansion was still in the future. For the moment, the Desert Air Force was still the uninhibited and flamboyant force that had swept the Italians from the skies in the early months under Collishaw. Now two flights of 213 Squadron were back under the command of this ebullient Canadian, who had commanded the Squadron for a

The Squadron pilots assemble for a mock scramble, Nicosia, Cyprus, Summer 1941. (J A Sowrey)

few weeks during the First World War.

Many of the hours flown by the aircraft at El Gerawla were devoted to long-range strafing sorties against the German supply lines, particularly along the much used Trigh Capuzzo. The loss of morale and equipment suffered by the Germans as a result of these raids is hard to measure, but it was probably the Desert Air Force's greatest contribution to the war in the summer of 1941. Sections of four aircraft would roam at will behind the enemy lines, without reference to intelligence reports or radio control, searching for enemy convoys and supply dumps. Attacks were also made on the German forward landing-grounds and, although casualties were heavy in this type of operation, "A" Flight came through with the loss of comparatively few pilots.

Another of the multitude of tasks was escorting naval vessels to the beleaguered garrison at Tobruk. Often this escort consisted of one solitary Hurricane flying for two-and-a-half hours at 12,000 feet, approximately twelve miles out to sea off the Libyan coast. However such "high" patrols often resulted in the Hurricane being chased by the far faster Bf 109s and Macchi MC 202s that were present in overwhelming numbers. The Hurricane I's position deteriorated seriously in the summer of 1941 as the Luftwaffe in North Africa received supplies of the latest Messerschmitt - the Bf 109F-2/Trop.

When crews were not in the air, the difficult conditions, accentuated by the unpalatable rations and insufferable sandstorms, were relieved by two great compensations. First and foremost were the generous supplies of Australian and Canadian beer that did much to lubricate sand-parched throats. Secondly, there was the Mediterranean close by, with its sandy beaches and crystal clear waters. When not at readiness everyone piled into the waiting three-tonner and headed for the beach, there to cast off the sandy uniforms and plunge into the sea.

Another pleasant interlude, when the moon was full, was to fly south deep into the desert and to disperse the aircraft on a salt pan, far away from the attentions of any wily Ju 88 that might well be abroad on such a night. These trips not only proved effective in reducing damage through bombing, but also provided a pleasant "boozy" party. Each pilot packed into his flare-chute, gun-panels and tail-locker as many pint bottles of beer as possible. Here, deep in the desert, the Flight met pilots of No.1 SAAF Squadron who had been flying in the desert since early in the war. Over bottles of cold beer in the cool moonlit nights, many stories were swapped concerning the Hun and how to out-wit him. Apart from all these sorties "A" Flight, together with "C" operating with 73 Squadron from Sidi Haneish, was also engaged in Operation Battleaxe, which was launched in June 1941.

On 24 May, even before "A" Flight moved up to El Gerawla, it had been divided into two, and Fg Off Temlett, Plt Off Douthwaite and Sgts Henderson, Lack White and Wilson flew into the desert to the airfield at Maaten Bagush to form "C" Flight of 73 Squadron, based at nearby Sidi Haneish. Their arrival coincided with a blinding sandstorm; nevertheless, all the pilots were able to land except Sgt Henderson, who had to put down some miles away in the desert. Now commanded by Sqn Ldr P G Wykeham-Barnes, DFC, 73 Squadron had been in the thick of the fighting both in the initial advance across the desert and subsequently as the British Army retreated in the face of the newly-arrived Afrika Corps. It had only recently flown out of the beleaguered town

Servicing a Hurricane, Nicosia, Cyprus, Summer 1941. (J A Sowrey)

The Squadron's pilots with a Hurricane I, Nicosia, Cyprus, 1941. (J A Sowrey)

of Tobruk. When Rommel had launched his offensive on 30 March 1941, only two Hurricane squadrons remained in the desert, Nos.73 and 3 RAAF, along with No.55 Squadron flying Blenheim IVs, and No.6 Squadron with Lysanders; all the other units had been withdrawn for use in Greece. Covering the retreating ground forces against great odds, the Squadron had been severely mauled, losing three COs in the space of two weeks. Daily their dwindling number of aircraft had taken off to intercept raids of seventy or more aircraft. Now, withdrawn to Sidi Haneish, 73 Squadron was still in the front line.

The time was one of great uncertainty. Greece had been over-run by the Germans and in their first, and last, use of mass paratroops Crete had been taken. In North Africa Rommel was attacking Tobruk. Initially Temlett and Douthwaite were reported as being attached for special duties over Crete, and on 28 May orders came that three of the most experienced pilots were to prepare to leave for Crete, but after two days of suspense this signal was cancelled. On the thirtieth of the month another signal arrived stating that 213 Squadron would join 258 Wing, and relieve 73 as soon as it was properly formed up, which it was anticipated would be in about a month's time.

On the morning of 26 May the pilots of "C" Flight had flown back to the Delta to bring out five more Hurricanes. In the afternoon emergency defensive patrols were called for commencing at 15.30 hours, to cover the badly-damaged aircraft carrier *Formidable*, that was approaching Mersa Matruh from Crete *en route* for Alexandria, with an escort of twelve destroyers and two cruisers. Temlett, Douthwaite and Plt Off Moss (a 73 Squadron pilot) flew the first of these patrols and, by the time the emergency was over, only one of the non-tropicalised Hurricanes that the 213 Squadron pilots had brought with them remained serviceable.

The over-stretched state of the RAF's resources was indicated when on 28 May five of 73 Squadron's pilots with experience on long range Hurricanes were detached to 274 Squadron. At the same time, orders were received for three of the 213 Squadron pilots to take non-tropicalised Hurricanes to attack one hundred and fifty Ju 88s reported to be arriving at Heraklion, Crete. By the time all the preparations had been made it was too late to take-off, and the orders were cancelled. By the end of the month 73 Squadron was reduced to eight of its own pilots, after three more had been detached to 274 Squadron, and the six pilots from 213 Squadron. With all this interchange going on, Group stepped in with a ruling that victories gained by attached pilots would be credited to the parent unit; at the same time it was ordered that non-tropicalised Hurricanes were not to be used in the desert but returned to the Delta. The aircrew situation eased somewhat two days later, when the pilots on attachment with 274 Squadron returned. It was now decided that Temlett, Douthwaite and Wilson would stay with 73 Squadron, and that Henderson, Lack and White would return to 213 Squadron. On 3 June the six pilots flew three tropicalised and three non-tropicalised Hurricanes back to the Delta, and Temlett, Douthwaite and Wilson returned with three replacement aircraft. 73 Squadron's ORB notes that the experienced 213 Squadron pilots were a big help.

On 6 June standing patrols were flown over Mersa Matruh, where 229 Squadron had landed its Hurricanes on the way from HMS *Ark Royal* to the Delta; while standing patrols were never popular, anything was better than the interminable shipping patrols. The major part of the operational flying, not only for 73 Squadron but also for 250 and 274 Squadrons, was the mounting of fighter protection patrols for the troops defending Tobruk.

In June 1941, the Army Commanders realised that the main battle for the Middle East would have to be fought across the sands of Libya. It was also evident that the battle would be one of supplies, and that the victory would to go to the side with the best defended lines of communication. So, in Egypt, "Operation Battleaxe" was planned with the dual object of relieving the garrison at Tobruk and securing the important airfields in the El Adem and Gambut areas. Despite his losses in Crete and Greece and the demands of the fighting in Syria, Tedder scraped together one hundred serviceable fighters to provide air cover for the operation. The Delta's defences were reduced to a minimum, and many units were operating at half-strength as they were still in the

A silver tankard was presented by Mr Morphitis to mark the destruction of the first enemy aircraft on Cypriot soil. From left to right: Fg Off A U Houle, Fg Off C B Temlett, DFC, Fg Off Allen (Intelligence Officer), Fg Off G H Westlake and Sqn Ldr D S MacDonald. (J A Sowrey)

Fg Off J A Sowrey seated in the cockpit of the "presentation" Hurricane Pride of Ceylon, *Nicosia, Cyprus, Summer 1941. (J A Sowrey)*

process of reforming. On 14 June the ill-starred "Operation Battleaxe" opened and "A" Flight, operating with 274 Squadron and the pilots forming "C" Flight of 73 Squadron, became involved in their first North African campaign. By 15 June, John Sowrey and Peter Pound had also arrived at Sidi Haneish after their trip across Africa and a short stay at Abu Sueir.

The Army's initial drive on 15 June, the opening day of the battle, was against the positions photographed in the immediately preceding days. The 11th Indian Infantry Brigade Group advanced along the coast road towards Halfaya and Sollum, while the tanks of the 7th Armoured Division, together with the 22nd Guards Brigade, set off across the desert and then turned north on to the Fort Capuzzo - Sollum defences. Forming part of the umbrella over the advancing troops, both Flights became heavily engaged from the outset. Leading his section of "C" Flight, which was airborne at 10.00 hours, Sowrey encountered two Bf 109s, one of which he shot down. This was possibly a reconnaissance aircraft of 2(H)/14 flown by Feldwebel Herbert Schaedlich. Temlett destroyed another, as well as damaging a Bf 110.

Some ninety minutes later, Temlett took-off with his Section "obviously intending to equal Sowrey's score even if he had to go to the 109 production line to do so". As matters turned out this was unnecessary, as the section was attacked by four Bf 109s, which were soon joined by a further eight. Temlett and Wilson claimed one each, but Plt Off Pound was shot down and the Hurricanes of Temlett and Wilson were badly shot up. Two days later, Pound turned up in Mersa Matruh hospital with shrapnel from one of our own ack-ack guns in his leg. At 16.55 hours Sowrey was again on patrol with his Section of "C" Flight, and shot down his second Bf 109 of the day.

For "A" Flight, the main action of the day took place when eight aircraft of 274 Squadron were sent to strafe German motor transport along the Gazala - Tobruk road as far as Sidi Azeiz. A camp fifteen miles east of Gazala was the first target, after which their attention was turned to a large concentration of vehicles and tanks nearby. On the return trip Briggs shot down a CR 42, the first Italian fighter seen for some weeks.

In view of the disparity in numbers when combat was joined, Wykeham-Barnes suggested that in future patrols should be flown in Squadron strength and the next day, 16 June, an order to this effect was received, causing general jubilation.

After initial successes, the Army ran into trouble against a much stronger enemy, with a marked superiority in equipment, especially in armoured vehicles. By the afternoon of 17 June, the British troops were consequently once again back behind the Egyptian border on the Sidi Barrani - Sofafi line. With the Army endeavouring to disengage itself from strong German counter-attacks, the Air Force was called upon to mount ground-attack sorties against the German armour and supply lines. In the afternoon of the same day a formation from 73 Squadron took off, with Sowrey and Temlett leading two sections, to strafe transport along the roads around Bardia. Once over the target area, Sowrey's section peeled off to attack eight trucks and a motorcycle, all of which were successfully accounted for. Temlett led his three aircraft onto four trucks and a tank, which were left disabled by the side of the road. The next day, as the battle continued, a sandstorm blew up and restricted all flying to the late evening. But the battle was nearly over, and the radio announced that the objectives had been reached, so it was assumed by the slightly mystified aircrew that the task had merely been to see just how strong the enemy forces were. In fact it had been recognised that "Battleaxe" had failed. After this hectic flurry of combat the pace slackened and, while one flight remained at readiness, the rest of the Squadron was released.

On 25 June four of the 213 Squadron pilots left for the Delta, and it was assumed that the rest would soon follow, much to 73 Squadron's regret at the loss of such experienced and effective pilots. As a parting gesture, on 26 June, Temlett found a lone Ju 88 while on escort duty over Tobruk and damaged it sufficiently to claim it as a probable. The assumption concerning the remaining 213 Squadron pilots turned into reality on 27 June, when Temlett, Sowrey and Chatfield left for leave in the Delta, prior to moving up into Palestine to join up with the rest of the Squadron.

The actual move to Palestine took some time to prepare, and it was not until 2 July that the party left for Abu Sueir where orders were waiting to proceed to Lydda the very next day. Here the party would join "B" Flight, which was attached to 80 Squadron commanded by Sqn Ldr Gordon-Jones. The trip from the Canal Zone was made in a Blenheim piloted by Flt Lt Olivier, the brother of Laurence Olivier, and

Flt Lt C B Temlett, DFC, OC "A" Flight, (still wearing Flying Officer's tapes), Cyprus, Summer 1941. (J A Sowrey)

Fg Off G H Westlake, "The scourge of the Cyprus skies", wearing the hornet on his left breast pocket, an unofficial addition to the uniform. Cyprus, Summer 1941. (J A Sowrey)

the whole party nearly came to grief when both engines cut out on take-off. It transpired that, when flying a Blenheim, the inboard fuel tanks, which contained 100 octane fuel, had to be used for take-off; this had not been done and it was only when the engines began to cut out that the correct selection was made. Eventually, after a stop at Aqir, Lydda was reached in the evening. Unfortunately the elusive 80 Squadron was not to be found, Lydda being the home of 3 RAAF Squadron equipped with Tomahawks. Finally the party moved on to Haifa and was there reunited with the other half of the Squadron.

For over a month, before they were joined by "A" and "C" Flights, "B" flight had been operating with 80 Squadron in the Syrian Campaign against the Vichy French. The pilots, headed by Flt Lt R Lockhart, moved up to Palestine late in May but, to their disgust, without their Hurricanes, which were left behind at Abu Sueir. The initial base of operations as the campaign opened was Aqir, but after a few days the Squadron moved to the airfield at Haifa. The nearby airstrip at Ramat David, now Israel's major airport, was also used but the conditions were primitive. The aerodrome was a field of chaff, while the living quarters were tents pitched in a nearby orange grove. Near the airfield was a kibbutz school, run by a retired Belgian cavalry officer, complete with horse.

The Syrian Campaign lasted a matter of five weeks and saw some very bitter fighting, especially when Free French troops met their Vichy fellow-countrymen. The campaign opened on 8 June 1941 as leaflets and broadcasts told the people of Syria that General Catroux, in the name of Free France, had come to end the Mandate under which the French had governed Syria and make them free and independent.

For the pilots with 80 Squadron, the campaign opened in style. Supporting the advance of the Army up the coast were the ships of the 15th Cruiser Squadron, and it was the main task of the Hurricanes to maintain an aerial umbrella over this force. On 9 June four patrols were flown in this role. Westlake, in a section of three led by Roald Dahl, saw the whole affair off to a flying start when, on the first patrol, he successfully engaged a Potez 631. The speed of this aircraft caused some surprise and it nearly escaped before he shot it down into the sea forty miles west of Tyre. The second patrol was airborne during the naval battle between the cruiser squadron and the French naval forces from Beirut harbour. The last patrol of the day intercepted a force of Dewoitine D 520 fighters and, in the general dog-fight that ensued, shot down four. The Dewoitine D 520 was a fast, manoeuvrable and delightful fighter, but under-armed and in this theatre of operations poorly flown. The pilots had come from Morocco via Italy and Greece, and they were inexperienced with between only one hundred and fifty and two hundred hours of flying time. This inexperience, allied to poor fighting tactics, led them into heavy losses; in contrast, 80 Squadron itself lost only four pilots in the whole campaign.

Not surprisingly the following days did not keep up the hectic pace of the opening day, although combat was a frequent occurrence. A routine of Fleet patrols soon became established, interspersed with patrols over Beirut itself. This city contained the Headquarters of General Dentz, the Vichy

"The Hornet's Nest Inn", the scene for many parties, Nicosia, Cyprus. The Potez 29 sign was taken from a French aircraft captured at Palmyra whilst operating against the Vichy French in Syria. Above it is a piece of an Italian aircraft shot down by FG Off G H Westlake over Cyprus. From left to right: Fg Off Allen (Intelligence Officer), Fg Off A U Houle, Fg Off G H Westlake, Sqn Ldr D S MacDonald and the Squadron Medical Officer "Doc" Chris Brocklebank.
(J A Sowrey)

"A" Flight dug-out, Nicosia, Cyprus, Summer 1941. Fg Off J A Sowrey on the left poised to make a quick descent.

French leader, and was the objective of the Allied troops moving up the coast.

Apart from these patrols, the main weight of the aerial campaign was directed against various airfields throughout Syria, notably Ras Baalbeck, Baalbeck, Rayak and Talia. The first trip to one of these was made as escort to some Blenheims, which kept the Hurricanes orbiting for eighty minutes while they carried out photographic runs over the airfield at Rayak. The round trip took two hours and ten minutes and the long-range tanks were proving a mixed blessing, as more than two hours in a Hurricane's confined cockpit was considerably less than comfortable.

The third week in June saw the strengthening of the air forces in Syria by squadrons released from "Operation Battleaxe". With this increase, fighter sweeps could now be added to the weight of bomber attacks against Vichy airfields. On 24 June, in company with the newly-arrived Hurricanes of 260 Squadron, attacks were made on Talia and Rayak airfields. At Talia, fires were started among Glenn Martin and Potez bombers parked on the field. At Rayak, the French had considerately parked five Dewoitines in a nice straight line which proved an attractive target. The success of this raid prompted a repeat two days later, but this time only to Rayak. Once again the aircraft were found parked cozily in a corner of the field, and were left blazing fiercely. These sorties provided welcome relief from the more mundane work of Fleet protection, and were greeted with appropriate enthusiasm.

The routine of fleet protection was again interrupted on 29 June when the two Squadrons escorted six Blenheims to Beirut to bomb the Headquarters of General Dentz, located on Beirut race-course. Of the fifteen bombs dropped, thirteen were direct hits on the Headquarters' buildings, a most impressive piece of medium-level bombing.

By the end of the first week of July, as the whole Squadron was once more reunited, (though still attached to 80 Squadron), the Syrian Campaign was drawing to its hectic close and large-scale operations were directed against the Vichy airfield at Aleppo. On 9 July the two Squadrons, 80 and 260, were to strafe the airfield at Meshine and then go on to Aleppo to repeat the dose; however this was later revised with 80 Squadron taking Meshine and 260 Squadron, led by Sqn Ldr Mount, attacking Aleppo. The next day an even bigger raid was mounted against the landing grounds at Talia, Rayak, Baalbia and Ras Baalbia. Four or five biplanes were found on the field at Talia and a good deal of ammunition expended on them. Unfortunately, as the supplies of de Wilde ammunition were limited, no fires resulted. Plenty of flak was experienced over the target and, although the formation broke up, individual aircraft proceeded to Rayak, just north of Damascus, where more aircraft were destroyed.

The approach to these airfields was from the south and across the Beka'a Valley, the mountains on the eastern side of the valley shielding the approach. The airfields were usually packed with aircraft, German as well as French, as at that time Germany was seeking to gain influence in Iraq by providing that country with He 111s and Ju 88s routed through bases in Syria. The success of these raids was phenomenal; the targets were virtually undefended, or perhaps the defenders were so surprised that they put up little resistance. Whatever the reason, the raids were more successful than anyone could have imagined.

The Squadron's third task, in addition to Fleet protection patrols and attacking airfields, was to prevent the movement of the Vichy ground forces by strafing convoys on the roads, which generally ran through the mountains with a steep precipice on one side. At times it was sufficient simply to point the Hurricane at the convoy of trucks and, as if mesmerised, the drivers ran the lorries off the road, disgorging troops all the way down to the bottom of the valley.

Another somewhat incongruous action took place when the Squadron flew as cover for what was probably the last cavalry charge made in any war. The Free French cavalry had been ordered to move up the Damascus-Beirut road. Previously a column of Vichy tanks had been reported by the Squadron on the self-same road but, as all too often happened, the report was ignored. Despite the urgent pleas of the pilots not to go, the column of cavalry set off with its fighter cover. To the horror of the pilots, when the tanks came in sight the cavalry charged; the resulting massacre was predictable.

Perhaps the most successful operation in which the

Squadron was engaged was yet another raid on Aleppo airfield on 11 July. The aircraft arrived at Palmyra for refuelling just after the Vichy French had strafed the airfield, leaving numerous fires burning among the petrol bowsers and parked aircraft. Nevertheless the refuelling was completed and the formation took-off with a feeling for vengeance about it. Once at Aleppo, the Squadrons pressed home their attacks; two large fires were started among some heavy bombers and the airfield installations were extensively shot-up. On the return trip 3 RAAF Squadron, which had joined the raid at Palmyra in its Tomahawks, fired at practically anything that moved.

This raid turned out to be the last of the campaign, as news came through to Ramat David later that day that hostilities were to cease by 21.00 hours. The formal armistice was signed by the French Commander three days later on 14 July and the first mission of the peace was flown as escort to nine Blenheims in a show of force over Beirut and Tripoli.

It was now learned, as hostilities ceased, that Plt Off Crowther, who had been lost on one of the earlier raids, was in Beirut hospital recovering from wounds. The CO of the hospital in question had been a room-mate of Crowther at Oxford before the war and so, instead of sending him off with the other prisoners-of-war, he had made him official interpreter and kept him in Beirut.

While the Syrian campaign was drawing to a close, three of the Squadron's pilots were once more on the move, with a detachment of 80 Squadron, to provide fighter-cover for the island of Cyprus. The German occupation of Greece and Crete led the High Command to suspect that the Germans would now step up their raids against the island in preparation for another airborne landing.

On the island the boot was initially on the other foot. Instead of mounting fighter sweeps against the enemy, the fighters at Nicosia found themselves under attack daily at 09.00, 11.00 and 16.00 from German and Italian bombers based in the Dodecanese. Twice on 7 July the flight was scrambled as bombs burst on the airfield. On the second raid, the bombs were exploding on either side of the runway as the Hurricanes strained to attack the Ju 88s which were bombing from about 8,000 feet. The effort was, of course, in vain, and the raiders were gone by the time the necessary height had been gained. The same disquieting experience was repeated on 9 July, and it seemed that the enemy attacks were in earnest. The Italians were operating Cant Z 1007s and Savoia Marchetti S 79s, and in the course of these attacks Westlake shot down a sample of each type.

On 18 July, even as the bombs were bursting once more, Westlake was scrambled to intercept a raid by four Ju 88s. At first no contact was made and then, purely by chance, two Ju 88s were spotted low over the water heading west in the Morphou Bay area. Chase was given on a cut-off vector and Westlake finally delivered his attack at about fifty feet immediately above some fishing boats, Greek or Cypriot caiques. The first burst produced spectacular results, it probably hit the oxygen cylinders in the rear of the fuselage, because there was a huge explosion and the Ju 88 disintegrated in a fire-ball. To avoid the centre of this conflagration, Westlake was forced to break upwards and in doing so lost sight of the other raider. He was also by now some forty or fifty miles out to sea, and there was the possibility that his aircraft had been damaged by the flying debris so he climbed to 5,000 feet, to facilitate a quick exit if necessary, and returned to base. The fishing boats, over which the attack had been delivered, confirmed the claim of one destroyed but were able to find no survivors. The exploit was rewarded with a bottle of whisky from the Governor - with the promise of a crate of whisky for the next one.

The pace of the German raids on Cyprus had indeed quickened, and taking-off with bombs bursting on the airfield had become an all-too-common experience. So, on 19 July, with the campaign in Syria well and truly over, the remainder of the Squadron came out to join up with the detachment. The arrival was marked by an extended beat-up of the towns of Nicosia and Famagusta. Thoughts of another Crete were strong in everyone's mind as Italian aircraft were found to be active over the island. Particularly persistent were the torpedo bombers operating in and around Famagusta harbour. "A" Flight, consisting of five Hurricanes, was therefore temporarily established in a dry lake-bed just outside the town to provide quick-reaction interceptions.

Initially, the Main Party of the Squadron moved into a camp sited in a dry wadi just off the edge of the airfield, but this location had obvious objections in the rainy season. Soon therefore the Main Party moved to the camp on Nicosia airfield, sharing it with 80 Squadron to which 213 was still officially attached. On 30 July, the somewhat tardy news arrived that the ground party had arrived in Egypt, and that the Squadron would reform as an independent unit on 12 August 1941. Two days before this, 80 Squadron returned to Palestine, minus their Hurricanes, leaving 213 Squadron as the fighter defence of the island with their dilapidated aircraft.

It was only on 3 August that the groundcrew, still digging slit-trenches in Egypt, heard that they were to move to Cyprus; by 5 August the date of the move had been postponed until further notice. The following Saturday night was celebrated in the usual fashion in Ismailia, and Jack Walton, recorded in the diary which he kept that he "had an occasional drink". On 10 August Sqn Ldr MacDonald addressed a parade at 06.00 hours detailing the move to Cyprus, and stressing its secrecy. By the next day the heavy kit was loaded, and at 01.30 hours on 13 August the party entrained at Kasfareet Station *en route* to Ismailia. Interrupted by two Italian air raids, the journey of thirty miles took over twelve hours, and the train remained outside Ismailia as a precaution against being hit. The next day, the train arrived at Port Said and the sea journey to Cyprus aboard HMS *Abdiel* began. After an uncomfortable journey, where the only place to attempt to sleep was on deck, Famagusta was reached at 02.00 hours, and a train took everyone to a nearby camp. The final leg of the journey to Nicosia was completed at 05.30 hours the next morning, after nearly forty-eight hours of constant travelling with little or no sleep.

The air defence of Cyprus was beset with difficulties. Radio communications were poor and the fighter controllers very inexperienced compared with those of the Battle of Britain days. As for radar, such modern aid had not yet arrived on the island; the only proper airfield was at Nicosia, which was supplemented by three other landing grounds. Throughout the early part of August the German and Italian raids continued with considerable frequency and, although the raiders were often reported, interceptions were frustratingly rare. On 12 August five Italian S 79s bombed the field at Nicosia, but fortunately caused no damage. As the alert sounded, Briggs and Sgt Sissons were scrambled although control was unreadable. Only Briggs actually became airborne, as his number two sprang a glycol leak on take-off and had to force land on the end of the runway. With his windscreen covered in glycol, Sissons hit the end of the strip and bounced through three anti-tank ditches at one hundred and forty miles per hour. Surprisingly enough the only damage to the Hurricane was a bent tail-wheel assembly, while Sissons emerged unscathed. Briggs's sortie also proved abortive since no contact was made with the raiders.

In anticipation of continued raids, a new system of readiness was evolved in the hope that it would increase the chances of interceptions. On receipt of an alarm, four aircraft from the Readiness Flight and two others would become airborne; the first pair of the Readiness Flight were designated Yellow Section and the other pair Red Section. Yellow One was to patrol Morphou Bay at 11,000 feet with Yellow Two 2,000 feet above as top cover. Red Section was to be held in readiness at the same height to be vectored on to any likely targets. White Section, the remaining pair, would be held orbiting the base in case of a surprise attack. This system did not of course solve all the problems and, when the Squadron put up nine aircraft two evenings later, control picked up the formation over Kyrenia and then vectored it on to itself - no mean achievement!

When the Governor of Cyprus, Sir William Battershill, left the island on 25 August, two sections took-off to carry out "radio tests". These "tests" involved flying in very close formation with the Lockheed in which he was travelling, as far as Limassol. His departure was viewed with a particular sadness by the Squadron, as with him went the chance of a crate of whisky. The whole event assumed even more tragic proportions the very next day when Westlake found a Cant Z 1007. He was airborne on a practice trip, orbiting over the positions of the Sherwood Foresters and studying their efforts at camouflage, when he heard over the radio Red Section being scrambled for "a bandit over Famagusta at 13,000 feet". Being already at 6,000 feet, he had a head start on Temlett and Plt Off Marshall and so he set course for Famagusta at maximum speed. The Cant was picked up heading south at 18,000 feet. As the Hurricane closed in, the top rear-gunner opened fire at about one thousand yards in sheer panic, and in no fashion to deter Westlake. Coming in on a quarter-attack, with the starboard engine as the target, the first burst hit the main-plane and blew off the starboard aileron. The Cant promptly flicked over and headed downwards rotating, but not spinning, and falling apart as it did so. The wreckage was found on the foreshore between Cape Greco and Cape Napa, and the bodies of the crew were buried by a company of the Royal Scots.

Under the headline "Shot to pieces by RAF fighter" the local press article reprinted the official Headquarters, Troops, communiqué which was brief and to the point; "One enemy aircraft was over the Island this morning. A few bombs were dropped in open country. The aircraft was shot down by RAF fighters at 11.15 am". The victory was hailed in the Cyprus press as the first enemy bomber to crash to destruction on Cyprus soil - a nice distinction between the fate of the Cant and the Ju 88 destroyed earlier in the month. Unfortunately, as the Governor had left the Island the day before, no crate of whisky was forthcoming.

The raids by the Italian and German bombers had brought the war unexpectedly close to the islanders, and these two victories did a great deal to bolster civilian morale. The aerial fighting thus made the headlines in the local Cypriot newspapers and, although no names or numbers were mentioned, the Squadron was given a great write-up (see Appendix).

The destruction of this first enemy aircraft over Cypriot soil moved one islander to write to the CO asking if he could present a cup to the Squadron to mark this auspicious occasion. The offer was naturally accepted, and on 24 September Mr Morphitis came to Nicosia and presented a tankard to Westlake which was suitably christened. For the remainder of the stay in Cyprus this handsome silver tankard lent an extra air of distinction to the Squadron bar, which ran under the name of "The Hornet's Nest". Unfortunately during the move later in the year from the island to Egypt, the tankard was stolen from its case, along with much of the rest of the Squadron silver, when in Port Said harbour.

No sooner had the Squadron settled down in Nicosia than a signal arrived asking for the immediate posting of Lockhart, Westlake, Lack and Wilson to 80 Squadron in Palestine. This signal might have caused some apprehension but for the fact that the original had been received almost a month previously, and it was considered that their actual departure was most unlikely. In fact, the Squadron was still building up to strength itself, and many of the pilots now arriving came from the Dominion of Canada. Among these was Fg Off A U Houle, who was to prove a first class pilot. This influx of Canadians turned out to be the first of three such "invasions" experienced by the Squadron while in the Middle East. Later on, in the Western Desert, a large number of Australian pilots arrived and, when stationed in Italy, a similar influx of South African pilots flew under the Hornet crest.

Together once more as a complete unit, the Squadron began to develop its own characteristics. A non-standard addition was made to the khaki uniforms in the shape of a small gold hornet worn on the tunic pocket below the pilot's brevet. For the moment the aircraft, apart from the Squadron identification letters AK, were only distinguished in the not unusual fashion of "A" Flight sporting red spinners and "B" Flight blue. A more artistic approach was deferred until the Squadron moved into the desert.

On two occasions, whilst in Cyprus, "The Hornet's Nest" was visited by Turkish pilots who were ferrying Tomahawks into Turkey. On both occasions formations with RAF markings approached from the south. Once on the ground, the Turkish pilots set to with pails of water and removed the RAF roundels, revealing underneath Turkish national markings.

To add to the international air that prevailed towards the end of the year, the Squadron was informed that one of the newly-arrived Hurricanes had been presented by the people of Ceylon, and that by an Air Ministry Order the title 'Ceylon' was to be added to the Squadron's name. Hurriedly an appropriate insignia was painted on the aircraft, and all was made ready for a photographic session to record the event. With the pilots casually grouped around it, and the silhouette of the photographer mounted on a step ladder caught in the evening sun against its nose, the special aircraft was duly recorded for posterity. In fact this name never came into general use, and all such designations were abolished in 1952.

After a series of air raids early in September, the Squadron was scrambled at 08.00 hours on 16 September, and three hours later all the aircraft returned claiming three Italian raiders destroyed. In the latter part of September flying was somewhat restricted due to - of all things - a tail-wheel famine, which was aggravated by a great shortage of tail-wheel covers. This unserviceability therefore limited the contribution that could be made to the anti-invasion manoeuvres held by the Army on 11 October. The results of this exercise in fact inspired the Squadron with little confidence. Early in the morning the serviceable Hurricanes converged on the naval airfield at Lakatamia to strafe the enemy column reported in the area. Unfortunately the column could not be located. During the remainder of the morning, the defending forces kept all the available aircraft in the air, and serviceability gradually dropped until only two aircraft per flight remained. Ultimately, with the GOC screaming for a section to strafe enemy troops climbing over the defences, no aircraft at all were available. It was generally assumed at Nicosia that the position had fallen, and it came as something of a surprise to hear later that the invasion had been successfully repulsed.

While this training was going on, the finishing touches were put to a training manual compiled by the CO and illustrated by Temlett, who was a brilliant cartoonist. Under the title *Don't Look Know*, the manual was forwarded to the AOC for official consideration. Unfortunately for the future of the work, a similar publication arrived from 13 Group in England a few days later and, although generally held to be an inferior production, it was adopted and issued. A copy of the original *Don't Look Know* was held on the Squadron until its final disbandment and its advice still applied.

Towards the end of October rumours were once more rife of an impending move. Considerable conjecture was caused when a signal arrived ordering an immediate move to Port Sudan. Later it transpired that the signal really meant Port Said. However the signal was cancelled and other conjectures replaced it. Ultimately definite orders were received sending "A" Flight to Ismailia on 21 October, and "B" Flight to Idku on the following day - just in time for the rainy season in the Nile Delta.

The warm summer days were also well in the past in Cyprus. A particularly bad sand-storm on 16 October blew down three of the Squadron tents, depositing one in the next valley a mile away; to add to everyone's discomfort it also rained all day. Following the move of "A" and "B" Flights to Egypt, the fighter defence of Cyprus now devolved upon the newly-created "C" Flight, commanded by Plt Off G H Westlake. The Flight had no doubts about its ability to carry out this task, and the Cypriots were still impressed by the display laid on by the Squadron a few days earlier. Selected dignitaries had been invited to the airfield at Nicosia, and then treated to an extended beat-up by the whole Squadron. Their departing remarks were heard to be "Before we had the fear, now we have the confidence". In fact November turned out to be a very quiet month, and no enemy aircraft appeared over the island.

In the middle of the month a detachment from 261 Squadron, commanded by Sqn Ldr "Imshi" Mason, came to Cyprus to provide extra cover for shipping moving to and from the island. A signal sent by Mason, about the great shortage of tail-wheel covers that still persisted, resulted in the despatch of a destroyer from Haifa with one cover, one tin of glycol and two blinkers for night-flying.

The only foreign aircraft to appear in the skies was a Russian-built Catalina, flown by a deserting mechanic, that was forced down in Morphou Bay.

The Soviet Union had been building American Catalinas under licence. Eleven Catalinas were based at Sevastopol. Generals, Commissars and high-level Russians were using them to take gold, furs, mistresses and families out of Sevastopol to the other end of the Black Sea and to safety. Sevastopol itself was being pounded to destruction by the German Army. The deserter, a non-pilot, was allowed access to the flying boats anchored in the harbour but one night, instead of going ashore, he stayed on board waiting for the dawn. He then slipped his mooring, opened up the engines and took-off, erratically, as he managed to dip his starboard wing-tip into the water nearly ripping off the wing-tip float. He knew enough to set course on a southerly heading, hoping to reach Egypt. The Turkish Air Force intercepted him, but then did nothing to stop him. Westlake was carrying out an air-test north of Kyrenia when he spotted this stranger

No. 213's squadron dispersal at Nicosia

wearing red stars. He made a couple of menacing passes, without opening fire, and then forced him to let down for a landing. Well out to sea over Morphou Bay, Westlake was surprised when the Catalina slowed right down and appeared to be attempting to land - it was still at about forty or fifty feet. At that time, of course, it was not known that the "pilot" could not fly.

After the aircraft was beached, (it had sprung its plates in the splash landing), it was discovered sure enough that it was packed full of gold ingots and furs as well as hundreds of boxes of silk stockings. Unfortunately, Intelligence Staff from Middle East Command arrived and commandeered everything.

The deserter was questioned by a White Russian doctor living in Cyprus and the Squadron Intelligence Officer Fg. Off Bill Allen. He then lived in the Sergeant's Mess for a few weeks, but eventually he had to be handed over. Later it was heard that he had been shot. The Catalina itself ended up with the RAF in Egypt and was used, spasmodically, by the Sea Rescue Flight until it sank in a gale at at Alexandria in February 1943.

For the next two months, until replaced by 261 Squadron on 23 December, "C" Flight remained on guard at Nicosia. On the fifth of the month, the new Governor of the Island visited the airfield, and seemed somewhat surprised to find that the defence of his realm rested on the four Hurricanes of 213 Squadron. He would probably have been even more surprised had he watched a soccer match two days later, when the second half had to be abandoned suddenly for the aircraft to be scrambled to investigate a mysterious plot.

On 23 December 1941, with the arrival of 261 Squadron, "C" Flight relinquished its lonely vigil and its aircraft flew south to join the rest of the Squadron in Egypt. The groundcrew's journey was somewhat more protracted, with an initial flight in a DC-2 to Haifa and then on to Cairo, which was reached on the evening of 24 December.

A Squadron Hurricane in desert camouflage and with forty-five gallon long-range tanks, Spring/Summer 1942.

CHAPTER EIGHT - THE DESERT AIR FORCE

A few days after the surrender of the Vichy French forces in Syria, the Defence Committee of the War Cabinet met in London to consider future plans for the war in the Middle East. The situation in North Africa had changed dramatically since the early days when General Wavell and Air Commodore Collishaw had pushed the Italians half-way across Libya. The Afrika Corps now stood where Graziani's Legions had once camped. Tobruk was a beleaguered fortress behind the German lines, and Rommel was gathering his strength for the final assault on the Nile Delta.

In June 1941, "Operation Battleaxe" to relieve Tobruk had failed ingloriously in three days. Not surprisingly the Prime Minister wanted yet another offensive against the German positions, and he wanted it quickly. In London, the idea of an offensive in September 1941 gained general approval. In the Middle East, the idea had less general acceptance; both Auchinleck and Tedder pointed out that a considerable increase in their forces was to be expected in October, while the German strength would remain relatively static. The strength of the argument was realised in London and "Operation Crusader" was finally scheduled for early November 1941.

After the successive defeats in Cyrenaica, Greece and Crete, much needed attention was given to prepare both the land and air forces for the coming battle. The Squadron had come close to being involved in the fighting in Greece; in fact the groundcrews were lined-up waiting to board a transport aircraft somewhere in Egypt when, after a long wait, they were told that Kos had fallen and the move was cancelled. Perhaps the most momentous of the many changes in the command organisation was the elevation of No.204 Group in the forward area of Egypt to become Air Headquarters Western Desert. The squadrons were stripped of all unnecessary encumbrances and grouped into small mobile Wings. In everything but name, the legendary Desert Air Force had come into being. Part of the fifty percent increase in strength that Tedder was expecting in October was provided by the two flights of 213 Squadron, which arrived at Ismailia and Idku direct from Nicosia on 22 and 23 October 1941. The Squadron had returned to the desert, this time to stay until the final battle had been won.

The Squadron's Hurricanes were now in the new camouflage, more suited to the desert terrain, that had been introduced in August 1941 after experiments at the Royal Aircraft Establishment. This Middle East (i.e. Desert) Camouflage was approved on 22 August 1941. On the red dope base which tautened the fabric covering of the fuselage, Midstone and Dark Earth colours were applied to the upper surfaces, the undersides being painted Azure Blue. Code letters were very light grey or white; later red was commonly used. At this time the Squadron, along with 43 and 112 Squadrons, acquired its own distinctive markings when Sgt "Wally" Lack and Cpl Frank "Wilbur" Wright painted "Crabro" - the Hornet - into the fuselage roundels on all the Squadron's aircraft. In keeping with the individual style of the Desert Air Force, this distinctive but unauthorised marking continued to be used well into the desert campaign. In its time the artistry was much photographed, even by Cecil Beaton, and admired by all, including the Duke of Gloucester on a visit to Idku on 22 March 1942. The highlight of the visit was an outstanding aerobatic display by Flt Lt C B Temlett DFC in one of the Squadron's Hurricane IIcs. This was followed a superb display by Wg Cdr G Stainforth in a Beaufighter, who did everything that Temlett did and at the same altitude.

The Squadron's immediate task on its arrival in Egypt was the defence of the shipping in and around Alexandria harbour, and the town of Alexandria itself. Although Cairo had never been declared an open city as the Egyptians wished, the Luftwaffe and the Regia Aeronautica refrained

New arrivals LACs D S Goldswain and A J Henry, Abu Sueir, Canal Zone, Summer 1941. (A J Henry)

Flt Sgt George Hersey with Sgts Wally Lack and "Hank" J Hancock standing by Crabro. Wally Lack painted Crabro into the roundels on all the Squadron Hurricanes at Idku, Egypt, April 1942. (G H Westlake)

from bombing the Egyptian capital in anticipation of an early occupation. Thus Alexandria stood not only as the main port of the Delta, but also as the largest town that provided a target for the Axis bombers.

Settling in proved to be a somewhat protracted business for the Squadron, as the flights were moved with bewildering speed from one to another of the many airfields and landing grounds that circled Alexandria to the west. The move to the landing ground at Kilo 8 was frustrated when it was decided that the Squadron could not operate there without tropicalised Hurricanes, those in use were still the basic Hurricane Is as brought out from England.

Although the Squadron was officially one of the four Hurricane squadrons that made up No.243 Wing of No.211 Group under the command of Air Headquarters Western Desert, the Squadron's situation on the perimeter of Alexandria meant that much of the operational flying was carried out under the direction of Air Headquarters, Egypt - the authority charged with the defence of Alexandria. Thus it was that, after a German night raid on Burg-el-Arab, a town on the coast to the west of Alexandria, a detachment was sent to Amriya for its defence. Bad weather in November and December made flying very unpleasant and, after a particularly heavy rainstorm, dispersals soon became flooded and the landing strips unserviceable.

On 3 December Flt Lt J Lockhart, who had joined the Squadron at Tangmere in September 1940, was promoted to Squadron Leader and assumed command. The latter days of December saw the arrival of the Squadron's third flight from Cyprus and the initial establishment of Squadron Headquarters at LG 90, which was some sixty-five miles out in the desert south-south-west of Alexandria and which, on arrival, proved to be a vast expanse of "damn all". While HQ was battling with the mud and lack of supplies, the Squadron's aircraft were flying from El Khanka and Dekheila. "A" Flight shared the airfield at El Khanka near Cairo with No.216 Squadron, a transport squadron whose Hawker Hardy some of the pilots took the opportunity to fly. More relevantly, the pilots also had the chance to fly their Hurricanes in mock combat with a captured Bf 109.

Whilst "B" Flight was at Dekheila, which was operated by the Navy, Italian miniature submarines, using the first known "frog-men", carried out their audacious raid on Alexandria harbour and sank Admiral Cunningham's two battleships, *Valiant* and *Queen Elizabeth*, in shallow water. The Squadron was given orders "to prevent at all costs" any reconnaissance aircraft taking photographs of the two crippled ships. Early that January, Westlake and Hancock were scrambled when a Ju 88 was reported approaching the harbour. All too soon, Westlake had to return to base with engine trouble; Hancock proceeded alone but was misdirected and failed to make contact. A second section was scrambled, but it was too late and also failed to make contact. It was subsequently shown that the Ju 88 actually turned away before taking any pictures. However this was not known at the time, and Admiral Cunningham's displeasure was shown

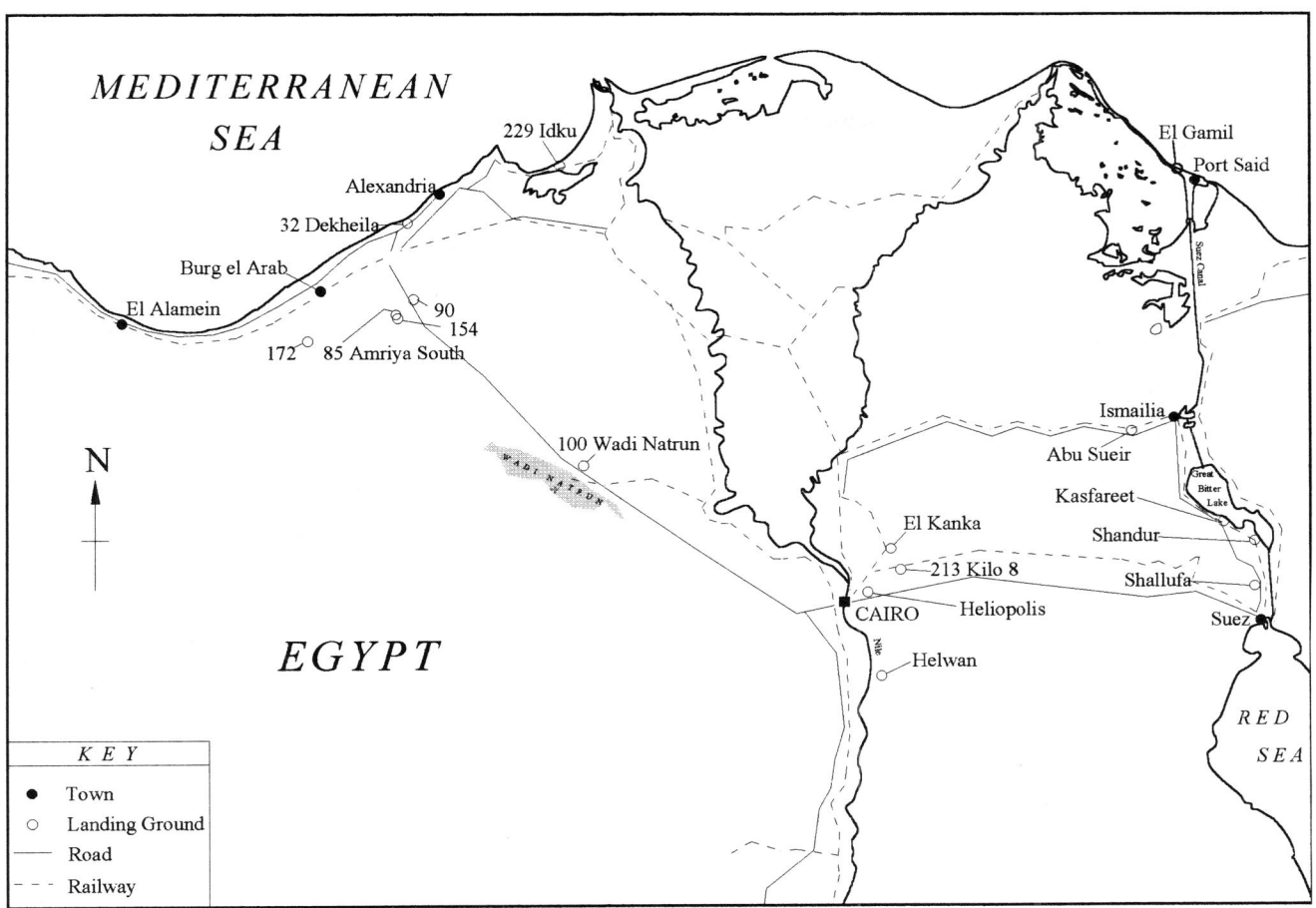

by the removal of Gp Capt The Duke of Newcastle, Sector Commander Seagull Sector (Alexandria), Wg Cdr R Budd, Chief Controller, and Sqn Ldr J Lockhart, OC 213 Squadron, from their commands. On 21 January 1942 Sqn Ldr G V Kettlewell arrived from 80 Squadron to take command.

Thus between 18 November 1941 and 18 January 1942, while "Operation Crusader" was pushing the Axis forces back beyond Agedabia to El Agheila on the Gulf of Sirte, the Squadron was rotating slowly around the periphery of Alexandria, providing fighter defence against an enemy which proved all too loath to appear. The Italian raid on Alexandria, and its aftermath, had started the Squadron on a private campaign that would last until the move out into the desert in June. The Squadron's objective was to prevent Alexandria harbour from being photographed by anyone. From January 1942, standing patrols of two aircraft were flown from dawn until dusk. Flying time mounted rapidly, in one month topping one thousand hours, with a monthly average of eight hundred plus. Heights for the patrols went up from 20,000 feet to 25,000 feet, and then to 30,000 feet and more. However even the Hurricane IIc, with which the Squadron re-equipped in March 1942, could not go above 34,000 feet.

Nevertheless the patrols proved effective since the Ju 88s had to go higher and higher, or be shot down. Finally the Luftwaffe introduced the very high-flying specially pressurised Ju 86P-2s of 2(F)/Aufkl.Gr 123. To combat these aircraft, Spitfire Vs from Aboukir, specially prepared with all but two guns taken out, no armour plating, screw-down cockpits and miniaturised radios etc., were used. At the end of May, Plt Off G E Genders flying one of these stripped-down Spitfires attacked a Ju 86P-2 at 45,000 feet. Later, another was shot down at 50,000 feet by Fg Off G W H Reynolds, a record height for this period of the war. After two more were lost, the German reconnaissance flights over the Canal Zone ceased. For something like four months no reconnaissance aircraft flew over Alexandria in daylight, a record that was not equalled in any other war zone. The Italians had to wait until the end of the war to discover the results of their miniature submarine attack on Alexandria harbour.

During this period, while operating from Idku, Bert Houle suffered an enforced absence from the Squadron in unfortunate circumstances. When engaged upon the standing patrols over Alexandria and operating at maximum altitude, the aircraft became super-cooled, especially the windscreen and the thick bullet-proof glass. Then, when descending into the warm, humid air of the Nile Delta, the hood iced-up badly and forward visibility became practically nil. Flying around at a low altitude eventually cleared the ice, but the pilot's patience was put to the test waiting for this to happen; invariably it was the thick bullet-proof glass forming the windshield that was the last to clear. It was of course possible to slide the hood back, and as the perspex side-panels cleared more quickly than the glass the pilot was not flying completely blind. Returning from one sortie, Bert Houle did not wait for his windscreen to clear and came in to land with considerably reduced visibility. As a result he dropped his Hurricane in and bent the undercarriage. In the Flight Commander's accident report, George Westlake referred to the pilot being over-zealous and guilty of gross carelessness. Much to his and the CO's amazement and chagrin, HQ Middle East grounded Bert and posted him to a Maintenance Unit near Cairo, where he became the "test pilot" for repaired aircraft. As Bert was one of the best and most aggressive pilots in "B" Flight, this was the last thing that anyone wanted to happen. However for the moment all appeals for clemency

Flt Lt J Logan Briggs who, as a Flying Officer, served with the Squadron in the Middle East 1941/1942.
(Mrs J Campbell Grant)

Fg Off J A Sowrey, Egypt, 1942. (J A Sowrey)

fell on deaf ears, and Bert did not rejoin the Squadron until just before the break-out from El Alamein.

Training and Army Co-operation flights now provided much of the flying, interspersed by numerous scrambles over the town with the contact all too often disappearing before an interception could be made. Amongst the training sorties that were carried out, those that pointed most dramatically to the future were the dive-bombing and air-to-ground gunnery practices carried out over Helwan and Heliopolis airfields.

Out at LG 90, one of a dozen or more landing grounds located on the edge of the Western Desert due south of Dekheila and clustered around Amriya, the Squadron HQ was fighting its own personal battle with sand, mud and the local natives, whose pilfering activities were all-encompassing. On the night of 8 January, a passing band of tribesmen with their donkeys and camels stole two tents and two kitbags. The move back to Idku on 13 January 1942 was accordingly welcomed by all, especially as the Squadron was re-equipped with new transport and made fully mobile. Also, as the month passed, the un-tropicalised Hurricanes were exchanged for tropical versions. In one respect this was a mixed blessing, as the large air-scoop under the nose detracted even further from the aircraft's performance.

As "Operation Crusader" pushed forward, the lessons learnt at the front were promptly included in the training programme. The Hurricane I, to an even greater extent than the Mk.II, was out-performed by the Bf 109s and the Italian Macchi MC 202s, which were taking a heavy toll of the "weavers". These were the aircraft that covered the flanks of a flight from the wing positions. The training programme was improved to contain a new practice which consisted of the whole Squadron flying in fluid sixes, thus increasing its manoeuvrability and effectiveness as a fighting unit. So, although the flying was largely directed towards training, and the operational flying was often frustrating due to the limitations of the GCI stations, the Squadron was absorbing that background of experience and desert lore that would be so essential in the hectic days ahead.

In March, much to everyone's relief, the Squadron was re-equipped with the Hurricane IIc with four 20mm cannons. The improvement in performance was in fact marginal, the IIc having a top speed 315 miles per hour at 18,000 feet and a service ceiling of 30,000 feet, compared with 312 miles per hour at 16,250 feet and a service ceiling of 28,000 feet for the Hurricane I. In neither respect did the Hurricane IIc compare with the improved Messerschmitt Bf 109F-2/Trop that was coming into service with the front line Jagdgeschwadern of the Luftwaffe. This aircraft had a top speed of 373 miles per hour at 19,700 feet and a service ceiling of 37,700 feet.

In the months ahead, the new armament was unfortunately to prove a mixed blessing as the cannons were plagued with stoppages, a most unhappy state of affairs. Throughout the campaigns ahead, many kills went begging as either one or both pairs of guns jammed at the crucial moment. Not only were kills missed, but it was always a nerve-wracking experience to be in the middle of a hectic dog-fight with Bf 109s, and suddenly to find that the harsh jarring note of the cannons had ceased. For the successes that were achieved, a tribute must be paid to all the armourers, particularly Cpl "Alf" Angell, an ex-Guardsman and a tower

Hurricane W9291 during night flying in Egypt. The badge carried under the cockpit on AK-M has not been identified

of strength, who worked unceasingly in appalling conditions to make the cannons as reliable as possible. The poor diet also made the armourers particularly susceptible to desert sores on their hands, when they damaged them on the alclad when pulling back the cannon breech-blocks. The practice combat with the captured Bf 109F from Helwan earlier in the month had shown all too clearly the Hurricane's limitations in speed and rate of climb.

Nevertheless the re-equipment had taken place just in time. By February 1942 "Operation Crusader" had come to a final halt along the front at Gazala after the initial advance as far as El Agheila. For a while, the exhausted armies settled down in their positions to gain strength and re-equip for the next round in the battle. In the air however, though activity over the front diminished, it was only because aircraft were turned to other duties. In April the Luftwaffe, released from its close support duties at the front, turned more of its attention towards the Nile Delta, and the Squadron's own personal war entered another phase of considerable activity.

Operating from the group of airfields around Martuba, Ju 88s began to appear more frequently in the skies over Alexandria. Difficulties with control and the small margin in speed of the Hurricane over the Ju 88 meant that interceptions required a great deal of skill and not a little luck. Nevertheless on 9 April Sgt "Lofty" Horn intercepted one of these aircraft over the harbour and shot it down into the sea fifteen miles off the coast.

Tragically a few days later on his twenty-first birthday, while coming in to land at Idku, his engine failed and his aircraft turned over in the shallow water at the edge of the lake as his wheels sank into the mud. The whole flight, pilots and groundcrew, rushed out to the aircraft and it was quickly realised that if one wing of the Hurricane could be raised then the cockpit hood could be opened. Everyone gathered round the wing, up to their chests in water, and started to lift working their way towards the fuselage. However, before anything could be achieved, the Station Engineering Officer called everyone back as he had ordered a crane out to lift the Hurricane. At first there was relief as the unconscious body was lifted from the cockpit and it could be seen that the oxygen mask was still in place. On returning to the dispersal, one of the pilots took the unopened bottle of champagne that was to have celebrated Lofty Horn's coming of age and smashed it against the wall of the hut, expressing the frustration and anger that everyone felt at the delay in rescuing him. Although he was alive when pulled from his aircraft, he died later in the night in hospital.

The Squadron's contribution to the defence of Alexandria during the month of April was 830 hours flown, three enemy aircraft destroyed and a further three damaged. The three aircraft destroyed were part of the total of seven enemy aircraft brought down in the course of a particularly heavy raid on the night of 28 April. In addition to the Squadron's victories, two were brought down by 272 Squadron and two by ack-ack fire. The promise of April was however not fulfilled, and the month of May saw even less to show for another massive flying effort.

Throughout May, as German air activity increased, operations were maintained at a high level and numerous encounters with Ju 88s kept the Squadron on its toes. Early on the morning of 5 May a loud explosion rocked the camp. An He 111, shot down by Sgt Peters of a Beaufighter squadron, had crashed on to the foreshore just north of the Squadron's quarters. The two survivors of the crew of four

Sgt R Halvorsen, an American pilot serving with the RAF, who was shot down and wounded on Friday, 13 June 1941, by Leut F Koerner of I JG/27.

From left to right: Plt Off A J Hancock, Flt Sgt Wally Lack, Fg Off W W Swinden, Plt Off G R S MacKay, Plt Off W Ismay and Jonah (Sgt J D Newick?). Emerging from "B" Flight's Nissen hut on the extreme left is Flt Sgt George Hersey, who as a Wing Commander was Engineering Officer to the Meteor High Speed Flight at Tangmere when the World Speed Record was broken.

were captured by Plt Off Henwood, the Defence Officer, though one of them later died from his injuries. As to the treatment of the survivor two schools of thought existed. In the event, the noble-minded policy prevailed and George Westlake's carefully-prepared breakfast was carried in state across to the Defence Tent. Although this involuntary sacrifice was haughtily refused, the amount of information the German disclosed more than made up for the lost breakfast.

On 13 May the Squadron provided an escort for General Smuts, who was going up to Daba from Heliopolis. Six aircraft from "B" Flight led by Westlake were detached for the whole week it took the General to visit the South African troops in the desert. The five aircraft on duty on the first day were led by WO R J "Wally" Wallace, one of the most respected pilots on the Squadron, who on occasions led the whole Wing in the air. He had joined the RAF as an Halton apprentice then, selected for flying training, he had qualified as a pilot and served as a Sergeant and Flight Sergeant. As the estimated time of arrival for the return of the escort arrived, the waiting groundcrew were surprised to see only four aircraft come into the circuit. It transpired that Wallace had landed at Daba with the General's aeroplane. Sometime later AK-S, Wallace's aircraft, was seen approaching on finals and comment was made upon the particularly smooth landing that was executed. Each aircraft on the Squadron had its own Airframe and Engine Fitters while the more specialised tradesmen, Armourers, Instrument Fitters and Wireless Technicians covered a number of aircraft. Thus as LAC Henry, who as an Airframe Fitter looked after AK-S together with Desmond Goldswain who took care of the engine, guided it into dispersal and then slid back the hood, it became apparent that Wallace had enjoyed his time on the ground at Daba. He asked Henry for his screwdriver and began to make his way somewhat unsteadily down off the mainplane and along the side of the Hurricane towards the tailplane. It was soon clear that Wallace was intending to undo the small access plate situated above the tail-wheel. However not wishing to see his precious Hurricane damaged as seemed likely, Henry retrieved the screwdriver and removed the plate himself. Inside, resting on the main fuselage girders, completely loose and unprotected lay a bottle of whisky, a testimony to Wallace's smooth landing even under adverse conditions.

In the middle of May, Sqn Ldr M H Young DFC took command of the Squadron, thus clinching rumours that the unit was westward bound for the desert. Young was ex-73 Squadron and had a great deal of front-line desert combat experience. Between his arrival and the departure of Sqn Ldr G V W Kettlewell, the Squadron was commanded for a three week period by Sqn Ldr G. Reid, who was subsequently posted to a Beaufighter squadron and was shot down north of Crete by three Arado float-planes.

The next day, as if to mark the arrival of the new CO, Plt Off "Hindoo" Henderson damaged a Ju 88 in the morning, and in the afternoon Sowrey and Sgt W H Stephenson, a Canadian, shot down another into Alexandria harbour. While patrolling the harbour area, Sowrey and Stephenson were vectored onto a bandit coming in at high level; then suddenly

WO "Wally" Wallace, beating up in a Hawker Hardy borrowed from No.216 Squadron, El Khanka, Alexandria, Egypt, December 1941.

Gambut West June 1942. Watching the Squadron return one by one from a dog-fight. Left to right, Sqn Ldr M H Young, DFC (facing the camera), Flt Lt G H Westlake, Fg Off W W Swinden and Plt Off D R Redhill.

operations called up to say that the plot had disappeared and that they could give no more information. This normally meant that the raider had dived below the radar cover and was coming in at low level. So, from their perch at 30,000 feet, Sowrey and Stephenson looked down over the harbour area. From that height it was impossible to pick out an aircraft as such, but the two plumes on the surface of the sea formed by the slipstream from the Ju 88's engines gave it away. Once seen the German's fate was sealed, and he was shot down into the harbour; had he been flying a few feet higher he would have escaped.

Two days later, the same team picked up another Ju 88 at 30,000 feet and gave chase. The German was pointing out to sea, and it looked as if a long stern chase was in the offing. For a while the Hurricanes made no impression on the German and it seemed that he would escape. Then suddenly he half-rolled and went into a vertical dive right down to deck level. Sowrey and Stephenson followed him down but lost him as their windscreens misted up in the descent. Looking out of his side panel, Sowrey caught sight of a shadow on the desert; it was the Ju 88 and Stephenson was with it. After a chase around the sand-dunes, the Ju 88 was shot down south-west of Burg-el-Arab, where it belly-landed in the desert. Although the Germans survived the landing, they did not escape the Arabs who caught them. As a result of these two victories, Sowrey and Stephenson were whisked off to the offices of the Egyptian State Broadcasting Company in Cairo to recount the stories of their exploits - the last the Squadron were to achieve in the defence of Alexandria.

To the west, the line at Gazala was about to erupt into flame and smoke. While Malta was ceaselessly attacked from the air by the Luftwaffe in Sicily, German convoys had made the passage from Italy to Libya. Now, restocked and primed for battle, Rommel was ready to attack. On 26 May 1942 while four Italian Divisions contained the British forces on the coast, the crack divisions of the Panzer Armee Afrika struck against Bir Hacheim, the southern terminus of the fortified line garrisoned by the Free French. Battle was joined once more. As the defences of Alexandria were stripped down to one squadron of Beaufighters, the Squadron was ordered westward to LG 12, near the coastal town of Sidi Haneish. After another considerable re-equipment, the Advance Party set out on 29 May. Almost at once new orders were received making LG 12 merely a staging post, with the final destination being Gambut Main another two hundred miles to the west.

As the Squadron prepared to move up to the front line the Nominal Roll of its pilots was:-

Sqn Ldr M H Young, DFC

"A" Flight	"B " Flight
Flt Lt C B Temlett, DFC	Flt Lt G H Westlake
Fg Off J A Sowrey	Fg Off J C Edmunds
Fg Off J L Briggs	Plt Off F A W J Wilson
Plt Off P P Wilson	Plt Off A J Hancock
Plt Off W H Thomlinson	Plt Off G R S McKay
Plt Off W R Henderson	Plt Off W W Swinden
Plt Off K N R Sissons	Plt Off D Redhill
Plt Off L D H Boucher	Plt Off C D A Smith
Plt Off J Avise	WO R J Wallace
Flt Sgt W H Stephenson	Flt Sgt W A Lack
Flt Sgt H M Compton	Flt Sgt J Edwards
Sgt J D Ritchie	Flt Sgt R H Halvorsen
Sgt H A Aitken	Sgt J F C Ballantyne
Sgt Jackson	Sgt J D Newick
Sgt R W Jones	
Sgt G S Bolton	

Though slightly farther from the front line than the airfields at Gazala itself, which was the German's favourite fighter base, or El Adem, Gambut had been developed as the main fighter complex to cover the front line. The numerous airfields there had been built on a dry dusty plateau, and were linked together by a full-scale communications network - something of a rarity in the desert. The fighters at Gambut were also conveniently close to the light bomber base at Bir-el-Baheira. While the dispersal of aircraft and airfields remained a first principle in the desert war, when conditions became relatively static the concentration of airfields at one site meant that strong anti-aircraft defences could be provided. At Gambut there was the main airfield plus three satellites and also a dummy field, especially built for the Germans to bomb. This decoy field was at least realistic enough to induce a squadron of Kittyhawks to land there. On the airfields themselves, protective pens for the aircraft and operations tents were constructed of sand-filled fifty-gallon drums piled two high. Here the Squadron came under the control of No.211 Group, which had been newly formed to work the leap-frog principle with No.212 Group while controlling the forward offensive fighter wings.

When the Advance Party of the Squadron set out from Idku at 23.00 hours, the immediate destination was still the town and airfield at Sidi Haneish. Even though much of the travelling was done under the cover of darkness, dawn found the party between Daba and Fuka, where it was attacked by a German fighter. Not surprisingly the CO's shooting-brake received most of the fighter's attention. While everyone rested at LG 12, outside Sidi Haneish, the CO and Temlett flew up to Gambut Main to see exactly what the situation there was, and discovered that the Squadron was to occupy the north-west corner of the airfield at Gambut West. The personnel remaining behind at Sidi Haneish took the opportunity to wash off some of the dust of travel in the Mediterranean. On 3 June, the Advance Party under Fg Off Barrett-Atkin, the Squadron Engineering Officer, set off at 06.00 hours for Gambut West where they arrived without incident at 19.00 hours. The Main Party left the next day, and moved up past Bardia, Sollum and Halfaya without an enemy aircraft in sight, although gun-fire was heard in the distance. Their arrival at Gambut on 5 June coincided with one of the biggest tank battles fought up to that date. With the move into the desert, the Officers' Mess as such ceased to exist and a new Officers' and Aircrew Mess was set up.

On 4 June, the Squadron's aircraft took-off from LG 12 and flew into Gambut West to join the Advance Party which was already in residence. Almost at once action was joined and the Squadron was given a hint of things to come. Temlett led six Hurricanes on an offensive sweep between Acroma and Gazala where they were jumped by five Bf 109s; after an indecisive turn-about with the Germans all six of the aircraft returned to base. The pattern, however, had been set and seldom in the coming battles was the Squadron to go into action with height advantage over the redoubtable Bf 109Fs. The next two days saw repeated sweeps over the heavy fighting going on below but no action was joined.

The importance of holding Bir Hacheim, and thus preventing the Germans from launching a right-hook towards Tobruk, was constantly reiterated in the newspapers of the day and it was a vital point in the defensive line. Nevertheless, for the Army Commanders involved in the battle, the need to keep their small armoured force intact to prevent a complete German break-through into Egypt was of even greater importance. If the tanks and armour were to be committed, then it had to be in a battle that could not be lost. So it came about that the defence of the Free French troops in the fortress of Bir Hacheim against the attacks of the German Panzers was allotted to the Desert Air Force. From 8 June until 11 June, these operations were given top priority by the squadrons in the front line. Whilst the fighters held the ring against the Bf 109s, the fighter-bomber and tank-buster squadrons attacked the German armour below.

The first sortie at 06.45 hours on 8 June did not see things off to an auspicious start since the aircraft flew in too tight formation and too close together so that when they were jumped by Bf 109s, a shambles resulted. The lesson was quickly learned. At midday a sweep was flown over the battle field at Knightsbridge and no enemy aircraft were seen. In the evening the Squadron flew as top cover to 73 Squadron over Bir Hacheim; this time all was in order although again no enemy aircraft were seen. Newly into the front line, the Squadron was having a difficult time as Flt Lt P Olver - just out from England and on temporary attachment - noticed in the short period before he moved on to become a Flight Commander with 238 Squadron. Before arriving in the Middle East, he had already completed one fighter tour in the UK, flying Spitfires with Nos.603 and 66 Squadrons in the Battle of Britain, during which he had a number of victories.

At 17.00 hours on 9 June, eleven Hurricanes of 73 Squadron, covered by 213 Squadron, carried out a sweep over Bir Hacheim, where they were jumped by twelve Bf 109s and some Macchi MC 202s. The squadrons turned into their attackers and in the resulting engagement each claimed two victims, 213 claiming one Macchi and one Bf 109. The Squadron returned without loss.

On the next day at 07.50 hours, twelve Hurricanes of 73 Squadron, once again covered by 213, took off on another sweep over the fortress, with a top cover of Spitfires. The first action occurred when the Hurricanes were jumped by five Macchi MC 202s; three times the Hurricanes turned into them and drove them off. They then saw two formations of Ju 87s and Ju 88s escorted by Bf 109s. The Squadron's Hurricanes immediately engaged the fighter escort and were forced into a defensive circle, just going round and round with the 109s like silvery fish above them. During this impasse the Stukas flew sedately past in close formation of threes, line astern. For Sowrey and Hancock the temptation was too much and, although the manoeuvre was really suicidal, they broke away from the circle and attacked the rearmost of the Ju 87s. Before they could really come to grips with the dive-bombers, the Bf 109s were upon them. Hancock, who was probably one of the finest pilots on the Squadron at the time, and who had just been commissioned, was hit in the arm by an explosive bullet. He was then chased some twenty miles to the emergency landing ground at Bir-el-Gubbi where, though faint from the loss of blood, he made a perfect landing before his Hurricane was strafed to destruction by the three pursuing Bf 109s. For this action he was awarded the DFC.

A number of the Squadron pilots had stocked up with tinned food, especially tinned fruit, against any prolonged period on hard rations in the desert. Alan Hancock, along with Plt Offs Henderson, G R S McKay and K N R Sissons, had been commissioned shortly before the move into the desert, and his uniform was brand new. This explains his first words when he came out of the anaesthetic after his wound had been operated on which were "Tell Freddie (Plt Off F A W J Wilson) he can have my tinned fruit but not my bullshit hat". Unhappily this was his last trip with the Squadron as on recovering from his wounds he returned to the UK. He was later killed flying a Mustang over Cherbourg; on D-Day he destroyed two Focke-Wulf FW 190s, the first enemy aircraft to be destroyed on that day.

Sowrey also had his problems. Although he himself was not wounded his aircraft was so badly damaged that he was forced to land close to the battle front. Once on the ground, the wreckage of his Hurricane was strafed by the 109s which had followed him down. Even then his troubles were not over as he had to cross a minefield to reach the Allied lines.

At 15.40 hours another combined sweep with 73 Squadron was again jumped by twelve Bf 109s from III/JG 53, which were on escort duty to a formation of Ju 87s. In the ensuing dog-fight one enemy aircraft was damaged and two claimed as probables, with all the Squadron's aircraft returning safely to Gambut.

On 11 June Bir Hacheim fell, and the DAF covered the retreat of the two thousand men who escaped. The resolute defence on the ground and the daily battles in the air had not been in vain as a German battle appreciation makes clear:

"Field Marshal Rommel's supply position was such that an advance into Egypt with the Suez Canal as its first objective seemed possible. The battle of Bir Hacheim

The C O, Sqn Ldr Jimmy Kettlewell, distributes the mail to George Westlake (half hidden), the Armament Officer, Chris Brocklebank (MO), Tommy Thomlinson, John Sowrey and "Tem" Temlett. (J A Sowrey)

deprived this offensive of its desired result. This fortress held out for nine whole days against an attack of nearly three divisions and three reconnaissance battalions, supported by about 15,000 air sorties. This meant nine days' gain for the enemy, and for our army and air force nine days of losses in material, personnel, aircraft and petrol. Those nine days were irrecoverable."

Continuous sweeps over the battle area brought the Squadron into daily contact with the Bf 109s. On a reconnaissance sortie over El Adem and Bir-el-Gubbi on 11 June, Westlake shot down a Bf 109 and damaged a Ju 87. The prolonged resistance of the Free French garrison at Bir Hacheim had seriously upset Rommel's timetable. This initial setback was in danger of jeopardising his whole offensive, and on 12 June the battle still remained in the balance. It was a busy day and offensive patrols were flown over El Adem and Knightsbridge at 08.47, 12.35 and 15.55 hours; on two occasions pairs of Bf 109s were seen, but they kept their distance.

At 19.35 hours, Nos.33, 73, 213, 238 and 274 Squadrons, covered by the Spitfires of 145 Squadron, were scrambled to intercept a large force of Ju 87s and Ju 88s, which was escorted by eight Bf 109s of I Gruppe and ten from III/JG 27, as well as some Macchi MC 202s. In the ensuing battle, Fg Off Edmonds was killed, and Flt Sgt Edwards had to bale out of his damaged aircraft. Edwards was flying as No.2 to Westlake and they had become separated from the rest of the Squadron in the general melée of the first attack. They were then bounced by four Bf 109s and Westlake saw Edwards bale out. Covering his descent, Westlake was able to attack the Bf 109s as they sought to pinpoint where the parachute was going to land. He saw one explode and go down as his cannon shells went right into the cockpit and hit the main fuel tank. He lost sight of the others and never saw them again - very worrying in an "empty" sky.

Friday 13 June 1942 proved to be the decisive day in the overall battle. Rommel's 90th Light Division attacked once more, and this time broke through and captured El Adem. The British armour suffered heavily in the battles in the Knightsbridge area, and fell back towards the coast. Sandstorms during the day restricted air operations, but nevertheless at 07.00 hours the Squadron carried out a sweep over the Tobruk - Gazala road and saw the South Africans pulling out. Twelve Bf 109s of I/JG 27 had taken off to escort a Bf 110 on a reconnaissance mission over the Acroma - El Adem area, and six of these bounced the Squadron north of Acroma. Lt Koerner claimed two Hurricanes and Lt Stahlschmidt one. In fact two Squadron aircraft were lost; Plt Off P P Wilson was seen to crash into the sea, and Flt Sgt D Halvorsen baled out and finished up in 62nd Field Hospital with burns to his chest and hands.

Halvorsen's recollection was that he was flying as Number Six in Blue Section, and acting as "weaver" as the Flight was returning to base at 13,000 feet after the initial dog-fight, when they were attacked by four Bf 109s. After the initial diving attack of the first pair, Halvorsen broke to the right and saw the two other enemy aircraft diving past one hundred yards away. Suddenly little holes "like hemstitching" appeared in his starboard wing. As he broke into a turn to port, he realised that his controls and rudder were damaged as the Hurricane responded only sluggishly. Three more cannon shells hit the propeller, spinner and engine cowling. As he prepared to bale out, another shell hit just above the windscreen and burst into the reserve fuel tank forward of the instrument panel. The exploding shell tore the tank apart and burning fuel poured into the cockpit. As he desperately clawed at his harness release with his right hand, he noticed that his left hand, still firmly holding the spade grip of the control column, was on fire. So also were his trousers and desert shoes, and the flames spread up his tunic and on to his right hand. Inverting his aircraft, he fell free and, after a pause to avoid contact with the rudder, opened his parachute. Looking down he saw below him a brown mist and knew that a sandstorm was blowing across the desert.

The remaining four aircraft of Blue Section had formed a protective ring around the descending parachute and were keeping the Bf 109s at bay. This was not fully appreciated by Halvorsen, as it seemed to him that this merely ensured that the airspace around him was full of flying shells and bullets. Eventually only one Messerschmitt remained and Halvorsen saw it coming towards him with its flaps lowered, throttle back, hood open and the pilot with his goggles back off his forehead. The German pilot smiled and gave him a thumbs up, followed by a wave, which Halvorsen took to mean "Good luck". He was eventually picked up by a Bren-gun carrier, crewed by the Scots Guards and taken to hospital. The German pilot who had shot him down was Leut Friedrich Koerner of I/JG 27.

What Dickie Halvorsen probably did not know was that the wing loading on the Hurricane he was flying was somewhat higher than usual. The aircraft, AK-W, was in fact Westlake's and all the spare space was filled with cans of beer and Westlake's kit. Among the retreating troops, Barrett-Atkin had found the NAAFI abandoning one of its depots and destroying tins of food, fruit, beer, etc. He organised a shuttle service of three-tonners and rescued certain items - in fact enough was rescued to last the Squadron for a further three months. Westlake's share went to the bottom of the Mediterranean.

On 14 June conflicting reports concerning the land battle were received. The Army was said to be holding the enemy at El Adem, but nevertheless the Squadron was due to move east - the wrong way! Bir Hacheim was in fact finally over-run by the Germans at around 13.10 hours. Sowrey remembers being on patrol late in the afternoon and seeing the German forces advancing in a big right hook about half-way to the coast. It was clear that the ground battle had been lost, and that Tobruk would again be cut off. For two days the Gazala - Tobruk road was packed with convoys of slowly-moving lorries and men, an inviting target for the Stukas and fighter-bombers of the German Air Force. However, during those two days the retreating armies lost only six men, rather than the hundreds that could have fallen to air attacks. General Freyberg spoke for all the troops when he said "Thank God you didn't let the Hun Stuka us, because we were an appalling target".

On the early morning sweep over Knightsbridge, the patrol had again been jumped by Bf 109s and the CO claimed one damaged. At 11.48 hours the Squadron was scrambled over base, as bandits were reported twenty miles to the north, but they turned out to be Kittyhawks escorting a convoy into Tobruk. Half of the Squadron's groundcrew, designated "B" Party, left Gambut West for LG 75 in the afternoon.

The early morning sweep on 15 June was carried out over the Acroma - Gazala - Knightsbridge triangle as bandits had been reported in that area, but no enemy aircraft were seen. Later in the morning, a sweep was carried out some six miles out to sea off Tobruk, and heavy movement eastwards from the town was seen. In the evening, Gambut Main was bombed by Bf 109s and an airman from 33 Squadron was killed. A dogfight took place immediately over the heads of the party from the Squadron who had gone to the airfield to draw water at a well to augment the usual supplies of unpalatable desalinated water. This desalinated water was horrible to drink even at only one bottle per day. However a way was found to use it only for washing. Somebody remembered that the fire tender had been filled with good water back in the Delta. The problem was that the only "tap" was the very large pipe used to connect up the hoses and to use this would lead to great wastage. The solution was to climb onto the trailer and dangle a small bottle, fastened with a string around its neck, through the vent on top. This produced a very slow and warm drink - but better than desalinated water. The question as to whether or not drinking from the fire tender was a chargeable offence was never resolved.

During the disorder of the retreat from Gazala, it was often necessary for the groundcrews to exist on emergency rations, which were generous in amount and sustaining rather than nourishing. Virtually everything came in tins. The basis of most meals - and popular despite their repetitiveness - were the versatile large round biscuits, a type of arrowroot, that were extremely hard and full of weevils. The biscuits were floated in shallow water until they doubled in size and were soft but not breaking up. They were then fried on a flat tin in "Oleo" margarine until crisp, and eaten with "McConachies Brown Stew" or the ubiquitous bully beef and beans. Alternatively, for "dessert", they could be spread with the anonymous jam that also came in large tins.

Evenings and nights in the desert could be very cold so, for heating and cooking, the top was cut off one of the four-gallon petrol cans, which was filled to the brim with sand and then soaked with 100-octane petrol. A little later, the surface could be lit and would burn with a blue flame for quite a long time. If extinguished, a light poking of the surface would usually persuade it to re-ignite. If this failed, great caution had to be observed as a cloud of heavy petrol vapour would spread around the floor of the tent when the "desert fire" was being used as a heater. The danger in relighting them was clear, since the whole floor area of the tent could momentarily become a sheet of flame.

By 16 June the position at Gambut West was becoming critical, and the epic fighting withdrawal to the El Alamein line commenced. For the first time since the beginning of "Crusader", the Tactical HQs of the 8th Army and the DAF split up as the army HQ moved back to Sollum. Advanced Air HQ Western Desert, however, stayed on at Gambut despite the risks involved. Close forward control was essential; Tobruk had not yet fallen, and the defenders of the El Adem box, under strong pressure from the advancing German armour, needed all the aerial support available at maximum intensity.

The initial move for "A" party was only as far as Gambut Satellite, since German tanks and infantry were seen in the vicinity of the main airfields. While at Gambut West, the armourers had had to bury some ammunition, which they marked by fixing a cross over the top inscribed RIP. Unfortunately, the very next day they had to return under the noses of the Germans and dig some up, as the Squadron had been in combat and the Hurricanes needed rearming. From Gambut Satellite, an evening scramble between Tobruk and El Adem saw the usual situation reversed, when a section jumped three Bf 109s which had been strafing. This was the only time Westlake ever remembers being above a Bf 109. Only one survived, with Westlake and Fg Off J L Briggs accounting for the other two. The whole performance had been watched by the top brass of No.211 Wing, Air Cdre Carter and Wg Cdr Rosier.

In the evening of the second day at Gambut Satellite, the order came once more to move, this time to Sidi Azeiz. As the Squadron flew in, Kittyhawks were already on the field. That night the pilots slept under the wings of their Hurricanes. The crews of the two vehicles that failed to make the airfield were awakened in the night by Free French troops with alarming stories of Germans in close proximity. The German successes continued and the El Adem box had to be abandoned.

Dawn the following day - 18 June - arrived with yet more orders brought by a despatch rider to move to LG 75, Sidi Barrani South. Initially, however, all the aircraft assembled at LG 155 (after maintenance had stayed behind to service a new Hurricane that had "pranged" on landing at Sidi Azeiz) before staging through to LG 75, their final destination. Jack Walton recorded in his diary - "I really can't make anything out in this desert warfare, first we make a good push and then something goes wrong; three days ago I counted 780 vehicles on the main road of the desert, all supplies for our front, and before we know where we are, scramble came through, and the day of evacuating Gambut. Jerry practically tore the drome to pieces. To speak of our fortunate break-away, all I can say (is) Thank God Jerry is a poor shot or we and our Squadron would have been no longer a Squadron".

About this time the Squadron's supplies were once again replenished, when it was heard over the land line that the NAAFI was about to blow up stores in the area. Three-tonners were once again despatched to load up, which they did to no mean effect, tinned fruit and rum being the prize pickings. The NAAFI depots that were being abandoned were used to supply units in bulk when transport could be arranged. At this time LAC Henry found himself not only a Fitter (Airframe) but also i/c Airmen's Shop. So, taking a three-tonner, he went to the depot where he found that it was a matter of loading up as quickly as possible from the hundreds of boxes that were strewn around on the ground - most of them with no means of identifying the contents. He was fortunate and returned with six large crates of rum. For the rest of the retreat he used them to build a blast wall round the two-man bivouac tent that he shared with Des Goldswain and which was always pitched near "their" aircraft. Other units were not so lucky, and one found that its main haul consisted of tins of boot polish.

The Squadron ground personnel were now operating in

Sgt W H Stephenson and Fg Off J A Sowrey at the studios of the Egyptian Broadcasting Company describe how they destroyed a Ju 88, May 1942. (J A Sowrey)

accordance with the plans laid back in the Delta; "A" and "B" Parties leap-frogging each other to service the aircraft as they fell back from airfield to airfield, a Main Party with the Squadron HQ and a Rear Party. The chief task for the Airframe Fitters was repairing the holes in the fabric covering of the Hurricane's fuselage and tailplane. A suitable-sized piece of fabric and a pot of glue soon restored a damaged aircraft to operational condition. On 20 June "A" Party moved to LG 76, and was joined there later by the Main Party and all the aircraft. During the night, at 23.45 hours, a lone Ju 88 strafed the decoy light; unfortunately it missed the light and the bullets tore up the ground perilously close to the Squadron's tents.

As Tobruk surrendered late on 21 June, the Advance Party left LG 76 for LG 12 at Sidi Haneish, where it arrived the next day, having travelled all night. During all these moves, which varied from Flight to Flight and even pilot to pilot, operational sorties, consisting of both fighter sweeps and reconnaissance missions, were flown over the confused battle area. These were the days when the Desert Air Force reached the peak of its achievements. There now seemed to be nothing between Tobruk and the Delta to stop Rommel, and speculation was rife as to what would happen to the Squadron. There seemed to be two alternatives - either to go to Russia up through the Caucasus, or go down to South Africa. The forces that had not been cut-off and captured in Tobruk seemed pathetically small, and were falling back in disorder to the Delta.

At this time Flt Lt J A Sowrey was called to the Wing HQ to report to Wg Cdr Rosier, who told him that he was to be posted to 80 Squadron to take over a Flight. On being asked where the Allies were going to stop, Rosier took out a map and pointed to the small front between the Qattara Depression and the Mediterranean Sea and said "That's where we are going to stop". During his time with the Squadron, Sowrey destroyed a total of four enemy aircraft (counting the two Ju 88s he shared with Stephenson as one) and damaged one; subsequently, while serving as a Flight Commander with 80 Squadron, he destroyed a further two Ju 87s, both on 4 July.

The patrols flown over Sollum and Bardia on 22 June saw the battle raging beneath them. In the evening "B" party also pulled back to LG 12 at Sidi Haneish, which the Squadron had passed through on the first two days of June as it moved up to the Gazala line.

As the Army prepared to make a stand at Mersa Matruh in order to salvage as much equipment as possible, orders arrived on 23 June for "A" Party and the aircraft to move forward to LG 07. All sections of the party were bombed and strafed by enemy aircraft while on the move.

On 24 June, Rommel's armoured columns crossed into Egypt and Auchinleck took over direct command of the 8th Army. The Squadron's mid-morning reconnaissance patrol was jumped by four Bf 109s and, although no losses were suffered on either side, the recce was abandoned. In the evening, with another reconnaissance patrol airborne, a message was received that a German armoured column was eighteen miles to the west, and that "A" Party should at once pull back to LG 12. Temlett took off to investigate and, although no enemy column was seen, the pull back to LG 12 took place as it was clear that the move up to LG 07 had been precipitate.

In the evening of the next day, news was received that enemy aircraft, Ju 88s and Bf 109s, were on LG 07, and twelve aircraft were scrambled to strafe the field. However no aircraft were seen, and the Squadron contented itself with shooting up some transport seen nearby. It was later realised that this transport could have been friendly and the error was put down to "duff gen".

On 26 June, the air fighting reached a climax as the Desert Air Force made a series of heavy attacks on the advancing German columns. The first patrol at 09.50 was over the new line forming at Mersa Matruh, and no enemy aircraft were seen. At mid-day a rapid scramble over base found the Squadron jumped by four Bf 109s, but no damage was done on either side.

Airborne again at 15.15 hours, two flights led by the CO and Temlett carried out an offensive sweep over the Charing Cross area. After almost an hour on patrol, and while flying at 19,000 feet on a heading of 290 degrees, eight Bf 109s were seen some three miles away at 14,000 feet flying in echelon starboard and stepped up in pairs. The 109s were passing from right to left below. Temlett leading "A" Flight was flying stepped up and behind "B" Flight, and he reported the bandits. Normally the leading flight would have attacked but, as the 109s were passing under the nose of the CO's aircraft and he was unsighted, he ordered "A" Flight to attack before the enemy escaped. Exultant at this rare chance to turn the tables on the 109s, "A" Flight bounced the Messerschmitts with "astronomical results". Temlett selected the second aircraft from the end on the right and closed to twenty yards, firing a five-second burst. He saw strikes all along the right mainplane from the tip to the root, then it just crumpled and fell away; the enemy aircraft burst into flames, rolled to the left and plunged into the ground. Thomlinson, flying as Red Two on Temlett's wing, identified the 109s by their white wing tips and saw pieces fly off his target, after which it crashed.

Henderson flying as Yellow One took the third aircraft from the right as his target; as he closed in, the 109 pulled up almost vertically and from one hundred yards, closing to seventy-five, he fired a two-second burst. "Chunks" flew off the engine and cockpit and black smoke "belched forth"; the damaged fighter then went down in five spiral turns before straightening out momentarily at 4,000 feet. From a range of one hundred yards Henderson fired another two-second burst, following which the Messerschmitt plunged into the ground south-west of LG 07. Sgt Ritchie, as Yellow Two, hit another Bf 109 in the tail section, which disintegrated and fell off, causing the fighter to roll over into a spiral dive which continued until it hit the deck. Ken Sissons, White One, picked out a target on the extreme left of the enemy formation; when he was six hundred yards behind it and 5,000 feet above, the enemy fighter pulled up in a steep climbing turn to the left. As Sissons turned with it, the 109 ran right through his line of sight; he fired a two-second burst and saw strikes all along the cockpit. As pieces broke off, the enemy aircraft rolled on to its back and then barrelled out, pulled up again, half rolled and then dived into the ground.

No German losses of this magnitude have been found recorded for this day, and it has been suggested in some quarters that the aircraft were in fact Macchi MC 202s. Given the detailed combat reports, and the experience of the pilots engaged, such a mistake appears unlikely. Whatever the identity of the victims, the successes put the section waiting at readiness on its mettle and, when later it ran into a formation of twenty Ju 87s on a bombing run over Mersa Matruh, Westlake led them into an attack that destroyed three and damaged a further four. This concluded a record day for the Squadron in the Middle East. While jubilation ran high, news came that the Germans had broken through at Mersa Matruh and "B" Party was ordered to LG 05. Once again the ground party was strafed *en route*.

On 27 June, "A" party was also ordered up to LG 05, while the Squadron's twelve aircraft flew an offensive sweep over Mersa Matruh and landed at LG 05 just after midday. As the Germans had moved up rapidly, an uncomfortable night was spent in the slit-trenches. As explained by the Army Liaison Officer, Capt Clifford Field, in a phrase that was to become famous on the Squadron, "the position which had solidified had become fluid again". On 28 June, the news came that Mersa Matruh had fallen.

As the last remnants of the Army were evacuated from the town on 29 June, the Squadron fell back rapidly to LG 154. On a sweep over the town, with "A" Flight at 6,000 feet and "B" Flight flying as top cover at 10,000 feet, the Squadron's twelve aircraft were once more on the receiving end and were jumped by four Bf 109s. Peter Olver was leading "B" Flight and was preparing to return to base when he saw two Bf 109s diving onto the port section of his flight. He gave the command "Duck" and turned right; as the first two attackers pulled out he saw two more come down, one of which turned towards him and then pulled up straight in front of him. As the range closed from one hundred yards down to fifty, he fired eighteen rounds from each gun, seeing strikes on the nose of the 109 and pieces flying off. However the damaged German fighter managed to pull up and escape.

Plt Off D W Beedham, flying as Blue Two, heard the order "Duck" and then saw a Hurricane behind him and so fell back to join up. Almost immediately they were attacked by three Bf 109s and pulled round into a circle. As one of the 109s gained on him, Beedham turned south and dived with the 109 firing constantly. At about 500 feet the 109 overshot and from five yards range Beedham fired, but only three guns operated; after the first burst only one gun was firing but Beedham continued his attack, pieces flew off the enemy fighter and it dived into the ground, exploding on impact. Due to the damage sustained by his aircraft in this engagement, Beedham had to land at LG 06.

No combat took place on 30 June, the day being largely one of repositioning. As the new line was finally stabilised at El Alamein, the Squadron found itself back at LG 154, near Amriya, after one of the most eventful periods in its history. The ground crews arrived at 10.05 hours, pitched their tents, slept all the afternoon and worked on the aircraft all night, to be ready for strafing the German positions in the morning. During the month, five new pilots had been posted in - Flt Lt P Olver, Fg Offs N Green and D W Beedham and Plt Offs D F Chadwick and J M Cochrane.

The Squadron was back on the edge of the Western Desert and the 8th Army was digging in at El Alamein, still just a little-known railway halt on the North African coast. The retreat was over for the moment - there was nowhere else to go. The Prime Minister told the House of Commons "When we retreated all those hundreds of miles from Tobruk at such speed, what saved us was superior air power". The telegram he sent to Tedder said:-

"I am watching with enthusiasm the brilliant supreme exertions of the Royal Air Force in the battle now proceeding in Egypt. From every quarter the reports come in of the vital part which your officers and men are playing in the Homeric struggle for the Nile Valley. The days of the Battle of Britain are being repeated far from home. We are sure you will be to our glorious Army the friend that endureth to the end."

As Rommel entered Egypt, the Luftwaffe in North Africa was nearing the end of its tether. Its great effort over Bir Hacheim, and the even greater one leading to the fall of Tobruk, had brought it to the point of exhaustion. It was not only combat losses but also the strain of the intensive operations on the crews and aircraft, the serviceability of which dropped catastrophically. Rommel thus decided to continue his advance "without the Luftwaffe". This was not particularly evident to the Squadron's pilots as they continued to be jumped in their now seriously out-performed Hurricanes by the Bf 109Fs of I/JG 27.

Plt Off 'Hindoo' Henderson, Egypt 1941

A Squadron Hurricane IIc, with two of its cannons removed, undergoing first line servicing at Misurata, Libya.

CHAPTER NINE - VICTORY IN THE DESERT

The darkest hour, it is said, comes just before dawn - and the last days of June 1942 were certainly the darkest hours for the Eighth Army. After the defeat on the Gazala Line, the retreat back into Egypt and to El Alamein had at times been near to a rout. That the Army had not suffered greater losses had, as the Prime Minister recognised, been due in no small measure to the close and effective air cover provided by the DAF. The techniques of tactical air support for the Army, worked out by Auchinleck and Tedder in the weeks and months before "Crusader", had not only been proved effective but had also been honed to a state of near-perfection. These techniques were light-years away from Army Co-operation, the old specialist art practised before the war, when Audaxes with sticks fixed to their undercarriages had been used to pick up messages over the notional battlefield. Joint operations now meant the three Services fighting as one, with a joint command structure at all levels. Now the flexibility of the air forces could be used to its fullest effect and maximum power could be switched with the minimum of delay to the point of greatest need.

In the DAF itself, the system of supply and servicing had been transformed in the latter part of 1941 and early 1942. Under the overall command of Air Vice-Marshal Dawson, the systems for the recovery of damaged aircraft and their subsequent refurbishment had helped to transform the supply situation. Serviceability increased as the campaign progressed, rising from 67% for single-engined fighters in the first week to just over 84% in the last week of June. At the time it did not appear that all of this would be enough.

The first battle of El Alamein and the battle of Alam Halfa had yet to be fought and, as June drew to a close, Rommel thought that he would be in Cairo in a matter of a few days. This view was apparently shared by Mussolini, who is said to have sent his favourite white charger out to North Africa so that he could ride it in the triumphal entry parade into Cairo; the existence of this animal was however never verified. The view from Cairo was not much different from Rommel's, and those at Royal Air Force HQ, entrusted with the task of ensuring that important papers should not fall into enemy hands, sought to destroy so many documents that the air became full of charred paper and the day came to be known as "Ash Wednesday".

The line itself at El Alamein, just thirty miles from the sea to the Qattara Depression, had three strong points, El Alamein itself, one covering the Ruweisat Ridge and the third north-west of the Depression. Holding this line were just four divisions, the 50th (Lowland) and 1st (South African) Divisions to the north, and the New Zealanders and 5th (Indian) Division to the south. As the eve of the first battle of El Alamein (fought from 1 July until 22 July) approached, air operations returned to their old intensity, even though the weather intervened on the first two days of July with blinding

Four of the Squadron's long serving pilots. Left to right: Bert Houle, G R S MacKay, "Tigger" Smith and Bill Swinden. Western Desert 1941.

dust storms covering the coastal areas.

The Squadron moved up to LG 39 and stood at readiness all day but the weather prevented any flying other than the move back to LG 154 in the evening. On 2 July, cover was provided for Blenheims bombing the attacking German forces. No enemy aircraft were encountered as the same sandstorms were blowing over Fuka and Daba where the forward elements of the Luftwaffe were located, just ten minutes flying time from the El Alamein positions. The patrol landed back at Idku due to the poor visibility nearer the front.

On the following day, 3 July, the mid-morning sweep over the northern sector of the front line provided a foretaste of things to come on what was to be a black day for the Squadron. Airborne at 10.47 hours, the Squadron was jumped by eleven Bf 109s at 12,000 feet. One was damaged by Sgt H A Aitken, but Plt Off L O H Boucher was missing, Plt Off J M Cochrane had his tailplane shot up and landed at Amriya while Plt Off W Henderson crash-landed thirty miles away at Burg-el-Arab.

The patrol scrambled over the front at 15.35 hours was, in the words of G R S McKay, "a shambles from the start". Concern was expressed at the outset that only one squadron was being used for a predicted Stuka Party. It was clear that the escorting Bf 109s would keep one squadron busy while the Ju 87s went about their work. The CO, who was leading the Squadron with "B" Flight, had R/T trouble and had to pull out, so Temlett with "A" Flight took over. Flt Lt D F Chadwick, leading "B" Flight, provided top-cover. Early into the patrol Beedham had engine trouble and had to return, thus leaving "B" Flight with only four aircraft and the same thing happened to Plt Off W H Thomlinson, thus reducing "A" Flight to five aircraft. Over Burg-el-Arab the patrol was jumped by six aircraft coming out of the sun but as "B" Flight turned to engage, it was seen that they were Hurricanes. However the damage had been done and "A" Flight was now on its own - five aircraft with no cover. When the Flight was jumped by six genuine Bf 109s, the outcome was catastrophic and only Plt Off J E Avise returned unscathed. Flt Lt C B Temlett DFC, Sgts G S Bolton and D C Ritchie were killed, and Plt Off K N R Sissons was wounded in the leg. Four of the attacking Bf 109s were from I/JG 27; Ltn Stahlschmidt claimed two Hurricanes shot down, and Ltns Koerner and von Lieres one each.

The death of "Tem" Temlett cast a particular gloom over the Squadron. He was a cheerful, vibrant character with a mop of red hair, always immaculately dressed - the epitome of the dashing leader, and one of the best pilots. His Flight had such tremendous faith in him that, when he was killed, for a time the bottom seemed to go out of everything. Indeed it seemed that Thomlinson lost all will to live and his disappearance the next day remains something of a mystery.

The main action on 4 July took place in mid-morning when the Squadron was scrambled at 10.17 hours to intercept a formation of Ju 87s; however none were seen and the Hurricanes were jumped by six Bf 109s from I/JG 27 near Burg-el-Arab. In the ensuing dog-fight, G R S McKay and WO R J Wallace claimed one probable each and Plt Offs D R Redhill and W R Thomlinson failed to return.

Later in the month, John Sowrey received a letter from Ken Sissons recovering in No.2 General Hospital, which indicated just what a rough time the Squadron was having and what had happened on 3 July.

P/O Sissons K N R
No 2 General Hospital
Middle East.
21st July

Dear John,
About a week ago a young F/O Walsh of 92 was admitted to the ward in which Boucher and myself are gracefully recovering from a 109 complex. He told me that you had had to bale out again, so I thought that I would drop you a line to say how pleased I am that you fooled the Hun. As you may know Temmy, Ritchie and Bolton were killed on the same show as me. Avise was the only one to get back. I was wounded in the leg but managed to crash land. Butch was put in the same Ambulance as me (he had been shot down earlier in the day along with Hindoo) and we have been together since then. Today I got a letter from Hindoo who is suffering from concussion in RAF Abassia Hosp.

We hope to go to Convalescent Centre together. Thomlinson was killed the day after Tem, and Don Redhill is also dead. Bally was missing when Slater wrote to me on the 16th. I am so sorry about Tem, just before he got it I was chatting to him on the blower and we were dealing very effectively with the Huns. (Originally they were 25+ to our five). Someone straggled and was attacked, I turned to poop at the attacker and unfortunately ran through the bullet stream which was not intended for me. Tem rallied the boys, and the last words I heard him say were "Come on lads, cover Siss, cover Siss". Bolton crashed almost on top of me, and the other two were about half a mile away, flamers. Would like to hear from you John. Butch sends his very best wishes and that goes for me too.

Siss

The news from the front line was however more promising, as Rommel had been forced to give up his attack on the Alamein line after twenty of his tanks had been destroyed by the British armour. A skeleton Advance Party moved up to LG 39 and was held in readiness to move up to Daba. However this proved over-optimistic and everyone moved back to LG 154 two days later. It was now the Squadron's turn to act as host and Sqn Ldr Hartley, who had flown one of the Malta "Faith", "Hope" and "Charity" Gladiators, and six pilots of 134 Squadron, were affiliated. Most of the pilots Hartley brought with him from the UK had been flying Spitfires, and they did not take kindly to flying the Squadron's tired-out Hurricane IICs.

In addition to coming to terms with flying war-weary Hurricanes, the pilots of 134 Squadron also had to learn to

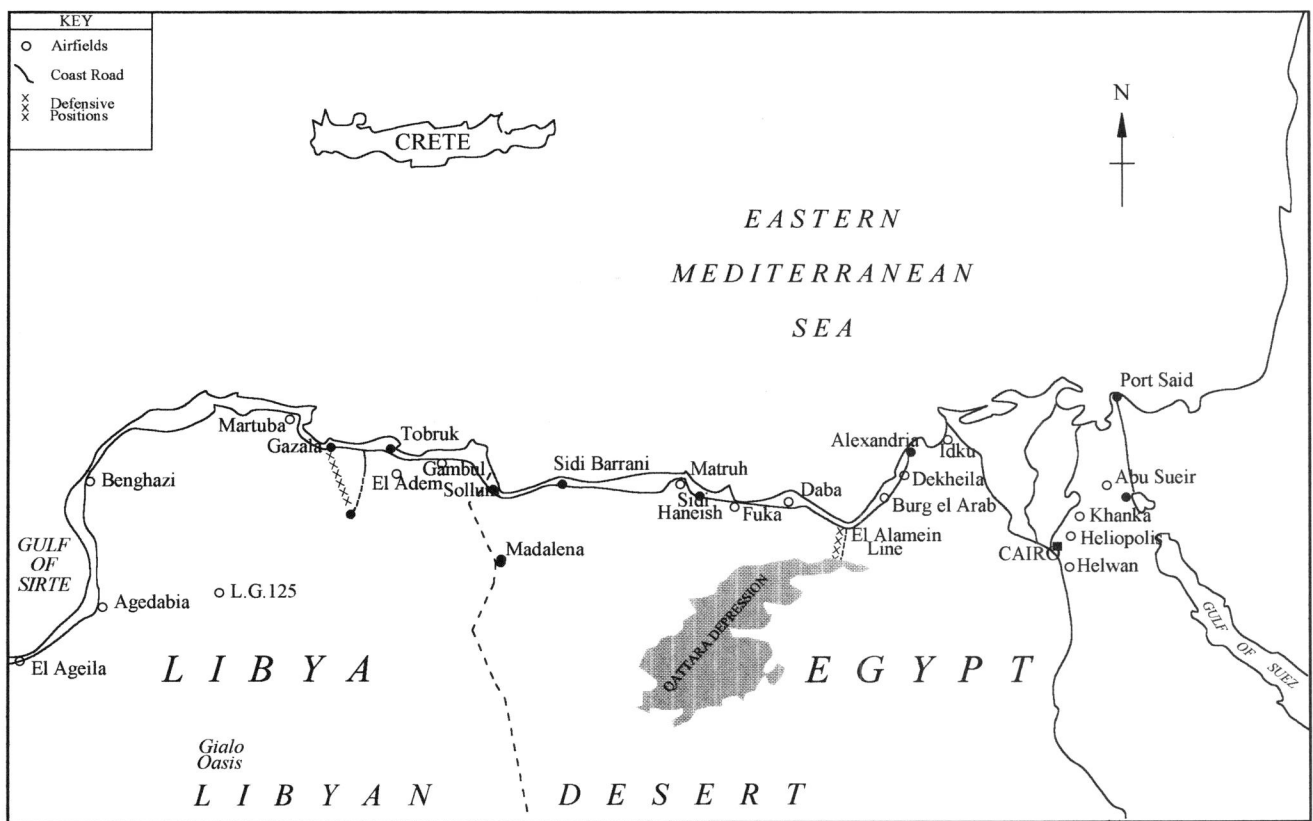

live with other unwelcome facts of life. Not only was there the hard and uncomfortable existence in the desert, but also operational flying took place under particularly disadvantageous conditions. At this time, the Hurricane force in the Western Desert was under a directive to fly at about 10,000 feet, which made it very vulnerable to the German and Italian fighters. The reason for this imposition was that the High Command wanted the Army to be able to see that it was being protected, especially from the Ju 87s. At the same time, the RAF squadrons received very little advanced warning of the presence of enemy aircraft due to the poor radar cover. Certainly the army was protected from the full force of the Luftwaffe's attacks, but the price paid by the Hurricane squadrons was high.

When attacked from above, the invariable tactic used by the Hurricane pilots was to turn into the enemy aircraft while they were still in their initial attacking dive. The engagement then broke up into a series of individual dogfights where the Hurricane's main advantage, its manoeuvrability, could be used to the full. The German and Italian tactics were to dive from above, selecting the rearmost aircraft as a target and then, using their superior speed, climb up again for a further diving attack. With such a large speed differential in favour of the Bf 109 and Macchi MC 202, it was very difficult for a Hurricane to take offensive action.

Additionally the Hurricane IIc had a weapon system that was unreliable in the conditions found in the desert, the 20mm cannons being plagued with stoppages and jamming. There is no doubt that, with more reliable armament, the Squadron's record in the Western Desert would have been even more impressive.

At 09.05 hours on 5 July, eleven of the Squadron's Hurricanes were airborne over the battle area, flying north-east over the westerly El Alamein track, when "bandits" were spotted at 12,000 feet flying south-east along the coast. The CO was leading "A" Flight at 13,000 feet, with "B" Flight led by George Westlake stepped up behind at 14,000 feet. The German formation consisted of two sections of aircraft, four Bf 109s leading four Ju 88s. Mike Young led his flight down onto the rear section, and opened fire from 150 yards; pieces broke off the fuselage and starboard mainplane of his target, but the Ju 88 then broke away and was lost. "Tigger" Smith, flying as Black One, also picked out a Ju 88 but lost it after his initial attack. Bill Stephenson, White One, closed to within 300 yards of a Bf 110, which broke away as he opened fire. He then saw two more Bf 110s flying in line astern. A Hurricane, diving at the leader, was being fired at by the Number Two which Smith then attacked, forcing it to break away and dive down almost to ground level. Closing from 150 to 100 yards, he fired two three-second bursts which caused the 110 to dive as if it was trying to force-land. Stephenson noted that the port engine of the leading Bf 110 had been set on fire by the attacking Hurricane.

As the CO attacked the rear formation, so Westlake led his flight down onto the leading group of Bf 110s. Picking out the lead aircraft, he fired a fairly long burst from fifty yards but saw no result; then, as he was being fired at by the second German fighter, he broke away to port. He soon saw another Bf 110 break away, heading west and diving to ground level; after a chase of five or six miles, during which the enemy aircraft was weaving violently, Westlake fired a steady burst from 250 yards dead astern, setting the port engine on fire. After a second burst, the starboard engine also burst into flames and the aircraft attempted to land; however intense light ack-ack fire opened up and when he was only some twenty yards behind the badly damaged German fighter it was hit and blew up, crashing into the desert.

Sgt J F C Ballantyne was flying as Green Two and, as his radio had packed up, the first he knew of the presence of the enemy was when he saw his leader diving to attack two aircraft half-a-mile away on the port side. As he dived on the last aircraft, he identified it as a Ju 88. It dived away and he followed it down, putting in a three-second burst from fifty yards. The port engine began to give off black smoke, strikes on both wings caused pieces to fly off, and it eventually crashed in flames into the desert.

The midday patrol saw eight Macchi MC 202s flying in pairs line abreast at 17,000 feet, with two more detached off to one side. As the Squadron climbed to attack, the enemy aircraft broke into a starboard turn and then flew off in a westerly direction, taking evasive action. To round off a most satisfactory day, eight new Hurricanes arrived from Kilo 8.

The patrol airborne at 08.45 hours on 6 July observed a big tank battle taking place. It was reported later that the military situation had deteriorated enough to lead to the withdrawal of the advance Party from LG 39. The Squadron was released for training until noon, when the welcome news was received that Boucher, who had been reported missing on 3 July, was only wounded and in hospital in Alexandria.

The day of 7 July was one of violent dust storms, and the first patrol was not airborne until 12.50 hours. Unfortunately the five Italian CR 42s that were intercepted were attacked by 73 Squadron, while 213 was left to deal with the accompanying Bf 109s, an encounter that left both sides even and without losses. The evening sweep led by Wg Cdr Fenton, OC No.243 Wing, returned with nothing to report.

During the first week of July, the DAF had flown 5,458 sorties. The single-engine fighters bore the brunt of this action, and their wastage rate was becoming a serious matter. By 7 July, in the six weeks since the battle along the Gazala line had erupted, no fewer than 202 had been lost on operations. Some of the Kittyhawk squadrons had lost 100% of their original establishment. The appreciation set down by General von Waldau, Fliegerfuehrer Afrika, should be seen against this background:-

"Although the enemy has lost a great many fighter aircraft in the last two months, there has been so far no apparent sign of a decrease in flying ability or combat performance. Combat effectiveness has been maintained, and indeed increased, by the assignment of new and excellently trained Spitfire squadrons from England. The employment of the Spitfires has given the enemy the confidence he needs to hold his own against our Me 109s."

However the Spitfires were still few in number, just over twenty, and it was with aircraft such as the outmatched Hurricane IICs and the Kittyhawks that the unremitting effort of the fighter force was maintained. There certainly was a feeling among the pilots that the Spitfires should be allocated to the squadrons with desert experience, rather than sending complete new squadrons out from the UK. Several planned operations, using the Hurricane squadrons as decoys to be bounced by the Bf 109s or Macchi MC 202s and 205s, which in turn would be bounced by the Spitfires, turned into debacles because the Spitfires were unable to find the rendezvous.

After the first week of July, the greatest danger was over and Egypt was no longer threatened with immediate capitulation. The front line had however by no means stabilised, and the battle still had two weeks to run before Rommel would be decisively held and the retreat from Gazala finally and irrevocably brought to an end.

None of this was immediately apparent on the ground. One of the two daytime sweeps on 8 July met Bf 109s as usual and, during the night, the airfield was attacked by German bombers with incendiaries, which fell uncomfortably close to "B" Flight's dispersal. Two straws in the wind appeared the next day as the Squadron was released in the morning for training, and Alexandria was once again put within bounds.

When the Squadron was based at LG 154, Alexandria was only a two-hour drive away. The contrast between the well appointed rooms of the Cecil Hotel and the dust and flies of a six-man tent in the desert could not have been more marked. A deep debt of gratitude was felt by all of the Squadron pilots to Mr and Mrs Metzger, who ran the Cecil Hotel, for the fantastic hospitality and kindness they showed. While the Squadron was in the desert, they converted one large bedroom in the hotel into a multiple bedroom and numbered it "213"; the furnishings came from Mary's House brothel in Alexandria. Any pilot on leave, or just in Alexandria for a day and a night, could use the room, have breakfast and have his laundry done free of charge. The chances were that they would also have lunch and dinner with the Metzgers.

The first battle of El Alamein consisted of a series of holding and probing operations. These were spread over a three week period as Rommel's advance was first halted, and then the front line stabilised. On 10 July, the 9th Australian Division attacked in the northern sector, precipitating an upsurge in the air fighting. The Squadron flew three sorties that day, at 07.15, 12.55 and 17.55 hours respectively; however only the last saw any action when it was jumped by five Bf 109s, one of which was damaged. It was noted that on the ground the Australians were giving a good account of themselves.

A similar pattern unfolded the next day when again it was only the evening patrol of twelve aircraft, airborne at 19.05 hours with four Spitfires of 145 Squadron as top cover, that saw any action. The patrol found forty plus Ju 87s escorted by Bf 109s but, in the ensuing engagement, the Stukas were not effectively intercepted and managed to make their bombing run. It was noted that "the bomb line which had been seriously dented Alexwards now bulges healthily the other way". Although no aircraft were lost in the actual combat, Sgt Newick "pranged" on landing and Briggs force-landed near LG 30. Personnel changes saw Plt Off D W Beedham leave for 238 Squadron as a Flight Commander, and the return of Bert Houle from his period of enforced penance with the MU.

During the next two days of very bad weather and dust storms, few patrols were flown although the squadron stayed at readiness from 05.30 hours on the second day, 13 July. At this time it was calculated that the Squadron's total for the Third Libyan Campaign was twenty enemy aircraft destroyed, three probables and nineteen damaged, thus putting the Squadron second only to 73 Squadron which had been in the Campaign for a month longer.

The bad weather was followed by a day of extreme heat on 14 July, and no activity took place until the evening. The sweep led by Wg Cdr Fenton was vectored by control onto a formation of twenty-plus "bandits", which was soon joined by a further ten-plus. Still climbing, the Squadron was jumped by the twenty-plus fighters and while the dogfight took place, the ten Ju 87s carried out their bombing attack. No losses were recorded on either side.

On 15 July, Group HQ let it be known that it was not pleased with the results of the sweep carried out the day before, but while an inquest was being instituted the Squadron was redeeming itself in the air. The patrol, airborne at 10.25 hours, met six Macchi MC 202s and four Bf 109s. The four

Fg Off Bert Houle and WO Wally Wallace find an alternative use for the 20mm cannon of the newly-acquired Hurricane IIcs.

Bf 109s were from the redoubtable I/JG 27. In view of the quality of the opposition, the result of the encounter was most encouraging, with Wallace destroying one Macchi and damaging another and Fg Off L E Barnes and Aitken each damaging a Bf 109. Sgt J D Newick who had been attacked by Ltn Stahlschmidt, one of the best of the German pilots flying in North Africa, was wounded and had to force-land a few miles west of Hamman.

The mid-morning sweep on 16 July started badly when one of the Spitfires of 145 Squadron, which was to provide top-cover with 33 Squadron, ran into one of the Hurricanes of 33 Squadron as it was taking-off. The pilots of both aircraft were killed and the runway was blocked. What had happened was that the two squadrons were taking-off from opposite sides of the airfield. No.145 Squadron was supposed to take-off with twelve aircraft and the CO of 33 Squadron thought this had happened, so he rolled the twelve Hurricanes of 33 Squadron into the dust and took-off. Unfortunately only six Spitfires had taken to the air, and the second flight met 33 Squadron in the dust. No.213 Squadron was taking-off at right-angles to 33 and 145 Squadrons and became airborne over the carnage below. It meant, however, that the Squadron patrolled without any top-cover. When jumped by one Macchi MC 202 and one Bf 109, Sgt J F C Ballantyne failed to return; when last seen he had the Bf 109 on his tail.

In the evening six more pilots of 134 Squadron arrived viz.:- Flt Lt L E Price, Fg Off T A McCann, Plt Off G P Waite and Flt Sgts S R Fry, R Griffiths and W D Gwynne. A few days earlier, on 14 July, Flt Lt R M Chatfield had arrived from 73 Squadron as "A" Flight commander. To complete the series of personnel changes three days later, Plt Off D J Thrift arrived from 243 Wing for flying duties.

The next two days provided something of a lull as bad weather and a lack of enemy air activity brought some respite. Just to demonstrate that the normal problems of life continued, a Mess Meeting was called in the evening of 17 July to sort out the bar deficit that had arisen "due to frequent movement and a breakdown in organisation". When the weather did improve on 19 July, 73 Squadron, which was to provide top-cover for the early afternoon patrol, took off before 213 and contact was never made, so two separate patrols were flown, each returning with nothing to report. On the next day, unbeknown to all at LG 154, Mussolini left North Africa and returned to Italy, having grown tired of waiting for his triumphal entry into Cairo.

On 21 July, the first Battle of El Alamein ended as General Auchinleck launched a counter-attack in force in an attempt to push the Germans back to the Egyptian Frontier. This offensive fared badly the following day, and eventually ground to a halt as the Allied forces lost forty out of the one hundred tanks used in the attack. For the Squadron, the two days were ones of great anticipation but little activity. All leave was cancelled on 21 July, but no flying took place until 19.15 hours, when a patrol was flown over the northern sector of the battle front. "A" flight was ordered to be at readiness to move at one hour's notice as from dawn the next day. Nobody knew where the Flight would be going but it was generally believed that it would be in the right direction. The Squadron felt that this was the lull before the storm. Distant rumbles were heard in the night suggesting that the big push had started. However neither of the two patrols flown on 22 July encountered any enemy aircraft, although much ground activity was observed.

In the air, it was not at all apparent that any particularly significant point had been reached in the fighting. The busy day promised by Wing did not materialise and it was clear that the Army's push was not going too well. This made it all the more curious that at 15.00 hours the Advance Party of the Squadron was ordered forward to LG 172, twelve miles from Burg-el-Arab. Two sorties were flown from LG 154 but, while one was jumped by four Bf 109s, no serious action took place.

The next morning, the rest of the Squadron moved up to LG 172 and, after a quick lunch of cheese and bully, came to readiness. The aircraft were scrambled at 15.00 hours, with 33 Squadron as top cover, to patrol the centre section of the line. Two Bf 109s made lunges at the formation and were then joined by another two. Eventually the formation broke up and McKay, finding himself alone, climbed into sun. A 109 came down on his tail and McKay swung round and passed underneath his attacker as he pulled up without firing. Suddenly McKay's port wing and radiator erupted; he had fallen into the old trap of seeing one of a pair but not his wing-man. Thinking he was on fire, he prepared to bale out but as the smoke cleared he saw that he was still being attacked. However, with zero oil pressure, he had to switch off his engine, and so was faced with a most unusual dog-fight, losing height all the time and with a stationary propeller. The attacking 109 gave McKay a final burst before he managed to land, and then strafed the stricken Hurricane on the ground, making eight passes as McKay dodged from one side of the engine to the other. Eventually he was picked up by the Army, and returned to LG 172 by ambulance the next day; as the Squadron Operations Record Book records "not with his head tucked underneath his arm but more or less unscathed". The CO gave him a few days leave in Alexandria to recover, and it was in the bar of the "Monseigneur" that he heard of the "hacking on take-off" suffered by the Squadron on Monday 27 July 1942.

The worst dust storms experienced so far had prevented all flying on 26 July, and the next day things went from bad to worse. At 13.00 hours the Squadron was on Red Alert since an imminent raid was expected. When the Squadron was scrambled, control was completely unaware that a force of Bf 109s was directly over the airfield, having come in undetected behind 33 Squadron on its return from a patrol. "B" flight was first airborne and so took the brunt of the attack. Plt Off T A McCann and Flt Sgt R Griffiths, who had flown with 134 Squadron in Russia in the winter of 1941, were killed together with Sgt J D Newick. Wallace had to bale out and landed unhurt. It was now realised that LG 172 was too near the front line, so the Squadron moved back to LG 154 the next day.

The ground party left at 22.05 hours and arrived back at LG 145 at 12.45 hours on 29 July. Jack Walton just took his ground-sheet and blanket off the lorry and slept in the open, noting that this was the sixty-first occasion on which he had had neither the time nor inclination to put up his bivouac tent. The move back to Amriya came just in time, since the next day, LG 172 was bombed by a formation of Ju 88s from 10,000 feet; in the event the only casualty was one donkey.

The last three days of the month saw little flying as both sides rested and re-equipped, and a quieter period ensued. On 29 and 30 July the Squadron was released to enable work to be carried out on the cannons, which were continually jamming, and on the last day of the month the worst sandstorm to date prevented all flying. The time was however put to good use as the Mess accounts were investigated and to everyone's surprise, instead of a deficit, a credit materialised. On the personnel front, news arrived confirming that Plt Off W H Thomlinson had been killed on 4 July, his aircraft having crashed ten miles west of LG 172. To add to the Squadron's numbers, Sgts K G Brookes and A Garrood arrived from Wing.

August opened with the more than usually interesting rumour that, at an important conference at Burg-el-Arab, it had been decided that 243 Wing was to be rested. This made little difference to the events of the following day when the evening patrol, flown as top cover to 33 Squadron, was jumped by Bf 109s. Twice they dived and then pulled up; the second time the Squadron turned into sun. For some reason one Hurricane was unable to keep up. Immediately it was attacked and went spiralling down and as it tried to pull out, it spun and crashed. At the end of the patrol WO R J Wallace did not return. His loss was deeply deplored, especially because he had been interviewed for a commission only that morning.

The very next day it was confirmed that the Squadron was indeed to move to Kilo 8 for three weeks rest and training; the Advance Party left the same afternoon. There was one last patrol to fly and at 13.25 hours the Squadron was airborne, as top cover to 33 Squadron, awaiting the return of a force of Baltimores, Kittyhawks and Spitfires which had bombed the German and Italian landing grounds near Daba. Jumped by two Macchi MC 202s, R Fry was shot down and force-landed north of El Hamman unhurt, while Plt Off B J Campbell had to land at Burg-el-Arab short of petrol. In the evening, when scrambled to protect some returning Bostons, the patrol was jumped by a mixed force of Macchi MC 202s and Bf 109s. Sgt D J McKay was shot down by a Macchi MC 202 and suffered from burns, although he landed safely.

At 09.00 hours on 5 August the Main Party left for Kilo 8 with the promise of five days leave; on arrival the CO was summoned to Group to have lunch with the Prime Minister. Training continued for the new pilots while the rest departed for Cairo. At this juncture, the Squadron Adjutant, Flt Lt A R Joyce, departed and was replaced by Flt Lt B Webb, who had first joined the Squadron at Tangmere and had stayed with it until Cyprus. As the five days leave drew to an end, news came that twelve pilots were to be fully trained for night duties. With what purpose in view, it was asked? No answer ever came.

During the rest period, a substantial change came over the Squadron, as many of the long-serving members left. Flt Lt G H Westlake, who had been with the Squadron since the Battle of Britain, was promoted to Sqn Ldr and went to take over his own Squadron. In something over two years of flying and fighting, his aircraft had not once been hit by an enemy bullet or by shrapnel; indeed he maintained this amazing record until the end of the war. The Squadron's popular and long-serving Engineering Officer, Fg Off H Barrett-Atkin, also left on a posting to Wing. On 13 August, Wg Cdr Fenton came to lunch, bringing the news that the Squadron was not to go up to Palestine, as the "cook-house" rumours had it, but was to return to the desert. It also transpired that he had been promoted Group Captain and was to take over a Group. Sqn Ldr Hartley and the pilots of 134 Squadron also departed on leave and, although the Squadron went on up to Palestine, many of the pilots returned to 213, and their attachment became an official posting. Contact with the High Command continued on 16 July with a visit from the Air Officer Commanding-in-Chief, Air Marshal Tedder.

The night training was brought to a sudden end on 21 August, as was the three weeks rest period, when the Squadron was ordered up to LG 85, Amriya South. The very next day, 73 Squadron also arrived to begin night operations again, thus perhaps taking over the role for which the

Plt Off G R S MacKay.

Fg Offs Freddie Wilson and Bill Ismay, two of the many Canadian pilots who flew with the Squadron.

Squadron's night flying practice had been introduced. As the Squadron prepared to resume operations, the CO discussed with the pilots the merits of removing two of the cannons to improve the Hurricane's manoeuvrability and performance; with four cannons the Hurricane had a tendency to go into a spin off a high speed turn. It was decided the idea was worth a try, and the outboard cannon on two aircraft were accordingly removed. Subsequently this became the standard operating procedure, although occasionally an aircraft would be fitted with two cannon and two machine-guns.

A warning was given by the Army to expect an attack by paratroops, since the Germans had over four thousand and enough Gotha Go 242s to carry them. To prepare for such an attack at night, the Army laid on a searchlight exercise. Unfortunately the beam was full on just as enemy aircraft were reported overhead. Although the beam was doused two minutes later, bombs started falling. One Squadron aircraft received Cat 3 damage and another Cat 1, three of No.145 Squadron's Spitfires being also damaged; anti-personnel bombs injured eight members of the ack-ack post.

The reason for the shortened rest period and the move up to LG 85 became clear on 24 August when Wg Cdr J Darwen, the new CO of 243 Wing, addressed all the officers and pilots. He revealed that the Germans were bringing up reinforcements, including a whole new division, and that an attack was expected to be launched the next day in the southern sector. The writer of the Squadron's ORB records that "We were all exhorted to show more of the offensive spirit". In fact the Allies had learned through Ultra that Rommel intended to launch an offensive on 26 August. At 11.50 hours the Squadron was scrambled as top cover for 274 Squadron strafing enemy tank carriers, and was told to fly at 10,000 feet. As 274 pulled out of its strafing run it was bounced by four Bf 109s; one aircraft was lost to ack-ack fire and three to the 109s, albeit that all three pilots of the latter aircraft were safe.

To replace the departing George Westlake, Plt Off F A W J Wilson was promoted acting Flight Lieutenant, and took over as OC "B" Flight. Wilson, from Thunder Bay, Ontario, had joined the Squadron in January 1941 at Driffield, and on arrival in the Middle East had gone up into Syria with the 80 Squadron detachment. By August 1942 he had destroyed six enemy aircraft in combat and four more on the ground, as well as damaging three and claiming another probable. In the air, he had shot down a Potez 63, a Dewoitine 520, two Bf 109s, two Ju 87s and a probable Macchi MC 202. As matters turned out, Westlake returned on 31 August to take over as temporary Commanding Officer from Sqn Ldr Young, who had gone into hospital on 27 August with sinus trouble.

The new Wing Commander, Jackie Darwen, was soon living up to his reputation as a forceful leader, and on 28 August he led a two-aircraft recce at zero feet to find out what was going on. The same procedure was repeated the next day. These were two of a series of such patrols which could become very exciting. On one such patrol, G R S McKay remembered that it seemed as if every soldier in the Afrika Korps had fired at him. On 30 August it was announced that 134 Squadron, previously affiliated, was now to be fully incorporated into the Squadron, with the official establishment being reduced from twenty-two officers and

351 men to nineteen officers and 208 men. The day also saw one of the heaviest German raids on the airfield complex lasting for over four hours, with twenty-nine bombs falling near the camp; one of the raiding Ju 88s was brought down.

During August 1942 it was not only in the close-knit world of 213 Squadron that personnel changes were taking place. On 15 August General Sir Harold Alexander replaced Auchinleck as GOC-in-C, Middle East, and Lieutenant General Sir Bernard Montgomery arrived to take command of the Eighth Army. Powerful materiel reinforcements also arrived in the shape of three hundred American Sherman tanks, the type that would prove to be the work-horse of the Allied forces for the rest of the war. Other reinforcements in men and materiel, together with the grave weaknesses in the Axis forces exhausted by their great efforts in June and July, meant that August was something of a turning point in the war in North Africa. The arrival of Montgomery also meant that co-operation with the RAF was put first in the order of priority. He immediately located his HQ alongside that of Air Marshal Sir Arthur Coningham, AOC Western Desert, thus restoring the situation that had obtained before the retreat from Gazala. This time the arrangements remained intact, and indeed were added to, for in future the Army "G" Operations Room and Air Operations Room were always sited adjacent to one another, and maintained a continuous liaison.

All of these changes were put to their first test at the battle of Alam Halfa, which was fought between 31 August and 6 September 1942. This battle was Rommel's last attempt to break the deadlock reached in July. In many respects this little-known battle was the climax of army/air co-operation in the Western Desert. The battle was a classic of its kind, demonstrating the use of air power, on efficient and economical lines, in direct support of the army in the field. Practically all of the offensive operations were carried out by the RAF; the Army, sensibly in the light of previous experience, remained on the defensive. The fighters of the Desert Air Force, twenty-two squadrons in all including ten Hurricane squadrons, three of Spitfire Vs and three of Kittyhawks, cleared the way for the bombers - Bostons, Baltimores and Mitchells. The Wellingtons of No.205 Group, accompanied by the Fleet Air Arm's Albacores, operated at night.

As dawn broke over the desert on 31 August 1942, Rommel's offensive, in the shape of a three-pronged attack against the north, centre and south of the line, began. The first of the Squadron's four sorties on this opening day was a dawn reconnaissance patrol over the southern sector as far as the Qattara Depression. On the return trip, German aircraft were found parked around the perimeter of LG 20; Flt Lt N Green damaged one Bf 109 and Gwynne four others. At 07.00 hours there was a hurried scramble as bandits were reported over the airfield, but in the event none were seen.

The main action of the day was fought at 10.25 hours, after the Squadron was scrambled to intercept a Stuka raid reported just east of El Alamein. Flt Lt Neil Cameron (later Marshal of the Royal Air Force, the Lord Cameron of Balhousie, KT, GCB, CBE, DSO, DFC, AE, FKC, LL D), who had arrived on the Squadron with the first party of 134 Squadron pilots, was leading with Red Section, Plt Off F W J Barnes was above with Blue Section and G R S McKay provided top cover with White Section. Red and Blue Sections dived head-on into the Stukas, while White Section took on the twenty or so Macchi MC 202s and Bf 109s providing the escort. Nine of the Messerschmitts were from I/JG 27, led by Oberleutnant H Marseille and eight from III/JG 53. Nevertheless the Squadron was by now well practised at its tasks and although not scoring any hits, the four Hurricanes of White Section engaged the escorting fighters as Red and Blue Sections made their attack. The Stukas immediately jettisoned their bombs over their own troops and fled westwards. One Bf 109, flown by Oberfeldwebel Kronschnabel, was destroyed by German ack-ack fire and one Ju 87 each by Barnes, Stephenson and Flt Sgt J R Rebstock. Both Barnes, who baled out, and Stephenson were shot down by Oberleutnant Marseille, with "Binnie" Barnes dying later from the burns he received.

On the evening patrol, all but six of the aircraft were prevented from returning to base by a violent sandstorm and the remainder landed at Dekheila. During the day Sqn Ldr G H Westlake arrived to take temporary command of the Squadron until 11 September, when Young returned from hospital. In the course of his service with the Squadron Westlake destroyed nine enemy aircraft with two shared; he also damaged a further three and claimed one probable.

The first three days of September contained the crisis of the battle and saw the complete defeat of Rommel's offensive intentions, leading to his decision to break off the action. For the Squadron, 1 September was a day of intense activity and mixed fortunes.

At 09.15 hours a patrol was scrambled onto fifteen Ju 87s. However Punnet Leader was flying with his hood open and, as he led the Squadron into the attack, his goggles were whipped off and he was blinded with dust from the cockpit. As a result, the attack went in too low and missed the Ju 87s. However, one Section met up with the escorting Bf 109s and Plt Off C D A Smith damaged one. Owing to the dust storms, which continued to hamper operations, the patrol returned to Idku where it was learned that a joint patrol with 33 and 145 Squadrons was to be mounted. In fact 33 Squadron never arrived and only one Flight of 145 Squadron put in an appearance; it hardly mattered though as the patrol, over Burg-el-Arab, returned with nothing to report.

The evening patrol at 18.00 hours, again over Burg-el-Arab, was more successful. The rendezvous with the accompanying Spitfires was made, and the joint patrol then met up with a force of Ju 87s and 88s, escorted by Bf 109s. As the Spitfires took on the escort, the bombers were severely mauled - three Ju 88s being destroyed by Houle, Avise and Waite, and two damaged by Garwood and Sgt W J Steele. At first this success looked costly as five pilots were missing, but eventually three returned, leaving Fg Off R F Wollaston, a former rubber planter from Malaya, killed in action and Sgt F G Potter missing. Garrood had had to bale out and landed unhurt, and Avise crash-landed.

On the next two days of the battle, offensive patrols were flown over the front and on three occasions the Squadron was jumped by German and Italian fighters, not suffering any damage but not scoring any victories. By 2 September it was clear which way the battle was going, when it was seen that much movement eastwards was eliminating the bulge in the line that had been occupied by the Axis forces. The same pattern repeated itself on the remaining four days of the battle, with the last serious engagement being fought on 4 September when the early morning patrol was jumped by five Bf 109s, four of which Houle attacked in succession. The patrol, scrambled at 13.40 hours together with 33 Squadron, took off in the middle of a sandstorm and on landing was scattered amongst five different landing grounds. With timing appropriate to a politician, Wendell Wilkie visited Group on 5 September, with the CO and Flt Lt E Price representing the Squadron at the reception held for him. Back at LG 85, another heavy German raid left three aircraft damaged and

Fg Off A E Houle, a first-class Canadian pilot who served with the Squadron in Cyprus and the Western Desert, winning the DFC.

Flt Lt R M Chatfield who flew as a Flight Commander with the Squadron in the Western Desert.

four airmen injured.

As the battle closed, the Squadron records were checked and it was seen that, having destroyed 133 enemy aircraft while based in the UK and another 54 in the Middle East, only thirteen more were required to reach the two hundred mark - and the justification for a terrific thrash! Prayers were said for a Stuka Party.

The war in the air was finally and irrevocably turning in favour of the DAF. The losses suffered and the months of operating in increasingly outmatched aircraft and under operational handicaps were now reaping their reward. With an increasing degree of air superiority, and with more Spitfire squadrons joining the battle, the strain on the German fighter units was becoming unbearable. A patrol flown on 7 September illustrated a number of aspects of this change. The Squadron, together with 33 Squadron, was escorting a Tac.R (tactical reconnaissance) aircraft, with seven Spitfires of 601 Squadron providing top cover. At 14.50 hours the top cover engaged four Bf 109s of I/JG 27; two were claimed as destroyed, two damaged and one probable. These were no ordinary losses. Ltn von Lieres, who crash-landed, was one of the unit's leading pilots and Ltn Hans-Arnold Stahlschmidt, who was killed, was the third-ranking German pilot of the whole desert campaign. Attrition is a two-edged weapon, and the Axis forces in North Africa were now less able to replace their losses.

As the front line settled down, changes came both on the ground and in the air. On the ground, the days of the Pilots Mess came to an end as two separate Messes were formed - one for the Sergeant Pilots and NCOs and another for the Officers. On 11 September, Sqn Ldr M H Young returned from hospital and resumed command of the Squadron. Also, after a number of protests, the Squadron establishment was increased up to 248, so that many who were scheduled to leave found themselves staying on. It was also felt that there should be a general tightening up of discipline. On 14 September the CO assembled all the Squadron pilots and warned of the serious view that would be taken of the indiscriminate "pranging" of aeroplanes. Culprits would be required to sit in the cockpit until the R&SU vehicles arrived, or would have to walk round the airfield in full flying kit.

By the middle of the month the Eighth Army was preparing to go onto the offensive. This time the advantages lay with the Allies and the plans were carefully laid. In the air, as the armies waited for the next encounter, most of the flying revolved around escorting Tac.R aircraft which were making a composite picture of the German positions, or low-level fighter sweeps against ground targets. Before the end of the month a reorganisation saw Nos.601 and 145 Squadrons leave No.243 Wing to be replaced by Nos.238 and 1 SAAF Squadrons, making the Wing once more an all-Hurricane unit.

On a Tac.R escort sortie on 16 September it was noted that, when jumped by four Bf 109s, 33 Squadron "stooged off" home covering the Tac.R aircraft, but leaving 213 Squadron to deal with the enemy fighters. The CO found himself alone with two 109s and engaged them for twenty minutes; once again the Hurricane's manoeuvrability in the hands of an experienced pilot proved sufficient. Eventually the 109s broke off the engagement and, although Young's aircraft was damaged, he claimed one Bf 109 as damaged also. On yet another escort patrol two days later, Brookes was hit when the patrol was bounced by Bf 109s, and landed in no-man's-land. The race that then developed between a German armoured car and an Allied tank to pick him up was, fortunately for Brookes, won by the tank. By 21 September, after yet another escort sortie with 33 Squadron and 601 Squadron as top cover, it seemed that all the tactical reconnaissance had been worthwhile, since it was announced that the elusive 91st Light Division had been found in the centre section, when it was previously believed to have been up in the north.

The decoy patrol, flown with 33 Squadron on 22 September, produced no enemy aircraft for the covering Spitfires despite radio silence being broken. Nevertheless it ended unfortunately for Sgt W G Sweney, who hit a barrel whilst taxying and duly walked around the airfield in full flying kit. Four days later, the Messerschmitts of I/JG 27 were found once again on a Tac.R escort patrol, with 33 Squadron and 92 Squadron as top cover. The Bf 109 flown by the now-promoted Hauptmann H Marseille broke through the Spitfire screen and shot down Plt Off C Luxton, who crash-landed but returned safely. After remaining at a wearisome "Readiness" all day, Thrift when scrambled at 16.40 hours "pranged" Sgt D C Usher's tail and starboard mainplane, and was therefore obliged to remain in his Hurricane, with only five minutes relief each hour, until midday the next day when his aircraft was made serviceable.

The news that the Wing was to move up to LG 172 was received with mixed feelings. On the one hand it was welcomed as it would put the Squadron closer to any Stuka Parties that developed, but on the other hand it revived the bad memories of 27 July when it had been scrambled directly into the guns of the waiting Bf 109s. The move was made on 28 September, together with Nos 238 and 1 SAAF Squadron, putting the Wing, which also included 33 Squadron, in Gp Cpt Fenton's new No.212 Group. The misgivings over LG 172 were rendered null and void by a series of violent sandstorms, which necessitated the immediate return to LG 85, Amriya South. During the month of September, as the situation on the ground resulted in stalemate, the increasing strength of the Desert Air Force and the continuous combat wore down the strength of the Luftwaffe, and the crack fighter unit, I/JG 27, lost its three leading pilots - Marseille, Stahlschmidt and von Lieres, who between them had claimed over two hundred victories in combat over the desert.

The opening days of the new month saw a continuation of the Tac.R escort duties, and also a succession of sandstorms which prevented all flying on a number of days. However, on 9 October, an Allied reconnaissance aircraft reported the Axis airfields at Daba to be under water and those at Fuka to be scarcely usable due to recent heavy rain. In an effort to take advantage of this situation and destroy the Axis air force on the ground, a maximum effort was made with five hundred sorties being flown against these targets. Seven heavy bomber attacks were launched and many fighter-bomber attacks and fighter strafes. 243 Wing carried out a fighter strafe late in the afternoon.

It was airborne at 16.48 hours, 238 Squadron leading with 213, and 33 Squadron led by Darwen with 1 SAAF; 601 Squadron in its Spitfires provided top cover. Flying in fluid sixes, the whole formation steered a course of 290 degrees for ten minutes to take it out over the sea, then on to 280 degrees for a further twenty-one minutes, taking it behind the enemy front line, while a final short leg of four-and-a-half minutes on a course of 265 degrees brought it back over land. However before landfall was made, contact with 238 Squadron was lost and the Squadron proceeded independently. Once over the coast, scattered transport was seen and, of more consequence, three Bf 109s sporting yellow spinners were encountered flying east at 800 feet. These then proceeded to follow the Squadron, firing intermittently. Their presence raised doubts as to the water-logged state of the German airfields and in fact little evidence of flooding could be seen. Plt Off C F A Cantin, whose aircraft was struggling to keep up, went down in flames. The Messerschmitts were engaged by Cameron, Houle and Gwynne but no claims were made.

Over the target area it proved impossible to identify LG 21, but much heavy black smoke was seen in the area. No aircraft were seen on nearby LG 09, nor any sign of flooding, thus leaving the Squadron to attack targets of opportunity. For the next hour and ten minutes, the area behind the German lines was subjected to a very close scrutiny and numerous attacks were delivered against a variety of targets in the shape of enemy lorries, a staff car, a twin-tailed aircraft with pinkish camouflage (destroyed by Sgt J T Field) and tents. Throughout the time over the target area, intense ground fire was experienced and the CO, Cameron, Usher and Field were all hit but returned safely. Plt Off B J McClelland however was lost when his wing-tip hit the ground and his aircraft crashed. Some one hundred and five minutes after setting out, the aircraft returned to Amriya South, although five aircraft had to land at LG 28 short of fuel. Initially the Wing Commander was also missing, having had to force-land in the desert, but he was picked up there by a party of the 11th (Prince Albert's Own) Hussars. He returned to LG 172 just in time to take part in a Wing debate, which asked the question "Should we show mercy to the Hun?".

During the next two days, the usual rumours which preceded any important event were heard to the effect that Sqn Ldr M H Young was leaving and Sqn Ldr P Olver was coming to replace him. Peter Olver was clearly no stranger to the Squadron; since his first spell of service in June 1942, he had served as a Flight Commander with 238 Squadron. The rumours duly proved correct when the new CO arrived on 12 October, along with 80 Squadron who were old friends from the Palestine days. Their arrival proved less than fortuitous for them as two days later, while still moving in and with 213 Squadron airborne, the airfield was strafed and bombed, leaving 80 Squadron to bear the brunt of the raid.

Suggesting that something was in the air, 15 October was marked by a visit from the AOC, Air Vice-Marshal Coningham, who, after talking to the airmen, then addressed the officers and pilots. The AOC appeared confident of the outcome of the impending battle. The ORB records that "his goal appears to be the complete annihilation of the enemy, the opening of the Med, the capture of Tunis and an attack on Italy as a second front". The next day a visit from Lord Trenchard was expected to "instil a policy of destroying everything German". The major flying effort of the day was an escort, in Squadron strength and led by the new CO, for 6 Squadron's tank-busting Hurricane IIDs.

A Wing parade was ordered for 13.30 hours on 16 October, engendering some debate as to whether or not this was really a good plan. It was considered that, if the Germans were to try such an idea, the RAF would surely seek to intervene. As it turned out, any such intervention was precluded by the sandstorm, which almost drowned

Fg Off W W "Bill" Swinden, one of the many Canadian pilots who served with the Squadron.

Flt Lt N Cameron, who joined the Squadron in the desert from 134 Squadron. Later Marshal of the Royal Air Force the Lord Cameron of Balhousie, KT, GCB, CBE, DSO, DFC, AE, FKC, LL D.

Trenchard's speech but failed to obscure his driving force which came through strongly. The parade was over by 14.15 hours but the sandstorm remained cloaking everything in a yellow cloud reminiscent of a foggy day in London. In the evening, as the wind howled through what the setting sun had transformed into an orange haze and the Mess Tents flapped, the pilots made their way back through the rain, hoping that their own tents would still be standing at the end of what had been a memorable day.

With the sandstorm continuing overnight, Arthur Henry decided to check the moorings and chocks on "his" Hurricane AK-S. Leaving his bivouac, which was pitched close to the aircraft, he made his way to it and checked that all was in order. However so dark was the night and so thick the air with blowing sand that he missed his tent on the way back. After wandering about for a while, and being able to see absolutely nothing, he caught his foot on a cable which he picked up and followed. It duly led him to a nearby ack-ack dugout, where he waited until he could make his way back to his bivouac during a lull in the storm.

To round off the series of visits by the top brass, the AOC-in-C, Air Chief Marshal Sir Arthur Tedder, appeared in the doorway of the Squadron's brand new "Ops" trailer at 15.50 hours on 18 October, together with Gp Cpt Fenton and Wg Cdr Darwen. After the visit it was generally reckoned by all concerned that the AOC-in-C gave a very good informal talk. Only two hours later, while everyone was at dinner, a Bf 109 came in at low level and dropped an anti-personnel bomb, filling the air with shrapnel and persuading everyone to flatten themselves on the ground. A couple of minutes later the raider returned - and the rat-tat-tat of his machine guns echoed from the other side of the airfield. The raid concluded with another anti-personnel bomb on the next-door camp which injured two airmen.

On 19 October, the Desert Air Force opened its air offensive prior to the impending Allied ground offensive. The Squadron, together with 33 Squadron, was patrolling the front line and, fifteen miles east of Alamein, was attacked by Bf 109s diving from above; no losses were suffered and Smith claimed one damaged. After a quiet day on 20 October, the next day brought heavy cloud cover which generally limited operations but the Squadron was in action early on. At 09.30 hours a patrol was flown as top cover to 33 Squadron, which was providing close escort for a Tac.R aircraft. Nine Bf 109s of II Gruppe were scrambled to intercept and three were engaged. No claims were registered and Plt Off W H Stephenson was shot down by Lt Kientsch near Daba 1.

Later in the day, news came that the Wing had been ordered up to LG 172 at Burg-el-Arab, some five miles from the front line. Leaving at 11.15 hours, the Squadron's Advance Party arrived by 15.00 hours, later to be joined by 238, 33 and 1 SAAF Squadrons - but not the Aerodrome Control Officer who was to direct the squadrons to their operating areas. The Advance Parties thus spent an uncomfortable night in their vehicles until Fg Off McSwene was finally located the next day and the Squadron established itself on the north side of the field. By the time Darwen flew in to see how the move had gone, the slit trenches were dug and everything was ready for the Main Party, which was still at LG 85, Amriya South. In the evening George Westlake dropped in for a chin-wag. By 18.30 hours on 23 October 1942 the Squadron, along with the rest of 243 Wing, was in residence at LG 172, Burg-el-Arab. Among a number of changes made by the new CO was the restoration of the Pilots Mess. At 21.40 hours more than one thousand guns of the Eighth Army opened fire in the greatest barrage since the First World War, all along the thirty-five miles of the front line. The second battle of El Alamein had begun.

Although not clear to those involved at the time, the tide had in fact turned and would carry the fighting all the way across Libya to the final defeat of the Axis forces in Tunisia. The men and materiel resources of the Allies would continue to grow, whilst those of the Axis partners would slowly but inevitably ebb away. The first signs of this change came in the air. The air superiority gained at Alam Halfa was now fully established. On some patrols over the battle front, the only aircraft seen were other squadrons of the Desert Air Force. When Bf 109s and Macchi MC 202s were encountered, they frequently made only one diving attack before breaking away or avoided combat altogether. Finally, on those occasions when combat was joined, the presence or early arrival of a Spitfire squadron tilted the balance.

On the opening day of the battle, 24 October 1942, the Squadron flew three sorties. At 08.00 hours twelve aircraft patrolled the front east of Daba, with 33 Squadron as top cover, which engaged the only enemy aircraft seen. At 11.05 hours when the second patrol was carried out as top cover to 238 Squadron over the northern sector of the front, six Bf 109s came in from the east, made one pass and then disappeared. The evening sortie, scrambled at 18.20 hours to patrol ten miles west of El Alamein, saw only two other Hurricane formations. On the ground, the opening attack by the infantry of 30 Corps, which was to clear a way through the enemy minefields for the armour of 10 Corps, had become bogged down in front of Kidney Ridge and on the flank of Miteiriya Ridge.

With dominance in the air well and truly established over the battle front, and passing trade thus reduced to a minimum, a more ambitious operation was launched in the pre-dawn of 26 October. Six aircraft, led by "Borneo" Price, set out to strafe LG 104 near Daba. Airborne at 05.50 hours, and without navigation lights, the formation lost contact with each other and only one aircraft, flown by "Lucky" Luxton, made it to the target area only to suffer from the old problem of having its guns jam. The remaining aircraft attacked targets of opportunity, and Flt Lt S P V Bird shot up a Ju 88 on the ground. Many early morning fires were seen, and the breakfast preparations of at least one German were disturbed as he was shot up on the beach.

In the evening a more elaborate stratagem was planned to attract some business, when Intelligence reported that Ju 87s would be coming over at dusk in the belief that the Allied fighters would have landed. At 17.35 hours the CO and G R S McKay took off on a decoy patrol, flying up and down the line deliberately breaking radio silence. Indeed considerable chatter was generated to give the impression that the whole of 213 and 238 Squadrons were airborne, McKay chipping in with a variety of English, Canadian and Australian accents. Eventually one of these calls told the story that he was running short of fuel and the CO gave the order for the formation to land, which it did at 18.20 hours. Ten minutes earlier, the remaining twelve aircraft of the Squadron together with 238 Squadron led by the Wing Commander had taken off. The only slight hitch in the operation was that the Stukas managed to drop their bombs before they were intercepted. The interception was finally made as the light was fading fast and the Stukas were seen low-down flying west. Darwen and Carrick destroyed one each, but the real success fell to "Bert" Houle, one of the best pilots to fly with the Squadron, who destroyed two, damaged another two and claimed one probable.

By the evening of 26 October, the forces on both sides had come to a standstill. 1 Armoured Division was still halted in front of Kidney Ridge but had successfully beaten off a German counter-attack the previous day, while in the south 4th Light Armoured Brigade had run into mines and heavy anti-tank fire, and 13 Corps had gone onto the defence. Only the South Africans and New Zealanders managed to make some ground on Miteiriya Ridge; apart from this the great offensive was stuck.

On 27 October the morning patrol, flown as top cover to 238 Squadron, encountered no enemy aircraft. In the afternoon enemy aircraft were reported ten miles west of El Alamein and the Squadron was scrambled at 15.45 hours, with 33 Squadron as top cover. Initially no contact was made and the patrol turned west along the coast at 14,000 feet towards Daba, where more enemy aircraft were reported. In earlier days Hurricane pilots might have been a little dubious about flying so far behind the German lines, but now enemy aircraft were pursued wherever they could be found. "B" Flight was leading and, as the flight leader had had to return early, the whole Squadron was led by Plt Off C D A Smith, an unprecedented state of affairs. G R S McKay finally reported bandits at twelve o'clock and below, and Smith led the formation over the top of the enemy aircraft and down into the attack. The target was twenty-four CR 42s in six vics of four flying line astern, escorted by eight Macchi MC 202s at 15,000 feet and five miles away to the south. As the CR 42s dived away, G R S McKay claimed one destroyed and one damaged, Luxton claimed one damaged and Smith and Sweney one probable each. When the Squadron returned to base, the CO was understandably annoyed that the whole enemy formation had not been destroyed, given the favourable circumstances, and that the escorting Macchi MC 202s had been successfully intercepted by 33 Squadron. After the formation had broken up under the first attack, it proved incredibly difficult to stay on the tail of a CR 42 long enough to fire an effective burst. Once having jettisoned their bombs, these biplanes twisted and turned all over the place, and some even tried to come in on the tails of the Hurricanes. For once the roles were reversed and the advantage in manoeuvrability lay with the enemy. Flt Sgt S G Brooks failed to return from this encounter, and it was later heard that he had been captured and was a prisoner-of-war.

The land battle remained at stalemate as Montgomery reorganised his forces and Rommel flew back from sick-leave in Austria to resume command of the Axis armies. The fighting showed once more the superiority of defence over attack, with 21st and 15th Panzer Divisions suffering heavy losses in further attacks on 1 Armoured Division around Kidney Ridge, attacks which reduced their petrol stocks almost to zero.

After a quiet day on 28 October, when the only flying was a sea search carried out by two aircraft, the next day saw more action. At 13.00 hours the Squadron was scrambled as top cover to 1 SAAF Squadron west of El Alamein at 10,000 feet. Initial contact was made with four Bf 109 bombers, which quickly dropped their bombs and headed off westwards towards Daba. The next engagement was with eight Bf 109s when, after the initial contact, a dog-fight ensued with no

Plt Off L E "Binnie" Barnes who was shot down and killed 31 August 1942.

results on either side. The fight was brought to a premature end when a Spitfire squadron came in from the east at 14,000 feet and the 109s made off in the opposite direction. Later six Macchi MC 202s were seen but, before combat could be joined, they dived away using their superior speed to escape.

At 17.00 hours in the evening the Squadron was airborne, with 1 SAAF Squadron as top cover, east of El Alamein at 15,000 feet. Usher spun from 13,000 feet down to 300 feet, before strafing some lorries. Two Bf 109s coming in from above dived away before the rest of the Squadron could attack, while a further eight Bf 109s made several passes before they too broke away and flew off westwards.

With his initial attack stalled, Montgomery conjured up a new plan on 29 October, with the code name "Supercharge". The attempts to break through in the north would be halted, but with enough pressure maintained to hold the German 29th and 90th Light Divisions in place. Meantime the New Zealanders of 30 Division in the centre would open a gap right through the Axis defences to enable 10 Corps to pass through into open country.

By the last two days of October, while diversionary attacks and counter attacks took place on the ground as the Allies reorganised for "Supercharge", the outcome of the fighting in the air was clear. Four patrols were flown over the battle line with 1 SAAF Squadron, but no contact was made with enemy aircraft nor was any ack-ack fire encountered. On both days the patrols commented on the number of friendly aircraft seen. The pattern varied only slightly as November opened. At 07.10 hours on the first day of the month, the Squadron led a patrol, with 33 Squadron, as top cover but again no contact made. Just after midday, with the CO leading and 33 Squadron again as top cover, the Squadron was scrambled over El Alamein. No contact was made initially, and then the patrol was attacked by three Bf 109s, which quickly dived away into cloud. The Squadron gave chase but, although diving in pursuit at 380 miles per hour, the Messerschmitts could not be caught. As the weather deteriorated, with eight-tenths cumulus cloud from three to ten thousand feet, the aircraft were recalled.

The early morning patrol on 2 November saw twelve aircraft flying top cover for 1 SAAF Squadron west of El Alamein, while on the ground below "Supercharge" went into operation. Flying north at 10,000 feet, the formation was attacked by six Bf 109s; however after the initial turn-about, they departed westwards when a squadron of Spitfires appeared. At 11.00 hours a patrol of the battle area, with 1 SAAF Squadron as top cover, encountered no enemy aircraft. Below, in the centre of the line, the New Zealanders had broken through the mine-fields and the first defensive line, but an armoured screen prevented 1 Armoured Division from making the final break-out into open country. The last great tank battle of the desert campaign took place in front of Tel El Aqqaqir, when the overwhelming numerical superiority of the Allied forces finally prevailed, and by the evening Rommel had decided to withdraw.

In the northern sector of the front, the Australians were still maintaining their pressure on the German 164th Division. At 15.40 hours twelve aircraft were scrambled as top cover to 1 SAAF Squadron over Sidi Abd-el-Rahman, where the Australians had reached the track leading west, when control reported twenty plus bandits approaching from the west at 17,000 feet. The enemy formation was seen initially by White Section at twelve o'clock, moving round to nine o'clock eight miles away on an easterly heading. This information was passed to Wombat Leader, the call-sign of 1 SAAF, as the Squadron climbed to engage the enemy formation of twenty Ju 87s, with an escort of Bf 109s flying 3,000 feet above. As action was joined, the vulnerability of the Stuka was once again confirmed; the CO claimed one destroyed, one damaged and one probable, Usher one destroyed and Carrick another, while Luxton and Sgt. R W Jones each claimed probables and Aitken another damaged. Bird claimed a Bf 109 as a probable. It was agreed that the day's work had ended on a most satisfactory note, particularly as all the Squadron's aircraft returned to base

As the armour of 10 Corps and the medium bombers of the DAF continued to batter the anti-tank screen, which was still holding up progress in the centre, a lull came over the rest of the battlefield on 3 November. The main air activity in the latter part of the day was concentrated against enemy transport moving west along the coast road. Thus, after an early morning scramble to intercept a reported force of Stukas that made off before they could be engaged, the Squadron was airborne again at 13.35 hours, with 1 SAAF Squadron as top cover, to strafe anything moving on the road east of Daba. A repeat performance at 16.10 hours by eleven aircraft led by Cameron, as top cover to 1 SAAF Squadron, returned without Luxton and Aitken. Luxton had been hit by ack-ack fire after attacking a staff car and a lorry, and had crash-landed among the 2/24 Battalion Australian infantry. Although his aircraft tipped over on landing, he escaped with nothing worse than scratches to his face and a swollen jaw.

Aitken's troubles started when he attacked a lorry from 20 feet. It exploded in a ball of fire, which he was unable to avoid and which first rocked his aircraft and then threw it upwards a further two hundred feet. While struggling to regain control, his aircraft was hit by anti-aircraft fire; oil and glycol streamed into the cockpit and over the windscreen, temporarily blinding him. From about 100 feet he was just able to make out that he was still over land. As his engine began to give clear signs of failing he switched off and made preparations to force-land. Then, realising that he might still be over enemy territory, he switched back on and was relieved to hear the engine pick up straight away as he dropped even lower and headed for the coast through a hail of small arms fire, which confirmed his worst fears. Once over the sea and safe from further ground fire, the main problem continued to be his damaged engine, which threatened to fail completely at any moment. As it was obviously going to be necessary to force-land sooner rather than later, Aitken turned towards the coast and, after parallelling the shore for a few moments, his engine finally cut out completely. Landing on the beach, he grabbed the code card from the cockpit and dived for the nearest slit trench, still sure he was in German territory. Shelling had commenced as soon as he landed although, unbeknown to him, this came from Australian troops putting up a protective barrage. As darkness fell, he returned to his aircraft, removed the water bottle and struck out eastwards. Exhausted after several hours travelling, he finally saw some figures outlined against the sky and, still uncertain of his position, he hid once more in a slit-trench and dozed fitfully until dawn. Finally a cry of "What's for breakfast, George?" positively identified the figures in greatcoats as Australian infantrymen, and Aitken was soon sharing what there was for breakfast.

On 4 November 1942, the second battle of El Alamein drew to a close. The hard-won break-out was finally achieved as 51st (Highland) and 4th (Indian) Divisions cleared the anti-tank screen, allowing 1st Armoured Division to break out into the desert beyond. In the south, the New Zealanders and 7 Armoured Division broke through and 10 Corps set off after the retreating Germans, leaving 13 Corps to round up the Italian troops who had been left without supplies or transport. Rommel ordered a general withdrawal to Fuka where the next stand was planned. On this day the Squadron flew only one patrol, at 15.35 hours as top cover for 238 Squadron, when it was scrambled over Ghazal Station some twenty miles west of El Alamein. The formation was attacked by three Bf 109s, which dived in to attack from astern. As ever the Squadron turned into the attackers, who drew off westwards after only one pass, and all the aircraft landed safely at 16.25 hours.

No operational flying took place on 5 November as the Squadron prepared to move forward. In the middle of the morning, the AOC-in-C Air Chief Marshal A W Tedder suddenly appeared in the doorway of the Ops Trailer with Wg Cdr Darwen. He spoke quietly and confidently and put everyone at their ease. He also delivered a special pat on the back for 213 and 238 Squadrons for the part they had played in the recent air fighting.

The next morning Darwen, Olver and G R S McKay took off to reconnoitre LG 105 near Daba. It proved to be flooded by the heavy rain that had turned the whole of the desert in the war zone into a quagmire, and the Squadron's aircraft remained at LG 172 for a further day. The ground party arrived at El Daba on 6 November, having camped the previous night in a wadi. Given the water-logged state of the airfield, which had been in use by the Luftwaffe until two days previously, the party moved on a further two miles, and camped near the road to be ready for an early start the next morning.

On 7 November 10 Armoured Division was ordered to advance on Mersa Matruh along the coast road, but made slow progress in the face of an effective rear-guard action fought by the German armour. The Squadron's progress towards LG 20, Qotafiya I, was hampered more mundanely - but just as effectively - by the heavy traffic clogging the road westwards, and by nightfall the Main Party was only two to three miles past El Alamein. It was already noted however that the Spitfire and Kittyhawk squadrons were well ahead in the race westward. By the next day the forward elements of the Eighth Army had reached Mersa Matruh, where Montgomery was to establish his Headquarters. The Squadron's main party finally made it to LG 20 by 08.30 hours, having started at 06.00 hours, indicating an improvement in conditions along the road.

On the airfields around Daba, the scale of the Allied victory and the precipitate nature of the German retreat could be clearly seen. At LG 20, there were eighty-seven German aircraft, disabled Bf 109s and Ju 88s as well as serviceable aircraft abandoned through lack of fuel, all over the airfield. At nearby LG 104 over one hundred aircraft littered the field. The German aircraft recovery system obviously could not compare with that of the DAF, which on the retreat to El Alamein had left only two of the Squadron's aircraft behind.

While sections of two aircraft patrolled the line from the airfield to Maaten Bagush from 09.30 hours until 14.00 hours, the remaining aircrew and groundcrew spent the day picking up supplies and souvenirs left behind in profusion by the retreating Germans. Particular care had to be taken for booby traps, and although many chances were taken few casualties resulted. Motor-cycles, trucks, revolvers and rifles, all the things that would attract interest, were the main items booby-trapped. At times the airfield sounded as if it was still near the front line with the sound of machine-guns, rifles, revolvers and even a twenty-five pounder shooting out to sea. The more adventurous took the caps off Italian red-devil hand grenades, which they then threw over the cliffs. Bert Houle picked up a Mauser rifle, which he kept for some time afterwards and which, on quiet afternoons, he would take out into the desert for target practice. Any further flying was limited by rumours of another move the next day and by eight aircraft being fitted with long-range tanks.

On 9 November, two patrols were flown over Matruh by the aircraft fitted with long-range tanks in order to protect the minesweepers clearing the harbour, while another pair of aircraft carried out a patrol designed to prevent a Fieseler Storch from picking up some encircled German Generals. In the afternoon the Main Party set off for LG 101 outside Sidi Haneish, which was littered with yet more abandoned German aircraft. The roads were blocked by German and Italian soldiers making their own way to the wire-fenced compounds where they would be fed. Some drove to the compounds in their own transport, others stopped passers-by on the road and asked to be taken prisoner. They were in the main a pitiful, beaten and disillusioned group wandering aimlessly in the desert looking for food and shelter. For the Allied forces, who had known the bitterness of defeat and now the elation of victory, morale was sky high.

A Squadron Hurricane, fitted with long-range tanks, prepares to taxy out at LG 125, November 1942.

CHAPTER TEN - A VERY SPECIAL OPERATION

On 11 November the Squadron aircraft left LG 20, Qotafiya I, west of Daba, and flew up to LG 13, Sidi Haneish South, a satellite of LG 101. In the evening, the CO gathered the pilots together and gave them the first news of an highly unorthodox operation to be mounted far behind the enemy lines in the best traditions of the DAF. The intention was to establish a secret base deep inside enemy territory from where the routed Axis forces could be most effectively attacked. To some of the pilots it sounded like a "suicide do", and they went away from the briefing not knowing what to think. Letters home were written saying not to worry as everything was alright, but that this might be the last letter for some time.

"Operation Chocolate", although that name was hardly known to the pilots taking part, was perhaps the most celebrated and audacious special operation carried out by the Desert Air Force during the North African campaigns. Those involved in the operation were awarded a clasp to the Desert Star campaign decoration. It was a simple but carefully-conceived plan to disrupt the German retreat from Benghazi to the regrouping point at El Agheila. Down the eastern side of the Gulf of Sirte, and round the broad sweep where the coast once again swings westward, vast quantities of German and Italian transport were in orderly retreat. Just east of El Agheila itself, the coastal road runs through an area of salt pans and marshes, thus restricting all traffic to the narrow ribbon of the hard-surfaced road. While this section of road was well out of range of the fighters based on the airfields immediately behind the front-line at El Adem, strikes could be flown from an old landing ground deep in the desert, some 145 miles south-west of Tobruk and well inside Axis-held territory. The plan was to base two Hurricane squadrons, experienced in ground strafing, at this landing ground for a short period to mount surprise attacks against the retreating German columns.

At a joint briefing with 238 Squadron the chosen pilots - Sqn Ldr P Olver, Flt Lt N Cameron, Fg Off R H Furneaux, Fg Off C D A Smith, Plt Off B J Campbell, Plt Off G Carrick, Plt Off A U Houle, Plt Off P A Knapton, Plt Off G R S McKay, Plt Off G P Waite, Flt Sgt H M Compton, Flt Sgt J T Field, Flt Sgt G A Wilson, Sgt R V Baxter, Sgt R J Breheny, Sgt D J McKay and Sgt D C Usher - were told that eighteen of the Squadron's aircraft, together with eighteen from 238 Squadron, would make up the strike force. One of the Squadron's Hurricanes would be flown by Wg Cdr J Darwen, who would lead the operation. The whole unit, commanded by Gp Cpt Whiteley, DSO, DFC, who had operated from the desert strip some years before, was to fly down to LG 125 escorting the Hudsons, which would carry nearly everything the party would require for its brief stay, including plentiful supplies of ammunition. Some of the groundcrew, together with supplies of petrol in four-gallon cans, would make the journey in the backs of open three-tonners. When sufficient destruction had been inflicted on the retreating Germans, or the risk of detection and an attack on the airfield became too great, the party was to withdraw to LG 101.

The next day at LG 101 everyone going on the trip was busy testing his aircraft, especially the long-range tanks that had now been fitted to all eighteen Hurricanes. Some stores and rations were also flown out and dumped at LG 125. Those pilots not going wore faces long with disappointment, and spent the time seeking to persuade someone that they should go. The CO would lead the Squadron, and of the two Flight Commanders one would be Cameron, and the other Houle, who was standing in for Price, ill in hospital with jaundice. In the evening, as the loading of the Hudsons and Bombays continued, some of the pilots paid a visit to their counterparts in 274 Squadron, who had a supply of beer and with whom G R S McKay's brother, who had spent a short time with 213 Squadron earlier in the desert campaign, was serving.

Even before the preparation of the aircraft for the operation had started, the Long Range Desert Group had carried out a reconnaissance of the area and the RAF's No.2 Armoured Car Company had been selected to provide ground support. This unit traced its origins back to the Armoured Car Companies, founded by Lord Trenchard between the wars to control the Bedouin Tribes in Iraq. No.2 Company was commanded by Sqn Ldr Casano, who had been in one desert or another for many years, and who knew the Libyan desert especially well. At 12.15 hours on 11 November 1942 his company received its orders to proceed to a secret forward landing ground well behind the enemy lines; the Company moved off at 12.30 hours. The "wire", the border between Egypt and Libya, was crossed at Fort Maddalena on 12 November, and the armoured cars arrived at LG 125 at 12.00 hours on 14 November. Immediately a defensive screen, some fifty miles from the landing ground, was established to observe hostile air or surface forces.

Early on the morning of 13 November, the selected pilots ate their breakfast largely in silence, and hastily stowed their bedding into their Hurricanes - some also found some space for a few bottles of beer. At 09.20 hours the eighteen Hurricanes, together with same number from 238 Squadron, took off and formed up as escort to the Hudsons carrying some of the groundcrew. Among these was Sgt R.M.McHugh, in charge of the Armament Party, who had joined the Squadron, on transfer from 238 Squadron, just before El Alamein. Others, including Arthur Henry, had already set off in open three-ton lorries, surrounded by the universal four-gallon cans of fuel. One of the major problems was clearly going to be navigation, since LG 125 was in reality just another piece of desert marked out by a few old rusty oil drums. In theory it was easy to locate; the key was to fly west-south-west to two conical sand dunes in an otherwise level expanse of sand, and from there a course of 030 degrees for twenty miles would bring the aircraft over the landing-ground. This route south-west was much too far inland for any signs of war to be seen and, as the aircraft flew deeper and deeper into the sandy wastes, there were no eyes to mark their passing. The Squadron pilots' hope was that the navigators of the Hudsons also knew the key to finding their destination.

After some two hours flying, without seeing any other aircraft, the whole formation was circling over the landing-ground. The Hudsons landed first, and then the fighters went in when and where they could. Here yet another virtue of the Hurricane showed itself, as with its wide-track undercarriage it was possible for it to operate from virtually any expanse of flat hard sand. The surface at LG 125 in fact consisted of compacted small round stones about the size of a small finger nail, half-white and half-black. Once on the ground, the first task was to disperse and refuel the aircraft from the four-gallon drums that had been quickly unloaded from the Hudsons. With their aircraft unloaded, the pilots of the Hudsons refused a hastily-proffered cup of tea, took off and departed rapidly for the "right" side of the front line.

One member of the groundcrew was assigned to each aircraft and the pilot assisted him with the refuelling. This was carried out in some cases with the aid of a stirrup-pump, originally designed to put out fires in the Blitz. Even with the ingenious aid of this device, it still took sometime to transfer over one hundred gallons from the drums into the Hurricane's tanks. The next task was to dig slit-trenches to provide some protection in the flat desert, which afforded no natural cover itself.

Immediately after a quick lunch, Darwen called the pilots together to brief them for the first sortie. The two squadrons, flying in independent sections of four aircraft, were to hit the coast road at seven points between Benghazi and El Agheila. The positions were marked on the maps, and vectors and distances drawn in. Radio transmission switches were not even to be switched on and under no circumstances whatsoever was the R/T to be used, whether it was a matter of life or death or not. After strafing the road, the aircraft were to keep to absolute ground level before heading for home, so that the Germans could not plot their line of flight and thus find the landing-ground.

Houle's section, consisting of McKay, Compton and Carrick, was first away at 13.45 hours, flying in loose formation at ground level. After about an hour's flying the landscape became greener. Then, in the distance, the German lorries could be seen - hundreds of them rolling along the road heading for safety behind the El Agheila line. The section hit the road about ten miles north of Agedabia and then turned north, following the road along the coast, weaving from side to side and shooting up any targets that presented themselves. As soon as a few vehicles were knocked out, a pile-up occurred and that gave the Hurricanes a field day. There were big six-wheeled lorries, jammed with troops and packed so tightly that only a few managed to escape before the cannon shells tore into them. Then both Houle and McKay spotted a Fieseler Storch flying at low-level down the road towards them. As the aircraft banked, McKay thought it was the barrel of a large gun being elevated to shoot at them. He soon saw that it was the wing of an aircraft banking and his first reaction was "109s - this is going to be difficult". He then quickly realised that it was a Storch and went after it at full throttle. He noticed that he had had only one gun firing after his last attack and therefore made due allowance. He was therefore gratified when, having fired only six rounds, he saw strikes on the engine and cockpit causing the Storch to fall away and crash underneath him. Following this interruption, both Houle and McKay went back to shooting-up the stranded transports. There was virtually no return fire, at least nothing to worry about. When their ammunition was exhausted, the section turned for home and found the landing-ground without too much trouble.

The section led by Cameron had a somewhat more eventful trip. Its target was also the coast road in the

Wrecked German aircraft, He 111s, Ju 87s and Bf 109s, litter Derna airfield

Agedabia area. For about forty-five minutes the aircraft flew low across the desert in loose formation. Then, approaching the target area, the aircraft closed up and, with about ten miles to go, Cameron took them down to 200 feet so that the radar at the nearby Agedabia airfield would not pick them up. A certain amount of ground fire was being experienced and, as the aircraft descended, one Hurricane flew straight into the ground. As the section approached the road, gunsights were switched on and the firing button on the control column put to 'Fire'. Soon targets appeared in profusion - the retreating vehicles of the Afrika Korps were nose to tail along the road. Attacks were launched on groups of vehicles, and soon explosions turned into fires. It was never wise to go back for a second attack and so the flight turned north where further soft-skinned vehicles could be seen. Anti-aircraft fire, particularly from heavy machine-guns, was now criss-crossing the sky and a further aircraft was lost. As ammunition was now exhausted or very low, Cameron turned to starboard back into the desert, breaking radio silence for one call, to commence the journey back to LG 125. Fortunately it was a clear day, and navigating by dead reckoning, he brought the remaining aircraft of his section safely to the golden sugar-loaf landmark which was the distinguishing feature close to the airfield when approaching from the west.

The CO, leading another section, hit the airfield at Agedabia just as six CR 42s were taking off. The hand of the Italian section leader was raised to signal the take-off as Olver pressed home his attack through heavy ground fire. The hits scored on the leading aircraft caused it to swerve, and the remaining aircraft ran into it destroying or damaging each other. Smith destroyed another CR 42 in the dispersal area.

The only damage suffered by the section occurred when the CO, while strafing the road through a cutting, was suddenly confronted by a line of telegraph poles as he crested the ridge. Too late to take avoiding action, he felt his starboard main-plane strike one of the poles and it sliced through the metal skin as far as the main-spar. The aircraft twisted to the right and with his wing-tip almost on the ground, it took all his strength to keep the Hurricane in the air. This he managed to do, but on returning to base he had to land his aircraft at high speed to prevent it diving into the ground, since it was inclined to stall at one hundred and eighty knots. Apart from this all the aircraft returned safely.

Back at LG 125, after all the sections had returned to their camp in the desert, a buoyant spirit and a great feeling of comradeship reigned, dimmed only by the loss of "Burt" Campbell and "Gordie" Waite, both of whom it later transpired had become prisoners-of-war. After an evening spent digging-in and being briefed for the following days operations, some of the pilots slept in their cockpits, while others spread their bedding on the open desert floor.

The next morning, 14 November, the CO led twelve aircraft, operating as two flights, on another attack on the airfield at Agedabia. As the Squadron approached the airfield at approximately 09.30 hours, a Savoia Marchetti S 79 was seen orbiting above the eastern LG at 400 feet and Cameron, who was leading the second flight, was ordered to deal with it. This he did in an head-on attack, firing an eight-second burst which set the central engine on fire and caused the bomber to crash into the desert. Once over the airfield, six CR 42s were seen on the tarmac, and a further three neatly arranged in line abreast in the dispersal. One was just beginning to taxi when Peter Olver sprayed all three of them on the first sweep across the field. He scored a direct hit on one of them, which exploded so violently that his aircraft was engulfed in the flames that shot up from it. The other CR 42s, already damaged in the CO's attack, were destroyed in the explosion. During this attack his port long-range tank exploded. When he finally returned to base, his groundcrew told him that his Hurricane had been hit by five different-sized projectiles. Attention was then turned towards the airfield buildings and installations, after which the formation swept across the town shooting up troops relaxing in the main square. On the landing ground to the west of the road, the CO damaged a Ju 87B, while Furneaux and Smith destroyed another CR 42. Having passed over the complex of landing-grounds and the town, the CO's flight continued to strafe the main coast road for a further ten miles, knocking out over thirty vehicles. Over the airfield there was intense anti-aircraft fire and the two flights separated, each of which then had an eventful and protracted return to LG 125.

Having used all of its ammunition, the section led by the CO turned into the desert for the return trip. As the aircraft flew on, the sky became overcast and the desert turned a uniform grey. The weakness of using a distinctive coloured dune or patch of sand as a turning point then became apparent. With the dead reckoning time for the return flight passed, fuel running low and still no landing ground in sight, Olver selected what looked like a suitable piece of desert and put his Hurricane down without mishap. Soon the rest of the section were safely down also, but exactly where nobody quite knew. As he stepped out of his aircraft, Knapton nearly trod on the skeleton of a dead gazelle and wondered if he would be like that in a few days time. In fact the six aircraft had landed approximately fifty miles north-north-west of base.

The flight of six aircraft led by Cameron was also having some difficulty in finding the distinctive dark belt of sand that was the key identification point. Even before the difficulties with navigation arose, the return flight had had its problems. As one of Cameron's wing-men came abreast of him after turning into the desert, he could see that his port long-range fuel tank was on fire. The Hurricane was leaving a trail of smoke across the desert but the greater danger was that the fire would spread to the main fuel system and that the aircraft would explode. Fortunately, before Cameron had to decide what advice to give, an explosion in the burning tank blew it off the wing and the aircraft continued to fly, though with what damage nobody knew. With this crisis over, the problem of finding LG 125 remained. Again, with no landing ground in sight after the dead reckoning flight time had expired, Cameron instituted a square search - still nothing. With the fuel state now low, he decided that the only thing to do was to turn north in the hope that they would cross the front line of the advancing 8th Army, and be able to refuel at one of the forward landing-grounds. The aircraft that had been on fire appeared to be flying satisfactorily, so the section set off with Cameron hoping that, even if they missed the front line, they would hit the coast somewhere near Tobruk if they had enough fuel. A little height was gained to improve visibility, the fuel mixture was set to weak and the engines were throttled back to conserve fuel. The flight had now been airborne for around four hours instead of the planned two. Then, after some anxious minutes, the coast appeared through the desert haze and the aircraft struggled into one of the recently-captured Gambut airfields, after being airborne for four hours and ten minutes. The aircraft that had been on fire was a write-off.

At LG 125 the morning wore on, and no returning aircraft appeared. Reason had it that the aircraft must be lost; it was impossible for a whole squadron to be wiped out, wasn't it? Midday came and went with still no sign of any aircraft. At 14.35 hours Darwen and Houle set off to search the desert for the missing aircraft, flying out to Giarabub, then along the Egypt/Libya border as far as Fort Maddalena and so back to base, returning after a two-hour flight with no sign of the missing formation. Shortly after landing a dust cloud appeared on the horizon and Houle set off to investigate; it turned out to be Sqn Ldr Casano and his armoured cars arriving to set up their protective screen. Two aircraft of 238 Squadron had also set out on a search patrol, and fortunately had located the six Hurricanes that had landed in the desert. Almost simultaneously, four of the aircraft led by Cameron returned from Gambut. At the same time, literally out of the blue, one of the six Hurricanes of Peter Olver's flight flew in. The Hurricane's gravity tanks had been filled from the long-range tanks of the other five aircraft. Once airborne the pilot had made radio contact with a South African armoured column moving up to occupy the landing ground at Martuba; the column had given him his correct position and from this he had been able to make his way back to base. Out in the desert the remaining pilots settled down for a bitterly cold and uncomfortable night. A number of aircraft passed overhead and concern arose that the landing-ground had been captured by German parachute troops.

During the flight back from Gambut, Cameron had begun to feel a little apprehensive about the reception he might receive after becoming lost. He was therefore surprised and a little relieved to find that the CO's flight had also had a small navigation problem. At 09.10 hours the following day, with full fuel tanks and equipped with the ubiquitous stirrup pumps, he took off again with Baxter to ferry fuel out to the aircraft in the desert. All the aircraft finally returned at 11.50 hours after an unduly protracted sortie.

At LG 101, all that was known of these events out in the desert was the news brought back by Breheny to the effect that Cameron had destroyed an S 79, and that Campbell and Waite were missing on the first sortie. The next day, Bird and Sgt R W Jones set off with Breheny for LG 125 via Gambut to bring the detachment back up to full strength.

On the morning of the third day of the operation, 15 November, the first sortie, airborne at 09.00 hours, consisted of six aircraft led by Darwen on a strike against the Axis airfield at Gialo Oasis. This was some 150 miles due south, deeper into the desert on the edge of the Great Sand Sea. After only forty miles had been covered, Darwen spotted a dust cloud and went over to investigate. He identified five vehicles towing four field guns, which were attacked and immobilised, two being completely destroyed. The Germans had little chance against the cannons of the six Hurricanes. Further in the distance other dust clouds could be seen, and a further four armoured cars were spotted. Unfortunately these had to be left unmolested owing to the lack of ammunition. On the section's return to LG 125, Darwen's initial plan was for Casano's armoured cars to go out and mop up the remnants of the German column, and pick up prisoners. However, owing to the distance - sixty miles - and the rough nature of the ground to be covered, this plan was held to be impractical. It was decided that the column could more easily be destroyed from the air, and Darwen quickly organised relays of aircraft to attack the armoured cars. This resulted in the complete destruction of the entire column.

With this task accomplished, Houle took off at 11.35 hours with the six available 213 Squadron aircraft flown by Carrick, Compton, Furneaux, Wilson and Sqn Ldr J N

A Squadron Hurricane prepares for start-up, LG 125, November 1942.

Young, to complete the strike against Gialo. Soon the aircraft were flying over steep sand dunes, rising up two hundred feet and stretching as far as the eye could see. The oasis at Gialo was easy to find but the airfield was more difficult to identify, and the section was right overhead before Houle saw it. Surprise was complete, and the mechanics continued to work on the aircraft as the Hurricanes swept in from the desert. Houle destroyed one Cant Z 1007 and badly damaged another. One pilot noted that, as he fired at a parked aircraft, a mechanic was still wiping the windscreen. When the attack was over, burning wrecks were all that was left of the few Cant Z 1007s, Savoia Marchetti S 79s and a Ju 88 that were being worked on. One Savoia was destroyed by Carrick and another by the combined efforts of Furneaux and Wilson. Young destroyed a Ju 88, which blew up violently, killing the mechanics who were still working on it, and he also destroyed two other aircraft believed to be CR 42s. A column entering the oasis from the east was also attacked, resulting in two motor vehicles being destroyed and three immobilised. The surrounding desert was literally covered with dispersed armoured cars so the Hurricanes, experiencing virtually no return fire, carried out target practice until all the ammunition was exhausted. When the section returned with the news of the plentiful targets, a further visit was planned for the next morning, which was to be the last day of the operation.

Even as the section was taking off for the first strike on Gialo, Smith was airborne on his way to Western Desert HQ to obtain permission for the two Squadrons to withdraw, as it was felt that the element of surprise had been compromised. When Smith was in AVM Coningham's operations trailer, some photographs taken by a photo-reconnaissance Spitfire were brought in, and soon comments were being made on the dislocation being experienced by the retreating German columns near El Agheila. Smith was able to explain exactly what 213 and 238 Squadrons were doing.

While the aircraft of 213 Squadron were directing their attention to the airfield at Gialo, 238 Squadron set off to repeat the attack on the Benghazi-Agedabia road. However, on the way to the target, an Italian column of over fifty vehicles was spotted some sixty miles from LG 125. This was in fact the retreating garrison of Siwa Oasis, although from the air it looked like a column advancing on LG 125. It seemed as if the security of the operation was compromised, and that this column had been sent to deal with the intruders. 238 Squadron abandoned its attack on the road and set off to deal with the column. Other aircraft, still on the ground at LG 125, were called to join in the attack and soon that column no longer existed. However, finding it in the desert, apparently on its way to attack the landing-ground, appeared to have been a stroke of luck. Everyone spent a restless and vigilant night waiting for another possible attack. Time it was thought was clearly running out.

Just before dusk, the arrival of the ground party coincided with the warning from the observer screen that nine bombers were approaching from the west at 9,000 feet. The vehicles were rapidly dispersed and four of the Squadron's Hurricanes were scrambled on a defensive patrol, but no enemy aircraft were found. Nevertheless the report was taken to be an augury that the lack of any enemy interference had run its course. Consequently, although it caused some regret amongst the newly-arrived ground party, the decision was made to withdraw the next day.

Permission was given for the withdrawal after a further strike against the airfield at Gialo on the morning of 16

November. This was carried out by ten of the Squadron's aircraft led by Darwen, without meeting any serious opposition. Once again there were few aircraft on the ground, but considerable amounts of transport and many very surprised troops. It seemed possible that the oasis was the HQ of an enemy long-range desert group. Thirty miles north-west of Gialo, a large stationary column of five hundred motor vehicles was observed and strafed; the vehicles with red strips laid across their bonnets, suggesting they were carrying casualties, were not attacked, but sixteen other vehicles were destroyed and eleven knocked out.

While the aircraft were away at Gialo, the camp at LG 125 had been packing up. By the time the aircraft from Gialo had returned, the two Hudsons that had flown in earlier in the day had already left, escorted by Furneaux and Usher. After refuelling, the last thirteen serviceable Hurricanes (one was left behind with a glycol leak) were airborne at 12.35 hours, together with 238 Squadron, escorting eight more Hudsons carrying the personnel and equipment not returning with the ground party. The formation landed at LG 101 at 14.20 hours.

So the special operation was over, and it had been a resounding success. It was estimated that one hundred and thirty-eight lorries and armoured cars had been destroyed, one hundred and seventy-three damaged, as well as fifteen aircraft destroyed or damaged on the ground and two in the air. The Squadron's score-sheet was:-

Pilot	Aircraft destroyed	Aircraft damaged	M/T destroyed	M/T damaged
S/L Olver	3 x CR 42	Ju 87	6	13
S/L Young	Ju 88			
	2 x CR 42			
Flt Lt Cameron	S 79		1	3
Plt Off Houle	Z-1007	Z-1007	4	12
Plt Off McKay	Storch		1	11
Fg Off Smith	½ CR 42			3
Plt Off Carrick	½ SM 79		1	8
Fg Off Furneaux	½ CR 42		4	6
	½ SM 79			
Plt Off Knapton			1	3
Flt Sgt Compton			6	
Flt Sgt Wilson	½ S 79			9
Sgt Usher			2	14
Sgt Baxter			4	7
Flt Sgt Field			3	4
Sgt MacKay			2	
Sgt Breheny			3	
Total		12 2	32	99

The Squadron's losses were three aircraft and two pilots; a total of seventy-five sorties was flown excluding the flights to and from LG 125.

The success of the operation was due not only to its daring concept and the enthusiasm of the pilots, but also to the Trojan efforts of the maintenance crews who, under the supervision of Flt Lt Barratt-Atkin, the Wing Engineering Officer - and working against great odds - maintained a unique standard of serviceability. Bird, Jones and Breheny never did return to LG 125 as, while they were waiting overnight at Gambut, Gp Cpt Fenton told them that the operation was being closed down and they duly flew back to LG 101 on 16 November.

At LG 101, while there was little Hurricane flying with the bulk of the aircraft away, a new type was added to the Squadron's establishment. Among the many destroyed and damaged aircraft littering the airfield there was S7+LL, a Ju 87D-1/Trop, the latest model Stuka, abandoned by 3 Staffel /SG G3 in the middle of an engine-change, with the new engine, the more powerful Jumo 211J, standing alongside waiting to be installed. The Germans had developed a system whereby every pipe and connection was marked by a colour that corresponded to the part to which it had to be joined; thus the skilled and experienced groundcrews found it possible to complete the engine-change on this new foreign type. By 16 November the Stuka was serviceable, the engine was run-up and, after taxying around for a short period to gain a feel for the machine, Plt Off H A Aitken took off for the first flight at 14.10 hours. Coincidentally, while he was in the air, the Squadron aircraft approached the field on their return from LG 125; not surprisingly, they gave the Stuka a very close inspection before coming in to land.

To the surprise and dismay of those who had worked so hard completing the engine change, when the Stuka landed oil was pouring from every part of it and there was a strong smell of fuel. Larry Flowerdew, the Squadron Engineering Officer, went over every inch of the fuel and oil system, and announced to everyone's surprise that no leak could be found. Drawing on his three terms of studying German at school before the war, G R S McKay announced that he would translate all the instructions relating to the various controls. After some intensive study of the mysteries of the Stuka's fuel system, the problem was solved. The engine drew its fuel from the main tanks but, on long flights, these could be topped up from reserve tanks in the wings. Thus the fuel leakage was explained; the already-full main tanks were being topped up from the reserve tanks. Once the controls for this operation, which were beside the main fuel controls, were re-set, the overflow was cured.

Later the Luftwaffe markings were painted out and RAF roundels, together with the Squadron identification letters AK, were painted on the side, followed by a large question mark instead of the individual aircraft letter. In the weeks that followed many of the pilots flew the Stuka, but with the new "type" in their log-book, they lost interest; not so G R S McKay, who was a Stuka enthusiast from the start. The first point he noticed, the same as on his first trip in a Spitfire later on in the year, was the light touch required on the controls, which induced a tendency to over-control. Visibility from the cockpit was excellent and the whole aircraft suggested power and strength. Once in the air the aircraft's excellent flying qualities were evident; it was fully aerobatic, and could be thrown around like a fighter. For the Squadron it proved to be a very useful, go-anywhere, do-anything communications aircraft.

McKay completed nine trips in it in December, totalling about three hours, while in January he amassed 15¼ flying hours, including the Squadron's move from Martuba to Misurata, and in February another 15½ hours. February's total included a 6½ hour trip covering the 1,300 miles back to Alexandria to collect a load of bar stocks. The return trip took an extra hour due to the four refuelling stops that had to be made, instead of the three necessary on the outward leg. In March, McKay's last month with the Squadron, he flew the Stuka for 8½ hours, including acting as a target for section attacks and carrying out mock dive-bombing attacks on the airfield to give the Bofors gunners some practice. As a result of his dedication to the Stuka, McKay was universally known for his last months on the Squadron as "The Baron". The Stuka registered some 250 hours in all, flying between the desert airfields and Alexandria, ferrying pilots going on leave and bringing back crates of beer and other necessities for the Squadron. Once all the armour-plating had been removed, the performance was considered very reasonable.

Much of the work on the Stuka was carried out by Arthur Henry and Des Goldswain, who were McKay's regular groundcrew, servicing his Hurricane AK-S. As such they had occasional flights in the Stuka. On one occasion, after having spent the morning painting the underside of the Stuka yellow to ensure recognition by ground forces, Henry was airborne in the rear cockpit with McKay at the controls. Realising that the Stuka still had German camouflage on the upper surfaces, Henry was shocked when he saw a Spitfire approaching from above and behind. His concern was all the greater as there was no communication between the front and rear cockpits. Fortunately the Spitfire pilot realised that this particular Stuka was no longer a part of the Luftwaffe and flew on. The Egyptian anti-aircraft guns around Alexandria always fired as it approached the town, but as they were always so far off target they were ignored. The Stuka not only provided a link with civilisation, but it also proved good for morale. Peter Knapton remembers flying back from a week's leave in Alexandria with Larry Flowerdew, the Squadron Engineering Officer, in the gunner's rear cockpit, and with either Aitken or MacKay as the pilot. Once having found the aircraft's ignition key, which was a usual item on German aircraft and which had been left behind in the Cecil Hotel, the troubles really started after becoming airborne. Notwithstanding the fact that the Ops Room in Alexandria had been informed that a "friendly" Stuka was about to take-off, this did not prevent an anti-aircraft barrage from being let loose. Having survived this, when abeam Gazala, the Greek squadron based there took a "dirty stab" at the intruder and, as the oil pressure was dropping fast, a landing was made. Neil Cameron, who was now commanding the Greek squadron, commented on the three white faces peering out of the cockpit windows as the Stuka taxied in. Flying in an enemy aircraft was clearly an acquired taste, particularly with a hangover.

On 17 November the aircraft flew to El Adem, the Squadron's new base, which the ground party reached at 19.30 hours after three days and nights on the severely flooded road, to be greeted by a bomb which fell only one 150 yards from the Armoury. This badly battered airfield had changed hands a number of times during the fighting in the desert, and the walls of the buildings were covered in English, German and Italian graffiti. In the afternoon, while waiting for the ground party to arrive, a number of the pilots visited the nearby town of Tobruk to see the effects of the many bombs dropped on it while the Allied forces were encircled there.

With the road north of Agedabia now in range, a series of raids was arranged. Darwen flew to HQ Western Desert to advise against it. The reason for the objection was clear. It was a cardinal rule never to follow another aircraft while on a strafing run and, as importantly, never to follow one raid with another over the same route. However the planners were adamant and, despite the CO's objections and Darwen's advice, the orders remained. The first attack was launched by 33 Squadron and they were met by Bf 109s and a heavy barrage of ack-ack fire, which caused a number of casualties including their CO. The omens were not good and ten minutes after 213 Squadron's Hurricanes had taken off, the raid was cancelled, but too late.

Twelve aircraft were airborne at 10.30 hours and flew on a course of 250 degrees for an hour, when they saw the water tower at Saunnu. The road was crossed ten miles north of Agedabia and immediately between forty and fifty motor vehicles were seen. Olver, leading, blew up a three-tonner and four others behind it before damaging a Ju 87 parked on the airfield. In two flights the Squadron passed either side of the town, encountering intense fire from the Breda guns. Seeing one aircraft go down, Olver went over to see if he could land and pick up the pilot. From the frantic hand signals, he realised that this would not be advisable as the Hurricane had come down in a minefield.

Hardly had the attack begun when Bert Houle heard one of his section say that he had been hit and was going down. Houle took a shot at a lorry, and then telephone lines appeared right in front of him. Frantically he pulled back on the control column in an effort to miss them. The next thing he knew he was at five hundred feet over the airfield at Agedabia West, right in the box of the ground defence anti-aircraft guns. He see-sawed his aircraft down to ground level, turned east, took another shot at some transport and found himself in the box over Agedabia East. Shells were pouring at him from every direction and he could hear them striking his aircraft. More frightened than at any time in his life, he expected any minute to be hit himself. Flying as low as he dared, he put the throttle through the "gate" to escape as quickly as possible. Suddenly he was clear and he immediately checked the aircraft's instruments, fearing that his engine might not have fared as well as he had. Sweat was pouring from him and his hands were shaking on the controls from the terrific strain. He was alone and all was in order with his aircraft so, keeping as close to the ground as possible for comfort and safety, he flew the 200 miles back to base. After Houle had landed, the groundcrew were amazed that his aircraft had been able to fly back from the raid. Although the wheels came down for the landing, the airframe was so badly riddled with bullet holes that it could not be repaired.

Of Houle's section of four, Compton and Baines were missing, and Thrift's aircraft had received almost as rough treatment as his own. Of the other eight pilots on the raid, Luxton and Rebstock were also missing. Baines and Luxton were prisoners-of-war and Sgt J R Rebstock died of wounds in a German field hospital near Marble Arch while being taken to the rear. His grave was discovered when the Squadron's ground party moved up to Misurata in January 1943.

Harry Compton's troubles started when his Hurricane was hit by anti-aircraft fire. Oil and glycol poured into the cockpit and he reckoned that he had only about ten minutes flying time left. Immediately he turned east and, once over the desert, pumped down his undercarriage and force-landed at about 12.45 hours. Carefully he removed the desert rations, which consisted of one tin of bully beef, one packet of biscuits, two bars of chocolate, one jar of water and the emergency rations, from the aircraft. Then taking the Very pistol and some cartridges, and after destroying the IFF equipment, he set off with the aid of a small escape compass and a silk map. During the night it rained heavily, which added to his discomfort but eased his water problem. It continued to rain all of the next day and he saw three aircraft pass overhead, as well as a staff car and some armoured cars driving by, all of which he avoided. Once more it rained heavily during the night. He started walking again at first light and saw some vehicles in the distance. On this his third day in the desert, he stopped walking earlier in the day and made a shelter in which to pass the coming night. Nevertheless, after a few hours sleep, he still woke up and had to move about to keep warm. Once more he set off and travelled north all day, not seeing any vehicles until the evening, and these he once again avoided. On 21 November, while travelling NNE, he saw some Kittyhawks flying east and apparently following a track, towards which he began to make his way. At 16.00 hours he could make out dust plumes thrown up by vehicles on the track, which he finally reached at 18.00 hours. His water was finished and all he had left from his rations were two biscuits and a Horlicks tablet. He had also run out of cigarettes. As he approached three stationary vehicles parked by the side of the track, they started to move off westwards and he fired his Very pistol. The vehicles stopped and three men dismounted and came towards him, one carrying a rifle which, at approximately one hundred yards, he raised and pointed in Compton's direction. In the circumstances he decided to give himself up. The man with the rifle turned out to be Staff Sergeant Jack Turner of the RAOC, who thought he was dealing with a stranded German soldier due to Compton's blond hair. After four days in the desert, Compton had been picked up some thirty miles east of Msus.

While Harry Compton was slowly making his way back to El Adem, Houle had been sent back to Alexandria by the CO to arrange with Mr and Mrs Metzger for the purchase of the Squadron's Christmas turkeys and other festive provisions. After two days in the comfort of the Cecil Hotel, he set off back to El Adem from Aboukir. Having left all the ammunition behind, he had been able to load his Hurricane with ten cases of canned beer, 4,300 cigarettes and numerous special parcels for the other pilots. Much of the beer was stowed in the mainplanes where the ammunition was normally carried. There was insufficient room for cases of beer and the bottles had to be packed separately. For weeks after Christmas, while the groundcrew worked on AK-S they were liable to find loose bottles of beer. The airmen at Aboukir bet him that the Hurricane would not fly. Nevertheless it did, and two hours twenty-five minutes later he had covered the five hundred miles back to El Adem, having stopped at Sidi Haneish to refuel and collect five new pilots and aircraft, who were on their way to join the Squadron.

At El Adem, the only flying involved the familiarisation trips carried out by the new pilots - Plt Off C H Phipps, WO Hoffreins and Sgts Steward, J E Oliff, RCAF and P T Temple-Murray. The next day saw a Wing Parade to say goodbye to Wg Cdr Darwen, who was handing over 243 Wing to Wg Cdr Burton. The Squadron also said goodbye to Sqn Ldr J N Young who left for 244 Wing; Jackie Young had come up from Rhodesia, where he had been an instructor on Tiger Moths, for a short attachment to the Squadron. He had wanted to do some operational flying "in case his son asked him what he had done in the war". Fg Off Bert Houle was also leaving to become a Flight Commander on 145 Squadron, flying Spitfires with 244 Wing, Wg Cdr Darwen's new command.

On 25 November the Squadron moved up to the landing-grounds at Martuba, finally settling in at Martuba No.2, where the ground party arrived on 29 November. Another era in the Squadron's history was coming to an end; the air-fighting over the El Alamein battlefields, and the special operation from LG 125, marked one of the most intense periods of fighting in the Squadron's history. The Hurricane, for all its fine qualities, was becoming seriously outclassed as a pure fighter aircraft, and was withdrawn from the front-line fighting as more Spitfire squadrons came out from the UK. From its entry into the air-fighting in the Western Desert, the Squadron had played its part in securing and maintaining aerial superiority. The Stukas and Ju 88s of Fliegerkorps Afrika had never been able to disrupt the operations of the 8th Army, either in attack or retreat, as the medium bombers of the Desert Air Force had disrupted those of Rommel's Afrika Korps. This was the true measure of aerial superiority.

The cost however had been high, particularly among the single-engine fighters. Throughout the whole of the Squadron's time in the desert, its Hurricane IICs were outperformed offensively by the Bf 109s it met in combat. Certainly the Hurricane was more manoeuvrable and more ruggedly built, attributes that were exploited to the full, but which left its pilots largely on the defensive, as did the tactics pursued by either side.

In carrying out the role of protecting the army fighting below, and remembering the criticism at Dunkirk, the Hurricanes invariably flew at about 10,000 feet so that they could be seen. Their role was to command the air from the ground upwards and this they did up to 10,000 feet, where the German 88mm anti-aircraft gun was least effective. However this left them well below the high-flying Messerschmitts.

On the other hand, the favourite mission of the German fighter pilot was the "Freie Jagd" - the free hunt - in which a small force of Bf 109s flying in pairs at over 15,000 feet, swept the sky looking for targets below. Once a formation of Hurricanes was seen, the Messerschmitts would dive down, the lead aircraft firing at the chosen target, for preference a lone damaged Hurricane, prior to pulling up again for another attack. All the time they maintained as high a speed as practical as a measure of self-preservation, but at the same time becoming tight on their ailerons. When bounced, the Hurricane pilots turned 180 degrees into their attackers, turning gently to starboard if the attack was coming from above, as it invariable was, and from the right. Then, when the attacker was nearly in firing range or had started firing, on the order "Go" the gentle turn was reversed, and the Hurricane thrown into as tight a turn as possible in the opposite direction. While the Bf 109 attempted to follow, invariably overshooting and was still scrambling for height, the Hurricane pilot had his chance with his cannon. The Hurricane IIC with its four cannon had a tendency to spin off this turn and slow to the point of a stall, and it was for this reason that the outer two cannon were removed. Particularly in the later stages of the campaign, the Bf 109s would not enter into a dog-fight where they were at a disadvantage.

It should be remembered that the experience levels of the German pilots rose rapidly, since they were not rotated to other duties after a tour, as were the RAF pilots, but remained in the desert with perhaps only a short leave break.

The hardships faced by both sides were the sand and the climate - adverse conditions which certainly affected the performance of the Hurricane. In anything but a new aircraft, it was common practice to fly with the hood open to improve visibility since the perspex windshield became almost opaque from the effects of the driven sand. However the abiding memory for the majority of those who fought in North Africa was the spirit and camaraderie, equally among both air and ground crew, for which the Desert Air Force has become a byword.

Plt Off R Jackson poses in front of Hurricane IIC, AK-A, Idku, October 1943. (A Thomas)

CHAPTER ELEVEN - A WAITING GAME

A glance at the map immediately makes it clear that the position of the Martuba landing-grounds is particularly advantageous for shipping protection duties. Here the Libyan coast sweeps farthest north, forming a funnel with the island of Crete some two hundred miles away to the north. In December 1942, the Germans made their determined stand at El Agheila in an effort to keep the 8th Army out of Tripolitania and Tripoli itself. Once again the Allied forces were operating at the end of over-long supply lines. The bases and supply dumps of the Delta had been left a thousand miles to the east. The problems of supplies - petrol, ammunition and food - had perhaps more than anything else slowed the momentum of advances in the past. "Crusader" had come to a stop at the Gazala Line. Rommel's last effort had failed at El Alamein far from his supply dumps and the port of Benghazi. This time the momentum was not going to be allowed to die. Supplying the front line over the rough desert roads was costly in both vehicles and petrol, neither of which could easily be spared from the fighting along the front line. If convoys could pass unscathed along the North African coast from the ports of Egypt to Tobruk, Benghazi and later Tripoli, the problems would be largely solved. The war in the desert had always been largely a war for supply lines and the army with the best-protected lines was bound eventually to triumph. The Squadron was now to be part of the aerial umbrella that covered those vital sea routes.

By the beginning of December the Squadron was well established at landing ground Martuba No.2, where it had arrived on 25 November. Wg Cdr Burton visited the airfield on the second of the month, and dashed many hopes when he suggested that re-equipment with Spitfires was a somewhat unlikely event. As the year drew to a close amid numerous difficulties, almost daily patrols were flown over a continuous stream of convoys, each with its more or less exotic code name, proceeding to and from the port of Benghazi. Long hours were flown with little reward. Fg Off Thrift and Sgt Steward escorted a Hudson from El Adem to Soluch and flew back without landing, a round trip of three hours thirty minutes. Heavy rain rendered the landing grounds unserviceable on numerous occasions, and aircraft passing through on their way up to the front, or returning to Egypt, depleted the already limited stocks of petrol. Life consisted of uneventful shipping patrols, scrambles after elusive bandits and rain and mud.

Four days before Christmas the news was received that the CO had been awarded the DFC. However this was quickly followed by the less welcome news that he had been posted to command No.1 SAAF Squadron, which had recently been re-equipped with Spitfire Vs, and which he left to join on 29 December. The New Year thus brought not only a new Commanding Officer in the person of Sqn Ldr V C Woodward, DFC, but also a new command, when No.243 Wing moved forward with the Army to Beda Littoria and the

The Squadron Stuka, captured at LG 101, November 1942.

The Squadron Stuka airborne.

Squadron came under the control of Air Headquarters Egypt. The new CO, who came from Victoria, British Columbia, had first arrived in North Africa in May 1939, straight from No.6 FTS in the UK. Flying Gladiators with 33 Squadron, he scored seven victories over the Libyan front, largely against CR 42s of the Regia Aeronautica following the entry of Italy into the war in June 1940. The award of the DFC for his part in this fighting was not gazetted until 9 May 1941, by which time he had moved with the squadron to Greece and then on to Crete. In June he fought with the reformed squadron in the air fighting supporting Operation "Battleaxe". His tour with 33 Squadron ended on 11 September 1942, from which time he served as a flying instructor in Rhodesia, until his return to North Africa to take command of 213 Squadron. It was not until almost the end of his time with the Squadron that the Bar to his DFC, for his activities in Greece, was gazetted. As CO, he normally led "B" Flight in the air, with "A" Flight being led by Neil Cameron. Vernon Woodward, quiet, reserved and somewhat unapproachable, had the clear blue all-seeing eyes of the legendary fighter pilot and also the fast reactions in the air that made him an outstanding combat pilot. By September 1943, he had been credited with twenty-two victories, second only in the Mediterranean theatre of operations to the thirty-six enemy aircraft destroyed by Flt Lt Pattle, another Hurricane pilot.

As the flying hours piled up week by week in endless patrols over the Mediterranean, the discomforts of life in the desert made themselves felt. By mid-January the battle front had moved westwards, yet again nearer Tripoli, and on 14 January the battle for the town opened. This action brought yet another move for the Squadron. Ten days before this, the Advance Party had set out through the mountain area of the Djebel *en route* for Agedabia, the first staging point on the journey to Misurata West. On 17 January, the Squadron stood down from operations and the Main Party was ready to move. The vehicles were on the road by 08.00 hours in heavy rain and with a coating of ice on the windscreens. The road led through wooded country with many trees and rich red soil, a great contrast to the dry sandy wastes of the Libyan Desert where so many months had been spent. Having covered 226 miles in two days, the Main Party refuelled north of Benghazi and camped overnight near Agedabia. The next day, the road party was encouraged to see the Squadron's Hurricanes and the Stuka pass overhead *en route* for Misurata West, the final destination. Once past Marble Arch, that triumphal monument built in the desert by Mussolini on the border between Tripolitania and Cyrenaica, the two parties joined together. All along the road, signs of the recent fighting were evident, and numerous notices proclaimed the ever present danger of German minefields. On 23 January all the transport arrived, more or less safely, to join the aircraft after a journey lasting a less - than - comfortable nine days.

The flying from Misurata brought a change of scenery, but no change in operations as a routine of further shipping patrols commenced. These patrols were to provide a protective screen against German aircraft operating from Tunisia and, to a lesser extent, Sicily. On a visit to the Squadron the SASO, Air Headquarters, Egypt, stressed the importance of convoys reaching the 8th Army via Tripoli, and thus the importance of convoy protection. The good news at the end of the month was that Luxton, Baines and Stephenson, missing since 18 November, were prisoners-of-war, and that "Steve" Stephenson had been awarded the DFC. Three days later the sad news came that Flt Sgt J R Rebstock, who had been lost on the same raid, had died from burns in a German prisoner-of-war camp.

As February opened with another period of bad weather rendering the landing ground unserviceable, such interest as there was came from elsewhere. On 8 February a visit from the AOC, Egypt, Air Vice-Marshal R E Saul, brought hope that re-equipment with Spitfires, which would put the Squadron back in the front line, was in prospect. This hope for a change from the doubtlessly essential, but nevertheless boring, shipping patrols was kindled further by the news of the creation of a new Group formation, No.210 Group, of which 213 Squadron was to be a part. Reality intruded the next day when a Hurricane was vectored on to a Ju 88, but proved unable to catch up with it. The reality on the ground was that winter in Tripolitania could be very wet, and that the two-man bivouac tents, in which some of the airmen were living, were not proof against the rain and the mud. As only a small minority of personnel were issued with gum-boots, moving about for the majority meant slipping and sliding through mud, up to the knees in some places.

A diversion from routine flying came in the middle of the month when, on 17 February, six aircraft were detached for night flying duties to Castel Benito, which was the main airfield for Tripoli, built by the Italians some twenty-three miles inland from the town. After two nights of practice, patrols were flown over the town on each of the subsequent nights during the detachment, but no positive contact was made with any enemy aircraft. Despite the lack of material success, the detachment was repeated again towards the end of March, providing a welcome change from the desert at Misurata. By the end of the month, over fifty hours of operational night flying had been logged - far exceeding the total for any other month. During the month, two departures were indicative of the change that was coming over the

Flg Off T G Steinberg, who flew with the Star of David painted on the cowling of his aircraft, despite warnings from the CO as to the probable consequences if he was shot down and captured by the Germans. (Jack Walton)

WO P C "Red" Haslam with Hurricane IIC, AK-I, Idku, October 1943. (A Thomas)

Squadron, as long-serving pilots came to the end of their tours. "Baron" G R S McKay, so named because of his predilection for flying the Squadron's Stuka, and WO Harry Compton, who was much respected and admired particularly after his long walk in the desert to rejoin the Squadron, left to go to No.22 PTC as instructors. Flying the Squadron's Stuka was very much an acquired taste and, apart from G R S McKay, only Tony Smailes seemed to take to it with enthusiasm. He remembers that many of his fellow pilots thought he was mad to want to fly in such a machine, which was eventually left at Misurata when the squadron moved on, since the time spent on servicing it became unsupportable.

Sgt A A Smailes (later Wg Cdr A A Smailes) had formally joined the Squadron at Martuba in January 1943, but had been flying with the Hurricane Support Wing, which provided major servicing, stores function, transport pool etc for all the Hurricane Squadrons. He had however been on the same airfield as the Squadron since October 1942, and thus knew many of the aircrew.

As the month ended news came that, far to the west in Tunisia, the Mareth Line had been breached.

April passed with a continuous routine of shipping patrols. On 17 April, two aircraft were scrambled to intercept a Blenheim and a French Potez; the plot was inspected carefully and the aircraft reported as friendly. Almost immediately Spitfires arrived, and it was noted that the Blenheim hurriedly fired off the colours of the day. The ORB notes that "No further comment is necessary". The Squadron's aircraft were perhaps outmoded, but its professionalism and pride were very much intact.

The Germans in North Africa surrendered on 14 May and the war in the desert came to an end. At Misurata, the routine continued much as before. Crete was still in German hands, and the convoys proceeding up to Tripoli and Malta still needed fighter protection. So, as the summer wore on, the flying programme consisted of convoy patrols and practice flying in almost equal parts, although June and July saw less and less operational flying. The normal hazards remained and on a practice flight during a tail-chase at 20,000 feet, Tony Smailes, flying as No.2, had the unnerving experience of seeing his leader, Sgt Arthur Garwood, roll and fly straight into the ground. There was no simple explanation other than oxygen failure. This was Smailes's first experience of being so close to a fatal accident involving a friend - and he flew very straight and level on his way back to Misurata.

On the ground the Squadron's sporting activities, which had continued all through the fighting and had played an important part in maintaining morale, still prospered. The soccer team had made an enviable reputation for itself on the field, and this was well and truly upheld when it beat a team representing the rest of 210 Group by ten goals to nil. At various times, as the war permitted, the Squadron also fielded a rugby football team and a cricket eleven.

Towards the end of July, hopes were once more raised of a change in fortunes and "some real action" as the Squadron was ordered back to Egypt. On 28 July eighteen aircraft set off, followed by a technical party in a Wellington and a Lockheed. All the aircraft, apart from two Hurricanes and one of the transports, reached Idku the same afternoon. The journey, that had taken the 8th Army and the Desert Air Force three months travelling from east to west, had been covered in the opposite direction in less than one day. The Advance and Main ground parties, which had left Misurata separately, linked up again at Martuba. By 3 August they were heading east past Tobruk, reaching Sidi Haneish on 4 August, and completing the journey of 1,250 miles in eight days, reaching Idku in the evening of 5 August.

The first full day back at Idku was inevitably spent in siting the various Messes and generally making the place look like home again. This was the Squadron's third stay there since its arrival in the Middle East. In the evening the last two vehicles, the office and cooking trailers, arrived. All that were now missing was the Squadron pilots, who had been taking some well-deserved leave since their arrival eight days previously. Although no operational flying took place on 9 August, all the aircraft were cannon-tested and the air defence of Alexandria was once again in the Squadron's safe hands.

In truth, the hopes of encountering any enemy aircraft at all were now more remote than ever before. The nearest German formations were no longer just down the road to the west, but on the other side of the Mediterranean Sea, in Crete and the islands of the Greek archipelago. However, no sooner had the Squadron returned to operational readiness than a party of eight pilots and sixty ground personnel departed for an unknown destination on instructions from HQ Middle East. It soon transpired that the detachment had gone to Cyprus, an omen for the future, whence it returned in September after an uneventful stay.

Soon a routine began to establish itself as convoys, with a wide variety of very anonymous code names, were covered

From left to right: Sgt T A Jowett, Flt Sgt J E Oliff, RCAF, Flt Sgt P T Temple-Murray and Sgt A A Smailes, at Misurata, Libya. Summer 1943. (A A Smailes)

Flt Lt G Carrick's Hurricane IIC, HW798, Paphos, Cyprus, September 1943. (A Thomas)

as they made their way in and out of the Suez Canal and along the North African coast. The Squadron was now operating with 74 Squadron, which was based outside Alexandria in the desert at LG 106. Wing sweeps and formation flying over the town provided a fine show of force, particularly when the whole Wing, which included the Squadron's old sparring partners 238 Squadron and 451 Squadron, late of 241 Wing in the Levant, was airborne. On 23 August a new Commanding Officer, Sqn Ldr S R Whiting, arrived from 94 Squadron to take over from Woodward, who left to attend a staff course at the Middle East Staff College, Haifa. Sqn Ldr Whiting, a South African, was to lead the Squadron for well over a year, during which its role and equipment underwent a complete and eagerly-awaited change. However, for the present, it was back to the familiar and frustrating work of convoy protection. Daily patrols were mounted over the numerous vessels that plied to and fro and the report "Patrol returned without incident" became as usual as sand in the tea.

The frustration of trying to intercept the high flying Ju 88s in a Hurricane II had been experienced by Whiting even before he joined 213 Squadron. He had accordingly, in the week before he arrived, borrowed a Spitfire IX to test it against the high-flying German photo-reconnaissance aircraft. On 20 August he had reached 42,000 feet only to find that the Ju 88 was still above him at something like 44-45,000 feet. Faced with this situation, he decided on a plan that he would put into effect when the Squadron was re-equipped.

The Squadron's eternal optimism that real operations were just around the corner was roused once more when the CO left Idku with twelve aircraft on 8 September, bound for Paphos on the western coast of Cyprus. The prospect of "mysterious ops" caused subdued excitement throughout the detachment, but a convoy patrol the next day soon managed to dissolve these hopes. Soon the Squadron HQ was all that remained at Idku, as all the aircraft, the Operations HQ and all the groundcrews moved to Paphos. Shipping patrols over the seas around Cyprus now became the mainstay of the Squadron's flying and all that remained to relieve the boredom was a change of surroundings - or almost all! When the war had broken out, most of the girls working in the cabarets in the Middle East were from the Balkans, Rumania, Bulgaria and Hungary. As soon as the German Army moved south-eastwards towards the Black Sea, they became enemy aliens. The problem of what to do with them had been solved by interning them in Cyprus - Nicosia in particular - allowing them their full freedom other than not being allowed to leave the island. Soon a strict rota for two-day passes to Nicosia had to be introduced to limit the numbers away from duty at any one time. Prior to the arrival of the Squadron, the girls' main entertainment, apart from the locals, had been provided by the resident Army units, who were seen as distinctly second best to "the boys in blue" (khaki actually), and fighter pilots to boot.

On 19 September, the Squadron received a visit from the Air Officer Commanding-in-Chief, Air Chief Marshal Sir Sholto Douglas, who chatted to the pilots before leaving for Limassol. Stan Pickford recalls that the NCO pilots were sent off to pick some fresh figs to sustain him on his journey.

The record of never having lost a CO was nearly broken on 22 September when it was reported that a Hurricane was on fire near a refuelling point on the emergency runway. As the flames died down, following a general rush to the scene, there was a violent explosion that killed LAC S S Mowat and from which the CO received chest wounds that required his prompt despatch by air to No.57 General Hospital. Back at Idku it was clear that some things remained unchanged and unchanging as one of "B" Flights domestic tents was stolen by the local natives. The British forces were a natural target for the "klefties" and the lengths to which their ingenuity took them beggared belief. The story goes that the cable connecting the two hundred yards of dubious lead-in lights, perched on poles over the lake at Idku, was stolen so often that it was eventually replaced with barbed wire, which must have caused a considerable energy loss but kept the lights burning.

On yet another shipping patrol, and while sixty miles out to sea, the Hurricane of the now-promoted Plt Off P T P Temple-Murray (Tee-Emm to all who knew him) developed a severe glycol leak and he had to bale out. Having lost his dinghy, it was necessary for Carrick and Steinberg to circle overhead and drop theirs. Fortunately Temple-Murray recovered one of these and was eventually picked up by an ASR Walrus. Sqn Ldr Whiting returned to resume command on 2 October, and on 6 October the first of a long series of patrols over Castelrosso, now the Greek island of Kastellorizon, a small island just off the southern coast of Turkey, was flown at his instigation. These patrols were introduced as being of more practical value than the sweeps in the local area, which had hitherto absorbed most of the Squadron's energies. Sections of four aircraft, fitted with long-range tanks, flew out on a heading of 303 degrees for 195 miles, and then patrolled Castelrosso and the harbour

Going on leave, three pilots in the rear gunner's cockpit of the Squadron's Stuka. Sgt J M Dixon, Sgt L P Geoffrion, RCAF and Flt Sgt J T Field, RCAF(?), to be flown by Fg Off G R S MacKay.

Squadron pilots, Idku, Spring 1944.

area for forty minutes before returning to Paphos on a heading of 121 degrees, gradually losing height. These patrols lasted some two and three-quarter hours, and in this way it was possible to put aircraft in the area where the enemy might be encountered for he seemed very loath to appear over Cyprus itself.

Just before 11.00 hours on 18 October 1943, as the six aircraft which had taken off for Castelrosso at 07.50 hours that morning were heard returning, the usual crowd gathered to watch them come in and land. As the aircraft approached interest quickened as it was seen that several of the long-range tanks had been jettisoned. The first aircraft into dispersal was soon surrounded by an eager crowd. It soon transpired that over Castelrosso, with one section at 6,000 feet and another at 8,000 feet, twelve Ju 88s had been seen flying in three vics of four. The second vic was attacked and three aircraft destroyed, one each by Flt Lt H R Rowlands (Red Leader), Plt Off R Jackson, whose victim was last seen by Sgt Stan Pickford, his Number Two, as it headed into Turkey with an engine on fire, and WO P C Haslam. Another Ju 88, attacked by WO T A Jowett, was not claimed since the result of his attack could not be verified. With hindsight, it seems likely that the use of Enigma and local intelligence played their part, because soon after this success the patrols once again reverted to pairs of aircraft.

Under the headline "Hurricanes Notch 200th Kill - Met careless Huns" an English newspaper recorded the incident thus:

"The 200th victim of a famous Hurricane squadron went down in flames over the tiny Mediterranean island of Castelrosso.

The Hurricanes were on a routine patrol when they encountered a formation of twelve Junkers 88s.

'My pilots were doubly lucky' said Squadron Leader S R Whiting, of Johannesburg, the squadron commander, 'First, that they just happened to be there when Jerry came along; and second that the Junkers flew over them without apparently seeing them'.

Flight Lieutenant H R Rowlands of Sydney N.S.W., who led the formation added 'We had time to get up high and were able to dive and intercept them after their bombing run. 'Red' Haslam got the first'. Flight Sergeant Peter Haslam, of Belmont, near Bolton, Lancs., said 'My man apparently failed to drop his bombs and turned back for a second run. As he turned he saw me for the first time but I was able to turn inside him to get the first squirt. I then got close in and he went down in flames. Yes, they gave me a bit of a party for the 200th.' An Australian pilot pointed out that the honour was missed by a tenth of a second by a fellow countryman, Pilot Officer Raymond Jackson, of Cardiff, N.S.W., who bagged another of the Junkers

The next victim fell to Flight Lieutenant Rowlands, the formation leader. 'I think my bloke must have been in the clouds and have come down to join Jackson's fight or to look at his baled out victims' he said. 'There would be forty-eight Huns in those twelve kites, and it's really amazing that not one of them saw us until so late. But it was okay by us.'

Three quarters of the Squadron's "kills" were made in England, in the early days of the war, and during the Battle of Britain.

The remainder were claimed in the desert war and in the defence of Alexandria last year."

At last the great day had arrived - the Squadron's total had reached the two hundred mark. Even though it had been necessary to go a long way in search of that elusive last victim, he had been found and the chance had been taken with both hands. Although withdrawn from the front-line after the second Battle of El Alamein, the Squadron could still show its prowess, and the capabilities of the Hurricane in the hands of a skilled and experienced pilot, when the opportunity arose.

For the six aircraft on the afternoon sweep there were eighteen pilots clamouring to go. Almost inevitably the patrol returned without incident. The same could not be said of the of the manner in which the evening was passed, when the double century was celebrated in no mean manner. The trip to Castelrosso now became a daily routine when the weather and aircraft state permitted but, although hope sprang eternal, no like occurrence came to pass.

The action of 18 October had whetted the Squadron's appetite and left it more discontented than ever with the daily round of convoy patrols. These however were shown not to be without danger when, on 30 October, Plt Off L P T Geoffrion was picked up by a French sloop after he was forced to bale out over the sea. Discovering that he was not only a French-Canadian but that it was also his birthday, the French Navy treated him to the best meal he had had for some time before transferring him to an Air Sea Rescue launch, which returned him to Paphos in the shortest possible time. This second engine failure over the sea prompted a keen interest by the pilots in the state of their parachutes, and a warm appreciation of the speed and efficiency of the Air Sea Rescue services based on the island. Nevertheless, as the winter approached and the temperature of the sea dropped, the price of an engine failure far from base was high and, despite all the efforts of the rescue services, both WO P C 'Red' Haslam and Fg Off T G 'Steiny' Steinberg were reported as missing after such incidents.

More convoy patrols and practice flying saw out the month during which the events of the eighteenth had given morale a bigger boost than any pep talk.

On 8 November the Squadron was ordered back to Idku; the aircraft flew back on 9 November, and the ground party travelled back in a Dakota. Once again the mirage of re-equipment shimmered before the Squadron's eyes. However there were no new aircraft - just new convoys to patrol. The middle of the month saw another detachment depart, when eight aircraft flew off to St Jean d'Acre in Palestine to share yet more shipping protection patrols with 127 Squadron. Here again there was little enough activity, although the aircraft were maintained at readiness.

At Idku, the Squadron took over buildings, with a proper operations room, from 74 Squadron. On 16 October four aircraft left Idku for Sidi Barrani to carry out a "rhubarb" over Crete. On the day, low cloud obscured the main target, but the secondary target was attacked and strikes were seen on the gun emplacements at Tymbaki. When still some thirty miles off the Egyptian coast on the return journey, Blue Two developed engine trouble and had to bale out. For 2½ hours he was covered by Blue One until picked up by an HSL. Hardly had the three remaining aircraft returned to Idku, when all the Squadron aircraft and the ground-crews departed once more for Paphos, to be joined there on 19 November by the detachment from St Jean.

In 1943 Paphos, where in legend Aphrodite arose from the sea, was a sleepy coastal fishing village with just one hotel, the Olympus, which had quickly become the Squadron's off-duty base. The Greek owner was assisted by his daughter Katie, a well-built eighteen or nineteen year old, whose forty-egg omelettes, served at the bar, had became quite famous - as indeed had Katie herself. Putting patriotic zeal above self-interest, the Squadron pilots persuaded Katie that she ought to become a WAAF, and with a considerable fanfare she was despatched to Haifa for basic training. Some six weeks later she was back in Paphos, the WAAFs having found her too much of a handful. The forty-egg omelettes returned to the menu at the Olympus Hotel.

December found the Squadron's Hurricanes once more over Castelrosso, and again the patrols returned with nothing to report. A scramble over base on 2 December failed to reach its target due to a lack of height and speed. The Squadron ORB lamented "What would we give for even two Spitfire IXs. We always seem to be beaten by superior height and speed, and although the pilots are keen to a degree a feeling of frustration is sensed at times." No doubt the entry contains a good deal of understatement.

On the evening of 11 December, the Squadron was stood down from operations and the pilots repaired to the Olympus Hotel for a beer or two. The evening was developing nicely when, at about seven o'clock, a signal arrived from Wing to the effect that an unidentified vessel had been located some forty miles off-shore. It was approaching the island and the Squadron was to investigate at once since an attack was expected. It was immediately apparent that there were three objections to this course of action, (a) the Squadron was stood down, (b) it was a black, black night and only a few paraffin flares were available for emergency lighting and (c) everyone was well over the limit. The CO had a distinct problem as there was no way he could order any of his pilots into the air, but at the same time he could not ignore the order from Wing. He decided to resolve the matter by going himself. Becoming airborne was comparatively easy and despite the dark night he found the vessel and made a low pass with his landing lights on which showed it to be a large caique. Afterwards he realised that, had he been completely sober, he would never have flown that low over the sea on such a black night and that, had the intruder been an enemy warship, it could hardly have asked for a more inviting target than a low, slow-flying Hurricane with its landing lights on.

Having successfully intercepted Wing's unidentified vessel, he returned to Paphos to be faced with the difficult task of landing. Even at the best of times Hurricanes and Spitfires were not the easiest of aircraft to land at night, with the flames from the exhaust ports glaring straight into the pilots eyes. Initially, on returning to the circuit, Whiting could not see the runway at all, then someone showing great initiative parked a couple of trucks at the end of it with their headlights shining across the threshold. After several attempts he finally made a successful landing, vowing never to go flying again either by day or night in such a condition.

As the month drew on and thoughts of Christmas arose, a twelve-bore shotgun and some clay pigeon targets arrived. The Squadron's acquaintances and influence in the Paphos area were by now well established. Indeed it had become a regular event for the local villages to invite groups of ten or so to visit them on a Saturday or Sunday for a splendid locally produced meal, and then to shoot over the surrounding area. The favourite quarry was pigeon, as they were so fast on the wing when flushed, but there was also francolin, pheasant, grouse etc. Nearer at hand, a walk on the airfield would produce a bag of quail and assorted ducks, all of which proved excellent supplements to the standard Mess rations.

A particularly dull period of flying saw the Squadron reduced to anti-aircraft co-operation flights, which seemed to sum up all that was most boring. On 21 December the CO chased an intruding bandit all the way up to 29,000 feet, but at that height the Ju 88 was still above him and he was unable to attack. The answer seemed obvious, better aircraft were needed.

The CO's summary for the end of the year assessed the situation. "Looking back the Squadron is not sorry to see the end of 1943. From the moment we left Martuba about the middle of last January and moving up to Misurata, operational life virtually ceased and an albatross-like existence began. While the value of convoy patrols is fully appreciated and everyone is perpetually and painfully conscious of the need for more and more training hours, we feel a whole year directed to just this is more than our fair share. In short we see no sign of progress from an equipment or operational point of view during 1943, and look to the New Year to revive the past glories of 213."

Thus the old year passed with some lamentations concerning the Squadron's lack of action, and the hope that 1944 would see this remedied. Initially all the New Year brought was a spell of prolonged bad weather, which rendered the airfield at Paphos unserviceable, forcing some aircraft to operate from Lakatamia, one of the three airfields around Nicosia. On 10 January the whole detachment moved there, only to have flying disrupted by a snow storm and continuing cold wet weather. Such flying as was possible

The Squadron re-equips with Spitfire Mk Vs and IXs, Idku, Egypt, February 1944.

The Squadron converts to Mustang IIIs, Idku, Egypt, May 1944. Mustang AK-D flown by Sgt A A Smailes.
(A A Smailes)

consisted largely of army co-operation exercises. The few raiders that did appear remained too high and departed at too great a speed to give the well-worn Hurricanes any chance of intercepting them. To the pilots the answer remained obvious; all the Squadron needed was to be re-equipped with Spitfire IXs. As 127 Squadron became operational at Lakatamia late in January and took over the readiness commitment, preparations were put in hand for another move back to Idku. On 2 February the long-awaited signal arrived, and fifteen aircraft rapidly formed up over Lakatamia in neat formation and departed from Cyprus for the last time, *en route* once more for Idku.

At last on 13 February the pilots' prayers were answered, with no prior notice and more surprisingly with no preceding rumours. Out of the blue came eight brand new Spitfire IXs, soon to be followed by eight more. The Squadron's five years of service with the Hurricane were over. From Dunkirk to Tripoli and through two of the fiercest passages of air fighting in the war, the Battle of Britain and the Western Desert, the Hurricane had borne the heat and burden of the day. Two hundred enemy aircraft had fallen to its guns, and the Squadron's part in the Second World War will always be indelibly linked with the Hurricane.

For the rest of the month every pilot was busy converting to the new type and becoming operational. Height climbs to 40,000 feet only served to show what the Squadron had been missing in Cyprus. Initially it was hoped and believed that the re-equipment would be entirely with Mark IX Spitfires, because this would be a sure sign that the Squadron was to return to operations. However, on 13 March the Squadron handed over six of its Spitfire IXs to 127 Squadron, which was defending Cyprus, and received in return six Spitfire Mark Vs. As the month wore on, a mixture of Mark Vs and Mark IXs arrived, producing at one time a tally of eleven Spitfire IXs, three Vbs and two Vcs. The Mark IX Spitfire was in essence a Mark Vc airframe fitted with the newer and more powerful Merlin 61 series engine, which had been introduced with the Spitfire Mark VIII. This latter aircraft, fitted with a retractable tail-wheel and slightly lengthened wings, entered operational service in large numbers and was used mainly in the Mediterranean and Far East

As the new aircraft arrived, so another move took place. On 24 February the Main ground party set off for El Gamil to enable the Squadron to provide close air defence to Port Said and the Suez Canal. After spending the night at Mence, they arrived at 15.00 hours to find the airfield largely flooded by the overflow from the nearby lake. Nevertheless, as the aircraft arrived, they were able to land and dawn-to-dusk readiness was instituted.

El Gamil was a two-squadron base, with one set of buildings on the Mediterranean or north side of the airfield and another on the south side. As the Squadron moved in and settled down on the Mediterranean shore, the buildings on the south side of the airfield were empty. In mid-March the CO received a signal from HQ RAF Middle East informing him that a party of some eighty or so WAAFs was due to arrive shortly at Port Said, and that the only accommodation immediately available was that provided by the buildings on the south side of El Gamil. The signal confirmed that their stay would be purely temporary and that it would not interfere with the Squadron's operations. Sqn Ldr Whiting's reactions to the signal were mixed. On the one hand what could be nicer than the company of some young girls fresh out from England, but on the other hand he doubted HQ's assessment of the situation. When the party arrived, the CO explained to the two officers in charge that a notice had been put up placing the south side of the airfield out of bounds to the Squadron personnel. He also explained that, while he would do all he could to prevent an invasion of the south side of the airfield, there were obvious limits to what he could do, since no-one had met any English girls for some time.

The next morning, a very agitated Adjutant rushed into the CO's office to ask him to come and see what was happening. Coming across the middle of the airfield, on which the Squadron was supposed to be at readiness, was a large group of very scantily dressed females with towels over their shoulders, heading for the north beach and a swim in the Mediterranean. There was a noticeable lack of activity in the Squadron's dispersals - but the beach was crowded! The CO quickly drafted a signal to HQ RAF, Middle East, advising that the Squadron was no longer operational due to an invasion of scantily dressed women. Back came the reply in no time at all, "Lucky b.........s, you sort it out and get back operational pronto". After this first invasion, the swimming parties agreed to go around and not across the airfield, and for the remainder of the WAAFs' stay the Squadron personnel were much cleaner than usual, and swimming suddenly became a popular pastime.

At El Gamil, another change came over the squadron as six South African pilots - 2Lts L J Leach, V Vorster, R E Rorvik, S W Pienaar, J W Moor and H B Helm - were posted in from Air HQ, Middle East, soon to be followed by many more of the CO's fellow countrymen as tour-expired pilots departed for pastures new. As a reminder of the "old days",

Flt Lt C D A "Tigger" Smith, a popular member of the Squadron from the days in Libya, arrived from 74 Squadron to become "A" Flight Commander. Also, on 8 March, Sgts Harry Howard and Eric Firmin arrived from the OTU at Abu Sueir for their first tours.

The move to El Gamil was marked by the issue of Africa Stars, dozens of them, to all Squadron personnel who qualified. At a party two days later, a not-so-subtle mixture of egg-nog, crème-de-menthe and cherry brandy was evolved, and passed on to posterity under the name of that hard-won campaign star.

In no time at all the Squadron was spread widely around the eastern end of the Mediterranean Sea, with detachments of three aircraft at St.Jean and two at Lakatamia being established on 9 March. By 20 April the detachment at St. Jean had run dry, and a Spitfire Mk.IX was despatched to Lakatamia to replenish supplies. After a shopping expedition into the nearby town, the aircraft's ammunition tanks were emptied and then refilled with marginally less dangerous materiel; the radio compartment and map case were also packed and the remaining bottles stood around on the floor of the cockpit. A smooth flight back to Palestine ensured that not a drop was spilled.

Now re-equipped, the urge to be back on "real ops" was even stronger and two successes by the Cyprus detachment - one against a Ju 188, the first to be destroyed over the island - only served to make the pilots more aware of what they were missing. On 2 April, the Squadron acquired a Fairchild Argus for communications flying, which was soon being put to good use ferrying to and from the detachments, until "pranged" by Plt Off J M "Dicky" Dixon. Towards the end of the month rumours were once more rife of a move, to Idku initially, prior to a further move back to the UK or conversion to Liberators! The move to Idku duly took place on 9 May, but was not followed either by a move to the UK, or conversion to Liberators.

By this time the CO had been able to put into effect the plan he had decided upon way back in August 1943. Two of the Spitfire IXs were modified to carry out two very specific roles. One, the attack aircraft, was stripped of everything possible - radio, IFF, armour plating and literally everything that could be removed including two of its four Browning .303 machine-guns, and the concrete stabilising block in the tail, which meant that two airmen had to sit on the tailplane while the aircraft was taxying. The second aircraft, also with its armour plating removed, had a radio and a full complement of guns. When a photo-reconnaissance Ju 88 was reported, the two Spitfires would be scrambled, with the radio-equipped aircraft in the lead. Once contact had been established, the attack aircraft would break off and climb the extra few thousand feet with a view to piercing the pressure bubble of the specially modified Ju 88, thus forcing it down to an altitude where the second aircraft would finish it off.

When this plan was first put into operation, it was found that some of the pilots were particularly susceptible to the "bends" if they descended too quickly, suffering from nausea, vomiting and severe headaches. It was clear however that all pilots did not suffer to the same extent. In order to identify those who most suitable for this type of operation, the pilots flew up to Aqir from Idku to undergo de-compression tests. In the end it was found that only Stan Pickford and Lt J W Moore, SAAF were really suitable for this type of operation, and they found themselves on stand-by with two Spitfire VHF (Very High Flying) IXs. The engines of these Spitfires were boosted for extra power, which limited their flying time between services to six hours. As matters turned out, this pair of specialised aircraft was never scrambled, and Stan Pickford's total flying time on this very special mark of Spitfire amounted to two twenty-minute air tests.

Flt Lt H R Rowlands, who was tour-expired, was delegated by HQ RAF, Middle East, to form a sub-flight, not attached to the Squadron and based at Heliopolis, to carry through this work. About ten days later, he went into a near vertical dive and must have been near the speed of sound when his aircraft hit the ground; it seems clear that he had passed out at altitude. The Spitfires were not, of course, pressurised and at that altitude, above 40,000 feet, could stall when the guns were fired. The unit eventually shot down the aircraft, identified as a Ju 86P, which was believed to be the only one flying in the area.

On 12 May the CO picked up a Harvard for training purposes and then on 17 May, without any forewarning, two Mustang IIIs arrived and the Squadron became only the second RAF unit in the Mediterranean theatre to be equipped with this famous aircraft. In April 1944 No.260 Squadron, operating from Cutella in Italy, had become the first when it exchanged its Kittyhawks for Mustangs. The next day, the CO took off for the first flight in this formidable aircraft, which was to equip the Squadron until the war's end. It was noted that, with four different aircraft types on the establishment and two different Marks of Spitfire, the Squadron resembled a training unit. Whatever the appearances, the arrival of the Mustangs clearly meant serious business. The detachments at Lakatamia and St. Jean were accordingly withdrawn and the Squadron, once again being re-equipped, was reunited. By the end of the month, the pilot strength had been pruned from thirty-four to twenty-two and everyone was restless to return to operational flying.

To assist with the conversion, Flt Lt E H Marshal, DFC, arrived from 203 Group and everyone was only too anxious to try out this incredible new aircraft. A display by the CO on 19 May showed off its capabilities to the full, and everyone agreed that it really was as fast as its reputation promised. The Merlin-powered Mustang was indeed the best low-level and ground-attack fighter of the Second World War, probably the best overall fighter aircraft, although this remains a matter of some dispute. The Mustang's greater speed, thirty to forty miles per hour at all altitudes, gave it an advantage over the Spitfire, and it also had much quicker acceleration. Its rate of roll was very much faster, a great advantage in a dog-fight, and its better flight envelope at altitude, when clean, would invariably place the Spitfire at a disadvantage. The Spitfire had a much better turning circle at all levels and at lower levels a much better rate of climb; these were its real advantages. Overall, the Mustang had most of the advantages in terms of performance, except when the Mustang's fuselage fuel tank was full when it could be heavy and tended to spin out of a tight turn. Much of the information concerning the Mustang and its armament, which was available to the units operating it in Europe, never made it to the Balkan Air Force. For instance, RAF Mustang units flying from the UK were in fact forbidden to undertake low-level sweeps on their way back from bomber escort duties because losses were too great. Yet such low-level sweeps were to become the daily operational role of the Squadron when it formed part of the Balkan Air Force, which helps to explain why the Squadron's losses became in due time the highest of any RAF Mustang squadron.

A few days later the CO, in a Spitfire IX, and Flt Lt C S Vos, in a Mustang III, compared the two aircraft's capabilities. As everyone expected, the Mustang had the

The Squadron pilots, Paphos, Cyprus, 1 January 1944. (A A Smailes)

advantage in speed, but the Spitfire remained the more manoeuvrable and seemed to outclass it in every respect except diving. It was very quickly found that the enclosed cockpit of the Mustang was very hot at low level. The CO soon fitted his own experimental modification, consisting of a small protruding vent forward of the wind-shield on top of the cowling. It proved highly successful, and was even more effective once a filter was fitted.

At the end of the month when the Squadron was operational with both Spitfires and Mustangs, Group Operations rang up during the night and asked for a sortie to provide visual confirmation of a ship unloading supplies in Candia Harbour, Crete, by dawn the following day.

It was about midnight when Scot Vos woke Tony Smailes to ask him to go and have a look; Stan Pickford and WO F E Mitchell tossed a coin to decide who should accompany him and Mitchell lost. So they proceeded down to the Ops tent to plan the route, timings, height to fly, etc. Although neither of them had flown a Mustang at night before, they agreed to operate at the lowest feasible altitude and at 04.00 hours they took off with a full internal fuel load. They planned that, as they arrived over the coast of Crete at dawn, Smailes would turn off his navigation lights which he had burned until then to assist Pickford to keep station. In the event these proved of little assistance, and Stan Pickford spent the next hour sweating blood as he formated on his leader's exhaust flames. As they approached the tip of the island, Pickford began to weave to cover his leader's tail. Suddenly he was alone; Smailes had dropped down to ground level and the Mustang's camouflage was so good that Pickford was unable to pick him up against the dull island terrain. Having lost contact, he returned to Idku. Swinging round to port, Smailes flew along the north coast of the island where anti-aircraft fire soon alerted him to the fact that he was approaching Candia harbour, rather earlier than he had expected. Sure enough, there in the middle of the harbour was a ship which, although he had been given no description other than it was a 1,200 tonner, he presumed to be the vessel he had been sent to observe. He therefore transmitted the code word "Bingo" for a successful sighting. Although he did not know it the message was not received, and he flew on westward around the northern tip of the island and back to the forward landing ground at Bu Amud to refuel before returning to Idku. The satisfaction of having completed the Squadron's first Mustang operation successfully was sadly diminished when Vos informed him that "they" required photo-reconnaissance confirmation, since a single sighting by one pilot was not sufficient.

With PR confirmation obtained on 1 June, ten aircraft, six Spitfires fitted with long-range tanks and four Mustangs, flew up to the advanced landing ground at Bu Amud for a special mission. They were assigned the task of escorting twelve Marauders and eighteen Baltimores of Nos.24 and 15 Squadrons SAAF, plus thirty-two Beaufighters, on a shipping strike off the coast of Crete. On the next day the convoy, which was the target of this considerable force, was successfully located and severely mauled by the medium level bombers and the rocket-firing Beaufighters. This time Tony Smailes saw "his" ship from the cockpit of a Spitfire. The only enemy aircraft seen were eight Bf 109s and three Arado 196s, which flew off rapidly as soon as contact was made. All the aircraft returned safely and, although it was hoped that the exercise would be repeated, it was not and on 3 June all the aircraft returned to Idku.

Both the reconnaissance flight, which lasted around four hours, and the escort duty typified the long-range opportunity sortie that the Squadron would undertake in the future. There seems to be some doubt about the operational value of the recce flight. The briefing was sketchy, no cameras were fitted, the requirement that the harbour must be viewed at first light seemed unnecessary, while to require a No.2 to formate in the dark at low level for over an hour across the sea was stretching the capability of even the best of pilots. There was in any event an efficient photo-reconnaissance unit based in the Delta, so it was presumed that Group Operations just wanted an excuse to use the newly-acquired Mustangs.

The Squadron expected to be fully operational with the Mustangs by 9 June, but flying was restricted due to a shortage of spares. The aircraft also all became due for their forty-hour check at more or less the same time, most of them having flown some twenty-five hours before arriving. After nearly four weeks of flying the Mustang III, Sqn Ldr Whiting reported to Group on a number of operational aspects. He noted that, with the fuselage tank full, the aircraft was longitudinally unstable at speeds below 200 miles per hour, and there was considerable difficulty in holding position when flying in formation at 170 miles per hour. The aircraft also stalled if pulled into a turn at 150 miles per hour. Partly as a result of the rarity of the Mustang in the Eastern Mediterranean, difficulty was encountered in distinguishing it from the Bf 109. It was therefore recommended that six-inch-wide white bands be painted from the leading to trailing edge of the mainplanes eighteen inches from the wing-tip, and four-inch bands be painted around the tail and rudder above the markings. He particularly noted that the cockpit provided poor visibility, making it necessary to fly in line abreast. He added "The rear mirror is useful for doing one's hair, but not much else, being situated inside the cockpit".

The news arrived on 6 June that the invasion of Europe had taken place and this engendered a wave of good spirit, and enthusiasm. The very next day a movement order arrived with the destination El Adem, but the CO took the precaution of hinting at a long sea voyage in order to prevent the accumulation of undue baggage. Maintaining a sense of reality, the readiness section was airborne at 14.19 hours to investigate a plot sixty miles off the coast. A Ju 88 was attacked from astern and strikes seen; it was therefore claimed as a probable. But the prospects were of more exciting flying, ground strafing and long-range cover. As a further indication of the capabilities of the new aircraft, two Mustangs flown by Vos and Pienaar carried out a reconnaissance of Rhodes harbour on 14 June, the sortie lasting three hours forty-five minutes. The next day the CO led four Mustangs as top cover for light bombers attacking the harbour, and a similar mission was mounted in the afternoon. These were the last operational sorties flown from North Africa. On 18 June flying ceased. The Fairchild and Texan were returned to Heliopolis and the last of the Spitfires flown to No.132 Maintenance Unit.

On 19 June, a convoy consisting of all the Squadron's ground personnel and transport left Idku for No.24 PTC at Aboukir. The pilots were distributed amongst SHQ, 294, 162 and 45 Squadrons' Messes. The next day, the transport moved up to Port Said for loading but still the destination remained unknown - given the normal fertility of the "cookhouse" rumours, an unprecedented state of affairs. In suspended animation, a special sense of the importance of events pervaded the Squadron. The ORB entry for 28 June illustrates the sense of anticipation:-

"The day was probably one of the most significant in the history of the Squadron. A new era is being embarked upon with adventure untold before it. By 08.00 the Squadron had en-trucked and by the turn of the half hour the convoy began the first part of its long journey to Italy.

The harbour of Alexandria was well filled with shipping of every size and description and some minutes passed before the vehicles of 24 PTC drew alongside the gallant 2,000-ton ship *Princess Kathleen*.

The scene very much like that of all embarkations with covered derricks, bales and other paraphernalia of war stacked at random as far as one chose to look. There was little glamour to the first stages of our new mission of active service and yet one could not but feel relieved at leaving the dull routine and monotony of the outcast Middle East to those who appear to revel in it.

The men of the Squadron were bitter about the comfort or rather lack of it which they were forced to endure. Conditions in the holds were deplorable and most of them decided to escape the heat and clammy air by sleeping on deck in the most convenient positions.

The Officer's quarters were crowded and unpleasant even though comparisons with other wartime voyages were made. The war must go on and 213 goes forward to deal the coup-de-grace together with other front line Squadrons."

The CO's summary for the month of June strikes a more reflective note. "So ends the Squadron's tour in the Middle East, taken all round a successful time for the Squadron and, except for the last year spent mainly on routine work, one of excitement and record."

Sqn Ldr SR Whiting, DFC, the CO, says "Goodbye" to Flt Lt H Rowlands, RAAF, a Flight Commander in 1943/44. Harry Rowlands was awarded the DFC after completing his tour with the Squadron.

A section of Mustangs providing an escort for Beaufighters over the mountains of Bosnia, 1944.

CHAPTER TWELVE - THE BALKAN AIR FORCE

In the June of 1944, the Allied advance up the Italian peninsula had reached as far as Rome, and the Allied and German armies stood facing each other across the Gothic Line. In Yugoslavia, Marshal Tito with his Yugoslav Partisan Army was containing the bulk of twenty German and six Bulgarian Divisions under the overall command of Feldmarshal von Weichs. The German Air Force in Yugoslavia was considerably weaker, consisting of some thirty to forty Bf 109s and forty to fifty Ju 87s based at Belgrade and Zagreb, and also operating from advanced landing grounds at Sarajevo and Mostar. These front-line aircraft were augmented by approximately fifty CR 42s and Henschel Hs 126 reconnaissance aircraft.

In Yugoslavia, as the year progressed, the Germans held the towns, and the communication routes between them, in the face of numerous, but ill-coordinated, Partisan attacks. The Partisans were provided with arms and equipment by the Allies and supported by small Allied raiding parties, which again were less effective than they might have been with an overall co-ordinating HQ. In May 1944, German paratroops and airborne troops in gliders had attacked Tito's Headquarters at Drvar in Bosnia, and had forced him to move to the island of Vis.

Early in June, Tito had been flown out of Yugoslavia to meet Air Marshal Slessor, C-in-C RAF Mediterranean and Middle East, at Bari in Italy. Here the future policy for the aerial support of Tito's quarter-of-a-million guerrilla fighters was discussed. The first and most important of Tito's demands was that the domination of the skies over Yugoslavia by the Luftwaffe should be ended, and that more effective and regular close support should be provided for the actions of his partisan forces. Facilities for the aerial evacuation of his wounded and increased supplies were also requested.

Since early April, Slessor had been advocating a single overall command to direct land, sea and air operations in this theatre of the war. In June came the news that his scheme had been approved, albeit that there would be three co-equal commanders, with Air Vice-Marshal W Elliot, CB, CBE, DFC, who was appointed Air Officer Commanding the Balkan Air Force on 16 June, operating in the role of coordinator from his Headquarters at Bari. Elliot had long inter-service planning experience in the War Cabinet Offices, and as a member of the Joint Planning Committee had attended meetings with the Prime Minister and the President of the USA. Thus, in addition to his role as an RAF commander, Elliot had two further functions, one as coordinator of all operations carried out across the Adriatic by all three services and the other dealing with the political

A Mustang III modified for straight fighter operations. Armed with four 0.5-in machine guns, a bubble canopy and with its fuselage fuel tank removed. In the background is a Mustang IV, or P-51K

problems inseparable from waging war in the Balkans.

The Balkan Air Force, which officially commenced operations on 1 July 1944, was a cosmopolitan outfit. Its fifteen different types of aircraft, including Italian Cants and Savoia-Marchettis, were operated by crews from eight different countries. Its main operational strength was made up of three Wings of fighters and fighter/bombers. No.254 Wing consisted initially of No.13 Squadron Royal Hellenic Air Force flying Baltimores, No.281 Wing consisted of Nos.32, 73, 249 and 283 Squadrons flying Spitfires, and No.283 Wing with No.213 Squadron being the only Mustang unit and No.39 Squadron flying Beaufighters armed with rockets.

1 July 1944 found the Squadron split into three sections; the aircraft together with the pilots and a skeleton ground party were still at Idku, the Main Party was on board the *Princess Kathleen* somewhere in the Mediterranean bound for Taranto, while an Advance MT Party, consisting of drivers and vehicles, had already arrived at Brindisi.

It was agreed by all who endured the five days at sea that the standards of sea transport had deteriorated considerably in the past year, and that bully beef and biscuits three times a day made for a very uninteresting diet. Once on board there was some dismay when it was learned that, on orders from the Captain, all officers below the rank of Major would receive their food from hay-boxes in the first-class lounge. Within twenty-four hours he realised that this order effectively excluded all RAF officers on board from the Wardroom, so he relented and extended an invitation to the officer in charge, the Adjutant Fg Off L Robins, and the next senior officer, the MO "Doc" Holgate. Thereafter these two dined in style, while some of the pilots who were left with the hay-boxes caused embarrassment by shouting ribald remarks from a companionway above the Wardroom. The Captain later told the Adjutant that he could always tell whether there were RAF personnel on board by the reports received on the bridge from the sentries on the watertight doors. The sailors invariably said "Aye Aye, Sir", the Army "Yes, Sir", and the RAF "OK".

On 2 July the Main Party arrived at Taranto, and by the evening had picked up its transport and joined the Advance Party at Brindisi to await further developments. Here it was learned that the Squadron was to be the first unit in the newly-formed 283 Wing of the Balkan Air Force, which was however not to operate from Brindisi but from airfields further south at Lecce in the heel of Italy. The now reunited Squadron ground parties moved off from Brindisi at 13.10 hours on 6 July for the two-day journey to the Squadron's new base. It had finally been decided that this was to be at Leverano, some ten miles west of Lecce in the very centre of the heel of Italy. On arrival, the bleak prospect that greeted them was not so much an airfield as a very large former wheat field. Nevertheless by 8 July all was ready to receive the aircraft, tents had been erected, and bathing parties organised to wash off some of the dust and sweat generated by the hard work of setting up the Squadron's new base in the middle of a hot Italian summer. In the evening Wg Cdr D S MacDonald, who had commanded the Squadron during the Battle of Britain, dropped in to meet this part of his new command.

Back at Idku, on 2 July, Air Marshal Sir Keith Park, MC and Bar, DFC, visited the station and spent half-an-hour with the Squadron pilots providing a brief summary of the war situation in the Balkans, and outlining the future operations allocated to 213 Squadron - a briefing that was much appreciated. At 07.30 hours on 5 July, Red Section, led by the CO and consisting of Fg Off S Chappell, Lt H B Helm,

THE BALKANS 1944 - 1945

Squadron pilots and 2Lt V O Stock, SAAF (Squadron Intelligence Officer), Biferno, Italy, July 1944.
Standing from left: Flt Sgt Firman, Fg Off Garwood, Fg Off Anthony, Flt Lt Smith, WO Mitchell (seated on propeller boss), WO Pickford, Sqn Ldr Whiting, Flt Lt Voss, 2Lt Stock, SAAF, Lt Pienaar, SAAF, WO Cook, Fg Off Chappell, Sgt Howard.
Front Row:- Lt Rorvick, SAAF, Fg Off Purchase, WO Watkins, Lt Vorster, SAAF, Lt Helm, SAAF, Lt Leach, SAAF.

2Lt S W Pienaar, WOs D E Cooke and F E Mitchell, dipped in salute over the airfield and then set off for Castel Benito to refuel before continuing on to Malta; all that is except Pienaar who remained at Castel Benito with hydraulic problems. At 08.00 hours Blue Section, with Flt Lt C D A Smith leading Fg Off T E G Purchas, Plt Off A A Smailes and WOs K A L Ford, S G Pickord and J P G Watkins, set off only to have two aircraft return with hydraulic trouble, but the remainder successfully joined up with Red Section at Castel Benito. Green Section, Flt Lt C S Voss, Fg Offs R Anthony and R H Garwood and Plt Off A R Bootherstone, took off at 08.30 hours bound for the airfield at Marble Arch to refuel before continuing onwards.

On 6 July, ten of the sixteen Mustangs that had set out arrived at Brindisi. Four others were expected to arrive within days, while the remaining two required spares, the provision of which might delay their arrival indefinitely. It was decided that the aircraft should remain at Brindisi for four days until the airfield at Leverano was serviceable. Finally at 14.30 hours on 9 July 1944, with sixteen aircraft crossing the airfield at Leverano in tight formation before landing, the Squadron had well and truly arrived in its new operational theatre. Ford had some difficulty in lowering his undercarriage and it was not until he had jettisoned his long range tanks and then turned onto his back, as directed by the CO who spent some thirty-five minutes alongside helping him, that his hydraulics functioned.

Later in the day, Air Marshal Jackman of HQ BAF visited the Squadron with the news that it was to move up to Biferno before starting operations. For the pilots, who were glad to be back "home", there was some disappointment that they were not staying at Leverano, which was located in pleasant countryside and bordered by vineyards. A lovely manor house close to the airfield had been requisitioned as the Mess, and under it a bricked-up cellar was discovered. When un-bricked it was found to be stocked to the ceiling with Spumante and numerous other wines. As the house was empty when taken over, the find was treated as the spoils of war - and the Squadron lived well for some weeks afterwards.

By the evening of the next day all was ready for the move, and a convoy of the Squadron's MT set off early in the morning of 11 July, expecting to reach Biferno the next day. After an overnight stop ten miles north of Canosa, when everyone was cheered up by a good meal and plenty of mail, the arrival at Biferno was something of an anti-climax. The beauty of the countryside could not compensate for the group of flea-infested huts, some three miles from the airfield, that were supposed to be the Squadron's new quarters. At 15.00 hours, about two hours after the ground party arrived, the aircraft flew in and then all was hard work again to prepare for operations. The move to Biferno meant a change of command, since the Squadron now became a part of 254 Wing.

It now became clear why the Spitfires, which had been operated for such a short time, had been exchanged for the longer-range Mustangs. Operating from the east coast of

WO J P G "Johnny" Watkins and his "self preservation". His Mustang III, minus a section of its port mainplane, which was lost on a low-level strafing attack, 7 October 1944.

Italy, the Squadron's aircraft were to range over the whole of Yugoslavia, into Albania, Bulgaria, Greece and even up into Austria. During its time with the BAF, the Squadron flew both Mark III and Mark IV versions of the Mustang. The Mark IV, or P-51K, was identical to the P-51D flown by the USAAF, other than for its Aeromatic propeller. The Mark III had been modified in the UK, mainly for straight fighter interception work. It had four 0.5" machine guns, and some later versions had a very pleasant bubble canopy which replaced the standard fold over clip-down "cottage pane" type of canopy, which was probably the worst feature of the Mustang. This canopy had two small sliding windows which could only be opened from outside the aircraft, or jettisoned altogether. It was also difficult to turn in, and hampered any rear view.

Later a number of the aircraft also had the fuselage tank removed to increase manoeuvrability, and this also allowed a large quantity of personal bits and pieces to be carried behind the pilot. Fuelling the aircraft for a sortie was critical, especially for a short-range mission. The two factors to be borne in mind were, firstly, that any sharp turn involving considerable G forces was highly dangerous with a full fuselage tank and, secondly, that it was forbidden to land with the tank full. This tank was used first, and it was soon found that leaving the tank approximately one-quarter full improved the Mustang's turning capabilities, and thus its manoeuvrability in a dog fight; however such tactics required experience. Also having that amount of fuel, or vapour which was worse, just behind the cockpit was something the pilots put well to the back of their minds. Not only was the Mustang the ultimate long-range escort fighter, but it was ideally suited to the role of fighter-bomber which had been evolved in the hard school of the desert. The flying and fighting on which the Squadron embarked in the second half of July set the pattern for its operations during the course of the rest of the war.

In mid-July, two German divisions launched an attack into Montenegro against the Partisan II Corps. In order to disrupt the German supply lines and support the Partisan counter-attack, Spitfires and Mustangs of the BAF attacked the main north-south Zagreb-Belgrade-Skopje railway and German troop concentrations.

Two days after arriving at Biferno the Squadron was ready to return to operations. Prior to the first sorties, a briefing session was held to discuss the best tactics. In view of the German radar cove, and the lack of any accurate information as to what opposition could be expected the other side of the Dalmatian Mountains, it was decided to fly at zero feet all the way. The fluid-four formation was flown, with the aircraft approximately two hundred feet apart, with the numbers three and four a further two hundred feet back and to one side, allowing them to weave and look around as well as keeping an eye on the ground. The leader was responsible for navigation and avoiding obstacles such as power lines. When carrying out turns, it was soon discovered that the leader had to pull up to one hundred feet because of the danger that the inner wing man would hit the ground, since he could not see his leader when turning if the leader kept too low. The Squadron's two flights were still each divided into two sections, Red and Yellow for "A" Flight and Blue and Green for "B" Flight, but now each section consisted of four aircraft.

Radio silence was maintained until the aircraft were well the other side of the Dalmatian Mountains, when the specially-allocated frequency was used as it was essential for the attacking aircraft to maintain constant communication while over the target area, using the Squadron's call-sign "Late-lunch". The aircraft could also contact "Big Fence", which was the military radio control frequency covering the whole of Italy.

At 09.15 hours on 14 July 1944, the CO led eight aircraft, flown by Moore, Bootherstone, Howard, Smith, Vorster, Purchas and Watkins, on a two-hour forty-minute raid, strafing road and rail targets. Having crossed the Adriatic at zero feet, the aircraft pulled up over the Yugoslav coast at 09.45 hours, and arrived in the target area east of Brod some thirty-five minutes later. It was an incredible sight to emerge from the foothills of the mountains into an area teeming with trains, transports etc, and an enemy oblivious to what was about to happen. Immediately a goods train heading east was attacked and severely damaged, as was another in some sidings at Andrijevki. Another west-bound train was attacked and a hay truck in the centre of the train and two petrol tankers at the rear were set on fire, the smoke reaching up to 4-5,000 feet. Later a passenger train was attacked, and it was noted that, while there was heavy but inaccurate 40mm anti-aircraft fire in the area around Brod, no flak was encountered from the trains. In the excitement of that first sortie, the Mustangs shot up everything there was to be seen; the net result was that all the aircraft ran out of ammunition in a short space of time. However, all the aircraft returned safely and the raid was a success and, as importantly, lessons had been learned that would make future sorties even more effective.

In the afternoon, Smith led four Mustangs flown by

Sqn Ldr P E Vaughan-Fowler, DFC and Bar at high speed, Biferno, Italy, 1944.

Mustang III on the Squadron dispersal at the north end of the airstrip at Biferno, Italy. Beyond the sand-dunes and visible behind the aircraft's tail-fin is the Adriatic. This aircraft was flown several times by Roy Ashley and it eventually crashed into the sea. (Roy Ashley)

Helm, Mitchell and Pickford, escorting four Beaufighters to attack trains on the Brod-Belgrade line. In the course of the four-hour sortie, twelve trains were attacked and one section gave chase to a single-engine aircraft which could not be identified. All the aircraft returned safely to base apart from Pickford who, believing he was short of fuel, landed at Vasto, where his Mustang turned onto its back and suffered Cat 3 damage. Here his slim build came to his rescue, as upside down in the sand, and unable to open the coffin-lid cockpit hood, he squeezed himself out through the small sliding window.

On 15 July, despite bad weather over Yugoslavia, which reduced visibility at times to half-a-mile, three attacks were mounted once more against road and rail targets. At 06.55 hours Garwood, Firmin, Chappell and Pienaar were airborne as escort for three Beaufighters, which set out to bomb an oil refinery. Due to the bad weather, the Beaufighters turned back but the four Mustangs pressed on and attacked targets of opportunity as they appeared.

At 07.05 hours, Whiting, Anthony, Cooke and Ford set off for a raid that took them across Montenegro and Bosnia-Herzegovina before, they started to sweep north-east along the railway line from Osijek to Vukovar on the Croatia-Vojvodina border. Two trains were attacked and brought to a halt. In the Vukovar area, a formation of six single-engine biplanes was attacked and four were shot down; these were probably Bucker Jungmeisters or Jungmanns and represented the largest force of enemy aircraft to be encountered. Evidence of the Luftwaffe's domination of Yugoslavian airspace was difficult to find. After this aerial diversion, the section returned to the main task of ground strafing and incapacitated two more trains. Sweeps along two more sections of railway produced no sightings, so the aircraft turned onto a heading of 220 degrees and climbed to 9,000 feet over Sarajevo. At 09.15 hours seven aircraft were seen on the airfield near the town and two of the Mustangs attacked a Do 17, setting it on fire. From Sarajevo the section flew to Hvar Island, and then headed for base where the aircraft landed at 10.00 hours after a patrol lasting nearly three hours.

Off the western tip of Hvar lay the island of Vis, which was occupied by the Partisans. Half of this island had been blasted away so that an emergency landing strip could be built to provide a safe haven for any crippled aircraft returning from operations. The strip was in constant use, and irreparably damaged aircraft were just bulldozed over the cliffs into the sea. The Squadron was asked to provide two aircraft to augment the two Spitfires, which were on detachment there to provide fighter cover, but it was argued that the range and effectiveness of the Mustang made it too valuable to use in this role.

The patrol airborne at 07.35 hours, consisting of Smith, Rorvik and Smailes, was unable to carry out its briefed mission to attack ground targets in southern Yugoslavia due to bad weather, so it turned north and flew inland, finally reaching the coast again at Fiume. Only one train with three rail tankers was seen and attacked. The aircraft then flew south-east along the Dalmatian Coast before recrossing the Adriatic Sea and returning to base.

The flying on 16 July repeated the pattern of the previous day except that the main effort was mounted in the evening. Only one raid was mounted in the morning when Purchas, Moor, Bootherstone and Howard were scheduled to escort some Beaufighters. However only one turned up, so the Mustangs set off alone to strafe ground targets and the airfield at Zagreb. After crossing the coast and the mountains of Bosnia-Herzegovina, the patrol picked up the railway line from Sisak to Zagreb and shot up five locomotives and many trucks. Three attacks were made on a concentration of three locomotives; on the second and third attacks two aircraft were hit by 20mm anti-aircraft fire from a stationary flak truck. Moor and Bootherstone called up to say that they had zero oil pressure and that they were going to force-land. They were last seen, three minutes after calling up, under control but trailing smoke and over country that was suitable for a forced landing. A third aircraft was hit in the crank-case but Purchas made it back to base, while the fourth Mustang suffered nothing worse than a cracked windscreen. Clearly the old maxim "Never go round for a second attack" still applied.

In the evening Vos led four aircraft on the first patrol, and seven locomotives and numerous trucks were set on fire on a route that finally took them west along the River Sava to Brod, and then on to Vincovci on the Brod - Belgrade railway line. Garwood's section of four aircraft, airborne five minutes later, attacked the main airfield at Sarajevo, destroying two single-engine biplanes and damaging three more. South of Sarajevo more trains were attacked.

Not only were operations now in full swing but the Squadron was also settling down in its new quarters despite

Impressive dive-bombing, all eight bombs from a section of four Mustangs burst within the area of the shipyard at Kraljevica, Yugoslavia, 11 March 1945. Photograph by Fg Off Welch.

the lack of some basic requirements, such as tables and chairs in the Operations Room. For the pilots this was not too much of an hardship because after three or four hours in the uncomfortable seat of a single-engine fighter, they were not particularly keen to sit down, and normally spent the next couple of hours standing up.

On 17 July, worsening weather completely frustrated the two early morning patrols. The four aircraft which took off at 16.00 hours, led by the CO on an offensive sweep over south-eastern Yugoslavia, had to return at 26,000 feet owing to a bank of cloud resting on the Dinaric Alps. The intense flying programme seriously curtailed the Squadron's sporting activities. However, as the airfield was practically on the beach, swimming became the major relaxation for the ground-crew, and the length of the patrols meant that this could be enjoyed while the aircraft were in the air.

When operating over Greece and the southern Balkans, use was made of the landing-ground at Leverano. On 18 July Vos led a section of four aircraft from there on an offensive sweep, strafing road and rail targets around Skopje in the southern province of Macedonia. During the patrol the weather closed in and, despite thick cloud from 2,000 feet to 20,000 feet, the airfield at Shijak was attacked and a Ju 52 destroyed. The first of the missions to pick up wounded partisans took place later in the day, when Smith led six Mustangs as escort for two Dakotas to the airfield at Vrgn Most in Yugoslavia. Once the Dakotas had landed, four of the Mustangs covered the airfield for twenty-five minutes and then escorted them back to Italy without any interference. The two other aircraft meanwhile carried out attacks on road and rail transport in the area.

Direct support for the activities of the partisans was provided on 19 July when four aircraft, led by Gp Capt Powell, the CO of 254 Wing, took off from Leverano to strafe the gun emplacements surrounding the chrome mines at Lake Xinias in preparation for a partisan raid. Despite the potentially dangerous nature of the mission, it was carried out successfully and all the aircraft returned safely. Large-scale demolition activity on the part of the partisans was noted by the pilots of an offensive sweep in the Karlovac - Metlika area earlier in the day, many short stretches of railway line having completely disappeared.

The next day saw the most intense flying since operations had restarted, and both the pilots and groundcrew were fully occupied from dawn until dusk. For the first time sections began to operate in pairs, a practice that would become standard operating procedure as time went on. The first section of two, airborne at 05.20 hours, was briefed to act as escort to two Beaufighters on a shipping strike off the Yugoslav coast. However, despite the escort role, when a target was sighted the first attack was made by the two Mustangs. The next two morning sorties were both offensive sweeps against ground targets, and both saw groups of partisans, one about to launch an ambush and another in the

A goods train carrying motor vehicles in the Zagreb area, 21 April 1945. Photograph by Lt Owen Jones, SAAF.

Dubrovnik area.

In the Rozaj area, the section of four that had taken off at 11.15 hours met twelve Henschel Hs 126s escorted by seven Bf 109s. The Mustangs attacked from below and astern, and the CO destroyed one Bf 109 and claimed one probable, while Cooke also claimed a probable and Watkins damaged a further two. After four or five minutes it seemed that the German fighters were anxious to break away. During the course of the action the two sections separated, and Helm and Watkins headed for base. The CO and Cooke searched the area for a few minutes and then followed the roads leading north-east. At 12.05 hours they found the twelve Henschels, now unescorted, flying in four vics of three in line astern. In the ensuing attack, initially on the rear vic, one was destroyed and one damaged by the CO, and two were damaged by Cooke. It was noted that the Bf 109s carried either long-range tanks or bombs slung under the fuselage, which they did not attempt to jettison. Two more patrols by pairs of aircraft in the afternoon attacked locomotives and mule trains between Skopje and Pristina, and barges in Albania.

On 21 July, a total of six offensive patrols were flown, strafing ground targets in south-west Serbia and Montenegro. It was noted that, while reports were received of enemy air activity, no Squadron aircraft had yet been attacked, although operating as much as three hundred miles from base. After only a week of operations, the novelty of reporting locomotives as severely damaged had also worn off and the Squadron Intelligence Officer complained that now pilots merely remarked somewhat nonchalantly that "a loco was hit there, another there and another there" with their index finger on the map. On the third mission however, as if to remind everyone that the war was still a serious affair, Anthony's aircraft received two direct hits from 20mm flak, the first in the centre of the rudder severing the left rudder cable, and the second exploded inside the fuselage between the cockpit and the tail-fin. He was unhurt and was able to bring his aircraft back to base, but it was clear that the German anti-aircraft gunners were becoming quicker to respond and more aircraft were being hit.

In response to reports of considerable German air activity, fifty sorties per day for a three-day period in the Berana area, the Squadron mounted patrols over this part of southern Montenegro. Nothing was found in the air, but a Do 17 and two Ju 87s were damaged on the ground and hits were recorded on a further four Ju 87s.

After two relatively quiet days, 26 July provided a record return for the three missions flown. On the first, twelve locomotives were damaged or severely damaged, on the second, fourteen and on the last, twelve or more. One of the trains was clearly a troop train as evidenced by the soldiers sitting on the roof; the attack caused unlimited havoc and large numbers of soldiers were seen to fall. In the course of the day thirty-eight trains had been incapacitated to some degree or another.

Given the versatility of the Mustang and the nature of the operations, it was clear that it would only be a matter of time before the aircraft were modified to carry bombs, and that a further string would be added to the Squadron's offensive bow. However, until that time, ground strafing operations continued, and on the first mission on 27 July a Ju 52 was left burning on Nis airfield. On the second mission, while strafing trains near Urosevac, Tony Smailes was shot down by flak. He was seen to land near the village and was last observed making for the nearby hills. Unfortunately he was found by the Germans and not the partisans and so became a a prisoner-of-war. During August, September and part of October, he was taken via Budapest, Vienna, Munich, Frankfurt-am-Main and Leipzig to Stalagluft III at Sagan in Silesia. With other prisoners he set out from there in January 1945, just keeping ahead of the advancing Russians. By April 1945 he was "resting" at a farm near Lubeck, having walked most of the way from Sagan via Berlin, Bremen and Hamburg. By the Spring of 1945 the Germans were only too anxious to keep away from the Russians, and in many ways the prisoners controlled their captors; the prisoners had no intention of walking any further east. He was finally liberated on 8 May by a troop of Comet tanks of 11th Armoured Division, which was on its way to capture Lubeck.

Fg Off A G R Ashley with three LAC armourers and Cpl Frank Wright, Engine Fitter and water colour artist, standing in front of Ashley's Mustang III. Note the armourer sitting on the wing of the taxying Mustang in the background.
(Roy Ashley)

In the afternoon of 26 July, the AOC of the Balkan Air Force, Air Vice-Marshal Elliot, visited the Squadron and created an excellent impression as he chatted informally with the pilots. In response to his question as to whether there were any difficulties or snags the three requests were:-

(1) the early arrival of the bombs;
(2) something to be done about the defective ammunition which caused stoppages; and
(3) an expert to be provided who could give a talk on how to dislocate a locomotive and how to assess the damage.

The AOC was no doubt impressed by the offensive spirit of the Squadron.

The next day Gp Capt Powell, who was essentially a bomber and light bomber pilot, and only flew a Mustang a couple of times, preferring (rather naturally) the Beaufighter, led six aircraft on a mission over Sarajevo. On his return something of a difference of opinion arose with the CO as to tactics. Powell advocated flying strafing missions at 4,000 feet in order not to cross the targets too quickly, and also to avoid the worst of the light flak. The CO was not impressed by these arguments believing that, at 4,000 feet, the element of surprise was lost, and that to make an attack it would be necessary to fly right down the barrels of the defenders' machine-guns, which would give them time to line up on the aircraft. Both schools of thought had their supporters and both remained unconvinced of the other's arguments.

On 30 July, a new record was set when, on one mission, sixteen locomotives were severely damaged and a further two damaged. However it was realised, for the first time, that flak wagons were now being regularly attached to trains and were now carrying 40mm anti-aircraft guns. The last day of the month started well, but ended badly. On the first mission of the day, Vos and Pienaar had been forced back from their original target by thick cloud associated with a cold front over the area. However, at 8,000 feet over the Gulf of Fiume, they encountered a S 79 and shot it down into the sea. "It was all over far too quickly" said Pienaar, "after one burst it exploded in flames and crashed into the sea." The second operation was an offensive sweep, north of the Brod - Zagreb railway line as far as the Danube, where it was reported that the Germans were dropping hand-grenades on the partisans.

WO Brown with a Mustang IV in peacetime silver finish, Italy, 1945.

On the return journey, while breaking away from an attack on a train, Fg Off R Anthony's aircraft was hit by flak and the cockpit filled with petrol vapour, which had a suffocating effect. He asked for a course for base and began climbing to 3,500 feet on a course of 220 degrees. While in the climb, his aircraft performed a perfect loop and then dived vertically into the ground where it burst into flames. Other aircraft had been hit on operations, but in all cases the pilots had been seen to bale out. This was the Squadron's first confirmed fatal loss on operations in the Balkans.

As the month closed, marking the end of the first two weeks of operations, two facts stood out. The first was that successful operations were very dependent on the weather, and forecasts of weather conditions over the Balkans were unreliable to say the least. The second was the phenomenal range of the Mustang, which still astounded everyone on the Squadron. A sortie on 2 August illustrated both points, when Scot Vos, the Squadron's ace navigator, spent the best part of three hours over enemy territory without knowing exactly where he was. He was exonerated from any blame due to the low cloud and poor visibility over the target area. From the debriefing that followed the operation, it appeared that he had flown almost as far as Vienna and back.

With the new month came new tactics, since all the trains now carried anti-aircraft guns mounted on an open flak wagon at the rear. In the past, all four aircraft in a section had attacked simultaneously; this was now modified with the leading pair attacking the flak wagon to silence the guns, and leaving the train to the second pair. This modified attack worked well on the first four trains on which it was tried. It was also recommended that the Squadron pilots should attend joint briefings with the Beaufighter and Baltimore crews when on a combined operation, since confusion had occurred when the bombers attacked different targets from those advised to the escort pilots at a separate briefing.

With operations continuing, despite the bad weather, two more aircraft were lost on 4 August when both Chappell and 2Lt S W Pienaar were hit by ground fire. Chappell's aircraft was not seriously damaged but Pienaar, who was flying Number Two to Stan Pickford, was hit while strafing a train. His aircraft shot past his leader, trailing vapour which Pickford suspected was petrol. As Pienaar climbed away to gain height, Pickford called him on the R/T to see if he was going to bale-out. His reply was "No I can't; I've been hit". He then attempted to make a wheels-up forced landing but his aircraft burst into flames as it hit the ground.

With bad weather still limiting operations, the CO tried

out the newly-fitted bomb-racks by dropping 1,000-lb bombs on an aluminium sea-marker just off the coast. Somewhat unnervingly, one of the bombs fell off on take-off at the first attempt. On the second occasion everything went as planned, and a technique of dive-bombing from 8,000 feet, pulling out at 4,000 feet, was developed. Soon bombing tactics were the main topic of conversation, and so keen were the pilots that the CO was pressed into agreeing that bombs should be carried on strafing missions to give the pilots live practice. The first mission with bombs was flown when the CO and Vos attacked the defences around the oil plant at Ilice on the Gulf of Kotor, which left the storage tanks burning. No flak was encountered and the attack was rated as a success.

Such was the spirit on the Squadron and the desire to know what was going on over the "other side" that for some time the CO had been under pressure from Lt V G Stock, the Intelligence Officer, who was also responsible for writing up the Operation's Record Book, Fg Off Robins, the Administration Officer, and the Padre to organise a trip over enemy territory. As a Mustang had only a single seat, Whiting borrowed a Baltimore and on 11 August they all set off for Yugoslavia. The sight-seeing tour went via Vis and then swept down the coast to Dubrovnik, where Whiting felt they were guaranteed to find some flak, albeit highly inaccurate. The party returned safely having greatly enjoyed its flirtation with operations, and was duly sworn to secrecy. On his subsequent return to South Africa, the CO was somewhat surprised to receive a scathing letter from Lt Stock's sister upbraiding him for exposing her brother to danger!

Another new role for the Mustang, and one that was greeted with less enthusiasm by the pilots, was that of de-flakking the target area for some 800 yards ahead of the Beaufighters. While the arrangement worked well - and it certainly persuaded the German gunners to keep their heads down - it was unpopular since it entailed flying at such a slow speed to keep abreast of the Beaufighters that the Mustang became awkward to fly. As the Germans learned to respond more rapidly and effectively to the strafing raids, and operations continued at a high level, losses began to mount. On 9 August, Lt L J Leach received a direct hit as he pulled up after attacking a train; a flash was seen in the cockpit and his aircraft heeled over and dived vertically into the ground. Two days later Chappell was again hit and had to bale out. He left his aircraft at 7,000 feet and, while his parachute was seen to open, no-one saw where he landed. On the third bombing and strafing mission, on 14 August, Cooke's aircraft was hit while he was shooting-up a gun position after completing his bombing run. After five minutes he was seen to bale out and land safely.

The return on 15 August of 2Lt J Moore, who had been shot down and had baled out on 17 July, was therefore not only welcome in itself but also as an indication that other missing pilots might return. Moore was in fact the first of a steady stream of pilots who, after having force-landed on the other side of the Adriatic Sea, made their way back to Biferno with the aid of the Partisans and the operations flown by a specialised formation at Bari. The fastest return was that accomplished by "B" Flight Commander, Flt Lt C S Vos, who crash-landed near the village of Turopulse, south of Zagreb, on 26 August, and by the end of the month was back with the Squadron flying operations.

By the middle of the month, the strafing of roads and railways gave way to attacks on German airfields in an attempt to reduce the aerial support available to the German troops attacking the Partisan II Corps. On 18 August, four Mustangs accompanied four Beaufighters of No.16 SAAF Squadron in an attack on Banja Luka airfield. The formation flew to the target area at 7,000 feet and then descended to ground level. The Mustangs went in just ahead of the Beaufighters, crossing the airfield from the south, shooting up all observed gun positions and starting fires in the only hangar that was visible. Although no aircraft were seen during the first attack, Gp Capt. Powell, who was leading the section of Beaufighters, was convinced that there were enemy aircraft somewhere on the airfield. So, breaking the cardinal rule, he then decided to make a second strike at the target preceded by only one section of Mustangs on a de-flakking run. The disastrous consequences produced by this practice in the past were repeated, as the defenders were by then wide awake. Soon, one of the Beaufighter pilots called up to say that one of his engines had been hit and Powell, cool as a cucumber, said that both of his had been hit. The first aircraft crashed into the bed of a dried-up stream, while Powell's aircraft crashed onto the side of a hill and disintegrated. The loss of the Wing's Commanding Officer was a severe blow felt by all. When Wg Cdr D S MacDonald, the CO from the Battle of Britain days, dropped in on his way to join No.283 Wing, he found a very subdued Squadron. Happily, it was subsequently learned that the Group Captain had survived and had been captured by the Chetniks.

In July 1944, the German Prinz Eugen Division and the 21st Mountain Division began to take the offensive against the Partisan II Corps in Montenegro. The German attacks soon resulted in a greatly increased number of wounded and 37 Military Mission, operating with the Partisans, asked for RAF personnel to establish a landing strip, so that some of the wounded could be flown out to hospitals in Italy. The landing ground party arrived in Montenegro on 11 August, but the strong German pressure forced the Partisans to move out of the area. For four days the Partisan group and the RAF party marched through the hills towards Brezner carrying the wounded. When they arrived the site of the proposed landing ground, it was found to be an open corn field which had to be cleared of obstacles. This was quickly achieved by the Partisan group, including women and children. Although the Partisan leader initially said that he could not hold out for more than two days, the required number of aircraft could not be made available due to other commitments until 22 August, when the rescue operation took place.

The Squadron became involved in this operation on 21 August when, after two missions in the morning, twelve aircraft, together with a Dakota carrying the ground-crews and spares, left for the main airfield at Brindisi in order to be ready for an early start the next morning. At 06.50 hours the twelve Mustangs were airborne, escorting six C-47s of the 60th Troop Carrier Group, USAAF to the landing ground approximately fifty miles east of Dubrovnik, where some thirteen hundred sick and wounded were awaiting evacuation. Within twenty minutes of landing, two hundred wounded had been loaded onto the six C-47s and evacuated. The turn-around would have been quicker but for the actions of members of the Garibaldi Division, who swarmed all over the aircraft looking for a berth that would take them back to Italy. Some had to be ejected at the point of a revolver. After the C-47s had taken off, a Spitfire dropped a message to the effect that another twenty-four were on their way. The first six of these, again escorted by the Squadron's Mustangs, arrived at 14.30 hours and thereafter formations of six aircraft continued to arrive, until over one thousand sick and wounded had been brought out with no enemy interference. The Partisans, who were being flown out, had to leave their arms

Belgrade, 28 February 1945. Photograph taken by Flt Lt F M Gamble, RAAF

and clothing for use by their comrades who remained behind, and were given blankets in which to wrap themselves. As priority was to be given to the evacuation of female Partisans, and since it was impossible on arrival to distinguish a male from a female Partisan, this change of clothing assisted in the identification process.

The sense of satisfaction with a job well done was somewhat diminished, when the pilots were ordered not to return to base at Biferno until after a visit by Air Chief Marshal Sir Charles Portal, Chief of the Air Staff, was over. This order was given on the grounds that the pilots would not have time to wash and "groom" themselves before meeting the Air Chief Marshal - a poor appreciation of the work being done. As the Squadron's Operations Record Book somewhat caustically noted "Fine feathers do not make fine birds". As it was, the Squadron was represented by four recently-arrived pilots, who had not yet commenced operational flying. The operational strength of the Squadron was increased even further on 24 August, when five more pilots arrived to join the four recent additions. With this increase in numbers also came a change in command structure when the Squadron returned to No.283 Wing. In practice little enough changed; the Wing HQ remained at Campomarino, and the operations room and Intelligence Section of No.254 Wing continued to be used. The reason for the change was that in future No.254 Wing was to operate as a purely bombing formation. No.283 Wing was also strengthened by the arrival of Nos.16 and 19 Squadrons SAAF, both flying Beaufighters.

As the month drew to a close, operations were restricted by the lack of spares and the limited number of pilots who were operational. At the same time, the German Air Force had to abandon operations from the advanced landing grounds at Mostar, Sarajevo, Banja Luka and Bihac. For future operations, all the Bf 109s were to be concentrated at Zagreb. On 24 August, five new pilots arrived, but on the next day's operations Sgt Liudzius was hit by ack-ack fire and baled out over southern Greece, and on the following day Flt Lt Vos had to force-land south of Zagreb.

On 29 August, WO A MacFarlane, one of the new arrivals, was killed in a flying accident; his hood blew off on take-off and, coming in to land, his aircraft stalled at fifty feet, hit the ground and burst into flames. He was buried with full military honours in the nearby River Sangro Military Cemetery. In another incident, a few days earlier, Helm had been more fortunate when his aircraft had swung off the runway and, after bouncing over the dunes on the edge of the airfield, had broken in two as it skidded across the beach. The engine and the airframe came to rest twenty yards apart and some fifty yards off-shore. Helm climbed into his dinghy and was pulled to shore by a party of airmen who were swimming nearby. On the more positive side, Scot Vos returned to operations on 30 August after his brief five-day stop-over with the Partisans.

The end of the month provided an opportunity to take stock. It was established that the change to bombing attacks, while less effective than ground strafing in terms of the destruction caused, was also less dangerous in terms of casualties. During the month over eight hundred hours of operational flying had been achieved with only ten pilots, thus averaging eighty hours each - a considerable achievement. Of the 318 sorties flown, only five had been affected by technical faults. On the ground, the MT (Motor Transport) Section had covered over 3,300 miles. They had also carried some one hundred and sixty tons of steel plates; as preparations were made for the coming winter, these perforated steel plates were laid to provide a hard surface for the runway and perimeter-tracks. Since joining the Balkan Air Force the Squadron's carefully kept score amounted to:-

Enemy aircraft destroyed in combat	8
Probables	2
Damaged	3
Enemy aircraft destroyed on the ground	4
Damaged	11
Locomotives	289
Motor Transport	203
Rail cars	93 plus
AA Guns	18
Caiques etc	18

At the beginning of September 1944, the sudden collapse of Rumania and Bulgaria, in the face of the advancing Red Army, had put the German forces in the Balkans in a perilous position, which necessitated a large scale withdrawal from the Aegean Sea, Greece and southern Yugoslavia. The two most important rail links for the retreating German forces were the Skopje - Belgrade - Brod line and that from Mostar through Sarajevo to Zagreb. During the first week of September, a special co-ordinated operation, code named "Ratweek", was mounted both on the ground and in the air by the Partisans and Land Forces Adriatic, supported by the BAF and the US 15th Air Force, to interrupt the enemy's rail, road, air and sea communications. In this operation, the Squadron assumed yet another role by providing tactical reconnaissance for the medium bombers of the American 15th Air Force. On the initial sortie of the first day of the month, the arrangements worked to perfection. Having reconnoitred north and west of Belgrade, the returning Mustangs reported the dispositions of the retreating Germans to the American bombers on their outbound journey over the mountains of Bosnia-Herzegovina. Such perfect co-ordination produced disastrous results for the German motor convoys. Later in the day, HQ BAF passed on the Americans' thanks for the excellent reconnaissance work. By the end of the month no through traffic was possible on any railway line in Yugoslavia; this forced the Germans onto the roads, thus consuming precious fuel reserves. Soon, even on the roads, movement was only possible at night, increasing the risk of Partisan attacks.

The Fighter Group forming part of the American 15th Air Force was one of their few coloured units, and it operated uncamouflaged Mustangs and some P-38s as long-range escort fighters for the bombers raiding as far north as Poland. In this role they were often in the air for four or five hours at a time, and quickly found that sitting on a parachute in a Mustang for this length of time was pretty uncomfortable. To ease the problem, tail-wheel inner-tubes were introduced as air cushions. These worked well on the ground, but on the first sortie sixty out of sixty aircraft had to return in a state of some embarrassment with the pilots jammed hard against the cockpit's canopy. It had been overlooked that at altitude the inner-tubes would expand. On another occasion the CO, Sqn Ldr Whiting, was returning with his section at ground level over Yugoslavia, when his number four called up to say that they were about to be attacked by fifty-plus bandits diving in from the rear. The section whipped round into a defensive circle and found itself being wildly attacked by fifty uncamouflaged Mustangs. Fortunately the attackers were not too experienced, and a call to "Big Fence" soon had the attack called off. In the evening, when the American CO and his No.2 came over to apologise, he explained that they had never seen camouflaged Mustangs before and had taken them for Bf 109s.

Further reconnaissance patrols over the next two days unfortunately returned with nothing to report, and by the fourth of the month a day free from operational flying allowed urgent servicing work to be carried out. It was felt that the arrival of the Russian forces on the eastern border of Yugoslavia had put HQ BAF in a dilemma, since the Squadron had aircraft ready but Command had nowhere to send them. That this situation would end the really long-range sorties was seen to be wishful thinking when, on 5 September, Gp Capt D S MacDonald, now promoted to command No.283 Wing, set out to lead a section on an armed reconnaissance patrol over the Danube. Ten-tenths cloud in the target area, however, led to the patrol being aborted.

As the Germans sought to use air transport to alleviate the pressure on the much-disrupted ground communications network, more aerial encounters ensued. On 6 September a patrol with Smith leading Vorster, Pickford and Sgt D E Firman, found a formation of four Bf 110s that had just taken off from airfield S52, south-east of Sombor. Closing fast from astern at 1,800 feet, the element of surprise was complete and three of the Messerschmitts were seen to hit the ground. Smith and Vorster claimed one jointly, and Firman and Pickford one each. As Pickford dived on one of the Bf 110s, its camouflage made it barely distinguishable from the landscape below; concentrating hard on his target as he closed from astern, he suddenly became aware that he was flying wing-tip to wing-tip with its Number Two. In the circumstances, one quick burst was all he had time for before breaking away; the one attack was sufficient.

The next day, Rorvik shot down an Hs 126 over the Danube while on an armed patrol; he first saw the enemy aircraft at 6,000 feet and a short burst sent it crashing down on the bank of the river. The day of 8 September turned out to be even more productive for an offensive sweep led by Smith with Vorster, Moor and Rorvik. Having attacked a Ju 52 over Belgrade, they then encountered two He 111s towing two Gotha Go 242 gliders. As the section attacked, both Heinkels were seen to crash along with one of the gliders. The other glider cast loose and made for a nearby field and, when it came into land, it was effectively strafed and attacked again as it came to rest in a hedge. None of the four Mustangs received any damage.

On the next day, Sqn Ldr S R Whiting flew his last mission with the Squadron, completing his third operational tour. His period in command had been one of the longest since the outbreak of the war. He had seen the Squadron through two re-equipments, moving from the pre-war designed Hurricane to the pinnacle of piston-engined fighter production, the North American Mustang. On operations, he had taken the Squadron from convoy protection work at Martuba to ground attack, fighter-bomber interdiction and armed reconnaissance work throughout the entire Balkan theatre of operations. During that time, and through a long frustrating period, he had maintained a high standard of efficiency and discipline that was the Squadron's hall-mark; it was clear that he would be missed. His value as a leader was emphasised, a few months after his departure, when he was awarded the DSO.

Leading a section of four aircraft over Greek Macedonia the next day, Smith found a Ju 52 heading south and shot it down in flames. Later in the patrol, they encountered an He 111 and chased it for twenty-five miles before forcing it

Sqn Ldr P E Vaughan-Fowler, DFC and Bar, FG Off A G R Ashley and Lt H B Helm, SAAF, standing outside a tent at Biferno, Winter 1944. (Roy Ashley)

down. During the course of the chase, another newcomer on the Squadron, Sgt Brierley, was lost. His aircraft was last seen in a steep turn after an attack, and it was presumed that he had been hit by return fire from the He 111. As the bulk of the flying still fell on the shoulders of the reduced number of operational pilots, some of them were certainly beginning to feel the strain of operations every day.

On 11 September, Vos and Fg Off F A E Penson attacked a Ju 52 which crashed into a hillside; then, on a second sweep near Belgrade, Flt Lt J Fairbairn destroyed another Ju 52 and Sgt D H Bell shot down an Hs 126. It was clear that the policy of mounting dawn sweeps in selected areas was paying rich dividends. If no ground targets presented themselves, enemy aircraft could often be found, particularly in the area around Belgrade and between Nis and Salonika (Thessaloniki) in the south. The next day, Garwood, leading a section of four aircraft, severely damaged a Do 17 as it completed its landing run at Pacevo airfield just north of Belgrade. Firman, his Number Two, scored several direct hits on a taxying Ju 88 and probably destroyed another Do 17 on the ground. During the attack Garwood, engrossed with his target, hit the flag-staff on top of the Air Traffic Control building which tore a hole in his mainplane; nevertheless he managed to return to base without too much difficulty.

In contrast to the preceding few days, the middle of the month proved to be a difficult time as a spell of bad weather and intensive operational flying brought a spate of losses. On 13 September, a section of four aircraft, flown by Flt Lt J H Fairbairn, Sgt A A Dowling, Lt H B Helm and Flt Sgt F Heard, split up in bad weather crossing the Adriatic. Helm and Heard returned to base after an hour. Fairbairn and Dowling, having persevered through bad weather, found a Savoia 79 in the Belgrade area. Pressing home his attack, Fairbairn's wing-tip hit an obstacle and his aircraft cart-wheeled into the ground before bursting into flames. Dowling carried on with the attack and the Italian bomber was last seen at about ten feet trailing smoke. On returning to Biferno, Dowling reported the details of Fairbairn's crash and as there was no way anyone could have survived such an accident he was confirmed as killed in action. Amazingly, Fairbairn had survived the crash, the details of which remained a total blank for him. His first memory on regaining consciousness was of lying on the ground unable to move, badly cut and bruised, and with an under-carriage leg lying alongside his head. He was then captured by the Germans and taken to a hospital with a broken leg.

For the next two days, bad weather prevented all operational flying. It was little better on 16 September when Lt J W Moore failed to return from a patrol; he was last seen entering thick cloud that extended from 400 feet to 10,000 feet and, although he was called up on the radio, no reply was received. It was feared that he had spun in. This sad period ended on a better note when, on a close support mission with 249 Squadron, backing up partisans in the hills around Prilep in the Yugoslav province of Macedonia, Rorvik attacked a Do 217, which was last seen diving steeply with one engine on fire; it was claimed as a probable.

On 19 September 1944, WO K M J Clarkson arrived on the Squadron from the Kittyhawk conversion unit at Fayid in Egypt. Having carried out his flying training at No. 2 BFTS at Lancaster, California, he had then spent six months back in the UK towing drogues before going out to Egypt. He stayed with the Squadron until the end of the war, flying seventy-two operational sorties, during which, apart from a brush with a tree, his aircraft never sustained any damage. Ken Clarkson's experience represents that of the majority of the pilots who flew with the Squadron during the war, men who flew on operations and, although not involved in any incidents which were recorded in the ORB, whose bravery and skill contributed to the final victory over the enemy, and the Squadron's proud war record.

As operational flying hours mounted and further preparations were made for the coming winter, with Nissen huts replacing the tents as living quarters, the news came that Flt Lt C S Vos, the popular commander of "B" Flight, was to take command of the Squadron as from 22 September. After a successful day's operations on 21 September, during which Pickford shot down a Bf 109 that had just taken off from Tirana airfield and damaged another, a large party was held in the evening to say "Good-bye" to the departing CO and to welcome the new. An antidote to the cold wet weather, which limited operations and depressed everyone's spirits, was provided when Plt Off R A Bootherstone returned to the Squadron. He had been shot down over Yugoslavia on 16 July, only his second day of operations, and having injured his spine during his forced landing had spent much of the intervening period in hospital. During the next two days missions were flown providing cover for British troops and Commandos being put ashore north of Saradne which was on the Albanian coast opposite the northern tip of Corfu.

During this period of bad weather, the Adjutant was kept busy and worried - dealing with the difficult question of the missing jam jar. This essential piece of equipment had apparently been borrowed from the army by the detachment at Lakatamia, back in November 1943. Although those involved swore that it had been returned, very carelessly the receipt had been lost and the ensuing correspondence had been going on ever since!

The centre-piece of this period of bad weather was a raging storm on 29 September with accompanying thunder and lightning. The winds flattened the remaining tents and even the Nissen huts leaked. Everyone and everything became thoroughly wet and it was noted that the canvas beds were particularly efficient in catching and holding the rainwater. The weather over Yugoslavia was equally bad, and on 27 September Sgt A A Dowling, leading a section, entered thick cloud at 400 feet and was not seen again.

By October the German position was untenable. Belgrade had been freed by a strong Partisan force, Tito's units had linked up with the Russians, and a strong British force was moving north from Athens. For the seven German divisions remaining in the Balkans, the only hope of survival lay in a

A typical sight at Biferno, Squadron Mustangs taxying out for a strike/armed recce. The armourers rode on the wings to take-off point before arming the bombs.

rapid retreat. However, all rail communications south of Belgrade had been severed and the only escape route lay across the Partisan-infested roads of Bosnia. For the first week of October, when rain and low cloud cleared long enough for the airfield to dry out and for operations to be mounted, support was given to the British forces pushing up from the south, and offensive sweeps were flown against the remaining communication routes leading north out of Albania. During October, the Germans best ally turned out to be the weather, which greatly curtailed operations. This lack of flying, and the limited scope of such operations as were possible, together with the growing feeling that the task of the Balkan Air Force had really been completed and that its continued activity was merely a political manoeuvre, led to a growing feeling of frustration. It seemed to some that sending four Mustangs and four Beaufighters to attack fifteen hundred troops quartered in a town was an unproductive use of air power. It was recognised that HQ BAF was in a predicament. For some of the ground-crew the frustration was alleviated when the first party of airmen were put "on the boat" for home, the first to return to the UK after a three-and-a-half years' absence.

During a brief spell of good weather on 7 October, WO Johnny Watkins had a particularly narrow escape while leading a formation of ten aircraft operating from Brindisi on an offensive sweep to attack a concentration of six troop trains north-west of Gorgpoe-Salonika. Flying at zero feet down the western side of the railway lines, he came across a train, which they strafed, severely damaging the locomotive. As the patrol was resumed, the target they were briefed to attack was seen to starboard; the Mustangs turned in to attack, flying straight down the railway line at three hundred miles per hour. Once again the locomotive was severely damaged and numbers of troops were caught in a hail of fire. The section of four led by Johnny Watkins continued to strafe the other trains. While doing so, Watkin's aircraft was seen to shudder, go out of control momentarily and have its port wing strike an object. Four feet of the wing was torn off and all but a foot of the aileron. The windscreen was shattered. The aircraft slewed to the left but was brought under control by the application of full starboard aileron, and full revs and boost.

Calling up the formation, Watkins told them he intended to crash-land in the nearest field. However, to his amazement the aircraft continued to fly on, or as he reported, "Well it didn't actually fly in the true sense of the word, it just wallowed round the sky, so I tried to gain height in order to bale out". On reaching 1,000 feet he called up his No. 3 and gave him the course to fly to base, telling him to take the lead, and that he would try to follow. Taking stock of his situation, he found that there was a fifty-foot length of fencing wire wound round the spinner behind the blades of the propeller, which then trailed back under the starboard wing and over the tailplane. Another fifteen-foot length of wire trailed back from his port wing. He realised that, as either could tear a parachute to pieces, there was nothing to do but to fly on.

There were still the mountains, the enemy coast and the Adriatic Sea to cross. As the fuel-load diminished and he fired off the remainder of his ammunition to lighten his aircraft, he climbed to 12,000 feet to start the sea crossing back to Italy. The strain imposed by the physical effort of holding the controls over to counteract the drag from the damaged port wing was intense. In the absence of any means of lashing the control column in place, he had to put both legs on one side of it and then force it over, using all his body weight. An hour later he was approaching Brindisi but, as his VHF aerial had been torn away in the accident, he was unable to make contact; however his escort did so and, after clearance, he approached to land. He now discovered that his throttle was jammed open, but by lowering his wheels and flaps he brought his speed back and touched down, at one hundred and seventy knots, to make a perfect landing which was ample testimony to his skill as a pilot and the strength of

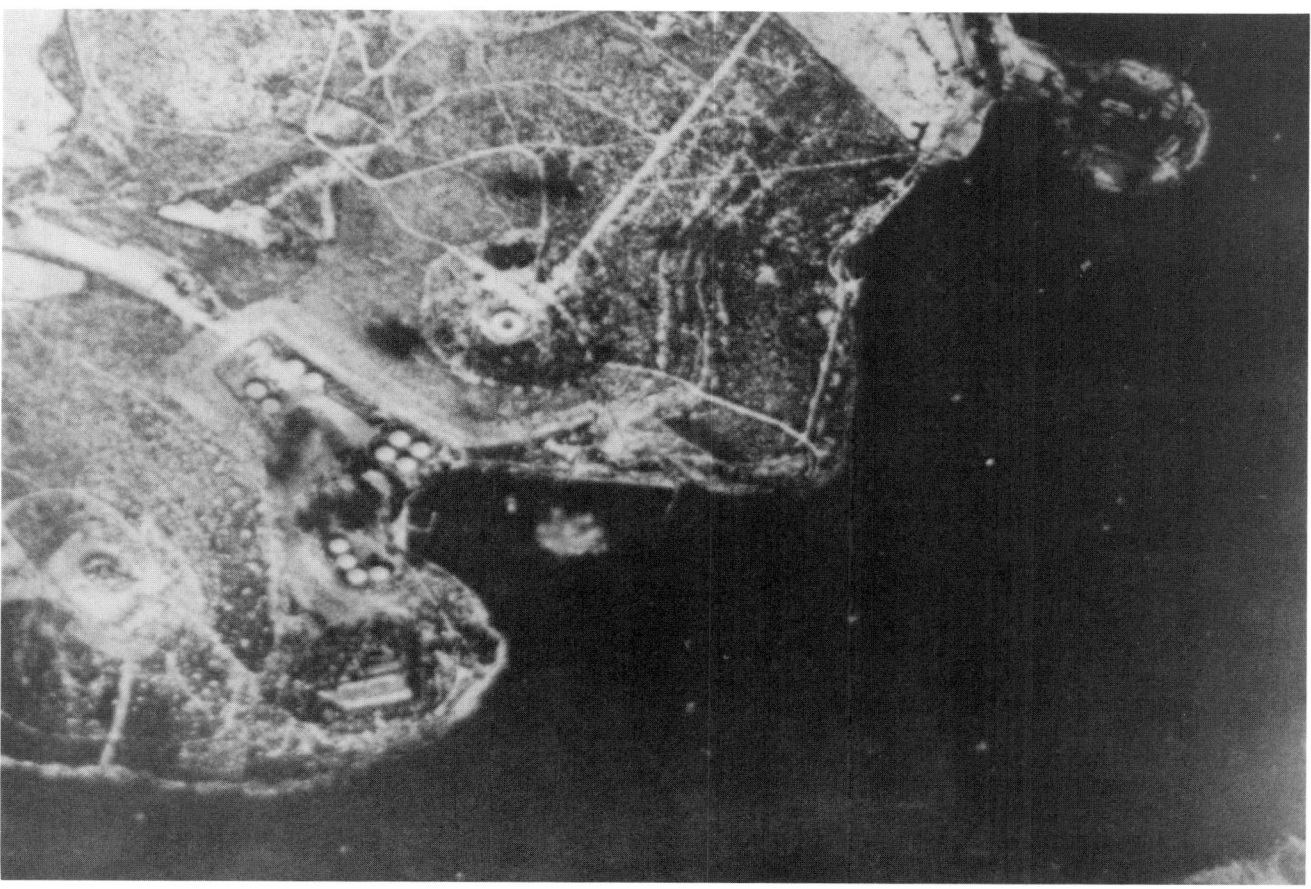
Oil storage tanks at Pola, south of Trieste, under attack. Fg Off A G R Ashley's bombs can be seen bursting among the tanks. Photograph taken by the CO who followed Ashley down. (Roy Ashley)

the Mustang. Inspection of the aircraft after landing revealed that ninety per cent of the rudder was missing as well as the top of the fin, the propeller was chipped and the spinner smashed in.

In addition to replacement aircraft, the urgent need was for experienced pilots and a signal to this effect arrived at 32 Squadron, which was then at Brindisi, *en route* for Greece as soon as the Germans had left. Four pilots were selected to join 213 Squadron, including Flt Lt E H MacLellan, Plt Off A G R Ashley and Flt Sgt N Stevenson. Roy Ashley, at least, felt enormously cheered by the move from 32 Squadron. Together with MacLellan and Stevenson, he had been with that unit for one month and had flown one operational mission. Having volunteered to become a pilot in late 1940, and following training in the USA, he had to his disgust been selected for further training to become an instructor on his return to the UK. It was not until March 1944 that his request for operational flying was granted and, together with MacLellan and Stevenson, he was posted to a Spitfire OTU at Abu Sueir, and then finally to Italy, on D-Day, 6 June 1944. He had completed one thousand hours flying. As they travelled north in a thirty-hundredweight truck, they felt flattered by the wording of the signal, which in turn induced a feeling of optimism that the boring times were over. They little realised just how fully that feeling was to be justified. A six-and-a-half-hour "in house" operational conversion course was undertaken, which included formation flying and dive-bombing on a sea-target with 100-lb bombs. The somewhat hurried nature of the course meant that some matters were passed over quickly, including the operation of the fuel tanks, which was to lead to a nasty moment while on operations.

In the four months of operations since arriving in Italy, the Squadron's Mustangs had been in action over four of the five capital cities in the Balkans, namely Athens, Belgrade, Sofia and Tirana. Hopes of reaching the fifth, Budapest, were fading daily as it seemed that before the Squadron made it there, the Russians would have arrived. With Greece cleared of German forces by 2 November and the continued advances of the Russians, the Squadron's sphere of operations was becoming drastically reduced. The news that the Mustangs were to be equipped with long-range tanks was however met with very mixed feelings. On the one hand, it gave the promise of operations in a new theatre but on the other hand - given that three to four hours in a Mustang was uncomfortable enough - the prospect of sorties of between six and seven hours was almost unimaginable. Water-filled cushions for all pilots seemed to be a useful suggestion but stores turned out to be particularly unhelpful, not being aware that such items existed.

At the same time, systems for the recognition of Russian aircraft and identification procedures for BAF aircraft were introduced. Aircraft would dip a port or starboard wing and fire a Very cartridge. This was simple enough, but it ignored the fact that the Squadron's Mustangs were not fitted with the necessary gadgets for firing flares.

Ashley's first operation was to strafe airfields north of Belgrade and, while crossing the Danube, he took the opportunity to strafe a barge moving up river. The attack is commemorated in a water-colour painted by Cpl Frank "Wilbur" Wright, an Engine Fitter on the Squadron, which is

Gp Cpt D S MacDonald's Fairchild Argus at Araxos with the three pilots who flew the escorting Mustangs.

reproduced on the back cover of this book.

With the liberation of Greece, more and more Allied aircraft were passing through Biferno, and the Squadron took on the air of a road-house for aircrews in transit. The task of escorting VIPs to Athens also fell to the Squadron pilots on numerous occasions and, although escort work itself was not popular, the accompanying stay in Athens afterwards generally made up for it. At one hundred and seventy knots, the cruising speed of the Dakota, the Mustang was not a comfortable aeroplane to fly. The constant weaving that was necessary to keep station was particularly hard work, as at that speed the controls were sloppy. On 25 October, Gp Cpt MacDonald led four Mustangs escorting General Maitland-Wilson to Athens, and the accompanying stop-over lasted four days. On a similar trip escorting Anthony Eden, Ken Clarkson remembers that, not having any local currency, they borrowed some money from the visiting dignitary to see them through the stop-over. The pilots noted that a flourishing black market existed; the rate of exchange was three million drachmae to the pound, but the best currency was cigarettes. These also had local purchasing power and Roy Ashley, who although a non-smoker still received his "free issue", came to an arrangement with a local Italian family to do his laundry for five Woodbines per week.

On 28 October, the Officers' Mess decided to become teetotal since, with the constant supply of visitors and the bad weather limiting flying, there were too many parties. The Mess was located in a Nissen hut and the bar consisted of a suitably modified Liberator tail-fin laid on its side. With strict rationing of beer and spirits from the UK, it had become necessary to supplement the meagre supplies from local sources. This led to such exotic creations as the "Balkan Caress", a mixture of gin Strega (a local seven-day vintage liqueur) diluted with enough orange juice to make it drinkable; the "Blue Train", a mixture of gin and Strega only, with a dash of Stevens ink, was less of a success and never really palatable.

The day after the teetotal ordinance saw the arrival of Flt Lt W J P "Bill" Straker (later Gp Cpt W J P Straker, AFC, MRAeS). Having already logged some one thousand flying hours as an instructor in the USA, and having completed a Hurricane/Spitfire OTU in Palestine, he was another of the experienced pilots to arrive on the Squadron. In the seven months that remained until the end of the war, he became a Flight Commander and was to fly sixty-two combat missions; thereafter he remained with the Squadron until June 1946. He quickly noted, amongst all ranks, the spirit of dogged determination to see the job through despite the drawbacks of a domestic life that had to contend with tented accommodation, Nissen huts, spam fritters, PSP (perforated steel planking) and mud. In contrast to these basic living conditions, the Mustang was a state of the art fighter, albeit that the Squadron had to devise its own type conversion programme for new arrivals. For some this would prove a dangerous transition. Additionally, the initiation into dive-bombing and strafing could not be rushed, if disproportionate losses were to be avoided. It was very clear that the success of missions was closely linked to the experience of the pilots involved. The combination of bad winter weather, flying over mountainous country and the need to attack targets at extremely low level, in the face of an aggressive and skillful enemy, all contributed to a relatively high loss rate in both pilots and aircraft. In all the close support operations in Italy and the Balkans, the RAF, RAAF and the SAAF lost one 161 Mustang IIIs in approximately one year of operations; the Squadron's losses were among the highest.

There was no doubt that, when flying did take place, the bad weather presented a real hazard, as was demonstrated by the events of 30 October. Ashley was detailed to carry out the dawn weather reconnaissance inland from the Albanian coast. He found ten/tenths dense cloud over the hills and in a continuous bank along the coast. It appeared suicide to attempt to fly inland among the mountains, so he called up "Watch-box", Biferno's call-sign, and gave the code-word "Oranges Sour". Later in the morning Fg Off G A Allan flew another weather reconnaissance sortie and reported a slight improvement; this latter report led to two strikes being mounted, unfortunately with tragic consequences. As soon as the aircraft were bombed-up, Lt R E Rorvik led four aircraft on a mission to Mitrovica when, shortly after take-off, the section ran into heavy weather at 1,000 feet. Rorvik ordered it to climb to 6,000 feet. Once again the section set course and once again it ran into cloud with visibility less than one hundred yards. The order was given to jettison the bombs and return to base. Rorvik's aircraft was last seen in a steep turn to port, and when his Number Two emerged from the cloud there was no sign of his leader.

The target was clearly of considerable importance, since notwithstanding the severe weather conditions and the fate of Rorvik's section from which only one aircraft returned, Roy Garwood was ordered to lead another section to attack the target. As he sat in his aircraft, with his section awaiting clearance to take off, he thought over the task ahead, not without some misgivings. While waiting, he heard over the R/T an American B-17, returning from a raid, calling up in some difficulty. The priority was sufficient for the American bomber to be given clearance to land immediately ahead of Garwood's section becoming airborne. The bomber's resulting forced landing on Biferno's only all-weather runway resolved Garwood's problems. Later in the afternoon, once the runway had been cleared, he carried out a search over the Adriatic for any sight of the missing aircraft from Rorvik's section, but without any success.

Shortly after, at 14.15 hours, four aircraft from the Squadron, together with four Mustangs from 249 Squadron, took off with MacDonald in the lead on an offensive sweep in the Prilep-Monastir area. The formation remained above cloud as far as Skopje, where it found a break in the otherwise ten-tenths cover and descended. On the way down, the formation split up and lost contact with the Group Captain. Once below cloud, Flt Lt E H MacLellan took five

Mustang IVs in peacetime silver finish, Italy, 1945.

of the aircraft north-west from Skopje into the Lipljan area. However, after one strafing run, MacLellan disappeared and it seemed that he had been hit by flak. The remaining four aircraft set course for base and flew into cloud over the coast at 5,000 feet. One of the 249 Squadron aircraft was last seen by Sgt W H Butterworth inverted, and Butterworth then found himself in a spin but fortunately managed to recover.

On a sad day, three pilots had been lost, but only one due directly to enemy action. Since operations over the Balkans had commenced in July, the Squadron had lost twenty-five Mustangs; three had been lost in accidents, one had hit the ground while attacking an enemy aircraft, one had been hit by return fire from a Fieseler Storch and was destroyed in the subsequent forced landing, and the remainder had been lost to ground fire.

Nine new pilots arrived on 30 October, but none with any Mustang or operational experience. In the evening, despite the teetotal ordinance, a party was held to celebrate Johnny Watkins receiving his commission.

November opened with the arrival of ten more new pilots. An eight-hour flying conversion programme was instituted for them, to be followed by escort duties and then shipping strikes, before they could achieve full operational status. A good deal of the non-operational flying was carried out at the nearby Nuova landing-ground. However, for the first three days of the month, both operational and training flying was seriously hampered by the bad weather. When flying was possible, the same round of escort duties, shipping strikes and ground attack missions was carried out. So serious had the position become, with some pilots not having flown for months, that a Harvard was borrowed to enable non-operational pilots to log some flying hours.

On 7 November, as the weather cleared, four aircraft set off on a bombing and ground strafing mission in the Scutari - Prizren area in northern Albania. A direct hit was scored on the bridge, which was the main target, and then Allen and Firman continued to strafe the roads in the area. During this phase of the operation, Firman's aircraft was hit by flak, and was seen to heel over and plunge into the marshy ground before bursting into flames. The same day also saw the arrival of Flt Lt P E Vaughan-Fowler, DFC and Bar, who was subsequently to succeed Sqn Ldr S C Vos as Squadron Commander and see the Squadron through until the end of hostilities.

After two days of bad weather, Sgt H Howard led a bombing mission to Knin on the morning of 12 November. The target was left a smoking ruin and all the aircraft returned safely. The afternoon mission was cancelled when an aircraft of 249 Squadron crashed, blocking the runway.

As the Germans continued to retreat northwards, Gp Cpt D S MacDonald led a combined formation of six Mustangs from 213 Squadron, led by Helm, and twelve from 249 Squadron to bomb and strafe a column of motor transport, which was trapped between the Albanian front line and a destroyed bridge south of Tirana. Experience was proving that the 500-lb bomb was at its most effective when used for attacking trains and columns of motor transport, where vertical error did not render bombing invalid and lateral error still resulted in damage to the chosen target. The role of the fighter-bomber, enhanced by the wider variety of weapons now available, was gradually becoming more sophisticated, but never less dangerous.

While dive-bombing was very effective in the mountainous regions, where the winding roads in narrow valleys made strafing suicidal - due both to enemy action and the likelihood of flying into the hillside - the terrain could also be used by the Germans to their advantage. On one occasion, when Ashley was flying as Number Two to Mackinnon, they came across a train sitting on the track in the bottom of a valley letting off steam. It appeared a sitting duck; however Mackinnon called up and said "I smell a rat", and he ordered Ashley to stand-off while he made as though to attack. The Germans opened fire prematurely from all the surrounding hillsides, and the trap was sprung harmlessly due to Mackinnon's experience and leadership.

On 20 November, after another period of bad weather, Sgt H Howard led eight aircraft, flown by Fg Off F M Gamble, WO I C Robinson, Flt Sgt K J Clarkson, Sgt R J Lawrence, WO F Heard, Fg Off F A E Penson and Fg Off A G R Ashley, on an offensive patrol. Airborne at 09.35 hours, the formation coasted in over Gradac *en route* to Skopje and, shortly after commencing its armed sweep eight miles east of Sarajevo, Howard found a convoy of about one hundred vehicles nose to tail on a mountain road. Fifteen 500-lb bombs were dropped on a three-quarter mile stretch of road, and twelve direct hits were scored, destroying approximately one-third of the convoy. Three days later on yet another offensive sweep, Flt Sgt A Liudzius was shot down and killed.

The month closed with a prolonged period of bad weather preventing all operations for six days. However, to brighten the gloom, the news came that Sqn Ldr S R Whiting had been awarded the DSO, and Flt Lts C S Vos, R H Garwood and C D A Smith the DFC. A month of mixed fortunes had ended on a high note. Aircraft serviceability had been maintained at a high eighty percent and, although five aircraft had been lost on operations and in accidents, this was the lowest monthly figure since operations commenced. The figure would clearly have been higher had bad weather not intervened, and was one that confirmed yet again the dangers inherent in the ground-attack role. In the circumstances it was gratifying that, as the month closed, all the new pilots bar one were fully operational.

With the CO absent in the UK on medical leave, December opened with Flt Lt R H Garwood in temporary command, Flt Lt J H M Mackinnon commanding "A" Flight and Flt Lt J A Mulcahy-Morgan commanding "B" Flight. The flight personnel were also reorganised so that it became possible for sections to consist of pilots from the same Flight, thus developing an increased sense of camaraderie. Flying was a mixture of operations and training, as the weather permitted and training hours were reduced to five, at which stage pilots were considered operational. As offensive sweeps were planned, and then cancelled, and then reinstated, the armourers came near to revolt as bombs were continually loaded, and then removed, and then reloaded, onto the under-wing racks. Intense periods of operations, when weather permitted, coupled with the wet ground led to a rapid deterioration in the state of the perforated steel plating, which reinforced the perimeter tracks and runways. This ultimately resulted in a nasty accident when an airman was thrown from the wing of a taxying Mustang, after it hit a particularly large hole in the PSP, and had to be taken to hospital.

On 2 December, sixteen sorties were flown in four sections to bomb the bridge at Bioce. In the morning, two sections of four aircraft led by Helm and Garwood attacked, but smoke from the exploding bombs made damage assessment difficult, and flak from emplacements on the bridge and in the surrounding hills made the area an uncomfortable place to stay. In addition to the Squadron's efforts, it was noted that the Mustangs of 249 Squadron were also in action. In the afternoon, Vaughan-Fowler led four more aircraft against the bridge, followed by Plt Off O Wilson-North with a further section of four aircraft, who reported that the bridge appeared to have been hit; his section accordingly concentrated on strafing the roads in the area. Weather conditions for once were ideal, with no cloud and fifty miles visibility.

While damaging bridges with 500-lb bombs was to prove notoriously difficult, the intense efforts of 2 December had clearly had some effect. Two missions on 4 December, when Garwood led eight Mustangs and Helm a further four, took advantage of the damage caused two days previously and attacked a column of over two hundred vehicles backed-up south-west of the bridge at Bioce.

The range of the Mustang and the versatility of the Squadron's capabilities were demonstrated by Vaughan-Fowler who, on 6 December, led a mission which commenced by escorting a Dakota from Bari to Niksic, then bombed MT concentrations at Klopot and finished off with an armed reconnaissance. The very next day, the news came that Sqn Ldr C S Vos would not be returning from the UK, and that Flt Lt P E Vaughan-Fowler would succeed him as Commanding Officer; his promotion to Squadron Leader came through two days later.

On 8 December, fourteen armed reconnaissance sorties were flown along the road between Brod and Doboj, and bombs were dropped on a motor transport convoy and railway sidings. Little return fire was experienced, but Flt Lt W J P Straker's aircraft was hit by debris and dented in numerous places when he hit an ammunition truck and had to fly through the resulting explosion. Three days later, in between periods of bad weather that seriously curtailed operations, a return visit was made to the Brod - Doboj road. Once again fourteen sorties were flown and again an enemy convoy was found. This time fate was not so kind. While strafing the convoy, Fg Off G F Allan was hit by return fire and glycol streamed from his engine. His initial thought was to force-land but then, deciding to bale out, he pulled up to 1,200 feet and inverted his aircraft. He fell free, but his parachute did not open and he was seen to fall on to the snow-covered ground below.

By the middle of the month, considerable German forces were trapped in the Podgorica pocket, north of Brod, by Partisans supported by Floydforce, one of the many special operation groups used in this theatre. On 15 December, twelve aircraft, along with a force from 249 Squadron and supported by Wellingtons, attacked ground troops in the Bioce - Matesevo area. Over the next three days, the fact that some fifty sorties were flown against the German forces, strung out in a convoy some thirty miles long, earned the congratulations of both Tito and the commander of Floydforce.

The old connections between the Squadron and the CO of the Wing resulted in the mutually satisfactory arrangement that the Squadron would have the use of his newly-arrived Fairchild Argus, a four-seat single-engine aircraft, in exchange for servicing both it and his own personal Mustang. The packing case in which the Fairchild arrived was also put to good use as a flight hut for the ground-crew airfield guard. To add yet another role to the Squadron's repertoire, the CO carried out experiments, which proved successful, in dropping supplies packed in the under-wing long-range tanks.

Just how rapidly the aircraft availability state could deteriorate was illustrated on 20 December, when four aircraft went out of service in one day. On the morning offensive sweep, WO F A O Ralph had most of his tailplane shot away. He quickly discovered that he could just about maintain a climbing attitude flying in a straight line with the stick in one corner, the rudder bar in another and with full power. Having climbed to 10,000 feet, he baled out and was seen to land safely and be taken into the nearby town by the Partisans. While taking off for an operational sweep, Sgt D H Bell swung off the runway and finished up in the sea. Finally, on the afternoon mission, Mulcahy-Morgan had to land at the emergency airstrip at Niksic with a bullet in his radiator, and the Group Captain came back with his aircraft so badly shot up that it had to be written off the Squadron's strength. The good news was that none of the pilots involved in these incidents was hurt. By the end of the month, when the weather again clamped in, the Squadron was down to five serviceable aircraft.

December overall proved to be a record month for strafing, despite there being nine non-flying days. The basis of the success was the large number of targets presented by the 21st Mountain Division, which was trapped in the

Some of the Squadron's armourers and fitters with the Squadron scoreboard for operations with the Balkan Air Force, Biferno, Italy, May 1945.

Podgorica (now Titograd) pocket and was attacked continuously from the twelfth of the month. The grand total at the end of the month was 183 motor vehicles destroyed and 279 damaged, considerably more than any other Squadron had achieved out of the overall total of over one thousand vehicles which had to be abandoned by the Germans in the area.

January 1944 opened with the Germans in full retreat through the snow-covered mountains of central Bosnia. Operations were fitful due to the bad weather, and were hampered by the low number of serviceable aircraft and the fact that there were only seven operational pilots per flight. Nevertheless, on the first three days of the month, offensive sweeps were flown in section strength harrying the retreating troops in and around Sarajevo. On 4 January, the first two sweeps along the Sarajevo - Doboj road found little to report. Two more sections, each of three aircraft, took off at 13.30 hours and 13.50 hours respectively, to attack targets in the same area. The lack of targets was repeated, and Mulcahy-Morgan received permission to sweep north of Brod. Near Deventa, his section caught a moving train in the open and he cut it in half with a neatly-placed 500-lb bomb. However, as he climbed away, his aircraft was hit by flak and crashed four hundred yards ahead of the train. Johnnie Morgan was a mild-mannered, popular and well liked Rhodesian, who had volunteered to join the RAF along with so many of his countrymen. He had no need to be involved in the war at all, and his selfless sacrifice was typical of so many of the men from the Dominions and Empire who flew with the RAF.

The other two aircraft destroyed the track ahead of another moving train, but it managed to pull up before it reached the danger spot. Between them the two sections claimed six locomotives destroyed and five damaged, plus sixty trucks destroyed and a further twenty damaged.

After four days with no operational flying due to bad weather, Fg Off "Jock" Donnelly scored an unusual "victory" on 12 January, when he flew a Mustang down to Bari for some spares. While coming in to land he saw ahead of him, on its final approach, an He 111 complete with German markings; when he taxied in everyone crowded round his aircraft, to his discomfort and amusement, asking him how he had managed to capture the German aircraft. Being one of the few Mustang squadrons in the Balkan Air Force made the procurement of spares the constant pre-occupation of the Squadron Engineering Officer, Fg Off "Pinky" White. The Maintenance Unit was at Naples, but a very fruitful source of spares was found to be the USAAF P-51 squadron based at Bari. The pilots were graduates of the all-black Tuskegee University, Alabama, and the going procurement rate for any one Mustang spare part, whether an elevator or a flap-jack, was one bottle of gin. On one occasion the Squadron's "negotiator" was particularly astute and acquired a 15-cwt Dodge truck for two bottles. Ownership of the vehicle was quickly assumed by Bill Straker, CO of "B" Flight, thus putting it on a par with the rival "A" Flight, which had the only other 15-cwt truck on the Squadron.

When operations resumed on 18 January, after four days of bad weather, eight Mustangs in two sections of four went to bomb E-boats in Pola harbour. Over the target WO F Heard spotted the 3,500-ton ship *Otto Leonhardt* and scored two direct hits, which caused great pleasure when reported to the Navy. Three days later, eight Mustangs returned to Pola to attack the oil storage tanks and depot there. On 21 January, as a further variation on normal operations, four Mustangs escorted two Beaufighters on operation "Tidal Wave" on 20 January. This mission was mounted to drop supplies, packed in long-range tanks, to an RAF Squadron Leader, who had been operating in the Klagenfurt area of Austria for the past fifteen months. Unfortunately, bad weather in the target area prevented location of the dropping zone, and the Beaufighters had to content themselves with releasing homing pigeons.

For two days, on 22 and 23 January, it snowed heavily, leaving everything covered in a twelve-inch thick white blanket. The only movement that took place was in the command structure, when the Squadron moved back once more under the control of No.254 Wing. The severe winter weather revised most people's ideas about sunny Italy, and the Officer's Mess Nissen hut was bitterly cold until a little know-how was applied in the construction of what came to be known as the V-2. This consisted of a "suitably-modified" forty-four gallon drum, with added pipe-work, which led into it through the wall of the hut from a petrol supply out in the open. The supply of fuel to the fire was controlled by a wing-tap; after a few drops of neat petrol were set alight, the flames engulfed the pipe-work, turning the petrol to vapour as it emerged from the spout. Being enclosed in a large drum, the whole contraption soon warmed up nicely and the Mess became a cosy refuge. Despite its somewhat Heath Robinson conception, the V-2 never gave the slightest problem.

On the next day the only mission flown was that carried out by a section of six aircraft, led by the CO, acting as anti-flak escort for sixteen Beaufighters attacking the barracks at Cigale Cove on Lussin Island. Two aircraft were forced to return early, and the remaining four found cloud down to 700 feet over the island. Nevertheless, the CO and WO I R H Iago attacked the flak positions and each scored direct hits, even though they were bombing from such a low level. The flak defences were totally destroyed. The Beaufighters made the most of such an effective introduction and destroyed three - and probably destroyed the remaining three - of the six motor torpedo boats pulled up on the beach. This fine piece of bombing not only pleased HQ BAF, but also earned the praise of the Beaufighter pilots.

As the weather partially cleared, operations returned to the normal offensive sweeps and armed reconnaissance patrols. On 26 January, Gamble and WO A W Hearndon were forced up to 32,000 feet while on their way to carry out an armed reconnaissance patrol in the Novska - Brod area. Substantial cloud cover remained over the target area and, as they turned back in cloud, Hearndon asked Max Gamble to throttle back; he did so but nevertheless saw that Hearndon had lost him. Over the radio, Gamble told Hearndon to maintain 12,000 feet and to steer 220 degrees, but he received no acknowledgment. When he broke cloud, there was no sign of his Number Two.

At the beginning of February, enemy resistance stiffened as the Germans made a last effort to withdraw their sorely tried troops northwards from around Sarajevo and Brod, and brought the Seventh SS Division in to Croatia to clear the escape routes to the north. Most of the Squadron's operations were now concentrated in the area north of Zagreb and up towards Maribor, and Graz in Austria, apart from an attack on the defences on Lusano Island, when napalm bombs were used for the first time. Harry Howard remembers flying on another sortie with Gp Capt MacDonald to drop seventy-five gallon drop-tanks, full of an inflammable "gunge" and armed with a fusing device, over Lussin Piccolo; unfortunately the "bombs" did not function. At the time there was no mention of napalm. The availability of the new bombs was of only limited advantage due to the embargo on carrying any bombs whatsoever on the new Mustang IVs then coming into service. As someone said "One good squirt with these six machine guns and a loco has had its time". The resulting emphasis on ground strafing confirmed just how much more dangerous this form of attack was as losses again mounted.

On 13 February, Flt Lt G P Elliot was hit by ground fire and had to bale out over enemy-held territory and, although hopes were not high of his avoiding capture, it was felt that he might have been able to escape into the surrounding hills. In fact, he was rescued by the Partisans after a fight in which they lost ten men to the rival Chetniks. To put the matter into some perspective, the Partisan leader told Elliot that he considered a pilot worth one hundred ground troops. On 15 February, while attacking the bridge at Celje, WO R Thomson was hit by flak and failed to return.

Leading three Mustangs *en route* for an offensive sweep in the Celje - Maribor area, MacKinnon saw a lorry full of troops and attacked it with his machine-guns. On the way back from the target area, he saw the same lorry being towed away and once again attacked, this time leaving both vehicles disabled. The next day, Flt Lt W J P Straker led three Mustangs on an armed reconnaissance sortie to Celje, scoring four direct hits on a convoy of trucks and the engine sheds on the edge of the town. The section then found a troop train in the open north of Maribor. While pulling up from an attack Straker's aircraft was hit, the engine began to stream glycol, the temperatures went off the clock and all the instruments sank to zero. The Germans had for some time put their formidable AA guns in flak-cars on their trains, for air defence against strafing fighters, and Straker assumed it was a shell from one of these that was responsible for the sickening thud that he felt in the bowels of his aircraft.

He climbed to 8,000 feet with the intention of selecting a site for a belly landing, but the surrounding country was very hilly and in any case things soon became very hot and smoke filled the cockpit, so he had no choice but to go over the side. As he baled out he lost his revolver and, even more seriously, struck the tailplane of his Mustang. However the rip-cord worked and he was soon experiencing his quietest moments of the war as he floated down to earth. Landing in three feet of snow, he was almost immediately confronted by a bearded giant bedecked with hand grenades and with a red star on his cap - a happy sight. Being able to walk only with difficulty, as a result of his collision with his tailplane, he was taken to a house full of Partisans, with whom he communicated in a mixture of school-boy French and German. He soon discovered that he was something of a hero, as his aircraft had crashed on a house used by the local Ustasi. After an issue of the local rot-gut, raki, he began to feel better and was given a bunk where, despite the bitter cold, he could keep warm wrapped up in his parachute. After four days in this house, it was a relief to move on and away from the dank thick atmosphere of cheap tobacco that filled all the rooms.

He had come down in the area of Slunj, about one hundred miles from Zara, where after a good deal of walking and lifts on the backs of motor-bikes and trucks he was delivered a week later. On one occasion, while on the back of a motor-bike, they ran into an ambush and Straker spent a couple of hours behind a rock in a ditch with bullets flying in all directions. While he expected to be shot at in the air, this experience he took to be a poor form of amusement. While *en*

WO Brown with a Mustang IV in peace-time silver finish, Italy, 1945

route to Zara he passed through a Partisan HQ Unit with an attached British liaison officer, who radioed Bari with the news of Straker's survival. The officer, Capt "Dickie" Bird, and his signals sergeant seemed to Straker to identify completely with the Partisans; despite incredibly difficult conditions, they appeared totally organised and were even able to offer him the luxury of a hot bath. Finally he was flown out of Zara in a Dakota, with a USAAF Liberator crew, to Bari for de-lousing and rehabilitation before being picked up by McKinnon, and flown back to the Squadron in Gp Capt MacDonald's Argus on 2 March 1945.

By 18 February, the damage to aircraft, and the losses being suffered, had become so critical that Gp Capt MacDonald put an embargo on all strafing unless it was known that the area was clear of flak.

On 16 February, MacKinnon and Ashley were detailed to fly to Bari where they picked up a Dakota carrying Dr Subasic, the Prime Minister in King Peter's Yugoslav Government-in-exile in London, and escorted it to Belgrade. A night out with the Partisans ended abruptly, when an argument began among friends and shots were fired. The casual approach to firearms was also evident the next day back at Belgrade airfield, which was full of Russian Yaks. Many of the aircraft were being serviced and, when the guns were tested, they were fired with the aircraft facing across the runway. Several times tracer shots passed just over MacKinnon and Ashley's heads; this they assumed to be what is now called friendly fire, and they took it as kindly meant. On the return journey to Biferno, the Dakota's passenger was Brigadier Fitzroy MacLean, Churchill's special emissary to Tito.

While the CO was away with five aircraft at Marcianise being briefed for a special mission to take place on 21 February, AV-M Elliot dropped in on a farewell visit prior to his handover as AOC Balkan Air Force to Air Vice-Marshal G M Mills, CBE, DFC. The auguries for the special mission were not good when WO F Heard's aircraft went missing over Naples; it was subsequently found buried in the ground fifteen miles north-east of the city. The special operation turned out to be nothing more than an escort duty, albeit an important one, which involved accompanying a Mitchell and a Dakota carrying Field Marshal Lord Alexander, Air Marshal Sir John Slessor and AV-M Mills to Belgrade. The CO and Iago returned the next day with the Mitchell, while Gamble and Fg Off D E Robertson stayed in Belgrade with the Dakota.

Towards the end of the month, three events conspired to lift everyone's spirits. One was the arrival of six brand-new Mustang IVs equipped to carry bombs; the second the news that Sgt D MacLelland, captain of the Hornets, the Squadrons' first eleven, had been picked to represent the RAF in the big football match against the Army in Naples and, last but not the least, the news that Elliot, who had baled out on 13 February, was safe. Less welcome was the realisation that about eighty airmen were due for "the boat" to take them back to the UK in May and June and that, to accommodate such a large change of personnel, many of them would have to move to other units by stages in the interim. This was particularly hard, as many of them had been with the Squadron since its embarkation in May 1941 - however the prospect of a berth on the boat back to the UK softened the blow! The end of February also saw the arrival of three more South African pilots in the persons of Lts B N Chiazzari, Owen Jones and W St C Thomson.

As March opened, and the front line moved ever further north, more and more use was made of the advanced landing ground at Prkos, in Yugoslavia. For some time Tito had wanted an airfield to be established in the vicinity of Zadar, but he refused to allow Allied troops to be based nearby to protect it, and was insisting that Partisan forces be used. Eventually, as the fighting moved north and the question of ground defence resolved itself, an airfield was established at Zara with a satellite at Prkos. Thus began the rather unsatisfactory arrangement, which lasted almost until the end of the month, of establishing a detachment of pilots overnight at Prkos to crew the Mustangs, which had taken off from Biferno on a morning mission, for another strike.

Operating from Zara on 1 March, the section led by MacKinnon showed the undoubted operational advantages of the new arrangements, when it destroyed seven locomotives in strafing attacks in the Zagreb - Varazdin - Maribor area on its first mission, and then returned and refuelled a further two times. While one section was operating from Zara, Fg Off A G R Ashley led an armed tactical reconnaissance mission from Biferno north of Zagreb. Running unaccountably short of fuel, and on his last tank, he told Donnelly and Robertson to go on while he returned to Zara to refuel. Ten minutes later, he called up to say that he was just south of Karlovac, down to his last twenty gallons and would have to bale out. The possibility of losing Ashley had more than the usual significance, since he was the Squadron Sports Officer and the organising force behind both the Hornets and the Wasps, the Squadron's highly successful first and second soccer teams.

The precise purpose of the reconnaissance mission was to establish the exact location of a football field outside Zagreb, on which it was reported there was a large concentration of German vehicles about to move north. Having located the field, Ashley was to radio the precise map reference back to base for the following bombers, which included Baltimores flown by Italian pilots. This was Ashley's first trip in a Mustang IV and, noticing the port wing tank showed five gallons less than full, he had his rigger physically check that all tanks were in fact full. Having taken off at first light, the section had just crossed the Dalmatian coast when his fuselage tank ran dry. Somewhat puzzled, since there was nothing to account for the situation, no black smoke and the mixture control was where it should have been, but not overly concerned he switched on to his starboard tank. The two wing tanks were ample for the task in hand. Just beyond Zagreb, and about to let down, the starboard tank ran dry also. The situation was now serious; he called up Donnelly, told him to take over and that he would try to make it back to Zara. As he flew south on the fuel in his port wing tank, he saw that this was dwindling at an excessive rate. At 10,000 feet over Karlovac, it became clear that he would not make it back to Zara and that he would have to bale out; the fuel gauge showed only twenty gallons.

Over the pine-clad hills south of the town, and with the fuel-gauge now showing only ten gallons, he called up Donnelly and told him that he was baling out. Having trimmed the Mustang and jettisoned the hood, he removed his helmet and undid his straps then, reducing the throttle setting to stop the fierce wind-flow, he climbed onto the seat. However, as the aircraft increased its speed in a terminal dive, Ashley found himself pinned against the armour plating behind the pilot's seat. There seemed to be no future in this so, giving a vicious wrench with his foot against the side of the cockpit, he made a racing dive for the trailing edge of the wing. This seemed to work well and on pulling the rip-cord his parachute opened; soon the noise of his aircraft died away. He landed near the summit of one of the hills, right into the trees bordering a clearing.

As he was slithering down an icy slope, a group of Partisans waylaid him and quickly hauled him into the cover of some tall scrub. One of the Serbs, who could speak French, explained that a Ustasi patrol had seen him come down and that the Partisans had had a fight with them, leaving one Ustasi dead and one captured. Two days of foot-slogging through the snow-covered countryside, devastated by the Germans scorched earth policy, brought the party to the local Partisan HQ at Koronica. The intervening night had been spent in a derelict village, where one building had been re-roofed and was used as sleeping quarters. The Partisan leader coyly offered Ashley a girl to keep him warm, but as the offer was sight unseen he politely declined.

His brief sleep at HQ was interrupted by the Italian doctor in whose care he had been placed with the words "Un avion avait tombé". The aircraft was a USAAF Liberator and, after some argument with the Partisans, arrangements were made for Ashley and the Liberator's crew, who had all been rounded up, to go to Lovinac where they were left outside the door of the British Military Mission. Eventually, after two more hair-raising rides through the mountains, they arrived at Zara. There to Ashley's surprise stood none other than AV-M Mills, who after a warm welcome told Ashley that the road he had travelled so recently to Lovinac was now back in German hands. Having spent a bitterly cold night at Zara, sleeping in the Medical Section's ambulance, he flew back to Italy the next day. After delousing and debriefing, he was delivered back to the Squadron, to be met by the CO, who said that he had never seen him looking so well. What exactly had caused the original problem remains something of a mystery, although the Packard-built Merlin did have a bad reputation for giving trouble and the Mustang IV was known for its siphoning effect.

On 2 March, Fg Off P Donnelly was lost north of Zagreb in initially mysterious circumstances. He had taken off, as Number Two to Gamble, to strafe transport along the main road leading north out of Zagreb towards Varazdin and Maribor. As Gamble was about to attack a bus, he saw that there were women among the passengers jumping out and therefore he aborted his attack, and told Donnelley to do the same. Donnelley acknowledged the call. Just one minute later Gamble could no longer see his No.2 and received no reply over the R/T. A search of the area at 100 feet revealed no sign as to what had happened; there had been no flak and, although there was low cloud, neither aircraft had flown into it. Gamble's radio had failed just after his final attempt to contact Donnelley so that, if there had been any further calls, he had been unable to receive them. In fact, whilst Gamble reported that there had been no flak, Donnelly's aircraft had been hit by heavy machine-gun fire and he had baled out about forty miles west of Zagreb. For nearly two days he avoided capture, but was finally picked up by the Ustasi and handed over to the Germans. He remained in Zagreb for ten days and was then put on a train bound for Stalag VII at Mooseberg in Germany. As the first part of the journey was enlivened by attacks on the train by the Squadron's aircraft, Donnelly rapidly divested himself of all RAF insignia, particularly those indicating that he was a pilot.

In the afternoon, Straker, who had been shot down on 16 February and picked up by the Partisans, returned to the Squadron. Shortly after his return, Straker took over as "B" Flight Commander when Max Gamble left for a leaders' course in Malta.

A combination of bad weather at the beginning of the month, the persistent shortage of aircraft and the long distance from Biferno to the main target areas, all conspired to reduce the number of operations flown. When the weather did clear on 11 March, operations resumed and so did the losses, which revealed the added danger of attempting to bale out of damaged aircraft at low level. During an operation to bomb landing-craft in the Baka Inlet, WO I A H Iago was hit by return fire from five machine-gun positions and, although he was able to bale out, his parachute did not have time to open and he was seen to hit the water. A Catalina, called up to the scene, failed to find any trace of him. On a second mission, led by the CO against the shipyards at Kraljevica and then strafing north of Zagreb, WO P M Johnston was hit by return fire while attacking a train and once again, although he was able to bale out, the parachute did not have time to open before he hit the ground.

On 12 March, while on an armed reconnaissance north of Zagreb, Chiazzari hit a tree, tearing off his mainplane at the point where the aileron started and the flap ended. He managed to make it back to base and wheeled the Mustang in under power at two hundred miles per hour on to the PSP strip, since he knew that under one hundred and eighty miles per hour the aircraft was not controllable. The next day, the BBC paid the Squadron an anonymous compliment, eulogising the efforts of a particular BAF squadron and featuring the efforts of Lt Chiazzari in taking away part of a tree with his mainplane. Plt Off P B Welch was severely shot-up while photographing the defences in the Cherso Inlet, where WO Iago had been killed, but he managed to return with some invaluable photographs. Apart from the mention on the BBC, the day was marked by the departure for the UK of the first batch of "old timers", some of whom had been with the Squadron for over four years.

By the middle of the month, the lack of any flying at all, whether operational or practice, due to a combination of poor weather and a shortage of aircraft, was more than compensated by the number of rumours that were circulating. The news of the breakthrough on the Western Front had pleased everyone, and the military strategists on the Squadron predicted that the war would be over by the end of April, or at least by June. The move of Gp Capt MacDonald sparked a series of rumours that No.283 Wing was to be dissolved, and that the Squadron was to return to the Desert Air Force, which was now operating over the Balkans. At a party thrown for the departing airmen, attended by the Group Captain and a number of "old boys", the rumour of a move to the airfield at Zara began to circulate. Although the weather remained poor from an operations point of view, there were signs of Spring in the air as the last snows disappeared from the distant hills surrounding the airfield and summer uniforms began to make their first cautious appearance.

Even though missions were now becoming almost routine, the results of poor planning were clearly demonstrated on 18 March, when a section of Mustangs took off to escort the Beaufighters of 16 SAAF Squadron on a mission to bomb the E-boat base on Lussin Piccolo Island. The rendezvous point with the Beaufighters was given as Ancona, which caused some surprise since this was an AA-gun defended area and a prohibited flying zone. Notwithstanding that at 3,000 feet both the Mustangs and Beaufighters were easily identifiable, the formation as it formed up was fired at by the naval guns defending the harbour. In the ensuing melée, contact with the Beaufighters was lost and the section went on to the target area alone. In the event, Straker and his section only arrived over the target after the Beaufighters had carried out their attack. Such incidents did nothing to encourage inter-service co-operation, and caused not a little ill-feeling.

Even though there were a few games still to play in the current season, the news that the Hornets had won the major trophy for the soccer season helped to restore the Squadron's equanimity. As pride comes before a fall, so the Squadron's reputation as the sporting king-pin in the area was immediately tarnished by a twelve-three loss at table tennis, although for some ping-pong hardly counted as a sport.

As the Germans continued to retreat through northern Croatia, travelling mainly at night, long stretches of road were found to be devoid of any traffic whatsoever during the day. In this context the use of the landing ground at Zara again proved useful, as aircraft arrived the night before for refuelling and so could be over the target area at first light. With the net closing in around the German forces in northern Croatia, Slovenia and the southern provinces of Austria, the Squadron operating in support of the Partisan 4th Army found itself flying with an intensity not seen since its first days in the Balkans.

The first mission of the day on 21 March took off from Zara before dawn. It was led by the CO, with Tommy Thomson as No.2, Bill Straker No.3 and Owen Jones No.4, to strafe road and rail communications north of Zagreb. The second section nearly came to grief, encountering intense anti-aircraft fire as they ran directly across Zagreb South airfield at first light. Ten locomotives were destroyed, together with a similar number of motor transports, and it was also noted that the Germans were now being forced to use more horse-drawn transport. Nine further sorties were flown during the day against the bridge at Litija, but with the same results as at Bioce. The nearest bomb fell some ten yards from the centre span and this confirmed the view, formed previously, that bridges were not good targets for fighter-bombers. During the day's operations, two aircraft were lost. The first was lost during the mission when Fg Off P B Welch was hit by small arms fire while attacking a tunnel thirty miles north-west of Zagreb; his aircraft was seen trailing smoke, but he baled out and landed safely. In the second incident, Ashley was not so lucky when his aircraft swung on landing and he was severely injured in the resulting crash. So, in the space of one afternoon, the Squadron had lost two experienced pilots, who were both potential Section Leaders.

On 23 March an old lesson was re-learned, when Flt Lt J H M MacKinnon was hit while leading a section of three aircraft on a morning offensive patrol, which destroyed and/or damaged ten locomotives and dispersed a number of troops. Going round for a second attack on one of the trains, MacKinnon's aircraft burst into flames and, although he was able to climb to 1,500 feet and bale out of his aircraft, he hit the ground before his parachute could open; his loss was particularly tragic as this was his last sortie before his tour expired.

Late in the evening of 23 March, reports were received that between forty and fifty German aircraft were on the ground at Gornje-Stupnik airfield, ten miles south-east of Zagreb, *en route* to Italy. Early the next morning Straker, with four 213 Squadron aircraft and four from 249 Squadron, took off for the target. Unfortunately only two aircraft were claimed as probables, including one FW 190, since most of them had already left. The attack on the airfield was launched from about 12,000 feet, with the eight aircraft in line abreast and from some distance away, to effect the greatest surprise. The aircraft were in a relatively steep dive, at about four hundred knots, ideally placed to cover the target, and Straker was just taking aim at a FW 190 when he became aware of Lt

W St C Thomson, flying as his No.2 on his starboard wing-tip, engulfed in flames. He yelled at him over the R/T to "pull up and get out", while he put in a short burst at the Focke-Wulf. However the formation was so low and fast that Staker thought Thomson must himself have been hit, as he saw his aircraft plough straight ahead into the ground.

The ground fire that hit Tommy Thomson had come from a train, that was crossing on a track just to the north of the airfield, as the Mustangs were delivering their attack. One of the anti-aircraft guns, mounted on the flak wagon, scored a direct hit, and his aircraft flew straight on into the ground at something like four hundred miles per hour. Miraculously, Thomson had managed to bale out by releasing his straps and helmet, jettisoning his canopy, winding the trim fully forward, pulling the stick back and bunting the aircraft - precisely the recommended procedure. He pulled his rip-cord as he left the aircraft, and his parachute opened just before he landed on the airfield where he was taken prisoner.

This incident gave rise to much debate in the Mess as to whether the losses were really warranted, if the operations being flown were just to serve political purposes. It was clear that to strafe the same target area over and over again was suicidal and that, for the moment, the losses being sustained were not thought to be commensurate with the damage being inflicted on the enemy. It was decided that it would be far more effective to move up to Zara, and from there mount bombing operations on selected enemy targets.

The old air of optimism was soon restored as the aircraft were fitted with racks to carry 1,000-lb bombs, which necessitated comparatively short-range operations. The Mustang's maximum all-up weight was 12,000 lbs so that, with two thousand pounds of bombs under its wings, the main fuel tank could only be partly filled. The Squadron also welcomed back Fg Off Johnny Purchas for a second tour of operations, his first tour having been completed in August the previous year. As yet more bad weather closed in, a further six South African pilots arrived in the persons of Lts C V Friendly, E Gardener, G R Holdsworth, I D Kenyon, D L A Peck and P C Thomson. The Squadron's pilots were now largely of South African origin, with a sprinkling of Australians and New Zealanders and a few from the British Isles.

By the beginning of April, with the Russians in Graz and the Squadron's sphere of operations shrinking daily, it became clear that the Balkan Front would either become a very significant part of the final stages of the war or dissolve into insignificance. In any event, it was obvious that the German retreat into Austria would significantly affect the Squadron's operations. By 4 April, all of the new pilots were operational and Straker and Penson had the dubious pleasure of being flown up to Bari to pick up two Tiger Moths, which they then flew over to Zara to enable Yugoslav pilots to be trained.

The next day, with the CO leading one section of three aircraft and Gamble another, a new 800-lb fire-bomb, dubbed the "Witches Brew", was used to bomb the villages of Otocac and Vrhovine. The results were seen to be very satisfactory. Vaughan-Fowler then led his section on a sweep over the roads leading north, during which Sgt E P Buchan, an experienced and first-class pilot, inexplicably hit a tree and his aircraft crashed and exploded.

As the bad weather once more clamped in, Flt Lt G S Hulse arrived to start his second tour as "A" Flight commander; as his first tour had been spent in operations over Greece he had considerable local knowledge. At the same time, 249 Squadron was re-equipped with Spitfires and the Squadron reverted to being the only Mustang unit in BAF. This, together with the arrival of four new aircraft, substantially eased the aircraft supply situation, eventually increasing the number on strength to sixteen, with a further four in the Wing pool.

On 10 April, Robinson led five aircraft on a bombing mission against the retreating German columns north of Brod. The first four aircraft completed their attacks successfully, but Lt E Gardener bringing up the rear was struck by a 20mm shell and his aircraft broke up at 2,000 feet. Although he was at the end of his bombing run, he managed to bale out. His parachute opened successfully and he landed in a tree; it was felt that he was almost certainly a prisoner-of-war. His was the first aircraft lost on a bombing run.

Concentrated attacks by 283 Wing, and the light bombers of 254 Wing, continued to harass the Germans retreating north from Sarajevo. During these operations, it became clear that bombing widely spaced MT convoys with 500-lb bombs was not a very profitable use of resources. On one mission, three aircraft dropped three thousand pounds of bombs on one convoy and claimed only one vehicle destroyed. More and more of the operations were being mounted from Prkos, and on 12 April Wilson-North and Friendly landed and refuelled there three times in between sorties and before returning to base. The repair facilities at Zara were also working well, as Johnson found when, having received a shell through his propeller, it was changed and he was back in the air within two hours.

On 17 April, six missions were flown from Prkos to harry the retreating Germans between Ljubljana and Celje. As the net closed ever tighter by the end of April, resistance was concentrated in two isolated areas north of Banja Luka and Zagreb. With a full establishment of aircraft, and increasing use of the landing ground at Prkos, the number of sorties flown reached new levels.

One of the many rumours circulating at this time also proved correct when, due to the overwhelming logic of mounting all operations from Prkos, the Squadron moved, lock, stock, and barrel, to the Dalmatian Coast on 25 April, and became part of No.281 Wing. Yet the move had come almost too late as it was increasingly clear that the Germans could not hold out for much longer and that, even when operating from Prkos, the target area was well to the north, and the biggest problem was now finding worthwhile targets.

By May, it had become clear that the war had but a few more days to run, and armed reconnaissance patrols began to push up more frequently into Austria; on 4 May such a patrol reached as far north as Linz. An armed reconnaissance mission in the Ljubljana - Zagreb area destroyed two trains in dramatic style. Blue Section, led by Straker, scored eight direct hits on one train, the resulting explosions severely damaging the tracks. The results obtained by Red Section were, if not more accurate, then at least more spectacular. Having already obtained direct hits on a suspension bridge spanning a narrow valley, Hulse led his section in to attack a train protruding from a tunnel, where two more direct hits cut the train in half. At once the rear half broke loose and, gathering speed, ran off in a southerly direction for some fifteen miles. During this unusual journey it was effectively strafed, setting more wagons carrying motor transport on fire. Its journey was only ended when the runaway wagons collided with the wreckage of a train that had been destroyed by the CO in an earlier raid and was now blocking the track. The explosion, resulting from this collision, destroyed another twelve wagons and blocked both tracks.

At 07.15 hours on 5 May, Flt Lt G S Hulse took off with

A goods train in the Zagreb area carrying motor vehicles, 21 April 1945. Just before the end of the war, the Germans petrol supplies were virtually exhausted, and most motor transport was being moved by rail. The infantry was supported by horse-drawn transport which made an unpleasant target. Photographed by Lt Owen Jones, SAAF.

WO F J Squire (RAAF), Fg Off F A E Penson and Flt Sgt W H Butterworth, on an armed reconnaissance patrol along the Ljubljana - Brod railway, which was completed without incident. Later in the day, Fg Off T E G Purchas led Lt G R Holdsworth, Lt O Jones and Flt Sgt W A Borthwick (RAAF), on a similar mission between Logatec - Ljubljana - Celje and Vransko, scoring two direct hits on some wagons. These were the Squadron's last two missions of the war as, in the afternoon, the unconditional surrender of Germany was announced, and the Squadron stood down from operations for the last time.

On 6 May, two cross-country flights were organised to view the destruction caused in the previous months. In 1942, the Yugoslav railway system had consisted of 6,420 miles of track, 2,411 locomotives and 61,000 units of rolling stock. In the course of its operations, the Balkan Air Force claimed 1,190 locomotives destroyed or damaged, which gives a fair indication of the damage done to the system and the dislocation caused to the occupying German forces.

Then for the next two days, as all flying ceased, the Squadron provided open house to visitors from all the neighbouring squadrons. On 11 May, the Commanders of all the units in the Wing met and together worked out a training programme of formation flying, aerobatics, and cross-country flights for as far as the range of the aircraft would allow.

By 14 May, the increasingly hostile attitude of the Yugoslavs led to all the units at Prkos moving back to Italy. They were, to all intents and purposes, forced out of the country they had helped to liberate. After all the effort put in by the Balkan Air Force to support the Partisans, it seemed inconceivable that the Squadron should be given just twenty-four hours notice to leave the country, but Communist political pressure was beginning to show itself. There was considerable ill-feeling, and most of the equipment that had to be left behind was burnt. By the end of the war the USAAF had also accumulated a large number of aircraft at Zara, in various states of unserviceability. Its solution to the problem was to fly in a couple of bulldozers, and crush the whole lot into one massive block of scrap metal. However, one item of great sentimental value to the Squadron was retrieved. One Squadron pilot had obtained a goat from a Yugoslav peasant, in exchange for a tin of fifty cigarettes, and it was decided that "Wallace" should become the Squadron mascot. Bill Straker flew one of the last Mustangs to leave Zara, and he recalls watching his wing-man with Wallace sitting behind him on the rear tank of the Mustang, with a blanket and some grass to nourish him on the journey.

North American Mustang IV KM348 at Nicosia, Cyprus, 1946.

CHAPTER THIRTEEN - THE MIDDLE EAST

Once the celebrations to mark the end of hostilities were over, there was an urgent need was to combat a feeling of anti-climax. A sense of being "in limbo" almost inevitably descended upon the Squadron. Everyone was elated that the war was over, but the contrast from intense operational activity, with its clearly defined objectives, to a life with an uncertain future gave rise to individual troubled thoughts.

The aircrew, all young men, were still possessed by the thrill of being fighter pilots on a squadron with a distinguished war record. Some may have wished the status quo to go on forever, but they knew in their heart of hearts that this could not be so, and that the Squadron's days in Italy were numbered. The officers all held volunteer reserve commissions and the RAF began to look for applicants for permanent commissions to fill the void of war-time recruitment. Direct entry into the universities was also available to those who had matriculated at school. The groundcrew and NCO aircrew were, almost to a man, studying the Release Groups, and were understandably anxious to return to the UK as soon as possible. All in all, it was a perplexing time for young men, pitched suddenly into the new environment of a world apparently at peace.

On 4 June, a new five-week training programme for all pilots was introduced; this required them to complete all the set exercises and fly a minimum of twenty hours per month. Each pilot also received instruction so that he was able to carry out his own Daily Inspection and rearm and bomb-up his aircraft. By the middle of the month, the pilots were also cleaning their own aircraft!

A new firing-range was established at the mouth of the River Biferno, and cross-country exercises were flown by sections of four aircraft, with a different pilot leading on each leg, as far north as the Po Valley. Courses also began to proliferate with remarkable speed. The CO left for an Army Co-operation course at Old Sarum, Bill Straker attended a Junior Commanders course in Malta, having just taken over command of "A" Flight from Max Gamble, who had returned to Australia on 2 June, while WOs I C Robinson and K J Clarkson, together with Flt Sgt W H Butterworth, attended an Instrument Flying course at No.5 Refresher Flying Unit. The flying training programme and the multiplicity of courses certainly helped to keep everyone busy, and to maintain Squadron morale.

On 10 June six new pilots arrived from the RFU at Gaudo, near Naples, Plt Off B H V T Powell, Flt Sgt J T Jennings and Sgts A E Balfour, A F Gundry, M Marshall and J I Williamson, bringing the Squadron up to full strength. This situation only lasted a couple of days, as on 12 June the first of the South African Air Force pilots, Lts D L A Peck, C V Friendly, P C Thomson and I D Kenyon, together with the Squadron Intelligence Officer Lt. Stock, were posted to a South African base prior to their return to the Union. On 13 June, four replacement pilots, Fg Off J R A Luckas, Flt Sgt W T F Hutcheson and Sgts J C T Clayton and J A W Jones arrived straight from an OTU in Egypt, to restore the situation, and the new IO, Fg Off R N Baldwin, three days later. By 17 June, Luckas and Hutcheson had completed their conversion to Mustangs at Madna, where the excellent long run-way with level sides, clear of obstacles, gave good allowance for the strong swing which tended to develop on

"Which One First?" "A" Flight line-up, Ramat David, Palestine, 1945/6. (J T Jennings)

take-off and landing. Amid all the comings and goings, Fg Off Robertson was posted home to New Zealand, having only recently returned from Yugoslavia.

Air Vice-Marshal G M Mills, CBE, DFC, visited the Squadron on 26 June and announced that the Balkan Air Force was to be disbanded by the middle of July. To everyone's relief he also added that, in view of its record, the Squadron would remain in service, and most likely become a part of the regular peace-time Royal Air Force.

After some days of rumours of a move back to the UK, or further afield to Burma, the issue was resolved when the Squadron moved down the coast to Brindisi and rejoined 281 Wing. The move took place on 28/30 June, and the excellent organisation and the smoothness of the move were, it was reflected, in strong contrast to the panic-stricken gyrations to and from Yugoslavia of the previous month. The move was in most respects for the better. The majority of the Squadron personnel were accommodated in barracks near the aircraft dispersals and only a few yards from the sea. The Sergeants' Mess was established in an old Italian Gas Centre, which some thought an admirable arrangement! The airmen were well established in their cool barracks, the Sergeants ship-shape in their gas centre, but the officers had drawn the short straw, having to Mess with the Wing, which was located approximately one mile from the Squadron and which meant catching a bus every mealtime.

July opened on a tragic note when, on 2 July, Fg Off O Wilson-North was killed when his Mustang flew into the ground while on a height climb exercise. It was suspected that his oxygen failed, as he went in from a considerable height in a high-speed dive which tore off a wing on the way down. It seemed that he was unconscious before his aircraft hit the ground, as no attempt was made to pull out. Once the Squadron had settled in at Brindisi, the CO decided to introduce night-flying into the training programme. However this radical new departure was greeted with incredulity, particularly by the long-serving NCO pilots, and as distinctly inappropriate for a day-fighter squadron! After a few sorties, flown largely by the more recently-arrived pilots, the matter was dropped.

Under the command of No.281 Wing there was no flying on Saturday or Sunday, and during the week sorties were restricted to the mornings, with take-offs timed for 06.45 hours or 09.15 hours to avoid the heat of the day. The temperature in the cockpit of the Mustang was still giving trouble, and the Engineering Officer was busy once again fitting improvised air-scoops above the coamings of the aircraft. Apart from completing the ballot papers for the General Election in the UK, which had been distributed on 5 July, there was plenty to do in Brindisi and an Information Room was established, in which Sunday newspapers were available. Life was further improved when, on 21 July, a rota for leave to the UK was instituted, with air transport available.

On 10 July, the last of the South Africans, Lts G R Holdsworth, B N Chiazzari, O Jones, Clement, Els and McGibbon, departed, leaving the Squadron with only seven General Duties Officers. Earlier in July, a departure of a different sort had taken place when Wallace the goat went missing, either stolen or just wandered off. Following the move to Brindisi he had been allowed greater freedom and it was surmised that this had led to his disappearance. There was considerable disappointment, as he had become quite civilised. Given the impoverished state of the south of Italy immediately after the war, it was assumed by everyone that he had finished up alongside the pasta on a local family's dinner table.

The Squadron's training programme was fully justified, when one of the many competitions designed to maintain flying proficiency, a Rover David Exercise, was held by Nos.213, 249 and 253 Squadrons. Some of the Squadron's NCO pilots were among the most experienced in flying time and operations, and the best team of four pilots that could be found was selected to represent the Squadron. The point was proved when the all-NCO team led by "Robbie" Robinson carried off the trophy.

In early August, the Squadron's old camouflaged Mustangs were exchanged for the shiny new silver aircraft

Squadron Soccer team versus A.Y.M.S Cyprus, 22 February 1947.
Left to right standing: Stringsby, Sgt Coulson, Flt Sgt Palmer, LAC Parncutt, Fg Off Knight, Cpl Ireland and Sqn Ldr Colebrook. Kneeling LAC Sim, Cpl Greenwood, LAC Watts, Cpl Hope, Cpl Adams and LAC Coomber.

being given up by 249 Squadron, which were due to be returned to the UK. When the sixteen new aircraft were taken over, they were repainted with the Squadron identification letters, with "A" Flight outlining theirs in red and "B" Flight theirs in yellow. Everyone agreed that this looked very smart against the silver background of the unpainted aircraft. On 16 August, a party was held to mark the departure of the very popular Adjutant, Leslie Robins.

The comfortable life, which had been so quickly established, was rudely shattered by a visit from Air Vice-Marshal Whitford, CB, CBE on 21 August. He brought the news that the Squadron was to move to Palestine, where a difficult situation was building up as refugees poured in from a war-torn and shattered Europe.

The Advance Party left for Palestine on 28 August via 54 PDC at Taranto, where it was delayed for some days. The Main Ground Party embarked on the liner *Winchester Castle* on 7 September. The excellent conditions on board ship, which promised a comfortable voyage, paled into insignificance when it was seen that there was a large contingent of WAAFs on board. Back at Brindisi, little flying took place for ten days while the aircraft were prepared for the flight to Ramat David by the few essential maintenance crews, who remained behind with the pilots. By 11 September, fourteen of the Squadron's sixteen aircraft had been air tested and serviceability was one hundred per cent, when the signal arrived on 12 September to depart the next day.

The departure of the first section of four aircraft, to be led by the CO and timed for 06.40 hours was delayed until 07.30 hours, since one of the aircraft had developed a glycol leak overnight. Even then the section's troubles were not over as another aircraft developed engine trouble after being airborne for about five minutes, and all four returned to Brindisi. The three remaining sections, led by Flt Lt G S Hulse, Flt Lt W J P Straker and Flt Sgt W M Monkman, encountered bad weather between Araxos and Athens, with cloud up to 28,000 feet, and several pilots blacked-out due to faulty oxygen equipment. The formation split up and all the aircraft finally landed at Hassani, Athens. As two aircraft had become unserviceable, Bill Straker's section remained on the ground and Hulse led the remaining eight aircraft on to Ramat David. The CO's section was finally airborne late in the afternoon, and landed at Nicosia for an overnight stop. This however extended into three nights, and it was not until 16 September that the section eventually arrived in Palestine, having taken part in the Battle of Britain fly-past at Nicosia *en route*. Bill Straker's section finally made it into Ramat David on 19 September, after an extended six-night stay in Athens.

Ramat David, which had changed considerably since the Squadron's first visit in 1941, now provided a comfortable home reminiscent of a regular RAF station. No sooner had Peter Vaughan-Fowler arrived there than he left for a Staff Course in the USA, and Hulse took temporary command. The day after the last 213 Squadron aircraft arrived, 32 Squadron moved out from Ramat David to the airfield at Petah Tiqva, and the Squadron hurriedly moved into their "Oh so nice" dispersals, taxying their aircraft in as 32 Squadron taxied out. The rest of the move, which was accomplished in record time, was only just complete when, thirty minutes later, the aircraft of 6 Squadron flew in. The hi-jacking of their accommodation was taken in good part, even when they saw what they had lost. Later a sign displaying the deathless couplet "Never falter, never fear / 213 fly around here" appeared over the Squadron Office.

Hopes of operations remained high as the Squadron

The Control Tower, Nicosia, Cyprus, 1946. (H Ayre)

Mustang IV AK-R at Ramat David, Palestine, 1946.

became the Garrison Squadron in Palestine, albeit that the establishment was reduced from 179 airmen to 115. These numbers were in fact rather academic, since by the end of October the Squadron's actual strength stood at only ninety. However, as many of the departing airmen had only been posted on to the strength of Ramat David, the situation was not as bad as it might have been, notwithstanding the increase in guard duties which the tense situation necessitated. These duties were shared by all ranks, including aircrew. The Guard bedded down in the hangar, and the Squadron settled into a routine of twenty-four-hour guard duties, as well as a full flying programme. The strain soon began to tell and, in response to the CO's request, a contingent of Grenadier Guards was drafted in to take over the security of the Squadron's aircraft. The Guards immediately dug fox-holes alongside each aircraft on the dispersal and secured the whole area. The pilots were most impressed with their new-found "Brown job" friends - life was a great deal more bearable, and there was more space in the hangar!

The Squadron's task in Palestine was two-fold, and both roles unfortunately involved long hours on patrol. On 1 October, a daily Pipe Line Patrol was instituted over the entire length of the oil-pipeline, from the port of Haifa to the Jordan Valley. This important link with the oil-fields of Iraq was receiving the attentions of saboteurs from dissident groups in Palestine, and the armed patrols were flown to act as a deterrent. Returning from such a patrol on 18 December, Fg Off Witteridge wrote off his Mustang when he made too tight a turn on his final approach and stalled. Fortunately he was only concussed and sustained a broken ankle and cuts and bruises to his face, although he did not return to duty with the Squadron. John Jennings (Gp Capt J T Jennings, DFC) recalls the background to this incident:-

"At morning briefing that day, Fg Off R C Willdey, OC "A" Flight, informed the Flight, all NCO pilots, that their circuits, and particularly the turns onto finals, were not tight enough in the true fighter tradition! He continued that Fg Off Witteridge would demonstrate the correct procedure. At the appointed time we all took our chairs outside in the sun, and awaited the demo. Witteridge roared in on the right hand side of the runway, pulled a split-arse turn all the way round until he flicked, stalled and went in short of the runway. We all came to our feet, and watched the fire truck and ambulance disappear into the distance, then picked up our chairs and returned to the crew-room. Not a word was uttered in the presence of Willdey, but once inside the comments covered a wide spectrum. 'So that's how it's done'. I don't think I like that method'. 'Christ, if that's how we are supposed to do it I'm putting in for a transfer'."

The subject of how to perform a proper approach in a Mustang was never raised again thereafter.

The second task allotted to the Squadron involved patrolling the eastern end of the Mediterranean, searching for illegal immigrant ships running refugees into Palestine. Despite the high level of operations, few ships were sighted. Such patrols seriously curtailed the traditional Christmas festivities of the first year at peace when, on 25 December, eight sorties were flown searching for a ship reported off the coast, but once again no contact was made. One outstanding success occurred on 17 January 1946 when Hulse set off, with Jennings as his Number Two, on an illegal shipping patrol. They duly found the ship, the *Enzo Sereni*, fixed its position, and then shadowed it until relieved by another section, led by Fg Off K A L Ford, which maintained the surveillance until a Royal Navy destroyer arrived four hours later.

Following this interception, Hulse, who was acting as CO, was named on the illegal Jewish radio station for retribution and he was therefore flown out of Palestine to Egypt on 27 January. John Jennings was praying that he would also be named, so that he too would be flown out of what was a most unpleasant situation. As far as he was concerned, the year in Palestine was the most uncomfortable year in his service career.

On 21 January Sqn Ldr R S Nash, DFC, arrived to take command.

The Squadron, on the whole, had great respect for the Israelis and their efforts to build a new country. Even more, perhaps, for the tenacity of the poor souls who, after a lifetime of persecution in Europe, risking their lives in small boats loaded to the gunwales, were now trying to reach their promised homeland in Palestine. It was no satisfaction for the RAF or the Royal Navy to be part of the procedure, which labelled them as "illegal immigrants" to be bundled into wired camps at Haifa for yet further incarceration. These however were the dying days of the Palestine Mandate. The Israelis wanted the British out, and while the wheels of diplomacy ground on, the extremists regarded any symbol of foreign authority as a legitimate target. Squadron personnel were restricted from going off base, which was allowed only in minimum groups of four, with each individual armed with personal weapons. It was not a pleasant atmosphere but, as the world has since learnt many times over, terrorism has to be opposed and hence the need for the armed patrols over the

Some NCO ground-crew and pilots, Ramat David, Palestine, 1945. (J T Jennings)

pipe-line and the police posts to "show the flag".

Despite the pleasant surroundings, the mounting tension and the general hostility towards the British forces clearly made Palestine a less than comfortable place to be in 1946. At the same time, the long hours in the air on patrol over the sea and desert led to a feeling of anti-climax after the active and dangerous role the Squadron had performed in the Balkans. As the year passed, the situation in Palestine became more and more difficult, and conditions reminiscent of wartime prevailed.

The routine of Pipe Line Patrols, Police Post Recces and illegal shipping patrols, absorbed most of the flying hours, with occasional diversions in the form of strafing demonstrations for the Army Liaison Officers' School. More and more of the "old timers" left, one being Bill Straker on 25 June, and on 2 July three new pilots, Fg Off Andrews, WO Williams and Flt Sgt Rumble, the latter two with Mustang experience, arrived. At the same time, three pilots were detached to Deversoir for Army Co-operation exercises. At Ramat David, practice Tactical Reconnaissance patrols were instituted, in conjunction with the Squadron's popular Army Liaison Officer, Capt "Steve" Gurteen; fighter affiliation sorties, with Lancasters of No.40 Squadron, were also introduced.

As the year drew on, conditions in Palestine became more and more difficult, so the news of a move to Cyprus in September was more than welcome. On 16 September, the rumours, which had been circulating for some time, were confirmed and the CO and WO Jennings flew to Nicosia to arrange the Squadron's new accommodation. The ground party's move commenced on 25 September, and the Main party arrived in Cyprus on 1 October, accompanied by the first rains of winter. By 5 October a busy flying programme was under way and two new Flight Commanders, in the persons of Flt Lts C J Barrey, DFC, AFC, DFM, and A E Johnson, had arrived. Together with the CO and John Jennings, now promoted to Plt Off, who served as Adjutant, these were the only four commissioned officer aircrew on the Squadron. The peaceful and friendly atmosphere of Nicosia was greatly appreciated, and by the end of the month the Squadron was at home in its new quarters. The long hours on patrol were no longer required, and under Sqn Ldr M C Wells, who assumed command on 5 November 1946, an extensive training programme was soon established.

Communications proved to be the greatest problem, since letters to HQ in Egypt seemed to take an inordinate length of time to arrive. Difficulties with transport also meant that, at times, the flying programme was seriously curtailed as supplies of fuel became exhausted. Where small items and essential spares were concerned, the Mustang again proved its worth when a "Pony Express" service was organised, the Squadron acting as its own transport unit. To increase the carrying capacity of the Mustang, the largest available under-wing drop-tanks were modified as cargo containers. The nose of the tank was cut off at the point of broadest cross-section, flanges with hinges fitted all round the cone, and bolts with wing nuts were fitted around the edge of the body of the tank to secure the nose cone when loaded.

On one memorable - and highly unofficial - occasion, the system was used to carry a passenger. On a trip for spares to Lydda, in Palestine, the section leader met an Australian Squadron Leader, who had been trying to return to Cyprus for three days. With hindsight, he all too readily accepted the casual offer of a lift back to Nicosia. When the time came to take off, the Squadron Leader inserted himself into the wing-tank, the nose-cone was screwed on, and the filler cap removed to provide some ventilation. All would have been well but for the fact that, as the aircraft set out across the Eastern Mediterranean, they had to climb to keep out of the cloud that covered the area. Having reached approximately ten thousand feet, it was clearly dangerous to go much higher and the aircraft entered the cloud and associated rain. There was, by now, considerable concern for the passenger who, if he had not succumbed to the cold or the lack of oxygen, might even have drowned! Fortunately it was a Wednesday afternoon and, as the aircraft landed at Nicosia, there were few ground-crew about. The dispersal was cleared of everyone apart from a senior NCO, and with considerable

Hawker Tempest VI with Sqn Ldr D C Colebrook at the controls, Shallufa, Egypt, 1947. (H Ayre)

trepidation the nose cone was removed. The passenger was almost literally frozen stiff, but after supporting him under his arms and running him up and down the dispersal a few times, he slowly thawed out and returned to full consciousness. It always remained something of a mystery as to what explanation he gave to his unit concerning his return to the island.

The days of the Mustang were however numbered, and re-equipment with the Hawker Tempest was scheduled for the end of the year. Soon the faithful Mustangs were standing forlornly around the edge of the airfield as the Squadron came to terms with its complex new aircraft.

The Hawker Tempest was perhaps the ultimate piston-engined fighter aircraft, and one of the fastest with a maximum speed of 440 miles per hour. The Tempest F Mark VI, with which the Squadron was equipped, was powered by a Napier Sabre 5A in-line engine. The Mark VI was in fact a tropicalised version of the Mark V. The essential modification was the removal of the oil-cooler from the aircraft's chin radiator and its relocation in the starboard mainplane, thus leaving the chin radiator solely for engine cooling. The Mark VI also had spring tab ailerons, the flying controls having no direct link with the ailerons, only with the tabs, which of course moved in the opposite sense to the ailerons; not only did this arrangement make the controls much lighter, but it also gave the aircraft a much faster rate of roll. With a wing-span of forty-one feet, a length of just over thirty-four feet and a height of fifteen feet ten inches, the Tempest was a large aeroplane for a single-seat fighter-bomber. Armed with four 20mm cannons and able to carry two thousand pounds of bombs or eight 60-pound rockets on under-wing pylons, the Tempest could also deliver a powerful punch.

On 7 January 1947, it was discovered that Sqn Ldr Wells had, in fact, been a Wing Commander since 1 November 1946; sad farewells were quickly said and the next day Sqn Ldr D C Colebrook, who had had considerable experience with both Tempests and Typhoons, arrived to take command.

On 25 January, the first two Tempests came off Flt Lt Bullock's production line. Flt Lt A E Johnson flew one for the first time and was heard to remark, "It's an awful lot of aeroplane - and it certainly makes Cyprus small". The latter part of this remark recognised the fact that the Tempest cruised at a speed some seventy miles per hour faster than the Mustang.

The Tempests ran into considerable teething problems in Cyprus. Overriding all others were the problems with the engine cooling system, which at times succeeded in grounding all the new aircraft, which were initially allotted to "B" Flight. Gradually the problems were overcome and an appreciation of the Tempest developed. Since the Squadron still had a ground-attack role, gunnery and dive-bombing practice absorbed most of the flying programme as the Squadron prepared itself, and its new aircraft, for any new contingency that might arise.

The good news surrounding Wg Cdr Well's departure was that he was to become the Deputy Senior Staff Officer i/c Movements at Ismailia. This was particularly encouraging in view of the communication difficulties and the fact that, in the age of radar and the atomic bomb, the Squadron's fuel supplies were transported from the mainland in a sailing ship!

Towards the end of January, a spell of bad weather with strong winds made the airfield unserviceable for single-engined aircraft and light twins, and revealed another problem with the Tempests. With its high fuselage profile and large

Plt Off J T Jennings's NX248 after the brakes locked on landing, Nicosia, Cyprus, 19 February 1947. (J T Jennings)

Pilot 2 Stephan Zagroba going back to turn off the fuel cock, Deversoir, Egypt, 1949. (Gordon Tripp)

tail-fin, the Tempest was vulnerable on the ground in strong winds and required strong ground-pickets, whereas the Mustang with its low centre of gravity, and with its radiator amidships, withstood high-speed gusts more easily.

As February wore on and the problems with the fuel supply remained, "A" Flight polished its new charges with almost industrial efficiency, while "B" Flight mourned as yet another Mustang was towed off to the dump, minus radio, guns, clock and compass, to be sold for scrap at £10 to £20 per ton. By the end of the month the change over to Tempests was complete and the "Pony Express" service was no more. Flt Lt Johnson predictably incurred the wrath of the CO when he was heard to express the view that the Squadron would be better off if it kept its Mustangs.

With the arrival of spring and the better weather, not only did the flying programme benefit but the delights of the island were also uncovered and frequent visits paid to the Dome and Empire in Kyrenia.

However, yet again, a pleasant summer was disrupted when the Squadron was once more on the move. Early on the morning of 4 September 1947, eight Tempests roared into the sky and, taking up formation over Nicosia, set course for Egypt. Two hours and five minutes later they were touching down and the pilots had their first look at the sandy wastes of Shallufa. Flt Lt H E A Douglas-Reid took the Harvard and proceeded via Amman where he picked up the CO. Due to the good back-up provided by the supporting Dakotas, flying recommenced only six days after the Main Party had arrived.

The initial sector reconnaissance flights all returned with the same reports - sand in all directions. Exploratory trips were also carried out on the ground, with a less operational objective. Regrettably, it soon became apparent that Shallufa did not come up to the standards of "sunny Cyprus" as far as off-duty recreation facilities were concerned. In the air, preparations were put in hand to establish low-flying areas, which were essential for the Squadron's ground-attack role. However, flying soon became somewhat restricted as priority for the limited supplies of fuel was given to the bomber squadron, which was a prior resident at Shallufa.

With Nos.6 and 213 Squadrons in residence, No.324 Wing was now fully established. The first occasion on which the Squadron was on show to the public was a mere week after its arrival, when it took part in the Battle of Britain fly-pasts. Flying at 1,000 feet, the Tempests did their best to stay in touch with a formation of Lancasters flying in open-box formation at one hundred and seventy knots. To achieve this, it was found necessary to fly as slowly as possible at forty-five degrees to the Lancasters and carry out ninety-degree cross-over turns every few minutes. Despite a complete lack of any rehearsals, the formation successfully flew over all the stations in the Canal Zone. The afternoon was marred by the first write-off of one of the Tempests, when WO E Leeson suffered complete engine failure due to a severe oil leak whilst flying near Ismailia. Although he managed to make it to the emergency airstrip at El Firdan, owing to obstructions he was forced to land across the runway and the engine was torn from its mountings. This and other damage reduced the aircraft to scrap.

Such was the low state of serviceability, which had again descended on the Tempests, that the only flying permitted consisted largely of Army Co-operation with the resident troops. A plentiful supply of rockets, plus a derelict Churchill tank in the desert, soon put the pilots in good heart. The highlight of the stay at Shallufa proved to be an Army Co-operation Exercise held at Ein Shemer. For the trip up to the range, the aircraft were armed with eight 60-lb semi-armour-piercing rockets and two hundred rounds of ammunition. The rocket target turned out to an old Arab house, and the strafing target a convoy of old trucks loaded with oil and flame-throwing material. As the whole convoy disappeared in a mass of flames and smoke, it was hoped that the "brown jobs", for whom the demonstration had been planned, were duly impressed.

As soon as this demonstration was over, news arrived that the Squadron was on the move again. Armed with rockets and with the gun-bays loaded with personal gear, the aircraft were prepared for take-off before dawn. By 06.00 hours on 22 October 1947, seven aircraft were airborne and setting course due south once more. Following closely the winding course of the Nile, two hours and twenty minutes flying time brought the pilots to Wadi Halfa. By mid-day they were "Way down in the sunny south" at their new home, Khartoum. Once again, in newer and hotter surroundings, the familiar process of settling in took place, and once again the desert stretched in all directions. The only feature for miles around was the junction of the Blue and White Niles, both of which looked remarkably brown. The airfield at Khartoum was situated on the eastern edge of the town after which it was named. In view of the considerable temperatures that were experienced, it was fortunate that the aircraft could be

Squadron Tempests, Deversoir, Egypt, 1948/49. The Station Commander, Gp Cpt A F Anderson, DSO, DFC, is in "B-Brenda" on the Squadron dispersal prior to a "Wing Ding".

kept in hangars. The heat also affected the flying programme. The first sortie of the day normally took off before breakfast and flying for the day finished before lunch. Once again rocket attacks at the local range were the order of the day, and a demonstration was laid on for the local army garrison.

Christmas 1947 proved a hard time for the Squadron personnel. The heat of the day, coupled with the normal festive celebrations and a hard round of athletic competitions between the Wing and the Station, caused many members to succumb before the expiry of the Christmas Grant. A particularly popular item, though not with the animals' owners, was a series of donkey races and a donkey-polo match between the various Messes. The first day's flying programme of the New Year after the break, which was to have been shallow dive-bombing, was altered to level bombing due to the prevalence of head colds! The other recreational pursuit, which occupied the Squadron's off-duty hours, was searching the banks of the Nile for crocodiles, under the leadership of the gallant Army Liaison Officer, Captain Histead. However, the total haul from the first two trips proved to be but one "croc", eighteen inches long.

On 18 March 1948, the new CO, Sqn Ldr P J Kelley, DFC, arrived to assume command. Towards the end of the month, long-range tanks were fitted to all the aircraft in preparation for a series of long-range cross-country flights. The first of these well-prepared trips unfortunately coincided with the local high wind, the Haboob, which made conditions very difficult. In fact, neither section claimed to be entirely sure of its position all the way round the three-hour trip, and Khartoum homer gave much appreciated assistance on the final leg. But much invaluable experience was acquired for the operations which were to occupy the Squadron in the next few months. Flying was now restricted to Tuesdays, Thursdays and Fridays, with the intervening days being given over to servicing the aircraft and keeping them on the top line in difficult conditions.

A satisfactory week's flying was rounded off in good style when a large party of pilots disappeared into the desert with the intrepid Captain, once again on a safari - this time to a nearby lake formed behind the dam at Jebel Aulia. Although most of the journey was across virgin desert, the surface proved to be smoother than some of the local roads. The primary object of the expedition was to introduce some variety into the menu in the Mess and, secondly, to have some sport shooting the duck which frequented the lake. By the evening the position had been reconnoitred and, as the ducks rose from the lake towards sunset, intermittent fire continued until the ammunition was nearly exhausted. At sunrise the next day Capt Histead located some geese and, with the limited rounds remaining from the previous evening, three were brought down. The week-end was voted a resounding success by all concerned, and resolutions were made to secure a more adequate supply of ammunition for the next venture.

On 24 March 1948, the Squadron received instructions to send a detachment to Asmara, since in Eritrea some of the local tribesmen were proving troublesome. After three days of intensive work, four aircraft, each with a full load of ammunition and the inevitable rockets, took off for Asmara, which lies about fifty miles inland from the Red Sea coast. The formation was led by Flt Lt L G Lunn, who was to command the detachment, while the three other aircraft were

Sqn Ldr D J A Roe, DSO, DFC. Squadron Commander 18 April 1949-14 September 1951.

Hawker Tempest, after its brakes locked on landing, pilot Plt Off J T Jennings, Nicosia, Cyprus, 1946. (H Ayre)

flown by Flt Lt R W G Austin and Fg Offs D A Hankin and P L N Poolman. As always, volunteers for the operation had far exceeded the number of personnel required. The supporting ground party moved up in a Dakota. At Khartoum the days of the Easter Grant seemed to drag by and, with the prospect of some real operations, every one was keen to be back at work as soon as possible. The immediate task was to fit long-range tanks to four more Tempests, in order to provide readily available replacements and a fast means of moving up spare parts. At this critical juncture, the Wing's Anson had become unserviceable and no routine flights were going to Asmara.

The trouble in Eritrea was being caused by wandering bands of tribesmen known as Shifta. More than usually lawless, these bands were robbing and terrorising the immediate vicinity of Asmara and the country to the south-west of the town. The terrain here consists of a very rugged plateau at about one thousand feet, grooved by many deep wadis and small dry streams emptying into the rivers Mareb and Bocra. The Mareb river bounds the plateau to the south, and also constitutes the border with Ethiopia. The ground forces operating against the Shifta were made up from the King's Own African Rifles and the local Tribal Force Levies. These troops were divided into light columns, which could travel relatively quickly over the rugged terrain, and whose object was to drive the Shifta towards the line of Police Posts established along the edge of the plateau. One of the most difficult, but essential, tasks was to stop the bands from slipping south over the border into Ethiopia, where the British forces could not operate. Due to the nature of the country, the greatest difficulty facing the ground forces lay in maintaining contact between headquarters and the columns in the field. It was in this connection that most of the detachment's flying was carried out.

The first few days were spent in flying sector reconnaissance patrols over what seemed impossible country. The four pilots soon realised that even to locate the columns would require the greatest accuracy in map-reading, and the proverbial hawk-eye look-out. Once having located the column or the Police Post, the actual dropping of the message proved relatively simple. The message was often the only contact the patrol would have with headquarters for days on end. The Squadron's tradition of excellence was well maintained, and the army was highly impressed with the standard of accuracy reached. At a party held in the Mess,

Inspector Burke of the Eritrean Police recounted how a message dropped to him in an isolated Police Post by Hankin had fallen literally right into his hands. Capt Histead, who was at Asmara as Liaison Officer, had such faith in the pilots' ability that he somewhat rashly made a wager with one of the local officers that a message would be dropped directly on to the roof of his bungalow on the first pass. The Captain's faith in the return of ten shillings was, for a short period, greater than that of the pilot involved. However the Squadron's honour was upheld, and the drinks were on the Captain for the rest of the evening.

Once having located the columns and having established a regular communications network, many other tasks came along. Pamphlet dropping over native villages offering rewards for information, and urging the villagers not to help the Shifta, also took up a good many sorties. Supply dropping was a new role for the Tempest, but bundles of bread and cigarettes - a somewhat limited diet - were dropped to some of the more isolated columns. The detachment's first contact with the Shifta came after about ten days when trouble was reported near Agordat, a town on the railway line roughly one hundred miles due west of Asmara. As the nearest army column would take some hours to reach the spot, Tempests with full long-range tanks took off to patrol the area at low-level, thus keeping the gang immobilised until the nearest column could come up. After two weeks of operations, the two biggest gangs, led by Hagos and Tegle, had been split up, but the danger remained that they would slip south over the border. One of the most unusual but effective of the Squadron's operations was mounted against Hagos' gang. Reports were received that between two and three hundred cattle had been stolen from the local tribes at the wells at Aclene, and that they were being driven south across the border into Ethiopia. The intention was that the Tempests should fly low over the herd and drive it back north-westwards. Although no really large herds were located, some cattle were successfully stampeded in a northerly direction, and confirmation arrived some days later that the operation had been very successful.

To mark St George's Day 1948, the detachment was asked to put on a rocket display for the assembled troops of the King's Own African Rifles and the Berkshire Regiment. The spectators were grouped on a large hill overlooking a smaller one on which the targets were erected. The targets were made at some personal sacrifice to Capt Histead, as they

Armament Practice Camp RAF, Nicosia, Cyprus, 26 May 1950. From left to right standing: Sgt Jock Stuart, Sgt Ted Sparks, Pilot 2 Stephan Zagroba, Sgt Frank Atkinson, Sgt Gordon Tripp, Pilot 4 Pete Hart, Sgt Guy Gibson, Sgt Chis Chiswick, Pilot 3 Harry Wragg, MP Jack Barnard. Front Row: Fg Off A L Twigg, Fg Off Jimmy Wilson, Flt Sgt Jimmy Walker, Pet Lee (APC), Sqn Ldr Derek Roe, Wg Cdr Elliott (APC), Pete Thorn (APC), Flt Lt Gus Davies, Flt Lt Tommy Ormiston, Fg Off Geoff Abel, Plt Off Herbie Sincock and WO Polly Perkins. (Gordon Tripp)

consisted of the sheets from his bed stretched over wooden frames! After a low pass over the spectators, Lunn pulled up for his attack and delivered his eight rockets neatly into the centre of Histead's bedclothes. Poolman following, raising an even greater cloud of dust as the hillside erupted into a smoking inferno. The soldiers were duly impressed, and expressed their appreciation of the fact that the Tempests were on their side rather than against them. The whole display was rounded off by a tail-chase, with Rankin joining in as the third aircraft, and some really close formation flying, before the three aircraft disappeared at ground level through a gap in the hills.

An extremely good working relationship had been built up very quickly with the officers and men of the King's Own African Rifles, and it came as something of a wrench when, on 4 May, a signal arrived indicating that there was "something in the wind" back at Khartoum. This was quickly followed by a further signal ordering the immediate return of all aircraft and personnel to base. Brief farewells were said and a passing Dakota on a training flight was loaded with much of the ground equipment. Soon the whole party had left the "lovely climate and sociable people" that had made the detachment so enjoyable. A letter from the officer commanding Eritrea District, Brigadier C M Gamble, OBE, to Group Captain A F Anderson, DSO, DFC, the commanding officer of No.324 Wing, Khartoum, indicated that the detachment's efforts had been well appreciated:-

"H. Q. Eritrea District,
Asmara, Eritrea

From Brigadier G. W. Gamble, O.B.E.
7th April, 1948.

My Dear Anderson,
I am writing to tell you how deeply I appreciate the valuable assistance given to us here in our operations against the Shifta by your fellows.
 They have been 100% cooperative and there is no doubt at all that the morale effect on the Shifta and others in the country has been considerable. From the point of view of communications, always very difficult in this mountainous country, their message dropping of astonishing accuracy has kept us continually in touch with outlying points and they have materially assisted us in our W/T communications.
Today they are dropping pamphlets urging the Shifta to surrender over a wide area - in fact there seems no limit to the ways in which they can help us!
I was sorry not to meet you when you came over the other day but had to stay at the helm here. I hope however that we shall meet next time you come to thank you personally for all your help.

Yours sincerely,

(Signed) G. M. Gamble.

Showing the flag. A Squadron Tempest being inspected by soldiers of the East African Rifles, Malakal, 1950. The Khartoum Detachment.

The Squadron re-equips, Deversoir, Egypt, 1949/50.

Back at Khartoum morale had risen considerably and, although flying was limited due to the demands at Asmara, serviceability rose to 100% and a new zest pervaded the Squadron. The only grouse was that not all the personnel could be up at Asmara taking a closer hand in the operations and benefiting from the ideal climate and the supplies of fresh food. A good deal of flying, by both the Tempests and the Anson, was carried out in keeping the detachment well supplied, and the crews normally managed a night-stop in Asmara. This was usually spent in a visit to the "San Georgio" restaurant, where a large meal in true Italian style was enjoyed. In the middle of the detachment, the new CO, Sqn Ldr P S Kelley, DFC, arrived from Headquarters, where he had been filling a staff post. With its aircraft now well and truly tried and tested and with a job to do, the Squadron was once again in fine fettle and eager for any new task.

June opened with a tragic accident, when Sgt Crighton crashed on Armil Island, off Massawa, while on a low-level cross-country exercise with Fg Off E Walker. The small island in the Red Sea was the turning point and, while carrying out a cross-over turn, his aircraft hit the ground and burnt out. His body was recovered later and he was buried with full military honours in the military cemetery at Asmara. As the month passed in the normal training routine, Sqn Ldr Kelley took command of the Wing temporarily when Gp Cpt Anderson left for the Delta. Being at the hub of things, the CO was able to give the Squadron advance news that a detachment could be expected to another trouble spot in the near future. Once again preparations were put in hand to be at readiness to move.

The trouble spot that was next expected to erupt was Somaliland. The centre of the trouble was forecast to be in the Ogaden, a strip of territory between Italian Somaliland and Ethiopia. Since the end of the war this area had been occupied by British Forces of Administration, as had former Italian Eritrea. Now, in accordance with the recommendations of the United Nations, the British Forces were to withdraw and the territory was to be handed over to Ethiopia. However various political parties had sprung up in this area and in Italian Somaliland itself, and the tribes which the parties represented wished neither to remain under British Administration nor to return to Ethiopia. As these tribes were Somali people, the cry became "Somaliland for the Somalis", an idea particularly fostered by the Somali Youth League. With such a touchy situation, it was expected that mob violence and other disturbances would mark the withdrawal of British Troops. The Squadron's role was to provide an element of air support to help protect British and Italian lives at the time of the hand-over. However, for the moment, no firm date had been fixed for the move and the normal flying training programme was continued.

At the beginning of July, the CO flew up to the Canal Zone to discuss arrangements for the move. His return trip to Khartoum was interrupted when he became part of a search and rescue operation. A civilian airline Dakota had reported that one of its engines was on fire, and it had subsequently force-landed in the desert south of Wadi Halfa. Flying in the Wing's Anson, the CO was asked to keep a look-out for the missing aircraft, which was carrying women and children amongst its passengers. Somewhere on the leg between Wadi Halfa and Khartoum, he picked out the wreckage of the Dakota, virtually intact, on a flat stretch of desert. After taking a good look at the surface, he put the Anson down and found the passengers and crew all safe though somewhat shaken by their experience. As the Anson was virtually empty and the desert surface looked to be good enough for a heavy-weight take off, the women and children were taken on board and were soon airborne again, bound for Khartoum. Much to their relief, and no doubt somewhat to their surprise, an unpleasant night in the desert had been avoided.

In the middle of the month, two pieces of definitive news arrived at Khartoum, which would affect the Squadron in the coming weeks and months. The date for the move to Mogadishu in Italian Somaliland was fixed for 7 August. Also, after many negotiations at Command and Group level, it had been decided to move No.324 Wing to Deversoir in the Canal Zone, and the date for this move was to be 1 September. For the moment, however, the detachment to Mogadishu held everyone's attention. Certain modifications to the aircraft were necessary. The under-wing hooks were designed for forty-five gallon tanks and a series of tests were carried out to check their ability to carry the ninety-gallon tanks being fitted for the trip to Mogadishu. Also the oxygen bottles only provided enough oxygen for 2½ hours, while the larger tanks gave the Tempests five hours endurance. The modification programme therefore included providing the aircraft with another oxygen bottle.

At last, on 16 August, after the passage of a very severe thunderstorm, thirteen Tempests took off for Khormaksar, Aden. *En route*, to recall to mind the very pleasant detachment at Asmara, the aircraft flew over the town and airfield in very close formation. The CO led five aircraft in a vic, as Red Leader, followed by two boxes of four. At Khormaksar the aircraft were met by No.8 Squadron, whose

The Squadron flight line, Deversoir, Egypt, 1950.

groundcrew looked after the necessary servicing. The next morning, the aircraft, minus one that had struck its propeller on the ground on take-off at Khartoum, were airborne for Mogadishu, via Djibouti and Belet Uen.

The first operation was flown two days after the arrival at Mogadishu. It was feared that an inter-tribal fight would break out at a village up the coast beyond Belet Uen. Two sections located the village and carried out an extensive "reconnaissance" of the small collection of houses, the second section arriving just as the first was leaving. The whole trip was something of an anti-climax as it appeared that the village was deserted. A reconnaissance of two advanced landing-grounds with sand runways along the coast showed that the surfaces would not support Tempest operations, so all the aircraft remained at Mogadishu. This news was not unwelcome as the station had many good features. Most appreciated was the delightful bathing beach, which was protected from the depredations of the local sharks by a barrier reef just off shore. As the operations were slow to commence and the airfield was right on the coast, full advantage was taken of the facilities. Visits were also exchanged with the local Army Mess, and a visit by the cruiser HMS *Birmingham* meant that a considerable round of social activities was undertaken.

As the date for the withdrawal drew near, a ground party moved inland to the landing-ground at Hargeisa, which boasted a gravel-surfaced runway of 2,200 yards. Operating from this strip, in territory where maps were inaccurate to say the least, posed certain navigational problems, even though a letter from the local Ethiopian Provincial Governor suggested that at least he was sure exactly where the border lay:-

"Provincial Office, Giggia,
Date:- 20th Nehase 1940 (26.8.48)
Ref: 8/797

H. E. The Governor of British Somaliland,
Hargeisa.

On 19th. Nehase 1940 (25.8.48.) at about quarter to twelve four British planes flew over Giggia for some twenty minutes at a height of 50 meters and returned.

I think that it is quite clear for you that this Planes should not operate in the Ethiopian Territory without first applying to Ethiopian Authorities and which is forbidden by international laws.

I am informing you that if in future such happens, any measure which will be given me by my Government will be taken against them, Having this opportunity I am sending you my best wishes.

Sgd. Demerke Retta,
Major,
Governor of Giggia Province.
H. Q. Office - Horar."

In practice, the withdrawal of the British troops from the various garrisons went off smoothly. The Squadron's part, repeated on numerous occasions, became fairly standard. As the troops, British and Ethiopian, paraded and the Union Jack was run-down, a flight of aircraft would dip low over the ceremony and make a couple of passes. The only two difficulties were firstly in keeping a large number of aircraft serviceable, since these ceremonies were fairly numerous and, secondly, in ensuring that the pilots arrived overhead at

Rising sand caused by aircraft taxying, Mafraq, Transjordan, April 1951. (W Menary)

Wheels-up landing, Khartoum, Sudan, November 1950. (W Menary)

the crucial moment as the flag was lowered. Both aims were achieved, at least to the satisfaction of the local army commander, and a series of congratulatory speeches sped the Squadron on its way when, on 20 October 1948, thirteen Tempests left Mogadishu for the Wing's new base at Deversoir.

The route back to the Canal Zone led the aircraft once more to Khormaksar, and then on to Port Sudan for another refuelling which took them as far as Fayid. There all personnel were checked for yellow fever before proceeding on to Deversoir. Once again it seemed that the change was for the better. The days were pleasantly warm and the nights cool. For the veterans of the wild south, items such as the radio and magazines provided a welcome touch of civilisation. Back at a regular RAF station, the Squadron personnel were soon adding to their record of athletic prowess, both in inter-squadron competitions and with numerous representatives in the station sides.

So the end of 1948 found the Squadron once more back in Egypt with No.324 Wing, and fully integrated as part of the defence of the Canal Zone. A full training programme gave particular attention to Wing formations with 6 Squadron and to night-flying, which had been non-existent for some months in Khartoum.

Trouble along the Palestine-Egyptian border in January 1949 meant that the Squadron was obliged to maintain its aircraft in a state of readiness in case of any incidents. On 7 January, the CO led a section of four aircraft as escort for a Mosquito of No.13 Squadron, which was on a photographic sortie along the border. In the afternoon, the pilots were hoping for a stand-down, but it was not to be. In fact it turned out to be a Black Friday.

Soon after lunch, it was reported that four Spitfires of 208 Squadron were missing on a tactical reconnaissance mission near the border. At 15.00 hours, seven of the Squadron's aircraft were airborne, with ten others from No.6 Squadron led by Sqn Ldr D Crowley-Milling (later Air Marshal Sir Denis Crowley-Milling, KCB, CBE, DSO, DFC), to carry out a search. The formation was bounced by a force of Israeli Spitfires near the border and, in the initial attack, Plt Off D Tattersfield was hit and his aircraft was seen by other members of the formation to dive into the ground and burst into flames.

The Tempests of both 6 Squadron, providing top-cover, and 213 Squadron, led by the wing commander Gp Capt Anderson, were at a double disadvantage in the combat that took place. The major problem was that the aircraft's guns were not cocked, in line with official policy. The second problem was that, due to the long distances to be covered in the Middle East, the Tempests always flew with long-range drop tanks and, as the Israelis attacked, the Tempest pilots found that they could not jettison these tanks however hard they tried. It later transpired that the release pins to the drop-tanks, which were operated by a Bowden cable to each wing, were too heavily loaded to be released without a superhuman effort to move the release lever in the cockpit.

Despite Crowley-Milling's warning, Tattersfield had been unable to take evasive action; perhaps his R/T was not functioning, but for the rest of the Squadron it became a case of down to deck-level and away back to the Canal area. In the process more than one aircraft exceeded its stipulated maximum speed, and the aircraft of Flt Sgt R G Waddington and Sgt R Heald were both holed in several places. So an unfortunate day ended, with the pilots still fuming over the question of the un-cocked guns and the loss of Plt Off Tattersfield. The Squadron's ORB records that "there were quite a number of very amazed pilots, due mainly to the gun-cocked question". This seems surprising in view of the "official policy". Perhaps nobody told the pilots.

Some months later, an Anson *en route* from Cyprus to Egypt was reported missing, and Deversoir was asked to send two Tempests to carry out a search in case it had been shot down. In the light of the previous experience, Gp Capt Anderson elected to fly one of the aircraft and Sqn Ldr Roe flew as his No 2. Before take-off the guns were loaded and cocked, Anderson remarking "I'm not getting caught like that again". Five more Tempests were held armed and ready on the dispersal in case back-up was needed. In the event it was not, as the Anson was found inside the Egyptian border, out of fuel, and with its radio unserviceable, but unharmed.

As the benefits of civilisation were quickly absorbed and then taken for granted, the existence of a permanent base began to lose some of its attraction. The Armament Practice Camp at Nicosia was therefore looked forward to with some anticipation. The old hands still remembered the haunts frequented during the Squadron's previous times on the island and these were quickly revisited when the move was made from Deversoir early in March. The flying was intensive and rewarding as the whole gamut of fighter operations was covered - air-to-ground firing, air-to-air firing, rocket firing and shallow dive-bombing. Hard work by the groundcrews produced an impressive standard of serviceability, and the flying hours mounted rapidly. On the return from Cyprus, a new commanding officer, Sqn Ldr D L A Roe, DSO, DFC, arrived to take command on 18 April 1949.

During 1948, 1949 and the major part of 1950 there

Part of the Squadron flight line, seven Vampires and three Meteors, Deversoir, Egypt, 1951. Vampire VZ309 was the aircraft of Flt Lt M P "Gus" Davies, "A" Flight Commander, which was serviced by Airframe Fitter Bill Menary. (W Menary)

appeared on the squadron NCO aircrew with the unfamiliar ranks Pilot 2 and Pilot 3, each with its own distinctive rank badge. These new ranks were the result of a new rank badge scheme recommended by a committee in July 1946. At the start of their training, cadets wore on each sleeve a wreath of blue leaves surmounted by an eagle denoting an Aircrew Cadet. At a fairly advanced stage of training, a single star was added inside the wreath and the rank P 4 assumed. With the award of the pilot's Wings, a second star was added, with promotion to the rank P 3. Approximately one year later, a third star marked the elevation to P 2. The penultimate step was to add a crown above the eagle which marked the rank of P 1. The ultimate step was to Master Pilot, signified by a badge on the cuff, as with the previous rank of Warrant Officer. These ranks applied to all NCO aircrew, pilots and navigators sporting blue stars, engineers, wireless operators and gunners white. The official form of address was "Pilot 1", "Navigator 2" etc, but when wearing a greatcoat with no rank badges visible, the form of address was "Airman Aircrew". It is not difficult to imagine how well this was received. The system was abandoned without regret on 1 September 1950, when the old ranks of Sergeant and Flight Sergeant were reintroduced. The only lasting vestige of the experiment remained with the ranks of Master Pilot and Master Navigator replacing that of Warrant Officer for aircrew. There was the suggestion that the change had been used to thin out the senior NCO ranks that had proliferated during the war, particularly Warrant Officers, most of whom dropped a rank.

The months of the summer slipped by under the blue skies of the Canal Zone, and the Wing's training programme produced some good results. The three units, Nos.6, 213 and 249 Squadrons, all equipped with Tempests, which made up No.324 Wing, participated in numerous exercises, and the Wing formation of twenty-four aircraft soon cut an immaculate figure in the skies over the other RAF stations in the Canal Zone.

The only event that disturbed the summer routine was the detachment of a section of eight aircraft, which left for Asmara, via Khartoum, on 15 July. The Shifta, a particularly warlike tribe in Italian Somaliland (now Eritrea), were once again causing trouble. A full scale armament demonstration was therefore laid on to show the flag, and to discourage would-be sympathisers. Six aircraft actually moved up to Asmara for the three-day attachment. With the airfield at 5,000 feet above sea-level, the Tempest's engine provided only +8lb boost on take-off, compared to the usual +15lb at Deversoir. The aircraft also carried drop-tanks for the whole time and, on one demonstration attack, one pilot flicked as he pulled up. He was lucky to recover; it could have quite spoilt the morning. The Tempest was in fact prone to a high-speed stall during the pull-out from a dive if excessive "G" was applied. With drop-tanks, it would flick onto its back with virtually no warning and, given the height of the mountainous terrain around Asmara, this characteristic was accentuated.

A message of congratulations from Major General L G Whistler, the local Army commander, indicated that the Squadron's demonstrations with its "monsters" had lost none of their effectiveness. The message read "The demonstration of attack, aerobatics and formation flying given by No.213 Squadron this morning was quite excellent. It was carried out with dash and precision and was a great credit to the pilots and groundcrews. It was a fine example of the RAF at its best". When the aircraft returned from the range, the

Keeping cool, dawn to dusk stand-by, Deversoir, Egypt.

The Squadron Gloster Meteor T.7, Deversoir, Egypt. (Gordon Tripp)

groundcrews also voiced their hearty approval of the whole show, which was very much appreciated by the pilots.

A few days after the detachment returned to Khartoum, four aircraft visited Atbara, approximately 150 miles to the north. Quite unexpectedly, the pilots were invited to the residence of the senior army officer in the area, where copious amounts of alcohol were pressed upon them. As they were about to leave, the officer's very attractive wife, either innocently or mischievously, said to Fg Off D A Hankin, who was leading the section, "You didn't come very low when you arrived, did you?". The remark served as a red rag to a bull as far as Hankin was concerned and he replied "Well, we'll try and do better on the way out". The aircraft took-off and turned back over the airfield, crossing it only a few feet above the ground. As he passed over, Gordon Tripp, who had joined the Squadron earlier in the year, remembers seeing the lady in question crouching low on the ground with her hands over her ears. Subsequently, he often wondered whether or not she regretted her remark to Hankin. The trip back to Khartoum was completed in very carefree fashion - and at very low level!

On 7 September, P2 Strobel, a Polish pilot who, along with his fellow countrymen P2s Dąbrowski and Zagroba, had joined the Squadron during the preceding months, was killed while carrying out front gun attacks at the Abu Sultan range. His aircraft flicked and he was too low to recover.

Towards the end of August, definite news was received regarding re-equipment. The Squadron was about to abandon propeller-driven aircraft and enter the new world of jet propulsion. The first Vampire FB.5s would arrive towards the end of the year. At the same time, permission was received for the aircraft to carry the markings that had distinguished the squadron's biplanes in the pre-war days of the late 1930s. These markings - two rectangles of three horizontal bars, black, gold, black, on either side of the Squadron's badge - were to be worn on the tail-plane of the Tempest and, at a latter date, on the nose of the Vampire. The Tempests were certainly now beginning to show their age and also the effects of the harsh climate and the desert sands in which they had operated. Major unserviceabilities hampered the training programme and the arrival of the Vampires was eagerly awaited. In terms of performance, the top speed of this first generation of jet aeroplanes was virtually the same as that of the Tempest, and its endurance considerably less. In terms of manoeuvrability however, and particularly visibility, the Vampire had the distinct advantage.

By December 1949, the change-over was complete and much hard work was put in to keep the Squadron's standards as high as ever with the new aircraft.

For many of the pilots, now well accustomed to the monster Tempest, the first flight in a Vampire was distinctly queer! There was no nose sticking out in front, the wings had moved back behind the cockpit and the whole experience was much quieter. Throughout January and the first half of February, the Tempests were ferried to Kasfareet, where they were stored prior to being returned to the UK. Gordon Tripp flew out the last one, appropriately AK-Z, on 15 February 1950.

Although during January 1950 the Squadron was officially non-operational, sorties were flown in the Army Co-operation Exercise that took place, and the pilots quickly appreciated the superb forward visibility that the Vampire provided. A large number of trial flights were also carried out at the instigation of 205 Group, and figures were recorded to provide graphs for operating limits. The value of the excellent forward visibility was amply demonstrated early in February. Two army trucks became lost in the desert west of Fayid, and the sixteen occupants were forced to survive on emergency rations of food and water for three days. The Squadron was asked to organise a search. Within two minutes of the first aircraft starting its search pattern, the unfortunate soldiers were located.

The first Vampire write-off occurred on 21 February when P3 "Harry" Wragg hit a lorry while on his landing run. He had become separated from his leader during a tail-chase when he discovered his radio was not working. All the desert looked the same so, concluding that he was west of the Suez Canal, he flew east. Unfortunately he had made the wrong choice and eventually he ran out of fuel near El Arish, close to the Israeli border. He made a successful forced landing, wheels down, on a road, but had the bad luck to collide with a lorry, whose occupants had baled out. The resulting damage caused the aircraft to be written-off.

The ferry pilots who delivered the Vampires were also due to take the Tempests back from Kasfareet to the UK. However this was not popular, as most of them had little Tempest experience and several aircraft were abandoned *en route* with low oil pressure. It was accordingly decided that the pilots of No.324 Wing would return the remainder of the aircraft, and special oil-filters were fitted to obviate the oil pressure problem. This, it had been discovered, was caused

The Commanding Officer's new Vampire FB.9, WR120

by the fact that when the engines were started up after having been standing for several months, the carbon deposits broke up and clogged the filters. The new filters were described as "big enough to shoot peas through". This solved the problem, but resulted in a thick black oily film being deposited down each side of the fuselage of the aircraft. This wiped off easily on to the pilots flying overalls where it remained.

On 30 April, four pilots proceeded to Kasfareet to airtest four Tempests and return them to the UK. The aircraft were fitted with ninety-gallon drop-tanks. However, on the aircraft air-tested by Gordon Tripp, the starboard tank refused to feed. After an hour he decided to land, notwithstanding the full drop-tank. The landing required full port aileron and a speed at touch down of one hundred and twenty knots. The landing was "hairy" but successful; to have jettisoned the tank would have prejudiced the chance of a few days leave in the UK. Fortunately one of the other pilots, P2 Chiswick, had been a boy-entrant mechanic before remustering as aircrew, and he cured the problem by hammering a piece of wood into the non-return valve.

By the time the Tempests reached Manston, the special filters had done their worst and the Tempests were covered with a black oily film. The Station Commander had seen the four Tempests in the circuit and had driven out to the dispersal to see them land. As they taxied in, he remarked to everyone in the vicinity "Those are the four filthiest aircraft I have ever seen" and, as the pilots climbed down, he added "And those are the four dirtiest pilots flying them". Without further ado, he climbed back into his staff car and left.

The return to Deversoir on 13 May was marred by the news of a particularly nasty accident. P2 Dabrowski had carried out a head-on attack on a Lincoln during a fighter affiliation exercise. The two aircraft collided and both crashed, killing Dabrowski and all seven on board the Lincoln, among whom, tragically, were two ATC Flight Sergeants out from the UK on Summer Camp.

Apart from the normal air-to-ground practices and fighter affiliation exercises carried out with the Lincolns from Shallufa, special emphasis was placed on weapons training as the time for the annual Armament Practice Camp in Cyprus drew near. Air-to-air firing and cine sorties at 30,000 feet introduced a new dimension into the Squadron's flying. Once again, the detachment to Cyprus was a great success and good results were obtained in all forms of firing and bomb dropping, especially in view of the recent change of aircraft.

Back in Deversoir, the Squadron was in good spirits when it heard that a trip to Greece, which had been in the air for some time, was finally going to take place in two months' time. The invasion of the CO's house by the officers, NCOs and aircrew, in search of the large quantities of alcoholic refreshment reported to be stored there, was doubtlessly a manifestation of this spirit. The excuse for the party that ensued was the impending departure of Fg Off G Abel and Sgt McDonald to England, and the fact that it was Sgt Stuart's birthday.

The latter days of July found the Squadron way out in the desert at El Adem for the exercise "Highway Two". This was a combined operation helping to defend the Royal Navy's Home Fleet, returning to the UK, from the US 6th Fleet based in Crete. The Americans were very active and the pilots had an enjoyable time intercepting such exotic aircraft as Corsairs, Bearcats, Skyraiders and Banshees. Interestingly the Vampire was superior in performance to the Banshee. Magnificent work on the part of the groundcrews ensured 100% serviceability during the whole exercise. The Royal Navy also scrambled Seafires from HMS *Glory*, but it was the general opinion on the Squadron that these were more of a hindrance than a help because they operated on a different radio frequency.

Much of the flying during August was devoted to

Close inspection by the Arab Legion while on detachment to Mafraq, Jordan. The real interest was in the cannons.

Khartoum, Sudan, November 1950. Left to right: Bill Menary, Cpl Davey, "Brummie" Hems, Jock White and Sgt Smith. (W Menary)

formation flying and aerobatics, in preparation for the coming visit to Greece. Two aerobatic teams were formed, led by the two Flight Commanders, and standards rose sharply; it was appreciated that nothing short of perfection would be good enough. The visit was only to last two days, but the display was to be a very high-powered affair.

On 29 September, nine Vampires took off bound for El Adem on the first leg of the journey to Greece. On landing at Ellenikon the following day, the Squadron was greeted by the Chief of the Air Staff of the Royal Hellenic Air Force. In the evening, a formation aerobatic practice was carried out over the promenade at Athens, in very bumpy conditions and with a strong cross-wind. So to the day of the big display before Their Majesties the King and Queen of the Hellenes, the British Ambassador, the Heads of the Greek Armed Forces and delegations from the French and American armed forces. The success of the rocket-firing demonstration was assured when Sgt Gibson shattered the target with his first rocket. The whole display was carried out with the Squadron's usual *élan* and a cocktail party in the evening concluded a most satisfactory day. Before leaving Ellenikon the next day, the Squadron was presented with a commemorative plaque from the Royal Hellenic Air Force, which continued to hang in the crew room from then on.

Towards the end of the year, the Vampires began to show less welcome characteristics and, at one stage, the Squadron was grounded for all the aircraft to be checked for cracked fuel pipes. A little later it was the turn of the fuel pumps to give trouble. At these times, flying was restricted to dual trips in the Meteor, which was normally used for check rides and conversion flights. The situation improved for a spell in November, and a fortnight's detachment showing the flag in Khartoum was successfully undertaken. The only incident occurred when, during a formation take-off, the hood blew off No.3 in the second section. Both pilots aborted their take-offs but unfortunately No.2 was so far committed that he had to raise his undercarriage to avoid running into a ditch at the far end of the runway. The aircraft was extensively damaged but the pilot, Sgt Sparkes, escaped without injury.

Another incident showed the strength of the Vampire which, like the Hurricane, was an aircraft of largely wooden construction. P 3 Wragg was returning from a sortie low over the Great Bitter Lake, flying parallel to the runway prior to pulling up into the circuit for a landing, when his fire-warning light came on. While pressing the Fire Extinguisher Button and turning off the High Pressure Fuel Cock, he allowed the nose of his aircraft to drop and it hit the water. The effect was, he said "...like a bow-wave in front of the cockpit". Jock Stuart was in a jeep waiting to cross the runway when he saw the Vampire bouncing off the lake, with flaps and undercarriage doors falling off, and water streaming everywhere. Wragg finally put the Vampire down on the sand

A Vampire FB.5 being armed up, Deversoir, Egypt.

Sgt Frank Atkinson seated in the cockpit of a Vampire FB.5, Deversoir, Egypt, 1950/51. (Gordon Tripp)

Armament Practice Camp, Nicosia, Cyprus, August 1951. Standing left to right: Sgt Jack Marshal, Sgt Mel Swann, Sgt Gordon Tripp, Sgt Tony Draper, Flt Lt Roy Radford, Sgt Bill King, MP Jack Barnard, Sgt Pete Gooding, Fg Off George Rogers. Seated: Fg Off Bob Ridley, Flt Lt Gus Davies, Pete Lee (APC), Wg Cdr Derek Roe, Wg Cdr Whitworth (CO APC), Flt Lt Pears (APC), Flt Sgt Johnny Walker, Flt Lt Ken Appleboom and Fg Off Bunny Bunyan. (Gordon Tripp)

alongside the runway, and stepped out unharmed. It was subsequently said that, if the angle at which the aircraft had struck the surface of the lake had been one degree less, the booms would have broken off, and if it had been one degree more the aircraft would have plunged to the depths.

During January and February 1951, several pilots took part in flights to Singapore as the RAF squadrons in the Far East re-equipped with Vampires. Ferry pilots would deliver eight aircraft from the UK to Egypt and then four of the pilots would return to the UK, to be replaced by Squadron pilots for the onward journey. The competition for these flights, and the opportunity to see new places, was severe. The route was from Egypt to Sharjah on the Persian Gulf, then on to Delhi, Calcutta, Rangoon, Bangkok, a refuelling stop at Butterworth and then on to Seletar, Singapore. The second ferry flight on which Sgt J Stuart flew consisted of six Vampires, led by a Mosquito providing navigational assistance; a Spitfire and a Brigand also attached themselves to the flight at various stages along the route. Apart from two occasions when the Mosquito lost an engine and the flight had to return to the last point of departure, the ten-day flight was uneventful, unlike some of the later convoys.

The early months of 1951 were spent in the normal training routine, and in dashing about over the Sinai Desert in co-operation with the Army Exercise "Sandgrouse". In April, the Squadron heard that it was to take part in yet another demonstration, this time for the benefit of King Abdullah of Transjordan at the Arab Legion Army Day. Carrying a full load of ammunition and fuel, nine Vampires led by the CO took off for Mafraq, an airfield some forty miles north-east of Amman. A successful demonstration was carried out before the King and numerous service chiefs, including Admiral Carney, USN, Commander-in-Chief Mediterranean and Eastern Atlantic. For the rest of the day, the Squadron was royally entertained by officers of the Arab Legion. Then it was back to Deversoir and the training routine once more. It was here that, after the conclusion of another Armament Practice Camp in Cyprus, Wg Cdr D J A Roe, DSO, DFC, relinquished command of the Squadron and was succeeded by Sqn Ldr D M Finn, DFC, on 12 September 1951.

With the introduction of modified hoods, the Vampires were cleared up to 40,000 feet and an intensive programme of high altitude work was undertaken. Cine work at that altitude was a new experience for most of the pilots and, although the Squadron was still basically a ground-attack unit, with the arrival of the Vampires more air-to-air work was undertaken. Someone had worked out that one disadvantage of operating at 40,000 feet was that, if one had to bale out, it was impossible to breathe at that altitude. In addition, if you elected to free-fall, you would be unconscious by the time you reached 20,000 feet and unable to pull the rip-cord. The problem was solved, officially, by the issue of ten-minute emergency oxygen bottles. The pilots believed that these were issued mainly for morale purposes, as the connection to the oxygen mask was a flimsy rubber pipe; it was reckoned that, even if the mask itself stayed in place during an ejection, the connection with the emergency bottle must have torn loose.

In the middle of October 1951, as the Squadron was preparing for a detachment to Shaibah on the Persian Gulf, news came that the Egyptian Cabinet had carried out its threat to abrogate the Anglo-Egyptian Treaty of 1936. Immediately a wave of unrest swept through the Canal Zone. Incidents increased and guards were doubled around the airfield. The aircraft and equipment were moved from the dispersals into No.2 Hangar, where a closer watch could be maintained. On 18 October, Gp Cpt Bowling, CBE, the Officer Commanding No.324 Wing, ordered all available aircraft to be prepared with high explosive rockets and operational ammunition. Twelve aircraft were rapidly armed and the pilots fully briefed. The reason for these preparations was that a force of

Squadron pilots kitted out with side arms at the time of the abrogation of the Anglo-Egyptian Treaty, October 1950. Left to right: Sgt Tony Draper, Sgt Jack Marshal, Sgt Bill King and MP Jack Barnard.

Squadron pilots outside the crew-room Deversoir, Egypt, 1950. From left to right: Sgt Gordon Tripp, Sgt Ted Sparks and Sgt Frank Atkinson. (Gordon Tripp)

Egyptian armour and infantry was reported moving along the Suez Canal road. Somewhat to the pilots' disappointment, the warning by the General Officer Commanding to the Egyptians not to cross a specified line was heeded and the incident passed off without any involvement on the Squadron's part. By the end of the month the crisis had passed, and the Squadron routine had returned to normal.

The only lasting result of the abrogation of the treaty was that a system of dawn-to-dusk stand-by was introduced which tied up both aircraft and pilots. While on such a standby, "Jock" Stuart was scrambled as one of a pair by the Ground Control Interception (GCI) unit to intercept an unidentified intruder in the Canal Zone airspace. The interception was successful and the intruder identified as a BOAC Argonaut, which had picked up a strong tail-wind and so was considerably ahead of its reported estimated time of arrival. The section closed in on the Argonaut, waved to the pilot and returned to Deversoir. If the intruder had in fact been an Egyptian aircraft, the Vampires would have had to return to base to have their 20mm cannons cocked before they could have taken any further action. Some things seem never to change!

As the political situation worsened again in the early months of the New Year, No 6 Squadron flew in from Habbaniya to Abu Sueir, and No.32 Squadron joined the Wing at Deversoir. At the same time the Squadron was re-equipped with Vampire FB.9s and brought up to full strength as a Mobile Day Fighter Squadron. This meant virtually doubling the number of personnel, which caused the accommodation situation to become acute. However, once the new personnel had been absorbed, the Squadron organisation was soon running smoothly and life at Deversoir returned to normal. The strong line taken had effectively calmed the situation in Egypt and, contrary to most people's fears, the Squadron was able to go to Cyprus for the annual Armament Practice Camp in the middle of the summer.

The course of 1953 ran smoothly along familiar lines until September, when the Squadron moved from Deversoir to Shallufa for a month's detachment. The start was inauspicious, to say the least, as two aircraft touched whilst practising formation flying for the Battle of Britain fly-past. Flt Lt Maddox, Blue Leader, found that, although his elevators were jammed, he could maintain height with eight thousand rpm set. By judicious use of the trimmers and the throttle, he made a successful emergency landing at Deversoir without further damage to his aircraft. Plt Off Buist, after a visual inspection of his nose-wheel had shown nothing untoward, landed safely at Shallufa. The final rehearsal for the parade and fly-past was held in very poor weather conditions, and the pilot of the aircraft in the box in the last section claimed that his altimeter was reading fathoms as the leader endeavoured to stay below the cloud over the Great Bitter Lake!

At the end of September, the Squadron was once more operating in two elements as five Vampires set out for Swartkop in South Africa. The journey down, flown in company with a Valetta, was routed via Wadi Halfa, Khartoum, Juba, Entebbe, Tabora, N'dola and Livingstone. The journey was beset with unserviceability problems, and the aircraft became scattered throughout the length of the African continent. However, hard work on the part of the supporting groundcrews soon rounded up all the miscreant aircraft, and the whole detachment proved to be a thoroughly enjoyable experience for all concerned. The trip was particularly welcome as, in contrast to the immediate post-war years, the Squadron was leading a fairly regular existence at its base in Egypt. Since the move up from Mogadishu in 1949, only the annual Armament Practice Camp had taken the Squadron away from Deversoir for more than a few days. Also, the greater level of ground support required by the Vampires prevented the pilots from dropping in at out-of-the-way places, as in the old days. All that the Tempest required was

Squadron Vampire FB.5s at Ellenikon, Athens, 1950. (Gordon Tripp)

a hard landing-strip and a supply of fuel but, unless electrical starter-trolleys were available, a Vampire could not be turned round.

The arrival of the new Commanding Officer, Sqn Ldr A J H Kitley, in March 1954 coincided with a special burst of activity. News came on the first of the month that severe rioting had broken out in the Sudan, and the Squadron was ordered to be ready to move at two hours' notice. However, the alarm proved false and the departure of the new CO with four aircraft on a long-range navigation exercise to Mafraq indicated that further trouble could not be expected. The middle of the month was marred by a fatal accident on the range near El Qantara, when Plt Off Coutts failed to pull out of a simulated rocket attack.

In April, the Squadron's strength at Deversoir was reduced to six pilots and aircraft. Two pilots, Fg Offs Buist and Swift, had left for Nicosia to represent the Squadron in the Imshi Mason Memorial Trophy, an annual weapons competition. A further detachment of four aircraft had also gone to Malta to take part in a large-scale combined operations exercise. This visit in fact foreshadowed the move of the whole Squadron to the island for its last exercise in August 1954. The summer had passed in the normal round of training, with no hint that this was to be the Squadron's last year in the Middle East.

Staging once more through El Adem, the Squadron arrived at Takali for the big exercise on 4 August. The attacking forces in this Defence Exercise were provided by the American Sixth Fleet, operating aircraft from the carrier *Coral Sea*. After working up for eight days, the exercise began in earnest on 12 August, when amphibious landings were attempted in the north of the island. The Squadron flew sixty-six sorties and the pilots returned with glowing reports of successful interceptions on Skyraiders and Banshees. In dog-fighting, the old story repeated itself as the Banshees were found to be considerably faster than the Vampires, but the latter were more manoeuvrable and normally finished up with the American aircraft firmly fixed in the gun-sights. The exercise finished with an attack by the Squadron and eight aircraft from No.78 Wing RAAF on the Sixth Fleet, the main target being the *Coral Sea*. However tactically unsound it may have seemed to send sixteen aircraft against an entire task force, the pilots all agreed that the exercise was a great success.

On arrival back at Deversoir, the CO was met by the Station Commander with the shattering news that the Squadron was to be disbanded. By the end of the month the news was confirmed and, with an all-pervading air of sadness, the pilots flew to Nicosia for the Squadron's swansong in the Battle of Britain Display. Thus the Squadron's last flights in the Middle East were appropriately enough in the Battle of Britain displays in Cyprus and the Canal Zone. A funeral pyre of cast-off equipment was topped off with the remains of the previous CO's derelict motor car. On 22 September 1954, the Air Officer Commanding 205 Group, Air Vice-Marshal Barnett, CBE, DFC, reviewed the Squadron's personnel at the disbandment parade. The aircraft were left wrapped in their covers and parked on the airfield. So ended the second phase of the life of the Squadron and, as many must have thought, the last.

The new machine - a brand new English Electric Canberra B(I).6 - still in its pristine silver finish straight from the factory. Fg Off N Hargreaves is at the controls, Ahlhorn, West Germany.

CHAPTER FOURTEEN - THE SECOND ALLIED TACTICAL AIR FORCE

After a year of silence, circumstances combined to put the Hornets back into the sky once more. The Air Ministry decided to create a specialised force of night interdictor squadrons, under the command of Royal Air Force, Germany, which itself was part of the Second Allied Tactical Air Force. These squadrons would fill a dual role immediately and have an even more important nuclear strike capability later on. When the Senior Air Staff Officer, RAF Germany, (later to be the Air Officer Commander-in-Chief), Sir Humphrey Edwardes Jones, KCB, CBE, DFC, AFC, was asked to provide a list of suitable squadron numbers for this force, No.213 Squadron appeared, not surprisingly, at the top.

The Squadron was consequently reformed at Ahlhorn, near Oldenburg in West Germany, as the first unit of this new specialised force on 22 July 1955. The Squadron's connection with its new formation was not only personal, through Sir Humphrey Edwardes Jones, but also organisational, since the Allied Tactical Air Force was the lineal descendant of the Desert Air Force. The first Tactical Air Force, a name not used before, was created on 18 February 1943, under the command of Air Marshal Sir Arthur Coningham, by bringing together No.242 Group, RAF, and the US XIIth Air Support Command. Within days, the unit was powerfully reinforced by the addition, on 23 February 1943, of the Desert Air Force. The Tactical Air Force, so created, was to finish the air fighting in North Africa, move up into Italy, and finally cover the landings in France and the ultimate assault on Germany.

On 31 December 1955, Wg Cdr H J Dodson, DFC, was appointed to command, having previously served as Squadron Leader Operations at Ahlhorn. The Squadron's establishment was fixed at sixty-one aircrew, and one hundred and thirty-four groundcrew, to fly and service sixteen English Electric Canberra B(I).6s and one Canberra T.4. In January 1956, a nucleus of experienced Canberra aircrew was posted to the Squadron from the Canberra Wing at Gutersloh in West Germany. This initial group included Flt Lts Brownlow and Hargreaves and Fg Offs Burley and Marlow, together with their navigators. John Brownlow (later Air Vice-Marshal J Brownlow, OBE, AFC) first flew in a Canberra, as a navigator, in October 1950 and made his last flight in one, as a pilot, on 3 June 1983.

The arrival of further aircrew was then halted until the middle of February because of the late delivery of the first aircraft. On 8 February, the two Flight Commanders, Sqn Ldrs S A Craigie, DFC, and C T Dalziel, picked up the Squadron's first aircraft, a Canberra T.4, WJ870, from Laarbruch. Meanwhile the groundcrews gained experience by servicing a Canberra from Wyton, which was based temporarily at Ahlhorn while carrying out photographic trials. By the beginning of February, eighteen aircrew and sixty-eight groundcrew had arrived. Much of the flying in the T.4 was taken up with flight commander's checks for both day

The CO with some of the first aircrew arrivals, Ahlhorn, West Germany, 1956.

and night flying. In the absence of the Squadron's operational aircraft, considerable use was made of the station's Meteor T.7 and a Prentice T.1. Some of the ex-Gutersloh pilots also managed to persuade the resident night-fighter squadrons, Nos.96 and 256, equipped with Meteor NF.11s, to allow a sortie or two in their aircraft. Since at that time practically all Canberra pilots had considerable Meteor experience, this flying could be arranged without too much difficulty.

In early March, the first two brand-new Canberra B(I).6s arrived, to be followed by two more in the middle of the month and a further two four days later. These arrivals, however, did nothing to increase the Squadron's flying hours, as all six aircraft and the T.4 were grounded while extensive modifications were carried out to the tail-plane trimmer. This first, and only major, technical problem had plagued the Canberra since early 1952, and a number of fatal crashes were attributed to "runaway" tail-plane trims. The fault was found to be the single-pole trim switch sticking in the "on" position, which caused the actuator to run to the full extent of its travel, forcing the aircraft into a dive which the pilot could not control. All aircraft were fitted with a dipole switch, improved wiring and a stop on the actuator. This, however, did not cure the problem, and in the later part of 1955 all aircraft were restricted to a speed of 250 knots below 10,000 feet. The problem came to a head in early 1956, when all aircraft were grounded until modifications could be carried out to the actuator system. The fine-trim control was moved to the control column and the coarse-trim switch on the console was made inoperative. Although this modification did not totally cure the problem, it did end the series of accidents which threatened to blacken the Canberra's otherwise spotless reputation. Once this problem had been overcome, the new Canberras, with their more powerful engines, were a joy to fly, particularly for the ex-Gutersloh pilots who had previously been operating cast-off Bomber Command Canberra B.2s.

The Canberra had been conceived by W E W Petter, then working for Westlands, in 1944, in response to the Ministry of Aircraft Production's requirement for a jet aircraft to replace the Whirlwind/Typhoon/Mosquito. Built eventually by the English Electric Company, which Petter joined later that year at Warton, near Preston in Lancashire, the first prototype flew on 13 May 1949 and deliveries to the RAF commenced in January 1951. The initial medium-bomber variant, the B.2, established the Canberra's reputation before numerous other Marks were developed, including the B.2's successor, the Canberra B.6, which first flew on 26 January 1954. It speaks volumes for the versatility of Petter's original design that the aircraft he conceived as a fast medium-level bomber could also be used successfully in the low-level interdictor and ground-attack role. The Canberra was designed to meet Air Ministry specification B.3/45 and was powered by two Rolls-Royce Avon engines.

Not only was the Canberra the Royal Air Force's first jet bomber, but it also established in its time a number of world performance records. On 29 August 1957 a Canberra, powered by two Bristol Olympus engines, gained the world altitude record at 65,890 feet, which was bettered on 28 August 1957 at 70,310 feet by an Avon-powered Canberra using a Napier Double Scorpion rocket motor.

The RAF planned to develop an entirely new Canberra variant, to be designated the Canberra B(I).8, for the night interdictor role. However, to allow the Force to commence operations at once and to gain experience, 213 Squadron, as the first unit to be formed, operated a heavily modified B.6. So it transpired that the Squadron was the only unit ever to fly the Canberra B(I).6.

The major modifications required were those necessary

The new CO, Wg Cdr H J Dodson, AFC.

Fg Off J A Hanson loses the hydraulics at Ahlhorn.

to enable the new mark of Canberra to operate in the interdictor role, and thus involved the armaments and related controls. To enable the aircraft to operate as a ground-attack fighter-bomber, modified bomb-doors could be fitted which allowed a Boulton and Paul ventral gun-pack, containing four 20mm Hispano Suiza cannons, to be located in the rear of the bomb-bay. Each gun was provided with 525 rounds, enough for fifty seconds of firing. No speed limit was set for firing the guns, although a micro-switch was sensibly fitted that prevented their operation when either the undercarriage was down or the bomb-doors were open. In addition to the three 1,000-lb bombs that could be carried in the bomb-bay ahead of the gun-pack, a further two could be carried on the underwing pylons. In the cockpit a Mk.3N reflector gun-sight was fitted above the pilot's instrument panel and a G.45 gun-camera in the starboard wing leading edge, while an F.95 forward-facing camera was carried in the perspex nose-cone. The control column hand-wheel was also modified to carry the gun, bomb and camera controls. The only major drawback suffered by the B(I).6 was that of poor visibility at low-level, a fault which was cured in the B(I).8 by the provision of an off-set bubble canopy.

Departing from the single-seat day-fighter role, the crew of the aircraft consisted of three, a pilot and two navigators. In both of the initial roles intended for the Squadron, that of a low-level medium bomber and that of a ground-attack fighter-bomber, pinpoint precision in navigation was essential. It was here, as experience proved, that the B(I).6 had the advantage over the later B(I).8, since the full skills of two navigators were required to operate effectively at night and in bad weather at low-level. As the full complement of aircraft built up during March, it was in the ground-attack role that the Squadron commenced flying operations. Even though the crews arriving at Ahlhorn all had previous experience on other Canberra squadrons, the type of flying now required was something completely new to them. Apart from the gunnery and dive-bombing techniques that had to be devised, as well as learnt, the all-important art of low-level navigation had to be developed and perfected.

In July, the arrival of a further twenty-five aircrew, mostly navigators, enabled the aircraft to be fully crewed. As soon as conversion flying by day and night had been completed, low-level flying training started in earnest, and the crews were shortly cleared to fly down to 500 feet above ground level, both by day and night. Long low-level cross-country flights became the order of the day. During this build-up to full strength, the initial problems that beset the introduction of any new mark of aircraft coming into squadron service were overcome. At Ahlhorn, the Squadron was situated in the heart of North Germany, but still within range of both the Baltic and North Seas over which the anti-shipping role, also allotted to it, was practised. Each sortie was something of an experiment, as facts and figures had to be gleaned to acquire not only operating data but also experience in all the other aspects of operating what was basically a conventional medium-level light bomber in this new role.

By July, the Squadron was up to full strength and fixed-gun ground-attack training started. For many Canberra aircrew this was their first experience of air-to-ground firing. A Vampire T.11, flown by a Pilot Attack Instructor, Flt Lt Loverspeed, was used to provide an introduction to this art. After one Vampire sortie, the Squadron pilots first fired their Canberra's guns over the sea and then used Stroehen Range for target firing. The Canberra proved a very stable gun platform and, considering that the Mk 3N Reflector Sight was such a crude device, quite respectable air-to-ground firing results were achieved by both day and night. The technique used was to fly at right-angles to the firing-line at 2,000 feet, then turn in and dive towards the target, commencing firing in a fifteen-degree dive at about two thousand yards. The navigator in the rear compartment was responsible for calling out the heights on the way down - a role that was not enjoyed!

Once the squadron was reasonably proficient at air-to-ground firing, it was tasked with "Light Strike" operations, flying from Valkenburg, a Dutch naval airfield near The Hague. The operational concept of "Light Strike" was to provide a counter to the threat of E-boats emerging from the Baltic into the North Sea at night. The Squadron would be tasked to patrol an allocated area of the North Sea and establish radio contact with a Shackleton. The Shackleton would identify the E-boat on radar and illuminate it with flares. A Canberra would then launch a visual attack with its guns in the light of the flares. Without exception the pilots found this a difficult task, since diving into a well-lit area over the sea with few visual references encouraged disorientation, and instantly degraded the pilot's night vision. The navigators in the back were also somewhat apprehensive in their now routine role of calling out the rapidly decreasing height during the attack - there was often a noticeable change in the voice tone when the altimeter reversed its movement and started to show a climb! At the same time, Valkenburg was not a very suitable airfield for night operations, since it

HRH The Duke of Edinburgh visited the Squadron, 11 March 1958. It had officially abandoned its ground attack role and become a Light Bomber (Intruder) Squadron, delivering tactical nuclear weapons by means of the new Low Altitude Bombing System (LABS).

had no approach lights and was difficult to identify, located as it was very close to large well-lit residential areas. Eventually the Squadron developed its own flare capability and was able to operate "Light Strike" missions in pairs, but the Shackleton was still needed to identify the targets by radar.

By September 1956, when the early snags had been ironed out and much-needed equipment arrived with a rush due to the Suez Crisis, the first Squadron Exercise was duly completed. Though fog and low cloud severely hampered operations in the earlier phases, the second night of the exercise saw attacks launched against a wide variety of tactical targets. Already the problems of successful air-to-ground firing at night were being overcome. Aircraft operated in pairs and, once over the target, whether it was a troop convoy or a ship, the same tactics were used. The first aircraft would fly over the selected target illuminating it with a series of flares; in the light provided, the second aircraft would deliver its attack out of the darkness. The flying by day was largely devoted to long-range low-level navigation exercises, with numerous black boxes mounted in the fuselage to record data for future operations. Such sorties often concluded with an air-to-ground attack at the nearby Stroehen Firing Range.

By the middle of 1957, the Squadron had recovered much of its old *esprit de corps* and now, with greater numbers of personnel than the fighter squadrons at Ahlhorn, a sporting record was achieved which was more impressive than ever before. The slightly amused curiosity that greeted the arrival of this apparently unorthodox unit, which operated a bomber aircraft in the night ground-attack role, soon therefore changed to one of respect.

As 1957 drew on, much of the information, that would be invaluable as the rest of the projected strike force formed, had been gathered. At the same time the Squadron's stay at Ahlhorn was coming to an end. As the German Air Force was being expanded, many ex-Luftwaffe bases, such as Ahlhorn, were being handed back to the Germans. Co-incidentally, the disbandment of many of the RAF fighter squadrons, then stationed at Bruggen, Laarbruch, Geilenkirchen and Wildenrath, meant that there was now room for the Canberra force at this group of airfields situated along the Dutch-German border. On 22 August 1957, the Squadron's aircraft left Ahlhorn for the last time and flew to their new base at Bruggen, just inside Germany. The first of the B(I).8 units had already come into existence when No.88 Squadron reformed at Wildenrath in January 1956. The second unit had been formed at Gutersloh as the lodger Bomber Command Canberra B.2 units there disbanded and 59 Squadron, having re-equipped with B(I).8s, moved to Geilenkirchen on 15 November 1957. The last of the four-squadron strike force came into being when No.16 Squadron moved into Laarbruch on 1 March 1958. As these squadrons formed up, some of the first crews to have been posted in to 213 Squadron, as it reformed, moved on to spread the gospel of low-level operations in the exacting roles allocated to this new Force.

Now that the Squadron was established at what was to be its permanent base, and at a respectable distance from the East German border, the primary role, for which the new force had been created, received much more attention.

Canberra XJ257 had its problems - Fg Off N Hargreaves suffered engine failure on take-off at Valkenburg.

A section of Canberras of "B" Flight, while based at Ahlhorn, West Germany.

Although the first months of its new existence had been spent in the conventional ground-attack role, it had always been intended that the force should have a nuclear-strike capability, operating the Low Altitude Bombing System (LABS).

During the planning of a tactical nuclear-strike force, it became clear that a new technique for the accurate delivery of a nuclear weapon and the safe escape of the aircraft delivering it, would be required. In the USA, work on such a system had commenced in the early 1950s by the USAF in conjunction with Minneapolis-Honeywell. It was designated the Low Altitude Bombing System and it became universally known by its acronym, LABS. By 1955 work was urgently undertaken to develop a similar system in the UK. This new technique gave an extra dimension to the Canberra as a strike aircraft and was brought to its maximum effectiveness in the RAF by the four strike squadrons in Germany. The concentration on LABS bombing in RAF, Germany, was such that, when a crew from the Squadron attended a LABS instructors course in the UK at Wittering in 1958, it was recorded on their return that "it would seem that knowledge of this subject is more advanced in 2ATAF than in Bomber Command".

The very precise flying required by this new technique, and the stresses imposed on the aircraft by the low-level high-speed flying, necessitated certain new items of equipment and the strengthening of the Canberra's airframe. The technique itself required an approach to the target to be made at the lowest possible level, the practical limitation being the height required to read a map accurately. In peace time (or rather Cold War time) in Germany in the late 1950s and early 1960s, the authorised altitude for low-level sorties was 250 feet, but the actual height flown depended more on the determination of the pilot to replicate combat conditions. If necessary, he climbed up to the set height for the final bombing run. During the flight planning before a sortie, a calculation was made as to how far the bomb would be tossed forward when released at a given speed and angle of climb. This calculation produced a Bomb Release Point at a given distance from the target. In order to arrive over the Bomb Release Point pointing in precisely the right direction, and at the correct altitude, the aircraft was flown on a timed run at 425 knots and 250 feet with the bomb-doors open from a distinctive land-mark designated the Initial Point (IP).

From this point, the pilot started an automatic timer, which indicated the precise moment at which the aircraft had to pull-up to obtain the pre-selected angle of release, either forty-five or sixty degrees, at which angle the bomb-release mechanism operated automatically. Once the bomb was released on a forward and upward trajectory, which would carry it 3,700 yards in distance and up to a height of 5,500 feet, the aircraft itself continued in a three-G loop until it reached the inverted position at approximately 7,000 feet and an airspeed of 170 knots, at which point it rolled out and returned the way it had come, diving back to ground level under full power. Although practised frequently with 25-lb bombs, and very occasionally with a mock-up of the nuclear device, no weapon was ever dropped in anger. This was probably just as well, as it appeared to the crews involved that, while the technique would ensure the accurate delivery of the weapon, performing simple aerobatics at slow speed and medium altitude over what would no doubt be strategically- placed missile sites was not conducive to the safe return of the aircraft.

When flown in clear weather conditions, the technique presented no particular problems other than those involved in arriving over the IP at the correct altitude and on the right heading. However, at night or in thick cloud, the situation was not so straight-forward, and the two accidents during 1959, when two experienced crews flew into the ground while practising in such conditions, illustrated the inherent dangers. The fact that was impressed on all new crews arriving on the Squadron was that, starting at 250 feet and pulling with a force of three "G", the Canberra would not complete a full loop before striking the ground, and the roll-out at the top of the manoeuvre was therefore essential.

With the commencement of this new role, a comprehensive training programme was put into operation, and another series of black boxes and dials made their appearance in the cockpit. The crews once again had new techniques to learn and new skills to master. It also now became clear why so much attention and effort had been devoted to the skills of very accurate and very low-level navigation. With the new role for the Squadron, there also arrived a new CO in the person of Wg Cdr I R Campbell, AFC.

The last month of 1957 was marred by the first of the three fatal accidents that occurred while the Squadron was operating this new and exacting procedure. On an inky black night, with low clouds scudding across the North German Plain, Flt Lt Clarke and his two navigators, Flt Lt McCarthy and Plt Off Milne, took-off on a low-level sortie that would take them down towards the mountains of southern Germany.

Wg Cdr P T Bayley and the Squadron, 29 July 1960, Bruggen, West Germany.

On the edge of the plain, as the hills begin to rise, the aircraft, still shrouded in cloud, struck the side of a mountain and all three of the crew were killed. The spot is marked today by a cairn of stones surmounted by a stone cross, erected by the children of the Deutscherötkreuzjugend (German Red Cross Youth) from Göttingen, and inscribed "To the memory of three officers of the Royal Air Force who died at this place on 30th December, 1957".

By May 1958, the Squadron was fully established in its new base and had reached operational efficiency with the new techniques. All that was lacking was the nuclear weapon itself and this was not to arrive until mid-1960. From its base in Germany, the Squadron's ties with the Middle East were regularly maintained, with LABS bombing attachments to Idris just outside Tripoli, the capital of Libya, and armament camps at Akrotiri, Cyprus. Thus "The Chanticleer" became known to another generation of 213 Squadron aircrew.

Idris, named after the then King of Libya, and also known as Tripoli International Airport, had started life as an Italian Air Force base, Castel Benito, and even in 1960 the walls of the dining-room were still decorated with ceramic blue and white tiles depicting Regia Aeronautica biplanes flying in massed formations. The operational attractions of this part of North Africa were the good flying weather and Tarhuna Bombing Range, which was set up for the practice of LABS bombing. Some twenty miles further out into the desert than the airfield, the range occupied an area of flat scrubby desert and was laid out with a target, an IP and a Bomb Release Point, all in a nice straight line and marked by large cairns that could be seen from a very considerable distance. Once the bomb-release calculations had been made, there was very little for the navigators to do but sit in the back of the aircraft as it thundered up and down the range at two hundred and fifty feet, hurling twenty-five pound bombs at the clearly marked target, which consisted of a forty-yard triangle of oil drums. The attraction of the range for the local Arab nomads was that they were paid a shilling for each bomb tail-unit recovered. To find them sitting on the bomb-release point was acceptable but for them to sit in the target area, with the presumption that this was a safe place to be, was considered bad form.

The more popular visit to the Mediterranean was the Armament Practice Camp that took place later in the year in Cyprus. Based at Akrotiri, in the large Sovereign Base Area, the facilities were good and the flying, again at least for the pilots, was interesting as air-to-ground firing and dive-bombing, both by day and night were practised. The air-to-ground firing range was over the beach at Larnaca, with the aircraft diving on to the targets on the beach and then pulling up out to sea. As the pilots set the aircraft up in the correct dive angle and fixed the target firmly in the gun-sight, the navigator in the back - with no view out - counted down the altimeter as it unwound, with firing to commence at 800 feet and cease at 400 hundred. With the normal pull-out at two hundred feet, if the barometric pressure had changed or the local pressure setting had not been accurately set, this could result in the altimeter reading a minus figure. Though this was never the most popular sport with the navigators, they managed to take such excitements in their stride.

The target for the dive-bombing practice was a barge moored out in the bay to the west of the base. The attractions of dive-bombing by day paled into insignificance once the crews graduated to night bombing. On at least one occasion, the night's work was brought to an early close when the first crew up scored a direct hit on the barge, thus extinguishing the light that illuminated the target in the otherwise total blackness of the surrounding sea.

In October 1960, Wg Cdr P T Bayley was commanding the Squadron when the American tactical nuclear weapons were delivered, and the Squadron finally became operational

Air Vice-Marshal John Brownlow, OBE, AFC, who was one of the first pilots to join the Squadron at Ahlhorn.
(J Brownlow)

Wg Cdr S Slater, DSO, OBE, DFC, Squadron Commander from 7 June 1960 - 24 April 1964.

in its main role. With this new low-level all-weather nuclear strike capability came the institution of the Quick Reaction Aircraft (QRA). One aircraft, fully armed and fuelled, was maintained at fifteen minutes readiness to take off and attack the designated target on the other side of the Iron Curtain. Crews lived for twenty-four hour periods in their flying suits in a room alongside the aircraft, being aware that they might be called upon to take off, and also being certain that, at some time in the twenty-four hours, the alarm bells would ring and they would have to be at the engines-start situation within the set time-limit. Each crew had to make a detailed study of the QRA (Quick Reaction Alert) Target and two automatic alternative targets, as well as prepare folders for secondary targets. Much of the twenty-four hours spent on fifteen minute stand-by was therefore usually spent in target study, in addition to playing cards, reading and sleeping. However, once the target-planning folder had been studied and checked and rechecked, there was all too little to do to while away the waiting hours.

In its conventional role, the Squadron took part with considerable success in the Cyprus air defence exercise, held in October 1960 and code-named "Jesse". Using the techniques developed over the past five years, attacks were successfully launched from low level on all the allotted targets. The defending fighters found themselves unable to make one successful interception, and it was clear that there was no effective defence against really low flying aircraft. Throughout the month of the detachment, only four sorties were lost through aircraft unserviceability and all four of the detachment's aircraft were in use all of the time, a tribute to the hard work of the groundcrew - and the rugged nature of the Canberra.

The third contact with Middle East, maintained by the Squadron whilst stationed in Germany, was the much sought-after Lone Ranger navigation exercise. Typically this exercise would take crew away from Bruggen for seven or eight days, and involved a week-end in Nairobi. The first leg would be a trip of nearly four hours down to El Adem. No doubt much improved since 1942, but still a desolate spot. Two further legs of between two and three hours to Khartoum and then on down the Nile Valley, over Lake Rudolph and on to Eastleigh, Nairobi, brought the first part of the exercise to a close in time for the week-end. Monday morning saw the aircraft over the still inhospitable mountains of the Ogaden in southern Ethiopia *en route* for Khormaksar in Aden. Two legs on Tuesday, back through Khartoum and on to Idris, ended in a rest for the navigators, since on the next day they "enjoyed" some LABS and dive-bombing on the range at Tarhuna. A three-hour trip the following day returned the crew to what could be a grey and chilly Germany.

In January 1961, No.87 Squadron was disbanded, and the Squadron found itself with more commodious accommodation as it took over one of the hangars relinquished by the departing Javelins. The Squadron was now operating on a one-flight basis, with four crews detailed for night-flying while the remainder worked a normal week. By May, with high levels of serviceability being maintained, the Squadron's flying hours were the highest since May 1957,

Air Vice-Marshal Graham and Mrs Graham in the garden of their house at Sannox, near Brodick, Arran. Photographed by a Squadron Canberra flown by Fg Off F M Leeson, 1961.

when sixteen aircraft had been available, compared with the current establishment in 1961 of twelve.

In the summer of 1961, the Squadron's primary nuclear strike role was interrupted, together with the routine trips to the Mediterranean for practice LABS bombing and Armament Camps, when trouble flared up in the small sheikdom of Kuwait in the Persian Gulf. General Kassem, the military ruler of nearby Iraq, laid claim to this small oil-rich state and the Neutral Zone between the two countries. The ruler of Kuwait called for military aid from Great Britain under the treaty then existing between the two countries. Here was just such a "brush fire" incident that the Squadron, and the other elements of the Canberra strike force in Germany, had been designed to meet in their ground-attack role.

The Squadron was stood down from exercise "Quo Vadis", which was about to commence, and the aircraft were quickly fitted with gun packs and long-range tanks. The lights in the hangars burned late into the night as the guns were harmonised and systems checked. Within forty-eight hours of the receipt of the order sending the Squadron to an, as yet, undisclosed destination in the Middle East, on Operation "Vantage", the first five aircraft were airborne at 19.30 hours on 30 June 1961 *en route* for Malta. After an overnight stop at Luqa, the aircraft flew the short distance to El Adem in Libya. The crews manning the aircraft were:-

Pilot	1st Navigator	2nd Navigator
Fg Off A J E Spain	Flt Lt M P Piddleton	Sqn Ldr W A S Harrison
Flt Lt A Wells	Flt Lt J Ford	Fg Off I Galletti
Fg Off C J Compton	Flt Lt G S Jones	Flt Lt R R Sharman
Fg Off T A Pearson	Flt Lt B W Woods	Flt Lt R M Leyland
Fg Off L Nel	Fg Off M G Brown	Fg Off M G Frankland

and the party was commanded by Sqn Ldr Harrison.

Early in the morning of 1 July a further section of three aircraft flown by:-

Pilot	1st Navigator	2nd Navigator
Sqn Ldr A Stroud	Flt Lt P Lane	Flt Lt T Hayward
Fg Off F M Leeson	Flt Lt K Darby	Fg Off C Merritt
Fg Off F L Rivett	Flt Lt S J Pratt	Flt Lt W L Gordon

with the CO and Sqn Ldr L C Swalwell riding on the rumble seats in two of the aircraft, took off and flew directly to El Adem. Here, as the two sections of aircraft met up, the new Squadron Commander, Wg Cdr S Slater, DSO, OBE, DFC, who had arrived only two weeks previously, briefed the entire

Six No. 213 Squadron Canberra B(I).6s and four No. 88 Squadron B(I).8s on the airfield at RAF, Sharjah, The Persian Gulf, July 1961, photographed by Fg Off L Nel.

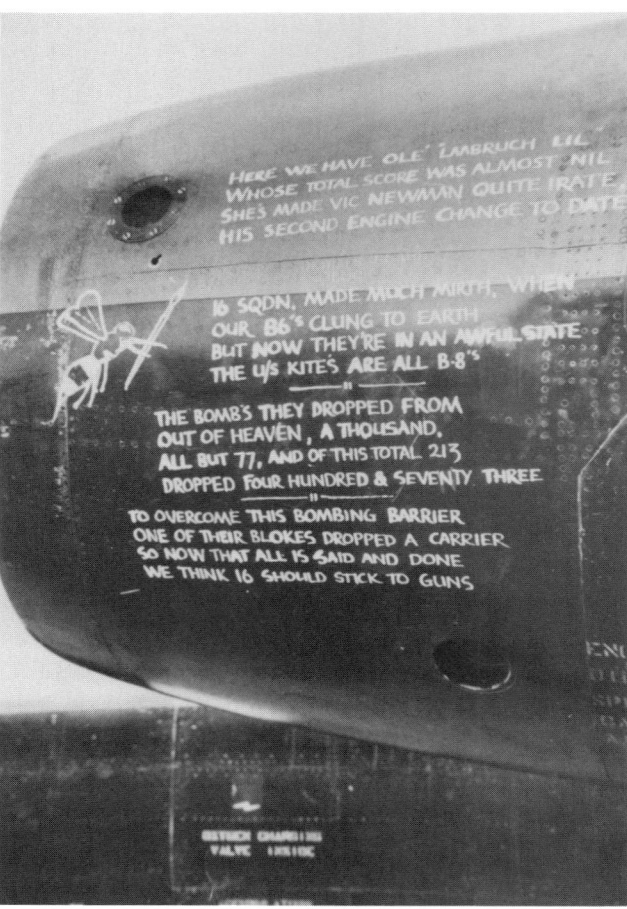

The Squadron ground-crews' epitaph to a combined bombing detachment, inscribed on a No. 16 Squadron aircraft, Idris, Libya, May 1962.

force and disclosed that the final destination was Sharjah in the Persian Gulf. Stan Slater had elected to fly out on the rumble seat with Arthur Stroud, partly because, in the short time he had been with the Squadron, he had not flown a B(I).6 at night and partly on the basis that, as a passenger, he could give some serious thought to the probable tasks that lay ahead and to any problems that might arise.

Late that same night, after a hurried meal and a brief rest, the aircraft, carrying the maximum fuel load (the aircraft's tanks had been topped up with cool fuel just before take-off) taxied out and one by one took off into the darkness of the desert bound for Khormaksar, Aden. The navigation briefing had stressed that the aircraft were not to infringe Egyptian air space. Therefore the most direct route could not be followed. Initially, the aircraft flew virtually due south to the south-western corner of Egypt, deep in the Libyan Desert. There they turned onto a south-easterly heading, across Ethiopia and on to Aden. Even with the long-range tip-tanks fuel would be short. As dawn broke, with the aircraft approaching the southern end of the Red Sea, all eyes searched to pick up some coastal features, which would positively identify the aircraft's positions. All that could be seen below was a swirling grey mist that could be shrouding land or sea in the early morning half-light. It was in fact wind-blown sand that obscured the whole area. As the fuel gauges dropped lower and lower, ears strained for the sound of the Aden Controller's voice until one by one the eight aircraft were eventually talked down onto the broad stretch of Khormaksar's runway. The flight of nearly five hours was the longest that most crews were to fly in a Canberra. The actual time spent in the air differed from crew to crew, depending upon the extent to which they had followed the navigation briefing, or had built in some insurance by cutting the corner over south-western Egypt.

The longest part of the journey was now over, and a short three-hour daylight flight saw the sandy strip of Sharjah's runway loom out of the desert. Once the aircraft had landed, the groundcrews, who had flown out earlier in a Transport Command Britannia, quickly refuelled, serviced and armed the aircraft ready for any eventuality. The Squadron's arrival coincided with the hottest part of the year, with the temperature on the airfield the next day reaching one hundred and sixty degrees Fahrenheit - the highest temperature for two years. The aircrew moved into accommodation vacated by the 11th (Prince Albert's Own) Hussars, who had moved up to Kuwait City in their armoured cars to provide armoured support for the infantry battalions deployed in the Sheikdom. The air component of the force sent to the Gulf to deter General Kassem consisted of the Squadron's eight B(I).6s and four B(I).8s of No. 88 Squadron based at Sharjah to provide the strike capability, and the Hunters of Nos. 8 and 208 Squadrons at Bahrein to provide air defence and close support.

On 3 July, the CO flew to Bahrein with Stroud and Harrison to be briefed on the local situation and on the role of the Canberra force if General Kassem attacked Kuwait. The

The Station Commander, Bruggen, West Germany, Gp Capt E D Crew, DSO, DFC and Bar, arrives at Sharjah, July 1961.

The Kuwait Crisis, July 1961. A Squadron Canberra bombed-up in case the Iraqis invaded.

welcoming words of Air Cdre Beresford, Senior Air Staff Officer, Bahrein - "I'd heard from the BBC that you were on your way from Germany" - suggested that he had received very little information from official sources. The existing plans were sketchy, certainly as far as the tasks allotted to the Canberras were concerned, and target priorities and weapon loads had to be worked out with the local Air Staff. Once back at Sharjah preparations were soon complete, targets were allocated and formation positions allotted to the various crews. Target briefings were particularly detailed, as some of the more senior pilots had actually been stationed at Basra airfield, the Squadron's first target. All that was missing was the actual flying, as the crews were held at readiness on the ground.

On 6 July, Beresford visited Sharjah to give an update on the political situation. It appeared from the tone of the Iraqi protests in the United Nations that they were rather taken aback by the speed of the UK's response, and were now doubting their ability to carry out their threat.

As soon as the situation stabilised, sorties were flown up the Gulf and low level reconnaissance was carried out over Kuwait itself. The take-off for the first of these missions will long be remembered by those who watched it, as well as by the crew taking part. It was clear that, with a heavy fuel load and full ammunition trays, the all-up weight of the aircraft was nearing its maximum. So Flt Lt Tony Wells held his aircraft on its brakes as he ran up to full power. The sight of large pieces of the runway flying out behind the jet-pipes suggested to the interested onlookers that the oiled-sand surface had not been prepared with modern jet aircraft in mind. As the aircraft slowly gathered speed down the runway, it became clear that it would be a close thing as to whether or not the aircraft would become airborne before the runway ended. In the end compromise took a hand since, although the aircraft was not airborne at the end of the runway, the desert remained flat and accommodating until it was.

A rapid return to the flight offices and some intense work with the flight calculators showed that an aircraft with a full fuel load and ammunition could not take off after about seven o'clock in the morning, or before something like six o'clock in the evening. The high daytime temperature, and the comparatively short runway, with a surface of rolled oiled sand, all imposed limitations. If war broke out between these times, some interesting decisions would have to be made. In the event no hostilities commenced and armed patrols - but without bombs - were flown daily over Kuwait. The routine patrol was to fly up the Persian Gulf at high level, 30,000 feet or so, letting down to 1,000 feet near Kuwait City, and then to continue the armed patrol at that height approximately fifteen miles inside the border of the country where it ran along those of Saudi Arabia and Iraq. Exactly where the border lay, in the sandy waste punctuated only by the occasional oil derrick with its plume of burning gas, was never very clear, but no other aircraft or any ground activity was ever seen.

On the return journey to Sharjah, again at high level, the most important consideration was to remember to fly with the cockpit heating turned off, notwithstanding the outside air temperature of minus forty degrees. The objective was to produce a refrigerator-like atmosphere in the cockpit for the groundcrew while they serviced and prepared the aircraft for its next sortie. The Canberra's fixed domed perspex canopy soon raised the temperature as the aircraft stood on the ground since, even with movable sunshades to screen the cockpit, the normal temperature in which the groundcrews worked was most uncomfortable. Within a few days the face of the desert and the various tracks and oil-rigs became surprisingly familiar to the Squadron pilots.

One of the lighter moments of the stay in the Gulf occurred when the Station Commander of Bruggen, Gp Capt E D Crew, DSO and Bar, DFC and Bar, flew out with Wg Cdr Ivan Whitaker, OC Technical Wing, and Sqn Ldr Dave Edwards, 80 Squadron's Navigation Leader. Such was Ed Crew's press-on spirit that they had flown continuously all the way from Germany, stopping only briefly for fuel: Dave Edwards was almost asleep at his navigation table when the aircraft landed. A small reception party consisting of Fg Offs Tony Pearson, Fred Rivett, Lou Nel and Clive Compton, kitted out as Arabs with the latter leading the donkey that was parked each day outside Air Traffic Control building whilst its owner was at work, and which had been specially hired for the occasion, was assembled to transport the Gp Capt to the Mess. The ceremony was only slightly delayed by the arrival of the station fire tenders, which attended very promptly to the brake fires that resulted from Ed Crew having to make a flapless landing due to hydraulic problems; the undercarriage had had to be pumped down by hand by the Officer Commanding, Technical Wing.

The boredom for the groundcrew was slightly relieved by the artistry practised on one of 88 Squadron's Canberra B(I).8s and other visiting aircraft, including the all-white

Fg Off T A Pearson lands with only two wheels locked down, Bruggen, 28 August 1961.

Canberra of the C-in-C Middle East Command, which were all mysteriously attacked by Hornets.

However it seemed that the action, in which the Squadron had flown so far to participate, was becoming less and less likely. On 11 July it was reported that the Iraqis were taking up defensive positions. When 14 July, the anniversary of the revolution that had brought General Kassem to power, passed without incident, the likelihood of armed operations receded even further. The plans to attack Basra airfield so carefully laid with 88 Squadron, which had also come out from Germany, remained just plans.

All that was left was the heat and the humidity of the summer, and a game of hockey for those determined to maintain the Squadron's sporting record. As the whole incident ceased to be newsworthy, the unwelcome feeling arose that the Squadron might be in for a long and uncomfortable stay. Longer sorties were flown down to Masirah Island in the Indian Ocean, and interesting reconnaissance missions flown in concert with the Trucial Oman Scouts, who seemed as much at home with aircraft as they did in their own element, the desert. This was in strong contrast to the disposed cavalry regiment which, although living on an RAF airfield, had instituted a system of demerits for unacceptable behaviour, which included reading *Flight* magazine.

On 18 July, the CO returned from a visit to Bahrein with the news that a prolonged stay was to be avoided. Events in Berlin and threats by Kruschev had lowered the temperature of the Cold War by a few degrees and the two Canberra Squadrons had been recalled to Germany. Leave was taken of the station's resident staff, whose hospitality had created a home in the desert, and within a few hours the Squadron was on the move. With only slightly less of the urgency which had brought the aircraft hurrying eastwards, the return journey was made in two days via Khormaksar, Khartoum and Idris, landing at Bruggen almost three weeks to the day from the start of the emergency.

The Kuwait Emergency gave justification to the Squadron's conventional operations role, and demonstrated the value of the Canberra as a long-range ground-attack fighter-bomber.

It was, nevertheless, as part of the North Atlantic Treaty Organisation's tactical nuclear strike force that the Squadron had its *raison d'être*. From 11 to 13 September, the Squadron took part for the first time in Exercise "Checkmate", the Annual Joint Atomic Air Defence Exercise sponsored by Strategic Air Command Europe (SACEUR). This exercise was designed to practise the implementation of SACEUR's Atomic Strike Plan and the Emergency Defence Plan. In the course of the Exercise, thirty sorties were flown by day and three by night.

In January 1962, one of the Squadron's Canberras, WT324, was forced to divert to Bremen Airport when its top hatch blew off. The hatch could not be replaced at Bremen and, because of the discomfort that would be caused to the navigators in the rear compartment with no top hatch, it was decided that a pilot would fly the aircraft back to Bruggen solo. The task was allotted to Flt Lt K J Wilson, who thus became one of the very few pilots to have flown a Canberra solo. Because the fuses for the aircraft's undercarriage are located in the rear compartment, the Canberra was flown with its undercarriage down and shepherded by a lead aircraft

A Squadron Canberra at Chaumont, France for the Aircent Tactical Weapons Meet, June 1965. (Bruce Robertson)

A less-than-restrained tail fin decoration appeared on Squadron Canberras. (Bruce Robertson)

during the one-hour flight.

The opening of the year 1962 was, however, marred when five aircrew and two aircraft were lost in a single accident. The two aircraft were flying as a pair on an interdictor sortie when they collided just south of Nordhorn Range. Flt Lt J E Abraham and Fg Offs J Hulland, K B Willings, R M Lear and D R Clarke were killed, while Flt Lt G Willis and Fg Off M Whittingham ejected and were taken to the RAF Hospital at Wegberg.

By this time the Squadron had reverted to the traditional two-Flight system, alternating on a weekly basis between day and night flying. Maintaining high levels of serviceability, flying hours reached new levels, with crews averaging nearly thirty hours per month. In February four crews at Idris, on a LABS bombing detail, dropped ninety bombs in three days.

A continuing matter of concern was the effect the constant low flying was having on the fatigue life of the Canberra's airframe, particularly the wings which had been designed for medium/high level operations. The rows of dials in the bomb-bay recorded very precisely the G forces inflicted on the aircraft during a low-level sortie, and the amount of the finite fatigue life of the airframe that had been used. With the LABS manoeuvre requiring a pull-up of 3.4 G and a speed of four hundred and thirty knots, and with the bomb-doors open at 250 feet, it was clear that the aircraft could easily be over-stressed. Training flights, when LABS manoeuvres were to be practised, had to be restricted if there was any significant ground turbulence. In Libya, for instance, bombing sorties were flown either in the early morning or late afternoon. The recently-introduced procedure of dropping the practice bombs from the under-wing pylons only marginally eased the problem.

During the summer, greater contact was made with the French Air Force than for some time when, in June and July, the CO and Fg Off Dyer and their crews took part in the first NATO Tactical Weapons meet at St. Dizier. This competition was won by the USAF, which formed part of 4 ATAF, highlighting the superiority of both their aircraft and the "lay down weapons system" they used compared with LABS. In September, Flt Lt Stephenson flew down to Colmar to take part in the French National Day Air Display at Mulhouse-Habsheim, where he made several low passes and carried out a LABS manoeuvre from two hundred and fifty feet.

Throughout most of October and the first few days of November, the Squadron was released from its primary nuclear strike role, and the long tradition of practice armament camps in Cyprus was continued. The aircraft were fitted with gun-packs and prepared for air-to-ground firing and shallow dive-bombing. For four weeks the firing range at Larnaca, and the bombing range at El Adem in Libya, were busy because of the intense rivalry between "A" and "B" Flights to achieve the best results. The contest was eventually settled decisively in favour of "A" Flight, with an average error of forty yards in dive-bombing and a score of thirty per cent in air-to-ground firing, compared to fifty-six yards and twenty-two per cent for "B" Flight.

More realism was given to the strike role when the CO and his crew dropped a full-size mock-up of the tactical nuclear weapon at Nordhorn range. The "shape" was considerably larger than anything dropped in normal practice, weighing 1,600 pounds. Such was the special nature of the event that the remainder of the Squadron's aircrew travelled to the range to watch the "shape" on its flight from release to impact. While, for the pilots, there was little doubt that the conventional ground-attack role provided the more interesting flying, it was clear to all that the first and most important task of the Squadron was its nuclear strike capability. In February 1963, the Squadron underwent its first NATO Tactical Evaluation, and later in the year an intra-Squadron competition, the Harrison Trophy was inaugurated for the crew carrying out the best First Run Attack. The first winners of the competition were Fg Off Wightman and his navigator, Fg Off Milligan. The Trophy had been presented for the competition by the Squadron's former Navigation Officer, Sqn Ldr Harrison, who had been awarded the MBE in November 1962, when he was also promoted to Wing Commander and posted to the Air Ministry in London.

The Squadron had always had a high reputation for the quality of its formation flying, and the move away from single-engined fighters had in no way impaired this reputation. So it was in keeping with past traditions that, on 26 June, four Canberras flown by the CO, Sqn Ldr T La Touche, Flt Lt F G Stephenson and Fg Off M H Wilson, led a formation of forty-two British, German, Dutch and Belgian aircraft in a fly-past to say farewell to the departing Commander-in-Chief, Air Marshal Sir John Grandy, KBE, CB, DSO.

Throughout the spring and summer of 1963, the Squadron's aircraft operated from the nearby airfield at Wildenrath, while the runway at Bruggen underwent extensive repairs and crash-barriers were installed at either end. Arrangements were made for the QRA aircraft to use the southern taxi-way in case of need. The move back to Bruggen coincided with the autumnal bird migration season, which inevitably led to an increase in bird-strikes. This phenomenon occurred both in the spring and autumn and eventually led to

Flt Lt E C Tilsley just after take-off. Eric Tilsley was nominated as the Canberra flying display pilot for the opening of the 1969 season.

some flying restrictions during these periods, since birdstrikes occurred at any height between 250 feet, the minimum authorised, and 3,000 feet, and in all the Dutch and German low-flying areas. Generally the damage suffered was only Cat.1, and fortunately strikes at night were fairly rare, but nevertheless disturbing enough when they did happen.

In February, the LABS bombing section of the Salmond Trophy was held and Flt Lt Collins, Flt Lt Travers and Fg Off Williams, together with their crews, successfully dropped all their bombs with a First Run Attack average of 160 yards. This achievement produced the highest score ever recorded by any squadron in any of the rounds of the Salmond Trophy to date. The performance actually secured the Trophy for the Squadron, because the final round had to be cancelled due to bad weather. The final scores, out of a total of twelve hundred, were 213 Squadron with 903 points, 3 Squadron with 653, 16 Squadron with 605 and 14 Squadron with 502. The trophy was presented by the Commander-in-Chief RAF Germany, Air Marshal Sir Ronald Lees, at a ceremony at Bruggen. He also presented Flt Lt Ken Wilson with the Briggs Trophy for the best all-round sportsman.

On 29 April 1964, Stan Slater was posted back to the UK to become President of the Aircrew Selection Board with the rank of Group Captain, and Wg Cdr R H Arscott arrived to assume command. No sooner had he arrived than the Squadron was plunged into the preparations for the presentation of the Standard, for which it had become eligible on 1 April 1961 in recognition of the completion of twenty-five years of service. During the first two weeks of July, the only flying that took place was practice formation flying for the big day, and considerable time was also spent on the parade ground practising for the presentation. On 15 July, the Standard was presented by Her Royal Highness The Princess Margaret, Countess of Snowden, together with the similar presentation to 80 Squadron, which echoed the time the two squadrons had operated together in the Middle East during the Second World War. The Standard was received by Fg Off A D Briscoe in front of some fifteen hundred visitors, including seven former Commanding Officers, Air Vice-Marshal R Graham, CB, CBE, DSO, DSC and Bar, DFC, Air Marshal Sir Humphrey Edwardes Jones, CB, CBE, DFC, AFC, Group Captain P E Vaughan-Fowler, DSO, DFC and Bar, AFC, Group Captain I R Campbell, OBE, DFC, Group Captain S Slater, DSO, OBE, DFC, Wing Commander P T Bayley and Squadron Leader D C Colebrook. The parade was immaculate, as was to be expected, and drew favourable comment from Her Royal Highness and the guests. The following day was one of the rare occasions when Bruggen was open to the public, and over four thousand visitors from The Netherlands and Germany came to see the static displays.

Even though LABS bombing practice was suspended in Germany during the autumn migratory season, this did not avoid the problem of bird-strikes entirely. In Libya, a Canberra flown by Sqn Ldr Huxley and Fg Off Thomas flew through a flock of large birds on the range at Tarhuna. The canopy was shattered and the skin of the aircraft was penetrated in fifteen places. Huxley suffered cuts and bruising on his face and arms, but was able to return to Idris and land safely.

An official evaluation of the Squadron's state of effectiveness had been awaited for over eighteen months, and it arrived before the end of the first month of the new year. At 05.50 hours on 26 January 1965, the sirens sounded, announcing that the Tactical Evaluation exercise had begun. The now well-rehearsed procedures swung into action as the aircraft were loaded with war reserve weapons. All Launch

HRH Princess Margaret, Countess of Snowden, presents Standards to Nos. 80 and 213 Squadrons at Bruggen, July 1964.

Wg Cdr M R T Chandler, the Squadron's last Commanding Officer.

Sequence Plan times were met and by 11.16 hours ten aircraft had been loaded. The aircrew were examined not only on their individual war missions, but also on aspects of the overall war plan. At 12.15 hours a General Alert was announced over the Tannoy, and at 13.30 hours the exercise QRA aircraft, manned by Flt Lt Underdown and his crew, was released by the Duty Operations Officer and became airborne at 13.36 hours. All the aircraft participating in the exercise reached their targets and on landing were briefed again for a re-strike; the aircraft turn-around time was one hour and twelve minutes. Thus far, on the first day, the TacEval Team had been impressed. At 05.30 hours on 27 January, eight re-strike aircraft were airborne, but bad weather in the local area caused all the aircraft to divert; one landed at Ahlhorn with only twelve hundred pounds of fuel. Despite the bad weather on the second day, the exercise had been a success and the Squadron had performed well. The Evaluation Team left with a favourable overall impression.

The only real problems faced by the Squadron were those due to the continual wear and tear on the aircraft, which were now beginning to show their age. Following an incident when the port undercarriage leg of WT313 subsided on landing, forcing Fg Off Wightman to perform a complete one hundred and eighty degree turn on the grass alongside the runway, cracks were also found in the undercarriages of WT314 and WT324.

Despite the age of the aircraft, the Squadron won the Salmond Trophy for 1964/65. Represented by Flt Lts Underdown, Travers and Webber and their crews, with Howells as reserve, the team scored 2,447 points as opposed to the 2,018 scored by 16 Squadron, 1,905 by 14 Squadron and 1,786 by 3 Squadron.

Flying low-level at night, sometimes in bad weather, was part and parcel of the Squadron's role as an all-weather interdictor force. Bird-strikes were one of the unwelcome interruptions to a night sortie, but even more disturbing, and fortunately less frequent, was a lightning strike. Such an incident occurred on the night of 26 April 1965 when Fg Off Peaty's aircraft was struck while in cloud some five miles north of the airfield. The lightning shattered the nose cone and melted the pitot static line, which is mounted in the centre of the nose, and this damage of course resulted in the loss of his air-speed indicator. Fortunately another aircraft was in the area, and Peaty was shepherded back to Bruggen in formation with Flt Lt Underdown.

When RAF Germany put up a formation of seventy-six aircraft in a fly-past to mark the visit of Her Majesty the Queen to Gutersloh, the Squadron occupied last place - rather than its usual lead position - as the aircraft flew in numerical order by squadron number. When it came to selection on merit, the placings were quite different. After its showing in the last two Salmond Trophy competitions, the Squadron was selected to represent RAF Germany at the Fourth Annual Tactical Weapons Meet held at a base, at Chaumont in France, of the United States Air Force, Europe. The competition was between two teams, one representing

Flt Lts Brian Stoat and Mike Cairns with Fg Off Garth Gardner, about to set off on an endurance test - target seven hours airborne time.

Gp Capt P T Bayley (left) and Air Marshal Sir Humphrey Edwardes Jones talk over old times at the Squadron's Fiftieth Anniversary celebrations.

2ATAF, consisting of British, Dutch, Belgian and German-north aircraft, flying against 4ATAF, represented by American, Canadian, French and German-south squadrons. The competition ran for most of the last two weeks of June and, although 4ATAF finally proved victorious, the Squadron's team performed better than any previous RAF representatives. In the course of the whole competition only two points were lost for navigation errors, an achievement which once again emphasised the effectiveness of the Canberra B(I).6 crew configuration of a pilot and two navigators, particularly when flying at low level at night.

The real danger posed by bird-trikes was illustrated all too tragically on 14 July when WT324, flown by Flt Lt L D Dingle, Fg Off T F Clapp and Fg Off H M Sime, crashed about four-and-a-half miles west of the airfield, after an asymmetric overshoot with the port engine shut down due to a bird-strike. With the undercarriage down, the aircraft was not able to reach its safety speed, and the crew ejected at less than three hundred feet, the navigators going out through the metal hatch. All three of the crew were killed, and it was only after this accident that the aircraft were fitted with the Mark 2 CA ejector seat with ground-level ejection capability.

The problems associated with the ageing aircraft were clearly illustrated in January 1966, when two aircraft were detached to Luqa, Malta, for LABS bombing at the Tarhuna range. Although one aircraft became unserviceable and had to have an engine-change, eighty bombs were dropped before noon on 20 January. On his last trip, Fg Off Naidoo took the CO of RAF Idris along on the sortie to see how things were done. After a normal landing, the Canberra's brakes failed completely at thirty-five knots and the aircraft, WT322, continued to the end of the runway, crossed the main road, narrowly missed the Station Warrant Officer's car and came to rest in an olive grove belonging to Ali Hag Hadi. The aircraft sustained category 3 damage. A Board of Inquiry was convened but the aircraft carrying the necessary papers from Bruggen to Idris itself became unserviceable, due to hydraulic problems, requiring yet another party to fly into Idris to carry out repairs. It was not until 28 January that all the personnel involved were able to return to Germany.

The early warm weather brought an early start to the bird migration season, and a Command Flight Safety Bird Warning was issued which restricted low-flying to two hundred and fifty knots, and kept LABS practice to a minimum. Towards the end of February 1966, the Non-destructive Testing Team of the Central Servicing Development Establishment also arrived at Bruggen to carry out ultra-sonic tests on the aircraft's mainframe. As a result of these tests, three aircraft were found to have stress corrosion cracks in their undercarriage legs and fuselage main beam and one in the undercarriage legs only. The surprising discovery was that the cracks were not due in any way to the manner in which the aircraft were operated, but were built-in during the initial casting and machining of the components. Their presence had only become apparent much later with the development of new screening techniques.

While these aircraft were being repaired, another aircraft was lost from use in early March when WT316 flew back to Marshals at Cambridge. This aircraft was to have the necessary modifications made to allow the Mark 43 Lay Down Nuclear Weapon to be delivered. Operating with this delivery system allowed the aircraft to fly across the target, at low level and high speed, without having to pull-up in the area of the target or slow down to drop the bomb. By the end of May, all crews had flown WT316 with the new delivery system and were familiar with its operation.

As Wg Cdr T E Benson assumed command, on 13 June 1966, following the posting of Wg Cdr R H Arscott to the College of Air Warfare at Manby, general flying became restricted. All available air time was devoted to the Weapon/Aircraft Training Programme, which emphasised Lay-Down Bombing Training and was designed to make the Squadron fully operational with the new weapons system.

At 08.55 hours, while on its fourth bombing run at Nordhorn Bombing range, Fg Off Hellyer's aircraft sustained a bird-strike which shattered the canopy. The citation for the award to Fg Off Hellyer of the Queen's Commendation for Valuable Services in the Air describes what happened:-

"On 1 July 1966 Fg Off C Hellyer and his crew of No. 213 Squadron were executing a bombing run in a Canberra B(I).6 on Nordhorn Range when a bird struck the aircraft's canopy. The canopy immediately disintegrated causing considerable damage to his aircraft.

Hellyer immediately decided to climb the aircraft and reduce speed. Even so he was still unable to see out of the cockpit and, having elected to divert to Hopsten airfield, he followed another B(I).6 which flew ahead and above so that Hellyer could sit low in the cockpit out of the slip-stream. The observer attempted to put his own helmet on the pilot's

The Squadron flight line and hangars at Bruggen, 1961.

head but this was also blown away; eventually however he succeeded in securing the plotter's helmet on the pilot. With the visor down, Hellyer's face had some protection but his eyes continued to stream and he had the greatest difficulty in reading the instruments and seeing out of the cockpit. Despite this Hellyer made a successful landing at Hopsten.

There is no doubt that by his presence of mind and extremely fine handling of this difficult situation, Hellyer prevented the loss of the aircraft."

The aircraft not only sustained a shattered canopy but had also suffered considerable damage to the port engine, engine intake, tail-fin, tailplane and navigator's hatch. A ground party consisting of Flt Lt Rolph, Chief Technician Howard, Sgt Blackwell and Sgt Berry, together with seven men, had the aircraft repaired and recovered by 5 July.

By August, the aircraft situation had become critical as increased stress fractures were found in the main-spars of five more aircraft, WT307, WT312, WT313, WT316 and WT319. All the aircraft were grounded and repairs were expected to take up to eight months per aircraft. The remaining five aircraft available for operational flying were restricted to a speed of two hundred and fifty knots, a minimum altitude of 1,000 feet and a force of 2G. Notwithstanding these restrictions, the Glorious Twelfth found the Squadron fully operational with the new Type 43 Lay-Down Bombing System and the Quick Reaction Aircraft were once more back at readiness with Sqn Ldr Knight and his crew, Flt Lt Wallington and Fg Off Michael, together with Fg Off Naidoo and Sgt Browne and Flt Sgt Young, taking the first turns with the new system. By the end of the month, 154 practice lay-down bombs had been dropped.

Although severely hampered by the loss of five aircraft and the restrictions imposed on flying, the normal round of exercises was carried out and, in October, the 2ATAF Tactical Evaluation Team arrived for a further very successful Squadron assessment. In November, it was not bird-strikes or mechanical failure but freak weather conditions that provided unwelcome surprises for Fg Off R J Milsom and Sqn Ldr E C Turner. Milsom was overshooting from a Ground Control Approach at Düsseldorf, and Turner was on his final approach after a GCA at Bruggen, when each experienced engine flame-outs; Milsom relit his engine and Turner carried on and made a single-engine landing. No technical fault was discovered, and the incidents were put down to the effects of the cold and very unstable air-stream over Germany, which was accompanied by heavy and prolonged showers. Flying through these showers produced severe icing in the forward section of the engine nacelle, which caused the engine malfunctions.

In December, the Squadron received a visit from the Chief of the Air Staff, Air Chief Marshal Sir Charles Elworthy, GCB, CBE, DSO, MVO, DFC, AFC, MA, as part of his tour of RAF Germany. A state of Re-enforced Alert was quickly followed by a state of General Alert as the Squadron went through its by-now well-practised war routine, and six aircraft were soon ready to go. Unfortunately, and as so often seemed to happen when senior officers were visiting, bad weather in the chosen target area prevented the full accomplishment of the exercise, and the alert finished with the anti-climax of a take-off, circuit and landing.

As the aircraft returned from being fitted with new main-spars, so bombing details at Nordhorn became more frequent. On 23 February 1967, Fg Off G W Wilkinson and his crew, Fg Off I G Chalk and Flt Lt D W J Harris, were killed when their aircraft unaccountably crashed sixteen miles north of the Rhine, while returning from its exercise in clear, but turbulent, conditions through Low Flying Area No.2. The aircraft was seen to start to roll, and then to enter a descending turn from which it never recovered. The subsequent inspection of the wreckage did not reveal any mechanical failure, and the findings of the Court of Inquiry were that control had been lost in turbulence. Some weeks later, Flt Lt Ray Passfield, the Squadron QFI, was returning to base when, on entering a turn, he found that the ailerons were jammed and he could not move them to stop the turn developing further. By skillful use of the rudder, he managed to regain some directional control over his aircraft and, having climbed to a safer height, the controls unaccountably freed themselves, allowing him to return to Bruggen and make a safe landing. Naturally enough, the informal view soon developed on the Squadron that Wilkinson's aircraft had suffered the same undiscovered and unproven fault as Ray Passfield's.

In June, the Squadron paid its last respects to its first-ever Commanding Officer, when Sqn Ldr E C Turner and Fg Off K D Richards attended the funeral of Air Vice-Marshal R Graham, CB, CBE, DSO, DSC and Bar, DFC, on 27 June 1967.

A certain amount of variety was introduced into the continuous bombing practice, when the Sixth Annual Tactical Weapons meet was held at Wildenrath in May, thereby restricting the use of the German and Dutch low-level flying routes and areas. The Squadron therefore used the bombing range at Wainfleet, off the Lincolnshire coast of the Wash. A detachment of four aircraft, under the command of Sqn Ldr K J Wilson, accompanied by twenty-seven NCOs and airmen, was also attached to the RCAF base at Zweibrücken for the whole of the month of July, and this provided an opportunity to use the French bombing range at Suippes in conjunction with 403 Squadron, RCAF, flying CF-104s. All of the pilots, and most of the navigators, enjoyed a trip in a TF-104; using only radar for navigation and target identification was both interesting and exciting, as was climbing at Mach 1.1. Flying from Zweibrücken also enabled the aircraft to carry out sorties into the 4ATAF low-flying areas and use the bombing range at Helchetern.

As the old year came to an end, a combination of bad weather, runway repairs at Bruggen and the continual shortage of aircraft restricted flying for all pilots. Even the attempt to escape to better weather in the Mediterranean in January 1968, when a detachment departed to El Adem, Libya, for conventional weapons training, was partly frustrated. The six Canberras and three accompanying Argosys, which all arrived on 6 January, were confronted by five days of sandstorms and high winds. Notwithstanding the restricted number of flying hours that were possible, the Squadron managed to maintain its traditional high standards. When the Joint Inspection Team arrived at Bruggen to evaluate the crews in lay-down bombing, armament and safety procedures, the results achieved were the best of any of the strike squadrons in RAF Germany.

On 23 May 1968, Wg Cdr M R T Chandler arrived from Bassingbourn to take command of the Squadron when Wg Cdr T E Benson was posted to the College of Air Warfare at Manby.

The highlight of the year was the weekend of celebrations which took place on 5 and 6 July 1968, to mark the Squadron's Fiftieth Anniversary. The parade, with which the celebrations commenced, was reviewed by Air Marshal Sir Humphrey Edwardes Jones, CB, CBE, DFC, AFC, and was followed by a flying display, which included four Hunters from 4 Squadron, a Lightning from 92 Squadron, and a formation of four Canberra B(I).6s led by the CO. To conclude the proceedings, Flt Lt E C F Tilsley, who had joined the Squadron from the Central Flying School, gave an aerobatic display. Six former Squadron Commanders attended the Ladies' Night held in the evening, namely Sir Humphrey Edwardes Jones, Gp Capt. I R Campbell, AFC, Gp Capt P T Bayley, Gp Capt H J Dodson, AFC, Gp Capt R H Arscott and Sqn Ldr D C Colebrook.

Later in the summer, the Squadron was reorganised on a one-flight basis, with the former "A" Flight Commander becoming the Senior Operations Officer, and "B " Flight Commander taking over as Weapons Officer.

During the three days of the fourth round of the Salmond Trophy in August, the problems caused by bomb hang-ups in previous rounds were overcome, and the crews' winning performance put the Squadron in second place, only seventeen points behind the leaders, 16 Squadron. However, a long shadow was cast over this achievement when the crew of one of the aircraft taking part were killed, in a mid-air collision during the night phase, over the little town of Holt in Norfolk. Flt Lt J Slabber and his crew, Fg Off S Cowie and Fg Off J H Woolnough, were climbing away from the range at Wainfleet when they collided with a Victor tanker and the crews of both aircraft were killed. The odds against this tragic collision ever taking place were incalculable. The subsequent Board of Enquiry found that no one had failed in his duty and that no person was to blame. The fatalities were the direct result of what was effectively a cockpit-to-cockpit collision, and did not reflect any failure of safety equipment, ejection seats or escape facilities on either aircraft. The Victor tanker was on a night exercise flight from Marham and was under the surveillance of Midland radar. However, such were the weather conditions, with a heavy storm over Marham itself, that aircraft identification was difficult. The "clutter" on the screens of the Eastern radar controllers was so heavy that it was only after asking the Canberra to identify itself specifically by a radio transmission, and switching to secondary radar, that they were able to identify it on their screens. Once the positive identification had been made, Jack Slabber and his crew were released to resume their own navigation. Some eighty seconds later, almost certainly in thick cloud which was solid from 2,000 to 25,000 feet, and on a dark night, the two aircraft collided.

On a visit to Bruggen later in the year, the Commander-in-Chief RAF Germany, Air Marshal C N Foxley-Norris, CB, DSO, OBE, MA, announced that it was intended to re-equip both Nos.213 and 80 Squadrons with Phantoms and Buccaneers respectively at an early date, thus ensuring that both squadrons would remain in service. The announcement was timely since, after the loss of WT325 in August and after WT313 being assessed as Category Five due to airframe fatigue, the Squadron was reduced to having only eleven aircraft. With a complement of eighteen pilots and crews, the shortage of aircraft and the restricted flying hours were an unfortunate fact of life.

In February 1969, four aircraft were detached to Larissa, the home of 324 Squadron of the Greek Air Force, to carry out joint exercises. The crews were accommodated in hotels in the town of Larissa and even, though the airfield closed at 13.00 hours each day, some 205 hours were flown.

As the month drew on, it was announced that the

Salmond Trophy Winners - September 1969.

Squadron had once more won the Salmond Trophy, beating 16 Squadron into second place by a margin of two hundred and thirteen points. A new Squadron trophy, The Henlow Shield, presented by the wives and parents of the crew killed in the accident in August to the crew scoring the highest number of points in the competition, was won by Fg Off N J Wilkinson and his crew, Flt Lt K Robertshaw and Fg Off J P Mullan. By September, the Salmond Trophy had been won yet again and so, for the second time in only six years, the premier bombing trophy in RAF Germany had been won by the Squadron in two successive years. The second and last holders of The Henlow Trophy were Wg Cdr M R T Chandler and his crew, Flt Lt J P Anderson and Fg Off G G Grumbridge.

Regrettably such success, and the Squadron's all-round high levels of performance, were not enough to ensure its continued existence. The confidence in the Squadron's future, occasioned by Air Marshal Foxley-Norris's visit in 1968, was rudely shattered later in the month, when it was announced that disbandment would take place in two months' time. Throughout December, flying largely consisted of delivery trips to Salmesbury and Warton, where the last remaining Canberra B(I).6s were handed over for sale abroad. On 5 December 1969, the Squadron paraded for the last time in front of the Deputy Commander-in-Chief, RAF Germany, Air Vice-Marshal Aitken, and the final Guest Night was attended by the Commander-in-Chief, Air Marshal C N Foxley-Norris. On 31 December 1969, at 14.00 hours, the last elements of the Squadron marched out of No.2 Hangar at Royal Air Force, Bruggen, West Germany, and the Squadron passed into the pages of history.

The Squadron says "Goodbye"

APPENDIX A

Battle Honours

Battle Honours of the Royal Air Force are, in the majority of cases, shown with dates indicating the period during which the unit served in the particular theatre of operations. Each of these Battle Honours has limiting dates prescribing the period to which the Battle Honour applies. The conditions of eligibility for those honours awarded to the Squadron are as follows. * Indicates those Battle Honours displayed on the Squadron Standard.

WESTERN FRONT 1914-1918 *
For operations in support of the Allied Armies in Belgium and France.

CHANNEL AND NORTH SEA 1939-1940
For ship attack, anti-submarine and mining operations over the English Channel and North Sea from the outbreak of war to VE-Day.

FRANCE AND THE LOW COUNTRIES 1939-1940 *
For operations in France and the Low Countries between the outbreak of war and the fall of France (3 September 1939 and 25 June 1940). Applicable both to squadrons operating from home and overseas bases.

DUNKIRK *
For operations covering the evacuation of the British Expeditionary Force from Dunkirk, 26 May to 4 June 1940.

BATTLE OF BRITAIN 1940 *
For interception operations by fighter squadrons in the Battle of Britain (August to October 1940).

HOME DEFENCE 1940-1945
For interception operations after the Battle of Britain, in defence of Great Britain and Northern Ireland against enemy aircraft and flying bombs (November 1940 to 1945).

EGYPT AND LIBYA 1940-1943 *
For operations in defence of Egypt and the conquest of Libya, from the outbreak of war against Italy to the retreat of the Axis Forces into Tunisia (10 June 1940 - 6 February 1943).

SYRIA 1941 *
For operations over Syria during the campaign against the Vichy French (8 June to 12 July 1941).

EL ALAMEIN *
For operations during the retreat to El Alamein and subsequent actions (June 1942 to November 1942).

MEDITERRANEAN 1942-1943
For operations over Italy, Sicily and the Mediterranean and Aegean Sea by aircraft based in the Mediterranean area (including reconnaissance, convoy protection, mining and attacks on enemy ports and shipping) between the entry of Italy into the war and the initiation of air action preparatory to the Sicilian Campaign (10 June 1940 to June 1943).

SOUTH EAST EUROPE 1942-1945 *
For operations over Yugoslavia, Hungary, Roumania, Bulgaria and Greece.

The Squadron, Nicosia, Cyprus, February 1947. (J T Jennings)

APPENDIX B

Commanding Officers

Sqn Cdr R Graham	3 July 1917	Sqn Ldr R S Nash, DFC	17 January 1946
Maj A G Tayler	21 November 1918	Sqn Ldr M C Wells	4 November 1946
Sqn Ldr J H Edwardes Jones	3 May 1937	Sqn Ldr D C Colebrook	2 January 1947
Sqn Ldr H Mc Gregor, DSO	27 May 1940	Sqn Ldr P J Kelley, DFC	18 March 1948
Sqn Ldr D S MacDonald	25 August 1940	Sqn Ldr D J A Roe, DSO, DFC	18 April 1949
Sqn Ldr R Lockhart	14 November 1941	Sqn Ldr D M Finn, DFC	14 September 1951
Sqn Ldr G V W Kettlewell	16 January 1942	Sqn Ldr A J H Kitley	31 March 1954
Sqn Ldr M H Young, DFC	18 May 1942	Wg Cdr H J Dodson, AFC	1 September 1955
Sqn Ldr P Olver	12 October 1942	Wg Cdr I R Campbell, AFC	29 December 1957
Sqn Ldr V C Woodward, DFC	1 January 1943	Wg Cdr P T Bayley	10 August 1959
Sqn Ldr S R Whiting, DFC	24 August 1943	Wg Cdr S Slater, DSO, OBE, DFC	7 June 1961
Sqn Ldr C S Vos, DFC	16 September 1944	Wg Cdr R H Arscott	24 April 1964
Sqn Ldr P E Vaughan-Fowler,		Wg Cdr T E Benson	13 June 1966
DFC & Bar	17 December 1944	Wg Cdr M R T Chandler	23 May 1968

APPENDIX C

Squadron Bases

Date	Unit	Base	Command
3 Jul 17	Sqdn	St. Pol, Dunkirk, France	61 Wing, 5 Group, Flanders Command
25 Jan 18	Sqdn	Bergues, Dunkirk, France	61 Wing, 5 Group, Flanders Command.
18 Mar 18	Sqdn	Bergues, Dunkirk, France	61 Wing, 5 Group, Dover/Dunkirk Cmd.
27 Nov 18	Sqdn	Stalhille, Ostend, Belgium	61 Wing, 5 Group, Dover/Dunkirk Cmd.
19 Mar 19	Cadre	Scopwick, Lincs., England	

Disbanded 31.12.1919.

Date	Unit	Base	Command
8 Mar 37	Sqdn	Northolt, Middlesex, England	11 Group, Fighter Command
1 Jul 37	Sqdn	Church Fenton, Yorks., England	12 Group, Fighter Command
18 May 38	Sqdn	Wittering, Northants, England	12 Group, Fighter Command
17 May 40	B Flt	Merville, France	British Air Forces in France
17 May 40	A Flt	Biggin Hill, Surrey, England	11 Group, Fighter Command
21 May 40	B Flt	Wittering, Northants, England	12 Group, Fighter Command
23 May 40	A Flt	Wittering, Northants, England	12 Group, Fighter Command
26 May 40	Sqdn	Biggin Hill, Surrey, England	11 Group, Fighter Command
18 Jun 40	Sqdn	Exeter, Devon, England	11 Group, Fighter Command
08 Jul 40	Sqdn	Exeter, Devon, England	10 Group, Fighter Command
7 Sep 40	Sqdn	Tangmere, Sussex, England	11 Group, Fighter Command
1 Dec 40	Sqdn	Leconfield, Yorks., England	12 Group, Fighter Command
15 Jan 41	Sqdn	Driffield, Yorks., England	13 Group, Fighter Command
20 Feb 41	Sqdn	Castletown, Caithness, Scotland	13 Group, Fighter Command
29 Mar 41	A Flt	Sumburgh, Shetland, Scotland	13 Group, Fighter Command
15 Apl 41	A Flt	Castletown, Caithness, Scotland	13 Group, Fighter Command
21 Apl 41	Sqdn	Turnhouse, Edinburgh, Scotland	13 Group, Fighter Command
11 May 41		HMS *Furious*	Liverpool to Mediterranean
21 May 41	Sqdn	Abu Sueir, Suez Canal, Egypt	Air Headquarters, Middle East
24 May 41	C Flt	Sidi Haneish, Egypt	Attached 73 Squadron
24 May 41	A Flt	LG 10, Gerawla, Egypt	Attached 274 Squadron
Jun 41	B Flt	Aqir, Palestine	Attached 80 Squadron
Jun 41	B Flt	Haifa, Palestine	Attached 80 Squadron
Jun 41	B Flt	Ramat David, Palestine	Attached 80 Squadron
20 Jul 41	Sqdn	Nicosia, Cyprus	Attached 80 Squadron
16 Aug 41	Sqdn	Nicosia, Cyprus	Air Headquarters, Middle East
22 Oct 41	A Flt	Ismailia, Egypt	Air Headquarters, Middle East
23 Oct 41	B Flt	LG 229, Idku, Egypt	Air Headquarters, Middle East
13 Dec 41	A Flt	Shandur, Egypt	Air Headquarters, Middle East

20 Dec 41	A Flt	El Khanka, Egypt	Air Headquarters, Middle East
29 Dec 41	B Flt	LG 32, Dekheila, Egypt	243 Wing, 212 Group, AHQ WD
30 Dec 41	HQ	LG 90, near Amriya, Egypt	243 Wing, 212 Group, AHQ WD
14 Jan 42	B Flt	LG 229, Idku, Egypt	243 Wing, 212 Group, AHQ WD
08 Mar 42	Sqdn	LG 229, Idku, Egypt	243 Wing, 212 Group, AHQ WD
04 Jun 42	Sqdn	Gambut West, Libya	243 Wing, 212 Group, AHQ WD
16 Jun 42	Sqdn	LG 142, Gambut No.2, Libya	243 Wing, 212 Group, AHQ WD
17 Jun 42	Sqdn	LG 148, Sidi Azeiz, Libya	243 Wing, 212 Group, AHQ WD
18 Jun 42	Sqdn	LG 155, Egypt	243 Wing, 212 Group, AHQ WD
19 Jun 42	Sqdn	LG 75, Sidi Barrani South, Egypt	243 Wing, 212 Group, AHQ WD
20 Jun 42	Sqdn	LG 76, Mischefa, Egypt	243 Wing, 211 Group, AHQ WD
23 Jun 42	Sqdn	LG 07, Mersa Matruh West, Egypt	243 Wing, 212 Group, AHQ WD
24 Jun 42	Sqdn	LG 12, Sidi Haneish North, Egypt	243 Wing, 212 Group, AHQ WD
27 Jun 42	Sqdn	LG 105, El Daba, Egypt	243 Wing, 212 Group, AHQ WD
29 Jun 42	Sqdn	LG 154, near Amriya, Egypt	243 Wing, 211 Group, AHQ WD
24 Jul 42	Sqdn	LG 172, near Burg-el-Arab, Egypt	243 Wing, 211 Group, AHQ WD
28 Jul 42	Sqdn	LG 154, near Amriya, Egypt	243 Wing, 211 Group, AHQ WD
5 Aug 42	Sqdn	LG 219, Kilo 8, Egypt	243 Wing, 211 Group, AHQ WD
21 Aug 42	Sqdn	LG 85, Amriya South, Egypt	243 Wing, 211 Group, AHQ WD
28 Sep 42	Sqdn	LG 172, near Burg-el-Arab, Egypt	243 Wing, 211 Group, AHQ WD
29 Sep 42	Sqdn	LG 85, Amriya South, Egypt	243 Wing, 211 Group, AHQ WD
21 Oct 42	Sqdn	LG 172, near Burg-el-Arab, Egypt	243 Wing, 211 Group, AHQ WD
8 Nov 42	Sqdn	LG 20, Qotafiya I, Egypt	243 Wing, 211 Group, AHQ WD
12 Nov 42	Sqdn	LG 101, near Sidi Haneish, Libya	243 Wing, 212 Group, AHQ WD
13 Nov 42	Detch	LG 125, Libya	243 Wing, 212 Group, AHQ WD
16 Nov 42	Sqdn	LG 101, near Sidi Haneish, Libya	243 Wing, 212 Grpop, AHQ WD
17 Nov 42	Sqdn	LG 164, El Adem, Tobruk, Libya	243 Wing, 212 Group, AHQ WD
24 Nov 42	Sqdn	Martuba No 2, Libya	243 Wing, 212 Group, AHQ WD
23 Jan 43	Sqdn	Misurata West, Libya	243 Wing, 219 Group, AHQ EGYPT
28 Jul 43	Sqdn	Idku, Egypt	243 Wing, 219 Group, AHQ EGYPT
8 Sep 43	Sqdn	Paphos, Cyprus	259 Wing, 219 Group, AHQ LEVANT
9 Nov 43	Sqdn	Idku, Egypt	243 Wing, 219 Group, AHQ EGYPT
13 Nov 43	Detch	St. Jean, Palestine	259 Wing, 219 Group, AHQ LEVANT
19 Nov 43	OpsHQ	Paphos, Cyprus	259 Wing, 219 Group, AHQ LEVANT
10 Jan 44	OpsHQ	Lakatamia, Cyprus	259 Wing, 219 Group, AHQ LEVANT
3 Feb 44	Sqdn	Idku, Egypt	243 Wing, 219 Group, AHQ EGYPT
24 Feb 44	Sqdn	El Gamil, near Port Said, Egypt	243 Wing, 219 Group, AHQ EGYPT
6 May 44	Sqdn	Idku, Egypt	243 Wing, 219 Group, AHQ EGYPT
3 Jul 44	Sqdn	Brindisi, Italy	283 Wing, Balkan Air Force
06 Jul 44	Sqdn	Leverano, Italy	283 Wing, Balkan Air Force
13 Jul 44	Sqdn	Biferno, Termoli, Italy	254 Wing, Balkan Air Force
26 Aug 44	Sqdn	Biferno, Termoli, Italy	283 Wing, Balkan Air Force
23 Jan 45	Sqdn	Biferno, Termoli, Italy	254 Wing, Balkan Air Force
27 Apr 45	Sqdn	Prkos, Zara, Yugoslavia	283 Wing, Balkan Air Force
14 May 45	Sqdn	Biferno, Termoli, Italy	281 Wing, Balkan Air Force
29 Jun 45	Sqdn	Brindisi, Italy	281 Wing, Balkan Air Force
13 Sep 45	Sqdn	Ramat David, Palestine	
Sep 46	Sqdn	Nicosia, Cyprus	
4 Sep 47	Sqdn	Shallufa, Egypt	324 Wing, 205 Group
22 Oct 47	Sqdn	Khartoum, Sudan	324 Wing, 205 Group
27 Mar 48	Detch	Asmara, Eritrea	324 Wing, 205 Group
16 Aug 48	Detch	Mogadishu, Italian Somaliland	324 Wing, 205 Group
	Detch	Hargeisa, British Somaliland	324 Wing, 205 Group
20 Oct 48	Sqdn	Deversoir, Egypt	324 Wing, 205 Group.
4 Mar 49	Detch	Nicosia, Cyprus	324 Wing, 205 Group
21 Apl 49	Sqdn	Deversoir, Egypt	324 Wing, 205 Group
15 Jul 49	Detch	Khartoum, Sudan	324 Wing, 205 Group
05 Aug 49	Sqdn	Deversoir, Egypt	324 Wing, 205 Group
Feb 51	Sqdn	Deversoir, Egypt	Canal Zone Fighter Defence Force.

Disbanded 22 September 1954

22 Jul 55	Sqdn	Ahlhorn, West Germany	RAF Germany, 2ATAF
22 Aug 57	Sqdn	Bruggen, West Germany	RAF Germany, 2ATAF
1 Jul 61	Detch	Sharjah, United Arab Emirates	
23 Jul 61	Sqdn	Bruggen, West Germany	RAF Germany, 2ATAF

Disbanded 31 December 1969

APPENDIX D

The Aircraft

* Denotes written off in an accident
+ Denotes lost to enemy action

Sopwith Pup
Flown by the Seaplane Defence Flight and the Seaplane Defence Squadron.

9744, 9900, 9916, 9929, N6171, N6179, N6203, N6206, N6335, N6345, N6348, N6349, N6368, N6435, N6436, N6437, N6459, N6478

Sopwith Baby

N1031.

Sopwith Camels

B3773, B3774, B3782, B3793, B3794, B3807, B3894, B3909, B3921, B3935, B3936*, B5687, B6202, B6212, B6239, B6240, B6357*, B6358+, B6378, B6390*, B6391*, B6397*, B6399, B6400, B6401, B6407, B6410, B6448*, B7175+, B7186+, B7192+, B7202*, B7215+, B7226, B7228*, B7229*, B7232*, B7233*, B7234+, B7245+, B7252+, B7254*, B7270, B7271+, B7272, B7274+, B7276+ C65+, C73*, C76, C200, D1871+, D3326+, D3331*, D3333*, D3341+, D3342*, D3351*, D3356+, D3358, D3360+, D3364+, D3369+, D3372+, D3378+, D3379, D3380+, D3383, D3397, D3398+, D3399*, D3400, D3407+, D3409+, D3411*, D3412+, D3413, D9490, D9627*, D9628*, D9647, D9648, D9649, D9675, D9677, D9678*, E1406, E4385+, E4397, E4406, E4419, E4421*, F3110, F3114*, F3118, F3120+, F3121, F3122*, F3126*, F3130, F3136, F3138, F3238, F3239*, F3240*, F3944, F3945, F3948+, F3950, F3951*, F3965, F3966, F3967, F5913*, F5966+, F8502, F8504, F8505, F8508, F8511, F8512, N6335*, N6345, N6348+, N6349+, N6363, N6376,

Gloster Gauntlet II

K5285, K5287, K5295, K5301, K5302*, K5306*, K5320, K5322, K5365, K5366, K7806, K7810, K7811, K7812, K7813, K7814, K7837 K7838, K7840*, K7857, K7864, K7879.

Miles Magister

L8057*, L8136*, L8263*

Hawker Hurricane I

L1584, L1600, L1605, L1770, L1771, L1772, L1777, L1780, L1783, L1784, L1785*, L1786, L1787*, L1789, L1790, L1800*, L1808, L1809*, L1810*, L1811*, L1812, L1817+, L1818, L1819, L1829, L1851, L1852, L1854, L1889, L1894, L1914, L1982, L2057, L2060, L2062, L2141, L2142+, L2146+, N2336+, N2344, N2396+, N2401+, N2473, N2476, N2479, N2489, N2490, N2520, N2521, N2536, N2537, N2538+,

N2539+, N2540, N2541+, N2544, N2548, \N2550, N2551, N2590, N2608*, N2620, N2630, N2631, N2645, N2646*, N2649*, N2650+, N2655+, N2661, N2665, N2668, N2708, P2397, P2557, P2558, P2647, P2673, P2721+, P2731, P2763+, P2766+, 2792+, P2802+, P2814, P2817+, P2834+, P2854+, P2954, P3057, P3091, P3092, P3113+, P3145, P3173+, P3200+, P3225, P3267+, P3314, P3348+, P3350, P3354+, P3361+, P3362, P3419+, P3474, P3480, P3522+, P3554, P3585, P3685, P3641, P3670, P3767, P3780+, P3789+, P3979, P5189, P5198, P5202, P6348+, P6349, P6463, P5189, P5198, P5202, P6348+, P6349, P6463, P4086, P4099, P4109*,V6533, V6541, V6544, V6558, V6603, V6609, V6643, V6667+, V6691+, V6697+, V6853, V6866, V6869, V6953, V6991, V6996, V7004, V7006, V7019, V7026, V7104, V7111, V7185, V7208, V7221+, V7224, V7226+, V7227+, V7228, V7287, V7306, V7314, V7403+, V7421, V7432+, V7602+, V7605, V7622*, V7625, V 7664*, V7679, V7725, V7736*, V7778, W3962*, W6667+, W6668, W6669, W9110, W9111, W9114, W9178, W9207, W9260, W9274, W9290, W9291, W9293*, W9309*, W9349, W9350, Z3507+, Z3514, Z4040*, Z4089, Z4095, Z4162, Z4163, Z4203*, Z4205*, Z4223*, Z4225, Z4242, Z4361, Z4366, Z4374, Z4861*, Z6998, Z7003, Z70098, Z7013*, AS987

Hurricane IIb

Z3590, Z5004, Z5005, BE200, BE701, BM966*

Hurricane IIc

BE200, BE336, BE337, BE340+, BE355, BE547, BE553, BE569, BE702, BM907, BM972+, BM981+, BM983, Bn117, BN128+, BN132+, BN133, BN134, BN136+, BN137+, BN139, BN141+, BN159+, BN184, BN186+, BN273+, BN276+, BN285+, BN286, BN290, BN337, BN349, BN354, BN361, BN367, BN368+, BN378+, BN404, BN527+, BN537+, BN539+, BN541, BN562+, BN597+, BN972, BP123, Bp128, BP180+, BP182+, BP189+, BP196+, BP197+, BP219, BP231+, BP237, BP239, BP331+, BP338+, BP341, Bp342+, BP345, BP351, BP354, BP355+, BP357, Bp359, BP401, BP450, BP451+, BP455+, BP460, BP462, BP499+, BP583+, BP599+, BP734, BS354, HL613+, HL628, HL630+, HL634+, HL678, HL680, HL704+, HL720, HL725, HL887, HL889, HL897, HL912, HL929, HL941+, HL970, HL987+, HL991+, HM122, HM131, HM143, HV290*. HV309+, HV340, HV344, HV347, HV349, HV401, HV440, HV444+, HV468, HV478, HV479, HV507, HV510, HV534, HV539, HV543, HV544, HV548, HV551, HV587*, HV609, HV965, HW241, HW408, HW553, HW797, Hw798, HW873, KW805, KW822, KW932*, KW934, KW953, KX830, KX854, KX888, KZ130, KZ487, KZ503, KZ522*, KZ542, KZ561

Supermarine Spitfire V

EP965, JG781, JK277, JK712.

Supermarine Spitfire IX

BS339, BS354, MA256, MH542, MH676, MJ385

North American Mustang III

FB298, FB302, FB303+, FB307, FB308, FB311+, FB313+, FB315+, FB316+, FB318*, FB319, FB322+, FB324+, FB328, FB329, FB331+, FB332, FB333, FB334, FB335+, FB336+, FB337+, FB342+, FB343, HB830, HB853+, HB854+, HB859, HB874, HB875+, HB879*, HB881+, HB888+, HB889, HB892, HB894*, HB895+, HB898, HB899*, HB901+, HB902, HB903+, HB905*, HB915+, HB916, HB919, HB921, HB932+, HB951, HB953,KH421+, KH423+, KH424, KH461+. KH465+, KH513*, KH520, KH534+, KH554+, KH591, KH596, KH598+, KH600* KH606, KH608. KH614+, KH6258, KH633+, KH637+, KH640.

North American Mustang IV

KH671. KH688, KH693+, KH751, KH757, KH780*, KH782+, KH797*, KH803+, KH804+, KH809+, KH*11, KH816+, KH823+, KH826, KH831*, KH840, KH846+, KH859, KH861*, KM101*, KM111*, KM116*, KM214*, KM262*, KM293, KM341, KM348, KM390

North American Harvard

EX814, KF287

Hawker Tempest F.VI

NX129, NX136, NX147, NX151, NX153, NX155, NX175, NX179, NX180*, NX181*, NX183, NX184, NX185, NX186, NX192*, NX193, NX204, NX206, NX207+, NX225, NX227, NX229*, NX230, NX241, NX244, NX248*, NX249*, NX252, NX254*, NX256, NX260.

De Havilland Vampire FB.5

VV554, VV562*, VV566, VV633, VV655*, VV668, VV691, VV694, VX983, VZ116, VZ127*, VZ173*, VZ174, VZ188*, VZ198, VZ214, VZ273, VZ309, VZ310, VZ322, VZ352, WA107, WA188*, WA622, WA624.

De Havilland Vampire FB.9

WG923, WG929, WL560, WL561*, WL562, WL571, WL573, WL574*, WL580*, WL585, WL603, WL605, WX207.

Gloster Meteor T.7

WA622, WA624, WF855, WH113

English Electric Canberra B.2

WH711, WK124.

English Electric Canberra T.4

WH814,WJ870.

English Electric Canberra B(I).6

WT304, WT310*, WT311, WT312, WT313, WT314, WT315*, WT316, WT317, WT318, WT319, WT320, WT321*, WT322*, WT323, WT324*, WT325*, XG554.

English Electric Canberra B.6

XJ249*, XJ257*

APPENDIX E

The First World War

Name	Rank	Date	From	Date	To
Graham R	Sqn Cdr	30.6.17	Seaplanes Dunkirk	20.11.18	233 Sqn Dover, to Command
Fisher P S	Flt Lt	30.6.17	Seaplanes Dunkirk	19.8.174	Sqn RNAS C Flight Cdr
Price G W	Flt Lt	30.6.17	Seaplanes Dunkirk	9.11.17	8 Squadron RNAS
Slatter L H	Flt-Sub Lt	2.7.17	Seaplanes Dunkirk	2.7.18	Pilots Pool, Wissant
Horstmann F G	Flt Lt	15.7.17	Seaplanes Dunkirk	11.5.18	Redcar
Pinscott L C	Flt- Sub-Lt	14.7.17	Seaplanes Dunkirk	28.8.17	Seaplanes Dunkirk
Allen J R	Flt Sub-Lt	6.7.17	Seaplanes Dunkirk	29.10.17	Killingholme Air Station
Duggan P	Flt Sub-Lt	21.8.17	Seaplanes Dunkirk	16.9.17	Admiralty & Seaplanes
Brown C P	Lt	29.8.17	Seaplanes Dunkirk	5.10.18	5 Group
Freeland R B	Lt	4.9.17	9 Squadron		RNAS; Discharged sick
Pinder J W	Lt	4.9.17	9 Squadron	14.12.17	RNAS; to England
Guidott W	Lt	19.9.17	Dover	20.9.17	Dunkirk Seaplanes
Lawson H	Flt Sub-Lt	19.7.17	10 Squadron RNAS	20.9.17	Dunkirk Seaplanes
Brice T G	2 Lt	27.9.17	Dover Aerodrome	21.5.17	To England
Greene J E	Lt	29.10.17	12 Squadron RNAS	14.6.18	To England
Moyle W A	Flt Sub-Lt	29.10.17	12 Squadron RNAS	20.3.18	3 Squadron RNAS
MacKay G C	Lt	2.11.17	12 Squadron RNAS	14.6.18	To England
Paynter J deC	Flt Sub-Lt	2.11.17	9 Squadron RNAS	5.6.18	Died of Wounds
Cooper M L	Flt Sub-Lt	7.11.17	9 Squadron RNAS	17.9.18	HQ 5 Group
Collishaw R	Flt Cdr	24.11.17	England	23.1.18	3 Squadron RNAS
Hay C M	Flt Cdr	27.11.17	Admiralty	14.1.18	1 Wing
Stevens G L E	Flt Lt	8.12.17	Dunkirk	27.12.17	6 Sqn RNAS, England
MacKenzie W J	Flt Sub-Lt	11.12.17	12 Squadron RNAS	27.3.18	9 Squadron RNAS
Goodchild P W	Lt	13.12.17	Eastchurch	16.12.17	Hospital in England
Beasley P E	Flt Lt	10.12.17	1 Squadron RNAS	8.3.18	11 Squadron RNAS
Gray W E	Lt	16.12.17	12 Squadron RNAS	19.10.18	471 Flight, Walmer
Windsor W A	Lt	19.12.17	12 Squadron RNAS	23.5.18	4 ASD Pool
Day M J G	Flt Lt	19.12.17	Isle of Grain	27.2.18	Reported Missing
Smith G D	Flt Sub-Lt	23.12.17	12 Squadron RNAS	11.8.18	4 ASD Pool

1918

Name	Rank	Date	From	Date	To
Hopewell G F C	Flt Sub-Lt	2.1.18	12 Squadron RNAS	17.8.18	471 Flight, Walmer
Beasley E F	Flt Sub-Lt	2.1.18	12 Squadron RNAS	2.5.18	Reported Missing
Hughes N W	Lt	6.1.18	5 Squadron RNAS	27.6.18	To England
Wesley J	WO II	21.1.18	Lee-on-Solent	17.3.19	11 Aircraft Park
Stovin F C	Flt Sub-Lt	29.1.18	12 Squadron RNAS	27.3.18	9 Squadron RNAS
Bell E V	Flt-Sub-Lt	29.1.18	12 Squadron RNAS	27.3.18	9 Squadron RNAS
Meyer C	Lt USN	22.2.18	Aviation Inst Centre	5.3.18	Aviation Inst Centre
Messiter L C	Flt Sub-Lt	24.2.18	12 Squadron RNAS	8.5.18	To hospital
Cole K R	Flt Sub-Lt	7.3.18	12 Squadron RNAS	7.4.18	Missing in Action
Ball R N	Flt Sub-Lt	9.3.18	12 Squadron RNAS	27.3.18	9 Squadron RNAS
Wilkinson E G	Flt Sub-Lt	9.3.18	12 Squadron RNAS	9.5.18	To hospital
Whiteley R I	Flt Sub-Lt	27.3.18	9 Squadron RNAS	9.5.18	Wounded
Haviland W B	Lt USN	29.3.18	US Navy Dunkirk	16.4.18	US Seaplanes, Dunkirk
Ingalls D L	Ens USN	29.3.18	US Navy Dunkirk	20.4.18	US Aerostation, Dunkirk
McLeish K	Ens USN	29.3.18	US Navy Dunkirk	20.4.18	US Aerostation, Dunkirk
Smith E T	Ens USN	29.3.18	US Navy Dunkirk	20.4.18	US Aerostation, Dunkirk
Tayler J A C	Lt	6.4.18	Freiston	7.8.18	Accidentally killed
Cattle F L	Lt	7.4.18	212 Squadron	29.6.18	Killed in a flying accident.
Denny C H	Lt	7.4.18	212 Squadron	15.8.18	Missing in Action
Reid J	Lt	7.4.18	212 Squadron	11.5.18	Missing in Action
Hancock S M N	Lt	9.4.18	Freiston	20.2.19	Demobilised on leave.
Pinder J W	Capt	29.3.18	Isle of Grain	20.8.18	To Air Ministry, app't Grand Fleet
Talbot R A	Lt	25.4.18	Dover	17.2.19	Spycker Camp
Nelson J N	Lt	10.5.18	Dover	12.6.18	Died of Wounds
Evans W G	Lt	10.5.18	Dover	27.6.18	Missing in Action
Jenner P C	Lt	11.5.18	Dover	19.9.18	210 Squadron
Nelson H E R	Lt	11.5.18	Dover	30.9.18	210 Squadron

Name	Rank	Date	From	Date	To
Sims C J	Lt	23.5.18	Dover	21.6.18	Missing in Action
Hall K W J	Lt	26.5.18	Dover	29.6.18	Killed whilst flying
Pemble F P	Lt	26.5.18	Dover	25.9.18	Missing in Action
Sparkes C P	Lt	26.5.18	Dover	19.9.18	210 Squadron
Hewett B A	Lt	12.5.18	Dover	17.3.19	11 Aircraft Park, Ghistelles
Fellows S H	2 Lt	1.5.18	208 Squadron	28.9.18	Missing in Action
Smith H C	Lt	7.6.18	4 ASD	28.9.18	Missing in Action
Rankin W A	Lt	7.6.18	4 ASD	4.10.18	Missing in Action
Upton W G	2 Lt	11.6.18	4 ASD	19.2.19	Crystal Palace for Dispersal
Chick A F	Lt	11.6.18	4 ASD	21.8.18	Missing in Action; POW
Wooding J	Lt	13.6.18	4 ASD	21.8.18	Missing in Action
Hodgson E A	Lt	13.6.18	4 ASD	13.3.19	7 Dispersal Area
Turner A H	Lt	14.6.18	204 Squadron	21.9.19	Crystal Palace for dispersal
Mayne F	Capt	22.6.18	Air Ministry	16.3.19	To Setques reposition pool
Pearce R A	2 Lt	28.6.18	4 ASD Pool	8.10.18	Transferred and struck off strength
Allott E N	2 Lt	26.9.18	4 ASD Pool	17.3.19	11 Aircraft Park, Ghistelles
Holden H E B	2 Lt	7.7.18	4 ASD Pool	25.8.18	Missing in Action
Toy E C	2 Lt	7.7.18	4 ASD Pool	15.7.18	Drowned at sea
Dawson W	Lt	10.7.18	4 ASD Pool	31.7.18	Medical Board. Dover
Wright C V C	2 Lt	17.7.18	4 ASD Pool	12.2.19	233 Squadron, Dover
Swanston J R	Capt	25.7.18	Manston	25.9.18	Missing in Action
Scroggie L C	Lt	5.8.18	4 ASD Pool	14.10.18	Killed in Action
Greene J E	Lt	12.8.18	471 Flight	15.9.18	Wounded, taken off strength
MacKay G C	Lt	12.8.18	471 Flight	25.9.18	Missing in Action
Sorley J C	2 Lt	23.8.18	4 ASD Pool	3.10.18	To US Air Station, Dunkirk
Ingalls D S	Lt USN	9.8.18	US Navy Dunkirk	29.9.18	Missing in Action
Iliff G	2 Lt	24.8.18	4 ASD Pool	17.3.18	11 Aircraft Park, Ghistelles
Hodson G S	Lt	29.8.18	4 ASD Pool	5.9.18	Missing in Action
Francis C E	2 Lt	29.8.18	4 ASD Pool	3.3.19	233 Squadron, Dover
Rosevear A B	2 Lt	1.9.18	4 ASD Pool	17.3.19	11 Aircraft Park, Ghistelles
Garner G C	2 Lt	6.9.18	4 ASD Pool	2.10.18	14 General Hospital, Wimereux
Pearson W G	2 Lt	16.9.18	4 ASD Pool	4.10.18	Missing in Action
Ibison K G	Lt	25.9.18	4 ASD Pool	28.9.18	Missing in Action
Fletcher A	2 Lt	25.9.18	4 ASD Pool	20.12.18	To Hospital, England
Stone J C	2 Lt	27.9.18	4 ASD Pool	28.9.18	Missing in Action
Jenner P C	Lt	27.9.18	210 Squadron	28.2.19	Temporary Attachment, Dover
Taylor A M	2 Lt	28.9.18	4 ASD Pool	17.3.19	11 Aircraft Park, Ghistelles
Radford F W	2 Lt	29.9.18	4 ASD Pool	2.10.18	Qn. Alexandra's Hospital
Herd W H	2 Lt	29.9.18	4 ASD Pool	4.10.18	14 General Hospital, Wimereux
Marchbank J N	2 Lt	29.9.18	4 ASD Pool		
Pownall A H	Lt	5.10.18	4 ASD Pool	14.10.18	Missing in Action
Owen W T	Lt	5.10.18	4 ASD Pool	14.10.18	Missing in Action
McDonald J C J	2 Lt	5.10.18	4 ASD Pool	16.3.19	233 Sqdn, Dover. For repatriation
MacKenzie W J	Lt	8.10.18	471 Flight, Walmer	14.10.18	Missing in Action
McMurty L B	2 Lt	9.10.18	4 ASD Pool	14.10.18	Missing in Action
Allen F L R	2 Lt	9.10.18	4 ASD Pool	14.10.18	Crashed; to Qn Alexandra's Hospital
Thorpe F L R	Lt	9.10.18	4 ASD Pool	25.10.18	To 4 ASD Pool
Marchbank J N	2 Lt	13.10.18	14 Gen. Hospital	5.11.18	Air Ministry
Fenn J F T	Lt	13.10.18	4 ASD Pool	14.10.18	Missing in Action
MacLeish K	Lt USN	13.10.18	US Navy Dunkirk	16.3.19	Setques, Repatriation Pool
Gilbert H H	Lt	14.10.18	4 ASD Pool	16.3.19	233 Sqn. To await repatriation
Webster R N	Lt	14.10.18	4 ASD Pool		
Shaw C	Lt	14.10.18	4 ASD Pool	17.10.18	Qn. Alexandra's Hospital
Whitewell E J	Lt	14.10.18	4 ASD Pool	13.1.18	Crashed; injured to hospital
McLean W S	Lt	14.10.18	4 ASD Pool	16.3.19	Scopwick, 213 Sqn Cadre
Stewart-Burton J P	Lt	14.10.18	4 ASD Pool	17.10.18	Qn. Alexandra's Hospital
Fleming W G	2 Lt	14.10.18	4 ASD Pool		
Coobes L A	2 Lt	17.10.18	4 ASD Pool	16.3.19	Setques, Repatriation Pool
Phelps W S	2 Lt	17.10.18	4 ASD Pool	14.11.18	US Northern Bombing Group
Williams T G	Lt USMC	17.10.18	USN Bombing Group	16.3.19	Setques, Repatriation Pool
Huston E R	Lt	26.10.18	4 ASD Pool	27.2.19	Air Ministry, for repatriation
Sargeant F T	2 Lt	26.10.18	4 ASD Pool	16.3.19	233 Sqn; to await repatriation
MacKay G C	Lt	27.10.18	Sick Leave	17.3.19	11 Aircraft Park, Ghistelles
Tayler A G	Maj	21.11.18			

France, Dunkirk and the Battle of Britain

Name	Rank	Event
Adair H H	Sgt	Killed 6.11.40
Adye	Fg Off	
Ailcock P O P	Plt Off	
Atkinson H D	Flt Lt, DFC	Killed 25.8.40
Atkinson A	Plt Off	Killed 17.10.40
Baker	Plt Off	
Barrow H I R	Sgt	Killed 28.11.40
Beamish	Sgt	
Beguin	Sgt	
Bigood I K	Sgt	Killed
Blackwood G D M	Flt Lt	
Bowen	Plt Off	
Boyd	Sgt	Missing
Bramah H G K	Sub-Lt	
Broughton	Sgt	
Bruce	Sgt	Killed
Buchin M S H C	Plt Off	Killed 15.8.40
Bullerfield S L	Sgt	Killed 11.8.40
Burton	Sgt	
Bushell G D	Sgt	Killed 31.12.40
Carthew G C T	Plt Off	
Chatfield	Plt Off	
Clark H D	Plt Off	
Cooke C A	Sgt	
Cooney	Sgt	
Cormack	Sgt	
Coflam H W	Plt Off	
Croskell M E	Sgt	
Czemin, Count M S	Plt Off	
David W D	Flt Lt	
Davies M P	Sgt	Killed
Denison R W	Fg Off	
Deport R	Flt Sgt	
Dewar J S	Wg Cdr	Killed 12.9.40
Dixon	Sgt	
Downie	Plt Off	POW 21.5.41
Drake B	Fg Off	
Dunscombe R D	Sgt	
Duryasz M	Flg Off	
Edwardes Jones H J	Sqn Ldr	
Fisher	Plt Off	
Gray W N	Fg Off	Missing
Grayson C	Flt Sgt	
Greasley G	Sgt	
Glover	Sgt	
Gould	Fg Off	
Grove H C	Sgt	Killed
Hallam	Flt Sgt	
Hanock A	Sgt	Killed 6.6.44
Howes	Sgt	
Hemingway	Sgt	
Holdaway D	Sgt	
Hutley R R	Plt Off	Killed 29.10.40
Janicki Z	Plt Off	
Jankiewiez J S	Fg Off	
Jeram D N	Sub Lt RN	
Kearsey P J	Plt Off	
Kelsey	Flt Lt	
Kellow R W	Plt Off	
Laricheliére J E P	Plt Off	Killed 16.8.40
Lindsell A M	Plt Off	
Lishman J A	Sgt	Wounded
Llewellyn R T	Sgt	Wounded 15.9.40
Lockhart J	Plt Off	
Lynch	Plt Off	
MacDonald D S	Sqn Ldr	
Marshal	Sgt	
McGregor H D	Sqn Ldr	
Miller	Plt Off	
Moss W J M	Sub Lt RN	
New	Fg Off	
Norris P P	Sgt	
Osmand A I	Plt Off	
Pain	Plt Off	
Phillipart J A L	Plt Off	Killed 25.8.40
Robinson K N G	Fg Off	
Pound P	Plt Off	
Savill	Sgt	
Schou	Plt Off	
Schwind L H	Fg Off	Killed 27.9.40
Sing J E J	Flt Lt, DFC	
Sizer W M	Plt Off, DFC	
Snowden E G	Sgt	
Sporny	Plt Off	
Stevens G	Sgt	
Stone L G E	Plt Off	Killed 28.5.40
Strickland J M	Fg Off	
Stuckey S G	Sgt	Killed 12.8.40
Sumner	Plt Off	
Talman J M	Plt Off, DFC	
Thomson T R	Plt Off	Wounded 28.10.40
Toyne W A	Fg Off	
Valentine A F C	Sgt	Wounded 17.5.40
Wallace T J	Sgt	
Weatherill	Fg Off	
Westlake G H	Plt Off	
Wight R D G	Flt Lt, DFC	Killed 11.8.40
Wilkes G N	Sgt	Killed 12.8.40
Wilson	Sgt	
Winning E G	Fg Off	Missing 28.5.40
Wlosnowalski B	Plt Off	Killed 29.10.40
Wojcicki A	Sgt	Killed 11.9.40

Western Desert, Syria, Cyprus and Egypt

Name	Rank	Event	Name	Rank	Event
Aitken H A	Plt Off		Horne	Flt Sgt	Killed
Anthony R	Fg Off		Houle A U	Fg Off	
Avise J E	Plt Off	Killed 17.10.42	Howard H	Sgt	
Baines R P	Plt Off	POW 18.11.42	Howell	Sgt	
Ballantyne J F C	Sgt	Killed 16.7.42	Humphries	Sgt	
Barnes L E	Plt Off	Killed 31.8.42	Ismay W H	Plt Off	
Baxter R V	Flt Sgt		Jackson	Sgt	POW
Beedham D W	Plt Off		Jackson R	Fg Off	
Bird S V	Flt Lt		Janes C L B	Sgt	Killed
Bolton G S	Sgt	Killed 3.7.42	Jowett T A	W O	
Bootherstone A R	Plt Off		Kettlewell G V W	Sqn Ldr	
Boucher L D M	Plt Off	Wounded 3.7.42	Knapton P W	Fg Off	
Bradley C F	Flt Lt		Lack W	Flt Sgt	Missing
Breheny R J	Sgt		Leach L J	Lt(SAAF)	
Brice E W L	Flg Off		Lee M S	Sgt	Killed 4.3.42
Briggs J L	Fg Off		Lockhart L J	Sqn Ldr	
Brook S G	Flt Sgt	POW 27.10.42	Luxton C	Plt Off	POW 18.11.42
Brookes K G	Sgt		Marshall	Plt Off	
Cameron N	Flt Lt		McAll C T	Sgt	
Campbell D J	Plt Off	POW 13.11.42	McAnn T A	Plt Off	Killed 27.7.42
Campbell	Sgt		McClelland B J	Plt Off	Killed 9.10.42
Cantin C F	Plt Off	Missing 9.10.42	MacDonald D S	Sqn Ldr	
Carrick G	Flt Lt		McGuire P E	Sgt	
Chadwick D F	Plt Off		McKay D J	Flt Sgt	
Chapman	Flt Lt		McKay D R S	Flt Lt	
Chappell S	Fg Off		McKay G R S	Fg Off	
Chatfield R M	Flt Lt		McKay R W	Sgt	
Cochrane J M	Plt Off		McKenzie J	Sgt	
Compton H M	W O		Mitchell F E	W O	
Cooke D E	W O		Moor J W	2Lt(SAAF)	
Crowther	Plt Off	Wounded	Newick J D	Sgt	Killed 27.7.42
Dixon J M	Plt Off		Nightingale A O	Sgt	
Double	Sgt		O'Halloran S M	Flt Lt	
Douthwaite	Fg Off		Oliff J E	Flt Sgt	
Downie	Plt Off	POW 21.5.41	Olver P	Sqn Ldr	
Duncan	Fg Off		Pain	Plt Off	
Du Pasquier	Plt Off	Killed	Phipps C H	Fg Off	
Edmonds	Fg Off	Missing 12.6.42	Pickford S G	W O	
Edwards	Flt Sgt	Missing 22.6.42	Pienaar S W	2Lt(SAAF)	
Etchells F A	Fg Off		Potter F G	Sgt	Missing 1.9.42
Field J T	Flt Sgt RCAF		Price L E	Flt Lt	
Firman D E	Sgt		Pound P	Plt Off	Wounded 15.6.41
Ford K A L	W O		Purchase T E G	Fg Off	
Fry S R	Flt Sgt		Rebstock J R	Flt Sgt	D of Wounds 18.11.42
Furneaux R H	Plt Off		Redhill D R	Plt Off	Killed 4.7.42
Garrood A	Flt Sgt	Killed	Ritchie J D	Sgt	Killed 3.7.42
Garwood R H	Fg Off		Rorvik R E	2Lt(SAAF)	
Geoffrion L P	Fg Off RCAF		Ross A D	Flt Sgt	
Gordon W I	Flt Lt		Rowlands H R	Flt Lt	
Gould	Flt Lt		Ryley R J	Fg Off	
Green N	Flt Lt		Sissons K N R	Plt Off	Wounded
Griffiths R	Flt Sgt	Killed	Smailes A A	Plt Off	
Gwynne W D	Flt Sgt		Smith C D A	Flt Lt	
Halvorsen R	Sgt	Wounded 13.6.42	Sowrey J A	Fg Off	
Hancock A J	Plt Off	Wounded 10.6.42	Steele J W	Sgt	
Hartley P W	Sqn Ldr		Steinberg T G	Fg Off	Killed 17.2.44
Haslam P C	W O	Missing	Stephenson W H	Plt Off	POW 21.10.42
Hay J F	Fg Off		Stevens T A	Flt Lt	
Helm H B	2Lt (SAAF)		Steward F H	Sgt	Killed
Henderson	Plt Off		Stratton W H	Sqn Ldr	
Hoffreins J A	W O	Killed	Stringer E A	Sgt	

Name	Rank	Event	Name	Rank	Event
Sweney W G	Sgt		Watkins J G	W O	
Swinden W W	Fg Off		Westlake G H	Sqn Ldr	
Temlett C B	Flt Lt DFC	Killed 3.6.42	White	Sgt	
Temple-Murray P T	Fg Off		Whiting S R	Sqn Ldr	
Thomlinson W H	Plt Off	Killed 4.6.42	Wilson D	Plt Off	
Thrift D J	Fg Off		Wilson F A W J	Flt Lt	
Turner E B	Flt Lt		Wilson F	Sgt	
Usher D C	Sgt		Wilson G A	Plt Off	
Vair-Turnbull S J	Fg Off		Wilson P P	Plt Off	Missing 13.6.42
Vorster C S	2Lt(SAAF)		Wollaston R F	Fg Off	Killed 1.9.42
Vos C S	Flt Lt		Woodward V C	Sqn Ldr	
Waite G A	Plt Off	POW 13.11.42	Wyatt-Smith	Flt Lt	
Wallace R J	W O	Missing 2.8.42	Young M	Sgt	
Walker P C	Plt Off		Young M H	Sqn Ldr	

The Balkans Air Force

Name	Rank	Event	Name	Rank	Event
Allan G F	Fg Off	Killed 11.12.44	Jones O	Lt(SAAF)	
Anthony R	Fg Off	Killed 30.7.44	Kenyon I D	Lt(SAAF)	
Ashley A G R	Fg Off	Wounded 21.3.45	Laurence R J	Flt Sgt	
Barrett F J	Fg Off		Leach L J	Lt(SAAF)	Killed 9.8.44
Bell D H	Sgt		Lludzius A	Flt Sgt	Killed 23.11.44
Bootherstone A R	Plt Off		MacFarlane A	Sgt	Killed 29.8.44
Borthwick W A	Flt Sgt(RAAF)		MacLellan E H	Flt Sgt	Missing 30.10.44
Brierley L W	Sgt	Killed 10.8.44	Mulcahy-Morgan J A	Flt Lt	Killed 4.1.45
Buchan E P	Sgt	Killed 5.4.45	Nethersole T O	Sgt	
Butterworth W H	Flt Sgt		Payne J	Sgt	Killed
Chappell S	Fg Off	Wounded	Peck D L A	Lt(SAAF)	
Chiazzari B N	Lt(SAAF)		Penson F A E	Fg Off	
Clarkson K M J	W O		Pickford F G	W O	
Cooke D E	Plt Off	Missing 11.7.44	Pienaar S W	Lt(SAAF)	Killed 4.8.44
Darling T K	Fg Off(RAAF)		Postlethwaite G	Flt Sgt	POW
Donnelly P	Fg Off	Missing 2.3.45	Purchase T E G	Fg Off	
Dowling A A	Sgt	Missing 27.9.44	Ralph F A O	Plt Off	
Elliott G P	Flt Lt		Robertson D E	Fg Off(RNZAF)	
Fairbairn J H	Flt Lt	Killed 13.9.44	Robinson I C	W O	
Farley S W	Sgt	Missing	Rorvik R E	Lt(SAAF)	Missing 30.10.44
Firmin D E	Sgt	Killed 7.11.44	Scarff C S	Flt Sgt(RAAF)	
Ford K A L	W O		Smailes A A	Plt Off	POW 27.11.44
Friendly C V	Lt(SAAF)		Smith C D A	Flt Lt	
Gamble F M	Flt Lt (RAAF)		Squire F J	Flt Sgt(RAAF)	
Gardener E	Lt(SAAF)	Missing 10.4.45	Stevenson N	Flt Sgt	Wounded
Garwood R H	Flt Lt		Straker W J P	Flt Lt	
Heard F	W O		Thomson A	W O	Missing 15.2.45
Hearndon A W	Flt Sgt	Missing 26.1.45	Thomson P C	Lt(SAAF)	
Helm H B	Lt(SAAF)		Thomson W	Lt(SAAF)	Killed 24.3.45
Holdsworth G R	Lt(SAAF)		Vaughan-Fowler P E	Sqn Ldr	
Howard H	Flt Sgt		Vorster V	Lt(SAAF)	
Hulse G S	Flt Lt		Vos C S	Sqn Ldr	
Hunt A F W W	Sgt		Watkins J P G	Plt Off	
Iago I R H	W O	Killed 11.3.45	Welch P N	Fg Off	Missing 21.3.45
Johnston P M	W O	Killed 11.3.45	Whiting S R	Sqn Ldr	
			Wilson-North O	Plt Off	

The Middle East 1945-1954

Name	Rank	Name	Rank	Name	Rank
Abel G	Fg Off	Gibson	Sgt	Radford R	Flt Lt
Anders	Flt Lt	Gooding P	Sgt	Ralph F A O	Fg Off
Andrews	Fg Off	Hambly	Fg Off	Raynor	Plt Off
Appelboom K	Flt Lt	Hand	Plt 2	Ridley R	Fg Off
Atkinson F	Sgt	Hankin D A	Plt Off	Rippin	Plt Off
Austin R W G	Flt Lt	Harrison M	Plt Off	Robinson I O	WO
Balfour A E	Sgt	Hart	Plt 4	Roe D J A	Sqn Ldr
Barker T I	Flt Lt	Heald R	Sgt	Rogers G	Fg Off
Barnard J	M Plt	Holman	Flt Lt	Rowe A D	Fg Off
Barrey C J	Flt Lt	Hudgel	Plt Off	Rumble	Flt Sgt
Bast	Flt Lt	Hulse G S	Flt Lt	Schaumburg O H	Fg Off
Bendeux	Fg Off	Hutchinson W T F	Flt Sgt	Searle M O	Fg Off
Biven	Plt Off	Jennings J	Plt Off	Sharpe J B	Plt Off
Blatch J	Fg Off	Johnson R E	Flt Lt	Sharrett G	Flt Lt
Bowley	Fg Off	Jolliffe	Fg Off	Simmons J S	Fg Off
Brannon	WO	Kelley P J	Sqn Ldr	Sincock H H	Plt Off
Brigham G C L	Flt Lt	Kilbansky M	Sgt	Smith A G	Fg Off
Brown D	WO	King W	Sgt	Sollitt S	WO
Buist	Fg Off	Kitley A J H	Sqn Ldr	Southon	Flt Lt
Bunyan	Fg Off	Knight S G	Fg Off	Sparks E	Sgt
Butterworth W H	Flt Sgt	Leach	Plt Off	Stares M J	Plt Off
Carter	Sgt	Leeson E	WO	Straker W J P	Flt Lt
Castagnola	Flt Lt	Leyshon	Sgt	Strobel	Plt 2
Chiswick	Sgt	Luckas J R A	Fg Off	Stuart J	Sgt
Clarke	Flt Sgt	Lunn L G	Flt Lt	Swann	Sgt
Clarkson K J	WO	MacGregor E M	Flt Lt	Swift	Fg Off
Claxton J C T	Sgt	Mackinson	Plt Off	Tatlersfield D	Plt Off
Colebeck R	Flt Lt	Maddox	Flt Lt	Taylor E M	Sgt
Colebrook D C	Sqn Ldr	Mandeville	Flt Lt	Taylor	Plt Off
Cooper	Flt Sgt	Marshal H	Sgt	Thirwell J D	Flt Lt
Coutts	Plt Off	Marshal	Plt Off	Tripp G	Sgt
Crighton	Sgt	Martin H T	Sgt	Tuck	WO
Curtiss C F A	Fg Off	May	Flt Sgt	Twigg A	Fg Off
Dabrowski	Plt 2	McDonald	Sgt	Vaughan-Fowler P E	Sqn Ldr
Davies M P	Flt Lt	Milligan	Plt Off	Waddington R G	Flt Lt
Day	Sgt	Mollan P F	Fg Off	Walker E	Fg Off
Deakin	Fg Off	Monkman W M	Flt Sgt	Walker J F	Flt Sgt
Deane	Sgt	Mott G	Fg Off	Wells M C	Sqn Ldr
Dennis	Flt Lt	Munford	Plt Off	West D R	Flt Lt
Douglas-Reid H E A	Flt Lt	Nash R S	Sqn Ldr	Willdey R C	Fg Off
Draper A	Sgt	Ormiston T M	Flt Lt	Williams	WO
Etheridge	Plt Off	Palmer F P	Flt Sgt	Williamson J I	Sgt
Ewing	Plt 2	Parish S C	Fg Off	Wilson J F	Fg Off
Finn D M	Sqn Ldr	Penson F A E	Fg Off	Wilson J G	Flt Lt
Ford K A L	Fg Off	Perkins	WO	Wilson-North O	Fg Off
Franklin	Plt Off	Poolman P C N	Flt Lt	Wittridge	Fg Off
Gardiner D A	Sgt	Powell B H V T	Plt Off	Wragg	Plt 3
Gatward	Fg Off	Purchase T E G	Flt Lt	Zagroba	Plt 2

Royal Air Force, Germany

Name	Rank	Name	Rank	Name	Rank
Abraham J E	Fg Off	Court A R	Fg Off	Hargreaves N	Fg Off
Ackersley S T	Fg Off	Court D J	Fg Off	Harrington R J	Plt Off, AFM
Alban G D	M N	Cowie S	Plt Off	Harris D W J	Fg Off
Anderson B M	Fg Off	Cox R T	Fg Off	Harris D W J	Flt Lt
Anderson J P	Fg Off	Cox S R	Fg Off	Harrison A J	Fg Off
Arscott R H	Wg Cdr	Craigie S A	Sqn Ldr, DFC	Harrison W A S	Sqn Ldr, MBE
Ashover D	Flt Lt	Cringle K	Flt Lt	Hatch L C	MN
Atkinson J C	Flt Lt	Crossley P D	Flt Lt	Hayward T	Fg Off
Austen	Plt Off	Cunningham M J	Plt Off	Hellyer C	Fg Off
Banfield M	Sqn Ldr	Dalziel C T	Sqn Ldr	Hill	MN
Banks W	Flt Lt, DFC	Darby K	Flt Lt	Hill I	Fg Off
Barnes S A	Fg Off	Darwin R B	Flt Lt	Hill W W	Fg Off
Barratt S G	Flt Lt	Davey A J	Flt Lt	Hitchen L S	Fg Off
Bayley P T	Wg Cdr	Davies C	MN	Hole P K	Plt Off
Beckingham R L	Flt Sgt	De Belle F A	Flt Lt	Holmes R M	Fg Off
Bedford R	Fg Off	Derbyshire E G	Fg Off	Hood	Flt Lt
Beggs B	Fg Off	Dineen M	Fg Off	Houghton A W	Fg Off
Benson T E	Wg Cdr	Dingle D	Flt Lt	Howarth P D	Plt Off
Blackburn G	Fg Off	Dodds P	Fg Off	Howell H T	Flt Lt
Bold G	Sqn Ldr	Dodson H J	Wg Cdr	Hughes J G	Plt Off
Boreham P M	Fg Off	Downes N J	Plt Off	Hughesden A	Flt Lt
Bosworth J	Fg Off	Draper A	Fg Off	Hulland J	Fg Off
Boyle E J	Fg Off	Draper A R	Fg Off	Hutchinson A S	Fg Off
Bridger D	Fg Off	DuFeu D F	Flt Lt	Huxley B	Sqn Ldr
Bridgstock A D	Plt Off	Dyer B H	Flt Lt	Huxley B	Sqn Ldr
Briggs F E	Plt Off	Dyer G L S	Fg Off	Jagger G A	Flt Sgt
Briscoe	Plt Off	Eagle J M	Lt RN	Jenkyn R A	Fg Off
Brown D C	Fg Off	Edge P M	Fg Off	Johnson D A J	Flt Lt
Brown E	MN	Ellis	MN	Johnston R A	Plt Off
Brown M G	Fg Off	Elton	Flt Sgt	Joiner C	Fg Off
Browne	Sgt	Everest K	Fg Off	Joiner K G	Flt Lt
Brownlow J	Flt Lt	Farmer M	Fg Off	Jones G C	Fg Off
Browse C R	Fg Off	Fewtrell C G	Fg Off	Jones G S	Flt Lt
Burke E S R	Fg Off	Filling W H	Flt Sgt	Jones K C	Flt Lt
Butterworth	Plt Off	Fillingham S	Fg Off	Jones P A R	Flt Lt
Cairns M	Flt Lt	Fisher B N M S	Fg Off	Joy R M	Fg Off
Callaghan J F	Fg Off	Fitzpatrick A G	Fg Off	Kaye D G	Fg Off
Campbell I R	Wg Cdr, DFC	Ford D L	Fg Off	Keaty J	Flt Lt
Carter R M	Fg Off	Ford J	Flt Lt	Kelley	M N
Carter R N	Fg Off	Foster A	Fg Off	King C W	Fg Off
Chalk I K	Fg Off	Frankland M R	Plt Off	Kirk J S	Fg Off
Chalkey K B	Fg Off	Fraser N N	Fg Off	Knight B C	Sqn Ldr
Chandler M R T	Wg Cdr	Gabriel D	Fg Off	La Touche T	Sqn Ldr
Chappell	Plt Off	Gale R C	Fg Off	Lane P	Flt Lt
Chessall M P	Fg Off	Galletti I	Fg Off	Lane P D	Flt Lt
Clappland F	Fg Off	Gardner G	Fg Off	Latcham P E	Fg Off
Clark D R	Fg Off	Gevaux W G	Flt Lt	Lear R W M	Fg Off
Clarke C E	Fg Off	Gifford G A	Fg Off	Leavey D	Fg Off
Clarke H W R	Flt Lt	Goodman B	Fg Off	LeComu C	Plt Off
Clayton-Jones G	Fg Off	Gordon W L	Fg Off	Lee J E	Flt Lt
Close J A	Fg Off	Gowing A J	Fg Off	Leefar B	Fg Off
Collins D	Flt Lt	Grainger J	Fg Off	Leeson F M	Fg Off
Compton C J	Fg Off	Green R	Fg Off	Leggett	Plt Off
Conway S D	Plt Off	Green W J C	Flt Lt, DFC	LeMarquand P M	Fg Off
Cook B M	Flt Lt	Greenaway P J	Fg Off	Levy M H	Sqn Ldr
Cooper	Sgt	Greenwood A N	Flt Lt	Lewis V B	Flt Sgt
Corduroy F G	Flt Lt	Greenwood A W	Flt Lt	Leyland R H	Flt Lt
Cornelius S J	Fg Off	Grumbridge G Q	Plt Off	Love J W	Flt Lt
Cotterill P	Flt Lt	Handforth P	Fg Off	Lowery W S	Fg Off
Coughlan D	Fg Off	Hanson J A	Fg Off	Lowry J	Fg Off

Name	Rank	Name	Rank	Name	Rank
Lyam D A	Fg Off	Polgreen R L T	Flt Lt	Trussler D	Fg Off
Macadam P A	Flt Lt	Povey K	Flt Lt	Turner E C	Sqn Ldr
Mair G H	Flt Sgt	Povey K C	Flt Lt	Turner E C	Sqn Ldr
Major D R	Fg Off	Pratt S J	Fg Off	Tustian D	Flt Lt
Manley T D W	Flt Lt	Preston	Plt Off	Twelftree J	Fg Off
Margreaves N	Fg Off	Price R	Fg Off	Twelvetree J C	Fg Off
Marlow R B	Fg Off	Pritchard A	Fg Off	Underdown P	Flt Lt
Matcham G M	Flt Lt	Rae W McC	Plt Off	Wade R A	Fg Off
McCarthy D J	Flt Lt	Rea N P C	Flt Lt	Walker G B	Flt Lt
McDonald J D	Fg Off	Redden S S K	Flt Sgt	Wallington W P	Flt Lt
McIntyre	Flt Lt	Richards K D	Fg Off	Walmsley M P J	Flt Lt
McLuggage W	Fg Off	Rivett F L	Fg Off	Warren R J	Fg Off
McNaughton J M	Fg Off	Robbie P J	Flt Lt	Webber F	Flt Lt
Merritt C	Fg Off	Robertshaw K	Flt Lt	Weir D M	Fg Off
Mibue B	Fg Off	Rogan	Fg Off	Wells A	Flt Lt
Michael C	Fg Off	Russell B E	Fg Off	West T A	Flt Lt
Miles J F	Fg Off	Schlidinger Z C	Flt Lt	Westbrooke L	Flt Lt
Milligan J	Fg Off	Scowen J	Flt Lt	Westcott D A	Flt Lt
Mills B W	Fg Off	Sharman R R	Flt Lt	Westwood C	Flt Lt
Milsom R J	Fg Off	Sheils	Sgt	Wheatley T M K	Fg Off
Mitchell J	Flt Lt	Sheridan K P	Fg Off	Whitby M S	Fg Off
Monkhouse K E J	Flt Lt	Sims A E	Flt Lt	Whitehead J	Fg Off
Moore	Fg Off	Slater S	Wg Cdr, DSO, OBE, DFC	Whitsun-Jones D D	Flt Lt
Mullan J P	Fg Off			Whittingham M F	Fg Off
Naidoo	Fg Off	Smith	Flt Lt	Wicks	MN
Nel L	Fg Off	Smith R J	Flt Lt	Wightman V	Fg Off
Newman A	Fg Off	Spackman D A	Sqn Ldr	Wilkes A	Fg Off
Newton G	Flt Lt	Spain A J E	Fg Off	Wilkinson G W	Fg Off
Nicholson E H	Flt Lt	Spear N J	Fg Off	Williams P A D	Fg Off
Nickson V J	Sqn Ldr	Sprent C	Sqn Ldr	Williams R J	Flt Lt
Nixon F	Flt Lt	Stannard E	Fg Off	Williamson H B	Flt Lt
Nixon F B	Fg Off	Steam	Flt Sgt	Willings K	Plt Off
Noad M A	Fg Off	Steel A J	Fg Off	Willis G	Flt Lt
Orr N W	Sqn Ldr	Steib P F	Sqn Ldr, DFC	Wilson	Plt Off
Parkinson D	Fg Off	Stephenson G G	Flt Lt	Wilson A J	Plt Off
Parkinson D	Flt Lt	Stoat B E	Flt Lt	Wilson K J	Flt Lt
Parratt D	Flt Lt	Stroud A	Sqn Ldr	Wilson K J	Sqn Ldr
Passfield R F	Flt Lt	Swalwell L C	Sqn Ldr	Wilson M H	Fg Off
Pearson T A	Fg Off	Syme H	Plt Off	Wilvox N H	Fg Off
Peaty B	Fg Off	Thomas C P	Fg Off	Woodacre R W	Fg Off
Pedder I M	Sqn Ldr	Thomas M	Plt Off	Woods B A	Flt Lt
Pegg J D	Fg Off	Thomas R	Fg Off	Woodward R	Fg Off
Pendleton G	Fg Off	Thompson G C	Plt Off	Woodward R C	Fg Off
Pendleton G	Plt Off	Thurnell D C	Fg Off	Woolnough J H	Plt Off
Piddleton M D	Flt Lt	Tilsley E C	Flt Lt	Wotherspoon A S	Fg Off
Pipe G K	Fg Off	Timbers M D	Plt Off	Wright J	Fg Off
Pitcher P C	Plt Off	Todd E	Fg Off	Yeo P	Fg Off
Pittard H	Plt Off	Tomkin R C	Fg Off	Young A W	Flt Lt
Plumb F	Flt Lt	Travers P	Flt Lt	Young	Sgt

APPENDIX F

As mentioned in Chapter Seven, the local Cypriot press carried a lengthy article on the doings of No.213 Squadron as follows:

RAF in Cyprus

One of the many anomalies of the censorship in Cyprus is that until to-day it has not been permitted to reveal that the RAF were based on this island, and that Hurricanes now regularly patrol our coasts and the approaches. While this ban existed it was not even possible to pay our tribute to one of the finest groups of men that ever came to Cyprus, men who have already established themselves with the island people, and whose keenness and modernity give a confidence in the ultimate victory over Nazi tyranny.

The roaring of the Hurricanes over Cyprus has been a common but very heartening sound to the people of this island for some weeks. They have in addition drawn first blood on such enemy machines that dared to approach these shores. In their own modest and unassuming way these men of the RAF will jocularly dismiss their achievements, but that does not mean that the people of Cyprus will not insist upon showing their gratitude and admiration for this most direct and continuous arm of Britain's offensive against the enemy. It needed at least a year of war in Britain for that revolution in war technique which placed the RAF in the forefront of our weapons of the offensive. Mr. Churchill may have coined that brilliant phrase about so many being indebted to the so few, but the war minds of Britain have now realised that the slogan of the future is that victory will be won by the very many in the skies. This has become an air war. Germany's first striking victories in the west were achieved only by superiority in the air. Since those early days of the war, it is not too much to say that Germany no longer has superiority in the air. The Luftwaffe has been held. It is now in the process of being soundly beaten. That is why in these days of great battles on the eastern front, it is the German Army that has been forced to show its powers, and the German Army still remains a mighty and most effective machine of Nazi aggression.

The victory of the RAF over the Luftwaffe is now being manifested daily. It is now accepted, probably even by the shrewd ones in Germany, that Britain's best chance of ultimate victory in this great war lies in the growing conquest of the skies by the RAF Germany may well claim to be the masters of European earth, but they have never controlled the seas and they have lost the mastery of the air. This achievement in the skies over Europe has been due to these young Englishmen, to young men from the far Dominions, with their vast sky horizons where flyers seem naturally born, and also to those valiant Allies Poles, Czechs, Free French, Belgians and many others. It is a new breed of fighting men that this war has produced, and it is good to have some of them here in Cyprus with the latest of their deadly and all conquering machines. Let us realise that in the great victory parade which will take place after this war has been won, the Army and the Navy, as they march past will receive great cheers for their magnificent achievements but the loudest cheers of all will be for those men of the RAF, the men who fought off the enemy at the time of Britain's greatest danger and who eventually carried the war deep into the enemy's country and brought him to his knees. We salute the men of the RAF now in Cyprus and we wish them the best of luck and always "a happy landing".

Nursed like Cars

Down they came gently, gradually onto the tarmac, each pilot nursing his machine as if it were a "Baby Austin". The ground-crews ran forward to meet the planes as they came to rest in their particular corners. Mechanics were ready to adjust myriads of screws and vital parts of the engines, and refill depleted tanks. The pilots climbed out and we were introduced to the mysteries of the cockpit, shown the baffling array of controls, clocks and gadgets. "How do you remember what to do with them all at the right time ?" someone asked.........How indeed ?

The men who build the Hurricanes leave nothing to chance. Each machine has every modern aeronautical device possible to help the pilot in his fight with enemy bombers. A part - and a very vital part - of the countless victories scored by Britain's fighters have been won in the workshops where the best that science and skill can produce is embodied in the construction of our aircraft.

Months before the Battle of Britain began I watched British aircraft workers building some of these fighter planes at a giant factory in the Midlands. After seeing them put through their paces over a Cyprus aerodrome I realise what a debt we also owe to the skill and intensity of those thousands of British workmen - and women - who have toiled ceaselessly in the race to establish air parity with the enemy.

Laughing before Battle

Back in the cosy dug-out we chatted about fighter tactics. I learned something of the plan which this famous fighter squadron has devised to keep the enemy bombers away from military objectives in Cyprus. It sounded pretty good to me. The walls of the dug-out are adorned with clever drawings, a mixture of Heath Robinson and Tom Webster, the funniest being a study of what happens to the fighter pilot on the morning after a night out in Cyprus.... All drawn by an unassuming young man with a strip of ribbon across his tunic - a memory of battles won in the sky.

These pilots have to make their own fun. They have to endure long hours of patient waiting, waiting which may end in an air battle in which every nerve must be strained to breaking pitch, every thought working in perfect unison with the speed at which his plane hurtles through the clouds.

But in the dug-out they relax and laugh over the pencilled humour of their comrade. All of which reminded me of a conversation six years ago on an outward bound New Zealand steamer with a young Dominion airman who had just completed his training at a famous Yorkshire RAF station. I asked him what had struck him most about his fellow airmen in the RAF Without hesitation he replied "Their astonishing sense of humour and high spirits...."

Well after two years of war, that astonishing sense of humour is still unbreakable. Round the corner, in the Hornets Nest, exclusive inn of this Hurricane squadron, I chatted with the breezy Scottish-born squadron leader who looks forward to the day when he sees the Kyles of Bute and the incomparable course at Gleneagles again; swapped yarns with a young pilot officer who will surely get Late Night blues when he returns to his office in Fleet Street after his air adventures, and tried to get a "story" out of two D.F.C. pilots in the squadron.

But, although they still remember what, to them, were the glorious days of the Battle of Britain, the days when they sent the remnants of the Luftwaffe staggering back to France, dripping with wounds, routed and defeated, the modest young men refused to "shoot a line". Theirs is a story in which the human element may never be told until the last Hurricane dips a final salute to Cyprus, an island at peace, until Cypriots drink a victory toast to the men of the Fighter Command. Then the klaxon blew reminding me forcibly of the shrill whistle of the 7 am buzzer in a Yorkshire mill-town, and I had to throw myself violently against the wall to avoid four pairs of limbs in a spontaneous dive towards the tiny doorway. I ducked to avoid contact with the roof, reached the surface and was just in time to, see the four young fighter pilots racing across the tarmac to their planes, whose propellers were already turning.

90 Seconds to the Sky

The deep throated drone of four Hurricane engines drowned the klaxon still wailing its warning to the aerodrome. Dozens of eyes scanned the skyline for enemy planes. Others watched the fighter pilots climb nimbly into their snug cockpits, watched the Hurricanes glide down the runway, a glide which developed into a hurtling race, until all four machines rose gracefully into the sky, each selecting its own course.

I glanced at the seconds' hand of my watch. The whole movement had taken less than 90 seconds. From the moment the klaxon blew until the fighters were soaring into the sky, well above our heads, something less than two minutes had elapsed. "Not bad going," remarked an old hand at my elbow, "although the take-off was rather bumpy."

To the layman's eye it had seemed a faultless take-off, one which would have satisfied the most exacting of Hollywood's stunt cameramen.

But the airmen-graduates of the Battle of Britain, men who have flown in a hundred dog-fights over the hopfields of Kent, the rolling downs of Dorset and the sluggish waters of the Thames Estuary, men whose trained eyes can spot the smallest fault, are satisfied only with perfection. Theirs is a life which demands no mistakes.

Still there was no sign of an enemy bombing fleet. It's a long time since we saw one in the daylight sky over Cyprus and we were not to see one that day. Through the courtesy of the O.C. RAF, Cyprus, island journalists were permitted to see a "Hurricane exhibition", staged especially for their benefit, a show rivalling any put up by Cobham's famous air circus in the days when aeroplanes were still regarded as friendly and not as the deadliest weapon of modern warfare.

Thrilling Dives

Fascinated, we watched the Hurricanes circle overhead the airfield, then held our breath as the pilots put them into a plunging power-dive pulling out only a few feet over our heads. Once it seemed certain that the leading fighter would hit the tops of the tent poles, streaking through the air at well over 300 m.p.h. Once, as another fighter swerved and twisted six thousand feet above us, finally plunging headlong towards the spot where we were standing, we felt for a nasty moment that we might have been mistaken for "military objectives... "

A man who had never seen a Hurricane fighter in his life before, certainly one diving straight towards him with screaming exhaust, flung himself on the ground. In a whirl of sand and dust the Hurricane swept over us, 30 feet from the ground and completed a perfect spiral run over the 'drome.

I realised what it must be like when our marauding daylight fighters visit enemy occupied bases in France Holland, Sicily and North Africa......

And so the show went on. We were treated to every trick of the fighter pilot, all faultlessly executed. In about ten minutes the Hurricane probably flew a distance further than from Cape Andreas to Paphos and back again, covering the distance at speeds six times as fast as Britain's fastest express train and using enough petrol to last a 10 h.p. car for months......

Watching the fighters swoop low preparatory to landing I wondered who it was who ever accused pilots of "shooting a line". The tallest story of aerial acrobatics fails to exaggerate the dizzy feats accomplished by these airmen. And then one thinks how paradoxically a Hurricane plane is a thing alive with beauty in the sky, yet on the ground, with its blunt nose and squat lines almost ugly and certainly less inspiring."

APPENDIX G

Copy of a "Blood Chit" carried by aircrew in the Western Desert, 1941/42.

الى كل عربى كريم

السلام عليكم ورحمة الله وبركاته وبعد، فحامل هذا الكتاب ضابط بالجيش البريطانى وهو صديق وفىٌ لكافة الشعوب العربية فنرجو أن تعاملوه بالعطف والاكرام.

وأن تحافظوا على حياته من كل طارىء. ونأمل عند الاضطرار أن تقدموا له ما يحتاج اليه من طعام وشراب.

وأن ترشدوه الى أقرب معسكر بريطانى.

وسنكافئكم مالياً بسخاء على ما تسدونه اليه من خدمات.

والسلام عليكم ورحمة الله وبركاته

القيادة البريطانية العامة فى الشرق

To All Arab Peoples — Greetings and Peace be upon you. The bearer of this letter is an Officer of the British Government and a friend of all Arabs. Treat him well, guard him from harm, give him food and drink, help him to return to the nearest British soldiers and you will be rewarded. Peace and the Mercy of God upon you.

The British High Command in the East.

Useful Words.

English	Arabic	English	Arabic
English.	Ingleezi.		
English Flying Officer.	Za-bit Ingleezi Tye-yar.	Water.	Moya.
Friend.	Sa-hib, Sa-deek.	Food.	A'-kl.

Take me to the English and you will be rewarded.
Hud-nee eind el Ingleez va ta-hud mu-ka-fa.

2672/PMEB/2,000-2/42.

Author's Note

In 1960, I was serving as a pilot, on a short service commission, with 213 Squadron at Bruggen in West Germany. Having enjoyed only three weeks basic training before starting flying training, there was very little I knew about the Royal Air Force other than how to fly an aeroplane. In the circumstances, the CO, Wing Commander P T Bayley, solved the problem of finding a Secondary Duty that he thought I might be able to carry out by giving me the task of writing the Squadron history; presumably he had seen from my records that I had read Politics and Modern History at university. I am only sorry that he is not still alive to see that his order was finally carried out; the Dedication recognises his initiative in the production of this book.

The first attempt at writing the Squadron's history was completed in 1964, and the manuscript was sent off to Bruggen; however difficulties in finding a publisher, and then the disbandment of the Squadron in 1969, meant that this first effort was lost. In 1996, having found the rough drafts of that first effort, together with the original Foreword written by Air Vice-Marshal R Graham, I decided to finish the task I had been given in 1960. The conditions for writing a comprehensive account of the life and times of the Squadron had greatly improved as, in the intervening years, the embargo on public access to the Squadron's Operation Record Books and combat reports had been lifted, and a considerable number of secondary sources detailing the crucial air battles in which the squadron fought had come into being.

No history book is the work of only one person, and this is particularly true of the history of a fighter squadron of the Royal Air Force. The pilots who fought the battles and flew the sorties were then required to make out their combat reports, and the Squadron Intelligence Officer wrote up the Operations Record Book which detailed, among other things, the *raison d'être* of a squadron, its performance in the air. So it is that the ORB and the combat reports form the very basis of this book. In the nineteen-sixties, I had the pleasure of talking to, or corresponding with, not only Ronnie Graham but also a number of the pilots who had flown in the Second World War, all of whom helped to fill out the somewhat bald official accounts of what had happened. The pilots who thus contributed to the story for a third time were J Logan Briggs, Sir Humphrey Edwardes Jones, Bert Houle, G R S MacKay, Jackie Sing, Wilf Sizer, Tigger Smith, John Sowrey and George Westlake. When contacted in 1996/7, Bert Houle, Wilf Sizer, John Sowery and George Westlake once again gave of their time and irreplaceable experience to help re-create the Squadron's life and times. In 1996/97 the contacts widened and Ken Clarkson, Mike Croskell, Roy Garwood, Owen Jones, Reg Llewellyn, Peter Olver, Stan Pickford, Leslie Robins, Tony Smailes, Geoffrey Stevens, Bill Straker, Denis Usher and Spencer Whiting, all of whom served with the Squadron during the Second World War provided details which cannot be found in the official sources. My thanks also go to Arthur Henry, Ted Smith and Jack Walton for providing some insights into the life of the groundcrews who kept the aircraft flying. For the period after the war Dick Arscott, Tom Benson, John Brownlow, John Jennings, Stan Slater, Gordon Tripp and Ken Wilson all added to the story from their own experience.

My belief that I could write reasonably correct prose was severely dented when my brother-in-law, John Gibson, offered to look the text over; for the substantial improvements which resulted I thank him unreservedly. I lay claim only to any errors which have resulted from additions I have made.

The final step in the journey that led to the publishing of the history was my fortuitous meeting with Michael Rice of Air-Britain, and the introduction he arranged for me to Jim Halley and Ray Sturtivant. Their experience, knowledge and helpfulness were all more than one could ever expect; the details of the Squadron's Camels all come from Ray's definitive book *The Camel File*.

A good story is helped immeasurably by good pictures. My thanks go to all those who generously entrusted their precious photographs to me for copying - thanks to my brother-in-law again - and particularly to Don Neate who conjured up from his many contacts over eighty photographs of the Squadron, and its predecessor units, from the First World War. My thanks also to Andy Thomas and to Tony Stevens, of the Air Historical Branch, who filled crucial holes in the pictorial record. Without maps, place names are almost meaningless, and for the excellent maps scattered through the book I give my warmest thanks to our son Ian who created them from the flimsiest outlines that I was able to produce. For the lists of the Squadron's aircrew which appear in the appendices, I thank my wife Joyce who, more than thirty years ago in our flat in the Netherlands, combed through the ORB and copied out, in an incredibly neat hand, the names of those who in the most fundamental sense wrote the Squadron's history.

Frank Leeson
Tonbridge
December 1997

A photograph of a painting by Cpl Frank Wright a Squadron engine fitter, depicting the incident when WO Johnnie Watkins struck a telephone pole while attacking a train, losing part of his port wing and tailplane.

SCRAPBOOK

Air Marshal Sir Leonard Slatter, KBE, CB, OBE, DSC and Bar, DFC.
(Air Historical Branch, Ministry of Defence)

Capt W J MacKenzie with his Sopwith Camel "Black Prince".

Three Squadron pilots standing in front of one of the Squadron's black Camels, "Black Cat".

Capt W J Mackenzie seated in his Camel with 2nd Lt F T Sargeant and 2nd Lt H E B Holden, winter 1918.

Lt C J Sims seated in the cockpit of his Sopwith Camel. Lt Sims joined the Squadron on 23 May 1918. (N Franks)

Major A G Taylor, Squadron Commander from the Armistice until disbandment in December 1919.

The Hornet, worn as an unofficial addition to their uniforms by the pilots of the Squadron, 1941. (Imperial War Museum)

Flt Sgt "Lofty" Horn, killed at Idku, April 1941.

Plt Off G R S MacKay spruces up in the desert.

Fg Off C D A "Tigger" Smith, who served two tours of duty with the Squadron.

Pilots at readiness Egypt 1942. From left to right: Flt Sgt "Lofty" Horn, killed March 1942, Plt Off Don Redhill, killed July 1942, Plt Off A J Hancock, shot down and wounded June 1942, awarded the DFC, killed D-Day 1944, Fg Off G H Westlake, Plt Off G R S MacKay and Plt Off Bill Ismay, killed El Adem, May 1942.

Flt Lt M D "Gus" Davies with a war time trophy.

Plt Off J E "Mike" Avise, an American pilot who served with the RAF.

Squadron personnel: Sqn Ldr D C Colebrook centre, Mustang IVs in the background, Nicosia, Cyprus, 1947.

Squadron personnel with newly-acquired Hawker Tempest F.VI. Nicosia, Cyprus, 1947.

Tempest F.6 NX192 running-up.

Squadron armourers, Khartoum, Sudan, May 1948. (Harold Stevenson)

Tempest F.VIs lined up at Nicosia in 1947.

Tempest FB.6 NX249 AK-Q at Khartoum.

Pilot 3 Harry Wragg's Vampire FB.5 after forcelanding on a road near El Arish, Egypt, 21 February 1950. (Gordon Tripp)

Squadron formation fly-past, Vampire FB.5s, Egypt, February 1950.

Turn around and re-fueling, Deversoir, Egypt.

Tempest FB.6 NX183 at Deversoir.

Vampire FB.9 with bombs, Deversoir.

Canberra B(I).6 WT312 with squadron bars on nose.

Air Vice-Marshal R Graham, standing left with Air Vice-Marshal Sir R Saundby and Air Marshal A T Harris right.
(Air Historical Branch, Ministry of Defence)

INDEX

Abassia, Egypt, 100
Abbeville, France, 41, 53
Abdiel, HMS, 84
Abdullah, King, 173
Abel, Flg Off G, 165, 171, 205
Aboukir, Egypt, 89
Abraham, Flt Lt J E, 187, 206
Abu Sueir, 75, 77, 78, 81, 82, 88, 174, 196
Abu Sultan, Egypt, 170
Achilles, LtzS, 28
Ackersley, Flg Off S T, 206
Acklington, Northumberland, 52
Aclene, Somaliland, 164
Acroma, Libya, 94, 95, 96
Adair, Sgt H H, 70, 202
Adams, Cpl, 158
Adem, El, Libya, 80, 93, 95, 96, 171, 172, 175, 182, 183, 187, 192, 197, 216
Aden, 78, 166, 182, 184
Adye, Flg Off, 202
Agedabia, Libya, 89
Agheila, El, Libya, 89, 91
Agordat, Eritrea, 164
Ahlhorn, Germany, 176, 177, 178, 179, 180, 182, 189, 197
Aitken, Fg Off H A, 93, 100, 103, 111, 112, 203
Aitken, AVM, 193
Akrotiri, Cyprus, 181
Alam Halfa, Egypt, 99, 106, 110
Alamein, El, Egypt, 90, 96, 98, 99, 100, 101, 102, 103, 106, 109, 110, 111, 112, 194
Albacore, Fairey, 171
Alban, M/Nav G D, 206
Albatros aircraft, 14, 15, 21, 24, 26
Alcombe, Kent, 57
Aldergrove, N Ireland, 37
Aldington, Kent, 54
Aleppo, Syria, 83, 84
Alexander, General Sir Harold, 106
Alexandria, Egypt, 80, 86, 87, 88, 89, 91, 92, 93, 102, 104
Allan, Fg Off G F, 71, 204
Allcock, Plt Off P O P, 44, 202
Allemand, Belgium, 27
Allen, FSLt 30, 201
Allen, FSLt J R, 10, 200
Allen, Fg Off W, 73, 81, 83, 86, 202
Amiens, France, 16, 40, 58
Amman, Transjordan, 162, 173
Amriya, Egypt, 77, 88, 90, 98, 100, 104, 108, 110, 197
Anders, Flt Lt, 205
Anderson, Gp Capt A F, 163, 165, 166, 168, 193, 206
Anderson, Fg Off B M, 206
Anderson, Fg Off J P, 193, 206
Andrews, Fg Off, 160, 205
Angell, Cpl A, 90
Anson, Avro, 164, 166, 168
Ansty, Warks., 11
Anthony, Olt Off R, 204
Antwerp (Anvers), Belgium, 27, 33
Appelboom, Flt Lt K, 173, 205
Aqir, Palestine, 82, 196
Arado Ar 196, 92
Araxos, Greece, 158
Ardoye, France, 17
Argonaut, Canadair, 174
Argosy, Armstrong Whitworth, 193
Argus, HMS, 77
Armil, Eritrea, 166
Armin, General Sixt von, 30
Arran, Scotland, 183
Arras, France, 41, 42, 43, 44, 46
Arscott, Wg Cdr R H, 188, 190, 192, 195, 206
Ashford, Kent, 69
Ashley, Fg Off A G R, 204
Ashover, Flt Lt D, 206
Asmara, Eritrea, 163, 164, 165, 166, 169, 197
Atbara, Egypt, 170
Athens, Greece, 158, 172, 175
Atkinson, Sgt F, 165, 172, 174, 206
Atkinson, Fg Off H D, 40, 41, 42, 43, 44, 48, 50, 51, 58, 59, 60, 61, 62, 63, 202
Atkinson, Flt Lt J C, 206
Atkinson, Plt Off R, 67, 202
Auchinleck, General Sir Claude, 87, 97, 99, 103, 106
Audax, Hawker, 99
Austen, Plt Off, 206
Austin, Flt Lt R W G, 164, 205
Avèsnes, France, 41, 42
Aviatik aircraft, 14
Avise, Fg Off J E, 93, 100, 106, 203, 216
Avon, Rolls-Royce, 177

Baalbeck, Syria, 83
Baalbia, Syria, 83
Baby, Sopwith, 7, 8, 9, 198, 210
Backmann, Leut, 8
Bacon, Admiral, 7
Bahrein, Trucial States, 184, 185, 186
Baines, Plt Off R P, 203
Bain-le-Compte, Belgium, 41
Baker, Plt Off, 202
Baldwin, Fg Off R N, 156
Balfour, Sgt A E, 156, 205
Balhousie, Lord Cameron of, 106, 109
Ball, FSLt R N, 16, 200

Ballantyne, Sgt J F C, 93, 101, 103, 203
Baltimore, Martin, 104, 106
Banfield, Sqn Ldr M, 206
Bangkok, Thailand, 173
Banks, Flt Lt W, 206
Banshee, McDonnell, 171, 175
Bardia, Libya, 81, 94, 97
Barker, Flt Lt T I, 205
Barnard, M/P H J, 165, 173, 174, 205
Barnes, Fg Off F W J, 106
Barnes, Fg Off L E, 103, 106, 203
Barnes, Fg Off S A, 206
Barnett, AVM, 175
Barratt, Flt Lt S G, 206
Barrett, Fg Off F J, 204
Barrett-Atkin, Fg Off C J, 94, 95, 104
Barrey, Flt Lt C J, 160, 205
Basra, Iraq, 185, 186
Bassingbourn, Cambs., 192
Bast, Flt Lt, 205
Bates, Sqn Ldr L A, 36
Battershill, Sir William, 85
Baxter, Flt Sgt R V, 203
Bayley, Wg Cdr P T, 181, 188, 190, 192, 195, 206
Bayonne, France, 60
Beachy Head, Sussex, 68
Beamish, Sgt, 202
Bearcat, Grumman, 171
Beasley, FSLt E F, 200
Beasley, Flt Lt P E, 16, 17, 200
Beaufighter, Bristol, 77, 87, 91, 92, 93
Beaumont-le-Roger, France,
Beckingham, Flt Sgt R L, 206
Bedford, Fg Off R, 206
Beedham, Plt Off D W, 98, 100, 102, 203
Beerst, Belgium, 30
Beggs, Fg Off B, 206
Beguin, Sgt, 56, 202
Beguin, Cdt, 70
Behrens, F/Obermaat, 17
Beirut, Lebanon,
Beka'a Valley, Lebanon, 83
Bell, Sgt D H, 204
Bell, FSLt E V, 15, 16, 200
Bembridge, Isle of Wight, 71
Bendeux, Plt Off, 205
Benson, Wg Cdr T E, 190, 192, 195, 206
Bentley engine, 11, 16
Beresford, Air Cdre, 185
Bergues, France, 11, 12, 13, 15, 16, 17, 18, 19, 20, 21, 23, 24, 25, 26, 30, 31, 32, 33, 34, 196
Berry, Sgt, 191
Béthune, France, 53
Bieber, Leut, 8
Biferno, Italy, 156, 197
Biggin Hill, Kent, 41, 42, 43, 44, 45, 46, 47, 48, 50, 51, 52, 53, 54, 57, 196
Bigood, Sgt I K, 202
Bir Hacheim, Libya, 93, 94, 95, 98
Birmingham, HMS, 167
Bir-el-Baheira, Libya, 93
Bir-el-Gubbi, Libya, 94, 95
Bismarck, battleship, 74, 77, 78
Biven, Plt Off, 205
Blackburn, Fg Off G, 206
Blackwell, Sgt, 191
Blackwood, Flt Lt G D M, 38, 41, 202
Blankenberghe, Belgium, 15, 16, 24, 27
Blatch, Fg Off J, 205
Blenheim, Bristol, 38, 41, 42, 43, 46, 47, 48, 53, 75, 80, 81, 82, 83, 84, 100
Blount, AVM C H B, 40
Bold, Sqn Ldr G, 206
Bolton, Sgt G S, 93, 100, 203
Bombay, Bristol, 40, 41, 46
Bombourg, France, 48
Bootherstone, Plt Off A R, 203, 204
Boreham, Fg Off P M, 206
Borthwick, Flt Sgt W A, 204
Boston, Douglas, 104, 106
Bosworth, Fg Off J, 206
Boucher, Plt Off L D, 93, 100, 102, 203
Boulogne, France, 34, 45, 46
Bourges, France, 55
Bowen, Plt Off, 44, 202
Bowley, Fg Off, 205
Bowling, Gp Capt, 173
Boyd, Sgt T, 48, 76, 202
Boyle, Fg Off E J, 206
Bône, Algeria, 76
Bradley, Flt Lt C F, 203
Bramah, FSLt H G K, 55, 56, 202
Brandenburg seaplanes, 8, 12
Brannon, WO, 205
Bray Dunes, France, 13, 28
Breheny, Sgt R J, 203
Bremen, Germany, 186
Brettmann, Leut, 12
Brice, Fg Off E W L, 203
Brice, 2Lt T G, 200
Bricy, France, 55, 59
Bridger, Fg Off D, 206
Bridgstock, Plt Off A D, 206
Bridport, Dorset, 59
Brierley, Sgt L W, 204
Brigand, Bristol, 173
Briggs, Plt Off F E, 73, 76, 77, 78, 81, 84, 85, 90, 93, 96, 102, 203

Brigham, Flt Lt G C L, 205
Brighton, Sussex, 58, 69
Brindisi, Italy, 157, 158, 197
Briscoe, Plt Off A D, 188, 206
Britannia, Bristol, 184
Broadhurst, Wg Cdr H, 44, 64
Brocklebank, Dr C, 73, 83, 95
Brodick, Scotland, 183
Brook, Flt Sgt W D, 100, 203
Brookes, Sgt K G, 104, 108, 203
Brooklands, Surrey, 26, 64
Broughton, Sgt, 202
Brown, Capt A R, 30
Brown, Lt C P, 10, 14, 16, 17, 18, 20, 21, 24, 25, 27, 28, 29, 200
Brown, Fg Off D C, 206
Brown, WO, 206
Brown, M/N E, 206
Brown, Fg Off M G, 183, 192, 206
Browne, Sgt, 191, 206
Brownlow, Flt Lt J, 176, 182, 206
Browse, Fg Off C R, 206
Bruce, Sgt, 187, 202
Bruges, Belgium, 13, 19, 23, 24, 26, 31
Bruggen, Germany, 179, 181, 182, 185, 186, 187, 188, 189, 190, 191, 192, 193, 197
Brussels, Belgium, 41
Buchan, Sgt E P, 204
Buchin, Plt Off M S H C, 55, 57, 60, 202
Budd, Wg Cdr R, 89
Buist, Flg Off, 174, 175, 205
Bullerfield, Sgt S L, 202
Bullock, Flt Lt, 161
Bunyan, Flg Off, 173, 205
Burgess, Plt Off, 74
Burg-el-Arab, Egypt, 88, 93, 100, 104, 106, 109, 110, 197
Burke, Fg Off E S R, 164, 206
Burley, Fg Off, 176
Burton, Sgt, 202
Bushell, Sgt G D, 55, 58, 60, 64, 66, 69, 72, 202
Butterfield, Sgt S L, 40, 41, 43, 44, 48, 52, 56, 57
Butterworth, Flt Sgt W H, 156, 204, 205
Butterworth, Plt Off, 206

Cairns, Flt Lt M, 190, 206
Cairo, Egypt, 86, 87, 88, 89, 93, 99, 103, 104
Calais, France, 11, 23, 31, 34, 53, 73
Calcutta, India, 173
Callaghan, Fg Off J F, 206
Camberley, Surrey, 68
Cambrai, France, 41, 43
Cambridge, Cambs., 61, 71, 190
Camel, Sopwith, 10, 11, 12, 14, 15, 17, 19, 20, 21, 24, 25, 26, 27, 28, 29, 30, 31, 32, 33, 34, 90, 198, 214
Cameron, Flt Lt N, 106, 108, 109, 111, 203
Camm, Sydney, 39
Campbell, Plt Off B, 104
Campbell, Plt Off D J, 203
Campbell, Sgt, 202
Campbell, Wg Cdr I R, 180, 188, 192, 195, 206
Canberra, English Electric, 176, 177, 178, 179, 180, 182, 183, 184, 185, 186, 187, 188, 190, 192, 193, 199, 219
Cant Z-1007, 84, 85
Cantin, Plt Off C F, 108, 203
Capuzzo, Fort, Libya, 79, 81
Carney, AC2 G, 40, 45
Carquebut, France, 55
Carrick, Flt Lt G, 110, 111, 203
Carter, Fg Off R M, 206
Carter, Fg Off R N, 206
Carter, Sgt, 205
Carthew, Plt Off G C T, 202
Castagnola, Flt Lt, 205
Castel Benito, Libya, 181
Castle Bromwich, Warks., 63
Castletown, Caithness, 72, 73, 196
Catroux, General, 82
Catterick, Yorks., 36
Cattle, Flt Lt F L, 18, 19, 24, 200
Chadwick, Plt Off D F, 98, 100, 203
Chalk, Fg Off I K, 192, 206
Chalkey, Fg Off K B, 206
Chandler, Wg Cdr M R T, 189, 192, 193, 195, 206
Chapman, Flt Lt, 203
Chappell, Plt Off S, 203, 204
Chappell, Plt Off, 206
Charing Cross, Libya, 97
Chartres, France, 55
Chatfield, Flt Lt R M, 81, 103, 107, 203
Chatfield, Plt Off, 202
Chaumont, France, 187, 189
Châteaudun, France,
Cherbourg, France, 55, 58, 59, 62, 64, 68, 94
Chesil Beach, Dorset, 56, 61, 63
Chessall, Plt Off M P, 206
Chiazzari, Lt B N, 157, 204
Chichester, Sussex, 70, 72
Chick, Lt A F, 28, 29, 30, 32, 33, 201
Chiswick, Sgt, 165, 171, 205
Church Fenton, Yorks., 34, 36, 37, 196
Churchill, Winston, 46, 78,
Clapp, Fg Off T F, 190
Clappland, Fg Off F, 206
Clark, Plt Off H D, 62, 202, 206

Clarke, Flg Off C E, 206
Clarke, Fg Off D R, 187, 206
Clarke, Flt Lt H W R, 206
Clarke, Flt Sgt, 205
Clarkson, WO K M, 156, 204, 205
Clayton, Sgt J C T, 11, 156, 205
Clayton-Jones, Fg Off G, 206
Clerget engine, 11
Cochrane, Plt Off J M, 98, 100, 203
Coflam, Plt Off H W, 202
Cole, FSLt K R, 18, 200
Colebeck, Flt Lt R, 205
Colebrook, Sqn Ldr D C, 158, 161, 188, 192, 195, 205, 217
Collins, Flt Lt D, 188, 206
Collishaw, Flt Cdr R, 12, 14, 15, 16, 78, 87, 200
Colmar, France, 187
Cologne, Germany, 27
Coltishall, Norfolk, 52
Compton, Fg Off C J, 183, 185, 206
Compton, WO H M, 92, 203
Condor, Focke-Wulf, 72
Conway, Plt Off S D, 206
Coobes, 2Lt W S, 201
Cook, Flt Lt B M, 206
Cooke, Sgt C A, 202
Cooke, WO D E, 203, 204
Coomber, LAC, 158
Coombes, Flt Lt L A, 26, 31, 33
Cooney, Sgt, 46, 202
Cooper, Capt M L, 14, 15, 17, 20, 24, 28, 29, 30, 200
Cooper, Flt Sgt, 205
Cooper, Sgt, 206
Corcieux, Belgium, 31
Cormack, Sgt, 202
Cornelius, Fg Off S J, 206
Corsair, Vought, 171
Cossack, HMS, 77
Cottam, Plt Off H W, 58, 65, 66, 68
Cotterill, Flt Lt P, 206
Coucy-le-Chateau, France, 42
Coudekerque, France, 24
Coughlan, Fg Off D, 206
Coulson, Sgt, 158
Court, Fg Off A R, 206
Court, Fg Off D J, 206
Courtemarck, France, 28
Courtrai, Belgium, 43
Coutts, Plt Off, 175, 205
Cowie, Plt Off S, 192, 206
Cox, Fg Off R T, 206
Coxyde, Belgium, 13
Craigie, Sqn Ldr S A, 176, 206
Cranwell, Lincs., 38, 62, 63, 73
Crete, Greece, 80, 84, 87, 92, 171
Crépon, France, 55
Cricklewood, Middlesex, 11
Crighton, Sgt, 166, 205
Cringle, Flt Lt K, 206
Croskell, Sgt M E, 41, 48, 50, 56, 64, 65, 66, 68, 72, 202
Crossley, Flt Lt P D, 206
Crowley-Milling, Sqn Ldr D, 168
Crowther, Plt Off, 76, 77, 84, 203
Croydon, Surrey, 73
Cunningham, Plt Off M J, 206
Curtiss, Fg Off C F A, 205
Czemin, Plt Off Count M S, 202

Daba, El, Egypt, 92, 94, 100, 104, 108, 109, 110, 111, 112, 197
Dabrowski, P2, 170, 171, 205
Dahl, Roald, 82
Daimler-Benz engines, 40
Dakota, Douglas, 162, 164, 165, 166
Dalziel, Sqn Ldr C T, 176, 206
Damascus, Syria, 83
Darby, Flt Lt K, 183, 206
Darling, Fg Off T K, 204
Darwen, Wg Cdr J, 105, 108, 109, 110, 112
Darwin, Flt Lt R B, 206
Davenport, Sgt D, 44, 45
Davey, Flt Lt A J, 172, 206
David, Flt Lt W D, 65, 69, 202
Davies, M/N C, 206
Davies, Sgt M P, 202, 206
Davies, Flt Lt W D, 65, 69, 202
Dawlish, Devon, 62
Dawson, Lt W, 99, 201
Day, Flt Lt M J G, 165, 169, 173, 200
Day, Sgt, 205
Deakin, Fg Off, 205
Deane, Sgt, 205
De Belle, Flt Lt F A, 206
Defiant, Boulton Paul, 50, 51, 52
Dekheila, Egypt, 88, 90, 106, 197
Delhi, India, 173
Demon, Hawker, 63
Denison, Fg Off R W, 36, 202
Dennis, Flt Lt, 205
Denny, Lt C H, 18, 27, 200
Dentz, General, 82, 83
Deport, Flt Sgt R, 70, 202
Derbyshire, Fg Off E G, 206
Deseronto, Canada, 31
Devesoir, Egypt, 160, 162, 163, 166-174, 197, 219
Dewar, Wg Cdr J S, 60, 61, 202
Dewoitine D 520, 82, 83, 105

Dhibban, Iraq, 67
Digby, Lincs., 34, 62
Dinant, Belgium, 55
Dinard, France, 55
Dineen, Fg Off M, 206
Dingle, Flt Lt D, 190, 206
Dixmude, Belgium, 24, 25, 27, 28, 29, 30
Dixon, Plt Off J M, 70, 203
Dixon, Sgt, 202
Djibouti, 167
Dodds, Fg Off P, 206
Dodson, Wg Cdr H J, 176, 178, 192, 195, 206
Donnelly, Fg Off P, 204
Dornier aircraft, 41, 42, 43, 44, 48, 51, 59, 66, 69
Dorsetshire, HMS, 78
Douai, France, 42, 43
Douglas-Reid, Flt Lt H E A, 162, 205
Douthwaite, Fg Off, 73, 76, 79, 80, 203
Dover, Kent, 7, 8, 9, 10, 18, 19, 21, 34, 45, 47, 48, 50, 51, 52, 56, 67, 196, 200, 201
Dowding, Air Marshal Sir Hugh, 40, 46
Dowling, Sgt A A, 204
Downes, Plt Off N J, 206
Downie, Plt Off, 76, 202, 203
Drake, Fg Off B, 70, 202
Draper, Sgt A, 205
Draper, Fg Off A, 206
Draper, Fg Off, A R, 206
Dreux, France, 55
Dreyer, Fgm, 15
Driffield, Yorks., 71, 72, 105, 196
DuFeu, Flt Lt, D E, 206
Duggan, Flt Sgt L P, 10, 200
Duncan, Fg Off, 73, 203
Dungeness, Kent, 64, 66
Dunkirk, France, 7, 8, 9, 10, 11, 12, 13, 14, 15, 16, 18, 21, 23, 24, 25, 27, 29, 32, 34, 37, 39, 41, 44, 45, 46, 47, 48, 50, 51, 52, 53, 55, 57, 63, 64, 66, 68, 71, 72, 194, 196, 200, 201, 202
Dunscombe, Sgt R D, 55, 65, 68, 202
Du Pasquier, Plt Off, 203
Durban, S Africa, 78
Duryasz, Flg Off M, 62, 64, 65, 66, 202
Düsseldorf, Germany, 191
Dyce, Aberdeenshire, 70
Dyck, Leut, 8, 9
Dyer, Flt Lt B H, 187
Dyer, Fg Off G L S, 206

Eagle, Lt J M, 206
Eastchurch, Kent, 31, 34, 200
Eastleigh, Hants., 30
Eastleigh, Kenya, 182
Eccloo, Belgium, 48
Edenbridge, Kent, 66
Edinburgh, Duke of, 179
Edmonds, Fg Off, 75, 95, 203
Edmunds, Fg Off J C, 73, 93
Edwardes Jones, Wg Cdr J H, 36, 38, 41, 46, 48, 50, 51, 52, 53, 72, 176, 188, 190, 192, 195, 202
Edwards, Sqn Ldr D, 185
Edwards, Flt Sgt J, 76, 93, 95, 203
Eesen, Belgium, 30
Ein Shemer, Palestine, 162
El Arish, Egypt, 170, 218
El Fasher, Sudan, 75
El Firdan, Egypt, 162
El Geneina, Sudan, 75
El Hamman, Egypt, 103, 104
El Khanka, Egypt, 88, 93, 197
Ellenikon, Greece, 172, 175
Elliott, Flt Lt G P, 204
Elliott, Wg Cdr, 165
Ellis, Fg Off J, 36
Ellis, M/Nav, 206
Els, Lt, 157
Elton, Flt Sgt, 206
Elworthy, ACM Sir Charles, 191
Ensign, Armstrong Whitworth, 40, 44
Entebbe, Uganda, 174
Enzo Sereni, SS, 159
Etampes, France, 55
Etchells, Fg Off F A, 203
Etheridge, Plt Off, 205
Evans, Lt W C, 24, 200
Everest, Fg Off K, 206
Evreux, France, 55
Ewing, P2, 205
Exeter, Devon, 3, 54, 55, 57, 58, 59, 60, 61, 62, 63, 64, 65, 77, 196
Exmouth, Devon, 62

Fairbairn, Flt Lt J H, 204
Famagusta, Cyprus, 84, 85
Fareham, Hants., 70
Farley, Sgt S W, 204
Farmer, Fg Off M, 206
Farnborough, Hants., 53, 59
Farr, Flt Lt T, 75
Fayid, Egypt, 168, 170
Fellows, 2Lt S H, 165, 201
Fenn, Lt J F T, 201
Fenton, Gp Capt, 102, 104, 105, 109
Fewtrell, Fg Off C G, 206
Field, Flt Sgt J T, 203
Fieseler Storch, 112
Filling, Flt Sgt W H, 203
Fillingham, Fg Off S, 206
Filton, Bristol, 54, 55, 63
Finn, Sqn Ldr D M, 173, 195, 205
Firefly, Fairey, 51
Firmin, Sgt D E, 203, 204
Fischer, Oberst, 58
Fisher, Fg Off B N M S, 206
Fisher, Flt Lt P S, 7, 9, 10, 200
Fisher, Plt Off, 46, 202
Fitzpatrick, Flg Off A G, 206
Fleming, 2Lt W G, 31, 201
Fletcher, 2Lt A, 28, 201
Focke-Wulf FW 190, 72, 94
Fokker aircraft, 15, 17, 25, 26, 27, 28, 29, 30, 31, 32, 33
Ford, Sussex, 69
Ford, Fg Off D L, 206
Ford, Flt Lt J, 183, 206
Ford, Fg Off K A L, 159, 203
Foster, Fg Off A, 206
Foxley-Norris, Air Marshal C N, 192, 193
Francis, 2Lt C E, 201
Frankland, Plt Off M R, 183, 206
Franklin, Plt Off, 205
Franklyn, Maj Gen H, 46
Franz, Leut, 15
Fraser, Fg Off N N, 206
Freeland, Lt R B, 200
Freetown, Sierra Leone, 78
Freiburg, Germany, 9
Freiston, Lincs., 18, 24, 200
Freyberg, General, 96
Fricke, Flugmaat, 17
Friedrichshafen aircraft, 8, 10, 12
Friendly, Lt C V, 204
Fry, Flt Sgt S R, 103, 104, 203
Fuka, Egypt, 94, 100, 108, 112
Fulmar, Fairey, 76
Furneaux, Plt Off R H, 203
Furnes, Belgium, 13, 41, 48

Gabriel, Fg Off D, 206
Gale, Fg Off C, 206
Galletti, Fg Off I, 183, 206
Gamble, Brig C M, 166
Gamble, Flt Lt F M, 156, 204
Gambut, Libya, 77, 80, 93, 94, 96, 197
Gamil, El, Egypt, 197
Gardener, Lt E, 204
Gardiner, Sgt D A, 205
Gardner, Fg Off G, 190, 206
Garner, Lt G C, 24, 28, 30, 33, 201
Garrood, Flt Sgt A, 104, 106, 203
Garwood, Fg Off R H, 106, 203, 204
Gatward, Fg Off, 205
Gatwick, Sussex, 67, 68
Gaudo, Italy, 156
Gauntlet, Gloster, 35, 36, 37, 38, 41, 67, 198
Gazala, Libya, 81, 91, 93, 94, 95, 96, 97, 99, 102, 106
Geilenkirchen, Germany, 179
General Craufurd, HMS, 29
Geoffrion, Flt Sgt L P, 203
Georgic, RMS, 77, 78
Gerawla, Egypt, 78, 79, 196
Gevaux, Flt Lt W G, 206
Ghazal, Egypt, 112
Ghent, Belgium, 27, 28, 30, 32, 33
Ghistelles, Belgium, 29, 34, 201
Gibraltar, 74, 76
Gibson, Sgt G, 165, 172, 205
Gifford, Fg Off G A, 206
Gilbert, Lt H H, 22, 24, 30, 32, 33, 201
Gladiator, Gloster, 66, 100
Gledhill, Sgt, 76
Glenn Martin 167F, 83
Glisy, France, 40
Glover, Sgt, 202
Goering, Hermann, 59, 64, 66
Goldswain, LAC D S, 88, 92, 96
Goodchild, Lt P W, 200
Gooding, Sgt P, 173, 205
Goodman, Fg Off B, 206
Gordon, Sgt G, 165, 170, 171, 172, 173, 174,
Gordon, Flt Lt W I, 203
Gordon, Fg Off W L 183, 206
Gordon-Jones, Sqn Ldr, 81
Gort, Lord, 51
Gosport, Hants., 16
Gotha aircraft, 10, 13, 25, 26, 105
Gould, Flt Lt, 76, 203
Gould, Fg Off, 78, 202
Göttingen, Germany, 181
Graham, Flt Lt/AVM R, 5, 7, 8, 9, 10, 11, 12, 15, 17, 20, 21, 23, 25, 27, 28, 29, 30, 31, 32, 33, 34, 183, 188, 192, 195, 200, 220
Grain, Isle of, Kent, 15, 200
Grainger, Fg Off J, 206
Grandy, Air Marshal Sir John, 187
Gravelines, France, 41, 48
Gravesend, Kent, 52
Gray, Lt W A, 41, 44, 48, 50, 202
Gray, Lt W E, 17, 18, 20, 22, 24, 25, 26, 27, 200
Gray, Fg Off W N, 52, 202
Grayson, Flt Sgt C, 36, 48, 50, 55, 58, 66, 68, 202
Greasley, Sgt G, 202
Green, Flt Lt N, 40, 98, 106, 203
Green, Fg Off R, 206
Green, Lt W, 9
Green, Flt Lt W J C, 206
Greenaway, Fg Off P J, 206
Greene, Lt J E, 15, 17, 20, 21, 23, 27, 28, 29, 30, 200
Greene, Capt W E, 30
Greenock, Renfrew, 77
Greenwood, Flt Lt A W, 206
Greenwood, Cpl, 158
Grice, Gp Capt, 53
Griffiths, Flt Sgt R, 103, 104, 203
Grove, Sgt H C, 82, 202
Groves, Plt Off, 77
Grumbridge, Plt Off G Q, 193, 206
Guernsey, Channel Is., 56
Guidott, Lt W, 200
Guildford, Surrey, 71
Guines, Belgium, 11, 31
Gundry, Sgt A F, 156
Gurteen, Capt S, 160
Gutersloh, Germany, 176, 179, 189
Gwynne, Flt Sgt W D, 103, 106, 108, 203

Habbaniya, Iraq, 174
Haifa, Palestine, 82, 86, 159, 196
Halfaya, Libya, 81, 94
Hall, Lt K W J, 201
Hallam, Flt Sgt, 202
Halvorsen, Flt Sgt R H, 92, 93, 95, 203
Hambly, Fg Off, 205
Hancock, Plt Off A J, 71, 73, 75, 76, 77, 88, 92, 93, 94, 203, 216
Hancock, Lt M H, 27
Hancock, Lt S M N, 18, 28, 33, 200
Hand, P2, 205
Handforth, Fg Off P, 206
Handley Page O/100, O/400, 13, 19, 24, 27
Hankin, Plt Off D A, 164, 170, 205
Hanock, Sgt A, 202
Hanson, Fg Off J A, 178, 206
Hardy, Hawker, 88, 93
Hargeisa, British Somaliland, 167, 197
Hargreaves, Fg Off N, 176, 180, 206
Harrington, Plt Off R J, 206
Harris, Air Marshal A T, 220
Harris, Flt Lt D W O, 192, 206
Harrison, Fg Off A J, 206
Harrison, Plt Off M O, 183, 205
Harrison, Sqn Ldr W A S, 183, 184, 187, 206
Hart, P4, 165, 205
Hartley, Sqn Ldr P W, 100, 104, 203
Harvard, North American, 162, 199
Haslam, WO P C, 203
Hassani, Greece, 158
Hatch, M/Nav L C, 206
Hauptvogel, Lt D R, 17
Haviland, Lt W B, 200
Havilland, Lt W P, 16, 17, 18
Hawarden, Flint, 55, 63
Hawkinge, Kent, 41, 44, 53, 70
Hawk, Curtiss, 43
Hay, F/Cdr C M, 200
Hay, Fg Off J F, 203
Hayward, Fg Off T, 183, 206
Heald, Sgt R, 168, 205
Heard, WO F, 204
Hearndon, Flt Sgt A W, 204
Heinkel aircraft, 50
Helchetern, Germany, 192
Heliopolis, Egypt, 57, 90, 92
Hellyer, Fg Off C, 190, 191, 206
Helm, 2Lt H B, 165, 203, 204
Helwan, Egypt, 90, 91
Hemingway, Sgt, 202
Henderson, Sgt/Plt Off W R, 73, 75, 76, 79, 80, 92, 93, 94, 97, 98, 100, 203
Hendon, Middlesex, 36, 38
Henlow, Beds., 52, 193
Henry, LAC A R, 55, 78,
Henry, LAC A J, 88, 92, 96, 109
Henschel Hs 126, 43, 44, 46
Henwood, Plt Off, 92
Heraklion, Crete, 80
Herd, 2Lt W H, 29, 201
Hersey, Flt Sgt G, 88, 92
Hewett, Lt B A, 26, 201
Hill, Fg Off I, 206
Hill, Fg Off W W, 206
Hill, M/Nav, 206
Histead, Capt, 163, 164, 165
Hitchen, Fg Off L S, 206
Hodgson, Lt E A, 201
Hodson, Lt G S, 19, 26, 27, 30, 33, 201
Hoffreins, WO J A, 203
Holdaway, Sgt D, 202
Holden, 2Lt H E B, 26, 28, 30, 32, 33, 201, 214
Holdsworth, Lt G R, 157, 204
Hole, Plt Off P K, 206
Holman, Flt Lt, 205
Holmes, Fg Off R M, 206
Holt, Norfolk, 192
Hondschoote, Belgium, 28
Hong Kong, 14
Honiton Clyst, Devon, 54, 55
Hood, HMS, 77
Hood, Flt Lt, 206
Hooglede, Belgium, 30
Hooton Park, Cheshire, 39
Hopewell, FSLt G F C, 16, 19, 20, 21, 200
Hopsten, Germany, 190, 191
Horn, Sgt 'Lofty', 91, 215, 216
Hornchurch, Essex, 50, 67
Horne, Flt Sgt, 203
Horstmann, 10, 17, 18, 19, 20, 200
Houghton, Fg Off A W, 206
Houle, Fg Off A U, 73, 81, 83, 85, 89, 100, 102, 103, 106, 108, 110, 112, 203
Houle, Fg Off A E, 107
Houtave, Belgium, 13, 21, 27
Houthulst, Belgium, 14, 28
Howard, Flt Sgt H, 191, 203, 204
Howarth, Plt Off P D, 206
Howe, Sgt, 38
Howell, Flt Lt H T, 206
Howell, Sgt, 203
Howes, Sgt, 202
Hudgel, Plt Off, 205
Hudson, Lockheed, 39
Hughes, Plt Off J G, 206
Hughes, Lt N W, 200
Hughesden, Flt Lt A, 206
Hulland, Fg Off J, 187, 206
Hullavington, Wilts., 56, 70
Hulse, Flt Lt G S, 158, 159, 204, 205
Humphries, Sgt, 203
Hunt, Sgt A F W W, 204
Hunter, Hawker, 184, 192
Hurricane, Hawker, 37 to 110, 172, 198, 199
Huston, Lt E R, 33, 201
Hutchinson, Flt Sgt W T F, 156, 205, 206
Hutley, Plt Off R R, 70, 202
Huxley, Sqn Ldr B, 188, 206

Iago, WO I R H, 204
Ibison, Lt K G, 30, 201
Ichteghem, Belgium, 27
Idku, Egypt, 86, 87, 88, 89, 90, 91, 94, 100, 106, 196, 197, 215
Idris, Libya, 181, 182, 184, 186, 187, 188, 190
Igoe, Fg Off W A K, 36
Iliff, 2Lt G, 28, 201
Ingalls, Lt D S, 12, 13, 16, 24, 26, 27, 28, 201
Ingalls, Ens D L, 200
Iphigenia, HMS, 20
Iseghem, Belgium, 30
Ismailia, Egypt, 78, 84, 86, 87, 161, 162, 196
Ismay, Plt Off W H, 92, 105, 203, 216

Jackson, Fg Off R, 203
Jackson, Sgt, 93, 203
Jagger, Flt Sgt G A, 206
Janes, Sgt C L B, 203
Janicki, Plt Off Z, 202
Jankiewiez, Fg Off J S, 202
Javelin, Gloster, 182
Jebel Aulia, Libya, 163
Jenkyn, Fg Off R A, 206
Jenner, Lt P C, 25, 28, 200, 201
Jennings, Flt Sgt/Plt Off J T, 156, 157, 159, 160, 162, 164, 195, 205
Jeram, S/Lt D, 55, 56, 66, 68, 202
Johnson, Flt Lt A E, 160, 161, 162, 205, 206,
Johnson, Flt Lt D A J, 206
Johnston, WO P M, 204
Johnston, Plt Off R A, 206
Joiner, Fg Off C, 206
Joiner, Flt Lt K G, 206
Jolliffe, Fg Off, 205
Jones, (see also under Edwardes Jones)
Jones, Fg Off G C, 206
Jones, Flt Lt G S, 183, 206
Jones, Sgt J A W, 156
Jones, Flt Lt K C, 206
Jones, Lt O, 151, 153, 155, 157, 204
Jones, Flt Lt P A R, 206
Jowett, WO T A, 203
Joy, Fg Off R M, 177, 206
Joyce, Flt Lt A R, 104
Juba, Sudan, 174
Junkers aircraft, 53, 62

Kano, Nigeria, 75
Kasfareet, Egypt, 78, 84, 170, 171
Kassem, General, 183, 184, 186
Kaye, Fg Off D G, 206
Kearsey, Plt Off P J, 202
Keaty, Flt Lt J, 206
Kelley, Sqn Ldr P, 166, 195, 205
Kelley, M/Nav, 206
Kellow, Plt Off R W, 41, 64, 65, 68, 69, 70, 71, 202
Kelsey, Flt Lt, 202
Kenley, Surrey, 52
Kenyon, Lt I D, 156, 204
Kerkhove, Belgium, 43
Kettlewell, Sqn Ldr G V W, 89, 92, 95, 195, 203
Keyes, Admiral, 7, 19, 23
Khartoum, Sudan, 75, 162, 163, 164, 165, 166, 167, 168, 169, 170, 172, 174, 182, 186, 197, 218
Khormaksar, Aden, 166, 168, 182, 184, 186
Kiel, Germany, 23, 27
Kientsch, Leut, 109
Kilbansky, Sgt M, 205
Killingholme, Lincs., 200
Kingston-upon-Hull, Yorks., 72
Kingston-upon-Thames, Surrey, 11
Kirk, Fg Off J S, 206
Kitley, Sqn Ldr A J H, 175, 195, 205
Kittyhawk, Curtiss, 93, 96, 102, 104, 106, 112
Knapton, Fg Off P W, 203
Knight, Sqn Ldr B C, 191, 206
Knight, Fg Off S G, 158, 205
Knightsbridge, Libya, 94, 95, 96
Koerner, Leut F, 92, 95, 100
Kos, Aegean, 87
Kronschnabel, Obfw, 106
Kruschev, Nikita, 186
Kuwait, Persian Gulf, 183, 184, 185, 186
Kyrenia, Cyprus, 85, 86, 162

Laarbruch, Germany, 176, 179
LABS system, 179, 180, 181, 182, 183, 187, 188, 190
Lack, Flt Sgt W, 203
Lagos, Nigeria, 75
Lahore, India, 71
Lakatamia, Cyprus, 85, 197
Lambe, Cdr C L, 8, 9
Lampernisse, Belgium, 28, 30
Lancaster, Avro, 160, 162
Landrecies, France, 41

Lane, Plt Off B J E, 36
Lane, Flt Lt P, 183, 206
Lannion, France, 60
La Panne, France, 30, 52
Larichelière, Plt Off J E P, 59, 61, 202
Larissa, Greece, 192
Larnaca, Cyprus, 181, 187
Latcham, Fg Off D E, 206
La Touche, Sqn Ldr T, 187, 206
Laurence, Flt Sgt R J, 81, 204
Laval, France, 55
Lawson, Flt Sgt L H, 14, 200
Leach, Lt L J, 203, 204
Leach, Plt Off, 205
Lear, Fg Off R W M, 187, 206
Leavey, Fg Off D, 206
LeCornu, Plt Off C, 206
Leconfield, Yorks., 71, 72, 196
Lee, Flt Lt J E, 206
Lee, Sgt M S, 203
Lee, Fg Off P, 165, 173
Leefar, Fg Off B, 206
Leeson, WO E, 162, 205
Leeson, Fg Off F M, 183, 206
Lee-on-Solent, Hants., 200
Leggett, Plt Off, 206
Legros, General, 63
Le Havre, France, 53, 55
Le Mans, France, 55
LeMarquand, Fg Off P M, 206
Le Touquet, France, 41, 46
Leuchars, Fife, 74
Leverano, Italy, 197
Levy, Sqn Ldr M H, 206
Lewis, Flt Sgt V B, 206
Leyland, Flt Lt R H, 183, 206
Leyshon, Sgt, 205
Lichtervelde, Belgium, 28, 30
Lieres, Leut von, 100, 107, 108
Ligescourt, France, 60
Lille, France, 33, 40, 41, 42, 43
Limassol, Cyprus, 85
Lincoln, Avro, 171
Lindsell, Plt Off A M, 202
Liphook, Hants., 70
Lishman, Sgt J A, 38, 40, 41, 42, 43, 44, 48, 202
Lisseweghe, Belgium, 21
Liverpool, Lancs., 74, 75, 76, 196
Llewellyn, Sgt R T, 50, 56, 59, 60, 62, 63, 64, 65, 66, 68, 202
Lludzius, Flt Sgt A, 204
Lockhart, Plt Off J, 67, 73, 76, 202
Lockhart, Sqn Ldr J, 88, 89, 203
Lockhart, Flt Lt R, 76, 82, 85, 195
Lockheed aircraft, 85
Love, Flt Lt J W, 206
Lovell-Greg, Sqn Ldr, 60
Loverspeed, Flt Lt, 178
Lowery, Flg Off W S, 206
Lowry, Fg Off J, 206
Luckas, Fg Off J R A, 156, 205
Lunn, Flt Lt L G, 163, 165, 205
Luqa, Malta, 76, 183, 190
Luxembourg, 40
Luxton, Plt Off C, 108, 110, 111, 203
LVG aircraft, 30, 31, 32, 33
Lyam, Fg Off D A, 207
Lydda, Palestine, 81, 82, 160
Lynch, Plt Off, 76, 78, 202
Lynes, Commodore, 21, 23
Lysander, Westland, 73, 80

Maaten Bagush, Egypt, 79, 112
Macadam, Flt Lt P A, 207
MacDonald, Sqn Ldr D S, 63, 64, 65, 68, 69, 70, 73, 76, 81, 83, 84, 132, 140, 142, 147, 150, 151, 153, 195, 202, 203
MacFarlane, Sgt A, 204
MacGregor, Flt Lt E M, 205
MacKay, Lt G C, 14, 15, 20, 21, 22, 23, 26, 27, 30, 32, 33, 200, 201
MacKay 92, 100, 105, 118, 119, 125, 216
MacKenzie, Capt F W, 27, 31, 32, 214
MacKenzie, Lt W J, 16, 22, 24, 25, 26, 33, 200, 201
Mackinson, Plt Off, 205
MacLeish, Lt K, 17, 30, 201
MacLellan, Flt Sgt E H, 204
Maddox, Flt Lt, 174, 205
Mafraq, Transjordan, 168, 172, 173, 175
Magister, Miles, 198
Maiduguri, Nigeria, 75
Maine, Capt, 24, 31, 33
Mair, Flt Sgt G H, 207
Malakal, Sudan, 166
Maldegem, Belgium, 48
Malo-les-Bains, France, 12, 13, 27
Malta, 74, 76, 77, 93, 100, 156, 175, 183, 190
Manby, Lincs., 190, 192
Mandeville, Flt Lt, 205
Manley, Flt Lt T D W, 207
Manston, Kent, 40, 43, 46, 48, 50, 52, 53, 67, 69, 171, 201
Marchbank, 2Lt J N, 30, 201
Marcq, France, 40, 41, 43
Margate, Kent, 50
Margreaves, Fg Off N, 207
Marham, Norfolk, 39, 192
Mariakerke-pres-de-Gand, Belgium, 27
Marlow, Fg Off R B, 176, 207
Marseille, France, 106, 108
Marshall, Sgt H, 85, 156, 205
Marshall, Sgt, 76, 78, 202
Marshall, Plt Off, 203
Martin, Sgt H T, 83, 205
Martlesham Heath, Suffolk, 36, 52, 57, 67
Martuba, Libya, 91, 197
Massawa, Eritrea, 166
Matcham, Flt Lt G M, 207
May, Flt Sgt, 205
Mayer, Hpt H-K, 63
Mayle, FSLt, 14
Mayne, Capt F, 201
McAll, Sgt C T, 203
McCann, Plt Off T A, 103, 104, 203
McCarthy, Flt Lt D J, 180, 207
McClelland, Plt Off B J, 108, 203
McDonald, 2Lt J C, 30, 201
McDonald, Fg Off J D, 207
McDonald, Sgt, 171, 205
McGibbon, Lt, 157
McGregor, Sqn Ldr H D, 47, 52, 56, 63, 202
McGuire, Sgt P E, 203
McIntyre, Flt Lt, 207
McKay, FSLt, 17
McKay, Flt Sgt D J, 104, 203
McKay, Flt Lt D R S, 203
McKay, Fg Off G R S, 92, 93, 94, 100, 104, 105, 106, 110, 112, 118, 119, 125, 203, 215, 216
McKay, Sgt R W, 203
McKenzie, Sgt J, 203
McLean, Lt W S, 201
McLeish, Ens K, 13, 16, 17, 18, 19, 30, 200
McLuggage, Fg Off W, 207
McMurtry, 2Lt L B, 30, 201
McNaughton, Fg Off J M, 207
McSwene, Fg Off, 109
Menary, W, 169, 172
Mercury, Bristol, 36
Merlin, Rolls-Royce, 37, 40
Merritt, Fg Off C, 183, 207
Mersa Matruh, Egypt, 77, 80, 81, 97, 98, 112, 197
Merville, France, 40, 41, 42, 43, 44, 45, 46, 196
Meshine, Syria, 83
Messerschmitt aircraft, 43, 48, 54, 56, 58, 61, 63, 69, 79, 90, 95, 97, 106, 108, 111
Messiter, FSLt L C, 16, 200
Meteor, Gloster, 92, 169, 170, 172, 177, 199
Metzger, Mr & Mrs, 102
Meyer, Lt C, 15, 200
Mélun, France, 55
Mibue, Fg Off B, 207
Michael, Fg Off C, 191, 207
Middelkerke, Belgium, 48
Middle Wallop, Hants., 55
Miles, Fg Off F, 207
Miller, Plt Off, 202
Milligan, Plt Off, 187, 205
Milligan, Fg Off, 207
Mills, Fg Off B W, 157, 207
Milne, Plt Off, 180
Milsom, Fg Off R J, 191, 207
Minna, Nigeria, 75
Mischefa, Egypt, 197
Misurata, Libya, 99, 197
Mitchell, WO F E, 203
Mitchell, Flt Lt J, 207
Mitchell, North American, 106
Miteiriya, Egypt, 110
Mitswaere, Belgium, 28
Mogadishu, Somaliland, 166, 167, 168, 174, 197
Mollan, Fg Off P F, 205
Monkhouse, Flt Lt K E J, 207
Monkman, Flt Sgt W M, 158, 205
Montgomery, General B, 106, 110, 111, 112
Montreal, Canada, 61
Moor, 2Lt J W, 203
Moore, Fg Off, 207
Moorslede, Belgium, 24
Morphou Bay, Cyprus, 84, 85, 86
Mosquito, de Havilland, 168, 173, 177
Moss, S/Lt W J M, 55, 61, 63, 80, 202
Mott, Fg Off G, 205
Mould, S/Lt, 76
Mount, Sqn Ldr, 83
Moyle, FSLt W A, 16, 200
Mulcahy-Morgan, Flt Lt J A, 204
Mulhouse-Habsheim, France, 187
Mullan, Fg Off J P, 193, 207
Munford, Plt Off, 205
Mustang, North American, 94, 156, 157, 159, 160, 161, 162, 199, 217

Naidoo, Fg Off, 190, 191, 207
Nairobi, Kenya, 182
Napier Sabre, 161, 177
Nash, Sqn Ldr R S, 159, 195, 205
Nel, Fg Off L, 183, 184, 185, 207
Nelson, Lt H E R, 26, 200
Nelson, Lt J N, 200
Nethersole, Sgt T D, 204
Neuville, France, 44
New, Fg Off, 202
Newick, Sgt J D, 92, 93, 102, 103, 104, 203
Newman, Fg Off A, 207
Newton Abbot, Devon, 62
Newton, Flt Lt G, 207
Nicholson, Flt Lt E H, 207
Nickson, Sqn Ldr V J, 207
Nicosia, Cyprus, 73, 75, 78, 79, 80, 81, 83, 84, 85, 86, 87, 156, 158, 159, 160, 162, 164, 165, 168, 173, 175, 195, 196, 197, 217, 218
Nieuport, Belgium, 8, 11, 12, 13, 14, 16, 24, 48
Nightingale, Sgt A O, 203
Nixon, Flt Lt F, 207
Nixon, Fg Off F B, 207
Noad, Fg Off M A, 207
Nomain, France, 43
Nordhorn, Germany, 187, 190, 192
Norris, Sgt P P, 41, 52, 55, 56, 59, 202
Northolt, Middlesex, 35, 36, 38, 44, 52, 65, 71, 196
N'dola, Rhodesia, 174

Odiham, Hants., 36, 59
Ogaden, Somaliland, 166, 182
Oldenburg, Germany, 176
Oliff, Flt Sgt J E, 203
Olivier, Flt Lt, 81
Olver, Sqn Ldr P, 94, 98, 108, 112, 195, 203
Olympus, Bristol, 177
Oostkerke, Belgium, 15
Orkney Islands, Scotland, 72
Orleans, France, 55, 59
Orly, France, 55
Ormiston, Flt Lt T M, 165, 205
Orr, Sqn Ldr N W, 207
Osmand, Plt Off A I, 55, 57, 59, 202
Ostend, Belgium, 7, 8, 9, 10, 12, 13, 14, 15, 16, 19, 20, 21, 23, 24, 25, 26, 27, 28, 31, 34, 47, 196
Oudenarde, Belgium, 43
Owen, Lt W T, 30, 201
O'Connor, Maj Gen R N, 78
O'Halloran, Flt Lt S M, 203

Paatz, Flugmaat, 10
Pain, Plt Off, 207
Paine, S/Lt L P, 8, 9
Palmer, Flt Sgt F P, 158, 205
Palmyra, Syria, 83, 84
Pantellaria, 76
Paphos, Cyprus, 197
Parish, Fg Off S C, 205
Park, AM Sir Keith, 132
Parkinson, Flt Lt D, 207
Parncutt, LAC, 158
Parratt, Flt Lt D, 207
Passchendaele, Belgium, 28
Passfield, Flt Lt R F, 192, 207
Payne, Sgt J, 204
Paynter, FSLt J deC, 14, 15, 19, 20, 21, 23, 24, 200
Pearce, 2Lt R A, 26, 28, 33, 201
Pears, Flt Lt, 173
Pearson, Fg Off T A, 183, 185, 186, 207
Pearson, 2Lt, 28, 201
Peaty, Fg Off B, 189, 207
Peck, Lt D L A, 156, 204
Pedder, Sqn Ldr I M, 207
Pegg, Fg Off J D, 207
Pemble, Lt F P, 24, 201
Pembrey, Carmarthen, 55
Pendleton, Fg Off G, 207
Penson, Fg Off F A E, 204, 205
Perkins, WO, 165, 205
Petah Tiqva, Palestine, 158
Peterborough, Northants., 55, 63, 71
Peters, Sgt, 91
Petite Synthe, France, 13
Petter, W E W, 177
Péronne, France, 42
Pfalz aircraft, 16, 24
Phantom, McDonnell, 192
Phelps, 2Lt H A, 26, 33, 201
Phillipart, Plt Off J A L, 55, 56, 57, 60, 62, 63, 202
Phipps, Flg Off C H, 203
Pickford, WO S G, 203, 204
Piddleton, Flt Lt M D, 183, 207
Pienaar, 2Lt S W, 203, 204
Pinder, Lt J W, 13, 14, 18, 20, 21, 24, 25, 26, 31, 200
Pinscott, FSLt L C, 10, 200
Pipe, Fg Off G K, 207
Pitcher, Plt Off P C, 207
Pittard, Plt Off H, 207
Plattenburg, Vfm, 12
Pluckley, Kent, 69
Plumb, Flt Lt F, 207
Plumetôt, France, 55
Plymouth, Devon, 60
Plynlimon, SS, 52
Polgreen, Flt Lt R L T, 207
Poolman, Flt Lt D C N, 164, 165, 205
Portland, Dorset, 56, 57, 58, 59, 60, 61, 63, 66, 68, 69
Portsmouth, Hants., 58, 64, 68, 70, 71
Port Tewfik, Egypt, 78
Postlethwaite, Flt Sgt G, 204
Potez aircraft, 82, 83, 105
Potter, Sgt F G, 106, 203
Potvin, FSLt J E, 7, 8
Pound, Fg Off, 74, 76, 181, 202, 203
Povey, Flt Lt K, 207
Powell, Plt Off B H V, 36, 156, 205
Pownall, Lt A H, 24, 26, 33, 201
Pratt, Fg Off S J, 183, 207
Preston, Plt Off, 207
Prestwick, Ayrshire, 70
Price, Flt Lt G W, 9, 10, 200,
Price, Flt Lt L E, 103, 106, 110, 203
Price, Fg Off, 207
Pritchard, Fg Off A, 207
Prkos, Yugoslavia, 197
Pup, Sopwith, 8, 9, 10, 11, 13, 31, 198
Purchase, Fg Off T E G, 203, 204, 205
Putz, Vfw, 10

Qantara, Egypt, 175
Qattara Depression, Egypt, 97, 99, 106
Qotafiya, Egypt, 112, 197
Queen Elizabeth, HMS, 88
Radford, 2Lt F W, 29, 30, 33, 34, 201
Radford, Flt Lt R, 173, 205
Rae, Plt Off W McC, 207
Raeder, Admiral, 56
Ralph, Plt Off F A O, 204, 205
Ramat David, Palestine, 82, 84, 157, 158, 159, 160, 196, 197
Ramsay, Vice Admiral B, 51
Rankin, Lt W A, 27, 28, 165, 201
Rapide, de Havilland, 54
Rayak, Syria, 83
Raynor, Plt Off, 205
Rea, Flt Lt N O C, 207
Rebstock, Flt Sgt J R, 106, 203
Redden, Flt Sgt S S K, 207
Redhill, Surrey, 66, 67
Redhill, Plt Off D R, 68, 93, 100, 203, 216
Reid, Sqn Ldr G, 92
Reid, Lt J, 18, 21, 23, 200
Rennes, France, 55
Reynaud, Paul, 40
Reynolds, Fg Off G W H, 89
Richards, Fg Off J D, 192, 207
Richthofen, M von, 30
Ridley, Fg Off R, 173, 205
Rippin, Plt Off, 205
Ritchie, Sgt J D, 73, 75, 93, 97, 100, 203
Rivett, Fg Off F L, 183, 185, 207
Robbie, Flt Lt P J, 207
Robertshaw, Flt Lt K, 193, 207
Robertson, Fg Off D E, 157, 187, 204
Robins, L, 158
Robinson, WO I C, 147, 156, 157, 204, 205
Robinson, Fg Off K N G, 52, 202
Rodgers, Lt T, 8
Rodney, HMS, 78
Roe, Sqn Ldr D J A, 164, 165, 168, 173, 195, 205
Rogan, Fg Off, 207
Rogers, Fg Off G, 173, 205
Rolph, Flt Lt, 191
Rommel, General Erwin, 46, 78, 80, 87, 93, 94, 95, 97, 98, 99, 100, 102, 105, 106, 110, 111, 112
Rorvik, 2Lt R E, 203, 204
Rosevear, 2Lt A B, 22, 24, 28, 30, 32, 33, 201
Rosier, LAC, 96, 97
Ross, Flt Lt A D, 203
Rotol propellers, 46, 60
Rouen, France, 53
Rougemont, France, 55
Roulers, Belgium, 27, 28, 29, 30, 31
Rowe, Fg Off A D, 205
Rowlands, Flt Lt H R, 203
Rumbeke, Belgium, 29
Rumble, Flt Sgt, 205
Rumpler aircraft, 15, 16, 24, 26, 28, 29, 31
Russell, Fg Off B E, 70, 207
Ruweisat Ridge, Egypt, 99
Ryley, Fg Off R J, 203

Sabre, Napier, 161
Sachsenburg, Oblt S G, 29
Salamander, Sopwith, 26
Salmesbury, Lancs., 193
Salmond Trophy, 188, 189, 192, 193
Sandford, Lt, 20
Sassoon Trophy, 36
Saundby, AVM Sir R, 220
Savill, Sgt, 202
Savoia-Marchetti aircraft, 84
Saxenburg, Flt Cdr, 27
Scapa Flow, Orkneys, 72
Schaedlich, Fw H, 81
Schaumburg, Fg Off O H, 205
Schlidinger, Flt Lt Z C, 207
Schou, Plt Off, 70, 202
Schwind, Fg Off L H, 67, 68, 202
Scopwick, Lincs., 34, 196, 201
Scowen, Flt Lt J, 207
Scroggie, Lt L C, 27, 201
Seafire, Supermarine, 171
Searle, Fg Off M O, 205
Seaton, Devon, 59
Sedan, France, 40
Seletar, Singapore, 173
Selsey Bill, Sussex, 55, 64, 65, 66, 68, 69, 70, 71
Sevastopol, Russia, 86
Sevenoaks, Kent, 67, 68
Shackleton, Avro, 178, 179
Shaibah, Persian Gulf, 173
Shallufa, Egypt, 161, 162, 171, 174, 197
Shandur, Egypt, 196
Sharjah, Trucial States, 173, 184, 185, 197
Sharman, Flt Lt R R, 183, 207
Sharpe, Plt Off J B, 205
Sharrett, Flt Lt G, 205
Shaw, Lt C, 201
Sheerness, Kent, 10
Sheffield, HMS, 76
Sheils, Sgt, 207
Shellhaven, Essex, 65
Sheppey, Isle of, Kent, 31, 34
Sheridan, Fg Off K P, 207
Shetland Islands, Scotland, 72, 196
Sidi Abd-el-Rahman, Egypt, 111
Sidi Azeiz, Egypt, 81, 96, 197
Sidi Barrani, Egypt, 81, 96, 197
Sidi Haneish, Egypt, 79, 80, 81, 93, 94, 97, 112, 196, 197
Sim, LAC, 158
Sime, Fg Off H M, 190
Simmons, Fg Off J S, 205
Simms, Lt C J, 30

Sims, Flt Lt A E, 207
Sims, Lt C J, 28, 31, 32, 201, 214
Sinai, Egypt, 173
Sincock, Plt Off H H, 165, 205
Sing, Flt Lt J E J, 36, 41, 56, 57, 58, 59, 60, 62, 64, 65, 66, 67, 68, 69, 70, 202
Sirte, Libya, 89
Sissons, Plt Off K N R, 73, 75, 76, 84, 85, 93, 94, 97, 98, 100, 203
Sizer, Plt Off W M, 38, 40, 43, 44, 48, 50, 52, 61, 65, 68, 70, 71, 202
Skyraider, Douglas, 171, 175
Slabber, Flt Lt J, 192
Slater, Sq Cdr S, 182, 183, 184, 188, 195, 207
Slatter, FSLt L H, 7, 9, 10, 12, 13, 14, 15, 16, 19, 20, 22, 200
Smailes, Plt Off A A, 203, 204
Smith, Flt Lt C D A, 93, 100, 101, 106, 109, 110, 113, 115, 116, 117, 118, 128, 134, 135, 136, 137, 142, 148, 203, 204
Smith, Ens E T, 13, 16, 17, 200
Smith, LAC E, 37, 45
Smith, FSLt G D, 15, 17, 19, 20, 200
Smith, Lt H C, 24, 26, 27, 28, 30, 201
Smith, Flt Lt R J, 207
Smith, Sgt, 172
Smuts, Jan, 92
Snipe, Sopwith, 26
Snowden, Sgt E G, 55, 56, 63, 65, 66, 67, 68, 69, 70, 202
Sollitt, WO S, 205
Sollum, Egypt, 81, 94, 96, 97
Somergem, Belgium, 31
Sopwith Triplane, 14
Sorley, 2Lt J C, 28, 201
Southampton, Hants., 64, 66, 68, 69, 70
Southon, Flt Lt, 205
Sowrey, Fg Off J A, 73, 74, 75, 76, 77, 81, 83, 90, 92, 93, 94, 95, 97, 100, 203
Spackman, Sqn Ldr D A, 207
Spad aircraft, 29
Sparkes, Lt C P, 25, 27, 28, 172, 201
Sparks, Sgt E, 165, 174, 205
Spear, Fg Off N J, 207
Spellings, Capt, 33
Sperrle, General, 55, 59
Spitfire, Supermarine, 36, 39, 40, 47, 48, 51, 55, 59, 61, 62, 63, 66, 67, 70, 89, 94, 95, 100, 102, 103, 104, 105, 106, 107, 108, 110, 111, 112, 168, 173, 199
Sporny, Plt Off, 202
Sprent, Sqn Ldr C, 207
Squire, Flt Sgt, 155, 204
Stahlschmidt, Leut H-A, 95, 100, 103, 107, 108
Stainforth, Wg Cdr G, 87
Stalhille, Belgium, 13, 25, 27, 29, 31, 33, 34, 196
St.André-de-l'Eure, France, 55
Stannard, Fg Off E, 207
Stares, Plt Off M J, 205
St.Armand, France, 43
Stavin, FSLt J C, 15
St.Catherine's Point, Isle of Wight, 58, 61, 68, 71
St.Denis Westrem, Belgium, 13, 27
St.Dizier, France, 187
Steel, Fg Off A J, 207
Steele, Sgt J W, 106, 204
Steib, Sqn Ldr P F, 207
Steinberg, Fg Off T G, 203
St.Eloi, France, 27
Stephenson, Flt Lt G G, 207
Stephenson, Plt Off W H, 73, 75, 92, 93, 97, 101, 106, 109, 187, 203
St.Eval, Cornwall, 55
Stevens, Sgt G, 62, 68, 69, 71, 202
Stevens, Flt Lt G L E, 200
Stevens, Flt Lt T A, 203
Stevenson, Flt Sgt N, 204
Steward, Sgt F H, 203
Stewart-Burton, Lt J P, 33, 201
St.Malo, France, 62
Stoat, Flt Lt B E, 190, 207
Stock, Lt V G, 134, 140
St.Omer, France, 47, 48
Stone, Lt C J, 28, 34, 201
Stone, Plt Off L G E, 41, 43, 48, 202
Storch, Fieseler, 112
Stoughton, Hants., 70
Stovin, FSLt F C, 16, 200
St.Pol, France, 8, 9, 11, 12, 13, 14, 15, 22, 46, 196

St.Quentin, France, 41
Staaker, Flt Lt W J P, 156, 158, 160, 204, 205
Stratton, Sqn Ldr W H, 203
Strickland, Fg Off J M, 40, 42, 43, 56, 59, 61, 62, 63, 65, 66, 67, 70, 202
Stringer, Sgt E A, 203
Strobel, P2, 170, 205
Strochen ranges, Germany, 178, 179
Stroud, Sqn Ldr A, 183, 184, 207
Stuart, Sgt J, 165, 172, 173, 174, 205
Stuckey, Sgt S G, 55, 58, 202
St.Valéry-en-Caux, France, 45
Suez, Egypt, 74, 78, 94, 170, 174, 179, 196
Suippes, France, 192
Sumburgh, Shetland Is., 72, 196
Sumner, Plt Off, 202
Sutton Bridge, Norfolk, 39, 53, 62, 72
Swalwell, Sqn Ldr L C, 183, 207
Swanage, Dorset, 58, 61
Swann, Sgt, 173, 205
Swanston, Capt J R, 26, 28, 33, 201
Swartkop, S Africa, 174
Sweney, Sgt W G, 108, 110, 204
Swinden, Fg Off W W, 92, 93, 100, 109, 204
Swift, Fg Off, 175, 205
Swyre, Dorset, 63
Sykes, Plt Off W N, 36
Syme, Plt Off H, 207

Takali, Malta, 175
Takoradi, Gold Coast, 74, 75, 77
Talbot, Lt R A, 18, 27, 200
Talia, Syria, 83
Taliaferro, Texas, USA, 31
Talman, Plt Off J M, 67, 68, 202
Tangiers, Morocco, 76
Tangmere, Sussex, 10, 52, 59, 62, 64, 65, 67, 68, 69, 70, 71, 88, 92, 104, 196
Taranto, Italy, 158
Tarhuna, Libya, 181, 182, 188, 190
Tattersfield, Plt Off D, 168, 205
Tayler, Lt J A C, 18, 20, 21, 24, 200
Taylor, Major A G, 33, 34, 195, 201, 214
Taylor, 2Lt A M, 33, 201
Taylor, Sgt E M, 205
Taylor, Plt Off, 205
Tedder, Air Marshal A W, 78, 80, 87, 98, 99, 104, 109, 112
Temlett, Flt Lt C B, 73, 76, 79, 80, 81, 82, 85, 86, 87, 93, 94, 95, 97, 100, 204
Tempest, Hawker, 161, 162, 163, 164, 165, 165, 167, 168, 169, 170, 171, 174, 199, 217, 218, 219
Temple-Murray, Fg Off P, 204
Termoli, Italy, 197
Thetis, HMS, 20
Thielt, Belgium, 31
Thirwell, Flt Lt J D, 205
Thomas, Fg Off C P, 207
Thomas, Plt Off M, 207
Thomas, Flg Off R, 207
Thomlinson, Plt Off W H, 93, 95, 97, 100, 104, 204
Thompson, Plt Off G C, 207
Thomson, WO A, 150, 204
Thomson, Flt Lt P C, 154, 156, 204
Thomson, Plt Off T R, 70, 202
Thomson, Lt W StC, 151, 153, 154, 204
Thorold, Gp Capt H K, 74
Thorpe, Lt F C A, 30, 201
Thourout, Belgium, 28, 30
Thurnell, Fg Off D C, 207
Tidworth, Wilts., 45
Ti Isley, Flt Lt E C, 188, 192, 207
Timbers, Plt Off M D, 207
Tobruk, Libya, 79, 80, 81, 87, 94, 95, 96, 97, 98, 197
Todd, Fg Off E, 207
Tomahawk, Curtiss, 74, 75, 82, 84, 85
Tomkin, Fg Off R C, 207
Tornau, LtzS, 17
Toronto, Canada, 14, 31
Tournai, Belgium, 43
Tours, France, 55
Toy, 2Lt E C, 25, 27, 201
Toyne, Fg Off W A, 39, 202
Travers, Flt Lt P, 188, 189, 207
Trenchard, Air Marshal, 108, 109
Tripoli, Libya, 84, 181
Tripp, Sgt G, 165, 170, 171, 173, 174, 205
Trussler, Fg Off D, 207
Tuck, WO, 205
Tunis, Tunisia, 108

Turnberry, Ayrshire, 16
Turner, Lt A H, 24, 25, 29, 30, 33, 201
Turner, Sqn Ldr E C, 191, 192, 207
Turner, Flt Lt E B, 204
Turnhouse, Midlothian, 64, 73, 74, 196
Tustian, Flt Lt D, 207
Twigg, Fg Off A, 165, 205
Typhoon, Hawker, 161, 177
Tyre, Lebanon, 82

Underdown, Flt Lt P, 189, 207
Upton, 2Lt W G, 30, 201
Upwood, Cambs., 63
Usher, Sgt D C, 204
Usworth, Co Durham, 67
Uxbridge, Middlesex, 55
Uytkerke, Belgium, 13, 21, 26, 27

Vair-Turnbull, Fg Off, S J, 204
Valentine, Sgt A F C, 40, 41, 202
Valetta, Vickers, 174
Valiant, HMS, 88
Valkenburg, Netherlands, 178, 180
Vampire, de Havilland, 169, 170, 171, 172, 173, 174, 175, 178, 199, 218, 219
Varssenaere, Belgium, 13, 24, 25, 26, 27, 29, 32, 33, 34
Vaughan-Fowler, Sqn Ldr P E, 158, 188, 195, 204, 205
Vaux-sur-Somme, France, 30
Ventnor, Isle of Wight, 62
Victor, Handley Page, 192
Villacoublay, France, 55
Vincent, Vickers, 67
Vindictive, HMS, 19, 21
Vlissinghem, Belgium, 13, 16, 27
Vorster, 2Lt C S, 204
Vorster, Lt V, 204
Vos, Flt Lt C S, 195, 204

Waddington, Flt Lt R G, 168, 205
Wade, Fg Off R A, 207
Wadi Halfa, Sudan, 75, 99, 106, 110, 162, 166, 174
Wadowski, Vfw, 24
Waite, Plt Off G A, 103, 106, 204
Walker, Fg Off E, 166, 205
Walker, Flt Sgt J F, 165, 173, 205
Walker, Plt Off P C, 204
Wall, Flt Lt G B, 207
Wallace, WO R J, 76, 77, 92, 93, 100, 204
Wallace, Sgt T J, 73, 75, 103, 104, 202
Wallingford, Berks., 71
Wallington, Flt Lt W P, 191, 207
Walmsley, Flt Lt M P J, 207
Walsh, Fg Off, 100
Walton, LAC, 74, 84, 96, 104
Warmwell, Dorset, 58, 59, 61, 62, 63
Warren, Fg Off R J, 207
Warton, Lancs., 177, 193
Wasigny, France, 41
Watkins, WO J G, 204
Watts, LAC, 158
Wavell, General, 87
Weatherill, Fg Off, 202
Webb, Flt Lt, 73, 104
Webber, Flt Lt F, 189, 207
Webster, Lt R N, 201
Wegberg, Germany, 187
Weir, Fg Off D M, 207
Welch, Fg Off P N, 204
Wellington, Vickers, 39, 106
Wells, Flt Lt A, 183, 185, 195, 207
Wells, Sqn Ldr M C, 160, 161, 164, 205
Wenduyne, Belgium, 14, 21
Wercken, Belgium, 28
Wesley, WO2 J, 14, 33, 200
West, Flt Lt D R E, 205
West, Flt Lt T A, 207
Westbrooke, Flt Lt L, 207
Westcott, Flt Lt D A, 207
Westlake, Plt Off G H, 64, 67, 70, 71, 72, 73, 76, 77, 81, 82, 83, 84, 85, 86, 88, 89, 92, 93, 95, 96, 98, 101, 104, 105, 106, 110, 202, 204
West Raynham, Norfolk, 38, 39
Westwood, Flt Lt C, 207
Weymouth, Dorset, 56
Wheatley, Fg Off T M K, 207
Whistler, Maj Gen L G, 169
Whitaker, Wg Cdr F, 185
Whitby, Fg Off M S, 207
White, Sgt, 79, 80, 204
White, Fg Off, 149

Whitehead, Fg Off J, 207
Whiteley, FSLt R I, 16, 17, 200
Whitewell, Lt E J, 31, 201
Whitford, AVM, 158
Whiting, Sqn Ldr S R, 195, 204
Whitsun-Jones, Flt Lt D D, 205
Whittingham, Fg Off M F, 187, 207
Whitworth, Wg Cdr, 173
Wick, Caithness, 52, 71, 72
Wicks, M/Nav, 207
Widley, Hants., 71
Wight, Isle of, 58, 61, 66, 70
Wight, Flt Lt R D G, 39, 40, 41, 202
Wightman, Fg Off V, 187, 189, 207
Wildenrath, Germany, 179, 187, 192
Wildernesse Golf Club, Kent, 67, 68
Wilhelmshaven, Germany, 23, 27
Wilkes, Fg Off A, 207
Wilkes, Sgt C N, 55, 58, 202
Wilkie, Wendell, 106
Wilkinson, FSLt E G, 200
Wilkinson, Fg Off G W, 192, 193, 207
Willdey, Fg Off R C, 159, 205
Williams, Fg Off P A D, 207
Williams, Flt Lt R, 207
Williams, Lt T G, 201
Williams, Fg Off, 188
Williams, WO, 160, 205
Williamson, Sgt J, 156, 205
Williamson, Flt Lt H B, 207
Willings, Plt Off K, 187, 207
Willis, Flt Lt G, 187, 207
Wilson, Plt Off A J, 207
Wilson, Plt Off D, 207
Wilson, Sgt F, 73, 75, 79, 80, 81, 85, 204
Wilson, Flt Lt F A W J, 76, 93, 94, 105, 204
Wilson, Plt Off G A, 113, 116, 117, 204
Wilson, Fg Off J F, 165, 205
Wilson, Flt Lt J G, 205
Wilson, Sqn Ldr K J, 186, 188, 192, 207
Wilson, Plt Off B, 66, 67, 70, 72, 204
Wilson, Sgt, 73, 75, 202
Wilson, Plt Off, 207
Wilson-MacDonald, Gp Capt D S, 63
Wilson-North, Plt Off O, 148, 154, 157, 204, 205
Wilvox, Fg Off N H, 207
Wimereux, France, 30, 201
Winchester Castle, RMS, 158
Windsor, Lt W A, 20, 21, 23, 200
Winning, Fg Off E G, 41, 46, 48, 202
Winnipeg, Canada, 17
Wissant, France, 31, 200
Witteridge, Fg Off, 159, 205
Wittering, Northants., 37, 38, 39, 40, 41, 44, 46, 47, 52, 53, 54, 60, 67, 180, 196
Wlasnowolski, Plt Off B, 66, 67, 70, 72, 202
Wojcicki, Sgt A, 62, 65, 202
Wollaston, Fg Off R F, 106, 204
Woodacre, Fg Off R W, 207
Wooding, Lt J, 27, 201
Woods, Flt Lt B A, 183, 207
Woods, Fg Off R, 207
Woodward, Sqn Ldr V C, 204
Woolnough, Plt Off J H, 192, 207
Wotherspoon, Fg Off A S, 207
Wragg, P3, 165, 170, 172, 205
Wright, 2Lt C V C, 201
Wright, Fg Off, 207
Wyatt-Smith, Flt Lt, 204
Wykeham-Barnes, Sqn Ldr P G, 79, 81
Wyton, Hunts., 176

Yarmouth, Isle of Wight, 61
Yaxley, Sqn Ldr R F, 77
Yeo, Fg Off P, 207
Yeovil, Somerset, 56
Young, Flt Lt A W, 207
Young, Sqn Ldr M H, 92, 93, 101, 105, 106, 107, 108, 156, 191, 195, 204
Young, Sgt, M, 204
Young, Sgt, 207
Ypres, Belgium, 27, 28, 29

Zagroba, P2 S, 162, 165, 170, 205
Zara, Italy (later Yugoslavia), 197
Zarren, Belgium, 28
Zeebrugge, Belgium, 7, 8, 11, 13, 14, 15, 16, 17, 18, 19, 20, 21, 23, 25, 26, 27, 47
Zenses, Flugmaat, 24, 28
Zevecote, Belgium, 30
Zweibrücken, Germany, 192